International Migration Outlook

Annual Report
2007 Edition

OECD

ORGANISATION FOR ECONOMIC CO-OPERATION AND DEVELOPMENT

ORGANISATION FOR ECONOMIC CO-OPERATION AND DEVELOPMENT

The OECD is a unique forum where the governments of 30 democracies work together to address the economic, social and environmental challenges of globalisation. The OECD is also at the forefront of efforts to understand and to help governments respond to new developments and concerns, such as corporate governance, the information economy and the challenges of an ageing population. The Organisation provides a setting where governments can compare policy experiences, seek answers to common problems, identify good practice and work to co-ordinate domestic and international policies.

The OECD member countries are: Australia, Austria, Belgium, Canada, the Czech Republic, Denmark, Finland, France, Germany, Greece, Hungary, Iceland, Ireland, Italy, Japan, Korea, Luxembourg, Mexico, the Netherlands, New Zealand, Norway, Poland, Portugal, the Slovak Republic, Spain, Sweden, Switzerland, Turkey, the United Kingdom and the United States. The Commission of the European Communities takes part in the work of the OECD.

OECD Publishing disseminates widely the results of the Organisation's statistics gathering and research on economic, social and environmental issues, as well as the conventions, guidelines and standards agreed by its members.

This work is published on the responsibility of the Secretary-General of the OECD. The opinions expressed and arguments employed herein do not necessarily reflect the official views of the Organisation or of the governments of its member countries.

Also available in French under the title:
Perspectives des migrations internationales
RAPPORT ANNUEL 2007

Foreword

*T*his publication constitutes the thirty first report of the OECD's Continuous Reporting System on migration (known by its French acronym SOPEMI). Formerly published as Trends in International Migration, the title was changed last year to the International Migration Outlook and, at the same time, its analytical scope broadened. This year's edition is a consolidation of the changes introduced last year, in particular with respect to standardised statistics on inflows and migration notes on individual countries.

The report is divided into four parts plus a statistical annex. Part I contains three subsections. The first of these provides a broad overview of trends in international migration movements, including a historical overview of migration over the last half century and a look at potential movements in response to future declines in the working age population. Net migration into OECD countries has tripled since the early seventies, with movements often driven by historical events such as the fall of the Iron Curtain. Asylum seeking is at a historical low since the early nineties, while the accession of the new members of the European Union in 2004 has resulted in a substantial increase in movements within Europe. Significant labour migration into southern Europe continues, most of it from outside OECD countries. The integration of immigrants and their children continues to be an issue of concern in many countries and the labour market section two provides for the first time an overview of labour force outcomes for children of immigrants in ten OECD countries for which data were available. The final section of Part I contains an overview of recent developments in migration policies, which includes a review of changes in migration restrictions with regard to EU enlargement countries, new measures to facilitate the migration of the highly skilled and the growing importance of migration issues in international relatio.

Parts II and III are devoted to special topics. The first examines the issue of overqualification among immigrant workers, namely the holding of jobs whose skill requirements are below their formal qualifications, and the possible reasons for this phenomenon. The second special chapter focuses on the international mobility of health professionals to OECD countries and presents the first broad based empirical results on this phenomenon, with implications for policy.

Part IV presents succinct country specific notes and statistics on developments in international migration movements and policies in OECD countries in recent years. Finally the statistical annex includes a broad selection of recent and historical statistics on immigrant flows, the foreign and foreign born populations, naturalisations and migrant workers.

Ce livre contient des...

 StatLinks

**Accédez aux fichiers Excel®
à partir des livres imprimés !**

En bas à droite des tableaux ou graphiques de cet ouvrage, vous trouverez des *StatLinks*.
Pour télécharger le fichier Excel® correspondant, il vous suffit de retranscrire dans votre
navigateur Internet le lien commençant par : *http://dx.doi.org*.
Si vous lisez la version PDF de l'ouvrage, et que votre ordinateur est connecté à Internet,
il vous suffit de cliquer sur le lien.
Les *StatLinks* sont de plus en plus répandus dans les publications de l'OCDE.

Table of Contents

Part II
MATCHING EDUCATIONAL BACKGROUND AND EMPLOYMENT:
A CHALLENGE FOR IMMIGRANTS IN HOST COUNTRIES

Part III
IMMIGRANT HEALTH WORKERS IN OECD COUNTRIES
IN THE BROADER CONTEXT OF HIGHLY SKILLED MIGRATION

INTERNATIONAL MIGRATION OUTLOOK: SOPEMI 2007 EDITION – ISBN 978-92-64-03285-9 – © OECD 2007

Part IV
RECENT CHANGES IN MIGRATION MOVEMENTS AND POLICIES
(COUNTRY NOTES)

STATISTICAL ANNEX

List of Charts, Tables and Boxes

Part I

RECENT TRENDS IN INTERNATIONAL MIGRATION

Charts

INTERNATIONAL MIGRATION OUTLOOK: SOPEMI 2007 EDITION – ISBN 978-92-64-03285-9 – © OECD 2007

Tables

Boxes

Part II

MATCHING EDUCATIONAL BACKGROUND AND EMPLOYMENT:
A CHALLENGE FOR IMMIGRANTS IN HOST COUNTRIES

Charts

Part III

IMMIGRANT HEALTH WORKERS IN OECD COUNTRIES
IN THE BROADER CONTEXT OF HIGHLY SKILLED MIGRATION

Part IV
RECENT CHANGES IN MIGRATION MOVEMENTS AND POLICIES

INTERNATIONAL MIGRATION OUTLOOK: SOPEMI 2007 EDITION – ISBN 978-92-64-03285-9 – © OECD 2007

STATISTICAL ANNEX

Acquisition of Nationality

Inflows of Foreign Workers

Stocks of Foreign and Foreign-Born Labour

INTERNATIONAL MIGRATION OUTLOOK: SOPEMI 2007 EDITION – ISBN 978-92-64-03285-9 – © OECD 2007

ISBN 978-92-64-03285-9
International Migration Outlook
Sopemi 2007 Edition
© OECD 2007

Editorial

The Medical Brain Drain: Myths and Realities

There are renewed fears of a "brain drain" from developing countries to the profit of OECD countries, especially with respect to health professionals

Increasing immigration of highly skilled workers into OECD countries over the past 10-15 years, often from developing countries, has refuelled fears of a "brain drain" from developing countries of much of their skilled labour, to the profit of OECD countries. This concern has been loudest in recent years concerning the recruitment of foreign doctors and nurses by OECD countries, and with ageing populations in OECD countries driving up the demand for health professionals, there are real fears that the health care sector in many developing countries could be severely damaged by the medical "brain drain".

This edition of the Outlook presents new evidence on this issue

Despite the heightened policy interest, solid evidence on the international mobility of health professionals has been limited and indeed often anecdotal. This has given rise to much speculation regarding what is a complex issue, and has hindered the development of effective policy responses. To fill the gap, one of the two special chapters in this year's edition of the Outlook presents an up-to-date and comprehensive picture of immigrants in the health sector in OECD countries. It provides answers to a number of basic questions that are at the heart of national and international debates on these issues.

What is the scope of the international mobility of health professionals in OECD countries? Which origin and receiving countries are the most concerned? To what extent has migration affected health-care systems in developing countries? What should governments do in both sending and receiving countries to adapt to the current international mobility patterns of health workers?

Health professionals are generally not over-represented among highly skilled migrants...

One claim not supported by the data is that health professionals are over-represented among highly skilled migrants. Results show that around the year 2000, 11% of employed nurses and 18% of employed doctors on average in the OECD were foreign-born. These figures are similar to those observed for professionals as a whole. There are, however, important variations across countries, which reflect in part differences in the characteristics of their health workforces and in historical migration patterns. For example, the percentage of foreign-born doctors ranges from less than 5% in Japan and Finland, to more than 30% in Ireland, the United Kingdom, Canada, Australia and New Zealand. Similarly, the percentage of foreign-born nurses is above 20% in Australia, Switzerland and New Zealand. And in absolute terms, the United States is the only net receiving vis-à-vis all other countries for both doctors and nurses. In many OECD countries, immigrants make an important contribution to health-care delivery, not only because of their numbers but also because they help ensure the continuity of service at night or during week-ends and the provision of care in under-served areas.

... and in large origin countries, such as India, China and the Philippines, the number of health professionals working abroad is low relative to the domestic supply

Some origin countries, such as the Philippines for nurses, or India for doctors, play a prominent role in providing health care workers to OECD countries. But intra-OECD mobility is also significant, particularly from the United Kingdom and Germany. And, there are important South-South migrations of health professionals, in particular from Africa and Asia to the Middle East and South Africa. Caribbean countries and a number of African countries have particularly high emigration rates of doctors. In some cases, relatively few doctors remain behind, making it difficult to deliver basic health care to the population. But for large origin countries such as India or China, the number of health professionals working overseas, although high, is low relative to the domestic supply and the number of doctors per person has not been strongly affected.

Stopping the outflows of doctors and nurses from low income countries would not solve the shortage of health professionals these countries face

The chapter also shows that the number of immigrant health workers in OECD countries represents only a small fraction of health sector needs for human resources in lower income countries, as estimated by the WHO (around 12% for Africa for example). In short, although stopping the flow, if this were indeed possible, would alleviate the problem, it would not by itself solve the shortage issue.

The rise in the immigration of health-care workers has occurred, even if there are no targeted recruitment programmes

Thus far, few OECD countries have specific migration programmes targeting health professionals, and bilateral agreements do not play an important role. Despite this, there has been an upward shift in immigration trends observed over the past five years, in parallel with that observed for the highly skilled in general. In addition to the continuing role played by the main origin countries (India, China and the Philippines), there have been increasing flows from smaller African countries and from Central and Eastern Europe.

To better mobilize the skills and competencies of foreign doctors and nurses and to ensure high-quality health care, OECD countries are emphasizing the recognition of qualifications

OECD countries are trying to mobilize the skills and competencies of newly arrived foreign doctors and nurses while ensuring high standards and quality in health-care delivery. A key issue concerns the recognition of foreign medical qualifications for health professionals. OECD countries have put in place a panoply of measures to address the skills' recognition question, among them theoretical and practical exams, language tests and most often, supervised periods of practice, but some countries are stricter than others. Several countries have also developed programmes to attract back into the health sector foreign-trained health professionals who are already settled in the country but work in other jobs.

The recent acceleration in flows calls for increased co-operation between origin and receiving countries to better share the benefits of the international mobility of health professionals

The fact that international migration has so far played a limited role in the current crisis for health human resources in developing countries, should not divert the attention of the international community, nor weaken its commitments towards better health for all. Because health is an international public good, because the health-related objectives of the Millennium Development Goals are key elements of international solidarity and because, above all, access to health can be considered as a basic right, origin and receiving countries need to work together towards providing health professionals with opportunities to use efficiently their skills where they are the most needed, while guaranteeing the individual right to move.

There is no unique response to the challenges posed by the international mobility of health care workers, but data are now available to ensure a more accurate diagnosis of what is at stake. In addition, a number of sound policy proposals to better share the benefits of the international mobility of the health workers have been made. The increase in Official Development Assistance to health and the current efforts devoted by the WHO to develop a global code of practice governing the international recruitment of health workers go in the right direction. However, these measures need to be accompanied, in both sending and receiving countries, by policies aimed at increasing domestic training capacity, improving retention, developing skill mix and coordinated care, and increasing productivity.

John P. Martin

Director for Employment, Labour and Social Affairs

ISBN 978-92-64-03285-9
International Migration Outlook
Sopemi 2007 Edition
© OECD 2007

Introduction

*2007 Edition of International Migration Outlook
shows an increase in migration flows to the
OECD...*

International migration of both permanent and temporary immigrants continued to increase in 2005. Overall, for the seventeen countries for which there exist comparable data on "permanent-type" legal immigration, inflows increased by about 11% in 2005 relative to 2004. Among the other OECD countries, there was an increase of about 10% between 2004 and 2005, largely due to greater inflows in Spain. At the same time, high temporary movements were observed in countries such as Australia, Canada, New Zealand, Switzerland and the United Kingdom, countries in which permanent migration is also high.

*... notably in family migration and migration
for employment...*

Family migration continues to dominate among the inflows of permanent-type immigrants. Although it represents only one third of all permanent-type migration in Japan and the United Kingdom, it reaches a high of 70% in the United States, whose migration regime is heavily family-based. Many European countries, among them Austria, Belgium, Denmark, Germany, Portugal, Sweden and the United Kingdom, appear as important labour migration countries, with some 30 to 40% of permanent-type immigrants arriving for work-related reasons.

*... while, the number of asylum seekers continues
to decline*

The number of asylum seekers continued to decline in OECD countries in 2005, falling by 15% overall. The 2005 level has almost halved compared to the number observed in 2000 and currently stands below 300 000. Absolute levels of asylum requests were at about 50 000 in France, followed by Germany and the United Kingdom at about 30 000 each, and Austria, Canada and the United States in the 20 000 to 25 000 range. However, relative to the population, it was Austria that received the most requests at more than 2 700 per million persons in the population.

*There are increasing inflows of international
students*

The number of foreign students in OECD countries has increased by more than 40% since 2000, with especially large increases in New Zealand, the Czech Republic and Korea. Other countries which have seen large increases (exceeding 50%) include the countries of southern Europe, Ireland, Australia, France, the Netherlands and Japan. The increase in the number of international students is most likely a response to signals which many OECD countries have been sending in recent years, concerning possibilities for work and residence following the completion of their education.

There are more immigrants from central
and eastern Europe, China and India…

In 2005, the major origin countries of migration remained relatively stable, with geographical proximity still being a major determinant in the choice of destination country. A change in origin countries is nevertheless evident in Europe, where movements have been largely influenced by the increase in flows from central and eastern European countries as a consequence of the enlargement of the European Union (May 2004) and the recent adhesion of Bulgaria and Romania (January 2007). Outside of Europe, in North America, Oceania, Japan and Korea, migrants from Asia are still dominant, with a significant growth in numbers of those from India and China.

… and destination countries for sub-Saharan
African migration have begun to diversify

Migration from Africa to OECD countries concerns mostly European countries due to historical links and geographic proximity. In Europe, North African migration is more frequent than migration from sub-Saharan Africa. Destination countries for African migration have begun to diversify, however, and Southern European countries have become an attractive destination as a result of new employment opportunities combined with geographical proximity. For instance, flows from Senegal and Nigeria to Spain increased on average by about 25 and 15% per year, respectively, over the past five years. Africans also emigrate to North America, especially those from English-speaking countries like Nigeria, Ghana and Kenya. In the United States, the number of persons from Africa obtaining legal permanent resident status increased by 30% in 2005 to reach 85 000.

The integration of immigrants into the labour
market is improving…

During the last 5 to 10 years, differences in participation rates between the native-born population and immigrants declined in most countries. This, however, conceals large differences regarding groups of origin and gender. Between 1995 and 2005, there was strong growth in employment in most OECD countries to which immigrants greatly contributed. In 15 out of the 18 countries for which data are available, the percentage of immigrants in net job creation between 1995 and 2005 was higher than the proportion of immigrants in the working population in 2005.

… but immigrants continue to be over-represented
among the unemployed

In 2004-2005, in all OECD countries, with the exception of Poland, Hungary and the United States, the unemployment rate of immigrants was higher than that of the native population. In the Nordic countries, Austria, Belgium, the Netherlands and Switzerland, immigrants are over-represented among the unemployed by a factor of at least two compared to their share in the labour force.

The report this year focuses on the labour market
integration of the children of immigrants...

Altogether, persons with a migration background account for more than 30% of the 20-29 year old in Australia, Canada and Switzerland (in descending order); between 30 and 20% in Sweden, the United States, the Netherlands, Germany, France and the United Kingdom; and around 15% in Denmark and Norway.

... which tends to be less favourable than for
the children of the native-born

A first glance at the employment rates of the children of immigrants reveals significant gaps for most countries. Although the second generation generally has a higher employment probability than young immigrants, the gaps vis-à-vis the children of the native-born are still large in European OECD countries. There is, however, a relatively strong improvement for second generation women. The large gaps in the employment rates of the second generation are partly due to the lower educational attainment of the former. In Denmark, for example, the gap would diminish by about half if the second generation had the same educational attainment as other natives. Nevertheless, even at given education levels, gaps remain large in all European countries with the exception of Switzerland.

This year's report provides a new approach
to migration policies

The report provides a new approach to presenting migration policies. A distinction is made between domestic policy issues such as the recruitment, reception and integration of immigrants on the one hand, and the international dimension of migration policies on the other hand. The domestic issues concern changes in migration policies which aim at responding to labour market needs (including in the context of EU enlargement), the introduction of more restrictive measures for family reunification, policies to enhance the human capital of immigrants, and recent changes in integration policies including a redefinition of responsibility sharing. This part also highlights recent regularisation programmes in OECD countries. The second more international set of issues deal with measures to combat irregular migration, the international co-operation for reinforcing border control and policies aiming at enhancing the links between international migration and development of origin countries.

Two special chapters deal with topical issues

The increase in the migration of highly skilled workers is one of the salient features of recent international migration trends in OECD countries. In this context, questions arise concerning the transferability and use of foreign skills in receiving countries' labour markets, and the impact of the international mobility of the highly skilled on origin countries.

The first chapter addresses the question of the mismatch between qualifications and jobs of immigrants in OECD countries...

Regardless of the definition used and the country concerned, immigrants are more likely than the native-born to hold jobs for which they are over-qualified. Foreign-born women seem to be at an even greater disadvantage. The analysis underlines the crucial importance of the place of education. This variable may translate differences in terms of the content and quality of schooling (at a given level of education), but it may also serve to distort employers' interpretation of education levels, given the lack of information available to them. In any case, the fact that in all of the countries considered, at least 25% (on average almost 50%) of skilled immigrants are inactive, unemployed or confined to jobs for which they are over-qualified, poses the question of finding ways to use more effectively on the human resources of skilled immigrants.

... and the second chapter presents an up-to-date and comprehensive picture of immigrants in the health sector in OECD countries

On average, around the year 2000, 11% of nurses and 18% of doctors employed in the OECD area were foreign-born. There are large variations in the size of the foreign-born health workforce across OECD countries, partly reflecting general migration patterns, notably of the highly skilled. In general, however, health professionals are not over-represented among highly skilled migrants. While there is a legitimate concern about the consequences of migration on origin countries, stopping the outflows of doctors and nurses especially from low income countries – if this were indeed possible – would by itself not solve the global health workforce crisis these countries face. The Chapter also emphasises the necessity to recognise that, in the long run, active international recruitment can hardly compensate for domestic solutions, especially when there is large pool of human resources that could be mobilised.

ISBN 978-92-64-03285-9
International Migration Outlook
Sopemi 2007 Edition
© OECD 2007

PART I

Recent Trends in International Migration

A. Developments in Migration Flows

1. A half-century of international migration

The increases in international migration to OECD countries observed in recent years are part of a trend that is interesting to view in a broader, historical context, dating from the post-war era to the present. There have been a number of developments during this period that have influenced international migration movements, among them post-war reconstruction, the end of the colonial era, the oil crisis in 1973, the rise and fall of the Iron Curtain, the ageing of the baby-boom generation, not to mention general demographic and economic imbalances between more and less developed countries. What has been the underlying trend in international migration over this period and how have specific events affected the scale and nature of movements within the OECD world?

Chart I.1 shows the evolution of net international migration for OECD countries from 1956 until recently. The movements shown here cover all international migration, including movements of nationals as well as persons of foreign nationality. For the purposes of the chart and the analysis, OECD countries have been divided into two groups, traditional immigration countries, on the one hand, and countries that were largely emigration countries or that saw limited movements of any kind in the first half of the period considered here. The latter include the countries of southern and central Europe,[1] Ireland, Japan and the Nordic countries except for Sweden. Not included among these are

Chart I.1. **Net migration rates, traditional immigration and emigration OECD countries, 1956-2003**

Net migration as a percent of total resident population

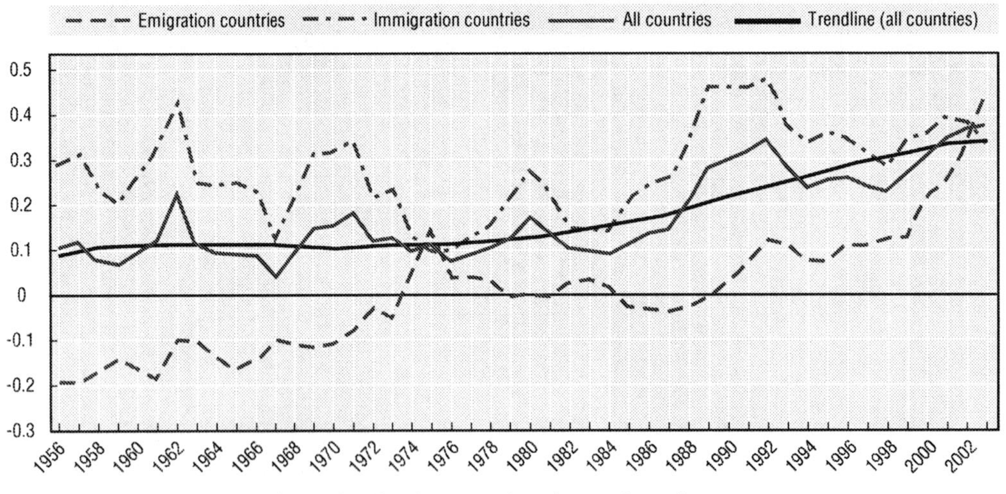

Note: For definition on immigration and emigration countries, please refer to the text.

Source: Labour Force Statistics, OECD, 2006.

StatLink ⬛⬛⬛ *http://dx.doi.org/10.1787/015200172027*

Korea, Mexico and Turkey, all of which would qualify as former or current emigration countries but for which net migration data are sparse or non-existent. All other OECD countries are categorised as immigration countries. Some of these, such as Germany, New Zealand and the United Kingdom have seen significant outflows of nationals as well over past decades, but they have been categorised here as immigration countries, because priority has been accorded to immigration and these countries already had significant immigrant populations in 1990 or earlier.

By definition, net migration within each country group is in principle zero, essentially because in-migration from any country in the group to any other country of the same group is cancelled out by the corresponding out-migration observed in the origin country. Thus the net migration rates shown for each group represent the net effect of movements between the group and the rest of the world. For the immigration country group, the net migration rate reflects the impact of movements to and from the emigration country group and the non-OECD world. Likewise, net migration within the all-country OECD group represents the net effect of movements to and from countries outside the OECD. Note that the absence of net migration data for Korea, Mexico and Turkey means that they are statistically considered to be part of the non-OECD world for the purposes of this analysis.

The trend net international migration rate for current OECD countries (that is, excluding Korea, Mexico and Turkey) was approximately 1 person per 1 000 persons in the population from 1956 until about the oil crisis or somewhat thereafter. This was the period of the so-called "guest workers", but the OECD net migration rate seems to have been relatively stable over this period, although with a number of peaks and troughs due to particular events (see below). The stable net rate masks considerable movements that were occurring within the OECD area, from "emigration" to "immigration" countries.

Since about the oil crisis, however, the net migration rate within the OECD has been increasing, with international migration contributing more and more to population growth, compared to natural increase (the excess of births over deaths) with each passing year (see Chart I.2 for the situation as of 2004). The increases in international migration during the nineties therefore would appear to be part of a broader underlying trend that dates back to the late seventies and early eighties.

Over the period considered, net migration from outside the OECD to OECD countries averaged 790 000 persons per year from 1956 to 1976, 1.24 million per year from 1977 to 1990 and 2.65 million per year thereafter up to 2003.

The net migration movements shown in Chart I.1 are also characterised by a number of peaks and troughs, which generally correspond to well-defined historical events or developments. The 1962 peak in the immigration countries series corresponds to the end of the Algerian War and the massive return of French citizens from Algeria; the 1969-1971 hump to the height of the "guest workers" era; the late seventies and early eighties increase to the migration of the boat-people; the late eighties and early nineties upswell to the appearance for the first time in United States statistics of large unauthorised movements from Mexico[2] as well as the general increase in movements following the fall of the Iron Curtain.[3]

Emigration countries show a steady increase over the period in the net migration rate that is perturbed in the mid-seventies by a combination of three events and their associated migration movements: the 1974 Portuguese revolution and the subsequent independence of the Portuguese colonies; the end of the Greek military junta in 1974 and

Chart I.2. **Components of population change, 2004,**
per thousand persons in the population

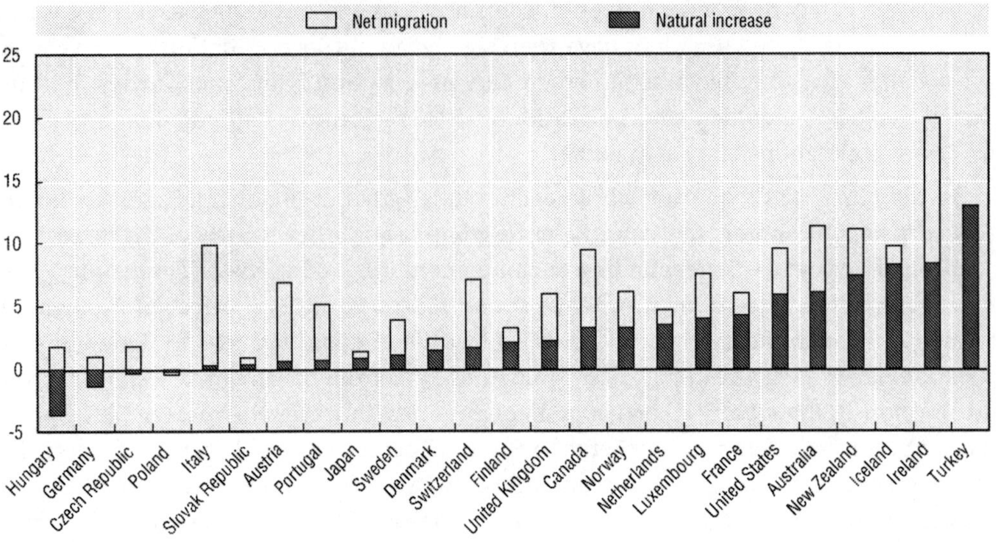

Note: Data for Japan are for 2000.
Source: *Labour Force Statistics*, OECD, 2006.

StatLink ☞ http://dx.doi.org/10.1787/015231465384

the death of Franco in 1975. All of these were associated with significant returns of citizens of the three countries concerned to their homeland, especially of Portuguese colonials.

Immigration countries appear to have actually undergone a decline in the net migration rate from the mid-fifties to the first oil-crisis, which witnessed a reversal despite the closing of borders to labour migration in many European countries. The general increase among emigration countries over the 1956-2003 period has accelerated since the turn of the century, to the point that the net migration rate of former emigration countries now exceeds that of traditional immigration countries.

2. Population ageing, the working-age population and international migration

Over the next few years OECD countries will be beginning to feel, if they have not done so already, the first consequences on the size of the working-age population of the fall in birth rates following the baby-boom period. The impact this is likely to have on international migration initially is as yet unclear, not only because there exist in every country sources of unutilised labour supply that can be mobilised in response to demand pressures, but also because entry and stay restrictions continue to exist in many countries and despite high levels of unauthorised migration in some, migration policy continues to have a significant impact on the magnitude of flows. Whether restrictive policies will and can continue into the future in the present of persistent labour shortages, however remains to be seen.

In 2005, the first cohort of baby-boomers born after World War II was entering its 60th year. Some of these persons had already retired from the workforce before 2005 and more have retired since then or will do so in the near future, to be followed by ever larger cohorts over the next fifteen years. Over time these cohorts will be larger than those entering the working-age population (15-64). In practice this means that without positive net migration, the working-age population at some stage will begin to decline. However, this phenomenon in itself cannot be considered a new and drastic change. OECD countries have been witnessing declines in the growth rate of the working-age population over the recent past and the crossing of the zero line does not introduce in itself anything fundamentally new. It is rather the fact that this decline will be occurring in the presence of continuing demand for goods and services, from both the growing number of retired persons who will continue to consume, albeit at reduced levels because of lower retirement incomes, and from the rest of the world. Satisfying this demand can be achieved in part through increases in productivity or by outsourcing production to other countries but may also require the recruitment of workers in certain sectors and occupations.

Chart I.3 shows the expected change in the working-age population, assuming zero net migration of persons in this group, over five-year periods beginning in 2005, expressed as a percentage of the working-age population in 2005. Note, first of all, that the size of the working-age population for 2005 used in estimating change in the chart reflects the impact of past migration, but that all estimated changes shown after that date reflect only the ageing of persons already resident in the country. Thus the working-age population 15-64 for the year 2010 was estimated by taking the population 10-59 observed in 2005 and ageing it five years under the assumption of no deaths and no net international migration. Of course, there is and there will be migration of persons of working-age even in the absence of labour migration, because of movements of persons arriving for family reunification and formation and for asylum, as well as movements of persons under a free circulation regime. But for most countries, these will be insufficient to compensate for the expected decline.

For the period, 2005-2010, only Japan, Germany, Italy, Spain, Greece, Portugal and the Czech Republic are expected to show a decrease or a marginal increase in the working-age population with no net migration. For some of these countries, migration over the 1995

Chart I.3. **Expected change in the working-age population assuming zero net migration over the periods indicated, 2005-2020**

As a percent of the 2005 population

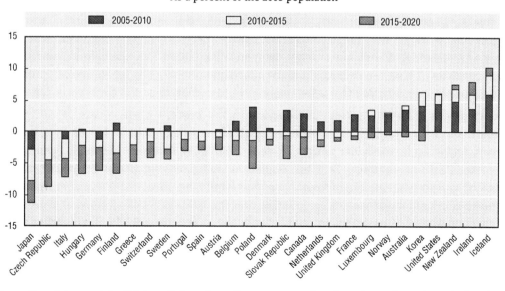

Source: Eurostat, except for Belgium, Italy and non-European countries where data refer to the United Nations Population Division.

StatLink ⌷⌷⌷ *http://dx.doi.org/10.1787/015240680655*

to 2005 period has already compensated at least in part for what would have been large declines or moderate increases in the working-age population over the 1995 to 2005 period. For example, in 1995 the decline from 1995 to 2005 in the working-age population in Germany was projected to be over 1.1 million, but as a result of international migration, the decline was about 700 000. In Italy the expected decline was over 1.2 million, but the working-age population actually declined by about 70 000 over the period. In Spain the working-age population was expected to increase by about one half million from 1995-2005; as a result of international migration, it actually increased by about 2.8 million in a period of strong economic growth.

For Japan over the 2005-2010 period, the decline in the working-age population is expected to be about 3%, for Germany and Italy over 1% and for the other countries shown, close to zero. To offset these declines, if that were indeed a sensible objective, would require a net migration of persons in the working-age population of about 500 000 per year for Japan, 150 000 for Germany and 100 000 for Italy. Net migration levels, however, are currently not zero and have been positive in most countries for some time.[4] For the total population in Japan, that is including children and older immigrants, for example, net migration has exceeded 100 000 only once since the year 2000. In Germany, it has declined strongly in recent years and is currently under 100 000. Italy, on the other hand, has seen net migration levels increase from around 180 000 in the year 2000 to apparently more than half a million in recent years.[5]

Situations thus differ considerably across countries and it is clear that demographic evolutions by themselves have not up to now always asserted a strong draw on migration flows, especially in the presence of migration policies which restrict possibilities for entry and stay as well as under conditions of weak economic growth. However, in the countries of southern Europe, where demographic ageing is more advanced than in many other European countries, control of illegal employment is weaker and the underground economy significant, employers have resorted to substantial hirings of unauthorised immigrants over the past decade to fill their needs. Japan, on the other hand, is currently undergoing a strong decline in its working-age population, without as yet a move in favour of freeing up possibilities for entry. If unemployment rates continue to decrease, however, pressures on wages may begin to operate, unless there is a significant mobilisation of unused domestic labour supply or other compensating factors (for example, the transfer of jobs overseas). There are indeed signs that participation rates in Japan are beginning to increase, although whether this is just a cyclical phenomenon or will continue is not clear.

Over the 2010-2015 period, the decline in the current stock of the working-age population will continue in the countries cited above, which will be joined by a further group, including in particular Finland, Sweden, Hungary, Switzerland and Belgium. The expected declines assuming zero net migration would average about 0.3 to 0.6% of the working-age population per year over the period for these countries. By way of comparison, actual net migration for the total population over the 2001-2005 period stood at about 0.3% in Sweden and at almost 0.6% in Switzerland, but at less than 0.15% in the other three countries (see Chart I.3). Thus some countries would appear to already be at immigration levels that ensure maintenance of the working-age population at current levels, while others would need to at least double or triple their current intake to achieve this objective.[6]

Finally between 2015 and 2020, all but six OECD countries can be expected to show declines in the working-age population without positive net migration.[7] Over the entire 2005-2020 period, the declines in the working-age population for some countries are expected to be as large as 5% or more and for many others in the vicinity of 3%, relative to the working-age population in 2005.

The size of the working-age population, however, is not the only element at play with respect to future labour force levels. A further issue is that of labour force participation. For some countries such as Belgium or Spain, the participation rate of younger women entering the workforce is significantly higher than those of older cohorts moving into retirement and this additional participation can be expected to counteract in part the effect of the decline in the cohort size. But in countries where women's participation has been high for some time, such as the Nordic countries, there is no countervailing effect and the decline in cohort sizes can be expected to exert its full effect on the size of the workforce.

3. International migration in 2005

In this context international migration of both permanent and temporary immigrants continued to increase in 2005. Overall, for the seventeen countries for which there exist reasonably comparable data on "permanent-type" legal immigration for both 2004 and 2005 (see Box I.1), inflows increased by about 11% in 2005 relative to 2004, following a relative increase of about 16% in 2004 (see Table I.1). Among countries for which national statistics are still being used, there was an increase of about 10% between 2004 and 2005, following a 25% increase in 2004, largely due to greater inflows in Spain.

The total additions to the legal permanent resident population amount to approximately 3.5 to 4 million persons over all OECD countries. However, these figures are incomplete because, with the exception of Spain, they only cover authorised movements and for some countries, in particular Italy, do not include persons who received work and residence permits under the 2002 regularisation procedure. Unauthorised migration for the United States alone, for example, is estimated to have been on the order of approximately 620 000 persons per year over the 2000 to 2004 period (Hoefer et al., 2006). In Italy applications for work permits in 2006 numbered 490 000 and based on past experience, a certain proportion of these undoubtedly concerned unauthorised immigrants already working in Italy who had entered in previous years. Table I.1 also does not include statistics for Greece, which do not exist even for legal movements, not to mention the large unauthorised movements which have characterised migration to that country over the last decade.

The largest increases in legal permanent-type immigration were observed in the United States (+164 000), the United Kingdom (+55 000) and Italy (+31 000). In relative terms, it was in the United Kingdom, Italy, and New Zealand that legal permanent-type immigrants increased the most. There was relative stability, on the other hand, in the magnitude of movements in France, Switzerland, Austria and Norway and a significant decline in Portugal. For countries where national statistics are being used, Ireland and Korea showed large increases in movements, as a result of developments related to EU enlargement in Ireland and of the introduction of a work permit system for less skilled migrants in Korea.

The extent of permanent-type immigration varies considerably, from less or close to two per thousand population in Japan, Portugal, Germany and Finland to close to eight in Australia and Canada, over ten in Switzerland and more than fourteen in New Zealand (See Chart I.4). Except for Switzerland, these latter three countries all have an active settlement migration policy with immigrants being selected on the basis of certain

Box I.1. **Standardised statistics on immigrant inflows**

This year, for the second time, the International Migration Outlook presents statistics on immigrant inflows for a large number of OECD countries on the basis of a standardised definition. An immigrant, by this definition, is a person of foreign nationality who enters the permanently resident population either from outside the country or by changing from a temporary to a permanent status in the country. This has generally been measured from statistics on residence permits by excluding situations in which a permit is granted that is not renewable or only renewable on a limited basis. Often persons in these situations also do not have the right to social security benefits. Persons arriving under a free movement regime with the intention of staying for a long period are also counted as permanent immigrants, although admittedly in such cases, the intentions of the persons concerned may not always be transparent.

More specifically, the categories of migrants that are not counted as "permanent immigrants" are generally familiar ones and considered as temporary by destination countries, namely international students, trainees, au pairs, seasonal and contract workers, persons on exchange programmes, in short any category of immigrants which the receiving country expects will be returning to their home country following the end of their stay authorization. Note that this does not preclude the possibility that an immigrant on a temporary status applies for permanent-type status and thus enters the population of interest. Such movements in general are not physical flows, however, but changes in status. They are, however, counted as permanent immigrants in the statistics presented here, because they need to be counted somewhere, if they are not at the actual time of entry.

Note that the definition given here does not correspond to the official international definition given in the UN recommendations on international migration statistics (UN, 1998). The reason is that, thus far, few countries have applied this definition and it is rarely possible to standardise publicly available national immigration data on the basis of the international definition. There are initiatives currently under way to encourage international data provision according to this definition, but progress on this front has been exceedingly slow.

The rationale for the approach adopted here is that it seems possible currently to arrive at reasonably comparable statistics on the basis of the concept of "permanent immigration" for a significant number of countries. Essentially, almost all countries distinguish between movements of persons who are expected to return to their home country after a limited stay and those who will be staying in the host country for the longer term. Immigration permit systems do not necessarily make this an easy matter to determine, however, because in many countries, especially in Europe, even permanent-type immigrants receive permits of limited duration upon entry, sometimes as short as one year. Indeed, certain forms of temporary migration, for example international study, may provide for permits of duration comparable to those given to "permanent" immigrants.

Because migration regulations and permit durations tend to differ from country to country, even for the same category of migration, a definition of a "permanent migrant" on the basis of an easily applicable objective criterion such as a duration is not possible. Still, the notion of "permanent migration" is one which is broadly understood and meaningful and it is clearly of interest to know how many persons in a given year are being admitted "for good", even in practice a certain fraction of these may eventually change their minds and leave the country or may not satisfy the conditions for a renewal of their permit.

The measures of immigrant inflows according to this definition generally differ from usual national statistics, essentially because they tend to exclude certain shorter term movements that are counted as immigration in many national data sources. These may include, in particular, international students and trainees and even contract or seasonal workers in some countries where persons entering even for relatively short periods are counted as immigrants. This is not to imply that national statistics are in any sense "incorrect" or "biased": they are simply based on a different definition, the rationale for which is equally defendable. Internationally comparable statistics require that a choice be made and inevitably, that choice will not always coincide with that made nationally for some countries.

Box I.1. **Standardised statistics on immigrant inflows** (cont.)

In this chapter, the statistics on inflows by nationality continue to make use of official national data, because statistics by nationality on the basis of a standardized definition do not yet exist.

For the sake of comparison, the Table below presents the statistics based on the standardised definition and those commonly used at the national level.

Inflows of foreign nationals in selected OECD countries, 2005
Standardised and official statistics

	Standardised flows 2005	Usually published statistics 2005	Difference	Percent difference relative to usually published statistics
Japan	81 300	372 300	−291 000	−78
Germany	198 600	579 300	−380 700	−66
Belgium	35 900	77 400	−41 500	−54
Portugal	13 300	28 100	−14 800	−53
Austria	56 800	101 500	−44 700	−44
United Kingdom	362 400	473 800	−111 400	−24
Norway	25 800	31 400	−5 600	−18
Switzerland	78 800	94 400	−15 600	−17
Netherlands	60 700	63 400	−2 700	−4
Canada	262 200	262 200	0	0
Finland	12 700	12 700	0	0
United States	1 122 400	1 122 400	0	0
Sweden	53 800	51 300	2 500	5
Australia	179 800	167 300	12 500	7
New Zealand	59 400	54 100	5 300	10
France	168 600	134 800	33 800	25
Italy	184 300	n.a.	n.a.	n.a.
Denmark	18 000	n.a.	n.a.	n.a.
Total (less Denmark and Italy)	**2 772 500**	**3 626 400**	**−853 900**	**−24**

"n.a." means not available.

Source: For information on the compilation of the standardised statistics, see *www.oecd.org/els/migration/imo2007*.

StatLink ▇▇▇ *http://dx.doi.org/10.1787/022288760708*

characteristics (age, educational attainment, work experience, etc.) which are awarded points, with candidates having more than a threshold value being invited to immigrate. Switzerland, by contrast, has signed a free circulation agreement with the European Union, which was implemented in 2004. It now exercises no discretionary authority with respect to immigrants from the European Union (with the temporary exception of citizens of the new accession states), and now receives most of its labour migrants, both low- and high-skilled from the European Union. The chart does not include several significant immigration countries over the past decade, namely, Greece, Ireland and Spain, because statistics of legal immigration on a standardised basis are not yet available for these countries.

Family migration continues to dominate among the inflows of permanent-type immigrants (see Chart I.5) in 2005. This consists of family reunification and family formation (marriage), as well as the accompanying family of immigrant workers. Family migration represents as little as one third of all permanent-type migration in Japan and the United Kingdom but as high as 70% in the United States, whose migration regime is heavily

Table I.1. **Inflows of foreign nationals, 2003-2005**
Permanent-type migration (standardised statistics)

	2003	2004	2005	2004-2005	Per cent change
Portugal	12 900	15 900	13 300	−2 500	−16
Germany	221 900	212 400	198 600	−13 800	−6
France	168 900	173 900	168 600	−5 200	−3
Switzerland	79 700	80 700	78 800	−2 000	−2
Austria	51 900	57 100	56 800	−300	−1
Norway	n.a.	24 900	25 800	900	4
Netherlands	60 800	57 000	60 700	3 800	7
Australia	150 000	167 300	179 800	12 500	7
Japan	72 100	75 300	81 300	6 000	8
Sweden	47 900	49 100	53 800	4 700	10
Denmark	17 400	16 400	18 000	1 700	10
Finland	9 400	11 500	12 700	1 200	10
Canada	221 400	235 800	262 200	26 400	11
United States	703 500	957 900	1 122 400	164 500	17
United Kingdom	258 200	307 300	362 400	55 100	18
Italy	120 100	153 100	184 300	31 200	20
New Zealand	48 400	41 600	59 400	17 700	43
Belgium	n.a.	n.a.	35 900	n.a.	–
Total (less Belgium and Norway)	**2 244 500**	**2 614 300**	**2 915 100**	**300 800**	**12**
Total (less Belgium)	**–**	**2 637 200**	**2 938 900**	**301 700**	**11**

Inflows according to national definitions (usually published statistics)

	2003	2004	2005	2004-2005	Per cent change
Turkey	152 200	155 500	131 600	−23 900	−15
Hungary	19 400	22 200	18 800	−3 400	−15
Slovak Republic	4 600	7 900	7 700	−300	−4
Poland	30 300	36 800	38 500	1 700	5
Spain	429 500	645 800	682 700	36 900	6
Luxembourg	11 500	12 500	13 500	1 000	8
Czech Republic	57 400	50 800	58 600	7 800	15
Korea	178 300	188 800	266 300	77 400	41
Ireland	33 000	33 200	51 000	17 800	54
Total	**916 200**	**1 153 500**	**1 268 700**	**115 000**	**10**

Note: Estimates exclude unauthorised migration (except for Spain) and large-scale regularisations.
Source: For information on the compilation of the standardised statistics, see *www.oecd.org/els/migration/imo2007.*

StatLink ⟡ *http://dx.doi.org/10.1787/022360657748*

family-based. In general, however, it accounts for between 45 and 60% of all permanent-type migration in most countries.

Many European countries, among them Austria, Belgium, Denmark, Germany, Portugal, Sweden and the United Kingdom, appear as important labour migration countries, with some 30 to 40% of permanent-type immigrants arriving for work-related reasons. This is larger than the percentages of labour migrants from some pro-active migration countries such as Canada and New Zealand. However, from half to three quarters of labour migration in many European countries consists of the free movement of citizens of the European Union. The proportion would be even higher if one were to include longer term movements of persons from the new accession countries, whose movements are not entirely unrestricted in many EU countries. Labour immigration from the rest of the world tends to be limited in EU countries except in the countries of southern Europe.

Chart I.4. **Permanent-type inflows, standardised statistics, 2005**
Number per thousand persons in the population

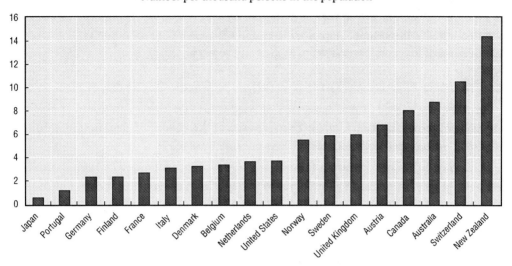

Note: For information on the compilation of the standardised statistics, see *www.oecd.org/els/migration/imo2007*.
StatLink ⌨ *http://dx.doi.org/10.1787/015258368022*

Chart I.5. **International migration by category of entry, selected OECD countries, 2005, standardised data**
Percentage of total inflows

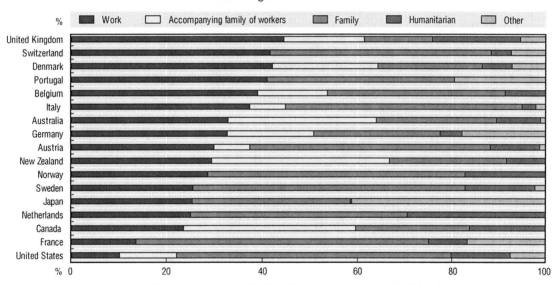

Note: For information on the compilation of the standardised statistics, see *www.oecd.org/els/migration/imo2007*.
StatLink ⌨ *http://dx.doi.org/10.1787/015262881585*

Since labour migrants tend to have better labour market outcomes than family or humanitarian migrants, one would expect the greater prevalence of these in European countries to be reflected in overall outcomes, all other things being equal. However, outcomes for European free movement migrants do not appear to be playing any strong compensating effects. The employment and unemployment rates of immigrants overall relative to those of the native-born do not appear especially favourable in many European countries compared to those of the so-called settlement countries (see Section I.B on Immigrants and the Labour Market).

Humanitarian migration (resettled refugees and asylum seekers recognised as refugees) accounts for between 15 and 20% of total movements in the United Kingdom, Norway, Sweden and Canada and almost 30% in the Netherlands. Elsewhere it is less important. Ethnic-based migration remains important in Japan and Germany (it appears under "other") and retirees and other persons of independent means in France and Portugal.

4. Regional aspects of international migration towards OECD countries

In 2005, the major origin countries of migration remained relatively stable, with geographical proximity still a major determinant in the choice of destination country in both OECD European countries and in those outside Europe.

A change in origin countries is nevertheless evident in Europe, where movements have been largely influenced by the increase in flows from eastern European countries as a consequence of the enlargement of the European Union or upcoming membership in the case of Bulgaria and Romania. Poland and Romania became by far the two main origin countries in 2005, even if they were already in the top 10 in 2000 (see Table I.2). The United Kingdom, Germany, Italy, Ireland and Austria were the main destination countries for Polish citizens (see next section).

Table I.2. **Top 10 source countries for immigration, 2000 and 2005**

OECD Europe

Thousands			
	2000		2005
Morocco	96	Poland	324
Ecuador	95	Romania	202
Poland	94	Morocco	128
Bulgaria	81	Bulgaria	82
Turkey	79	Germany	77
Romania	76	Ukraine	70
United States	64	Turkey	66
Germany	61	United Kingdom	65
France	60	Russian Federation	54
Italy	56	France	49

OECD outside of Europe

Thousands			
	2000		2005
China	238	China	297
Mexico	175	Mexico	164
Philippines	145	Philippines	158
India	78	India	134
Korea	49	United Kingdom	69
United States	47	Korea	57
Brazil	46	United States	53
United Kingdom	43	Viet Nam	52
Viet Nam	42	Russian Federation	39
Russian Federation	35	Cuba	36

Note: Data are not standardised and statistics for some countries may include many short-term flows. Data refer to the year 2003 for Korea and to 2004 for Denmark and Italy.
Source: See Table A1.1 in the Statistical Annex.

StatLink ⟶ *http://dx.doi.org/10.1787/022377568357*

Flows from Romania are highly concentred in Europe with 90% of movements towards three destination countries, namely Spain, Italy and Germany.

The United Kingdom, Ukraine and the Russian Federation figure among the top 10 origin countries in 2005. A large part of the flows from the United Kingdom are towards Spain and consist largely of retirees. Ukraine and the Russian Federation have appeared since the beginning of 2000 as major source countries for the Czech Republic, Germany but also for Italy and Spain.

Outside of Europe, in North America, Oceania, Japan and Korea, the top source countries were relatively stable with only one replacement (Brazil by Cuba) between 2000 and 2005. Migrants from Asia are still dominant, with a significant growth in those from India and China.

The United Kingdom is an exception to the rule of geographic proximity in the choice of destination country as its outflows are equally distributed between European and non-European OECD countries.

Chart I.6. illustrates for selected OECD countries the relative frequency of migration flows by country of origin, contrasting average inflows (dotted lines) over the 1990-2004 period with those (in blue) observed in 2005. For example, although Mexico continues to be the leading source country of immigration for the United States, the share of Mexicans in overall authorised flows has fallen from an average of 25% between 1990 and 2004 to less than 15% in 2005. Origin countries for legal migration have thus become more diverse in the United States.

Inflows from eastern Europe increased in 2005 following the enlargement of the European Union, with Poland being by far the top source country. Poland shows an increase in the share of inflows in 2005 compared to 1990-2004 for most of OECD countries, the change among countries shown in the chart being particularly large in Germany (from 13 to 26% in 2005), in the Netherlands and Norway (from 2 to 9 and 10%, respectively) and in Belgium and Sweden (from 2.5 to 6 and 7%, respectively).

High-growth Asian countries saw a further increase in their share of inflows in most OECD countries in 2005. With the increase in levels of education among young Asian adults, this trend is likely to continue in coming years.

Two countries are particularly prominent in the flows, namely China and India. Chinese inflows among the total entries in Canada increased from 10% for the average 1990-2004 to 16% in 2005, from 21 to 28% in Japan, and from 3 to 7% among total inflows for the United Kingdom (see Chart I.6). Migration from India increased as well in 2005 and accounted for almost 8% of total inflows in Australia compared to 5% for the period 1990-2004, for 13% in Canada compared to 8% previously, and for 8% in the United States compared to 5% previously.

Within European OECD countries, the situation is varied and origin countries are diverse. Movements depend, among other factors, on geography, linguistic proximity and historical links (see Chart I.6).

Chart I.6. **Inflows of migrants by country of origin, selected OECD countries, 1990-2004 and 2005**

2005 top ten countries of origin as percentage of total inflows

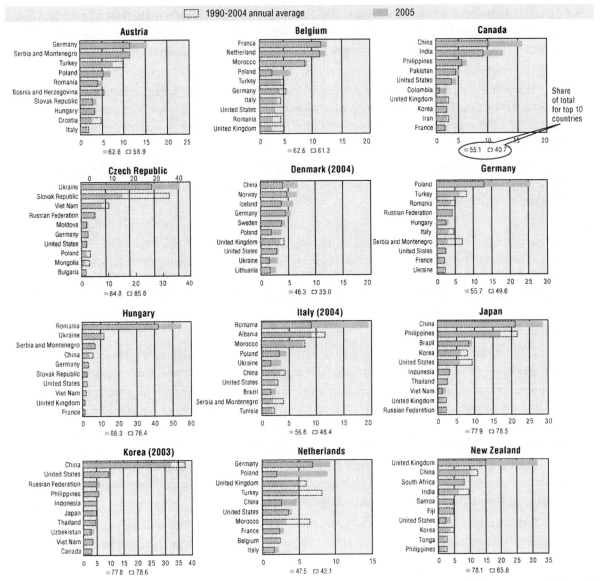

StatLink 〓〓 http://dx.doi.org/10.1787/015267228642

5. Recent trends in migration from new European Union members

Central and eastern Europe countries are traditional emigration countries and this characteristic was intensified by the inclusion of these countries in the European Union in May 2004. Ireland, Sweden and the United Kingdom, allowed workers from the new accession countries immediate access to their labour market and in the summer of 2006, Greece, Portugal, Finland and Spain also decided to open their labour market to the ten accession countries (see Section I.C on Migration Policies).

Ireland showed an increase of 50% in entries of foreign nationals, which reached 51 000 persons in 2005. This was largely attributable to citizens from the new EU10[8]

INTERNATIONAL MIGRATION OUTLOOK: SOPEMI 2007 EDITION – ISBN 978-92-64-03285-9 – © OECD 2007

Chart I.6. **Inflows of migrants by country of origin, selected OECD countries, 1990-2004 and 2005** (cont.)

2005 top ten countries of origin as percentage of total inflows

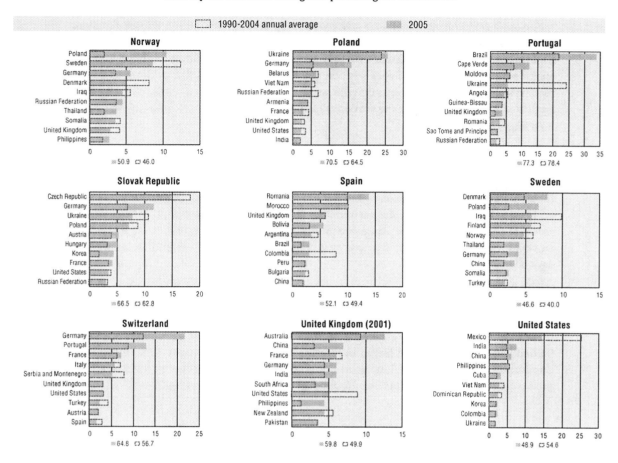

Note: The top 10 source countries are presented in decreasing order of the number of immigrants in 2005. Data for Canada, New Zealand and the United States refer to inflows of permanent settlers by country of birth, for Italy and Portugal to issues of certain types of permits. For the United Kingdom, the data are from the International Passenger Survey. For all other countries, figures are from Population registers or Registers of foreigners. The figures for the Netherlands, Norway and especially Germany include substantial numbers of asylum seekers. Annual average flows for the period 1990-2004 except for Austria, Poland, Spain (1998-2005), Italy (1998-2002), Portugal (2001-2004), the Slovak Republic (2003-2004), the United Kingdom (1990-2000) and Korea (2000-2002).

Sources: National Statistical Offices. For details on definitions and sources, refer to the metadata relative to Tables B.1.1. of the Statistical Annex.

StatLink ᴍ╔╗ *http://dx.doi.org/10.1787/015267228642*

countries (26 400 persons, of which most of were Polish citizens). The United Kingdom is the country which has seen the largest increase in movements (see Box I.2).

Among the Nordic countries, Sweden showed a large increase in new EU8 country arrivals. In 2005, inflows from these countries increased by almost 30% compared to the previous year and rose further while remaining modest at 8 900 persons in 2006 (of which three quarters were Polish citizens).

Between 2004 and 2005, Norway showed an increase of 80% in inflows of EU8 citizens to 4 700 persons and Iceland granted 2 800 works permits to EU8 citizens. Note that these movements do not include shorter-term movements, for example for seasonal work.

Polish citizens dominate in the flows, in particular in Iceland, Sweden and Norway, whereas in Finland the main origin country is Estonia. Denmark has approximately equal

Box I.2. **United Kingdom: Who are the new immigrants from the A8 countries?**

Nationals from A8 countries who wish to take up employment in the United Kingdom for a period of at least a month are generally required to register with the *Worker Registration Scheme*. Workers who are self-employed do not need to register and are therefore not included in *Worker Registration Scheme* data. In addition, there is no de-registration requirement, so people who work for a short time and then return to their country would be counted in the statistics in the same way as people who intend to stay on a long-term basis.

According to the *Worker Registration Scheme* data, most of the nationals from A8 countries came to the United Kingdom to work for more than 16 hours a week and the vast majority of workers were young people (82% aged between 18 and 34 years old). Men accounted for nearly 60% of the workers. Most of them (94%) stated that they had no dependents living with them in the United Kingdom when they registered. Nationals from the A8 countries came to work in the United Kingdom mainly as process operatives (that is, factory workers), warehouse operatives, packers, kitchen or catering assistants, as well as agricultural workers.

The Table shows the number of applicants approved (including dependents) by nationality since the enlargement on the European Union as well as the cumulative inflows since enlargement as a percentage of the population of the origin country. In 2006, more than 70% of A8 emigrants came from Poland. However, inflows from Lithuania to the United Kingdom were much larger in relative terms and represented 1.7% of the total population of Lithuania (and an even larger share of its labour force). This is a high proportion, especially since it is heavily concentrated among the young.

Immigration from the new EU accession countries to the United Kingdom
Nationality of approved applicants

	2004	2005	2006	Cumulative inflows as a percentage of the origin population (%)
Czech Republic	8 255	10 570	8 185	0.26
Estonia	1 860	2 560	1 460	0.44
Hungary	3 620	6 355	6 950	0.17
Latvia	8 670	12 960	9 380	1.35
Lithuania	19 270	22 985	16 810	1.74
Poland	71 025	127 320	159 855	0.94
Slovak Republic	13 020	22 035	21 370	1.05
Slovenia	160	170	180	0.03
Total	**125 880**	**204 955**	**224 195**	**0.76**

Note: Data refer to approved applicants rather than the total number of applications made. The figures refer to initial applications only (not multiple applications, *i.e.* an individual doing more than one job simultaneously, or re-registrations, *i.e.* cases in which an individual has changed employers). Data for 2004 refer to the period of May to December.
Source: Home Office, Accession and monitoring report, May 2004-December 2006.

StatLink [image] *http://dx.doi.org/10.1787/022338417860*

numbers of arrivals from the Baltic countries and from Poland. As in other European countries, these new EU member country migrants are mainly workers.

Chart I.7 shows inflows from the 8 new EU members of the European Union into OECD countries for which data were available. In order to better show data for other countries, Poland is presented on the right scale.

Chart I.7. **Migration from new EU member countries to selected OECD countries, 1998-2005**

Thousands

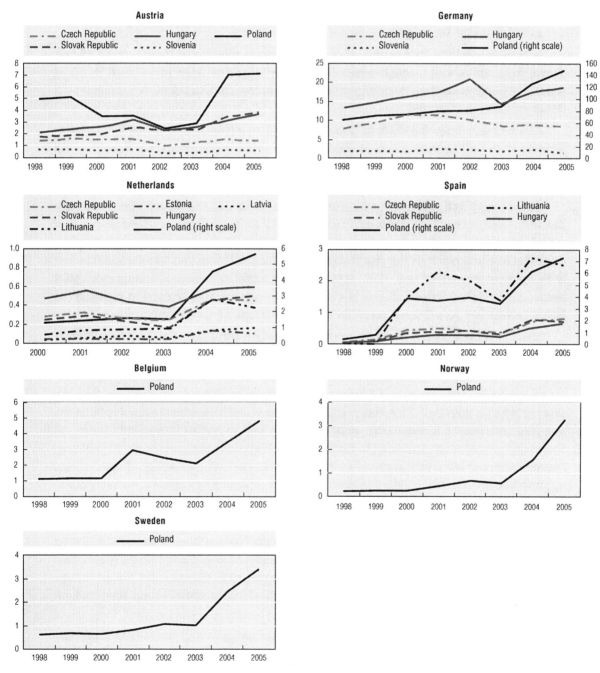

Sources: National Statistical Offices. For details on definitions and sources, refer to the metadata relative to Tables B.1.1. of the Statistical Annex.

StatLink ▮▮▮ http://dx.doi.org/10.1787/015140410036

These flows also include significant number of persons coming for short periods and returning thereafter to their countries of origin. In Austria for example, of permits granted to EU8 nationals in 2004, about 87% were issued for less than 6 months, and a similar situation was observed in 2005. In Italy 71% of the authorisations for work permits for A8 citizens were given to seasonal workers in 2005, proportions similar to those in France.

The increase in inflows from new EU members countries concerns not only countries which allowed them free access to their labour market but also other countries as well, among them Belgium, Norway, the Netherlands and Germany.

6. Indian and Chinese immigrants in OECD countries

At the time of the 2000 round of censuses, about 2 million migrants (aged 15 and above) from China and a roughly equal number of migrants from India lived in OECD countries. Immigrants from these two countries accounted for about 5.5% of immigrants in OECD countries at that time.

Chart I.8 illustrates the share of Chinese and Indian citizens in the stock of foreigners (blue bars) as well as their share in total inflows in 2005 (pink diamond). Note that the relative frequency of Chinese and Indians is higher in the flows than in the stocks of most OECD countries. This illustrates the recent increasing migration from these two countries.

In the traditional settlement countries (Canada, Australia, the United States and New Zealand), immigration from China and India accounts for a significant and growing part of overall immigration. In Canada, China and India have been by far the most important origin countries of immigration in the past decade. In the United States and Australia, China and India are now the second and third most important origin countries of immigration (after Mexico in the United States and after the United Kingdom and New Zealand in Australia). In Japan, immigrants from China account for almost one-fourth of new arrivals.

Despite some increase in recent years, immigration from China and India to Europe still accounts for a relatively small part of overall immigration into the region, except for the United Kingdom where strong historical links exist.

A particular characteristic of Chinese and Indian immigrants is the fact that they are relatively highly educated. This is especially the case of Indians, who are among the most qualified immigrants in the OECD, with more than half of Indian immigrants having at least tertiary education (according to the *OECD Database on the Foreign-born and Expatriates*). For example in the United Kingdom in 2005, India was the first nationality of applications approved among the *Highly Skilled Migrant Programme,* followed by Pakistan, and accounted for 40% of all approvals (with 6 716 persons). In Australia, Chinese and Indians accounted for about 30% of the General Skilled Migration Programme in 2005.

Chinese and Indians also account for an important part of foreign students studying abroad. China is the top origin country of foreign students in OECD countries (more than 15%). India is the second most important origin country (6%). Chinese and Indian foreign students are particularly present in Australia, the United States, Japan, Korea, New Zealand and the United Kingdom.

There are also significant populations of Indian emigrants in non-OECD countries, notably in the Persian Gulf region. The same is true for the Chinese, most recently in some African countries, accompanying the important flows of investment funds and the execution of large infrastructure projects. The new airport in Algiers, for example, was built by Chinese contractors.

Chart I.8. **Indian and Chinese immigrants in selected OECD countries in 2005**
Percentage of stock of foreigners and percentage of total inflows of foreigners

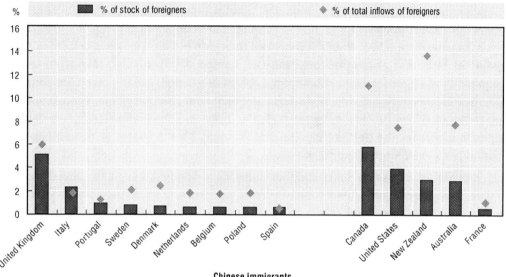

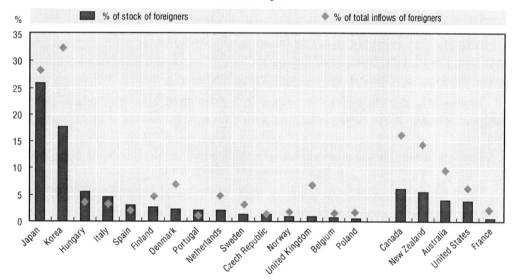

Note: Data refer to the foreign-born population for Australia, Canada (2001), France (1999), New Zealand (2001) and United States. Data refer to the year 2001 for United Kingdom, 2002 for Poland, 2003 for Korea, and 2004 for Denmark and Italy.

Source: OECD database on International Migration.

StatLink ⟨⟩ http://dx.doi.org/10.1787/015168874183

7. Africa and international migration

African migration to developed countries is marginal in relation to overall flows. Movements from sub-Saharan Africa are mostly intra-regional in character. The West African region is one of high mobility particularly, as exemplified by movements from Guinea to Senegal, from Ghana and Niger to Nigeria, and from Burkina and Mali to Côte d'Ivoire (these latter movements have slowed recently due to the political crisis in Côte d'Ivoire). Some countries such as Senegal or Mauritania are becoming transit regions for migration towards Europe or America. The transit migrants are mainly workers, refugees and persons displaced by conflicts or climatic crises. By contrast with West Africa, migration toward developed countries is more significant in North Africa than are intraregional movements.

Recent African migration flows towards OECD countries

Migration from Africa to OECD countries concerns mostly European countries due to historical links and geographic proximity. In Europe, North African migration is more frequent than migration from sub-Saharan Africa in general. Among countries for which African inflows are significant, flows from Maghreb countries are higher than those from sub-Saharan Africa in France, Belgium, Spain, Italy and the Netherlands, whereas the opposite is true for the United Kingdom and Portugal. This is related to movements from former British and Portuguese colonies.

Traditional migration flows such as those from Senegal, Mali and Côte d'Ivoire to France, from Nigeria and Ghana to the United Kingdom, and from Angola and Cape Verde to Portugal have remained stable in recent years. Destination countries for African migration have begun to diversify, however, and southern European countries have become an attractive destination as a result of their geographical location and employment opportunities. Thus flows from Senegal and Nigeria to Spain increased on average by about 25 and 15% per year, respectively for the past five years to reach 5 700 and 5 300 persons in 2005. To a lesser extent migration from Senegal increased in Italy as well.

Africans also emigrate to North America, especially those from English-speaking countries like Nigeria, Ghana and Kenya. In United States, the number of persons from Africa obtaining legal permanent resident status increased by 30% in 2005 to reach 85 000.

Among Maghreb countries, Morocco is by far the most important origin country in Europe, especially in Spain where inflows have increased for several years to reach 70 000

Chart I.9. Share of immigrants born in Africa in the foreign-born population in OECD countries, Circa 2000

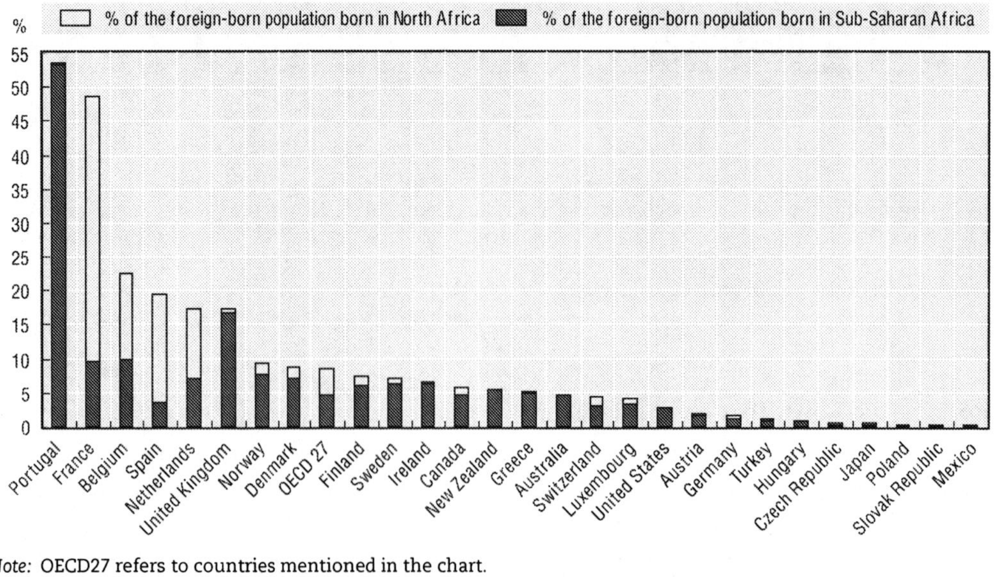

Note: OECD27 refers to countries mentioned in the chart.

Source: OECD database on Foreign-born and Expatriates; for more information, please refer to *www.oecd.org/els/ migration/censusdatabase.*

StatLink 🔗 http://dx.doi.org/10.1787/015186845138

in 2005. Stable levels are observed in France, Belgium and Germany for 2005 whereas the Netherlands shows a significant decrease of 50% in flows from Morocco in 2005 compared to levels observed at the beginning of the century.

Among a total inflow of 297 700 asylum seekers in OECD countries in 2005, 23% came from an African country, France and the United Kingdom being the main destinations. From Africa the first origin country of asylum seekers is the Democratic Republic of the Congo which totalised 4 400 requests in France and the United Kingdom, followed by Somalia in the United Kingdom and the Netherlands, which accounted for 3 400 requests.

Chart I.9 based on census population data illustrates the share of immigrants born from Africa in OECD countries as well as the breakdown between North African and Sub-Saharan countries. Africa accounts for a relatively small part of the total foreign-born population in OECD countries (9% for the 27 countries shown in the chart) with significant variation across countries, from as high as 54% of the foreign-born in Portugal to 0.2% in Mexico. Among the 7 millions immigrants born in Africa and living in OECD countries nearly half are from North Africa and reside essentially in France, Belgium, Spain and the Netherlands.

8. Unauthorised immigration

As noted above, the standardized statistics presented only cover legal migration, which strongly underestimates the total level of immigration for some countries, in particular the United States and southern Europe. For most other countries, it is difficult to assess the impact of the omission of unauthorised immigrants on the statistics. Certainly, in Australia and Japan, where there exist reliable estimates of the total unauthorised population,[9] the stock of irregular immigrants is relatively small. In Australia, the stock of unauthorised immigrants stands at less than one third of the annual inflows of permanent-type immigration. In Japan, the stock of unauthorised overstayers has been declining in recent years and at end-2005 amounted to 194 000, somewhat more than twice the number of legal permanent-type inflows. Expulsions of unauthorised immigrants in 2005 were some 57 000 which, with the decline in the stock of about 14 000, suggests a level of unauthorised (overstay) immigration for 2005 of approximately 43 000, a level approximately half that of permanent-type immigration.

In Europe, information on the level of unauthorised immigration is spotty, but semi-official estimates suggest cumulative numbers in the vicinity of about 1% of the domestic population or less in a number of countries (see the 2006 edition of this publication for estimates for the Netherlands and Switzerland). The levels would appear to be increasing, but they remain largely under those observed in southern Europe and in particular the United States in recent years, where almost 4% of the total population consists of unauthorised immigrants.

Although illegal entry, whether in overcrowded boats making their way to a landing point or across land borders at night with the aid of paid "smugglers", tends to attract the most media attention, this is not the only form of unauthorised immigration and indeed may not even be the most common one. Fraudulent entry with falsified documents is another means. But perhaps the most common form in many countries may be legal entry, whether as an asylum seeker, tourist or family visitor, followed by overstaying beyond the allowed period specified by law or on the entry visa. Most cases of unauthorised migration in European countries appear to be of this type. Even for the United States, which has a long land border with Mexico, it has been estimated that more than one-third of unauthorised immigrants in January 2000 were overstayers (GAO, 2003).[10] In Spain, for the most recent regularisation, almost 40% of applicants were from Latin America, who clearly entered Spain either directly by air or by various other means after entering another Schengen country. Many other entries from other parts of the world were likely of the same type. In Italy, in 2005, unauthorised immigrants apprehended were 60% overstayers, 25% persons having entered fraudulently (with false documents) and 14% sea landings in southern Italy. Corresponding percentages based on data from the 2002 regularisation were 75, 15 and 10%, respectively (MDI, 2006).

Indeed OECD countries generally issue visas and allow entry to persons from any country satisfying a number of conditions, in particular they must have a round-trip ticket and a plausible reason for visiting the country, they can demonstrate means of support during their stay and in some cases, they can supply the name and address of someone they are visiting. Opportunities for legal entry by means of a visa are significant. Italy, for example, granted almost 1.1 million entry visas in 2005. Some of these were for reasons of settlement, such as family reunification, adoption or some labour migrants, but over half a million were for tourism, almost 139 000 for business and 46 000 for study (MAE, 2006). In France, there were over 1.9 million short-term visas granted in 2005, of which about 1.3 million were for visits (tourism and family) to France, 500 000 for professional (business) reasons and 77 000 for study (HCI, 2007). France and Italy are fairly typical among OECD countries in this respect in granting significant numbers of visas for short-term stays unrelated to work.

Asylum seeking, whether legitimate or not, also provides possibilities for entry and stay because under the Geneva Convention, the dossier of the asylum seeker must be examined on the soil of the country where the asylum request is made, a process which in some cases takes many months and where a negative decision can be appealed, prolonging the stay even further. With high refusal rates and often long delays in the consideration of requests, the possibilities for possible employer/job seeker matching are heightened.

Because of the numerous possibilities for legal entry and overstay, what distinguishes countries with high levels of unauthorised migration from countries where the levels appear to be more limited may thus be less the efficacy of border control measures[11] or of strong repatriation measures for identified unauthorised immigrants or asylum seekers who are turned down than a more limited availability of jobs for potential immigrants or of employers willing and/or able to hire an immigrant without a work or residence permit (See Box I.3). The prospect of a regularisation downstream is a likely drawing card as well, but the holding of a job has generally been a precondition for an unauthorised immigrant to be regularised. Indeed it is characteristic of countries which have had high levels of unauthorised migration that employment growth has been high and employment rates of immigrants have tended to be higher than those of the native-born. This is true in all countries of southern Europe and in the United States. In addition, southern European countries are also among those generally considered to have large underground economies and the United States to have a growing one (OECD, 2004).

Whatever the merits of regularisations, which have been common in southern Europe, the process itself does allow the movements due to unauthorised entry or overstay to enter the immigration statistics and thus to provide some idea of the scale of movements. The Spanish regularisation procedure of 2005, for example, elicited some 692 000 applications,

---

Box I.3. **Recruitment of workers from abroad**

Not all countries or enterprises are faced with the same recruitment problems with respect to immigrant workers. For highly skilled jobs, employers and potential employees have rarely had difficulties "finding" each other across borders, at least for jobs in the international labour market. In these days of Internet job search and advertisement, this is likely to become even more common. Multinational enterprises which often have English as a working language and OECD countries for whose language there is a significant basin of language speakers outside the national borders (essentially French, English and Spanish) have a readily available supply of potential workers on which to draw.

For other countries, in particular those with languages hardly spoken outside their national borders, the situation is not quite so obvious, because the recruitment of workers directly into employment is not possible for jobs which require a certain minimum command of the language. This is generally the case for highly skilled jobs. In this situation, without prior knowledge of the host-country language, it may take a potential worker several years before acquiring sufficient proficiency in that language to work at a productive level. Thus, there may be some room for the national administration to become involved in immigrant recruitment of and language teaching for highly skilled immigrant workers.

Although native language proficiency may be less of an issue for lower skilled employment, recruitment may be more difficult, because the means whereby employers and potential employees can "meet" to "negotiate" are less obvious. In the "guest worker" era of the sixties and early seventies recruitment was often done directly in origin countries by agents or government intermediaries but also by means of "tourist" migration and on-site hiring in the host country, with the hiring being subsequently regularised. It is perhaps not entirely a coincidence that migration into southern Europe in recent years has been both low-skilled in nature and unauthorised. The high proportion of overstayers in the countries of southern Europe suggests that employers are resorting to informal means once again, in the ostensible absence of recruitment and work permit systems that operate efficiently across borders. Over time, one might expect such recourse to decline, at least in part, as employers use immigrant employees as a conduit for further recruitment.

---

which, given that the previous regularisation occurred in 2001 and under the assumption that all applicants had entered since then, suggests unauthorised immigration on the order of 175 000 per year. This amounts to about 0.4% of the Spanish population per year, which is higher than legal migration levels for many OECD countries.

9. Permanent settlement

Although the migration flows considered above have been labelled "permanent-type" and tend to exclude shorter term movement such as those of students, trainees, seasonal workers, etc., how many of these permanent inflows eventually turn into long-term settlement and how many leave, either returning to their home countries or migrating to other countries? Direct measures of this tend to be relatively scarce, but some exist. For the United States, it has been estimated that 30% of immigrants who arrived between 1900 and 1980 eventually left the United States (Warren and Kraly, 1985). In Norway as in other countries with central population registers, the movements of immigrants can be tracked over time. For Norway, the per cent of persons who immigrated to Norway over the period 1990 to 2005 and who were still there in January 2006 was 72%.[12] The directly measured

Norwegian figures are also available by category of entry. For international students, the stay rate for those who arrived before the year 2000 is about 18%, for labour migrants about 30% and for family migrants about 80%. Although students are not considered permanent-type immigrants in the standardised statistics presented in this chapter, they are generally registered in the Norwegian population register, because the entry criterion for registration is the intention to stay in Norway for at least six months.[13]

For countries with low unauthorized immigration levels, it is possible to obtain a residual estimate of departures of immigrants by subtracting from the net change in the number of foreign-born persons between two consecutive censuses (assumed to have the same rate of undercoverage), the number of entries of permanent-type immigrants in the intervening period less the number of deaths to immigrants.[14] This yields an estimate of the number of outflows of permanent-type immigrants over the period. Although the number of entries of which these departures are a fraction cannot be precisely determined, the departures over the period can be compared to permanent entries over the same period and the ratio of departures to entries estimated. This has been carried out for a number of OECD countries and the results appear in Table I.3. The estimates obtained are not fully comparable because the inflows used are not on a standardised basis for all countries (time-series of standardised inflow data do not yet exist). Consequently national inflow series were used. For Australia and Canada, data cover flows of persons receiving the right of permanent residence (plus New Zealand settler arrivals in the case of Australia). For other countries, the statistics count as immigrants persons entering who intend to stay or actually stay one-year in the host country, except for Norway for which the duration threshold is six months (see Statistical Annex of this publication for details of the definitions). With the exception of Norway, included here in order to compare results with the directly measured proportions of immigrants staying on cited above, the estimates have been restricted to countries having at least a one-year immigration criterion. Clearly, countries which count even short-term entries in their immigration numbers would show high departure rates. They have not been included here.

For the countries considered (see Table I.3), the ratio of outflows to inflows for the foreign-born population in the 1990s was less than 0.45, except for Switzerland, which at 0.68 is an outlier. The foreign-born population in Switzerland, however, is largely European

Table I.3. **Estimated ratio of outflows to inflows of the foreign-born population, 1990s**

Selected OECD countries

	Inflows	Estimated outflows	Ratio outflows to inflows
	Thousands		Per cent
Australia	1 160	260	22
Canada	2 230	670	30
Denmark	210	80	37
Norway	220	90	42
Sweden	420	140	33
Switzerland	890	610	68
United Kingdom	2 630	1 140	44

Note: Inflows are those of permanent residents in the case of Australia and Canada, of persons with an expected stay of one year in Sweden and the United Kingdom, of persons with one-year actual stay in Denmark, of six-months expected stay in Norway and of holders of permits of at least one year in Switzerland. In all cases, these correspond to the official national definitions of "immigrants".

StatLink ⟶ http://dx.doi.org/10.1787/022457626371

in origin and almost 60% of it comes from the European Union, almost one third of it from neighbouring countries. It would appear that many immigrants do not come to Switzerland to settle indefinitely.

In the Nordic countries and the United Kingdom, there are 33 to 44 foreign-born persons leaving for every 100 persons arriving, depending on the country, while in Canada and Australia, there are 30 and 22, respectively. Unlike Australia and Canada, however, both the Nordic countries and the United Kingdom count international students and other migrants coming for temporary stays as immigrants, which explains in part (and perhaps entirely) the higher departure rates observed for these countries.

These results are instructive in a number of other respects. First of all, they indicate that even apparently longer term migration movements are dynamic. Just as temporary migrants are sometimes accorded the right to modify their situation and to become permanent-type immigrants (see below, "Changes in status"), so also do permanent-type immigrants, even those that receive the right of permanent residence upon entry as in Australia and Canada, may not always have permanent-stay intentions or may change their minds about these following their arrival. Secondly, they suggest that the nature of the permit system appears to have little impact on eventual settlement. European countries tend to grant temporary permits upon arrival, even to those who are arriving for the long term, such as family reunification immigrants. These permits are generally renewed and, over time, are converted to longer term or permanent residence permits. Any uncertainty associated with this gradual approach to permanent status does not seem to effect the magnitude of settlement outcomes. Proportionally as many immigrants appear to stay on as in countries such as Australia and Canada which grant the right of permanent residence upon entry.

10. Temporary workers

Temporary worker migration covers an extremely broad array of different movements, conditions and durations, varying from *au pairs*, seasonal workers, trainees, intra-corporate transfers, contract workers, working holiday makers, exchange visitors, highly skilled professionals, cross-border service providers, installers, performing artists and sportspersons, etc. The statistics shown in Table I.4 do not cover all of these because the statistics are not always available. In addition, there are forms of temporary movements, for example international study, in which work is carried as an incidental part of the stay in the host country. For the categories shown in Table I.4, the increase in movements was about 7% from 2003 and 2004. If one restricts oneself to those categories and countries for which there are corresponding data for 2004 and 2005, the levels seem to have remained broadly unchanged in 2005, with entries standing at about 1.8 million workers.

However, this does not count the large movements associated with the new EU accession countries as well as the coming into force of the free circulation agreement between the European Union and Switzerland, which led to considerable influxes into Switzerland of EU nationals, for both long and shorter term jobs.

Generally, it is the case that countries with high permanent-type migration levels also tend to show high inflows of temporary workers, with some exceptions. The most obvious one is Germany, which has limited permanent-type labour immigrants, except for those under free circulation, but high temporary worker movements, in particular of seasonal and contract workers, essentially from Poland.

Table I.4. **Entries of temporary workers in selected OECD countries by principal categories, 2003-2005**

Thousands

	Trainees			Working holiday makers			Seasonal workers			Intra-company transfers			Other temporary workers		
	2003	2004	2005	2003	2004	2005	2003	2004	2005	2003	2004	2005	2003	2004	2005
Australia	6.9	7.0	7.0	88.8	93.8	104.4	..	..	..	..	..	..	56.1	58.6	71.6
Austria	1.7	0.8	..	..	..	..	17.4	15.7	..	0.2	0.2	..	10.5	9.8	..
Belgium	..	..	..	..	..	..	0.4	1.0	2.7	..	..	..	1.2	0.5	2.8
Canada	..	..	..	..	..	..	18.7	19.0	20.3	3.8	4.2	4.5	52.1	55.8	..
Denmark	1.4	1.5	1.9	..	..	..	..	..	..	..	..	..	3.6	3.4	2.6
France	1.0	0.5	0.4	..	..	..	14.6	15.7	16.2	..	..	..	10.2	10.0	10.5
Germany	2.3	2.3	..	..	..	..	309.5	324.0	320.4	2.1	2.3		43.9	34.2	21.9
Italy	..	..	..	0.1	0.3	0.4	68.0	77.0	70.2	..	..	..	..	..	..
Japan	64.8	75.4	83.3	..	..	..	..	..	..	3.4	3.6	4.2	143.7	146.6	110.2
Korea	58.8	46.7	51.6	..	..	..	..	..	..	7.8	8.5	8.4	7.2	8.3	11.9
Netherlands	..	..	..	..	..	..	..	..	..	..	..	..	38.0	44.1	46.1
New Zealand	2.0	2.4	1.8	20.7	21.4	29.0	..	..	2.9	..	..	..	40.3	43.7	44.3
Norway	0.5	0.5	0.3	..	..	..	17.9	25.4	20.9	..	..	..	2.5	2.1	1.1
Sweden	..	..	..	..	..	..	7.3	4.9	5.9	..	..	..	2.6	3.4	2.2
Switzerland	0.4	0.4	0.3	..	..	..	–	–	–	14.4	7.5	1.8	..	..	..
United Kingdom	..	..	..	46.5	62.4	56.6	..	19.8	15.7	..	..	..	98.0	113.4	111.2
United States	1.4	1.4	1.8	..	..	..	29.9	31.8	31.9	57.2	62.7	65.5	192.5	221.8	218.6

Note: The categories of temporary workers may differ from one country to another. Only the principal categories of temporary workers are presented in this table. Data on temporary workers generally do not cover workers who benefit from a free circulation agreement.

Sources: Residence or work permit data.

StatLink ᴍ⬚ *http://dx.doi.org/10.1787/022474603552*

More frequently, however, one sees high temporary movements in countries such as Australia, Canada, New Zealand, Switzerland and the United Kingdom which are high permanent migration countries. Indeed, as will be seen below, temporary worker migration is often a springboard into permanent migration in these countries. Although the numbers are not fully shown here, Japan and Korea have been high temporary worker migration countries, at least relative to the very low levels of permanent-type migration in these countries. Often this has taken the form of "traineeships", which more often than not have been a disguised form of lesser skilled migration. Entries of trainees into Japan, for example, have increased from 59 to 83 000 since 2001 and growing numbers of them are staying on for further employment after their traineeship ends (32 000 in 2005). Korea has recently introduced an explicit work permit regime, however, and temporary worker movements are increasingly being channelled into this regime. Some 60 000 foreign workers entered Korea under the employment permit scheme in 2005, while traineeships continued at the level of about 52 000.

The United States has always had a significant temporary worker system, to respond to temporary labour needs that can with difficulty be met through the largely family-based "green card" system. Indeed, certain categories such as the H1Bs, which provide for stays of up to six years, are almost an automatic channel into permanent migration as well as an entry point for highly qualified international students who stay on after the end of their studies.

The United Kingdom is scaling back its lower skilled seasonal agricultural worker and sector-based schemes, as most labour needs formerly met through these are now being filled by means of workers from the new accession states of the European Union.

INTERNATIONAL MIGRATION OUTLOOK: SOPEMI 2007 EDITION – ISBN 978-92-64-03285-9 – © OECD 2007

11. International students

It is difficult to get a clear picture of the evolution of international students in OECD countries, essentially because the data suffer from coverage problems. Historically, the data that have been most often supplied to the OECD cover foreign students, which can include students of foreign nationality who are permanently resident in the country as well as foreign students coming to the country to study. It is the latter that is the population of interest and for some countries data are only beginning to be supplied according to definitions that reasonably approximate this population. International students as shown in Table I.5 for countries for which statistics are shown, are defined as either non-resident students or as students who obtained their prior education in another country. Both cases do not exclude situations in which non-resident nationals return to their country of citizenship for study, but the numbers in this group are likely to be small.[15]

Table I.5. **International and/or foreign students in tertiary education, 2000 and 2004**

	International students as a percentage of tertiary enrolment in 2004		Foreign students as a percentage of tertiary enrolment in 2004		Index of change in the number of foreign students, total tertiary (2000 = 100)	Number of foreign students 2004
	Total tertiary	Advanced research programmes	Total tertiary	Advanced research programmes		
New Zealand	n.a.	n.a.	28.3	36.6	456	68 900
Australia[1]	16.6	17.8	19.9	26.4	158	167 000
Switzerland[3]	12.7	42.5	18.2	42.4	137	35 700
United Kingdom[1]	13.4	38.6	16.2	40.3	135	300 100
Austria[1]	11.3	16.8	14.1	21.3	111	33 700
Germany	n.a.	n.a.	11.2	n.a.	139	260 300
France	n.a.	n.a.	11.0	33.9	173	237 600
Canada[1,2]	8.8	23.3	10.6	34.1	116	133 000
Belgium[1]	6.0	20.0	9.6	31.3	114	44 300
Sweden[1]	4.0	4.5	8.5	19.9	143	36 500
Denmark[1]	4.6	7.0	7.9	20.4	133	17 200
Czech Republic	n.a.	n.a.	4.7	7.1	262	14 900
Norway[1]	1.7	3.5	4.5	18.2	142	12 400
Portugal	n.a.	n.a.	4.1	7.8	145	16 200
Netherlands[3]	4.8	n.a.	3.9	n.a.	152	21 300
United States[1]	3.4	n.a.	3.4	n.a.	120	572 500
Iceland	n.a.	n.a.	3.3	13.7	121	500
Hungary[1]	2.8	6.9	3.1	7.4	130	12 900
Japan[1]	2.7	n.a.	2.9	n.a.	177	117 900
Finland[3]	3.4	7.0	2.6	7.0	142	7 900
Greece	n.a.	n.a.	2.4	n.a.	167	14 400
Spain[1]	0.8	5.5	2.3	17.5	164	41 700
Italy	n.a.	n.a.	2.0	3.6	163	40 600
Slovak Republic	n.a.	n.a.	1.0	1.2	104	1 600
Turkey	n.a.	n.a.	0.8	n.a.	87	15 300
Poland	n.a.	n.a.	0.4	n.a.	133	8 100
Korea	n.a.	n.a.	0.3	n.a.	320	10 800
Ireland[3]	6.7	n.a.	n.a.	n.a.	171	12 700
OECD	**6.5**	**16.1**	**7.3**	**19.5**	**141**	**2 255 900**

"n.a." means not available.

1. International students for these countries are students with a permanent residence in another country.
2. Year of reference 2002.
3. International students for these countries are students whose prior education was obtained in another country.
Source: Education at a glance, OECD, 2006. See Annex 3 at www.oecd.org/edu/eag2006.

StatLink ᴧᴦᴤᴘ *http://dx.doi.org/10.1787/022522616558*

Generally international students account for at least three quarters of foreign students, with lower percentages in the Nordic countries and in Spain. The trend in foreign students can be expected to reflect in general that which would be observed for international students, were the data available.

The number of foreign students in OECD countries has increased by more than 40% since 2000, with especially large increases in New Zealand, the Czech Republic and Korea. Other countries which have seen large increases (in excess of 50%) include the countries of southern Europe, Ireland, Australia, France, the Netherlands and Japan. Turkey is the only country which has seen a decline, and relatively modest increases (in the vicinity of 10%) have been observed in Belgium, Canada and Austria.

The fields of study are rather broadly distributed, with social sciences, business and law accounting about one third of enrolments. Health fields, the sciences, humanities and the arts as well as engineering, manufacturing and construction each accounted for some 12-16% of all fields of study. International students are even more frequently enrolled in advanced research programmes than in regular university programmes. In Switzerland and the United Kingdom, almost 40% of persons in such programmes are international students and in Australia, Austria, Belgium and Canada it is between 15 and 25%.

China (close to 340 000 students), India (almost 125 000) and Korea (95 000) remain the principal source countries, with Germany, Japan, Morocco and France all clustered around 60 000 students each. The destination of the students tends to be heavily geographically oriented, with European students tending to stay in Europe and students from the rest of the world and Asia in particular tending to study in OECD countries outside of Europe, although clearly not absent from European universities. The only exceptions to this rule among the top 25 source countries are the United Kingdom and Brazil, which tend to send equivalent numbers of students to either zone.

The increase in the number of international students is likely a response to signals which many OECD countries have been sending in recent years concerning possibilities for work and residence following the completion of study. In the past, many countries had so-called "quarantine" provisions, which specified that students coming to OECD countries for study, in particular from developing countries, could only apply for residence or work a certain minimum number of years following the receipt of the degree or the diploma. The implication was that they should return to their countries of origin after graduation. These provisions were not completely effective, however, both because some students gained entry as spouses of citizens of the countries in which they studied and because the quarantine obviously did not apply to emigration to other countries than the country of study. Indeed, the latter was often facilitated by the fact that some programmes and courses were taught in a commonly used language, such as English, different from the national language and which facilitated migration to countries where this language was spoken. Partly as a result and because national migration policy is being formulated more and more in terms of national self-interest, many countries have or are abandoning such quarantine provisions to allow the migration of international students.

Japan, for example, for finishing international students, permits a passage into a residence status allowing work. Most of those who obtain a residence status do so as engineers (20%) or specialists in the humanities or international services (71%). As a percentage of the total number of international students, the number of international students who stay on has remained relatively steady over recent years at about 5%. As a percentage of finishing students, it is of course several times higher. In Australia, finishing student migrants numbered almost 20 600 in Australia in 2005, or about 11% of all international students for the 2005/2006 fiscal year. In Canada, former foreign students accepted as permanent residents accounted for a little under 6% of all foreign students. Almost one third of these were spouses of Canadian residents or citizens.[16] In Norway, the number of graduated students with new work or family permits remained steady throughout the 1990s, but as a percentage of all finishing students, declined from about 25 to close to 15% over the decade (Brekke, 2006). With the removal of the quarantine provision in 2001, the number of international students has risen strongly and the number of graduating students who stay on has begun to rise as well. Almost three quarters of those who stay on now do so on the basis of a work permit; ten years ago, it was for family reasons, that is, generally marriage.

12. Arrivals of asylum seekers

The number of asylum seekers continued to decline in OECD countries in 2005, falling by 15% overall and showing increases in excess of 5% only in the Netherlands, Greece and Korea. The 2005 level has almost halved relative to the number observed in the year 2000 and currently stands below 300 000 (see Table I.6). Recognition rates overall are in the vicinity of about 25% but vary considerably across countries from as low as a few percentage to over 50% in some countries. In practice, this means that asylum seeking has become a relatively minor source of immigrants in OECD countries. Since asylum seekers whose request is turned down do not always return to their home countries, it remains a source of unauthorised migration.

The falling figures reflect the more strict application of processing rules and the imposition of stricter visa requirements in many potential destination countries. In Europe, for example, under the Dublin Convention an asylum seeker can only make an asylum application in a single country, generally the first through which he/she has transited. The "safe-country-of-origin" rule also eliminates the possibilities of requests from countries that are considered to be "safe". Applications from citizens of such countries would normally be considered "manifestly unfounded".

Absolute levels of asylum requests were at about 50 000 in France, followed by Germany and the United Kingdom at close to about 30 000 each and Austria, Canada and the United States in the 20 000 to 25 000 range. However, relative to the population, it was Austria in particular that received the most requests at more than 2 700 per million persons in the population, a level comparable to permanent migration rates in countries such as France and Germany. Sweden, Belgium, Luxembourg and Switzerland also had relatively light rates of asylum seeking, at between 1 500 and 2 000 requests per million persons in the population. The Pacific rim countries of Australia, Japan, Korea and New Zealand attract few asylum seekers as is the case in Italy, Portugal and Spain, where unauthorised migration provides alternatives routes of entry and work for potential migrants. The exception in this regard is Greece which has seen a tripling of requests since the year 2000 and received more than 9 000 requests in 2005. Increases in requests for Greece were observed for many source countries, in particular Georgia and Pakistan and to a lesser extent Bangladesh.

Overall, the most important source countries for asylum requests were Serbia and Montenegro, the Russian Federation, China, Iraq, Turkey and Iran, all of which were the source of at least 10 000 requests for asylum and together accounted for almost a third of

Table I.6. **Inflows of asylum seekers in OECD countries, 2000-2005**

Trends and levels

	Index of the number of asylum seekers			Total number	Number per million population
	2000	2004	2005	2005	2005
Australia	100	25	25	3 200	158
Austria	100	135	123	22 500	2 728
Belgium	100	36	37	16 000	1 523
Canada	100	75	61	20 800	674
Czech Republic	100	62	47	4 200	407
Denmark	100	27	19	2 300	417
Finland	100	122	113	3 600	681
France	100	151	128	49 700	817
Germany	100	45	37	28 900	351
Greece	100	145	294	9 100	850
Hungary	100	21	21	1 600	160
Ireland	100	44	40	4 300	1 047
Italy	100	62	61	9 500	164
Japan	100	197	178	400	3
Korea	100	337	958	400	9
Luxembourg	100	254	129	800	1 763
Netherlands	100	22	28	12 300	757
New Zealand	100	37	22	300	85
Norway	100	73	50	5 400	1 168
Poland	100	176	149	6 900	180
Portugal	100	50	51	100	11
Slovak Republic	100	732	228	3 500	659
Spain	100	70	66	5 300	121
Sweden	100	142	108	17 500	1 941
Switzerland	100	81	57	10 100	1 349
Turkey	100	69	69	3 900	54
United Kingdom	100	41	31	30 800	512
United States	100	68	59	24 200	82
Total	**100**	**65**	**55**	**297 700**	**280**

Source: UNHCR database (*www.unhcr.org*).

StatLink 🔗 http://dx.doi.org/10.1787/022528358230

all requests. There is a certain continuity in source countries, with 11 out of the leading source countries already being in that situation in the year 2000. Among rising origin countries for asylum requests would appear to be the Russian Federation, Haiti and Colombia.

Most asylum requests (about 85%) are lodged with European countries, with the impact of geography being evident in the choice of destination. The top five source countries for European destination countries are all within Europe or in proximity (Serbia and Montenegro, Russian Federation, Iraq, Turkey, Iran). For OECD destination countries outside of Europe, Latin American and Caribbean countries, China and India figure among the more important source countries.

13. Changes in status

In all OECD countries, there are certain categories of immigrants who are admitted with the understanding or expectation that they will be returning to their countries of origin after the period or activity for which they have been admitted expires. Some obvious examples are seasonal workers, trainees, working holiday workers, international students as well as some categories of highly skilled workers. Often, however, there are possibilities for such persons to change their status before the end of their residence permits, in order to engage in a different activity in the host country, one which enables them to prolong their stay or even to make it permanent. The clearest example of this concerns persons in settlement countries (Australia, Canada, New Zealand, the United States) who enter the country on a temporary permit and apply for and are granted the right to permanent residence under the country's permanent migration regime.

Such situations are variously known as changes in status (France), adjustments (United States), transformations (Switzerland) or category jumping (Australia). Changes in status are easy to identify in the settlement countries because of the unambiguous distinction between the temporary and permanent migration regimes, with the latter granting residence permits of unlimited duration upon entry or acceptance as "permanent immigrants". Indeed, in Australia and Canada and in certain cases in the United States, immigrants in the past were not allowed to apply for the right of permanent residence while in the country on a temporary status. They were obliged to return to their country of origin or to a neighbouring country in order to file an application.

In many other countries, however, in particular the European countries, "permanent" permits are never granted upon entry, except perhaps to refugees resettled in the host country from overseas camps, and all entries into the country are on the basis of permits of limited duration, which can be as little as three months and as long as several years.

However, this clearly does not mean that in such countries all migration movements are considered to be temporary in the first instance. Every country distinguishes between, for example, movements of seasonal workers, on the one hand, and persons arriving for family reunification with a permanent resident, on the other. Both will be granted permits of limited duration upon or prior to entry, but in the former case, the permit will generally not be renewable or only renewable on a limited basis and the immigrants will generally not have the right to social benefits. For persons arriving on a "permanent track", however, the permit will generally be more or less indefinitely renewable, provided certain conditions are met, and the immigrant will generally benefit from many of the same social rights and benefits as established permanent residents. Over time, immigrants accumulate rights including eventually, the right to a longer term permit or even one of unlimited duration. Transitions from the temporary regime to the permanent one, however, may not be identified as such in the migration system, which concerns itself more with whether the conditions or criteria which must be met to change status are met, rather than whether or not an immigrant is formally recognised or not as a permanent resident as a result. Indeed in many cases, formal residency in the country is defined on the basis of enrolment in a population register, for which the entry criterion is an intended duration of stay (and the possession of a residence permit, if needed, in support of it), rather than any formal recognition by the host country of the permanent character of the stay. As a result, changes in status may not be specifically identifiable in the statistics, unless a historical record is kept of all permit changes.

There are certain forms of migration that automatically lead to status changes, provided they are accepted as legitimate by the host country. These are movements of asylum seekers, which are considered to be temporary in character, until such time as the request for asylum is recognised and the person is granted the right to stay in the country indefinitely. Regularisations are another example of a change in status of a particularly significant kind, from illegal to legal, although the regularisation may not necessarily confer the right to indefinite stay, either explicitly or implicitly.

In recent years, many OECD countries have provided opportunities for international students to stay on after the end of their studies to search for work during a specified period, for example six months. If a job is found during the period in an occupation deemed to be in shortage, the graduated student will be accorded a work or residence permit. Other examples include international students who marry residents or citizens of the host country and stay on after they have completed their degrees.

Table I.7 provides the prevalence of status changes to permanent-type family and worker migration in a number of OECD countries in 2005. It is evident that status changes of the kind described are relatively common in both categories of migration, especially in the United States and New Zealand. There are obvious advantages to this kind of migration, especially for family migration. Persons who are granted a permanent-type status have generally lived in the country for several years, speak the language and are familiar with societal customs and institutions. This should make for a more rapid integration and be associated with a less reliance on social transfers, to which permanent-type migrants generally have access.

Table I.7. **Changes in status from temporary to permanent in selected OECD countries, 2005**

Percent of immigrants in group having changed status

	Permanent migration category		
	Family	Employment	Both
Australia	25	33	30
Canada	23	11	15
Japan	n.a.	28	28
New Zealand	61	66	65
United Kingdom	n.a.	20	20
United States	52	89	62

Note: Data for Canada are for 2004. "n.a." means not available.
Changes in status for Australia and New Zealand correspond to "onshore" cases, in the United States to "adjustments of status", in Japan to changes from student to worker status at the end of studies and in the United Kingdom to "first permissions" as a percentage of the total of work permits, first permissions and highly skilled migrant programme admissions.
Sources: See Table I.1.

StatLink ᴍⳑ▄ http://dx.doi.org/10.1787/022540487052

Chart I.10 maps out the trends in changes in status in recent years for permanent-type worker migration. The data show that the changes in status for worker migrants are not a very recent phenomenon but have always been important in the United States, at least for the years shown on the chart. The temporary-to-permanent transition seems to be a normal one for employment migrants to the United States, who would appear to generally enter the country by means of a so-called "non-immigrant" visa, among which are the well-known H1B visas for high-skilled persons. This has also been a fairly common route in New Zealand, and has increased substantially since 2002, when extra points were given applicants for a relevant offer of employment or a New Zealand qualification. Changes in status in the skilled migrant stream have almost doubled in Australia since the year 2000, with most of the increase occurring from 2000 to 2001 when additional points were introduced for persons with an Australian qualification and international students were allowed to apply for immigration from within Australia.

Chart I.10. **Changes in status from temporary categories to permanent-type worker migration, selected OECD countries, 1996-2005**

Percentage of all permanent-type worker migration

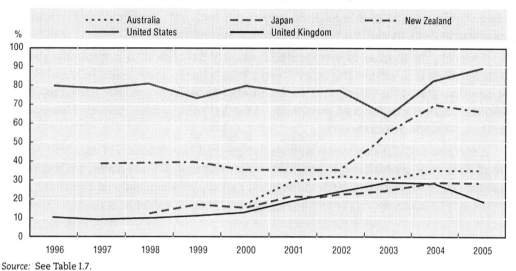

Source: See Table I.7.

StatLink 🔗 http://dx.doi.org/10.1787/014871247784

14. The immigrant population

With increasing immigration in recent years, it comes as no surprise that both the size and the relative frequency of the foreign-born population have increased in all OECD countries (see Chart I.11) since 1995. This is especially the case in the new migration countries of Italy,

Chart I.11. **Prevalence and evolution of the foreign-born population in OECD countries, 1995-2005**

Percentages

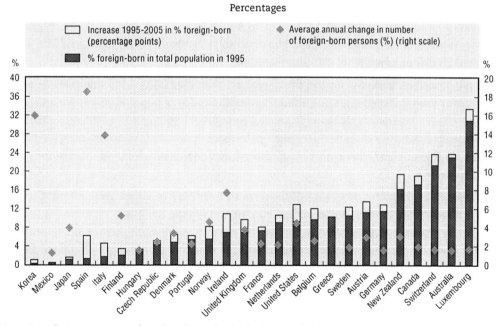

Notes: Data for Japan, Korea, Italy and Spain are for the foreign population. The earlier data year for Ireland and New Zealand is 1996, for Austria and the Czech Republic 1998 and for France 1999. The later data year for Germany is 2003.

Source: Please refer to the metadata for Table A.1.4 of the Statistical Annex.

StatLink 🔗 http://dx.doi.org/10.1787/015028624173

Spain, Norway, Denmark and Ireland. However large increases have also been observed in such traditional migration countries as the United States and New Zealand. Ireland has surpassed the United Kingdom as an immigration country over the past decade and France, which used to be a significant country of immigration, now finds itself with fewer immigrants in relative terms than Norway, Ireland, the United Kingdom and even Greece.

Generally, the number of immigrants in country has tended to increase the most in countries where their relative frequency was the lowest. Korea, Japan, Spain, Italy and Finland are cases in point. At the other end of the spectrum, relative increases have been small in the four countries with the highest prevalence of foreign-born persons, namely Luxembourg, Australia, Switzerland and Canada.

About half of OECD countries now have foreign-born populations that represent at least 10% of their total populations. If one adds in the offspring of immigrants, particularly in "mature" migration countries, such as Australia, Canada, New Zealand and Switzerland, the percentage of persons with an immigrant background almost doubles to reach percentages as high as 40% or more. In some countries such as Belgium, Germany and the Netherlands, the fertility rates of immigrant women have been higher than that of native-born women, so that the second generation represents even a higher proportion of their cohorts than does the parental generation.

15. Migration of the highly educated in perspective

The stock of immigrants as well as their characteristics for a particular country provide a snapshot of the accumulated impact of international migration, of arrivals, departures and mortality among persons in the foreign-born population over previous decades. International migration is not a static phenomenon, however. The conditions in origin countries may change, as may those in destination countries, so that the countries of origin, the choice of destination country, the reasons that motivated the migration and the cost/benefit trade-off of a movement may not necessarily be the same recently or currently as they were twenty or thirty years ago. Many countries that used to be largely source countries for migration movements are now receiving countries. The countries of southern Europe, Ireland and Korea are the most obvious example of this phenomenon.

In all countries, both within the OECD and outside the OECD area, there has been an increase over time in the educational attainment of the resident population. Notwithstanding this, most OECD countries expect to experience shortages of highly qualified immigrants in the near future, as their economies become more knowledge-based and manufacturing jobs move overseas. In this context, the evolution of the educational attainment of immigrants is of particular interest.

Chart I.12 depicts the percentage of persons with tertiary qualifications among persons having arrived within the past ten years (as observed in the year 2000) and those having arrived more than ten years ago, compared to that of the current native-born population as a whole. Note that these are not measures of actual arrivals of persons with these qualifications for the time periods shown, because some immigrants may have left the country in the interim.

The countries have been divided into two groups, those for which recent immigrants with a tertiary qualification are no more frequent in relative terms than those who arrived prior to the 1990s and those for which the percentage of recent immigrants with a tertiary qualification is significantly higher. The former group consists essentially of southern Europe, the Nordic countries with the exception of Sweden and Hungary, almost all of whose immigrants are

Chart I.12. **Percentage of immigrants and native-born persons aged 15 and above with a tertiary qualification, Circa 2000**

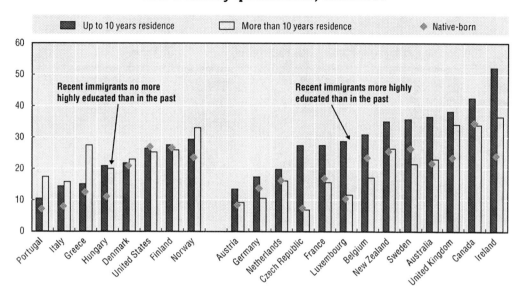

Source: OECD database on Foreign-born and Expatriates.

StatLink ᵐˢˢ *http://dx.doi.org/10.1787/015032154880*

persons of Hungarian origin, and the United States. Except for the United States, this group consists entirely of countries where immigration levels were relatively low until the 1990s.

The second group is composed of the older immigration countries, plus the Czech Republic (for which the Slovak portion of former Czechoslovakia was a source of immigrants in the past) and Ireland, whose booming economy during the nineties attracted immigration that was very highly qualified. The higher qualification level of immigrants arriving during the 1990s compared to the past was especially evident in Australia, Belgium, the Czech Republic, France, Ireland, Luxembourg and Sweden.

Generally, the education level of recent immigrants exceeds that of the native-born population as a whole, largely because of the difference in the age structure of the two populations. Immigrants are a younger group and therefore, all things being equal, will tend to be more highly educated than an older population. The educational level in origin countries and the extent to which emigration from source countries is selective can also influence the outcome.

There are a number of countries for which recent immigration is no more qualified that than that of the past, however, in particular Denmark, Finland and the United States. In the Czech Republic, Luxembourg and Ireland, by contrast, the percentage of recent immigrants with a tertiary qualification strongly exceeds the corresponding percentage for the native-born population.

The origin regions of highly qualified immigrants have changed significantly in the 1990s, compared to the past, but not in the same way in Europe and outside of Europe (see Chart I.13). The relative importance of Europe as a source of immigrants with tertiary qualifications increased strongly for European OECD countries in the 1990s, while the share of African immigrants with tertiary qualifications more than halved. The relative increase in European immigrants was accounted for by persons from central and eastern Europe (including the

Chart I.13. **Immigrants with a tertiary qualification in OECD countries by continent and duration of residence, Circa 2000**

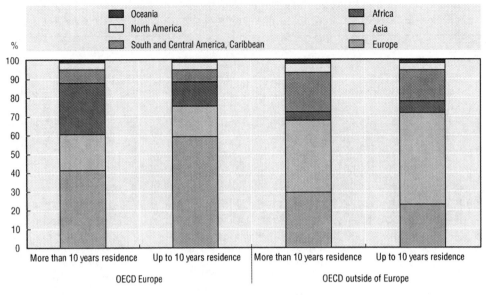

Source: OECD database on Foreign-born and Expatriates.

StatLink ⟨⟩ *http://dx.doi.org/10.1787/015131312336*

Russian Federation), although there was some increase as well in highly qualified migration from within the European Union itself. Migration from European countries accounted for over 60% of total migration of persons with tertiary qualifications in OECD Europe during the 1990s.

In OECD countries outside of Europe (Australia, Canada, New Zealand and the United States), the picture is different, with European migrants with tertiary qualifications declining in importance to between 20 and 25% of the total and the share of Asian immigrants increasing to almost 50%. In addition, the relative importance of immigrants from Latin America and the Caribbean has fallen. Migration from these areas, in particular from Mexico to the United States, has been strongly concentrated among lower educated persons.

B. *Immigrants and the Labour Market*

This section describes the situation of immigrants, *i.e.* persons of whatever nationality born abroad, on the labour market in OECD countries in 2004-2005. It is followed by a detailed analysis of the situation of young immigrants and the children of immigrants in relation to education and employment.

1. The situation of foreigners and immigrants in the labour market in OECD countries

There has been an improvement in labour market performance in the OECD area as a whole over the past decade: Unemployment has fallen while employment and activity rates have increased (see *OECD Employment Outlook, 2006*). The growth in employment – nearly 50 million more people in work over the period 1994-2004 – was slightly higher than the increase in the working-age population, with the result that the employment rate in the OECD area as a whole reached an all-time high (65.5% in 2005).

INTERNATIONAL MIGRATION OUTLOOK: SOPEMI 2007 EDITION – ISBN 978-92-64-03285-9 – © OECD 2007

More recently, economic growth in the OECD area has proved resilient in an environment characterised by geographical tensions, important current balance imbalances and high and volatile energy prices (OECD, 2006 *op. cit.*). In 2005, real GDP growth in the OECD area as a whole was 2.8% on average, slightly down on 2004 (3.3%). At the same time, employment continued to grow in 2005 at the moderate pace of 1.1%. Throughout the OECD area as a whole, the average unemployment rate was 6.5% in 2005, down 0.2% on the previous year.

Immigrants represent a large and growing share of the labour force...

In 2005, foreigners and immigrants accounted for an often large, though variable, proportion of the labour force in OECD countries (see Table I.8). While in Korea, Japan and

Table I.8. **Foreign or foreign-born labour force in selected OECD countries, 2000 and 2005**

Thousands and percentages

	Foreign-born labour force			Foreign labour force			Source
	2000	2005	% of total labour force in 2005	2000	2005	% of total labour force in 2005	
	Thousands			Thousands			
Australia	2 242	2 615	24.9	..	..	..	HS (1999)/ LFS (2005)
Austria	474	610	15.5	377	413	10.5	LFS
Belgium	455	562	12.3	366	385	8.5	LFS
Canada[1]	3 151	..	19.9	..	..	..	C
Czech Republic	..	101	2.0	28	42	0.8	LFS
Denmark	138	173	6.1	78	89	3.2	LFS
Finland[2]	54	70	2.7	31	37	1.4	LFS
France	3 014	2 992	11.2	1 549	1 379	5.2	LFS
Germany	4 412	5 896	14.9	3 430	3 828	9.5	LFS
Greece	263	420	8.8	163	322	6.7	LFS
Hungary	67	81	1.9	..	32	0.8	LFS
Ireland	136	232	11.8	64	159	8.1	LFS
Italy	240	1 954	8.1	..	..	..	LFS
Japan[3]	..	..	..	155	180	0.3	WP
Korea[4]	..	..	..	123	198	0.8	WP
Luxembourg	76	90	44.4	77	92	45.2	LFS
Netherlands	895	970	11.6	298	291	3.5	LFS
Norway	138	169	7.2	75	95	4.0	LFS
Portugal	273	407	7.8	101	182	3.5	LFS
Spain	565	2 761	13.3	255	2 308	11.1	LFS
Sweden	447	617	13.1	205	231	4.9	LFS
Switzerland	..	1 031	25.3	807	902	22.2	LFS
United Kingdom	2 392	2 919	10.1	1 248	1 642	5.7	LFS
United States	18 029	22 422	15.2	10 677	13 283	9.0	LFS
OECD[5]	..	..	12.4	..	..	8.6	

Note: Data based on Labour Force Surveys cover labour force aged 15 to 64 with the exception of Canada and the United States (labour force aged 15 and over). Data from other sources cover the labour force aged 15 and over.
1. Data refer to 2001.
2. Data refer to 1999.
3. Foreign residents with permission to work, excluding permanent and long-term residents whose activity is not restricted. Overstayers (most of whom are believed to work illegally) are not included.
4. Overstayers are included.
5. Only countries for which data on the foreign and foreign-born labour force are available are included.
Source: C: Census; HS: Household survey; LFS: Labour force survey; WP: Work permits.

StatLink 🔗 *http://dx.doi.org/10.1787/022174831538*

central European countries, fewer than 2% of workers were born abroad, the proportion is nearly 45% in Luxembourg, some 25% in Switzerland and Australia, and 20% in Canada. In the United States, New Zealand, Austria and Germany, about 15% of the workforce are immigrants. This figure is close to or over 12% in several other OECD European countries such as Sweden, Belgium and the Netherlands, as well as Spain and Ireland.

Numbers of foreign-born workers have increased greatly over the past five years. The growth rate is over 20% in nearly all OECD countries with the exception of Australia (17%), the Netherlands (8%) and France, where there was no perceptible increase in the employment survey statistics. Growth was particularly marked in south European countries, especially in Italy where there was an eight-fold increase in foreign-born workers, and in Spain, with an almost five-fold increase between 2000 and 2005. There was also a remarkable increase in Ireland and Greece too (70% and 60%, respectively).

... with constantly rising participation rates

In almost half of the countries for which data are available, foreign-born persons have a participation rate which is equivalent to or higher than the native-born population (see Chart I.14 and Table I.A1.1 of the Annex). This applies in particular to the "new" immigration countries of southern Europe, where employment-related migration predominates. In several European OECD countries, *e.g.* Austria, France and Switzerland, there is less than a 3% gap between the two groups.

In other countries, like Australia, Denmark, Norway, Netherlands and Sweden, the participation rate differential ranges from 8% to as high as 13%. However, these are the OECD countries with the highest overall activity rates. It is also these countries which have recorded the highest rises recently. Between 2000 and 2005, the gap between immigrants and native-born in terms of participation rate fell by 7% in Denmark, 6% in Finland and 3% in the Netherlands.

Chart I.14. **Participation rate by birth status in some OECD countries, 2004-2005**

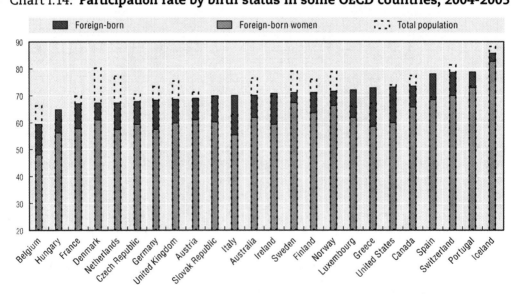

Sources: European Union Labour Force Survey (data provided by Eurostat); Australia (2005): Labour Force Survey; Canada (2003-2004): Survey of Labour and Income Dynamics; United States: Current Population Survey March Supplement.

StatLink ⧉ http://dx.doi.org/10.1787/014342316600

During the last 5 to 10 years, the participation rate difference between the native-born population and immigrants has tended to fall in most countries, with the exception of Austria. This, however, conceals large differences regarding groups of origin and gender.

For immigrant women, for example, participation rates in the labour market are systematically lower than for immigrant men, and usually lower than those for native-born women (see Chart I.14).

Important differences are noted by country of origin of migrants, but also for migrants from the same country, depending on the host country (see Chart I.15). Persons from ex-Yugoslavia residing in the United Kingdom or Denmark, for example, have a participation rate which is at least 40 percentage points lower than that of the native-born, whereas the difference is much smaller in Austria, France, Luxembourg and Switzerland.

Immigrants from sub-Saharan Africa provide another example where differences with the native-born population vary widely, or are even inverted, depending on the host country. In Spain, Luxembourg and Austria, persons born south of the Sahara have a higher activity rate than the native-born, whereas in France, Switzerland and the United Kingdom their participation rates are relatively similar. In contrast, in Norway and Denmark, there are very large differences (17 and 26 percentage points lower participation rates for immigrants, respectively). In Belgium, the difference between persons born in China and nationals is the smallest among host countries, whereas for Moroccans, it is the country where the difference is largest. The opposite is true in Switzerland, where immigrants from China have a relatively low participation rate and Moroccans a relatively high one.

The duration of residence, the institutional, historical, linguistic and cultural links between the host country and the country of origin, and the characteristics of the migrants themselves (reasons for entry, level of education, demographic composition, etc.) explain most of these differences.

Chart I.15. **Difference between the participation rates of native- and foreign-born by origin in selected European OECD countries, 2005**

Percentage points

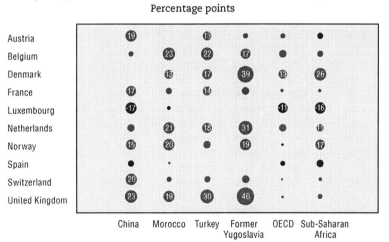

Note: The size of the bubble reflects the difference between the participation rate of the native-born compared to the foreign-born population.The greater the gap between the participation rate of the native-born and the foreign-born, the greater the size of the bubble will be. Differences above 10 percentage points are specified in the bubbles. Blue bubbles correspond to positive differences, black bubbles to negative ones.

Source: European Union Labour Force Survey (data provided by Eurostat).

StatLink ᴴᵗˢ⊨ *http://dx.doi.org/10.1787/014471868131*

Immigrant employment plays a key role in labour market dynamics in several OECD countries, due in particular to new entries of foreign workers

Between 1995 and 2005, there was strong growth in employment in most OECD countries. Thus, over the past ten years, the average annual increase in employment has been some 4% in Ireland and Spain, nearly 2% in Australia and Finland, for example, and more than 1% in most other Member countries. Over the period in question, net job creation amounted to nearly 7 million in Spain, 2.6 million in Italy, and more than 2 million in Australia, France and the United Kingdom. In the United States, net job creation was over 16 million.

Immigrants have made a large contribution to this dynamic (see Table I.9). In 15 out of the 18 countries for which data are available, the percentage of immigrants in net job creation between 1995 and 2005 was higher than the proportion of immigrants in the working population in 2005 and *a fortiori* in 1995, thus indicating much stronger growth in immigrant employment than in the labour market as a whole. In the United States, for example, more than half of the net job creation recorded over the past decade involves jobs held by persons born abroad, which is 3.5 times higher than their proportion of the total labour force in 2005. In Austria, Denmark, the United Kingdom, Sweden and the countries of southern Europe, the phenomenon is even more marked. In Germany, the increase in the number of immigrants in

Table I.9. Employment change, total and foreign-born, 1995-2005

	Employment (thousands)				Increase in employment (thousands)		Relative change over the period (%)	
	Foreign-born		Total		Foreign-born	Total	Foreign-born employment	Total employment
	1995	2005	1995	2005				
Australia	1 876	2 483	7 879	9 981	606	2 102	32.3	26.7
Austria	424	544	3 620	3 726	120	106	28.3	2.9
Belgium	306	466	3 769	4 187	159	418	52.0	11.1
Canada	2 007	2 343	12 636	14 352	336	1 716	16.8	13.6
Czech Republic	..	88	..	4 698	..	..	..	..
Denmark	80	156	2 569	2 686	75	118	93.6	4.6
Finland	–	57	1 926	2 379	..	453	..	23.5
France	2 336	2 552	21 927	24 205	216	2 278	9.3	10.4
Germany	4 199	4 892	36 208	35 705	693	–502	16.5	–1.4
Greece	148	377	3 693	4 301	229	608	154.2	16.5
Hungary	..	77	..	3 869	..	..	..	..
Iceland	3	9	133	156	6	23	170.5	17.7
Ireland	64	219	1 229	1 891	154	662	239.8	53.9
Italy	83	1 768	19 644	22 293	1 686	2 649	2 038.4	13.5
Luxembourg	62	85	161	193	23	32	37.3	20.1
Netherlands	499	864	6 727	7 953	366	1 227	73.3	18.2
Norway	88	151	2 007	2 240	64	233	72.6	11.6
Poland	..	49	..	13 683	..	..	..	..
Portugal	162	370	4 210	4 806	208	596	128.2	14.2
Slovak Republic	..	17	..	2 189	..	..	..	..
Spain	227	2 448	11 895	18 760	2 221	6 865	979.3	57.7
Sweden	230	525	4 064	4 280	296	216	128.7	5.3
Switzerland	..	942	..	3 883	..	..	..	..
United Kingdom	1 783	2 706	25 489	27 495	923	2 005	51.8	7.9
United States	12 410	21 276	122 764	138 943	8 866	16 179	71.4	13.2

Notes: 1994-1995 average and 2003 for Canada; 1994 for Australia; 1992 for Germany.
Sources: European Union Labour Force Survey (data provided by Eurostat); Australia: Labour Force Survey; Canada: Survey of Labour and Income Dynamics; United States: Current Population Survey March Supplement.

StatLink http://dx.doi.org/10.1787/022252560028

work has gone hand in hand with a corresponding fall in total employment between 1992 and 2005.

The growth in immigrant employment can be explained in part by the increase in the employment rate of immigrants but it is without any doubt the new entries of foreign workers which have played the bigger role over the period in question (see Chart I.16). With the exception of France and the Netherlands, the greater facility with which immigrants can find jobs accounts for less than 20% of the total increase in immigrant employment between 1995 and 2005, and this in spite of the sometimes remarkable progress made in terms of employment rates: +24 percentage points in Spain, +15 in Ireland and Portugal, +13 in the Netherlands and +11 in Greece. In the United Kingdom, for example, the immigrant employment rate grew by nearly 5 percentage points in 10 years, but this accounts for only about 150 000 of the new jobs for immigrants out of the more than 900 000 recorded.

Recent waves of immigration have been characterised by higher levels of skills. Many more of the immigrants in employment in 2005 who arrived within the last 10 years have a higher education diploma than those who arrived a decade before that (see Table I.10). In Belgium, Sweden and Denmark, more than 40% of the immigrants employed in 2005 and settled for less than 10 years have tertiary education. But it is in Austria that the increase in qualifications of new immigrants has been the most marked. This trend has been accompanied by a sharp fall in the arrival of unskilled immigrants, both absolute and relative terms. The trend recorded in southern European countries is a bit different as despite a sharp increase in entries of skilled workers, there has been a fall in their share of total entries.

The educational profile of recently arrived immigrants must also be compared, however, to that of young people entering the labour market at the end of their schooling. From this

Chart I.16. Change in the number of foreign-born employed in selected OECD countries, 1995-2005

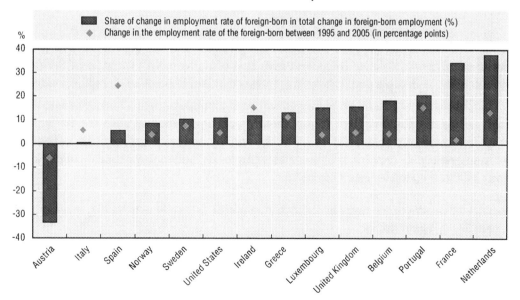

Note: For example in the United Kingdom, the employment rate of the foreign-born increased by 5 percentage points. This increase contributed to 15% of the total increase in foreign-born employment over that period.

Sources: European Union Labour Force Survey (data provided by Eurostat); United States: Current Population Survey March Supplement.

StatLink http://dx.doi.org/10.1787/014531521452

Table I.10. **Educational attainment of employed population by birth status**

Thousands and percentages

		Foreign-born employed						Native-born employed 2005		
		1995, present in the country for 10 years or less			2005, present in the country for 10 years or less			completed their studies 10 years ago or less		
		Below upper secondary	Upper secondary	Tertiary	Below upper secondary	Upper secondary	Tertiary	Below upper secondary	Upper secondary	Tertiary
Austria	Thousands	76.2	93.8	25.9	31.0	78.4	35.5	134.3	553.3	228.9
	%	39	48	13	21	54	24	15	60	25
Belgium	Thousands	14.2	11.2	21.0	41.1	33.0	69.7	88.8	374.8	472.2
	%	31	24	45	29	23	48	9	40	50
Denmark	Thousands	5.1	9.3	9.0	16.7	21.3	25.8	194.7	407.1	362.7
	%	22	40	38	26	33	40	20	42	38
France	Thousands	57.7	43.2	46.9	152.8	97.0	136.0	975.3	2 216.9	2 566.8
	%	39	29	32	40	25	35	17	38	45
Greece	Thousands	36.4	31.1	15.5	99.5	80.7	24.5	66.6	440.2	309.3
	%	44	38	19	49	39	12	8	54	38
Ireland	Thousands	3.4	4.0	9.6	16.5	43.2	55.6	11.1	53.6	77.0
	%	20	24	56	14	37	48	8	38	54
Italy	Thousands	32.6	14.8	14.6	385.9	386.8	94.1	536.4	2 196.9	1 238.2
	%	53	24	24	45	45	11	14	55	31
Luxembourg	Thousands	11.4	3.6	4.9	7.1	9.2	18.1	3.9	14.4	11.2
	%	57	18	25	21	27	53	13	49	38
Netherlands	Thousands	37.1	66.7	37.6	38.4	76.5	48.7	605.5	1 080.4	933.7
	%	26	47	27	23	47	30	23	41	36
Portugal	Thousands	17.4	8.3	5.1	70.2	34.9	21.6	423.2	276.6	325.1
	%	56	27	16	55	28	17	41	27	32
Spain	Thousands	20.3	9.1	19.3	709.4	635.6	381.7	1 132.1	981.1	2 318.4
	%	42	19	40	41	37	22	26	22	52
Sweden	Thousands	18.0	31.4	30.6	16.5	43.1	44.3	109.6	481.9	465.7
	%	23	39	38	16	41	43	10	46	44

Sources: European Union Labour Force Survey (data provided by Eurostat).

StatLink 🖩 *http://dx.doi.org/10.1787/022108871154*

standpoint, in spite of the fact that new immigrants are better qualified, their level of education still remains lower in general than that of native-born youngsters entering the labour market. This gap is particularly large in the countries of southern Europe, for example.

In addition, while having a higher educational attainment helps immigrants to find a job, it seems not to be enough to put them on an equal footing with the native-born population inasmuch as the difference in the employment rate between the native-born and immigrants also remains at higher education levels, and in some cases is widening, in nearly all OECD countries (see Chapter II).

Equality of employment rates is an objective which is partly attainable, subject to equality of opportunity

The situation of immigrants with regard to employment is the result of a complex combination of factors, involving, for example, the endowment with host-country specific human and social capital. In addition to studying these factors, the question is to what extent, accounting for the intrinsic dynamic of the labour market of each host country, policies aimed at promoting more equal access to employment can affect the differences recorded in terms of employment rates.

In other words, considering the differentials noted and assuming that from now on, all people with the same educational attainment have the same chance of losing or finding a job, irrespective of their place of birth, how long would it take for the difference between the employment rate of immigrants and that of native-born to disappear?

Logically, the reply to this question depends on both the initial difference between the employment rates and the number of jobs that are renewed each year, i.e. the job turnover rate. This in turn depends on the structure of the labour market and in particular the ratio of permanent to temporary jobs and their respective turnover rates. Based on the employment survey data (LFS) for the European countries of the OECD, turnover rates for different types of job can be estimated.[17]

It is assumed, for the purposes of calculating the employment rate of each group at each iteration, that there is no net job creation, that the labour market structure stays the same (the share of permanent jobs remains unchanged), and that each group, immigrants and native-born, has the same chance of losing or finding a job (see Box I.4).

Box I.4. **Trends in the employment rate of immigrants and native-born assuming an equal probability of losing or finding a job**

- i refers to the population in question, $i \in$ {immigrant, native-born}, j refers to the type of job, $j \in$ {temporary, permanent}, and h refers to the level of education $h \in$ {primary, secondary, tertiary}.

- $E_t^{i,j,h}$ is the number of jobs of type j held by persons from group i and with the level of education h on date t.

- $P^{i,h}$ is the working-age population of group i and level of education h, assumed to be constant and $P = \sum_h P^h = \sum_h P^{immigrant,h} + P^{native-born,h}$ the total population of working age.

- $e_t^{i,h}$ is the employment rates of persons from group i and with level of education h on date t.

- α^j is the turnover rate of jobs of type j, assumed to be constant and $NE^{j,h} = \alpha^j \cdot E^{j,h}$ the number of jobs of type j for persons of level of education h reallocated each year.

It is assumed that jobs are reallocated in accordance with the proportion of each group within the total population of working age.

It is also assumed that there is no net job creation and that the structure of jobs of each type remains the same, i.e. that the total number of jobs of each type $E^{j,h}$ and the average employment rate e^h remain constant.

$$E_{t+1}^{i,j,h} = \left(1-\alpha^j\right) \cdot E_t^{i,j,h} + NE^{j,h} \cdot \frac{P^{i,h}}{P^h} = \left(1-\alpha^j\right) \cdot E_t^{i,j,h} + \alpha^j \cdot E^{j,h} \cdot \frac{P^{i,h}}{P^h} \qquad [eq.1]$$

$E_t^{i,j,h}$ is therefore a series of type $x_{n+1} = a \cdot x_n + b$ where $a \neq 1$,

$$\text{thus } E_t^{i,j,h} = \left(1-\alpha^j\right)^t \cdot \left(E_0^{i,j,h} - E^{j,h} \cdot \frac{P^{i,h}}{P^h} \right) + E^{j,h} \cdot \frac{P^{i,h}}{P^h} \qquad [eq.2]$$

It can therefore be deduced that:

$$e_t^{i,h} = \frac{E_t^{i,h}}{P^{i,h}} = \sum_j \left(1-\alpha^j\right)^t \cdot \left(\frac{E_0^{i,j,h}}{P^{i,h}} - \frac{E^{j,h}}{P^h} \right) + \frac{E^h}{P^h} = \sum_j \left(1-\alpha^j\right)^t \cdot \left(e_0^{i,j,h} - \frac{E^{j,h}}{E^h} \cdot e^h \right) + e^h \qquad [eq.3]$$

$$e_t^i = \frac{\sum_h E_t^{i,h}}{P^i} = \sum_h \frac{E_t^{i,h}}{P^{i,h}} \cdot \frac{P^{i,h}}{P^i} = \sum_h e_t^{i,h} \cdot \frac{P^{i,h}}{P^i} \qquad [eq.4]$$

On the basis of these assumptions, estimates can be made of changes in the employment rate differential between immigrants and native-born. By definition, only the part of the differential attributable to differences in employment rates by educational level (not that relating to differences in educational profile) can be eliminated. This proportion of the total differential varies across countries. It varies from around 60% in Austria to 95% in the Netherlands. It is, for example, 65% in Germany, 80% in France, 85% in Belgium and over 90% in the United Kingdom and Sweden. It is therefore the larger part of employment rate differentials which is involved.

The results set out in Chart I.17 show that, on the basis of these assumptions, the differential initially noted between the employment rates of immigrants and nationals, for a given level of education, could normally be reduced by more than a third in three years and by more than half in ten years. As mentioned above, the speed with which rates converge depends on the structure of the labour market (job turnover rate, and ratio of temporary to permanent jobs) and on the part of the differential in employment rates attributable to differences in educational profile. Countries with the highest turnover rates, like the United Kingdom and Denmark, have the potential for rather rapid convergence. Countries where the proportion of permanent jobs is high and turnover low, on the other hand, such as France and the Netherlands, achieve limited convergence, even after 10 years.

The preceding simulation exercise suggests that when job turnover rates are high, the simple assumption that immigrants and native-born have the same probability of losing or finding a job leads to a relatively rapid convergence of their employment rates, even in the absence of net job creation. These results are intended to be illustrative, however, rather than predictive and need to be treated with some caution. The low turnover rate for permanent jobs in some countries, for example, may be due to frequent cases of promotion from temporary to permanent status and these situations would not appear in the data as hirings into permanent jobs. Also, the assumption that hirings are distributed in proportion to the presence of immigrants and non-immigrants among the unemployed rather than in the working-age population (as assumed here) would likely show a more rapid convergence of

Chart I.17. Evolution of the gap in the employment rate between the native- and foreign-born population over time assuming equal hiring and job loss probabilities for both groups, selected European OECD countries, 2005

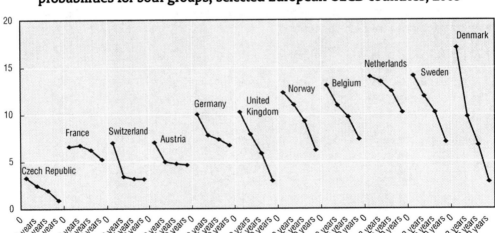

Source: European Union Labour Force Survey (data provided by Eurostat).

StatLink *http://dx.doi.org/10.1787/014553827303*

employment rates. On the other hand, if hirings depend on previous work experience and the latter is a source of human-capital development, then equal hiring treatment of persons of equal productivity might result in immigrant workers being hired less.

Immigrants usually continue to be over-represented among the unemployed, notably the long-term unemployed

As for employment, the difference in terms of unemployment between the native-born population and immigrants has, in most member countries, tended to decrease over the past ten years. Important differences nevertheless persist (see Chart I.18). In 2004-2005 in all OECD countries, with the exception of Poland, Hungary and the United States, the unemployment rate of immigrants was higher than that of the native population. In the Nordic countries, Austria, Belgium and Switzerland, immigrants are over-represented among the unemployed by a factor of at least two compared to their share in the labour force (in other words, their unemployment rate is at least twice that of the native-born). In France, Germany and the United Kingdom, those born abroad also suffer a notably higher rate of unemployment. On the other hand, i1n the main settlement countries (Australia, Canada and the United States) and recent immigration countries (Italy, Spain and Greece), place of birth makes little difference to the unemployment rate.

Compared to previous years, the situation has improved markedly in Denmark, Spain and Ireland, where the unemployment rate for immigrants has fallen by more than 10 percentage points in ten years (see Table I.A1.1 of the Annex). This favourable trend is generally observed even though, in the course of the last five years, the progress achieved has to some extent been reversed in several countries. This is the case for example in Austria, Norway, Belgium and Sweden. In the first two of these, the trend has been reversed both in real terms and relative to the native population.

Generally speaking, the situation of foreigners in terms of unemployment is less favourable than that of persons born abroad (see Table I.A1.2 of the Annex). This is particularly true in the Nordic countries, Italy, Portugal and France. In the latter two countries, the result observed for immigrants is partly influenced by the fact that

Chart I.18. **Unemployment rate of foreign-born and native-born, 2004-2005**

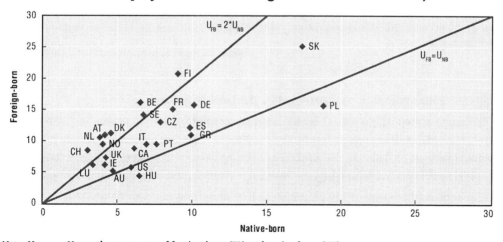

Note: $U_{FB, NB}$ = Unemployment rate of foreign-born (FB) and native-born (NB).

Sources: European Union Labour Force Survey (data provided by Eurostat); Australia 2005: Labour Force Survey; Canada 2003: Survey of Labour and Income Dynamics; United States: Current Population Survey March Supplement.

StatLink ⫘⊑⊒ http://dx.doi.org/10.1787/014623118568

repatriates form a large group and tend to perform rather well on the labour market. More generally, the difference between foreigners and the foreign-born can be explained in part by the fact that acquisition of the host country nationality reflects a *de facto* integration and that in some countries, certain categories of employment are not accessible to certain categories of foreigners (for example, jobs in the civil service for nationals of third countries in most European OECD countries).

In roughly half of the countries for which data are available, immigrants are relatively more exposed to long-term unemployment than are native-born (see Chart I.19). In Finland, the Czech Republic, the Netherlands, Norway and Switzerland, the difference exceeds 10 percentage points. It is also significant in Belgium, where more than 17% of immigrants are looking for work, 60% of them for over a year. In other countries like Germany and Denmark, the over-exposure of immigrants to unemployment does not go hand-in-hand with over-exposure to long-term unemployment.

Chart I.19. **Share of long-term unemployment (1 year or more) in total unemployment by birth status, 2005**

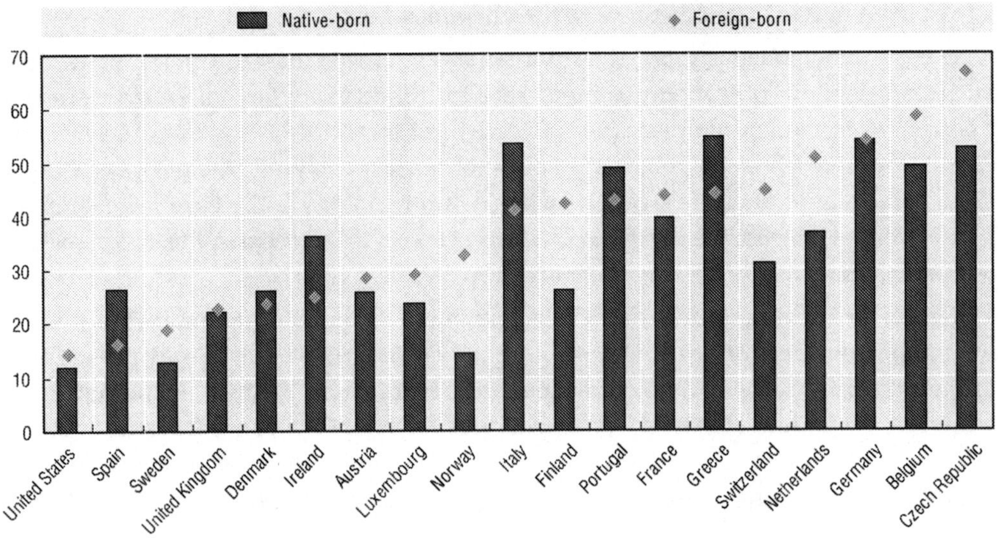

Sources: European Union Labour Force Survey (data provided by Eurostat); United States: Current Population Survey March Supplement.

StatLink ⌧ http://dx.doi.org/10.1787/014640521446

Immigrant employment is concentrated in the service sectors...

Table I.11 shows the sectoral breakdown of immigrant employment in 2004-2005 in the OECD countries. Immigrants tend to be over-represented in the construction, hotel and restaurant sectors, and also in the healthcare and social services sectors, where their share in employment is on the whole higher than their share in the overall labour force.

The sectoral breakdown varies considerably from one country to another, however. Remarkable is, in particular, that some 6% of immigrants work in agriculture in Spain, 29% in the mining and manufacturing industries in Germany, 29% are in construction in Greece, 15% in the wholesale and retail trade in Switzerland, 13% in hotels and restaurants in Ireland, 15% in education in the United States, 24% in healthcare and social services in Norway and 33% in other services in Canada.

INTERNATIONAL MIGRATION OUTLOOK: SOPEMI 2007 EDITION – ISBN 978-92-64-03285-9 – © OECD 2007

Table I.11. **Employment of foreign-born by sector, 2004-2005 average**
Percentage of total foreign-born employment

	Agriculture and fishing	Mining, Manufacturing and Energy	Construction	Wholesale and retail trade	Hotels and restaurants	Education	Health and other community services	Households	Admin. and ETO	Other services
Austria	1.2	**20.8**	**9.1**	14.6	**12.7**	4.2	8.8	**0.4**	3.7	**24.7**
Belgium	1.2	17.2	**6.8**	13.5	**7.9**	6.6	10.5	**0.6**	11.5	**24.3**
Canada (2003)	1.2	**19.8**	6.0	14.1	**7.8**	5.5	9.6	..	3.6	**32.5**
Czech Republic	3.2	29.2	**10.5**	16.4	**4.9**	4.9	6.9	–	4.1	**19.7**
Denmark	1.8	**19.3**	5.2	10.0	**6.2**	8.8	20.8	–	3.1	**24.9**
Finland	–	**20.4**	–	**14.8**	**7.4**	6.2	12.9	–	–	**29.2**
France	2.2	14.7	**10.9**	11.8	**5.8**	6.1	9.9	**5.8**	6.5	**26.5**
Germany	1.3	**29.3**	6.3	14.0	**7.0**	4.4	10.2	**0.7**	3.8	23.1
Greece	6.7	**15.3**	**28.5**	11.3	**9.7**	1.9	2.3	**13.2**	1.4	9.6
Hungary	3.0	21.4	**8.9**	18.0	**5.2**	8.5	8.8	–	4.3	**21.9**
Ireland	2.5	**16.2**	11.0	12.0	**12.5**	6.2	**11.4**	–	2.7	**24.7**
Italy	3.2	**24.5**	**12.4**	12.0	**8.7**	3.1	5.0	**9.4**	2.6	19.3
Japan	0.6	**54.4**	1.1	8.1	8.0	8.4	..	..	..	**19.4**
Luxembourg	1.0	**10.0**	**14.8**	10.7	**6.4**	2.4	7.2	**4.0**	12.8	**30.7**
Netherlands	1.5	**17.1**	4.2	12.5	**6.9**	5.7	15.6	–	7.3	**29.2**
Norway	–	12.3	4.4	11.6	**8.6**	8.9	24.2	–	3.7	**25.1**
Poland	**18.2**	13.0	–	**15.2**	–	17.9	–	–	–	**19.5**
Portugal	1.9	14.3	**14.7**	14.4	**6.7**	9.0	7.7	**5.1**	6.7	**19.4**
Slovak Republic	–	26.2	–	**13.0**	–	8.8	7.5	–	–	**21.8**
Spain	**5.6**	13.0	**18.2**	10.7	**13.8**	3.2	3.0	**13.6**	1.5	17.4
Sweden	0.7	**17.2**	2.8	11.5	**7.0**	11.1	18.6	–	3.8	**27.5**
Switzerland	1.2	**19.1**	**8.6**	14.9	**7.5**	6.3	13.3	**1.3**	3.5	24.4
United Kingdom	0.4	11.4	4.7	13.3	**8.6**	8.4	15.2	**0.9**	5.4	**31.7**
United States	**2.5**	13.6	**11.5**	13.7	**11.4**	15.0	..	..	2.4	**29.8**

Note: The numbers in bold indicate sectors where the foreign-born are over-represented (i.e., the share of foreign-born employment in the sector is larger than the share of foreign-born employment in total employment). The sign "–" indicates that the estimate is not reliable enough for publication. ETO means extra-territorial organisations. For Japan, "Health and other community services", "households" and "Admin. and ETO" sectors are included in other services. For the United States, "Health and other community services" is included in "Education", and "Households" in "Other services".
Sources: European countries: European Union Labour Force Survey (data provided by Eurostat), Japan: Labour force surveys; Canada: Survey of Labour and Income Dynamics; United States: Current Population Survey March Supplement.

StatLink ᘠᔈᔈᕗ *http://dx.doi.org/10.1787/022151356541*

... and in low or very highly skilled jobs

In most OECD countries, tertiary activities nowadays account for a preponderant share of employment in general and immigrant employment in particular. This applies to both extremes of the range of levels of skills. Chart I.20 shows some of the skilled and unskilled occupations in which immigrants are likely to be present in large numbers. These include new information and communication technologies, the health sector and secondary school teachers, but also waiters, domestic care workers and cleaners.

In most cases, persons born abroad are over-represented in these occupations. This applies in particular to cleaning, where more than 50% of jobs are held by immigrants in Switzerland, and more than 30% in Austria, Germany, Sweden, Italy, Greece and the United States. The proportion of immigrants working as waiters or cooks is twice as high as their share in the total labour force in Spain, Switzerland, Norway and Denmark. Such over-representation is less marked, on the other hand, in relation to domestic care workers for

Chart I.20. **Share of foreign-born employed within selected occupations in the service sector, 2004-2005**

In percent

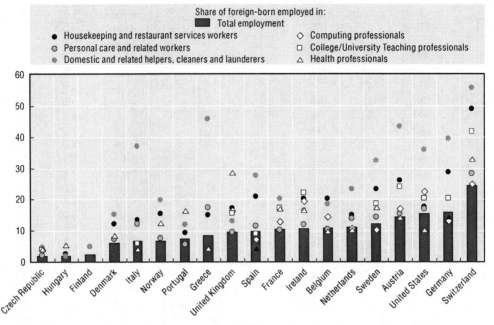

Note: In the International Standard Classification of Occupations (ISCO-88), Computing professionals refer to ISCO213; College, University and higher education teaching professionals refer to ISCO231; Health professionals refer to ISCO222 and 223; Housekeeping and restaurant services workers refer to ISCO512; Personal care and related workers refer to ISCO513; and Domestic and related helpers, cleaners and launderers refer to ISCO913.

Sources: European countries: European Union Labour Force Survey (data provided by Eurostat); United States: Current Population Survey March Supplement.

StatLink ⋘⋙ *http://dx.doi.org/10.1787/014666425174*

children and older people, with the exception of Greece and Italy. However, this situation could change quickly given the scale of the need for manpower in this domain.

Results concerning the most highly qualified professionals show greater variation, depending on the host country. Nevertheless, there is, somewhat surprisingly, less concentration than in the case of jobs requiring fewer skills. There are exceptions, however: teachers in Switzerland and Ireland, doctors and nurses in the United Kingdom (see Chapter III), and to a lesser extent, computer experts in the United States.

While there has been an important shortage of manpower in the most highly skilled service jobs in recent years, some have been filled by native-born, thereby reducing the over-representation. This has apparently not been the case with jobs requiring fewer skills, notably because working conditions are unattractive and young people entering the labour market are better qualified. Even though labour migration policies continue in part to target highly qualified immigrants, labour market requirements in OECD countries will no doubt retain this dualism, especially in the context of the ageing of the labour force and of the population as a whole.

Immigrant self-employment is on the increase

In almost all the countries for which data are available, self-employment among immigrants has increased over the past five years, both in numbers and as a percentage of overall self-employment (see Table I.12). In some countries, for example Germany, the trend can be seen in terms both of level and percentage. Foreign-born persons accounted in 2005 for some 12% of the self-employed in the United Kingdom, 13% in Belgium, France and Germany, and over 14% in Sweden, figures which are generally higher than the share of immigrants in the labour force.

This finding could reflect an improved position in host country society, but it could also be an illustration of the fact that, to cope with a growing difficulty of labour market entry (insufficient social capital, language difficulties, problems with the recognition of qualifications, etc.), some categories of immigrant worker are using self-employment as a fall-back solution.

Table I.12. **Foreign-born in self-employment in OECD countries, 2000 and 2005**

Percentages

	Share of foreign-born in total self-employment		Share of self-employment in total foreign-born employment	
	2000	2005	2000	2005
Australia	. .	26.7	. .	12.7
Austria	6.7	9.3	7.3	7.5
Belgium	10.2	12.7	17.0	15.1
Czech Republic	. .	3.0	. .	24.4
Denmark	4.8	6.3	9.1	8.5
France	11.1	12.7	11.4	11.6
Germany	9.7	12.8	8.6	10.1
Greece	2.0	3.7	13.7	12.6
Ireland	7.7	8.1	17.4	11.0
Luxembourg	33.5	38.9	7.5	6.9
Netherlands	10.3	10.3	10.4	10.8
Norway	6.0	7.4	7.6	7.6
Portugal	3.6	5.4	14.9	14.2
Spain	3.0	8.1	18.9	10.3
Sweden	11.4	14.4	12.0	11.3
Switzerland	. .	18.2	. .	10.1
United Kingdom	10.7	11.6	15.2	14.4
United States	. .	14.1	. .	9.6

Sources: European countries: European Union Labour Force Survey (data provided by Eurostat); United States: Current Population Survey, March Supplement; Australia: Survey of Education and Work, 2004.

StatLink ᴍᴤᴘ *http://dx.doi.org/10.1787/022174723861*

Working conditions for immigrants often continue to be less favourable than for the native population

Chart I.21a shows that in nearly all the countries under consideration, apart from Austria and Switzerland, immigrants are much more likely to have temporary jobs than are native-born. The proportion of temporary jobs among immigrants is nearly 56% in Spain and nearly 30% in Portugal, *i.e.* 25 and 12 percentage points, respectively, more than for the native-born. In some cases, it seems to reflect the growing precariousness of employment which affects immigrants disproportionately. In contrast, the incidence of part-time work (see Chart I.21b), more difficult to interpret, does not vary systematically by place of birth.

Chart I.21a. **Share of temporary employment in total employment by birth status, 2005**

Percentages

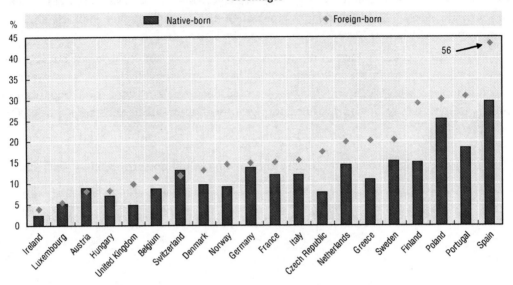

Source: European Union Labour Force Survey (data provided by Eurostat).

StatLink http://dx.doi.org/10.1787/014773561442

Chart I.21b. **Share of part-time employment in total employment by birth status, 2005**

Percentages

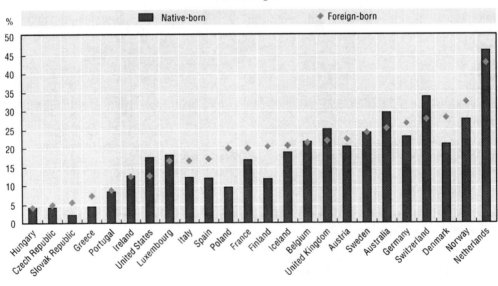

Sources: European Union Labour Force Survey (data provided by Eurostat); Australia 2004: Survey of Education and Work; United States: Current Population Survey March Supplement.

StatLink http://dx.doi.org/10.1787/014788525162

INTERNATIONAL MIGRATION OUTLOOK: SOPEMI 2007 EDITION – ISBN 978-92-64-03285-9 – © OECD 2007

2. The integration of the children of immigrants

There is a growing interest in the integration of native-born children of immigrants, and the integration issues for this group are not necessarily the same as for young immigrants

When analysing the integration of the children of immigrants, it is necessary to distinguish between young immigrants (foreign-born who have migrated, often with their parents) and the native-born children of foreign-born parents. The latter have been fully raised and educated in the host country, whereas this is not necessarily the case for young immigrants. Young immigrants may have arrived as young adults, and may have been educated abroad, at least in part. Depending on the country of origin, differences in education systems and in educational curricula could have an impact on their educational and labour market outcomes in the destination country if some prior schooling was obtained abroad. Likewise, other difficulties related to the migration process itself, such as language deficiencies or foreign work experience may affect their likelihood of finding employment or a job commensurate with their qualifications and experience.

One would expect such factors to matter less when immigrants arrived at a very young age and indeed, in many respects they are similar to native-born persons with foreign-born parents. However, the age of arrival after which this is no longer the case is not well-defined and early childhood education in the host country can have a significant impact on eventual outcomes. For many young immigrants, data do not permit a clear determination of whether all or part of the education was obtained in the origin country. This hampers comparisons with natives. One group for which this ambiguity does not exist consists of the native-born children of foreign-born parents. For this group, one would expect, at the least, outcomes that are similar to those of the children of native-born persons with a comparable socio-economic background.

There is no internationally recognised term for describing native-born persons, both of whose parents are foreign-born. Denmark and Norway, for example, generally refer to them as "descendants", but this term is rarely used elsewhere. For the sake of conciseness and convenience, the term "second generation" will be used below, in line with most of the literature in this area. The phrase is not ideal, however, because it does tend to suggest an "inheritance" of immigrant characteristics, which may be true to some extent, but does not reflect the fact that the person in other respects, including language, education and indeed cultural outlook, may be indistinguishable from other native-born persons.

A third group (in addition to young immigrants and the second generation) are native-born persons with one foreign-born parent. However, this group can be heterogeneous including, for example, native-born offspring of immigrants who marry someone from the country of origin of their parents.

The integration of the second generation is not a new issue. Already in the 1970s there was growing concern about the lower education and labour market outcomes of the second generation in those western European countries where low-educated labour migration had been prominent in the 1950s and 1960s (see, for example, Castro-Almeida 1979). However, empirical research on the second generation has been relatively rare until recently. This has been partly attributable to data limitations (see Box I.5). With information on the country of origin of the parents now becoming more often available from surveys and other sources, there has been a recent blossoming of research related to the labour market integration of the second generation.[18] However, international comparisons of the

Box I.5. **Data on the second generation**

Proper identification of native-born children of foreign-born parents requires information not only on the place of birth of the individual, but also on that of the parents. This information is not readily available in most commonly used datasets. In particular, the European Union Labour Force Survey from Eurostat does not collect data on parents' place of birth – except indirectly for those young persons still living in the same household as their parents, who themselves respond to questions on their own place of birth. Some other household-specific surveys have such information, but the sample sizes are generally too small to produce reliable figures in the aggregate.

Up to now, international surveys on educational outcomes have been the main source of information on the second generation for the purposes of international comparisons. The most comprehensive of these, covering all OECD countries, has been the OECD's Programme for International Student Assessment (PISA) (see OECD, 2006a). The PISA database provides information on the background characteristics and the educational outcomes of 15-year old students. Other international surveys of students which contain information on parents' place of birth are the Trends in International Mathematics and Science Study (TIMSS; covering 7th and 8th graders) and the Progress in International Reading Literacy Study (PIRLS; covering 4th graders) (see Schnepf, 2004). The International Adult Literacy Skills Survey (IALSS) has information on the country of origin of the parents for respondents for some countries, but the sample sizes are generally too small (see Chapter II).

Some basic data on the educational attainment and the labour market status of the second generation for 10 OECD countries are now available (OECD, 2007). There are three principal sources for these data: the 2000 round of censuses (Australia, Canada, France, Switzerland), population registers (Denmark, Norway and Sweden), and national labour force surveys (Germany, the United Kingdom, the United States). In some countries the second generation (i.e. native-born with two foreign-born parents) cannot not be identified precisely, so proxies have been used instead. For Australia, it was not possible to distinguish between native-born children with one or two foreign-born parents. For Switzerland, on the other hand, the second generation referred to in this section relate to native-born persons with a foreign nationality at birth. For the United Kingdom, the second generation refers to native-born who identified themselves as other than "white British".

educational attainment and labour market status of the children of immigrants have been notably lacking. To overcome this deficiency, data have been compiled on the educational attainment and the labour market situation of 20-29 year old immigrants, native-born children of immigrants, and children of the native-born. This information has been collected for 10 OECD countries for which the former two groups account for a significant proportion of young adults (OECD, 2007).

Children of immigrants now account for a large share of young people entering the labour market in many OECD countries

Persons with a migration background account for a large part of young people in many OECD countries (see Chart I.22). Immigrants generally account for a larger share of the 20-29 year old population than the second generation, due to student migrants and young labour migrants. Altogether, persons with a migration background account for more than

Chart I.22. **Share of persons with a migration background in the population aged 20-29**

Percentages

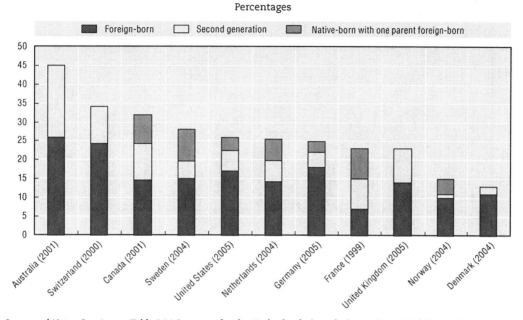

Source and Notes: See Annex Table I.A1.3, except for the Netherlands (population register 2004); "Second generation" refers to the second row of the table for each country. Slightly different definitions are used for Australia, Switzerland, the United Kingdom and Denmark, which do not allow for all distinctions to be made.

StatLink ⧉⧉ *http://dx.doi.org/10.1787/014814437360*

30% of the 20-29 year old in Australia, Canada and Switzerland (in descending order); between 30 and 20% in Sweden, the United States, the Netherlands, Germany, France and the United Kingdom and around 15% in Denmark and Norway.

Educational outcomes and attainment levels of the children of immigrants tend to lag behind those of the native-born without a migration background.

Much of the post-war labour migration to European OECD countries was low qualified, and the spouses of these immigrants also tended to be low qualified. Empirical data from many studies show some tendency towards the intergenerational transmission of human capital (*e.g.* Bauer and Riphahn, 2007). Because of the difference between the educational attainment of immigrant and native-born parents, one might thus anticipate somewhat lower educational outcomes for the children of immigrants.

This is confirmed by the OECD's Programme for International Student Assessment (PISA) which assessed student knowledge and skills in mathematics, science, reading and cross-curricular competencies at age 15, that is, towards the end of compulsory education. PISA data show strong linkages between the skills level of the migrant intake and the educational attainment of the second generation relative to that of natives. In OECD countries which have selected their immigrants based on qualifications and labour market needs, such as Australia and Canada, the average achievement level of the second generation (*i.e.* prior to controlling for the socio-economic background) is about the same as that of other natives or even slightly better (see Chart I.23).[19] At the other end of the spectrum are Germany and Belgium, where the recruitment of low-skilled labour was particularly pronounced.

Chart I.23. **PISA (2003) results in mathematics for the children of immigrants**

Points differences compared to children of native-born, children at aged 15

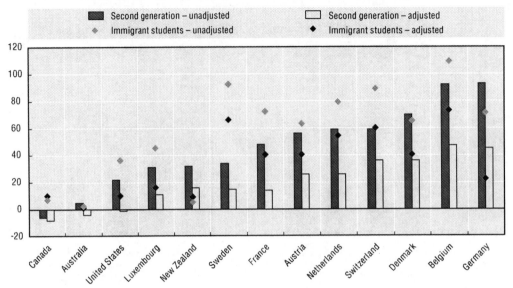

Note: "Adjusted" means taking into account parental education and occupational status. All figures for Australia are not significantly different from zero. This is also the case for the unadjusted figures for Canada (second generation and immigrants) and New Zealand (immigrants) and for the adjusted figure for immigrants in the United States.
Source: OECD PISA Database.

StatLink ⟨⟨⟩⟩ http://dx.doi.org/10.1787/014823628866

In general, the second generation tends to perform better than their immigrant counterparts. This is what one would expect, since the former were born and entirely educated in the country of assessment. In most countries for which data are available, there are nevertheless significant gaps between the children of natives and the second generation. This is particularly the case for Germany and Belgium, where the gaps in the raw scores for the second generation amount to the equivalent of about two years of schooling.[20] Gaps are also large in Denmark, Switzerland, the Netherlands, Austria and France.

If the differences in educational outcomes *vis-à-vis* the children of native-born were solely attributable to differences in the socio-economic background (including education of parents, but also other factors such as family wealth and educational resources at home), one would expect them to diminish after controlling for this. Indeed, controlling for socio-economic background reduces the gaps by about half. However, even then, second generation students often remain at a substantial disadvantage, particularly in Germany, Belgium, Switzerland and Austria. In contrast, in France and Sweden, the second generation's disadvantage is no longer significant. The school systems in these latter countries thus seem to be better able to provide for equitable outcomes than those in the former.

One factor specific to the children of immigrants is that they often speak a language at home which differs from that of the host country. Such children tend to have lower outcomes than other children with a migration background, particularly in Belgium and Germany (OECD, 2006a). Although this may indicate a multilingual environment which can be an advantageous, it can reflect limited exposure to the host-country language in students' personal lives.

The highest educational attainment is an important determinant of employment prospects. Although Annex Table I.A1.3 refers to a different cohort – the 20-29 year old for the most recent year available – there are many parallels with the PISA results on educational outcomes. Young immigrants have a lower educational attainment than the children of native-born in all countries except Australia and Canada. With the exception of the same two countries, the second generation has a higher educational attainment than young immigrants. The results are likely a consequence of the selective migration policy pursued in Australia and Canada, which seeks to attract young, high-qualified immigrants. Despite better outcomes for the second generation compared to immigrants, the second generation still lags behind the children of native-born in all European OECD countries except the United Kingdom.[21] Again, parental background characteristics seem to account for a significant part of this gap (see *e.g.* Nielsen *et al.*, 2003). The lower educational attainment is particularly apparent in Denmark and Germany – countries where the differences in the PISA scores are also higher than in the other countries for which comparable data are available.

For those countries for which data on the native-born persons with only one immigrant parent are available, these tend to have a higher educational attainment than those both of whose parents were foreign-born.

Annex Table I.A1.3 also reveals significant gender differences.[22] In all countries with the exception of the United States, native-born women with foreign-born parents have a higher educational attainment than their male counterparts. The difference is particularly pronounced in the Scandinavian countries. In contrast, young immigrant women often have a very low educational attainment. In Germany, France, Switzerland and the United Kingdom, their attainment level is lower than that of immigrant men. The generally observed improvement in attainment levels for the second generation *vis-à-vis* immigrants is thus much more pronounced for women than for men. In several OECD countries, this pattern has also been reported in econometric analyses after controlling for parental background characteristics (*e.g.* Van Ours and Veenman, 2004 for the Netherlands and Nielsen *et al.*, 2003 for Denmark).

Labour market outcomes tend to be unfavourable even after accounting for the generally lower educational background

A first glance at the employment rates of the children of immigrants (Annex Table I.A1.4) reveals significant gaps for most countries. Although the second generation generally has a higher employment probability than young immigrants, the gaps *vis-à-vis* the children of the native-born are still large in European OECD countries. The only exception is Switzerland, which could be linked to the fact that a significant proportion of the parents of the second generation came as labour migrants from neighbouring European countries, particularly from Italy. In contrast, gaps are largest in the Scandinavian countries, where much of past immigration has been from non-OECD countries and was of humanitarian nature. There is evidence that the country-of-origin of the immigrant parents is linked with the labour market outcomes of their children (*e.g.* Olsen, 2006; Meurs, Pailhe and Simon, 2006). In particular, native-born children of immigrants from African countries face more difficulties in the labour market than those whose parents came from European countries.

Immigrant women are generally the group with the least favourable outcomes in the labour market (see also OECD 2006b), both in absolute terms and relative to children of natives of the same gender. There is, however, a relatively strong improvement for second generation women. In all countries, one observes an increase in employment rates for second generation women compared to foreign-born women, and this increase is always stronger than among the respective groups of men. In Canada, women from the second generation have even significantly higher employment rates than the children of native-born.

The observed large gaps in the employment rates of the second generation *vis-à-vis* the children of natives in most European OECD countries are partly attributable to the lower educational attainment of the former. As Chart I.24 shows, differences would decrease significantly if the second generation had the same educational attainment as other natives. In Denmark, for example, the gap would diminish by about half. Nevertheless, gaps remain large in all European countries with the exception of Switzerland (see above).

Chart I.24 also indicates that higher educational attainment could particularly promote integration of second generation women in the labour market. Assuming the same educational attainment as for the children of natives, in France, Germany, Norway and the United States, the respective gaps in the employment rates would diminish more for second generation women than for men. In Switzerland, second generation women would even perform better than other native women if they had the same educational attainment structure.

Taking a closer look at the employment rates by educational attainment presented in Annex Table I.A1.4 reveals a rather uneven picture across countries, although the same ranking of employment outcomes tends to be observed across all attainment levels. The foreign-born generally have the least favourable outcomes, followed by native-born with

Chart I.24. **Differences in employment rates between native-born without migration background and the second generation by gender, latest available year**

20-29 years old and not in education, percentage points

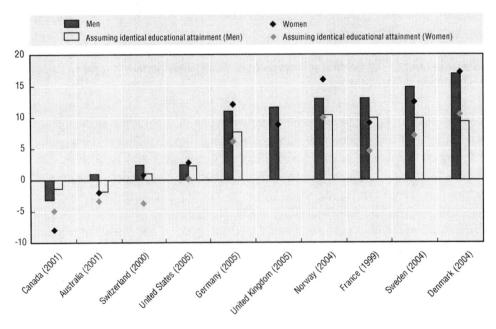

Source: See Annex Table I.A1.3; "Second generation" refers to the second row for each country.

StatLink ⌦ *http://dx.doi.org/10.1787/014832005472*

no, one or two native-born parents, respectively. For the second generation, gaps *vis-à-vis* comparable children of natives are often highest at the top end of the qualification scale. The exceptions to this pattern are Sweden and France, where the gaps between the second generation and their native counterparts are higher for the low-qualified. Significant gender differences in the gaps for the second generation compared to their respective native counterparts without a migration background are only observed for the low-qualified. At this qualification level, gaps tend to be smaller for women than for men.

The children of immigrants also generally face higher unemployment than the children of natives. Chart I.25 shows the unemployment rate of young immigrants and the second generation relative to the children of natives. In Denmark, Norway and Switzerland, the unemployment rate of young immigrants is more than twice as high as that of the children of natives. The situation is somewhat more favourable for the second generation. Nevertheless, except for Switzerland and Sweden, the improvement remains limited. In all European countries, the incidence of unemployment among the second generation is about 1.5 to 2 times higher than among the children of natives. In the United Kingdom and Germany, the second generation has even higher unemployment than young immigrants. However, this appears to be attributable to cohort effects specific to these two countries (*i.e.* recent labour migration in the United Kingdom and immigrants with an ethnic German background in Germany).

In contrast to the favourable situation regarding employment, the second generation in Switzerland has 1.7 times higher unemployment than the natives. For young immigrants, unemployment is even more than 3 times higher than that of natives. However, this has to be seen in the context of relatively low unemployment of young people in Switzerland. Native Swiss persons have an unemployment rate of only 3%.

Chart I.25. Unemployment rate of immigrants and the second generation relative to that of native-born

20-29 years old and not in education, latest available year

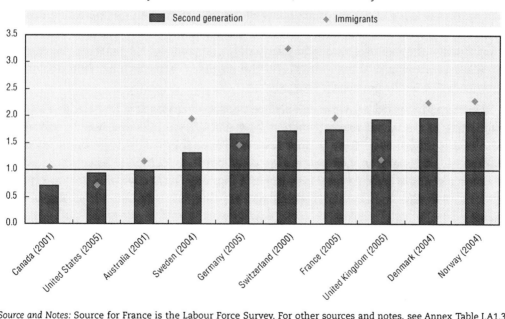

Source and Notes: Source for France is the Labour Force Survey. For other sources and notes, see Annex Table I.A1.3; "Second generation" refers to the second row for each country.

StatLink ⇨ *http://dx.doi.org/10.1787/014866430010*

Obstacles to the labour market integration of the children of immigrants... and possible remedies

Summing up the above, one observes that part of the lower employment outcomes of the children of immigrants is due to a lower educational attainment. Early participation in the residence country's educational institutions has proved important in raising educational attainment levels. For example, Caille (2001) has shown that kindergarten attendance at the age of 2 has an important impact on the school success of the children of immigrants – much stronger than on comparable natives. Policies targeted at improving educational achievement thus seem to yield the largest return as early ages, and several OECD countries – including Germany and Denmark – have recently introduced measures in this direction.

However, gaps in employment rates *vis-à-vis* children of natives remain large even for native-born children of immigrants who have a comparable educational attainment, which suggests that factors other than education are at work. There are several possible reasons for the observed lower employment rates of the second generation even for given education levels.

The first is lack of access to networks. A significant proportion of jobs in many OECD countries appears to be filled through contacts with friends or relatives (see OECD, 2007). Presumably, these personal contacts would be more extensive for the native-born than for the foreign-born. For the second generation, personal contacts to persons making employment decisions in domestic firms also tend to be more limited, due to the generally lower socio-economic status of their parents – many of whom have arrived either as low-skilled "guest workers" or as refugees. Measures aimed at bringing employers in contact with the adult offspring of immigrants seem to be relatively effective – although programmes have been rarely designed in a way to allow for a proper evaluation of their impact. Such tools include company fairs, internship programmes and mentoring. The latter is increasingly prominent – mentoring schemes have been introduced, for example, in Australia, Denmark, France and Germany – as it provides the children of immigrants with tacit knowledge about the functioning of the labour market. As mentoring involves the civic community and is relatively low cost, it is appealing to governments. Yet, in order to be effective, the mentors have to be adequately prepared and the matching be carefully organised to meet both the mentors' and the mentees' expectations. Finding suitable mentors has generally not been a problem.

Linked with limited networks can also be a more general lack of knowledge about the functioning of the labour market, such as how to apply for jobs and how to succeed in recruitment interviews. There is anecdotal evidence that this is a problem for many children of immigrants as their parents are often not in a position to assist them. Again, there are a series of training measures in place in many OECD countries (for example, in Belgium, Denmark and Germany) which address this, but it is difficult to assess their impact.

Discrimination on the basis of origin or class may be part of the explanation for the lower outcomes of the second generation. It is generally difficult to assess the incidence of discrimination among immigrants, because their qualifications and experience have often been obtained in another country and it is difficult to determine to what extent these are equivalent to those obtained in the host country or recognised by employers. Without a common measure of human capital, one can never be certain if the observed differences are in fact due to discrimination or rather to unmeasured human capital differences. For the second generation, this is not an issue. In a number of country studies sponsored by the ILO, testing procedures have been implemented in which persons whose characteristics are matched except for nationality/national origin as revealed by name, apply for job openings. Such tests are close to reality and focus on actual behaviour – rather than on subjective statements – of employers seeking to fill vacancies. These testing procedures have revealed the prevalence of discrimination in all countries in which they have been applied (for an overview, see Simeone, 2005).

Probably only a minor part of selective hiring is due to outright discrimination. As a consequence, mere anti-discrimination legislation is generally not sufficient to tackle the issue, although such legislation – if properly designed – is an important element. Anti-discrimination legislation has been complemented in OECD countries by other measures such as the use of anonymous CVs, mainly on a voluntary and trial basis, for example in Belgium, France, Sweden and the United Kingdom. In some of these countries, an evaluation of this measure is currently under way. Other promising measures in this respect have aimed at the diversification of recruitment channels and at enhancing employers' awareness of the particular obstacles which the children of immigrants face.

One would expect discrimination and lack of networks to be more of a problem under slack labour market conditions when employers have the luxury to hire selectively either directly by favouring applications from certain groups or indirectly by limiting recruitment to channels which are not accessible to everyone. However, even in countries with relatively open and flexible labour markets and a favourable economic environment such as Denmark and the United Kingdom, labour market outcomes for the second generation are not favourable.

In some member countries, notably in Denmark, there have been efforts to attract the children of immigrants into certain professions in the trades where there are current or expected labour shortages. Yet, these strategies have not always been successful as these occupations are often perceived by the second generation as being the type of work which their parents have done – and thus to be avoided.

In the past, the public sector has often played an important role in the labour market integration of the second generation. The public sector provides the government with a lever to aid labour market integration, as it has a more direct influence on its own employment decisions than those in the private sector. If in fact children of immigrants find employment in the public administration, this also increases the visibility of persons with a migration background in daily life and can contribute to enhancing the understanding of their needs by public institutions. Furthermore, by employing children of immigrants, the public administration acts as a role model for the private sector. However, children of immigrants tend to be largely under-represented in the public sector. This is often due to a lack of awareness of available opportunities (which are, in addition, more limited now than in the past). Encouraging applications of children of immigrants can already have a significant impact, as suggested by experiences in Germany. Several OECD countries – notably Belgium, Denmark and France – have also introduced targeted policies to promote employment of the children of immigrants in the public sector.

Annex Table I.A1.1. Labour market situation of foreign- and native-born populations in selected OECD countries, 1995, 2000 and 2004-2005

	Participation rate (%)								Unemployment rate (%)								Employment/population ratio (%)							
	Native-born				Foreign-born				Native-born				Foreign-born				Native-born				Foreign-born			
	1995	2000	2004	2005	1995	2000	2004	2005	1995	2000	2004	2005	1995	2000	2004	2005	1995	2000	2004	2005	1995	2000	2004	2005
Men																								
Austria	80.4	79.6	76.7	77.7	84.0	83.3	79.1	76.8	3.6	4.3	4.3	4.1	6.6	8.7	11.2	11.8	77.5	76.2	73.4	74.5	78.5	76.1	70.2	67.8
Belgium	72.4	73.9	73.0	73.4	70.9	72.9	70.8	71.7	6.3	4.2	5.6	6.3	16.9	14.7	14.9	14.8	67.8	70.8	68.9	68.7	58.9	62.2	60.3	61.1
Czech Republic	..	..	77.7	78.2	..	..	73.5	79.1	..	..	7.0	6.2	..	..	12.4	10.4	..	..	72.3	73.3	..	..	64.5	70.8
Denmark	84.2	83.8	82.9	84.2	64.4	65.2	63.3	74.8	6.4	3.4	4.6	4.0	20.5	9.5	11.8	7.2	78.9	80.9	79.1	80.8	51.2	59.0	55.8	69.4
Finland	75.1	79.4	78.2	76.6	..	78.9	83.4	76.0	17.7	10.3	9.9	8.0	..	-	21.3	16.6	61.8	71.2	70.5	70.5	..	50.4	65.7	63.4
France	75.0	75.6	75.1	74.7	78.8	78.0	77.3	76.2	9.1	7.7	8.0	8.1	16.6	14.5	13.8	13.3	68.2	69.8	69.1	68.7	65.7	66.7	66.6	66.1
Germany	..	79.3	79.2	80.7	..	76.2	77.7	80.0	..	6.9	10.3	10.6	..	12.9	18.3	17.5	..	73.8	70.4	72.2	..	66.3	63.5	66.0
Greece	77.0	76.6	78.4	78.4	81.9	86.3	87.1	88.3	6.1	7.4	6.5	5.9	14.0	9.5	6.5	6.4	72.3	70.9	73.3	73.8	70.4	78.1	81.4	82.7
Hungary	..	67.5	66.9	67.6	..	71.8	76.1	74.2	..	7.3	5.9	7.0	..	-	2.0	..	..	62.6	62.9	62.8	..	69.4	74.6	72.7
Ireland	76.0	79.1	79.1	79.4	76.7	79.2	79.6	83.8	12.0	4.4	4.9	4.5	16.8	6.5	6.7	6.0	66.9	75.6	75.3	75.8	63.9	74.9	74.3	78.8
Italy	72.4	73.6	74.6	73.9	84.8	88.2	86.0	86.9	9.3	8.4	6.4	6.2	-	-	6.2	6.1	65.6	67.4	69.8	69.4	78.9	82.4	80.7	81.6
Luxembourg	72.2	74.2	70.5	71.0	83.0	80.2	81.2	83.6	..	-	2.4	3.0	-	-	4.4	4.2	70.7	73.2	68.8	68.8	81.3	78.1	77.6	80.1
Netherlands	81.0	85.5	85.0	84.6	69.9	74.0	76.2	78.3	4.9	1.8	3.6	3.6	19.5	5.4	10.3	11.9	77.0	84.0	81.9	81.6	56.2	69.9	68.4	69.0
Norway	..	85.2	82.1	82.1	..	80.0	77.5	76.5	..	3.4	4.3	4.2	-	6.8	8.9	12.5	..	82.3	78.6	78.7	..	74.6	70.6	67.0
Portugal	76.5	78.0	78.6	78.4	73.0	83.7	85.5	85.7	6.6	3.1	5.7	6.8	-	3.9	9.8	8.5	71.5	75.5	74.2	73.1	65.4	80.5	77.1	78.4
Slovak Republic	..	..	76.5	74.0	..	..	81.2	78.3	..	..	17.8	15.7	..	..	17.9	23.0	..	..	62.9	64.1	..	..	66.7	66.1
Spain	74.2	78.3	79.4	80.0	78.9	85.9	89.0	87.9	18.0	9.5	7.8	7.0	24.4	12.4	11.4	9.5	60.8	70.8	73.2	74.4	59.7	75.2	78.8	79.5
Sweden	82.7	79.9	80.7	82.8	73.3	69.9	74.5	75.9	7.9	5.1	6.2	7.9	24.8	12.3	14.2	15.6	76.2	75.9	75.7	76.3	55.1	61.3	63.6	64.1
Switzerland	..	..	88.1	87.4	..	..	87.8	87.4	..	..	2.9	2.7	..	..	7.5	7.7	..	..	85.6	85.1	..	..	81.2	80.6
United Kingdom	83.7	83.5	82.0	81.8	78.5	78.7	78.5	78.2	9.9	5.9	4.7	4.7	14.2	9.6	7.3	7.4	75.4	78.6	78.1	77.9	67.4	71.1	72.8	72.4
Australia	85.3	84.3	85.3	84.4	80.1	77.8	80.6	78.2	8.4	6.6	5.6	4.7	10.6	6.5	5.5	5.0	78.2	78.7	80.6	80.5	71.6	72.7	76.2	74.3
Canada	83.0	82.1	..	..	84.4	82.0	..	..	8.6	5.7	..	..	10.4	6.1	..	..	75.9	77.4	..	..	75.6	77.0	..	..
United States	81.6	80.8	78.4	78.2	83.8	85.9	85.2	86.0	6.2	4.5	6.9	6.3	7.9	4.5	5.8	5.1	76.5	77.2	73.0	73.3	77.2	82.0	80.2	81.7

INTERNATIONAL MIGRATION OUTLOOK: SOPEMI 2007 EDITION – ISBN 978-92-64-03285-9 – © OECD 2007

Annex Table I.A1.1. Labour market situation of foreign- and native-born populations in selected OECD countries, 1995, 2000 and 2004-2005 (cont.)

| | Participation rate (%) | | | | | | | | Unemployment rate (%) | | | | | | | | Employment/population ratio (%) | | | | | | | |
| | Native-born | | | | Foreign-born | | | | Native-born | | | | Foreign-born | | | | Native-born | | | | Foreign-born | | | |
	1995	2000	2004	2005	1995	2000	2004	2005	1995	2000	2004	2005	1995	2000	2004	2005	1995	2000	2004	2005	1995	2000	2004	2005
Women																								
Austria	62.3	62.5	64.1	65.9	62.0	62.8	60.1	61.7	4.6	4.2	4.3	4.4	7.3	7.2	10.7	9.8	59.4	59.9	61.4	63.0	57.5	58.3	53.7	55.7
Belgium	52.9	58.1	59.3	61.3	41.8	45.2	47.2	48.7	11.2	7.4	7.5	7.5	23.8	17.5	15.0	20.3	46.9	53.8	54.9	56.7	31.9	37.3	40.1	38.8
Czech Republic	..	..	62.2	62.2	..	..	57.7	61.5	..	..	9.6	9.7	..	..	13.5	16.5	..	..	56.2	56.1	..	..	49.9	51.3
Denmark	75.9	77.3	77.6|	76.4	52.4	53.4	51.3|	60.2	8.4	4.3	5.2|	5.0	20.7	9.6	12.7|	12.4	69.5	73.9	73.5|	72.6	41.5	48.3	44.8|	52.7
Finland	69.6	74.2	74.5	73.2	..	–	63.1	64.2	16.1	12.0	10.2	8.3	..	–	25.3	20.2	58.4	65.3	66.8	67.1	..	–	47.1	51.3
France	62.0	63.8	64.5	64.7	54.4	56.8	58.0	57.6	13.6	11.3	9.9	9.2	19.0	19.7	17.4	16.5	53.6	56.6	58.1	58.7	44.1	45.6	47.9	48.1
Germany	..	64.8	66.9	68.7	..	53.0	54.9	57.3	..	8.0	9.6	10.2	..	12.1	15.2	16.3	..	59.6	60.5	61.7	..	46.6	46.5	48.0
Greece	43.8	49.2	53.8	54.2	53.7	56.9	58.3	58.7	13.7	16.6	15.7	15.3	20.8	21.1	19.1	15.9	37.8	41.1	45.3	45.9	42.5	44.9	47.2	49.4
Hungary	..	52.5	53.6	54.9	..	52.3	54.3	58.4	..	5.8	5.9	7.4	..	–	6.4	7.3	..	49.4	50.4	50.9	..	49.8	50.8	54.1
Ireland	46.9	55.5	58.1	60.2	49.5	58.8	57.0	61.4	11.9	4.2	3.7	3.5	15.4	–	5.3	6.0	41.3	53.1	56.0	58.0	41.9	55.2	54.0	57.7
Italy	42.5	46.2	50.1	49.9	49.1	51.4	56.6	54.7	16.3	14.9	10.1	9.2	23.5	21.2	13.2	14.6	35.6	39.3	45.0	45.3	37.5	40.5	49.1	46.7
Luxembourg	40.3	48.0	49.9	52.9	51.7	57.2	60.6	63.1	–	–	4.5	4.5	..	–	9.6	7.5	38.8	46.5	47.6	50.5	48.8	55.3	54.8	58.3
Netherlands	59.5	67.6	71.2	71.7	47.8	52.8	56.0	58.0	7.7	3.0	4.3	4.5	19.8	7.6	10.6	9.5	54.9	65.6	68.1	68.5	38.4	48.8	50.1	52.5
Norway	..	77.1	76.2	75.7	..	67.1	67.1	65.3	..	3.2	3.7	4.3	..	–	7.3	8.5	..	74.6	73.4	72.4	..	63.5	62.2	59.8
Portugal	59.1	63.3	66.4	67.1	58.0	66.5	70.9	74.7	7.8	4.9	7.4	8.4	–	5.4	9.6	9.7	54.5	60.3	61.5	61.5	49.9	62.9	64.1	67.5
Slovak Republic	..	..	63.0	61.3	..	..	62.2	57.6	..	..	19.5	17.0	..	..	30.5	28.6	..	..	50.7	50.9	..	..	43.3	41.2
Spain	44.8	51.6	55.7	56.8	51.5	57.9	65.2	69.9	30.5	20.5	15.1	12.0	30.5	20.7	17.1	13.5	31.1	41.0	47.3	50.0	35.8	45.9	54.1	60.4
Sweden	79.5	76.6	76.9	79.6	64.0	63.4	67.7	67.0	6.6	4.2	5.2	7.9	18.5	10.8	12.6	14.1	74.2	73.4	72.9	72.9	52.2	56.6	59.1	57.5
Switzerland	..	..	75.2	75.9	..	..	70.3	69.7	..	..	3.4	3.7	..	–	9.2	9.7	..	..	72.7	73.1	..	..	63.8	62.9
United Kingdom	66.8	68.9	69.6	69.6	57.7	57.5	59.3	60.3	6.7	4.6	3.9	3.8	10.9	7.8	7.3	7.1	62.3	65.7	66.9	67.0	51.4	53.0	55.0	56.0
Australia	66.7	68.1	69.9	71.9	57.1	58.2	61.0	61.8	7.7	5.8	5.7	5.0	9.6	7.0	5.6	5.2	69.8	71.4	65.9	68.3	61.8	63.5	57.6	58.6
Canada	68.8	70.4	..	..	63.4	65.3	..	..	9.8	6.2	..	..	13.3	8.7	..	..	62.0	66.0	..	..	55.0	59.6	..	..
United States	69.5	71.4	69.2	68.9	58.4	61.1	60.3	59.5	5.3	4.2	5.5	5.2	8.2	5.5	6.8	5.2	65.8	68.4	65.4	65.3	53.6	57.7	56.2	56.4

Annex Table I.A1.1. **Labour market situation of foreign- and native-born populations in selected OECD countries, 1995, 2000 and 2004-2005** (cont.)

| | Participation rate (%) | | | | | | | | Unemployment rate (%) | | | | | | | | Employment/population ratio (%) | | | | | | | |
| | Native-born | | | | Foreign-born | | | | Native-born | | | | Foreign-born | | | | Native-born | | | | Foreign-born | | | |
	1995	2000	2004	2005	1995	2000	2004	2005	1995	2000	2004	2005	1995	2000	2004	2005	1995	2000	2004	2005	1995	2000	2004	2005
Men and women																								
Austria	71.4	71.1	70.5	71.8	72.8	72.7	69.2	68.8	4.1	4.3	4.3	4.3	6.9	8.0	11.0	10.8	68.5	68.0	67.5	68.7	67.8	66.8	61.5	61.4
Belgium	62.7	66.0	66.2	67.4	56.3	59.0	58.9	59.8	8.4	5.6	6.4	6.9	19.5	15.8	14.9	17.1	57.5	62.4	62.0	62.8	45.3	49.7	50.1	49.6
Czech Republic	..	..	70.0	70.2	..	..	65.3	70.7	..	..	8.2	7.7	..	..	12.9	12.9	..	..	64.3	64.7	..	..	56.9	61.6
Denmark	80.1	80.6	80.3	80.4	58.5	59.3	57.3	66.5	7.3	3.9	4.9	4.5	20.6	9.5	12.2	9.8	74.2	77.5	76.3	76.8	46.4	53.6	50.3	59.9
Finland	72.4	76.8	76.4	74.9	..	65.8	72.6	69.8	17.0	11.1	10.1	8.2	..	–	23.1	18.3	60.1	68.3	68.7	68.8	..	45.1	55.8	57.0
France	68.4	69.6	69.8	69.6	66.7	67.4	67.5	66.6	11.2	9.4	9.0	8.6	17.6	16.7	15.4	14.7	60.7	63.1	63.5	63.6	55.0	56.2	57.1	56.8
Germany	..	72.1	73.0	74.8	..	64.8	66.3	68.7	..	7.4	10.0	10.4	..	12.6	17.0	17.0	..	66.7	65.8	67.0	..	56.7	55.1	57.0
Greece	59.9	62.6	66.0	66.3	66.0	70.3	72.4	73.3	9.0	11.1	10.3	9.7	17.1	14.6	11.6	10.2	54.5	55.6	59.3	59.8	54.7	60.0	64.0	65.8
Hungary	..	59.9	60.1	61.1	..	61.0	64.0	65.6	..	6.6	5.9	7.2	..	–	–	4.6	..	55.9	56.5	56.7	..	58.5	61.4	62.6
Ireland	61.6	67.3	68.7	69.8	62.6	68.9	68.1	73.0	12.0	4.3	4.4	4.1	16.2	5.7	6.1	6.0	54.2	64.4	65.7	67.0	52.4	64.9	63.9	68.7
Italy	57.3	59.8	62.3	61.9	66.7	69.3	70.0	70.1	11.9	10.9	7.9	7.4	13.1	12.1	9.3	9.5	50.4	53.3	57.4	57.3	58.0	60.9	63.5	63.5
Luxembourg	56.4	61.6	60.4	62.1	67.7	68.4	70.9	73.3	2.6	2.0	3.3	3.6	3.4	2.9	6.7	5.6	54.9	60.4	58.4	59.8	65.4	66.4	66.2	69.2
Netherlands	70.4	76.7	78.2	78.2	59.0	63.4	66.0	67.9	6.0	2.3	3.9	4.0	19.6	6.3	10.4	10.8	66.1	74.9	75.1	75.1	47.4	59.4	59.1	60.5
Norway	..	81.2	79.2	78.9	..	73.5	72.2	70.8	..	3.3	4.0	4.2	..	6.1	8.1	10.6	..	78.5	76.0	75.6	..	69.0	66.4	63.3
Portugal	67.5	70.4	72.5	72.7	65.2	75.8	77.6	79.9	7.2	3.9	6.5	7.5	12.1	4.5	9.7	9.0	62.7	67.6	67.8	67.2	57.3	72.4	70.1	72.7
Slovak Republic	..	..	69.7	68.6	..	..	69.7	70.2	..	..	18.6	16.3	..	..	24.7	25.5	..	..	56.8	57.5	..	..	52.4	52.3
Spain	59.4	64.9	67.6	68.6	64.2	71.4	76.8	78.7	22.8	13.9	10.8	9.1	27.0	15.9	13.8	11.3	45.8	55.9	60.3	62.3	46.8	60.0	66.2	69.8
Sweden	81.1	78.3	78.9	81.0	68.3	66.6	71.4	71.3	7.3	4.7	5.7	7.9	21.7	11.6	13.4	14.9	75.2	74.6	74.4	74.6	53.5	58.9	61.3	60.7
Switzerland	..	..	81.7	81.7	..	..	78.8	78.4	..	..	3.1	3.1	..	..	8.3	8.6	..	..	79.2	79.2	..	..	72.3	71.6
United Kingdom	75.3	76.3	75.7	75.6	67.7	67.7	68.4	68.8	8.5	5.3	4.3	4.3	12.8	8.8	7.3	7.3	68.9	72.2	72.4	72.4	59.0	61.8	63.4	63.8
Australia	76.0	76.2	77.6	78.2	68.8	68.1	70.7	70.1	8.1	6.2	5.6	4.8	10.2	6.7	5.6	5.1	69.8	71.4	73.2	74.4	61.8	63.5	66.8	66.5
Canada	75.9	76.2	..	..	73.7	73.3	..	..	9.1	6.0	..	..	11.7	7.3	..	..	68.9	71.7	..	..	65.1	68.0	..	..
United States	75.4	76.0	73.7	73.4	71.1	73.6	73.0	73.1	5.8	4.4	6.2	5.8	8.0	4.9	6.2	5.1	71.1	72.7	69.1	69.2	65.4	70.0	68.5	69.4

Note: The sign " .. " means not available, " _ " means insufficient sample sizes at B threshold, " | " means a break in series.

Sources: European countries: European Union Labour Force Survey, population aged 15 to 64 (data provided by Eurostat) except for Denmark (Population register (1995, 2000, 2004); United States (Population register (1995, 2000, 2004)); United States: Current Population Survey March Supplement; Australia: Labour Force Survey; Canada: Survey of Labour and Income Dynamics.

StatLink http://dx.doi.org/10.1787/022084606301

Annex Table I.A1.2. Labour market situation of foreigners and nationals in selected OECD countries, 1995, 2000 and 2004-2005

	Participation rate (%)								Unemployment rate (%)								Employment/population ratio (%)							
	Nationals				Foreigners				Nationals				Foreigners				Nationals				Foreigners			
	1995	2000	2004	2005	1995	2000	2004	2005	1995	2000	2004	2005	1995	2000	2004	2005	1995	2000	2004	2005	1995	2000	2004	2005
Men																								
Austria	80.3	79.5	76.8	77.5	85.6	85.2	78.9	77.9	3.7	4.4	4.6	4.4	6.2	8.6	10.0	12.7	77.3	76.0	73.3	74.1	80.3	77.9	71.0	68.0
Belgium	72.6	73.7	73.0	73.2	68.7	73.9	70.2	72.9	6.1	4.3	6.0	6.6	19.8	15.1	14.5	14.8	68.2	70.6	68.6	68.3	55.0	62.7	60.0	62.1
Czech Republic	..	78.9	77.6	78.1	..	90.1	83.1	88.6	..	7.4	7.2	6.3	..	7.7	2.5	–	..	73.1	72.0	73.2	..	83.2	81.0	86.6
Denmark	84.1	83.5	82.5	84.0	58.1	59.8	60.3	72.8	6.6	3.6	4.8	4.1	23.2	10.1	11.5	14.4	78.6	80.5	78.5	80.5	44.6	53.8	53.4	67.7
Finland	75.0	79.3	78.3	76.7	58.2	82.0	84.3	72.6	17.9	10.2	10.1	8.2	–	28.6	21.4	14.4	61.6	71.3	70.4	70.4	45.4	58.6	66.2	62.1
France	74.7	75.1	75.2	74.8	76.0	76.5	77.4	76.0	9.3	7.9	8.2	8.3	20.2	18.0	16.6	15.3	67.8	69.2	69.1	68.6	60.7	62.7	64.6	64.3
Germany	79.7	79.0	79.2	80.7	79.0	77.2	76.8	79.9	6.2	7.1	10.4	10.7	15.1	13.6	19.5	20.3	74.8	73.4	70.9	72.0	67.0	66.7	61.9	63.6
Greece	77.1	76.6	78.5	78.5	86.7	89.4	88.3	89.2	6.3	7.5	6.6	6.0	–	7.4	4.8	4.4	72.2	70.9	73.3	73.8	77.7	82.8	84.1	85.3
Hungary	..	..	67.0	67.6	..	..	78.6	76.7	..	..	5.9	7.0	..	..	1.0	–	..	..	63.1	62.9	..	..	77.8	76.3
Ireland	76.2	79.3	79.3	79.5	73.4	74.5	76.4	84.2	12.1	4.4	5.0	4.5	..	–	7.1	6.2	66.9	75.8	75.3	75.9	60.6	70.1	71.0	79.0
Italy	72.4	..	..	..	84.6	..	..	..	9.3	..	..	..	..	–	..	..	65.6	..	..	..	78.7	..	82.6	..
Luxembourg	73.6	75.8	72.3	72.4	80.1	77.4	78.4	81.0	–	–	2.2	2.6	–	–	4.7	4.6	72.2	75.0	70.7	70.5	78.0	75.0	74.7	77.2
Netherlands	80.8	84.6	84.5	84.2	63.9	70.1	71.5	74.1	5.4	2.0	4.2	4.2	23.2	–	9.1	13.4	76.5	82.9	80.9	80.7	49.0	66.3	65.0	64.2
Norway	..	84.9	81.8	81.8	..	82.5	80.6	79.8	..	3.6	4.3	4.5	..	..	12.9	13.5	..	81.9	78.3	78.1	..	78.1	70.1	69.0
Portugal	76.4	78.9	79.0	78.6	64.3	80.1	83.7	86.7	6.8	3.2	5.9	6.8	..	..	12.7	9.8	71.3	76.4	74.5	73.3	59.3	74.1	73.1	78.2
Slovak Republic	..	76.4	76.5	76.1	..	81.1	..	..	..	19.5	17.8	15.8	..	..	5.2	–	..	61.6	62.9	64.1	..	..	88.7	–
Spain	74.2	78.4	79.6	80.2	84.0	84.4	89.4	87.7	18.1	9.6	7.9	7.0	20.3	13.8	11.4	10.1	60.8	70.9	73.4	74.5	66.9	72.7	79.2	78.8
Sweden	82.6	78.0	80.2	82.3	69.7	63.1	71.7	74.8	8.3	5.5	6.8	8.4	23.5	16.1	17.2	18.5	75.8	73.7	74.8	75.4	53.3	52.9	59.4	61.0
Switzerland	..	89.6	88.2	87.4	..	88.5	87.4	87.4	..	1.4	2.9	2.8	..	5.0	7.6	7.6	..	88.3	85.7	85.0	..	84.0	80.7	80.7
United Kingdom	83.6	83.4	81.9	81.7	75.8	75.9	77.2	76.3	10.0	6.0	4.8	4.8	16.6	11.7	7.3	8.9	75.3	78.5	77.9	77.8	63.2	67.0	71.5	69.5

Annex Table I.A1.2. **Labour market situation of foreigners and nationals in selected OECD countries, 1995, 2000 and 2004-2005** (*Cont.*)

	Participation rate (%)								Unemployment rate (%)								Employment/population ratio (%)							
	Nationals				Foreigners				Nationals				Foreigners				Nationals				Foreigners			
	1995	2000	2004	2005	1995	2000	2004	2005	1995	2000	2004	2005	1995	2000	2004	2005	1995	2000	2004	2005	1995	2000	2004	2005
Women																								
Austria	62.1	62.4	64.0	65.6	64.2	64.4	57.4	61.7	4.7	4.1	4.4	4.6	7.8	9.1	13.7	10.7	59.2	59.8	61.2	62.5	59.1	58.5	49.5	55.1
Belgium	53.0	58.1	58.6	60.5	38.0	41.3	49.0	49.4	11.0	7.8	7.5	8.3	31.5	16.4	18.1	17.8	47.1	53.6	54.2	55.4	26.0	34.5	40.2	40.6
Czech Republic	..	63.6	62.2	62.1	..	52.8	58.3	65.1	..	10.6	9.7	9.8	..	..	9.9	14.1	..	56.9	56.1	56.1	..	49.3	52.5	55.9
Denmark	75.7	77.0	77.1|	76.1	44.3	45.5	47.2|	53.7	8.5	4.4	5.3|	5.4	25.5	11.3	12.9|	13.2	69.2	73.6	73.0|	72.0	33.0	40.4	41.1|	46.7
Finland	69.4	74.2	74.4	73.3	65.9	61.9	56.6	54.9	16.2	11.8	10.3	8.4	30.4	–	31.3	26.9	58.2	65.4	66.7	67.1	45.9	43.4	38.9	40.1
France	61.5	63.4	64.4	64.6	46.8	48.6	51.8	51.0	13.6	11.5	10.2	9.4	24.4	25.6	21.6	21.6	53.1	56.1	57.9	58.5	35.4	36.2	40.7	40.0
Germany	62.3	64.4	66.6	68.3	50.6	49.7	51.0	52.7	9.3	8.1	9.7	10.4	14.9	11.6	15.6	18.9	56.5	59.2	60.1	61.2	43.1	43.9	43.0	42.7
Greece	44.1	49.5	54.0	54.3	56.3	55.8	57.1	58.2	14.0	16.9	16.0	15.4	18.2	17.6	16.7	14.1	37.9	41.1	45.3	46.0	46.1	46.0	47.6	50.0
Hungary	..	55.8	53.6	54.9	..	..	51.8	62.2	..	..	5.9	7.4	..	..	6.3	6.3	..	..	50.5	50.9	..	..	48.6	57.3
Ireland	47.1	55.8	58.2	60.3	44.6	53.5	53.1	60.4	11.9	4.2	3.7	3.6	–	..	6.3	6.3	41.5	53.4	56.1	58.1	36.1	49.7	49.8	56.6
Italy	42.5	..	50.1	..	49.3	..	60.5	..	16.3	..	10.1	..	22.8	..	15.4	..	35.6	..	45.1	..	38.1	..	51.2	..
Luxembourg	40.2	47.8	50.6	53.4	51.2	56.8	59.3	62.0	–	–	4.2	4.2	–	..	10.0	7.8	38.7	46.7	48.5	51.1	48.5	54.6	53.4	57.2
Netherlands	59.2	66.7	70.1	70.9	39.8	46.1	49.5	47.6	8.2	3.3	4.8	4.9	24.3	9.7	11.3	10.0	54.3	64.5	66.8	67.4	30.1	41.6	43.9	42.8
Norway	..	76.7	75.9	75.2	..	68.3	66.8	66.2	..	3.3	3.8	4.5	..	..	8.3	7.4	..	74.2	73.0	71.9	..	65.3	61.2	61.3
Portugal	59.2	63.7	66.7	67.4	35.1	68.8	68.6	75.6	8.0	4.8	7.4	8.3	..	..	14.1	14.0	54.4	60.6	61.8	61.8	28.0	61.9	58.9	65.0
Slovak Republic	..	62.9	63.0	61.3	..	43.6	76.7	..	..	18.6	19.7	17.1	..	..	15.5	–	..	51.2	50.6	50.8	..	64.9	64.9	–
Spain	44.9	51.7	55.9	57.1	48.6	58.2	65.7	70.4	30.6	20.6	15.2	12.1	27.0	17.6	16.2	13.5	31.2	41.0	47.4	50.2	35.5	48.0	55.1	60.9
Sweden	79.2	74.2	76.2	78.2	60.2	60.3	64.6	62.0	7.1	4.6	5.8	8.4	15.6	13.0	15.1	14.2	73.6	70.8	71.8	71.6	50.8	52.4	54.8	53.1
Switzerland	..	72.8	74.9	75.4	..	66.4	70.2	69.9	..	2.4	3.3	3.8	..	6.5	10.8	10.8	..	71.1	72.4	72.6	..	62.1	62.6	62.4
United Kingdom	66.5	68.5	69.1	69.1	55.5	56.2	59.6	60.5	6.8	4.8	4.0	3.8	11.8	8.0	7.6	8.1	62.0	65.2	66.3	66.5	49.0	51.7	55.0	55.6

Annex Table I.A1.2. **Labour market situation of foreigners and nationals in selected OECD countries, 1995, 2000 and 2004-2005** (Cont.)

	Participation rate (%)								Unemployment rate (%)								Employment/population ratio (%)							
	Nationals				Foreigners				Nationals				Foreigners				Nationals				Foreigners			
	1995	2000	2004	2005	1995	2000	2004	2005	1995	2000	2004	2005	1995	2000	2004	2005	1995	2000	2004	2005	1995	2000	2004	2005
Men and women																								
Austria	71.1	70.9	70.4	71.5	75.5	74.7	68.6	69.7	4.1	4.3	4.5	4.5	6.8	8.8	11.5	11.8	68.2	67.9	67.2	68.3	70.4	68.2	60.6	61.5
Belgium	62.8	66.0	65.8	66.8	54.8	58.3	59.8	61.6	8.2	5.8	6.7	7.4	23.5	15.6	15.9	16.0	57.7	62.1	61.4	61.9	42.0	49.2	50.3	51.8
Czech Republic	..	71.2	69.9	70.1	..	73.0	70.6	77.7	..	8.8	8.3	7.9	..	7.3	5.6	6.9	..	64.9	64.1	64.6	..	67.6	66.6	72.3
Denmark	79.9	80.3	79.8|	80.1	51.4	52.6	53.6|	62.0	7.5	4.0	5.1|	4.7	24.2	10.6	12.1|	10.0	74.0	77.1	75.8|	76.3	39.0	47.0	47.1|	55.8
Finland	72.2	76.8	76.4	75.0	61.9	72.9	69.8	63.3	17.1	11.0	10.2	8.3	26.3	29.0	25.6	20.0	59.9	68.4	68.6	68.8	45.6	51.8	52.0	50.6
France	68.0	69.2	69.8	69.6	62.3	63.0	64.8	63.5	11.3	9.6	9.2	8.8	21.7	20.9	18.5	17.8	60.3	62.6	63.4	63.5	48.8	49.8	52.8	52.2
Germany	71.0	71.7	72.9	74.5	66.2	64.3	64.3	66.7	7.5	7.5	10.1	10.6	15.1	12.9	18.0	19.8	65.6	66.3	65.5	66.6	56.3	56.0	52.8	53.5
Greece	60.0	62.7	66.1	66.4	70.2	71.8	72.9	74.0	9.2	11.3	10.4	9.9	13.8	11.6	9.3	8.1	54.4	55.6	59.2	59.8	60.5	63.5	66.1	68.0
Hungary	..	..	60.1	61.1	..	..	64.8	69.0	..	..	5.9	7.2	..	..	..	–	..	..	56.6	56.7	..	..	62.7	66.2
Ireland	61.7	67.6	68.8	69.9	58.2	64.4	64.8	73.3	12.0	4.3	4.4	4.1	18.1	6.4	6.8	6.3	54.3	64.6	65.7	67.0	47.7	60.2	60.4	68.7
Italy	57.3	..	..	..	66.7	..	..	..	11.9	..	..	..	12.9	..	..	..	50.4	..	..	..	58.1	..	..	..
Luxembourg	57.2	62.6	61.6	63.0	65.9	66.7	68.9	71.5	2.5	1.6	3.0	3.3	3.6	3.4	7.0	6.0	55.7	61.6	59.8	60.9	63.5	64.4	64.1	67.3
Netherlands	70.1	75.8	77.4	77.6	53.1	58.1	60.5	60.7	6.5	2.6	4.4	4.5	23.6	7.2	10.0	12.0	65.5	73.8	73.9	74.1	40.6	53.9	54.5	53.4
Norway	..	80.8	78.9	78.6	..	75.5	73.4	72.5	..	3.4	4.1	4.5	..	..	10.7	10.6	..	78.1	75.7	75.1	..	71.8	65.5	64.9
Portugal	67.5	71.1	72.7	73.0	49.9	74.7	75.6	81.1	7.3	3.9	6.6	7.5	..	–	13.3	11.8	62.6	68.3	68.0	67.5	43.8	68.3	65.6	71.6
Slovak Republic	..	69.6	69.7	68.7	..	..	83.6	66.1	..	19.1	18.6	16.4	..	..	..	–	..	56.3	56.7	57.4	..	..	..	59.9
Spain	59.4	65.0	67.8	68.7	65.9	70.7	77.6	79.0	22.9	13.9	10.9	9.1	22.8	15.5	13.4	11.6	45.8	56.0	60.4	62.5	50.8	59.8	67.2	69.8
Sweden	81.0	76.2	78.3	80.3	64.7	61.7	68.1	68.2	7.7	5.1	6.3	8.4	19.7	14.6	16.2	16.5	74.7	72.3	73.3	73.5	52.0	52.7	57.1	56.9
Switzerland	..	81.1	81.4	81.3	..	78.3	79.3	79.2	..	1.9	3.1	3.3	..	5.6	8.9	8.9	..	79.6	78.9	78.7	..	74.0	72.2	72.2
United Kingdom	75.1	76.1	75.4	75.3	65.0	65.4	67.7	68.1	8.6	5.4	4.5	4.3	14.4	10.0	7.5	8.5	68.7	71.9	72.1	72.1	55.6	58.9	62.6	62.3

Note: The sign " .. " means not available, "–" means insufficient sample sizes at B threshold, "\|" means a break in series.
Source: European Union Labour Force Survey, population aged 15 to 64 (data provided by Eurostat) except for Denmark (Population register (1995, 2000, 2004).

StatLink ⌦ http://dx.doi.org/10.1787/022084212552

Annex Table I.A1.3. **Education levels for immigrants, the second generation, and other native-born, 20-29 and not in education, by gender, latest available year**

	Men			Women		
	Low	Medium	High	Low	Medium	High
Australia[1] (2001)						
Foreign-born	40	19	41	39	13	48
Native-born, at least one parent foreign-born	46	30	24	44	19	37
Native-born, both parents native-born	49	32	19	50	18	32
Canada[2] (2001)						
Foreign-born	22	18	60	19	16	66
Native-born, both parents foreign-born	16	19	65	9	12	78
Native-born, one parent foreign-born	19	21	61	13	16	71
Native-born, both parents native-born	27	20	53	20	16	65
Denmark (2004)						
Foreign-born	56	35	9	50	39	12
Native-born, both parents foreign-born	57	34	9	44	43	13
Native-born, at least one parent native-born	28	59	13	24	53	23
France (1999)						
Foreign-born[3]	40	44	16	45	37	18
Native-born, both parents foreign-born	29	55	17	26	53	21
Native-born, one parent foreign-born	22	52	26	21	45	34
Native-born, both parents native-born	20	54	26	19	48	34
Germany (2005)						
Foreign-born	39	46	15	42	41	17
Native-born, both parents foreign-born	36	52	12	35	49	16
Native-born, one parent foreign-born	30	56	14	23	56	20
Native-born, both parents native-born	18	62	19	17	57	26
Norway (2004)						
Foreign-born	14	74	12	14	66	21
Native-born, both parents foreign-born	12	75	13	8	73	19
Native-born, one parent foreign-born	6	73	21	5	64	31
Native-born, both parents native-born	5	75	19	4	64	33
Sweden (2004)						
Foreign-born	24	47	29	20	43	37
Native-born, both parents foreign-born	21	57	23	15	53	31
Native-born, one parent foreign-born	16	58	27	12	51	37
Native-born, both parents native-born	11	59	30	8	50	42

INTERNATIONAL MIGRATION OUTLOOK: SOPEMI 2007 EDITION – ISBN 978-92-64-03285-9 – © OECD 2007

Annex Table I.A1.3. **Education levels for immigrants, the second generation, and other native-born, 20-29 and not in education, by gender, latest available year** (Cont.)

	Men			Women		
	Low	Medium	High	Low	Medium	High
Switzerland (2000)						
Foreign-born	44	41	15	46	39	12
Native-born with foreign nationality at birth	14	69	17	13	75	12
Native-born with Swiss nationality at birth	7	74	20	7	81	15
United Kingdom (2005)						
Foreign-born	25	35	40	27	27	45
Native-born with other "ethnic background"	11	54	27	8	55	37
Native-born with "white British ethnic background"	8	65	27	9	60	31
United States (2005)						
Foreign-born	35	46	19	29	44	28
Native-born, both parents foreign-born	14	59	27	15	57	28
Native-born, one parent foreign-born	13	68	20	9	58	34
Native-born, both parents native-born	10	65	25	7	57	36

Notes: "Low" refers to below upper secondary; "medium" to upper secondary and post-secondary non-tertiary and "high" to tertiary education.

1. Qualification levels for Australia were classified as follows: Low: No (professional) qualifications; Medium: Certificate; High: Diploma and above.
2. Qualification levels for Canada were classified as follows: "low" refers to "no schooling or Grade 1 to 13", "medium" refers to "secondary school graduation certificate", "high" refers to "Trade non-university" and university.
3. Foreign-born for France excludes foreign-born with French nationality at birth.

Sources: Switzerland: Census (2000); Denmark, Norway and Sweden: Population register (2004); Germany: Microcensus (2005); Australia and Canada: Census (2001); France: Étude de l'histoire familiale (1999); United States: Current Population Survey March 2005 supplement; United Kingdom: Labour Force Survey (third quarter 2005).

StatLink ⫘⬚ *http://dx.doi.org/10.1787/022058503223*

Annex Table I.A1.4. **Employment rates for immigrants, the second generation, and other native-born, 20-29 and not in education, by gender, latest available year**

	Low		Medium		High		Total	
	Men	Women	Men	Women	Men	Women	Men	Women
Australia[1] (2001)								
Foreign-born	74	55	81	59	73	66	66	50
Native-born, at least one parent foreign-born	77	67	88	76	89	82	80	72
Native-born, both parents native-born	76	61	89	75	91	82	81	70
Canada[2] (2001)								
Foreign-born	75	49	78	59	84	71	81	65
Native-born, both parents foreign-born	74	62	84	76	90	87	86	83
Native-born, one parent foreign-born	75	59	86	77	90	86	86	81
Native-born, both parents native-born	71	50	84	71	89	84	83	76
Denmark (2004)								
Foreign-born	51	30	69	46	64	57	50	32
Native-born, both parents foreign-born	57	46	79	71	74	74	64	59
Native-born, at least one parent native-born	62	49	90	85	87	87	81	76
France (1999)								
Foreign-born[3]	63	32	66	50	83	72	67	44
Native-born, both parents foreign-born	55	40	70	63	86	80	68	60
Native-born, one parent foreign-born	69	49	78	67	85	81	77	67
Native-born, both parents native-born	67	45	84	68	88	85	81	69
Germany (2005)								
Foreign-born	62	27	76	54	82	61	71	43
Native-born, both parents foreign-born	52	43	76	69	78	74	68	60
Native-born, one parent foreign-born	:	:	:	:	:	:	69	70
Native-born, both parents native-born	57	42	81	73	90	86	79	72
Norway (2004)								
Foreign-born	55	40	66	63	75	74	64	50
Native-born, both parents foreign-born	58	50	73	67	75	74	69	63
Native-born, one parent foreign-born	59	54	75	71	82	82	74	73
Native-born, both parents native-born	65	53	82	75	89	89	82	79
Sweden (2004)								
Foreign-born	45	37	66	59	53	53	52	46
Native-born, both parents foreign-born	52	50	75	73	77	79	68	69
Native-born, one parent foreign-born	58	54	80	76	82	82	75	73
Native-born, both parents native-born	66	58	86	82	87	88	83	81

Annex Table I.A1.4. **Employment rates for immigrants, the second generation, and other native-born, 20-29 and not in education, by gender, latest available year** (Cont.)

	Low		Medium		High		Total	
	Men	Women	Men	Women	Men	Women	Men	Women
Switzerland (2000)								
Foreign-born	86	62	92	78	94	79	88	70
Native-born with foreign nationality at birth	78	71	94	89	93	89	91	86
Native-born with Swiss nationality at birth	76	68	95	88	95	91	94	87
United Kingdom (2005)								
Foreign-born	:	:	:	:	:	:	77	61
Native-born with other "ethnic background"	:	:	:	:	:	:	75	66
Native-born with "white British ethnic background"	:	:	:	:	:	:	87	74
United States (2005)								
Foreign-born	87	37	79	55	82	59	83	51
Native-born, both parents foreign-born	62	41	72	68	77	75	72	66
Native-born, one parent foreign-born	66	44	70	60	86	81	72	66
Native-born, both parents native-born	58	39	73	66	85	84	75	69

Source and notes: See Annex Table I.A1.3.

StatLink http://dx.doi.org/10.1787/022060177817

C. Migration Policies[23]

There are two broad categories of migration policy. The first category, connected mainly with domestic concerns, covers criteria for the recruitment of immigrants, their reception and their integration into the labour market and society as a whole. However, migration is also at the centre of international relations and the second category covers international co-operation for better management of flows, and the links between migration, regional integration and development.

1. Attract, receive and integrate: Domestic immigration policies

In domestic terms, a distinction must be made between policy choices relating to flows and actions relating to the integration of foreigners once they have reached a country. Recent policies confirm renewed interest in labour migration in response to market needs. New integration measures emphasise all the stages in the process, from the reception of first-generation immigrants to access to citizenship. These measures also emphasise the active role that immigrants should play as part of a redefinition of the responsibilities of the various actors involved.

Meeting labour market needs

The purpose of employment-oriented migration policies is to define the criteria for recruiting immigrants so as to meet labour market requirements. It is necessary, therefore, not only to attract and in some cases retain foreigners but also to make better use of the human capital they represent. Some countries have also decided to set up regularisation programmes targeting some categories of illegal immigrants.

a) Selective policies for recruiting skilled workers

Most OECD countries have introduced new measures to attract skilled workers in recent years. It is interesting to note that this trend can also be observed in the countries that have recently joined the European Union and in Mexico, even though they are still countries of emigration. Emigrants from these countries are drawn not only from the unskilled but also from educated sections of the active population. In the specific case of central European countries,[24] a rapidly ageing population and the scale of emigration make immigration even more necessary. Selective policies may also target less skilled workers. Korea, for example, has decided to replace its system of internships in industry by the recruitment of temporary workers issued with work permits.

Although there is a consensus on selection, there is considerable variation in the content of the measures taken. In the European OECD countries, where labour immigration was halted in the late 1970s because of the high level of unemployment, the first step was to ensure that labour market testing could not be used to refuse entry to the most highly skilled foreigners.[25] Researchers and executives working for multinationals were the first to benefit from these opportunities. It is generally employers who make the selection, but countries use a range of criteria to guide their choices, including qualifications, sponsorship by firms, salary level and an assessment of skills requirements. At the same time, the ways in which selective policies were implemented gave rise to systems of quotas, points and targeted programmes.

Towards the end of labour market testing. Since the early 2000s, the retirement of the first generations of the post-war baby-boom has increased labour market pressures which can affect some branches and professions more than others (they can also be amplified periodically by factors other than ageing). Initially, measures targeting these branches and professions were able to cushion the effects, as with nurses in France, or with the recruitment of IT operatives in several OECD countries, such as Germany. On the basis of a precise evaluation of the shortages in certain branches and professions, labour market testing has been lifted for a wider range of occupations. In France, for example, the Ministry of Employment publishes an annual "shortage occupation list", region by region, based on an indicator calculated by the ANPE (national employment service). Publication of the list of occupations where labour market testing no longer applies to immigrants from the new EU member states led to an increase in direct entries of permanent workers in 2005, especially for skilled jobs such as technicians, supervisors, managers and engineers, representing a total of approximately 10 000 individuals. In Belgium the regions, after consulting the social partners, publish lists of sectors and occupations for which immigrants are granted work permits. In the United Kingdom, there is a "shortage occupation list" for which foreigners can obtain a work permit if they meet a minimum level of qualification.

How are needs evaluated and how is selection performed?. Some countries, like Italy, have opted for quotas. The problem here is to ensure that the number of permits allocated *ex ante* matches labour market needs ascertained *ex post*.[26] Thus, Italy had to double its quotas between 2005 and 2006. Despite the increase, however, in 2006 the quota was reached within a few days and there was a considerable difference between the number of applications and the number of permits: 490 000 applications were submitted for 170 000 permits. Faced with this rush, in May 2006 the government decided to allow all immigrants who had completed an application to stay. However, it also announced a major overhaul of the system which parliament will debate in 2007.

Some countries have opted for a points system along the lines of the one long in use in Canada, Australia and New Zealand. In 2006, the Netherlands announced their intention of introducing such a system within the broader framework of a new migration policy. The main advantage of the system is that points can be modulated year by year by varying the criteria for obtaining bonus points, such as professional experience or the educational level of a spouse, as in the United Kingdom. Governments can thus easily steer the system.

Relatively straightforward in theory, the points system nevertheless has two major drawbacks. First, it implies the introduction of a system for verifying qualifications and diplomas awarded in countries of origin, which is not easy. Second, it assumes, for example, that a university degree has the same value as a qualification, whatever the country in which it is awarded. Qualification becomes equivalent to skill, the educational level guaranteeing the worker's competencies. To get round the problem, the United Kingdom has added a wage level requirement to its points system, determined by region of origin. For supporters of the system, a high salary may be regarded as an indicator of recognition of both qualification and skill. In a way, it is the labour market of the country of origin which organises the selection (see Box I.6).

More generally, the chief factor that guides countries' labour immigration choices is the objective they pursue. Countries that have introduced a points system are those which want foreigners to settle there. Other countries select immigrants to meet labour market

---

Box I.6. **The points system in the United Kingdom: Qualification and sponsorship**

The British system has two levels for skilled workers.

The first level, Tier 1, corresponds to the old points system (the Highly Skilled Migrant Programme, HSMP) but with new criteria. Under the previous system, professional experience and the spouse's educational level were taken into account in addition to qualification. Under the new system, the only criteria taken into account are the candidate's qualifications, salary level in country of origin and age, though bonus points are awarded to candidates who have previously studied or worked in the United Kingdom. Tier 1 candidates have six months in which to find a job entitling them to a work permit. The Tier 1 system will be introduced in the third quarter of 2007.

The second level, Tier 2, covers skilled workers with a job offer in the United Kingdom. If the job is in one of the occupations on the shortage occupation list, candidates are granted a permit without any formality other than a check on their qualifications and their level of English. If it is not, the company making the offer must fulfill a number of formalities. It must apply to the authorities for inclusion on the list of companies officially authorised to sponsor immigrant workers. For that purpose, at the start of the year the company is asked to estimate how many foreign workers it will need and must be able to prove that the position(s) cannot be filled by a British citizen or EU national. If these criteria are met, the company can send the candidate a certificate of sponsorship enabling him or her to start the process. In all events, selected candidates are given a 5-year residence permit (an initial 2-year permit and eventually a 3-year renewal), after which they can apply for a permanent residence permit.

The new system will be phased in between 2007 and 2009.

---

needs on a temporary basis. The issue is therefore not so much whether one system is more effective than the other but how a country can ensure that its selection criteria are consistent with the objectives it pursues. However, this distinction is tending to fade. The foreigners who integrate most easily are generally those who had a temporary permit before obtaining a permanent residence permit. In several countries it is now possible for temporary immigrants to become permanent residents.

Other countries try to encourage skilled immigration through programmes that target certain categories. Japan, for example, amended its Immigration Control and Refugee Recognition Act in 2006 in order to increase the opportunities for immigration of researchers and engineers specialising in information systems. It had been possible beforehand for immigrants in these two categories to obtain work permits, but only in certain regions included in structural reform programmes. The measure now applies throughout the whole of Japan.

The growing number of new types of residence permit: What legal status for immigrants?

With the new recruitment systems come new types of residence permit, raising the issue of the legal status of foreigners and changes of status. The legal certainty offered to foreigners may be regarded as a criterion for judging the effectiveness of selective policies. In a globalised economy, skilled workers can choose between several countries on the basis of criteria such as the stability of their situation and, for those granted a temporary permit, subsequent possibilities for access to permanent residence.

As an example of the proliferation of permits, the United States now has over 80 types of temporary visa, a certain number of them being for skilled workers. Several countries introduced new temporary residence permits in 2005 and 2006. In France, for example, the Immigration and Integration Act of 24 July 2006, designed to attract more highly skilled workers and facilitate temporary migration, created three new types of 3-year residence permit for highly skilled workers,[27] employees seconded to France by their employer and seasonal workers. In Ireland, the Employment Permits Act which came into effect in January 2007 introduced a new "green card" for skilled workers.[28] Like the points system in the United Kingdom (see Box I.6), qualification is measured *inter alia* by the salary in the country of origin. This must be over EUR 60 000 a year unless the application is for occupations in sectors where there is a shortage of skilled labour, in which case the salary requirement is reduced to EUR 30 000.

These new visas are generally granted for periods longer than one year (three years in France, five in the United Kingdom) and entitle the holder to apply for a permanent residence permit after a certain time (two years in Ireland). By offering these advantages, the host countries clearly signal their wish to see such immigrants take up long-term residence. There is therefore little risk that the introduction of new visas or residence permits will increase uncertainty as to the legal status of skilled foreign workers. Some countries, like Portugal, have even taken advantage of such developments to streamline procedures, make them more transparent and reduce the number of different types of visa.

b) Attracting temporary workers to alleviate sectoral shortages

Recruiting skilled workers is not sufficient to meet all labour market needs. In countries with ageing populations, sectoral shortages also appear in low-skilled or unskilled occupations. To deal with the problem, many countries have developed strategies for encouraging temporary immigration, with the underlying idea that the foreigners concerned will not settle and that recruiting them does not generate a long-term commitment on the part of the host country.

The methods for recruiting these temporary workers vary according to sector of activity, country of origin and policy choices in host countries. In agriculture, countries continue to prioritise seasonal work. In other sectors, they tend to conclude bilateral labour agreements or lift restrictions on the movement of citizens of border countries or member states of regional organisations.

Seasonal workers.   Several OECD countries have substantial seasonal labour needs for agriculture, viticulture, horticulture and fishing. This is the case in all countries where the primary sector is still important, either because it continues to occupy a significant proportion of the active population, as in Mexico and Poland, or because it represents an important resource for the agrifood industry (as in France, the United States and Spain) or for exports (in New Zealand in 2003, farm produce represented almost 50% of exports). Some countries, like Germany, take in as many as 300 000 seasonal workers a year.

Seasonal workers often come from neighbouring countries. In Mexico, most of them come from Guatemala and are hired to work on farms for a few weeks or months. Likewise, foreigners on Canada's Seasonal Agricultural Workers programme mainly come from Mexico and the Caribbean. For this type of farm worker and because the stay is so short, some countries simplify or even abolish administrative procedures for obtaining work permits. Poland, which itself provides large numbers of seasonal workers to its neighbours, especially Germany, has turned to Ukraine, Belarus and the Russia Federation for the necessary labour at harvest time and has abolished the work permit requirement for seasonal farm workers. New Zealand has also introduced a programme, the Recognised Seasonal Employer Policy, to make it easier for local employers to hire foreign seasonal workers. Labour market testing is no longer applied in horticulture and viticulture. Workers are recruited from Oceania: by giving priority to its neighbours, New Zealand hopes to contribute to development and regional stability.

As far as the type of work permit granted to seasonal workers is concerned, countries can be divided into two groups. Some, like Poland and Mexico, have opted to make an exception to the ordinary rules governing labour migration. Since September 2006, the Polish government has authorised farmers to hire seasonal workers with visas but not work permits. However, they may not stay longer than three months in any six-month period and the employer must have been approved by the local authorities. To make it easier to issue visas, employers must also provide the seasonal workers they plan to hire with documentation describing their future job before the application is submitted. Other countries have preferred to create a specific permit along the lines of the H-2A visa in the United States. This is the case in France, where the law of 24 July 2004 created a temporary residence permit for seasonal workers. It is issued for three years to holders of a seasonal work contract who undertake to maintain their customary place of residence outside France. Holders may not work for more than six months in any 12-month period and may not reside in France for more than six consecutive months.

Although most of these seasonal residence permits are not specifically reserved for farm workers, the jobs concerned are sufficiently limited. Countries have to find other ways of recruiting workers to alleviate their more structural labour shortages. In this context, there has been renewed interest in bilateral labour agreements and other forms of recruitment.[29]

Bilateral labour agreements. Labour agreements are either bilateral treaties relating specifically to the terms of immigration between the two countries or sections of broader treaties covering trade, for example.[30] New Zealand, for example, has entered into negotiations for future free-trade agreements with Malaysia and China which include migration. In legal terms, these agreements provide a framework in which flows can be authorised in proportions and forms that constitute an exception to the ordinary law of the country. They mean that host countries can meet their labour needs with a certain degree of flexibility, without having to alter their domestic legislation. For some countries where opportunities for immigration are limited, like Korea and Japan, such agreements may be the only way of enabling foreign workers to enter. In Korea, for example, the new work permit system (see above) applies only to citizens of countries with which such a bilateral agreement exists. In 2005 and 2006, Korea concluded a series of agreements with other Asian countries (China, Pakistan, Uzbekistan and Cambodia), covering all selection procedures for future workers. In 2006, the government planned to issue 105 000 work permits to citizens of signatory countries.

The interest of such agreements lies in the guarantees they offer with regard to the control of inflows and outflows. As a rule, the country of origin is responsible for selection formalities, which can be administratively onerous. They give better guarantees that immigrants will return, since they define the conditions for workers' readmission into their country of origin when their permit expires. In January 2007, Spain concluded an agreement with Ukraine setting out all the selection and readmission procedures to be implemented by Ukraine with Spanish support.

In some cases, agreements may include measures providing for the regularisation of illegal immigrants present in one of the countries entering into such an agreement. In 2005, the Portuguese government regularised several thousand Brazilians following a bilateral agreement. In addition to enabling the control of flows, such agreements often provide a framework for trade-offs not directly linked to immigration, such as investment and more open trade. The increase in the number of such agreements, and the resulting obligations for countries of origin, has caused a rapid rise in the number of private agencies which select candidates and take care of admission formalities for host countries. In Romania in 2004, for example, agencies of this type negotiated and organised around 100 000 temporary work contracts.

Extending freedom of movement. To make it easier to recruit both skilled and less skilled workers, countries can also create free movement areas within which people may settle without restriction. The European Union is one such area. Until recently, freedom of movement had only marginal effects on migration flows as a whole within EU15. However, this situation changed with the entry of ten new countries on 1 May 2004, followed by Romania and Bulgaria on 1 January 2007. The new member states have lower standards of living than the 15 longer-standing members and high unemployment rates, despite well-educated active populations. To give an example, GDP per capita was USD PPP 29 000 in EU15 in 2005 compared with only USD PPP 13 000 in Poland;[31] similarly the unemployment rate in EU15 was 8.3% compared with 17.7% in Poland.[32] In contrast, Poland's results in PISA tests in 2003 were close to the OECD average.

Fearing the consequences of CEEC nationals flooding into their labour markets, many countries chose to take up of the possibility offered by the treaty of membership of preserving restrictions on entry during a transition period for eight of the ten new member states.[33] In practice, the transition period is divided into three phases (2 years plus 3 plus 2), each phase being evaluated before restrictions are renewed or lifted in the following phase. Only Ireland, the United Kingdom and Sweden opted to fully open up their labour markets from 1 May 2004.[34] For the eight member states concerned, the first phase ended on 30 April 2006. The situation is both unusual and instructive, since membership caused two contradictory movements: some capital flowed east, while labour flowed west. So what conclusions can be drawn from the first phase?

The available data show massive entries of migrants from the eight new member states into Ireland and the United Kingdom, while flows into Sweden remained relatively small. Approximately 580 000 nationals[35] from the eight countries entered the United Kingdom between May 2004 and the end of April 2006 in order to work. However, this figure is probably overestimated since a significant number are assumed to have returned to their country of origin. Furthermore, the figures (see Table I.13) do not only count new entries but also include a percentage of migrants already in the country before May 2004, since the official opening of borders meant that residence permits could be issued to people already in the country illegally, especially in the United Kingdom.[36] Despite these reservations, the flows were substantial. In Ireland, an estimated 40% of entrants in 2005 were from one of the eight new member states. Polish official statistics show that almost 400 000 Poles left the country in the second quarter of 2006 to work in other countries for two months or more, 125 000 more than in the same period of the previous year.

However, flows were not on the same scale everywhere. Fewer than 2 000 citizens emigrated from the Slovak Republic in 2005, barely more than in the years before membership. These differences are partly due to the fact that one of the factors encouraging immigration is the existence of a home country community in the host country which can help new arrivals and hence contribute to "cut the cost" of immigration.[37] That is probably why not all the new member states are concerned to the same extent and why countries that have kept restrictions have also seen a rise in immigration. That is the case with Germany, which is traditionally a host country for Poles and continues to be the prime destination for Polish migrants.

What effect have these flows had on the labour market (see Table I.13)? From this standpoint, eastern European workers have not taken the place of local workers but alleviated labour shortages in certain sectors.[38] In economic terms, the influx has not caused wages to fall.[39] In Ireland, the United Kingdom and Sweden, the resulting increase in supply has been greater than the increase in demand, helping to reduce inflationary pressure despite sustained growth.[40] The outcome has been less clear-cut for the new member states. Remittances from migrants have increased, but the outflow of often employed and well-educated workers has created pressures in some sectors. The Baltic States have faced severe shortages in the healthcare professions, where wage differences with EU15 countries were substantial and the prospects of finding work high.[41]

Overall, the greater mobility of workers from the new EU member states may be seen as one stage in the process of integrating those countries into the European economy. In practice, although it is too soon to measure any great effect on the standard of living in the new member states, the overall efficiency of the labour market appears to have improved. Illegal work has diminished and labour shortages in certain sectors in host countries have been alleviated, albeit sometimes at the price of a relative devalorisation of immigrant workers (see Chapter 2 below). It is doubtless these positive results that have encouraged several governments to lift restrictions. Some have decided to open their labour markets completely (Spain, Finland, Greece, the Netherlands, Portugal), some have committed to gradually liberalising their legislation (France) and others have eased restrictions in the second phase (Belgium, Denmark, Luxembourg). However, this openness is not without limits: Ireland and the United Kingdom have not lifted restrictions on the free movement of workers from Bulgaria and Romania, which joined the EU in January 2007. In contrast, Bulgarian and Romanian workers have the same advantages granted to the eight new member states since May 2004 in countries where restrictions have not been entirely lifted but where exceptions are allowed in order to give easier access to certain occupations (see above).

c) Making the most of human capital: Facilitating student jobs and changes of status

Host countries often fail to make the most of the human resources provided by labour immigration (see Chapter 2 below). Several OECD countries have sought to take better advantage of this human capital, especially at a regional level. Host countries are also giving consideration to the future of foreign students and more generally to increasing the possibilities for changes of status.

Flow management taking local needs into account

Local authorities are playing an increasing role in the management of migratory flows in several OECD countries. For example, on 21 November 2005, Canada's federal

Table I.13. **Review of the first phase of the transition period in EU15, EEA and Switzerland**

Countries	National Measures for the First Period (2004-2006)	Labour Flows 01/05/04-30/04/06	Decision for the Second Period (2006-2009)
Austria	● Work permit scheme. ● Labour market test. ● Specific restrictions for some cross border services.	About 7 800 work permits with more than 6 months duration.	Maintenance of the restrictions.
Belgium	● Work permit scheme. ● Labour market test.	Estimated 7 000 for 2004 and 2005 in total.	Maintenance of the restrictions but some loosening in certain sectors and professions (determined regionally).
Denmark	● Work permit scheme. ● No labour market test. ● Limited to full-time employment.	10 700 work permits, including renewals.	Preservation of the restrictions but with a facilitated procedure and progressive easing of the restrictions on free movement.
Finland	● Work permit scheme. ● Labour market test.	6 000 work permits of more than three months duration.	● Removal of the restrictions and development of a worker registration scheme as in the United Kingdom. ● Strengthening of the controls on working conditions including those for sub-contractors and posted workers.
France	● Work permit scheme. ● Labour market test, but some occupations exempted.	7 000 work permits excluding seasonal workers.	Progressive easing of the restrictions on free movement by expanding the list of exempted occupations.
Germany	● Work permit scheme. ● Labour market test. ● Specific restrictions for certain cross border services.	63 700 during 2005.	Maintenance of the restrictions.
Greece	● Work permit scheme.		Removal of the restrictions.
Ireland	No restrictions but obligatory registration for workers.	186 000[1]	Maintenance of registration system.
Italy	● Work permit scheme. ● Special entry quota for workers from EU8 member states (79 500 for 2005).	About 78 000 01/05/04-31/12/05.	Removal of the restrictions as of July 2007.
Luxembourg	● Work permit scheme. ● Labour market test but simplified procedure for agriculture and viticulture.	53 during 2005.	Maintenance of the restrictions but with an easing of the procedure for specific sectors and professions with shortages.
Netherlands	● Work permit scheme. ● Easing of the procedures for some sectors/professions.	54 171[2] 01/01/04-31/12/05.	Removal of the restrictions as of 1 January 2007.
Portugal	● Work permit scheme. ● Special entry quota system.		Removal of the restrictions.
Spain	● Work permit scheme.		Removal of the restrictions.
Sweden	No restrictions.	11 000 permits of more than three months and 2 200 renewals.	Maintenance of no-restriction policy.
United Kingdom	● No restrictions but obligatory. ● Registration for workers.	580 000 from 01/05/04 to 31/12/06 including 183 000 re-registrations.	Maintenance of registration system.

European Economic Area

Countries	National Measures for the First Period (2004-2006)	Labour Flows 01/05/04-30/04/06	Decision for the Second Period (2006-2009)
Norway	Work permit scheme.	42 000 plus 27 000 renewals.[3]	Maintenance of restrictions.
Iceland	Work permit scheme.	6 000 plus 3 000 renewals.	Removal of the restrictions.

Switzerland

Country	Restrictions (1st April 2006-30 April 2011)	Transition System
Switzerland[4]	● Work permit scheme. ● Labour market test. ● Special entry quota system.	● Quota for annual permits: 700 (3 000 for 2010 and 2011). ● Quota for short-term permits: 15 800 (29 000 for 2010 and 2011).

1. Registration of EU8 citizens is compulsory but the number may be over estimated.
2. During the first transition period, the maximum number of work permits allowed annually was 22 000.
3. Switzerland is not a member of the EEA but linked with the EU through a series of bilateral agreements including one on free movement. As of 1 April 2006, Switzerland introduced a transition period for nationals from the 8 new EU member states from Central and Eastern Europe.
4. Dolvik, J.E., Eldring L. 2006.

Sources on flows: Austria: Austrian labour market service; Belgium: Data provided by SPF ETCS, INASTI; Denmark, Finland, Sweden, Norway, Iceland: Dolvik, J.E., Eldring L. 2006; France: Ministry of Labour; Germany: Federal Agency for Employment; Ireland: Department of Social and Family Affairs, Data on Personal Public Service Number; Italy: Ministry of Labour; Luxembourg: Report of The Ministry of Foreign Affairs; Netherlands: Statistics Netherlands; United Kingdom: Home Office, Data on Worker Registration Scheme and National Insurance Numbers.

government concluded an agreement with the province of Ontario (the biggest host region for foreigners in Canada) which contains a set of measures to facilitate the reception of migrants and their integration into the local labour market. The province must implement the measures but is free to adapt them to the situation. In a different register, Australia intends to use immigration to leverage local and regional development. In order to obtain certain visas, candidates can be sponsored by a region, giving them extra points. Similarly, for self-employed candidates, the number of points is reduced if they undertake to create a business in a sparsely populated area.

The need for a regional or local approach has also emerged in countries that have decided to lift labour market testing (see above) in sectors with labour shortages. In Belgium, the list of "shortage" occupations for which nationals of new member states can obtain a work permit, is drawn up on a regional basis and discussed by social partners at local level. In France, the national list drawn up by the Ministry of Employment is adjusted regionally to take account of local differences. In Australia, the Working Holiday-Maker programme now directs candidates towards sectors under pressure and regions where recruitment difficulties are particularly acute (see Box I.7).

Box I.7. **Developments in the Working Holiday-Maker programme**

Australia's Working Holiday-Maker programme (WHM) has been a great success, attracting some 120 000 beneficiaries in 2005-2006.

The WHM programme has been extended and adjusted to improve its contribution to business and the regions. Since 1 July 2006, WHMs can study for a maximum of four months and work for up to six months (the previous limit was three months). From November 2005, beneficiaries of the WHM programme who have done at least three months' seasonal work in an Australian region are authorised to reapply for the programme (WHM2). Some 2 000 people were able to take advantage of this option to renew their WHM visa in 2006. In July 2006, the list of industries accessible to holders of a WHM visa was extended to the entire primary sector and not just agriculture (slaughterhouses, forestry work, fishing).

These developments are intended to make it easier to direct labour towards seasonal work in sectors where there are shortages, especially in certain regions. By this means, the Australian government also wishes to encourage "green" tourism in non-coastal areas.

Students are increasingly regarded as potential skilled workers

With migration policies becoming more selective, foreign students are probably the category whose status has changed the most in recent years. More and more countries regard them as future skilled workers who should be encouraged to stay in the host country either long term or at least for a number of years after they graduate. Students have many advantages. They are already in the host country, which therefore does not have to do anything about selecting them. Those who have been educated there are considered easier to integrate, especially as regards language and social customs. Furthermore, in a globalised world it is anything but safe to assume that foreign students will go home once they graduate if their visa is not extended. Consequently, many OECD countries have introduced new measures, some of them relating to the integration of foreign students into the labour market during their studies, others relating to what becomes of them after they have finished.

In France, the law of 24 July 2006 made access to employment easier for foreign students since they can now work up to 60% of the annual working time specified in the Labour Code (1 607 hours). In Hungary, foreign students can work without having to obtain a work permit. In Canada, since April 2006 they can look for work outside the campus of the university they attend. Many countries have taken steps to allow students to stay in the host country after graduating. In many cases they have opted for a two-stage system. On completing their studies, foreign students of a certain level[42] can obtain a temporary permit (six months in Ireland and France) which authorises them to look for work. If they are then offered a job, they can apply for a change of status. In Italy, this is a means for candidates to obtain a work permit outside the quota system. The possibilities may be limited in time: in Canada, for example, changes of status[43] are allowed only for a one-year period renewable once.

However, the integration of foreign students into the labour market is not a foregone conclusion. In some countries, like France, the average time it takes for a recent higher education graduate to find a job (eight months) is longer than the length of the temporary visa (six months). For that reason, Finland has extended the temporary permit to ten months. Language problems may also arise.[44] Finland has thus decided to fund Finnish lessons for students wishing to stay on and work after they complete their studies. The effectiveness of such measures is amplified by the help given to students with administrative formalities and the search for a job.

Possibilities for changing status

Change of status occurs when persons with temporary status are granted permanent residence or another permit that can lead to permanent residence. Here, the term "temporary status" refers not to individuals who enter on a temporary permit but to those who enter on a visa that is non-renewable or renewable only under certain conditions. Similarly, permanent status does not mean that the individual is entitled to permanent residence but that he or she is granted a permit (which may be for a limited period) that can lead to permanent residence in the host country.[45]

In Switzerland, the law used to allow seasonal workers who had worked in the country for four years to change status. That option has now been abolished but the number of status changes remains substantial (30% of new entrants in 2005 have changed status; most of them are from European countries). There is no longer any specific legal mechanism: the possibility is left to the authorities' discretion. The number of status changes is due to the fact that when the limit on the number of long-term European permits is reached, EU citizens are granted a permit valid for less than a year. When such permits are renewed and the stay exceeds one year, EU citizens are considered long-term migrants. The problem will disappear in 2007 when the number of permits is increased: All EU citizens will be able to obtain a long-term permit on request. 10% of non-EU citizens (4 000 individuals) were able to change their status in 2005. Such changes are decided on a case-by-case basis.

In Australia, until recently changes were possible only in the specific case of family links. However, new possibilities for change of status have been introduced, especially for students. About 33 000 of the 143 000 permanent entries in 2005 concerned people changing status. The system in Belgium is similar to the system in Switzerland: There is no statutory mechanism but status changes are possible, especially for foreign students who find work on completing their studies. In Austria, new legislation allowing for status changes was introduced in 2006, albeit with a cap on numbers except for foreign students. The total number of changes remains small, though it is increasing.

In New Zealand, a study of a cohort of permanent residents who entered the country in 1996 shows that 78% of them were initially granted a temporary permit (see summary of flows below). In Norway, any person who has been in the country for more than nine months and meets the requirements may apply for a long-term permit. The entry permit remains valid until a decision is taken. In Canada, a person cannot change status without leaving the country, resulting in movements at the border with the United States in order to meet the requirements. Several studies have shown that persons who have had temporary status enter the labour market more easily once they have obtained resident status. Consequently, Canada is considering changing its current procedures.

The systems vary considerably from one country to another: Some, like New Zealand, offer considerable opportunities for changing status while others, like Austria, offer few. Many countries take a simple and pragmatic approach by granting a change of status when the criteria for access to permanent residence are fulfilled. Countries in which status changes were prohibited have changed their procedures or plan to do so in the near future. In all events, the number of status changes tends to increase as countries realise the advantages of allowing people who have studied or worked there to stay.

d) Towards targeted regularisation

Governments regard regularisation as an exceptional and generally discretionary procedure.[46] However, the question has arisen this year in almost a third of OECD countries, either because regularisation has taken place (Belgium, Greece, France, Mexico, etc.) or been completed (Spain, Portugal), or because a debate has begun (the United States, Germany, the Netherlands). Regularisation procedures generally tend to target certain categories of foreigner.

Targeted regularisation concerns specific categories of foreigners. As a rule, they are cases where the authorities acknowledge the legitimacy of residence despite the lack of authorisation. Such a situation may occur, for example, following changes to the law or when a residence permit expires and is not renewed. It may also occur as a result of shortcomings on the part of a country's authorities, for example if they fail to consider applications for asylum within a reasonable time, allowing applicants to settle and ultimately integrate. More generally, targeted regularisation is often inspired by the idea that such people have forged links with the society in which they have been living, sometimes for several years.

Belgium took measures in favour of asylum seekers whose applications had not been considered even after several years. Asylum seekers who had filed their application before 2001 and had not received an answer before the new, faster asylum procedure was introduced, were accepted for regularisation. In France, a procedure was introduced in the summer of 2006 to regularise certain illegal immigrants having strong links with the country. Parents with children at school in France since at least September 2005 were allowed one-year renewable residence permits. Some 7 000 applications from just under 30 000 submitted were ultimately regularised. Another possible criterion is the one chosen by the Portuguese government: Everyone without an authorised residence permit but affiliated to the social security system was allowed a legal permit.

In some cases, a large number of individuals can benefit from targeted regularisation. In 2005, Greece regularised two categories of foreigners: Those whose permit had expired before 23 August 2005 but who had neither renewed it nor left the country, and those who had never had a permit but could prove that they had been in the country since before 1 January 2005. One other condition had to be met in order to obtain a permit: Proof of having worked for 150 days (200 days if more than one employer). Spouses and children aged over 14 were issued with a personal residence permit. 142 000 applications were submitted, many fewer than had been expected. The Greek government attributes the lack of success of the campaign to cumbersome administrative procedures and the days worked requirement. For those reasons a bill was tabled in early 2007, extending and broadening the 2005 procedure. Various documents, like birth certificates for children born in Greece, are now accepted as proof of residence in the country. Workers unable to prove that they have worked for 200 days can add up to 40 days to their total by paying the relevant social security contributions. For some occupations the required number of days has been halved. Individuals who have attended primary or secondary school or an institution of higher education in Greece can also obtain a residence permit.

The Greek example shows that the administrative regularisation procedure can be an obstacle, especially if too many documents are required. That is the likely explanation for the fewer than expected applications submitted in the last regularisation campaign in Mexico, which began in September 2005 and ended in June 2006. Just over 4 000 applications were filed, two-thirds had been examined by the end of 2006 and most of them accepted; the remaining third are being examined. The small number of applications led the government to extend the procedure until 31 October 2006.

Some countries, like the Netherlands, are considering regularisation campaigns in the near future. In February 2007, the new Dutch government announced an identical plan to the Belgian one for asylum seekers from before 2001. Procedures for examining applications have been revised and streamlined. However, a substantial number of outstanding applications remain. The authorities estimate that this means of access to refugee status concerns between 24 000 and 30 000 individuals.

Germany's federal government has concluded an agreement with the interior ministries of the *Länder* concerning the regularisation of 180 000 individuals whose presence in Germany is "tolerated". They can obtain a residence permit if, before September 2009, they can prove that they are in work. In return, the *Länder* have been given powers to restrict such people's access to social assistance.

In the United States, a debate was sparked off by the publication in August 2006 of a survey of the number and characteristics of illegal immigrants by the Department of Homeland Security's office of immigration statistics. The study estimated that there were 10.5 million illegal immigrants in the United States in January 2005, significantly more than in January 2000, when the statistical office put the number at 8.5 million. This estimate put the annual net increase in the number of illegal immigrants at 480 000. In reaction, several plans for immigration policy reform are under discussion between the White House and the House of Representatives, including the establishment of a regularisation procedure, the terms and conditions of which diverge. Discussion centres less on the conditions (no criminal record, continuous employment or education, language test for eligibility for permanent residence) than on the type of visa that could be issued: Amount of the fine, duration of the work permit, possibilities for renewal or access to permanent residence.

I.2. *Better reception, better integration: redefining responsibilities for integration*

Although immigration is increasingly regarded as a solution for labour shortages, paradoxically immigrants and their children continue to encounter difficulties. In many host countries, they are more likely than nationals to be unemployed, especially long-term, or to suffer social exclusion. They are also more exposed to precarious employment and have fewer prospects for improving their situation. Often these difficulties continue into the following generation, including as a result of discrimination. To deal with the problems, which can generate further tension in host countries, governments are trying to implement policies that target all the dimensions of the integration process and the obstacles that can cause it to fail, such as reception, family reunification, access to employment, access to citizenship and discrimination.

Such policies can take very different forms in different countries, focusing on some stages of the process more than others according to the local situation, but they all emphasise that foreigners must play an active role. Recent actions not only seek answers to the problems of integration but also insist on the need for foreigners to take responsibility, the need to put them at the heart of the process and hence enable them to take possession of the sometimes radical changes in lifestyle that settlement in a host country implies.

a) *From reception obligation to obligatory reception*

The conditions of arrival in a country are seen as a special moment which can subsequently facilitate or complicate the process of long-term integration. That is why many OECD countries put the emphasis on welcoming new arrivals. Among recent measures, language courses seem to be increasingly widespread, as are information programmes which provide practical advice and describe the country's administrative systems and the formalities to be fulfilled.

The widespread introduction of language courses and information programmes. Germany introduced such measures in its 2005 Residence Act. Over 115 000 people attended language courses in 2006. In the Czech Republic, language courses were provided for the first time in 2006. In Austria and Australia, the length of language courses has been increased. In Austria, since 2005, such courses have been provided not only for adults but also for their accompanying children.

Immigrants do not all have the same needs for language training, nor are those needs the same in all countries. Some nationals of new EU member states who have settled in the United Kingdom or Ireland have relatively high-skill levels and a good knowledge of English. Likewise, in France many newcomers are French speakers: Only 25% attend language classes. In Norway, in contrast, since September 2005 foreigners settling there have to take 300 hours of Norwegian classes and that figure can be raised to as many as 3 000 hours in some cases.

In Australia, language training is included in an induction course for political and humanitarian refugees, the length of which was extended from three to five days in 2006. Through agreements with the provinces, Canada's federal government has also sought to encourage local reception and guidance platforms that include practical advice on settlement and language learning. The courses may be dispensed by private companies or public agencies. In France, a new national agency for the reception of foreigners and migration (ANAEM) was created in 2005, combining various administrative departments (including the Office of International Migration), and given the task of facilitating the reception and integration of foreigners.

The spread of targeted programmes and individual contracts. In response to the diversity of newcomers, linked to the variety of their cultural origins and status, countries try to adapt reception measures to people's needs. To do so, they may choose to target particular categories. In Australia, for example, certain courses are reserved for refugees and suitably adapted courses are offered to children under 12. Generally speaking, special attention is paid to minors, especially when they are not accompanied. In Belgium, the family courts assign them a tutor who accompanies them throughout their administrative, health and social formalities until they reach adulthood.

Children are also an important target for reception programmes, especially in schools, in order to facilitate their future integration. In Luxembourg, for example, very considerable differences in performance between Luxembourg and foreign schoolchildren, even when the family's socio-economic level is taken into account, have encouraged the government to introduce reforms. Multilingual preschool education in almost all communes should help to improve the results of children arriving in Luxembourg at an early age. The emphasis is placed on learning the three official languages (Luxembourgish, German and French) and on respecting the child's mother tongue. Reception and integration classes have been created in secondary schools.

So that needs can be met as precisely as possible, it is also possible to set up a system of contracts between the host country and foreigners wishing to settle there. This makes it possible to tailor reception to the individual, which in practice consists in adjusting the duration or amount of provision under the contract according to the individual's profile. By generalising its reception and integration contract (CAI) in the law of July 2006, France chose this option after a successful three-year experiment. Over 90% of newcomers offered a contract of this type in 2005 accepted it. All foreigners admitted for permanent residence must now sign a CAI, including minors over 16 years of age. The other advantage of this type of contract is to send a message that foreigners must play a part in their own integration. Reciprocal commitments are spelled out through such measures tailored to the individual. The incentives are such that in many cases immigrants have no option but to sign. That is the case when arrival in a country depends on passing an exam, as in the Netherlands, or when it is a condition for the granting of a permanent residence permit. As a rule, participation is quite simply compulsory (see Box I.8).

These features illustrate a growing awareness of the authorities' responsibility in the success of the integration process. However, insofar as an element of reciprocity on the part of migrants is expected or demanded, they also indicate a shift in responsibilities where integration is concerned.

b) Family reunification: Liberalisation or restriction?

Family reunification is undeniably a factor of integration for immigrants. From the immigrant standpoint, the fact of bringing over the family underlines the desire to stay in a country in the long-term and the presence of children helps to increase links with society

---

Box I.8. **Towards an obligation of result: the new Integration Act in the Netherlands**

Since March 2006, any foreigner wishing to immigrate into the Netherlands on a long-term permit must pass a civic integration test before entering. Organised by the host country embassy or consulate, the test includes a language exam and questions about some of the main characteristics of Dutch society. Private training firms dispense courses to prepare for the test, which candidates must pay for themselves. If they pass the test, foreigners can take other courses after arriving in the Netherlands to help them to integrate.

Several changes have taken place since 1 January 2007, when the new Integration Act came into force. It no longer requires foreigners to take all the courses offered to them but keeps the exam, passing which has become a precondition for obtaining a residence permit or receiving certain social benefits. However, the main innovation is the requirement in the new Act that the measures should be evaluated to assess their effectiveness, with the aim of striking a balance between the host country's obligations and those of the foreigner. By keeping the exam, it makes candidates for immigration prove their desire to integrate. At the same time, by requiring the state to evaluate its action, it emphasises the responsibility of public agencies in the process of reception and integration.

---

in the host country. An analysis of the maths scores of foreign pupils (PISA 2003, OECD) shows the influence of the age on arrival in the host country on their results. In some countries (Germany, Belgium, Denmark and France), each year spent in the country of origin after the parents had emigrated reduced test scores by four to six points. With one year's schooling representing 35 points, a child arriving at the age of ten will be on average between one and two years behind a child arriving at a younger age.[47]

Stricter conditions on family reunification for certain categories of foreigner. In several OECD countries, family reunification is conditional and contingent on the fulfilment of certain criteria. In Germany, last year the federal secretariat for integration announced its wish for applicants to attend language courses in their country of origin and to take a test before entering the country for family reunification purposes. In France, the law of 24 July 2006 restricted the possibilities for family reunification, *inter alia* by extending the required time of residence for the applicant from 12 to 18 months, imposing stricter resource requirements (now calculated without family and social benefits) and by making extension of the residence permit granted to the spouse uncertain in the event of a break-up. In Ireland, although the residence requirement is less (one year), a beneficiary of family reunification can seek a permanent residence permit only after being in the country for five years.

In some cases, restrictions may be designed to prevent forced marriage and to protect individuals, especially minors. In France and in Germany, the minimum age for women wishing to marry or to benefit from family reunification has been raised to 18. A debate has taken place on the same subject in Norway, where the government also wishes to increase the legal age for marrying and benefiting from family reunification in a bill to be discussed in parliament in 2007.

Some countries encourage and facilitate family reunification for certain categories of foreigners, especially skilled workers. In Germany, families of foreign researchers can settle after a short and quick procedure. In the Czech Republic, which encourages the immigration of skilled workers, streamlined procedures also exist for their families.

Another approach: Sponsorship. Some countries have preferred a different approach to the question of family reunification: Rather than ensuring that applicants fulfil various criteria, the aim is to make them responsible by asking them to sponsor the family member(s) they wish to bring (see Box I.9). It is up to them to ensure that the family members will be able to lead a normal life in the host country. Such a sponsorship system was introduced in Canada in 2003. More recently, in 2005, the government decided to release funds to facilitate procedures not only for spouses and dependent children but also for parents and grandparents. The extension seems to have borne fruit, since about 7 000 parents and grandparents were able to benefit from family reunification in 2005.

Box I.9. **Canada's sponsorship system**

Canadian citizens and permanent residents living in Canada aged over 18, whatever their status, may sponsor close relatives or family members who want to become permanent residents of Canada. The sponsor must promise to support the relative or family member and their accompanying family members for three to ten years depending on their age and relationship with the sponsor in order to help them settle in Canada.

This unconditional promise of support comprises two separate undertakings, the first between the sponsor and the Ministry of Citizenship and Immigration, the second with the sponsored person and all accompanying family members. The sponsorship agreement describes the commitment to meet the needs of the sponsored persons and their reciprocal commitment to do what they can to support themselves. Dependent children under 22 years of age do not have to sign a sponsorship agreement.

The duration of support varies according to age and relationship.

● For the spouse, common-law or conjugal partner, the support is for three years from the date at which the person concerned becomes a permanent resident.

● For a child under 22 years of age dependent on the sponsor, or on the spouse, common-law or conjugal partner, the support is for ten years from the date on which the person concerned becomes a permanent resident or until the child reaches the age of 25.

● For a child over 22 years of age dependent on the sponsored person or on the sponsor of the spouse, common-law or conjugal partner, the support is for three years from the date on which the person concerned becomes a permanent resident.

● For any person not mentioned above, the support is for ten years from the date on which the person concerned becomes a permanent resident.

On 18 February 2005, the system was extended to all permanent residents of Canada and the processing of applications was accelerated for all families.

New Zealand has a sponsorship system similar to Canada's, though the possibilities for reunification differ according to the type of beneficiary (spouses, siblings, dependent children, etc.). Two major changes were introduced in August 2006. First, for major children and siblings, the sponsor in New Zealand must be under 55 years of age. Second, for the spouse and dependent children of citizens and residents, there is no longer any limit on the number of reunifications, since the quota was deemed an excessive restriction of the right of residents and citizens to enjoy a normal family life. The measure will take effect in July 2007.

Austria has opted for a system that combines both regulation and sponsorship. Until 2005, the reunification or founding of a family with a non-European citizen was based on sponsorship. The law on immigration was reformed in 2005. It now stipulates that sponsors resident in Austria must prove their capacity to support their spouse, i.e. they must have income equal to or greater than the minimum wage. This new condition is a major barrier for the spouses of permanent residents or Austrian citizens receiving social benefits. The income criterion does not apply to minor children. In return, access to the labour market has been made easier for immigrants benefiting from family reunification. These new measures have reduced the number of long-term immigrants from non-EU countries.

c) Recognition of qualifications

Participation in the labour market is obviously one of the main criteria for assessing the extent of foreigners' integration into a country. In theory, the success of a process for integrating foreigners through the labour market means that as they become familiar with the host country's language and working practices, their professional results will tend to resemble those of natives with similar characteristics (age, sex, qualifications).[48]

Some countries have introduced arrangements for recognising immigrants' qualifications and professional experience or have extended existing systems. In Canada, for example, discussions are taking place between the authorities and the social partners over the creation of an independent agency for recognising references and qualifications earned abroad. Learning the host country's language quickly is a key factor for finding work. Although language courses have become widespread in recent years, few countries take measures directed specifically at vocational language training. In Germany, to facilitate the integration of foreigners, recipients of certain benefits such as unemployment benefit can now take such courses. In Canada, occupational and specialised language certificates are now available to qualified foreigners under the Enhanced Language Training Initiative.

These measures concern skilled workers, though it is unskilled immigrants who have the greatest difficulty in finding work. Furthermore, they do not remove certain obstacles that foreigners face on the labour market, one of the most important being immigrants' lack of social capital. Discrimination against immigrants is another obstacle to their integration. Discrimination also affects their children, even though they do not in principle face language difficulties or non-recognition of their diplomas.

d) Measures to combat discrimination and promote equal opportunity

The fight against discrimination has become a subject of great concern in OECD countries. The existence of forms of segregation, especially affecting residents of immigrant origin, is an avowal that integration policies have failed. Discrimination affects the chances of employment at all levels, and also concerns access to housing. Many OECD countries have introduced legislation to counter discrimination, making it easier for victims to seek redress and increasing the penalties for wrongdoers. Measuring the nature and scale of discrimination is also a subject of debate.

Stepping up legal measures against discrimination. The fight against discrimination in recent years initially took legal form. Case law has evolved in several European OECD countries, on the one hand by acknowledging that "testing"[49] can under certain conditions constitute evidence of discrimination and on the other by switching the burden of proof to the defendant. Employers have been convicted. Following these changes, some countries have strengthened their legal arsenal and introduced new measures to enable victims to defend themselves more easily.

In Norway, a new law came into force in January 2006. First, it defines the scope of the ban on discrimination, which may be direct or indirect, based on ethnic origin, national origin, sexual orientation, colour, religion, language, beliefs or gender.[50] To make the law more effective, Norway has also decided to set up an Equality and Anti-Discrimination Tribunal with an Equality and Anti-Discrimination Ombudsman. The Swedish government is considering similar legislation.

The fight against discrimination may also involve the creation of independent authorities[51] with extensive administrative powers, in particular to help victims. They are not tribunals as such, but structures situated at the interface between victims and the justice system. In 2005, the French government created HALDE, the Independent High Authority For Equality and Against Discrimination, to deal with complaints and inform complainants of their rights. If it finds evidence of discrimination it can examine the case and its decision can be presented in civil or criminal proceedings if the victim refers the matter to the prosecuting authorities. HALDE's analysis of complaints received in 2006 found a prevalence of discrimination based on origin (36%) and disability or health (17%), well ahead of age (6%). Almost half of the complaints related to employment (42%), followed by public services (22%), access to goods and services (9%) and housing (5%). Job discrimination occurred most frequently at important steps of the career such as recruitment or promotion.

Knowledge for action: The debate about statistics on origin. Alongside campaigns to promote equal opportunity and measures to increase penalties for discrimination, research has been carried out to improve knowledge of the nature and scale of discrimination. In Belgium, several employment and labour market surveys have confirmed the scale of discrimination, not only against foreigners from North Africa and Turkey but also against Belgian citizens of North African or Turkish origin. In France, a study by the International Labour Office carried out in 2006 and published in 2007[52] on the basis of 2 323 tests of low-skilled jobs in various towns and cities showed that four times out of five,[53] employers preferred to hire a young candidate of 20-25 years of age of "long-standing French origin" rather than a candidate with the same skills but of "North African or sub-Saharan origin". Only 11% of employers offered genuine equality of opportunity throughout the recruitment process. The study also highlights the discrimination barrier of first contact: Almost 90% of discrimination takes place when CVs are being considered, before the employer interviews candidates.

The results of a recent Swedish study of wage differentials between natives and workers of immigrant origin are somewhat less clear-cut. Wage differentials exist between natives and non-natives with the same skill level. However, these differences disappear with the introduction of the results obtained by individuals in army skill tests of young people doing their military service. The results seem to suggest that employers mainly take account of skills and not ethnic origin when setting wages. However, that does not mean there is no discrimination in access to employment: Differences do indeed exist between the employment rate of natives and non-natives which cannot be explained by the diverging skill levels measured by the scores obtained in army tests.

In view of the scale of the problem, questions have been raised openly about the possibility of authorising the collection of statistics on ethnicity in countries like France and Belgium where it is prohibited. Discrimination researchers and statisticians in these countries must make do with information about the parents' country of origin or use artefacts like the sound of a name. These rather heated and recurrent debates oppose those who wish to open up the possibility, albeit under strict rules, in order to properly identify the problem and hence develop more effective means of combating discrimination, and those who believe that such data would artificially define membership of a community and could exacerbate rather than relieve identity pressures.

e) Access to citizenship: Naturalisation and the right to vote

Access to citizenship for foreigners goes hand in hand with the process of integration into the host country. It often takes the form of naturalisation, citizenship being generally linked to nationality. From this standpoint, legislative changes in many countries in recent years have tended to tighten up the conditions of access to nationality. However, access to citizenship may also involve giving foreigners the right to vote without requiring them to obtain the nationality of their host country.

Naturalisation as a measure of the extent of the integration of foreigners. Several OECD countries changed their legislation on the acquisition of nationality in 2005 and 2006. Broadly speaking, the new rules are more restrictive than the old ones, especially in countries where naturalisation was relatively easy. The aim of the new legislation is to verify the extent of foreigners' integration before granting them nationality, though the criteria on which verification is based vary considerably from one country to another. The easiest criterion to change is length of residence: The longer the period of residence, the greater the degree of integration that can be assumed. That is the thrust of the bill tabled by the Australian government at the end of 2006. Four years of permanent residence are now required for access to nationality rather than the previous two.

The second criterion for verifying the extent of integration is fluency in the language of the host country. In 2005, the United Kingdom and Norway introduced measures to assess the linguistic skills of candidates for naturalisation. In the United Kingdom, since 1 November 2005 foreigners have had to pass a language exam, a measure which incidentally caused a 60% jump in applications in 2005 before the test became compulsory. In Norway, the new Nationality Act which came into force in September 2005 requires future citizens to have an adequate knowledge of Norwegian or Sami. In the United Kingdom and Australia, such tests also provide an opportunity for verifying candidates' knowledge of some fundamental aspects of the everyday life and culture of the host country. Taking a slightly different approach, some countries have chosen to make naturalisation more formal and to increase its symbolic dimension by organising naturalisation ceremonies. In the Netherlands, the first ceremony of this type took place on 1 October 2006 and it is now mandatory for all new citizens. In France, such events are increasingly popular with local authorities though they remain strictly voluntary.

One country, Hungary, chose to liberalise access to nationality in 2005. Almost 10 000 individuals acquired Hungarian nationality in that year, twice as many as in the previous year. By streamlining the formalities, the government wished to give easier access to Hungarian nationality to members of certain minorities of Hungarian origin living in neighbouring countries, who constitute the majority of foreigners settling in Hungary. 70% of the new Hungarian citizens were from Romania, 10% from Serbia Montenegro and 9% from Ukraine.

The *jus soli/jus sanguinis* dilemma. As regards access to nationality for the children of foreigners born in a host country, the debate continues between supporters of *jus soli* and supporters of *jus sanguinis*. The tendency is towards a gradual extension of the right of the soil. In Norway, the right of the blood continues to dominate the new Nationality Act since children automatically acquire their parents' nationality at birth, but if the parents have different nationalities and one of them is Norwegian, the child can obtain a Norwegian passport if he or she renounces the other parent's nationality.

The Portuguese government has opted for *jus soli* to give children born in Portugal of foreign parents' access to nationality. However, the right is not absolute unless one of the parents was also born in Portugal. In other cases, nationality is acquired only if one of the ascendants who has raised the child has lived in Portugal for more than five years without interruption, or if the child has attended school in Portugal for at least ten years before the age of 18.

The foreigners' right to vote. Naturalisation often requires candidates to renounce their nationality of origin. Many foreigners living in OECD countries are unwilling to do so but nevertheless take an interest in the political, economic and social life of the country in which they reside, in some cases for many years. Access to citizenship may involve granting the right to vote, as is the case (though only in local elections) for all European citizens living in an EU country.

Some countries have recently decided to liberalise their legislation. In New Zealand, permanent residents can vote in all elections, local and national. In fact, that is the reason why New Zealand has extended the residence period required for access to nationality: Naturalisation is thus more clearly distinguished from permanent residence. Belgium has also opted to allow non-EU immigrants to vote in local elections, for the first time in communal elections on 13 October 2006. The results were somewhat disappointing since only 17 000 foreigners registered to vote in municipal elections,[54] or 17% of the 100 000 potential voters. This low level of participation may be due to the fact that many of the immigrants most likely to take an interest in local political life (both the best integrated and those already resident in Belgium for a long period) have taken Belgian nationality. The cumbersome procedure and the lack of any national information campaign were further contributing factors. The participation of non-EU foreigners should also be compared with that of EU nationals: Only 7% of EU foreigners registered to vote in Belgium after the law allowed them to do so.

2. Immigration at the heart of international relations[55]

Immigration is increasingly becoming a key element of international relations. Host countries wishing to regulate migratory flows find it to their advantage to co-operate with countries of origin in order to limit illegal immigration as much as possible and make it easier for immigrants in an irregular situation arrested in host countries to be expelled or repatriated.

Two trends have emerged from recent developments. The first is the emphasis placed on combating illegal immigration. The second is the link between migration and development. Many OECD countries try to strike a balance between the need to recruit more immigrant workers, especially skilled workers, and the desire not to prejudice the development of countries of origin.

2.1. *The fight against illegal immigration and respect for basic human rights*

OECD countries regard the fight against illegal immigration as a fundamental issue. It can take several forms, including stricter controls on entry, measures to prevent document fraud and the conclusion of re-admission agreements. Governments are co-operating more and more closely in such matters. Co-operation does not only concern enforcement, since it also aims to ensure respect for basic human rights and to combat trafficking in human beings.

a) *Devoting more resources to controls*

At national level, controls are carried out not only at frontiers but also inland. Regional organisations and intergovernmental agreements between countries in the same geographical area can also play an important role. Co-operation has recently been reflected in the growing use of databases and the inclusion of biometric information in identity documents.

The Security Fence Act passed by the US Congress in December 2006 calls for the construction of a 1 200 kilometre fence along the border with Mexico. It also gives border guards additional resources for more vehicles, more patrols and high-technology surveillance material. Likewise, new detention centres will be created for those who cross the border illegally. An additional budget of USD 12 billion over several years has been voted. These measures follow the US administration's decision in May 2006 to step up controls at the frontier with Mexico, including the transfer of 6 000 national guardsmen (Operation Jumpstart).[56] At the same time, the government is continuing the close co-operation with the Mexican and Canadian governments begun at the Waco summit in Texas in March 2005. On that occasion the three heads of state signed a tripartite co-operation agreement (the Security and Prosperity Partnership of North America), providing amongst other things for the sharing of surveillance technologies, access to information in the three countries' databases relating to passengers crossing North America, exchanges of information about certain individuals and co-ordinated visa policies.

Mexico is also anxious to secure its southern frontier. The National Institute of Migrations in Mexico has proposed a plan to better manage regular flows, respect migrants' rights and increase the number of controls. The measures were phased in during the year 2006.

The European Union continues to step up its measures to counter illegal immigration, especially after the last two enlargements. In December 2006, the Council of Justice and Home Affairs Ministers adopted conclusions on "integrated border management", insisting *inter alia* on the four levels of control of access to Europe: Controls at the border, controls within the country, measures relating to third countries and co-operation with neighbouring countries.

The EU has adopted a Community Code on the rules governing the movement of persons across borders (the Schengen Borders Code), approved on 15 March 2006.[57] As it takes the form of a regulation replacing part of the Schengen *acquis*, a whole segment of member states' domestic law is now covered by a rule of Community law that applies uniformly to the entire Schengen area. On 19 July 2006, the Commission proposed a regulation establishing a mechanism for the creation of Rapid Border Intervention Teams (RABIT).[58] It authorises the European Agency for the Management of Operational Co-operation at the External Borders of the Member States of the European Union (Frontex) to deploy a team of border guards from different member states which could on request help a Member State under particular pressure (*e.g.* facing a large number of third country nationals trying to enter the EU illegally). Ultimately, the mechanism will allow for the creation of a European border guard corps. In view of the lack of resources allocated to Frontex, which nevertheless carried out various operations to control maritime borders around the Canary Islands in 2006,[59] at its meeting in December 2006, the European Council proposed the establishment of a permanent network of coastal patrols for the southern maritime border in co-operation with the member states of the region.

New technologies to support identity controls and prevent document fraud. The development of new technologies in recent years offers possibilities for making document checks more effective. In 2006, the United States introduced a new system of biometric passports to improve and facilitate controls. The new system addresses two main concerns: Homeland security and the fight against terrorism, and the prevention of illegal immigration. In Japan, the Immigration Control and Refugee Recognition Act was amended in May 2006. Document control procedures for passengers at airports have been expedited using a system of automatic portals.

Given their cost, such procedures are generally introduced in a multilateral and regional framework. Since March 2006, New Zealand, Australia and the United States have cooperated on the introduction of a pilot scheme for a Regional Movement Alert System, a new passport control system initiated within APEC (Asia-Pacific Economic Co-operation). It enables all the countries taking part in the system to detect when a passport is used fraudulently at any time during a journey.

In Europe, the Schengen Information System (SIS) is currently in operation in the 13 Schengen area member states plus the two associate countries (Norway and Iceland). Looking forward to the extension of the Schengen *acquis* to all EU countries and Switzerland, a new system, SIS II, will be phased in. SIS will continue to encourage judicial and police co-operation in criminal matters and to increase co-operation between countries relating to visas, immigration and the freedom of movement between member states. SIS II will include data on criminals and persons who fail to comply with foreigner entry and residence requirements. It will also have new functionalities, especially relating to the fight against terrorism.

In its communication on priorities in the fight against illegal immigration,[60] on 19 July 2006 the Commission launched the concept of "e-frontiers", an integrated technological approach which it proposes to develop in order to better fight illegal immigration. The approach is based on the use of computer databases of third country nationals containing biometric data. In addition to the Schengen Information System (SIS II) and Eurodac, a system for the comparison of fingerprints of asylum applicants and illegal immigrants, the aim is to establish the future Visa Information System (VIS) for applicants for short-stay visas, the legal basis for which was adopted on 8 June 2004[61] though it is not yet operational. The Commission is also planning to create a comprehensive, automated entry/exit system based on systematically recording third country nationals when they cross external borders instead of stamping passports.

These measures will help to increase the effectiveness of controls, though they are unlikely to put an end to illegal immigration. Only a minority of immigrants in an irregular situation enter OECD countries by sea or by illegally crossing borders (see chapter on flows below).

b) Co-operation in expulsions

The proportion of expulsions actually carried out is often rather small. In France, for example, despite an increase in the enforcement rate since 2001, expulsions performed in 2005 represented only a quarter of removal orders issued (17 000 out of 66 000). There are several reasons why such measures are difficult to implement, including inability to find the foreigners to be expelled or to identify their nationality, problems with the issuance of consular passes or the lack of transport links with the country of origin (for reasons of insecurity, for example). Most OECD countries are trying to improve the enforcement rate of expulsion orders, in particular by concluding readmission agreements either with countries of origin or with transit countries.

This was the case with Mexico between 2005 and 2006. Because it shares a border with the United States, Mexico is largely a transit country. Mexico has therefore negotiated and signed a set of bilateral agreements with its neighbours and the main countries of origin of illegal immigrants, providing for the immediate readmission of nationals from signatory country.

Readmission agreements may also be negotiated in a multilateral framework. Since the Tampere European Council meeting in October 1999, which defined the EU's broad strategy for combating illegal immigration, the importance of these agreements has been regularly called to mind. The Council has authorised the Commission to negotiate readmission agreements containing reciprocal co-operation commitments between the European Union and partner third countries. Eleven countries were initially concerned: Morocco, Sri Lanka, the Russian Federation, Pakistan, Hong Kong (China), Macao, Ukraine, Albania, Algeria, China and Turkey. Establishing the agreements was a lengthy process: The agreement with Hong Kong China, for example, was signed in November 2002 and concluded in December 2003 but did not take effect until 1 March 2004, the Community's very first readmission agreement. The agreement with Sri Lanka took effect on 1 May 2005. Under the terms of the agreement with Albania, which came into effect in 2006, the Greek authorities can help the Albanian government with enforcement. Negotiations with the Russian Federation, Pakistan, Morocco, Ukraine and Turkey are in progress. Negotiating mandates have also been granted for China and Algeria though no formal negotiations have begun. More recently, in December 2006, the Council mandated the Commission to negotiate a readmission agreement with Moldova in return for a promise by the EU to grant more visas to Moldovans. The aim is for the agreement, once signed, to come into force on 1 January 2008.

It has not been possible to negotiate agreements with some important transit countries like Belarus, either at European level or in a bilateral framework, even though Belarus is one of the main transit points for illegal immigrants seeking to enter the Baltic States. However, member states can always negotiate bilateral agreements and continue to apply existing agreements. For example, there are fifteen or so readmission agreements between France and member states, plus twenty or so with third countries that are still in effect.

Two specific cases should be mentioned: That of the new entrants into the EU in January 2007 (Romania and Bulgaria) and that of Switzerland. The membership treaties with Romania and Bulgaria provide for a transition phase during which readmission agreements with these two countries concluded prior to membership will continue to apply unless measures promoting greater openness are taken. For Switzerland, although the Swiss approved their country's participation in the Schengen area in September 2005, the treaty will not take effect until all the member states have ratified it (they should do so by the end of 2008). In the meantime, Switzerland's bilateral readmission agreements continue to apply. Since 2005, Switzerland has concluded such agreements with Nigeria, the Slovak Republic, Algeria, Greece and Afghanistan.

c) Developments in procedures for asylum applicants

Legislative changes have taken place recently relating to the processing of asylum applications and the conditions for obtaining refugee status. The authorities responsible for receiving and guiding asylum seekers and processing their applications have been reorganised in France (2004), Italy (2005) and Belgium (2006). Initial results indicate that in France and Italy the time taken to process applications has been significantly reduced. In Italy, applications are now often processed within two weeks. In France, the time was reduced from 258 days in 2003 to 108 days in 2005. Processing time varies considerably according to the complexity of the circumstances and in some cases a decision may not be reached for one or two years. A priority review procedure (23% of applications) allows certain applications to be processed more quickly (15 days in principle), especially when they involve a request for a decision to be reconsidered. The processing of applications has also been speeded up by the adoption in several OECD countries of a list of safe countries of origin, for which asylum applications are in principle not admissible.

d) Co-operation in the prevention of people trafficking

Respect for the human rights of illegal immigrants is an integral part of plans to combat illegal immigration. It is a matter that equally concerns host countries and transit countries. While legal procedures exist in OECD countries to regulate the expulsion of illegal immigrants, recognition of their rights has been improved recently by tougher action against networks that organise illegal immigration and people trafficking. Preventing criminal activity of this nature requires close co-operation between police forces, which is still in its infancy.

Following adoption by the Council of Ministers of the European Union in December 2005 of a plan to prevent and combat trafficking in human beings (see Box I.10), several countries have introduced legislation, especially in favour of victims. In Portugal, transposition of the European status of long-term resident was accompanied by measures to facilitate the reception of victims of people trafficking, who can now obtain long-term resident status. In Finland, a change to the Aliens Act came into effect in July 2006, giving victims priority access to permanent resident status through a streamlined procedure. An amendment to the Integration Act is due to be voted in 2007, providing victims with a set of benefits designed to facilitate their integration. However, these measures apply to relatively small numbers of people, not least because of the difficulty of proving that a crime has been committed.

Box I.10. **The European Union plan to prevent and combat trafficking in human beings**

In December 2005, the Council of Ministers adopted a plan to prevent and combat trafficking in human beings which lists best practice, standards and procedures. The approach is based on the inalienable rights of the human person and respect for victims' rights. It contains eight measures that member states are required to implement before the end of 2007:

1. Precise definition of trafficking in human beings and how it occurs in practice in the EU.

2. Reducing demand.

3. Improving investigation techniques.

4. Better legal protection for victims and more precise definition of offences to allow for prosecution.

5. Support for victims.

6. Assisted return.

7. Consideration given to people trafficking in the EU's relations with other countries.

8. Policy co-ordination.

An initial evaluation by the EU presidency at the end of 2006 concluded that implementation of the eight measures should continue and added that member states should designate a contact point to facilitate co-ordination between the national authorities concerned.

2.2. Migration policy: Between competition to recruit highly skilled workers and co-operation to promote development

OECD countries tend to compete with each other to attract the most highly skilled immigrants while endeavouring to co-operate with countries of origin in economic development matters.

a) Human capital, competition and the risk of a "brain drain"

A country's attractiveness, regularly invoked in a context of inward investment and the location of economic activity, is also a major issue in OECD countries' recruitment of skilled foreign workers. Human capital is increasingly regarded as a resource, like financial or natural resources, for which countries compete. That is why some countries have introduced incentives that are more or less complementary to selective policies. But it is the most highly qualified students who are the subject of greatest attention.

Tax incentives for certain categories. Taxation can be used as a means of attracting the most highly skilled foreign workers. Within the EU, a degree of competition exists in the sphere of corporate taxation, enabling small countries like the Baltic States and Ireland to attract large amounts of capital and reinvigorate their economies in recent years. High levels of economic growth, the establishment of many firms and the associated job creation have helped to attract workers, especially skilled workers. Ireland has been a particularly striking example of this phenomenon in recent years. Some countries, not wishing to cut their tax rates, have sought to introduce specific tax breaks, like the scheme introduced in France in 2005 for impatriates of multinationals. So as not to disadvantage the executives of such firms, they are taxed in line with the levels prevailing in the most favourable countries.

The foreign student "market".   Students are increasingly regarded as future highly skilled immigrants. Registering for courses in the sciences, law, economics and management, they have at least a bachelor's degree and come to a host country for a master's or a doctorate. Mostly from emerging countries, foreign students are the subject of particular attention, especially from the OECD countries that most recruit them (the United States, the United Kingdom, Germany, France, Australia and Canada). The flows are considerable (see below).

To attract foreign students, some OECD countries, like the Scandinavian countries and especially Finland, have opted to focus on courses taught in English. However, they face a new problem when they want to encourage graduates to stay by granting them a change of status. Mostly English-speaking, these students do not always speak the host country language well enough to join the labour market. Finland has introduced occupation-oriented language courses in order to induce such students to stay. In the main countries receiving foreign students, specialised agencies have been set up in order to recruit, select, guide and welcome these students. For several years, France has engaged in a series of reforms in this direction. All the various existing structures in charge of services to foreign students have been grouped to form a single network (Campus France) responsible for informing, guiding and facilitating administrative procedures for candidates.

Recognition of diplomas poses another problem, though progress has been made in recent years. In Europe, with the generalisation of the BMD system (bachelor, master, doctorate) and the ECTS (European Credit Transfer and Accumulation System) in the EU, EEA and associate countries of the Bologna process, the UNESCO/Council of Europe recognition mechanism (ENIC, European Network of Information Centres) merged with the EU mechanism (NARIC, National Academic Recognition Information Centres) in 2005. The ENIC-NARIC network now has national relays in all the countries that have signed up to the two networks' common charter, accessible both to the authorities responsible for checking students' applications and to the students themselves, to facilitate the administrative formalities for studying or working in another country.

Should and can the "brain drain" be stemmed?   The most frequent criticism of selective policies is that they cream off the results of the efforts made by developing countries to invest in the education of young people. Small countries and those with insufficient higher education structures are particularly hard hit. The consequences may differ depending on the economic sectors concerned. The international mobility of healthcare personnel is considered in this report (see Chapter III).

Complex interactions exist between trade flows, investment flows and the mobility of workers, especially the highly skilled. The case of South-East Asian countries shows that the emigration of workers from certain less developed countries to OECD countries, especially those that are geographically close, can support economic development and industrial specialisation (see Box I.11). The Asian experience proves that despite the costs incurred by such outflows, diasporas also make an important contribution, in particular through increased exports to the host country and remittances to the country of origin.

b) Greater attention to the links between migration and development

When co-operation between countries takes account of the development problems of regions of origin, it is likely to limit the risks raised by the "brain drain". For example, increasing budgets for education and training (possibly with outside support) can help to reconstitute the pool of skilled labour, as has happened in the Philippines. Likewise, coherent economic and social policies in countries of origin can attenuate the costs of emigration and bring certain advantages in terms of opening up national economies to trade and foreign direct investment. Several OECD countries have also recently introduced measures to encourage the return and integration of immigrants.

Question marks over the effectiveness of aid for return and reintegration. As part of the "Solidarity and management of migration flows" framework programme adopted on 2 May 2005, the European Commission proposed setting up a European Return Fund for the period covered by the inter-institutional agreement and financial perspective (2007-2013). The proposal was accepted by the European Parliament at the end of 2006 and the Fund will have an allocation of EUR 759 million over the period. It will start operation in January 2008. The European Refugee Fund, with an allocation of EUR 628 million for the period 2007-2013, continues to operate. Some of the money is intended to help asylum seekers, whose applications have been rejected, return to their country of origin.

At the other end of the chain, the return of emigrants may be facilitated to a greater or lesser extent by the situation in the country of origin and by training and employment policies. For example, among Turkish workers who have settled in another country after pursuing their studies there,[62] intentions to return diminish in times of economic crisis. Lengthy studies (*e.g.* an entire cycle) show a negative correlation with the desire to return, and the wish to return depends to a very large extent on the reasons for emigrating in the first place. Those wishing to return have seen their studies abroad as an opportunity for acquiring experience and qualifications of which they can then take advantage in their country of origin. Many foreign graduates residing in OECD countries will countenance a return to their country of origin only if it offers good career opportunities, in innovative sectors for example, and if it has a research and development capacity.[63] Greater investment in universities in countries of origin could encourage short study visits to foreign countries as a complement to initial studies, rather than continuing to encourage studies abroad for an entire cycle.

It is not so much the existence of assistance programmes that helps certain immigrants to return to their country of origin as the coherence between such measures, economic policies in the country of emigration and the migrants' own plans. It is therefore helpful to gain a better understanding of the links between migration and development if coherent and effective migration policies are to be implemented both in OECD countries and in developing countries. Coherence is measured more specifically at regional level.

The links between migration and regional integrated economic development. Taking account of the regional dimension of migration means that host countries and countries of origin can be considered as partners within coherent sets of geographical and economic entities. This approach has the advantage of emphasising the need for active co-operation where migratory flows are concerned. Of course, countries are not on equal footing. But thanks to economic integration and the expansion of trade, intermediate countries reap economic benefits and receive investment flows, and ultimately manage to train sufficient numbers of workers to make up for those who leave, with the result that migration accompanies regional economic development (see Box I.11).

The importance of the link between regional economic development and migration flows is underlined in the most recent free trade agreements. In the framework of trade negotiations between the ten ASEAN countries and Australia and New Zealand, there are plans for the agreements to include measures encouraging temporary migration and facilitating business travel.

Box I.11. **Economic policy coherence and migration of highly skilled workers: The case of East Asia**

The vigorous economies of the countries of East Asia and their interaction with migration provide instructive information about emigration from those countries and its multidimensional consequences.* Several lessons may be drawn.

The first concerns developments in the countries from which immigrants originate. Chinese, Filipino and Indonesian workers are now emigrating to Japan, Korea and Chinese Taipei on the one hand, and to North America and western Europe on the other. Malaysia and Thailand have become countries of immigration after having long been countries of emigration. The reversal of flows in these two countries is largely correlated with the rise in average income per capita and shows the influence of international trade specialisation and the economic effects of migratory flows. High growth levels there have reduced the outflow of unskilled labour and increased that of skilled workers.

The second concerns the factors that encourage the most highly skilled individuals to emigrate. There are many such factors and it is difficult to measure the respective importance of each one, whether under-utilisation of qualifications in countries of origin, the wage gap with host countries or better career prospects in foreign countries. Although a link can be identified between education policies and migration, the direction of cause and effect is not entirely clear. Does better training make it easier for educated workers to leave or does the scale of flows encourage countries to invest more in education?

Thirdly, intraregional immigration has probably gone hand in hand with the economic integration of East Asian markets as a result of an intensification of trade relations and investment between countries. The presence of immigrant communities in a country increases both imports from and exports to their countries of origin. Highly skilled migrants are generally employed by multinational firms and transferred according to investments. Consequently, the mobility of such workers is a complement to foreign direct investment and not a substitute.

The fourth lesson concerns the implications of labour mobility for countries of origin. A "brain drain" may cost a country dear in terms of the loss of dynamic, productive workers, wasted investment in education and training which benefits labour markets in neighbouring countries, and loss of tax revenue. However, a cost/benefit analysis must also take account of the opportunities created by the presence of diasporas in other countries, such as increased trade, financial transfers, remittances and returns of certain migrants. It is difficult to ascertain a net benefit or net cost to countries of emigration. In the long-term, they simply appear to benefit from an increase in economic exchanges which favours the consolidation of development.

* Chamalwong (2005).

c) Complementarity between migration and development

Remittances are one of the key elements of the relationship between migration and development. Because of the scale and effects of remittances, they generate considerable expectations in both OECD and developing countries. The annual report *OECD International Migration Outlook 2006* emphasises the links between migration, remittances and development while underlining that such transfers of funds are not always directed towards productive investment. Recent developments in the sphere of international co-operation have focused on a set of measures to facilitate low-cost transfers and promote better governance in order to attract more foreign direct investment. Lastly, there is a growing awareness of the importance of the mechanisms and resources needed to better mobilise and channel remittances from emigrants into the development of countries of origin. More generally speaking, greater attention is being paid to the flows of human and financial capital from diasporas.

Notes

1. Portugal, Spain, Italy, Greece, Poland, the Czech Republic, the Slovak Republic and Hungary.

2. These were recorded following the implementation of a large-scale legalisation provided for under the Immigration Reform and Control Act of 1986.

3. The trough observed in 1967 is largely attributable to a decline of about 300 000 in inflows in Germany, ostensibly a decline in recruitment of "guest workers" attributable to a recession at the time.

4. The statistics on net migration commonly available cover persons of all ages. Net migration for the working-age population will generally be lower. Working-age persons, however, tend to be over-represented among migrants, so net migration rates of working-age persons will tend to be somewhat higher than those for the total population.

5. The large net migration levels recorded in Italy in recent years may reflect the entry into the population statistics, as a result of a major regularisation, of movements that actually occurred over several years.

6. Immigration is of course not the only way of doing this; an effective mobilisation of the domestic labour supply is another, by means of increases in the participation of women and older workers, for example. See below.

7. Mexico and Turkey are not shown on the chart, because they show large working-age population increases (> 30%) over the 2005-2020 period.

8. A8/EU8 countries refer to the Czech Republic, Estonia, Hungary, Latvia, Lithuania, Poland, the Slovak Republic and Slovenia. EU10 countries refer to the countries previously mentioned plus Cyprus and Malta.

9. Both countries operate a double-card system in which arrivals (at airports or ocean ports) fill out two cards providing identification information, surrender one to the authorities and are required to return the second at the time of departure. The arrival and departure cards are then linked, and based on the number of non-matches, the number of unauthorised overstayers can be determined.

10. This is considered to be an underestimate because it does not include possible overstays by Mexican and Canadian visitors not filling in the double-card I-94 form, which serves as the basis of the overstay estimate.

11. The exceptions are countries like Australia and Japan which are islands and use this geographical advantage to good measure in limiting unauthorised entry and stay.

12. See www.ssb.no/english/subjects/02/01/10/innvgrunn_en/.

13. This entry criterion may also explain the low stay rate for labour migrants, which may include persons arriving for relatively short work assignments.

14. For the purpose of estimation, it was assumed that age-group-specific mortality rates for all persons in each country (from www3.who.int/whosis/life/life_tables/life_tables.cfm?path=life_tables) applied to the foreign-born population as well. A total mortality rate for the foreign-born population was then estimated by applying the age-group-specific rates to the distribution by age group of the foreign-born population for the 2000-round census.

15. The numbers shown in Table I.5 are for stocks of foreign students rather than flows.

16. The results cited here are taken from the national SOPEMI reports supplied to the OECD Secretariat.

17. On the basis of the LFS survey data for the month of March, we shall proceed as follows: i) for permanent jobs, the turnover rate is calculated by comparing the number of persons who have held a job for at least one year (less the net permanent job creation) to the number of permanent jobs a year previously; ii) for temporary jobs, an average turnover rate in calculated having regard to contract length structure (100% for contracts of less than one year, 50% for contracts of more

than one year but less than two, and 30% for other types of contract). The reference population used for calculating the "employment rate" does not include self-employed workers.

18. See, for example, Khoo *et al.* (2002) for Australia; Meurs, Pailhe and Simon (2006) for France; Van Ours and Veenman (2004) for the Netherlands; Aydemir and Sweetman (2006) for the United States and Canada; Dustmann and Theodoropoulos (2006) for the United Kingdom; Rooth and Ekberg (2003) for Sweden; Nielsen, Rosholm, Smith and Husted (2003) for Denmark; and Olsen (2006) for Norway.

19. The figure shows the points differences in the PISA (2003) scores for mathematical and reading literacy between native-born, on the one hand, and immigrant and second generation students on the other. "Immigrants" are students who are foreign-born and whose parents were also born in another country. "Second generation" are native-born students both of whose parents were foreign-born. "Unadjusted" refers to the point differences in the raw scores, "adjusted" to the differences after controlling for the socio-economic background of students. The socio-economic background was constructed on the basis of the following variables: The highest level of the student's parents on the International Socio-Economic Index of Occupational Status (ISEI), the highest level of education of the student's parents, the index of family wealth, the index of home educational resources and the index of possessions related to "classical culture" in the family home. For each test, the mean score across all OECD countries was set at 500 points, with a standard deviation of 100 points.

20. Although an exact translation of PISA-points into years of schooling is not possible, a rough approximation is that about 35 points amount to one year of schooling (see for details Willms, 2004).

21. The rather favourable educational level of the second generation in the United Kingdom has also been observed in several other studies using different and more comprehensive datasets (Wilson, Burgess and Briggs, 2005; Dustmann and Theodoropoulos, 2006).

22. For an in-depth discussion of the labour market integration of immigrant women, see OECD (2006b).

23. This sub-section C was written by Hélène Orain, ENA trainee at the OECD.

24. Fihel, Kaczmarczyk and Okolski (2006).

25. With labour market testing, a system more widespread in the European OECD countries, an employer wishing to hire a first-generation immigrant must first ensure that no resident (native or legally resident foreigner) looking for work can occupy the position concerned. Labour market testing has been phased out for the most highly skilled workers since the General Agreement on Trade in Services came into effect in 1995.

26. See the special chapter on "Managing migration" in OECD 2006e.

27. "Skills and talents" residence permit: *Decree 2007-372 of 21 March 2007* (J.O. of 22 March 2007).

28. Strictly speaking, this system is not comparable to the "green card" in the United States, which is a permanent permit. In Ireland, it can give access to resident status.

29. OECD (2004).

30. Idem.

31. OECD (2006a).

32. OECD (2006b).

33. Given the size of their populations, Malta and Cyprus already benefit from freedom of establishment.

34. All the other countries introduced restrictions, though real opportunities for immigration have opened up in several countries. In Italy, quotas for nationals of the new member states were doubled in 2005. Yet despite greater flows, and contrary to the situation of nationals of non-EU countries, the quotas were not filled in 2005 or 2006. In the Netherlands, the entry quota for EU8 countries was increased to 22 000 in 2005.

35. Including 180 000 renewals.

36. Fihel, Kaczmarczyk and Okolski, (2006).

37. Heinz and Ward-Warmedinger (2006).

38. Commission of the European Community (2006a).

39. Fihel, Kaczmarczyk, Okolski (2006).

40. Blanchflower, Saleheen and Shadforth (2007).

41. Fihel, Kaczmarczyk, Okolski (2006).

42. These possibilities are generally available only to higher education graduates, as is the case in Canada, Finland and Ireland, for example. The Netherlands are also considering introducing such measures. Some countries have sought to limit the possibilities to the highest levels. In France, for example, they apply only to those with a Master's degree (i.e. 5 years higher education).

43. The term "change of status" is generally used when a person with a temporary permit obtains a residence permit. Here it is used in a broader sense to mean all foreigners who change their type of permit.

44. In several Scandinavian countries, a lot of the teaching in certain university courses is in English.

45. The data given below derive from national rules on change of status, with definitions that vary from one country to another.

46. OECD (2006e).

47. OECD (2006b).

48. OECD (2006d).

49. Testing is a way of highlighting discrimination and is accepted as evidence by the courts. For example, two fictional CVs will be submitted in response to a job offer, identical except for the variable to be tested (ethnic origin, sex, age, etc.), with the aim of seeing if a link exists between rejections and the tested variable.

50. In fact it takes up the specific definition contained in the various EU directives on the subject.

51. Along the lines of the Commission for Racial Equality, which has existed for 30 years and has just merged with other independent authorities to form the Commission for Equality and Human Rights.

52. Centre for Strategic Analysis, 2007.

53. When employers chose between the two candidates on offer (which they did in 89% of cases), the majority candidate was chosen in almost four cases out of five (70/89 = 78.7%). Cediey and Foroni (2007).

54. Voting is compulsory in Belgium. For Belgians, inclusion on electoral lists is automatic. EU or non-EU foreigners have to initiate the procedure themselves, and once registered they are subject to the same obligation as nationals. It is therefore the registration rate that is relevant rather than the participation rate.

55. A contribution from Philippe de Bruycker (Brussels Open University) to the section dealing with migration policy in the European Union is gratefully acknowledged.

56. According to some estimates, over half the 11 to 12 million illegal immigrants living in the United States are from Mexico. Source: Pew Hispanic Center Estimates based on March 2005, Current Population Survey; DHS reports.

57. Official Journal of the European Union of 13 April 2006, Series L, No. 05, p. 1.

58. COM(2006)401.

59. Before the rapid response mechanism was implemented, between June and October 2006 almost 19 000 illegal immigrants tried to reach the Spanish coast on the Canary Islands. Drownings and the numbers involved attracted attention, although such immigrants represent a very small proportion of entries into Spain. Frontex has been able to use the rapid response mechanism in support of action taken by the Spanish coastguard. The previous year, Italy intercepted 22 000 illegal immigrants, mostly around the island of Lampedusa off the coast of Tunisia.

60. Commission of the European Community (2006b), pp. 6 and 7.

61. Official Journal of 15 June 2004, Series L, No. 213, p. 5.

62. Güngör and Tansel (2007).

63. This assertion comes with a caveat, since it implies that many foreign students remain in the host country after they have finished their studies and there is a lack of definite statistical evidence for such an assumption.

Bibliography   (Related to Section I.A. Developments in Migration Flows)

GAO (2003), "Overstay Tracking is a Key Component of a Layered Defense", Testimony before the House Subcommittee on Immigration, Border Security and Claims, United States general accounting Office, Washington, D.C.

HCI (2007), *Rapport statistique 2005 de l'Observatoire statistique de l'immigration et de l'intégration*, Haut Conseil à l'Intégration, Paris, janvier.

HOEFER, M., N. RYTINA and C. CAMPBELL (2006), "Estimates of the Unauthorized Immigrant Population Residing in the United States: January 2005"; DHS Office of Immigration Statistics, *http://149.101.23.2:graphics/shared/statistics/publications/index.htm.*

MAE (2006), *Annuario Statistico*, Ministero degli Affari Esteri, Rome.

MDI (2006), *Note sulla sicurezza in Italia 2005*, Ministero dell'interno, Rome.

OECD (2004), "Informal Employment and Promoting the Transition to a Salaried Economy", in *Employment Outlook*, Organisation for Economic Co-operation and Development, Paris.

United Nations (1998), Recommendations on Statistics of International Migration – Revision 1, United Nations Publication, New York.

WARREN, R. and E. KRALY (1985), "The Elusive Exodus: Emigration from the United States", Population Trends and Public Policy Occasional Paper No. 8, Population Reference Bureau: Washington, D.C.

Bibliography   (Related to Section I.B. Immigrants and the Labour Market)

AYDEMIR, A. and A. SWEETMAN (2006), "First and Second Generation Immigrant Educational Attainment and Labor Market Outcomes: A comparison of the United States and Canada", IZA Discussion Paper 2298, Bonn.

BAUER, P. and R. RIPHAHN (2007), "Heterogeneity in the Intergenerational Transmission of Educational Attainment: Evidence from Switzerland on Natives and Second Generation Immigrants", *Journal of Population Economics*, Vol. 20, No. 1, pp. 121-148.

CAILLE, J.-P. (2001), "Scolarisation à 2 ans et réussite de la carrière scolaire au début de l'école elémentaire", *Education and formations*, Vol. 60, pp. 7-18.

CASTRO-ALMEIDA, P. (1979), "Problems facing second generation migrants in Western Europe", *International Labour Review*, Vol. 188, No 6, pp. 763-775.

DUSTMANN, C. and N. THEODOROPOULOS (2006), "Ethnic Minority Immigrants and their Children in Britain", CReAM Discussion Paper No. 1006, University College London.

KHOO, S-K., P. McDONALD, D. GIORGAS and B. BIRRELL (2002), *Second generation Australians*, Report for the Department of Immigration and Multicultural and Indigenous Affairs, Canberra.

MEURS, D., A. PAILHE and P. SIMON (2006), "Persistance des inégalités entre générations liées à l'immigration : L'accès à l'emploi des immigrés et de leurs descendants en France", *Population* (édition française), Vol. 61, No. 5-6, pp. 763-801.

NIELSEN, H., M. ROSHOLM, N. SMITH and L. HUSTED (2003), "The school-to-work transition of 2nd generation immigrants in Denmark", *Journal of Population Economics*, Vol. 16, pp. 755-786.

OECD (2006a), *Where Immigrant Students Succeed. A Comparative Review of Performance and Engagement in PISA 2003*, Paris.

OECD (2006b), *International Migration Outlook*, Paris.

OECD (2007), *Jobs for immigrants: Labour market integration in Australia, Denmark, Germany and Sweden*, Paris.

OLSEN, B. (2006), "Are young immigrants a marginalised group?", *Samfunnsspeilet*, Vol. 4/2006. Statistics Norway: Oslo and Kongsvinger.

ROOTH, D-O. and J. EKBERG (2003), "Unemployment and earnings for second generation immigrants in Sweden. Ethnic background and parent composition", *Journal of Population Economics*, Vol. 16, pp. 787-814.

SCHNEPF, S. (2004), "How Different Are Immigrants? A Cross-Country and Cross-Survey Analysis of Educational Achievement", IZA Discussion Paper No. 1398, Bonn.

SIMEONE, L. (2005), Discrimination testing based on ILO methodology. International Labour Office, Geneva. Mimeographed.

VAN OURS, JC. and J. VEENMAN (2004), "From parent to child: early labor market experiences of second-generation immigrants in the Netherlands". *De Economist*, Vol. 152, No. 4, pp. 473-490.

WILLMS, D.J. (2004), Variation in Literacy Skills Among Canadian Provinces: Findings from the OECD PISA. Statistics Canada, Research Paper No. 12.

WILSON, D., S. BURGESS and A. BRIGGS (2005), "The Dynamics of School Attainment of England's Ethnic Minorities", Centre for Market and Public Organisation Working Paper 05/130, University of Bristol.

Bibliography   *(Related to Section I.C. Migration Policies)*

BECKOUCHE, P. and J-L. GUIGOU (2007), "Méditerranée: d'un Euromed en panne à une région industrielle Nord-Sud", in *Horizons stratégiques*, No. 3, January 2007, Paris.

BLANCHFLOWER, D.G., J. SALEHEEN and C. SHADFORTH (2007), "The impact of the recent migration from eastern Europe on the UK economy", *IZA, Discussion paper* No. 2615, Bonn.

CEDIEY, E. and F. FORONI (2007), *Discriminations en raison de l'origine dans les entreprises en France*, ILO, Genève.

CENTRE D'ANALYSE STRATEGIQUE (2007), "Discriminations à l'embauche dans 4 cas sur 5 en France, selon un testing du BIT", *La note de veille*, No. 50, 19 March 2007.

CHAMALWONG, Y. (2005), "The Migration of Highly Skilled Asian Worker in OECD Member Countries and Its Effects on Economic Development in East Asia", in FUKASAKU, K. (dir) *Policy Coherence Towards East Asia: Development Challenges for OECD Countries*, Paris, OECD Development Centre Study and Tokyo, Policy Research Institute, Ministry of Finance.

COMMISSION OF THE EUROPEAN COMMUNITY (2006a), Report on the Functioning of the Transitional Arrangements Set out in the 2003 Accession Treaty (period of 1 May 2004 to 30 April 2006), COM(2006)48 final, 8 February 2006, Brussels.

COMMISSION OF THE EUROPEAN COMMUNITY (2006b), Communication from the Commission on Policy Priorities in the Fight Against Illegal Immigration of Third Country Nationals, COM(2006)402, 19 July 2006, Brussels.

DENEUVE, C. (2006), "Quelles perspectives d'immigration à moyen terme ?", in *Regards sur l'actualité*, No. 326, December 2006, La Documentation Française, Paris.

DOLVIK, J.E. and L. ELDRING, (2006), "The Nordic labour market two years after the EU enlargement; mobility, effects and challenges", Nordic Council of Ministers, Copenhagen, *www.norden.org/pub/velfaerd/arbetsmarknad/sk/TN2006558.pdf*.

FIHEL, A., P. KACZMARCZYK and M. OKOLSKI (2006), "Labor migration from the new EU member States", *Quarterly Economic Report*, World Bank EU8, Part II: Special Topic, September 2006.

GÜNGÖR, N.D. and A. TANSEL (2007), "Brain Drain from Turkey: The Case of Professionals Abroad", IZA Discussion Paper No. 2617, OECD, Paris.

HEINZ, F.F. and M. WARD-WARMEDINGER, (2006), "Cross Border Labour Mobility within an Enlarged EU", *Occasional Paper Series*, No. 52, October 2006, European Central Bank.

OECD (2004), *Migration for Employment, Bilateral Agreements at a Crossroads*, Organisation for Economic Co-operation and Development, Paris.

OECD (2006a), *National Account of OECD countries*, Organisation for Economic Co-operation and Development, Paris.

OECD (2006b), *Where Immigrant Students Succeed? A Comparative Review of Performance and Engagement in PISA 2003*, Organisation for Economic Co-operation and Development, Paris.

OECD (2006c), "Employment and labour market statistics" in *OECD Employment Outlook*, Organisation for Economic Co-operation and Development, Paris.

OECD (2006d), "Policies targeted at specific workforce groups or labour market segments", in *OECD Employment Outlook*, Organisation for Economic Co-operation and Development, Paris.

OECD (2006e), *International Migration Outlook*, Organisation for Economic Co-operation and Development, Paris.

QUARTEY, P. (2006), "Migration, Aid and Development – A Ghana Country Case Study", *op. cit.* in "Migration, aide et commerce: plus de cohérence en faveur du développement" DAYTON-JOHNSON, J. and L. T. KATSELI (dir) *Cahier de politique économique* No. 28, Paris, Development Center, OECD.

WEIL, P. (2005), "Immigration, du contrôle à la régulation", in *La République et sa diversité. Immigration, intégration, discriminations*, Seuil, Paris.

WORLD BANK (2006), *Global Economic Prospects 2006. Economic implications of remittances and migration*, Washington D.C.

ISBN 978-92-64-03285-9
International Migration Outlook
Sopemi 2007 Edition
© OECD 2007

PART II

Matching Educational Background and Employment: A Challenge for Immigrants In Host Countries*

* This document was written by Jean-Christophe Dumont (OECD) and Olivier Monso (CREST-Université de Paris-I). It is based on a working paper (DELSA/ELSA(2005)12) co-authored with Ana Damas de Matos and on a report submitted by Céline Antonin.

Introduction

The growing migration of skilled workers is one of the salient features of recent international migratory trends in OECD countries, many of which have adopted measures to facilitate their recruitment, including tax incentives (OECD, 2004a). This trend is likely to persist, in light of the current and anticipated demographic changes at work in OECD countries. Even so, the processes of bringing skilled immigrants into the labour market are not always well understood and in some cases may entail particular difficulties.

As has been observed among the native-born population, immigrants (defined here as persons born abroad) with higher education degrees find it easier to enter the host-country labour market than do those with lower levels of education. This is the case overall in OECD countries, but the relative situation of immigrants vis-à-vis the native-born varies considerably. The discrepancies in terms of the employment and unemployment rates between the native-born and immigrants tend to increase with the level of education.

Labour market access is not measured solely by the yardstick of the unemployment rate, but is also assessed in terms of the match between qualifications and jobs. From this viewpoint, qualified immigrants encounter special difficulties in all OECD countries. This could be attributable to i) unobserved differences in the "value" of degrees or in intrinsic skills; ii) problems with the recognition of degrees acquired in the country of origin; iii) a lack of human and social capital specific to the host country (e.g. proficiency in the language); iv) the local labour market situation; and v) various forms of discrimination.

This chapter presents a measure of the occupational over-qualification of immigrants, together with some key factors that may explain why that level is higher or lower. It also looks at the differences observed according to immigrants' length of stay, their country of origin, their gender, the place where their diploma was earned, and their linguistic capabilities.

The first part gives an overview of the conditions surrounding immigrants' entry into the labour market in OECD countries. The second part presents the main theoretical approaches to over-qualification. The third part proposes a way of assessing occupational over-qualification, by place of birth and socio-demographic characteristics. The fourth part refines this analysis by attempting to control for certain cognitive and linguistic skills. The conclusion reviews the main results and highlights the policy issues related to addressing the over-qualification of immigrants.

1. Education: A labour market access factor which immigrants do not always benefit from

The immigrant population structure, by level of education, varies from one host country to another. Individuals born abroad tend however to be overrepresented at the highest and lowest levels (see Table II.1). In some OECD countries, nearly 50% of all immigrants between 25 and 64 years of age have not attended upper secondary school. Such is the case in France, for example, as well as in Italy, Portugal and Belgium. In contrast, in settlement countries (Australia, Canada, United States and New Zealand), which select some of their new

Table II.1. **Education level of foreign- and native-born populations aged 25 to 64 in OECD countries, 2003-2004**

Percentages

	Foreign-born			Native-born		
	Less than upper secondary (ISCED 0/1/2)	Upper secondary and post-secondary non-tertiary (ISCED 3/4)	Tertiary (ISCED 5/6)	Less than upper secondary (ISCED 0/1/2)	Upper secondary and post-secondary non-tertiary (ISCED 3/4)	Tertiary (ISCED 5/6)
Australia	24.1	40.1	**35.7**	32.3	41.5	26.2
Austria	**36.7**	44.7	**18.5**	18.3	63.7	18.0
Belgium	**47.5**	27.1	25.4	35.9	34.6	29.6
Canada	22.1	31.8	**46.1**	22.9	38.3	38.8
Czech Republic	**29.0**	55.4	**15.6**	10.8	77.2	12.0
Denmark	**23.8**	38.3	**37.9**	17.0	51.3	31.7
Finland	**24.3**	**47.9**	27.8	23.4	43.0	33.6
France	**51.1**	27.8	21.1	32.8	43.6	23.7
Germany	**37.4**	43.7	18.9	12.3	62.2	25.5
Greece	38.3	**42.3**	19.4	43.1	37.3	19.6
Hungary	16.4	56.0	**27.6**	25.6	58.7	15.7
Ireland	23.9	30.7	**45.4**	39.2	35.3	25.5
Italy	48.7	**40.0**	**11.3**	52.2	36.7	11.1
Luxembourg	**36.7**	40.5	**22.8**	18.3	65.7	16.0
Netherlands	**43.5**	32.3	24.2	30.6	44.4	25.0
New Zealand	15.9	**46.5**	**37.6**	28.2	39.5	32.2
Norway	**16.9**	46.7	**36.4**	12.8	56.0	31.2
Poland	**27.1**	50.4	**22.5**	16.5	68.3	15.3
Portugal	52.0	**25.8**	**22.2**	78.0	11.2	10.8
Slovak Republic	**21.0**	61.7	**17.3**	13.3	74.6	12.1
Spain	40.9	**29.3**	**29.8**	57.1	17.5	25.4
Sweden	**21.7**	48.7	**29.5**	16.8	55.9	27.3
Switzerland	**29.6**	42.8	27.6	7.2	65.2	27.6
United Kingdom	**22.1**	43.6	**34.3**	15.9	54.8	29.4
United States	**30.1**	34.9	35.0	8.5	51.6	39.9

Notes: Bold figures indicate an overrepresentation of foreign-born at that level of education. Data refer to the population aged 15-64 for Australia. Reference years are 2001 for Canada and New Zealand, 2002 for the Netherlands, 2003 for Australia and 2004 for the United States.
The ISCED variable specifies the level of education according to the International Standard Classification of Education.
Sources: European countries: European Union Labour Force Survey (data provided by Eurostat); United States: Current Population Survey March Supplement; Australia: Survey of Household, Income and Labour Dynamics; Canada and New Zealand: Population censuses.

StatLink ᵐˢᵖ *http://dx.doi.org/10.1787/021681308135*

immigrants according to their level of education, as well as in Ireland, the United Kingdom, Norway and Denmark, the proportion of immigrants with low education is significantly smaller, and that of higher-educated immigrants generally exceeds 33%.

With the exception of the countries of southern Europe (Portugal, Spain, Greece), where immigration is a recent phenomenon, and of Luxembourg and Hungary, the employment rate for immigrants is below that for the native-born in all OECD countries. Education differences explain only a limited portion of this differential, except in Austria and the United States. In France, for example, even if the educational level of immigrants were comparable to that of the native-born, over 60% of the employment rate gap would persist (see Chart II.1). In Ireland, where immigrants are relatively well educated, if immigrants had the same educational profile as the native-born, their employment-rate gap with nationals would be significantly higher.

Chart II.1. **Differences in employment rates of native- and foreign-born populations, 2003-2004**

Percentage points

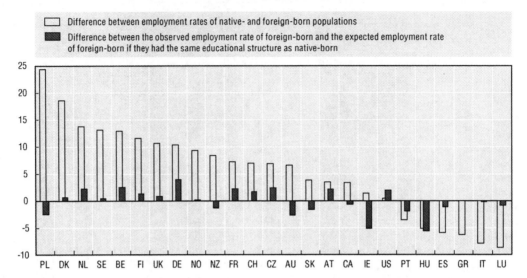

Note: 2001 for Canada and New Zealand, 2002 for the Netherlands, 2003 for Australia and 2004 for the United States.

Sources: European countries: European Union Labour Force Survey (data provided by Eurostat); United States: Current Population Survey March Supplement; Australia: Household, Income and Labour Dynamics; Canada and New Zealand: Population censuses.

Interpretation: In France difference between employment rates of natives and foreign-born is 7.3 percentage points. If the foreign-born had the same educational structure as the natives, their employment rate would be 2.3 points higher. In other words, 5 points, that is to say more than two third of the difference, cannot be explained directly by differences in qualifications.

StatLink ⟨⟨⟨⟩⟩⟩ http://dx.doi.org/10.1787/014267406755

The results presented in Annex II.A1. that the immigrant employment rate is often close to or higher than that of the native-born with low education (defined here as people who have not gone to secondary school). That finding does not hold, however, for people, particularly women, with higher levels of education (Dumont and Liebig, 2005). It seems true of immigrants and the native-born alike that a higher level of education facilitates access to the labour market. Yet the fact remains that the gap between the native-born and immigrants persists, and is indeed growing, in nearly all OECD countries. In Denmark, Germany and Finland the gap exceeds 15 percentage points. The outcome in terms of the unemployment rate is similar. These results, taken as a whole, suggest that immigrants face special difficulties in making effective use of their human capital in the labour market.

Among those who hold a job, there is also the question of whether their job reflects their qualifications. Difficulties in accessing the labour market can occur in the case of over-qualification, i.e. holding a job that requires lesser qualifications or that pays less than would theoretically be available to people having the same level of education.

2. Occupational over-qualification: A variety of approaches

Research into the over-qualification phenomenon dates back to the 1970s, at a time when the "universalisation" of access to higher education led some people to fear that a growing imbalance in the supply of and demand for skilled labour would dilute the value of diplomas

Box II.1. **Different approaches to the over-qualification problem**

The "normative" approach uses a presumed correspondence between education and job qualifications (*e.g.* Chevalier, 2003; McGoldrick and Robst, 1996). This is a measure used frequently in the literature, yet its arbitrary nature makes it debatable, especially if the same correspondence is imposed for all countries. Prior analysis may be needed to identify more closely the correspondence between diploma and job. The ISCO occupational classification system devised by the International Labour Office (ILO) can be used to establish linkages between levels of qualification and educational levels as designated by the International Standard Classification of Education ISCED),[1] using this normative approach.

The "statistical" approach consists in observing the "normal" correspondences between education and employment. Such statistical norms can be applied, for example, through contingency table analysis or by assuming that all individuals whose years of schooling exceed the national average by more than one standard deviation are over-qualified (Bauer, 2002; Rubb, 2002; Nauze-Fichet and Tomasini, 2002; McGoldrick and Robst, 1996). In the case of France, Lainé and Okba (2004) have estimated the probability that a young person leaving the education system will hold a low-skilled job, depending on the level and field of the person's diploma and where the person lives. "Over-qualified" persons are those relegated to unskilled jobs when the statistical norm (in this case the estimation from a logistic model) would not predict such employment.

Norms for over-qualifiaction entail being able to compare and classify two individuals against a criterion of labour market success, such as type of job or pay. The job categories used do not always allow such classification, or in some cases they can make it appear to be excessively arbitrary. The hourly wage, when available, constitutes an objective criterion for classifying two individuals working in two very different types of jobs (which cannot necessarily be ranked) or in the same category of employment. In this regard, the study of wage distribution by level of education can provide a criterion of over-qualification. This was the approach taken by Nauze-Fichet and Tomasini (2002), whereby an individual earning lower wages than two-thirds (or any other threshold determined) of people having the next-lowest level of education is deemed over-qualified. Nevertheless, this standard is sensitive to the threshold selected and to the educational categories used.

The statistical and normative approaches are *de facto* quite similar. A statistical approach entails prior stipulation of the relevant categories or standards (in the above examples, it is necessary to define an "unskilled" job or levels of education and qualification for the construction of matrices, etc.). In return, a statistical approach can facilitate the adaptation of standards to new socio-economic realities. The use of ISCO and ISCED classification systems has called into question some of the equivalencies initially set by the ILO (the classification systems themselves have also been changed) and provides an example of this adaptation effort (OECD, 2002).

The third option (the "self-declared" approach) consists in compiling individuals' opinions on whether their jobs match their education, either by means of a direct question, or by asking people about the prerequisites for their employment (*e.g.* Dorn and Sousa-Posa, 2005; Sicherman, 1991; Alba-Ramirez, 1993; Sloane, Battu and Seaman, 1999; McGoldrick and Robst, 1996). This "subjective" approach may be subject to several sources of bias, such as how the question is worded or the impact of external variables.[2]

1. Case studies on the United States generally use the Dictionary of Occupation Titles (DOT) to establish these correspondences.
2. In their study of young people from immigrant backgrounds in France, Lainé and Okba (2004) show that the feeling of over-qualification among young men of North African descent reflects a real discounting of their capabilities on the labour market, but is equally observed independent of their "objective" over-qualification situation. For the authors, there may be other socio-cultural factors at work, including the aspirations and demands specific to that population.

(Freeman, 1976). If this did not in fact happen, it is in part because technical progress helped sustain the demand for skilled labour (Krueger, 1993). In effect, the emergence and spread of new technologies in the 1980s and 1990s had considerable repercussions on the organisation of tasks and the upgrading of jobs in many sectors of the economy, helping thereby to rebalance the match between education levels and available jobs (Acemoglu, 1999; Autor, Levy and Murnane, 2003). These trends have sparked renewed interest in the question of over-qualification since the 1990s (see Groot and van der Brink, 2000 and Rubb, 2003 for a summary analysis).

The literature on over-qualification distinguishes between three types of approaches: "normative", "statistical" and "self-declared" (see Box II.1). Generally speaking, research has focused primarily on the return to investment in education, and has concluded that: i) for the same level of education, persons who are over-qualified are paid less than people who are not over-qualified; ii) for the same type of employment, persons who are over-qualified for their jobs are paid more than those who have a level of education that corresponds to the job; iii) over-qualified persons have greater occupational mobility, which over time allows for a better match between their job and their initial training;[1] iv) women are generally more likely to find themselves in jobs that do not reflect their qualifications; and, lastly v) over-qualification results at least in part from a lack of human capital acquired beyond initial training (professional experience, job experience, further training) and in some cases from less favourable intrinsic skills. With few exceptions, these studies have not sought to address the specific situation of immigrants. The following section attempts to assess immigrants' over-qualification relative to that of the native-born, on a comparative basis for several OECD countries.

3. An evaluation of immigrants' risk of occupational over-qualification

Over-qualification is examined here with a normative-type measure based on the correspondence between level of education and qualifications for the job held (see Annex II.A2). It has also been analysed from the viewpoint of wages (where the wage distribution by level of education indicates whether a person is over-qualified or not, see Annex II.A3). The results from these two types of measurement point in the same direction.

Education and job qualification levels are grouped into three broad categories: Low, intermediate and high. An over-qualified individual is one who holds a job that requires lesser qualifications than would theoretically be available to him at his education level. Over-qualification rates are calculated for individuals with an intermediate or higher education.

Immigrants are more over-qualified than the native-born

Table II.2 shows the proportions of persons born abroad who are over-qualified, for different OECD countries, and compares them with those obtained for the native-born using data from employment surveys and the population census. These two sources produce comparable results in terms of over-qualification by place of birth, but they occasionally differ in their level because they refer to slightly different periods and population groups. The employment survey data are used to examine over-qualification by gender and length of stay, while census data allow a detailed analysis by country of origin.

According to employment survey data, over-qualification rates vary sharply among countries, ranging from 5% (Czech Republic) to 26% (Spain). In Spain, Ireland, the United

Table II.2. **Over-qualification rates of native- and foreign-born populations in some OECD countries**

Percentages

Sources	Survey Data Population 15-64, 2003-2004				Censuses and Population Registers Population 15+, Circa 2000			
	Total	Native-born (A)	Foreign-born (B)	B/A	Total	Native-born (A)	Foreign-born (B)	B/A
Australia	20.4	19.0	24.6	**1.3**	14.5	12.9	18.9	**1.5**
Austria	11.5	10.3	21.1	**2.0**	10.9	9.9	20.0	**2.0**
Belgium	16.2	15.6	21.6	**1.4**	..	..	..	..
Canada	..	..	..	..	22.1	21.3	25.2	**1.2**
Czech Republic	5.2	5.2	10.0	**1.9**	5.8	5.6	9.6	**1.7**
Denmark	10.9	10.4	18.6	**1.8**	11.9	11.2	24.5	**2.2**
Finland	14.4	14.3	19.2	**1.3**	16.2	16.1	21.6	**1.3**
France	11.6	11.2	15.5	**1.4**	11.0	10.8	13.7	**1.3**
Germany	12.3	11.4	20.3	**1.8**	..	..	..	..
Greece	11.3	9.0	39.3	**4.4**	13.1	10.1	32.4	**3.2**
Hungary	6.4	6.3	9.7	**1.5**	5.1	5.0	7.4	**1.5**
Ireland	16.6	15.7	23.8	**1.5**	17.5	16.9	21.0	**1.2**
Italy	7.0	6.4	23.5	**3.6**	7.3	6.9	15.4	**2.2**
Luxembourg	5.5	3.4	9.1	**2.7**	7.6	5.4	11.7	**2.2**
Netherlands	10.1	9.3	16.8	**1.8**	..	..	..	..
New Zealand	..	..	..	..	18.6	18.9	17.2	**0.9**
Norway	9.2	8.4	20.3	**2.4**	..	..	..	..
Poland	..	..	..	..	7.8	7.8	9.0	**1.2**
Portugal	9.0	7.9	16.8	**2.1**	9.0	8.3	13.6	**1.6**
Slovak Republic	..	..	..	..	26.9	26.9	24.5	**0.9**
Spain	25.5	24.2	42.9	**1.8**	8.1	7.3	19.8	**2.7**
Sweden	7.6	6.5	16.1	**2.5**	8.7	7.6	18.6	**2.4**
Switzerland	10.5	10.0	12.5	**1.3**	7.8	7.2	10.6	**1.5**
United Kingdom	15.5	15.3	17.8	**1.2**	14.4	14.0	18.4	**1.3**
United States (2002)	14.0	13.4	18.1	**1.4**	14.4	14.0	17.3	**1.2**

Sources (left columns): European countries: European Union Labour Force Survey (data provided by Eurostat); 2005 for the Netherlands; Australia: Survey of Household, Income and Labour Dynamics; United States: Current Population Survey March Supplement.
Sources (right columns): Population Censuses and population registers for all countries.

StatLink ⟶ *http://dx.doi.org/10.1787/021687371867*

Kingdom and Belgium, the over-qualification rates are high for immigrants and for the native-born alike. Conversely, in Luxembourg, the Czech Republic, Hungary, and to a lesser extent Switzerland, the over-qualification rate is low for both categories.

In all OECD countries, regardless of the source used (except for New Zealand, with population census data), immigrants are more likely to be over-qualification than persons born in the country. These results are consistent with those of Battu and Sloane (2002) in the United Kingdom on over-qualification among ethnic minorities (particularly Indians) relating primarily to problems with diploma recognition and discrimination. This finding is mirrored in the case of France by Laine and Okba (*op cit.*), for young people of North African origin. Similarly, Buchel and Battu (2003) found that foreigners in Germany were more likely to be over-qualified, *ceteris paribus*, then Germans. On the other hand, Wirz and Atukeren (2005) found no evidence that national origin had any effect in Switzerland.

These results point to a particularly high degree of over-qualification among immigrants compared to the native-born in countries of southern Europe (Italy, Greece and to a lesser extent Portugal and Spain) and in some countries of northern Europe (Norway and Sweden). In southern Europe, immigration is a recent phenomenon, and consists essentially of workers who are apparently ready to accept unskilled jobs upon arrival, with the hope of subsequent upward professional mobility. One might well surmise that, for material and sociological reasons (with host country over-qualification standards being less of a consideration), immigrants are in fact less reluctant to accept jobs for which they are over-qualified.[2] Legal and regulatory aspects (e.g. requirements for work permits, region of settlement, and access to citizenship) can also limit the choice of jobs for new immigrants, at least temporarily. In this case, it could be expected that immigrants' over-qualification would diminish significantly as their stay lengthens (see below).

The situation is different in Norway and Sweden, where the proportion of migrants entering as workers is low and the proportion of refugees is substantial. These refugees are relatively highly skilled but face special problems arising from their status (sudden and fortuitous migration, no official certification of their education level and occupational qualifications, uncertainty as to the end of their stay, psychological complications, etc.), which may be compounded by significant language problems. Moreover, employers often have little or no information or knowledge about the validity of academic or occupational qualifications acquired abroad.

The discrepancies in relative over-qualification rates among countries may also reflect specific features of the labour market. Whereas some countries do a better job of integrating immigrants into employment but leave them at greater risk of being over-qualified (as in Italy, for example), others reveal a lower rate of immigrant over-qualification but have a high rate of immigrant unemployment (as in Belgium).[3] More generally, labour market characteristics, and especially those likely to affect the supply of low-skilled labour (e.g. existence of a minimum wage, prevalence of short-term temporary work, the laws governing contracts, the certification process), may be invoked to explain why some countries have a greater incidence of over-qualification. However, as will be demonstrated below, it is individual characteristics that generally explain a preponderant portion of the disadvantage observed for immigrants.

Women, recent immigrants, and those from outside the OECD area are most likely to be over-qualified

The very high over-qualification rates for immigrants in certain countries may be interpreted through the particular circumstances of immigrant women (see Table II.3).[4] This is especially the case in Greece, where the over-qualification rate for female immigrants is 53%, versus 9% for native Greek women, and in Italy (where the rates are respectively 27% and 7%). In the majority of cases, the over-qualification rate is higher for female immigrants than for male immigrants, although the United States, the United Kingdom, Portugal, New Zealand, Sweden and Ireland are exceptions. The relative over-qualification of women vis-à-vis men is more pronounced among immigrants: This is particularly so in Germany, Austria, Canada and Sweden, countries in which native-born women, by contrast, have lower over-qualification rates than do native-born men.

Given the presumed importance of human and social capital specific to the host country, one might expect, a priori, that the risk of over-qualification would decline with length of stay, in a manner similar to what Chiswick (1978) found regarding wage convergence between immigrants and the native-born in the United States. The results presented in Table II.4 seem in fact to indicate an improvement with length of stay in

Table II.3. **Over-qualification rate of native- and foreign-born populations by gender in some OECD countries, 2003-2004**

Percentages

	Foreign-born		Natives	
	Women	Men	Women	Men
Australia	21.6	17.4	13.7	12.3
Austria	24.8	18.1	9.3	11.1
Belgium	24.6	19.4	17.7	13.8
Canada	27.6	23.2	21.7	20.9
Czech Republic	12.8	7.8	6.6	4.0
Denmark	19.7	17.5	10.5	10.4
Finland	26.2	12.2	18.8	9.7
France	18.8	12.9	14.2	8.6
Germany	23.6	17.9	9.9	12.8
Greece	53.4	28.3	9.0	9.0
Hungary	10.5	9.0	7.3	5.5
Ireland	23.9	23.6	15.6	15.8
Italy	27.4	19.9	7.1	5.9
Luxembourg	14.1	5.6	3.2	3.6
Netherlands	16.6	16.9	9.9	8.7
New Zealand	16.0	18.3	23.3	14.4
Norway	25.1	16.1	10.6	6.3
Poland	9.3	8.8	9.1	6.5
Portugal	16.2	17.5	8.9	6.5
Slovak Republic	27.0	22.2	27.9	26.0
Spain	47.6	38.8	24.4	24.1
Sweden	15.3	16.9	7.2	5.7
Switzerland	13.8	11.4	7.6	12.0
United Kingdom	17.0	18.4	14.9	15.7
United States	17.0	19.0	11.2	15.5

Sources: European countries: European Community Labour Force Survey (data provided by Eurostat); 2005 for the Netherlands; United States: Current Population Survey March Supplement 2002; Australia, Canada, New Zealand, Poland and Slovak Republic: Population censuses, Circa 2001.

StatLink ᔡᓵ *http://dx.doi.org/10.1787/021705673073*

several OECD countries, and especially in Ireland and Norway, where the immigrant over-qualification rate among those settled for more than 10 years is half the rate for those who have been in the country for less than three years.

These results, as well as the over-qualification rates observed in certain economic sectors (hotels and catering, mining and manufacturing, household services) support the idea that newly arrived immigrants are more likely than the native-born to accept unskilled jobs, even arduous and low-paying ones, but that they tend to move on from such work as they stay longer in the host country and become fully integrated into the labour market.

A number of studies have examined the role of the time variable in correcting over-qualification situations for the population as a whole, and especially for new labour market entrants. In a study on Switzerland, Dorn and Sousa-Poza (2005) found that 44% of over-qualified persons were still in that status after one year, 20% after two years and fewer than 10% after four years. In the United States, Rubb (2003) showed that 26% of over-qualified persons are no longer in that situation the following year (see also Sicherman (1991) for the United States and Alba-Ramirez (1993) for Spain). Dolton and Vignoles (2000) showed that in the United Kingdom, 38% of people were over-qualified in their first job, and 30% after six years.

Table II.4. **Over-qualification rate of the foreign-born population according to their duration of stay in some OECD countries, 2003-2004**

Percentages

	≤ 3 years	≤ 5 years	≤ 10 years	≥ 11 years
Austria	28.6	21.8	20.5	20.3
Belgium	16.8	27.4	27.6	20.8
Czech Republic	15.5	19.6	12.6	7.2
Denmark	27.9	29.1	25.5	13.9
Finland	–	–	28.2	15.2
France	21.8	32.0	27.1	13.4
Germany	25.4	30.3	28.3	17.1
Greece	47.4	47.0	44.6	32.4
Hungary	–	–	–	8.9
Ireland	34.0	27.6	17.7	15.3
Italy	33.7	39.5	31.5	25.5
Luxembourg	8.2	8.5	11.1	8.5
Netherlands	42.5	36.7	28.0	13.9
Norway	31.8	35.4	17.1	17.2
Portugal	–	–	–	7.0
Slovak Republic	–	–	–	12.6
Spain	55.8	54.8	47.7	30.2
Sweden	26.2	25.8	23.2	12.7
United Kingdom	20.9	18.3	18.3	16.9
United States	24.7	22.5	21.7	16.3

Sources: European Union Labour Force Survey (data provided by Eurostat); 2005 for the Netherlands; United States: Current Population Survey March Supplement 2002.

StatLink ⬛⬛⬛ *http://dx.doi.org/10.1787/021737534444*

Any analysis of trends in the situation of immigrants over time requires specific precaution, however, recognising that entries and exits from the territory can cause selection bias: Immigrants who have been in the country longest may have greater capacity to enter the labour market than did those who left the country after a short stay (Edin, Lalonde and Aslund, 2000). Moreover, length of stay can potentially conceal cohort effects: Groups may differ by their level of education, their country of origin, the category under which they entered the host country, and the conditions in which they arrived on the labour market.

In any case, for all countries with the exception of Ireland and Portugal, immigrants still have a higher rate of over-qualification after 10 years than do the native-born. This gap reaches 10 percentage points in Austria and in Norway. The fact that convergence has not been fully achieved in many countries could suggest, then, that immigrants face difficulties in accumulating human and social capital specific to the host country, or that other, non-observed factors are behind this persistent situation.

Finally, a breakdown of immigration by geographic origin shows that individuals originally from outside the OECD area are on average at greater risk of over-qualification than other immigrants. For the OECD as a whole, some 15% of immigrants from an OECD country with an intermediate or higher education will be over-qualified, while the figure is close to 20% for people from outside the OECD area. Moreover, the change in over-qualification rates is much more limited for people from OECD countries than for those from non-member countries. This reflects in part a certain homogeneity in the education systems in OECD countries and the characteristics of migration between those countries.

A more detailed analysis reveals the variety of situations by region of origin. Chart II.2 shows, in the form of a "box plot" (see Box II.2), the distribution of average ratios of over-qualification for each country of birth within a given region. For example, among the new member countries of the European Union (EU), Lithuania appears as the country of origin for which the average ratio of the immigrant over-qualification rate to that for the native-born is highest (2.7). This tendency provides a more general illustration of the situation of immigrants from the former Soviet republics. The regional average for the new EU members is 1.7.

Chart II.2. **Dispersion in the over-qualification rates of the foreign-born by main regions of origin relative to those observed for the native-born, Circa 2000**

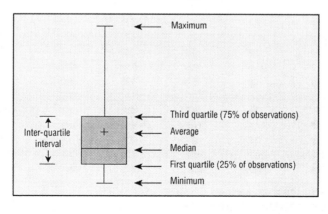

Sources: Censuses and population registers.

StatLink ᵐˢ *http://dx.doi.org/10.1787/014286628466*

Box II.2. **The "Box and Whiskers Plot"**

A "box and whiskers plot" is a graphic representation of several distribution parameters for a variable (here the average ratio of over-qualification rates between immigrants and the native-born). It should be read as indicated opposite.

Chart II.2 confirms, first, that people originating from the EU15, from Canada or from the United States, are on average no more over-qualified than persons born in the country in which they reside. On the other hand, it shows that immigrants from sub-Saharan Africa and European countries from outside the EU, and Asia as well, are particularly exposed to over-qualification. However, there are huge differences within these regions, by country of origin. According to the average figures for the OECD, people born in the Philippines are the most likely (4.3 times more likely) to be over-qualified compared to the native-born. Among immigrants from the Middle East, persons born in Iraq are especially exposed (on average, 2.3 times the rate for the native-born).

Detailed results by place of birth (see Table II.5) highlight the fact that certain groups of educated immigrants are particularly exposed to over-qualification compared with the average over-qualification rate for total immigrants in the given receiving country. This is especially pronounced for people born in Colombia, the Philippines, the former Soviet republics, and to a lesser extent the former Yugoslavia. On the other hand, some groups of migrants, such as those from Argentina and South Africa, despite the diversity of migration patterns, seem relatively unaffected by the problem wherever they go. Finally, Moroccans and Indians show the greatest differences in their profiles by host country.

A number of factors mentioned above can shed some light on this situation. For instance, immigrants from regions or countries that produce a greater proportion of

Table II.5. **Over-qualification rate of immigrants by country of birth and destination country, Circa 2000**

Percentages (in blue zone) and ratio (relative to the average over-qualification rate of immigrants in the given destination country)

Country of birth	Destination country						
	Australia	Canada	France	Spain	Sweden	United Kingdom	United States
Argentina	20.6	21.6	10.9	11.8	14.9	17.2	13.4
	1.1	0.9	0.8	0.6	0.8	0.9	0.8
China	31.5	24.5	19.7	16.3	19.3	25.3	13.4
	1.7	1.0	1.4	0.8	1.0	1.4	0.8
Colombia	44.9	30.8	24.6	33.3	24.6	35.1	21.3
	2.4	1.2	1.8	1.7	1.3	1.9	1.2
Former USSR	24.7	31.7	19.4	38.9	27.6	27.4	24.4
	1.3	1.3	1.4	2.0	1.5	1.5	1.4
Former Yugoslavia	26.3	26.4	17.8	18.3	25.5	23.5	21.2
	1.4	1.0	1.3	0.9	1.4	1.3	1.2
India	27.7	33.2	24.9	12.2	18.2	21.9	13.9
	1.5	1.3	1.8	0.6	1.0	1.2	0.8
Morocco	16.3*	21.1	14.3	18.3	32.5	24.6	20.7
	0.9	0.8	1.0	0.9	1.7	1.3	1.2
Philippines	43.3	45.0	46.6	37.9	48.9	27.7	24.8
	2.3	1.8	3.4	1.9	2.6	1.5	1.4
South Africa	12.4	16.4	11.7	9.0*	15.5*	14.3	13.6
	0.7	0.6	0.9	0.5	0.8	0.8	0.8
Turkey	22.3	21.3	14.8	9.6*	19.9	27.4	15.7
	1.2	0.8	1.1	0.5	1.1	1.5	0.9
Native-born	**12.9**	**21.3**	**10.8**	**7.3**	**7.6**	**14.0**	**14.0**
Foreign-born	**18.9**	**25.2**	**13.7**	**19.8**	**18.7**	**18.4**	**17.3**

* Population between 300 and 500 observations.
Sources: Population censuses and population registers.

StatLink ⟡ *http://dx.doi.org/10.1787/021852728204*

refugees may have higher over-qualification rates because they have entered the labour market under less favourable conditions. Another factor may have to do with the quality of educational systems in the country of origin, or the transferability of diplomas. Questions of the recognition and capitalisation of diplomas, or levels of study, no doubt play an important role in explaining the relative over-qualification of immigrants. Those questions may relate to information asymmetry (employers may question the curricula of a diploma earned in a foreign country), or the conditions under which knowledge can be transferred (inadequate mastery of the host country language can make it difficult to put to use the skills acquired in the country of origin, the certification process may be complex, certain jobs may be closed to foreigners), and in some cases the immigrant's knowledge may not be readily applicable in another country (law, customs, etc.).

Beyond the issue of diploma recognition, it can also be surmised that discrimination exists. It may be due to: *i)* a lack of information (especially on another country's education system and its diplomas); *ii)* a preference for hiring certain nationalities; or even *iii)* institutional frameworks, through restrictions on foreigners' access to certain occupations, particularly in the public sector.

A more thorough explanation of the determinants requires information on some generally unobserved aspects of skills, such as the place where the diploma was obtained, cognitive skills, or proficiency in the host country language. These aspects can be investigated for some OECD countries through an international literacy survey.

4. Interpretation of over-qualification by levels of literacy

The International Adult Literacy Survey, IALS (see Box II.3) uses tests of written, graphic and quantitative comprehension to classify people by the level of their cognitive and linguistic skills. Data on individual employment and training are also included in this survey, thereby enabling the estimation of occupational over-qualification indicators based on a definition comparable to that used in the previous section. Moreover, the survey provides relevant information on where the diploma was obtained (based on the highest diploma earned before immigrating and the highest diploma held at the time of the survey) and on the mother tongue which is used as a proxy to linguistic proficiency.

Bearing in mind sample size and other constraints on data availability, the estimates in this section are confined to Australia and to a pooled sample of European countries of the OECD (Germany, Ireland, the Netherlands, Sweden, the United Kingdom, Belgium, Italy, Finland, Portugal, Denmark, Norway and Switzerland).

Calculation of over-qualification rates by level of quantitative literacy (Chart II.3), which is presumably less directly affected by proficiency in the host country language, reveals a clear association between literacy and effective use of skills. In other words, people with the lowest literacy scores are those with the highest occupational over-qualification rates. This association is very strong in Australia, but has been validated only for the native-born in Europe. It tends however to be more pronounced if the sample is restricted to people with higher education. The other indicators of literacy included in the IALS survey produce similar results. Consequently, by controlling for cognitive skills as measured in the IALS, one can explain a portion of over-qualification and perhaps the effect specifically associated with the "immigrant" variable.

To this end, a logit model has been estimated, where the probability of being over-qualified, explained by individual characteristics, is the dependent variable. It includes the

Box II.3. **International Adult Literacy Survey, IALS**

The objective of the International Adult Literacy Survey is to measure literacy, defined as "the ability to understand and employ printed information in daily activities, at home, at work and in the community, to achieve one's goals and to develop one's knowledge and potential". It considers three categories of literacy: Prose literacy, document literacy and quantitative literacy.

In each category, tasks are assigned (understanding of prose text, interpreting a document, etc.) and rated according to difficulty on a scale from 0 to 500. The individual's score is calculated at the point where his probability of success in the task is 80%.

The 1994, survey was conducted in English- and French-speaking Canada, in France, Germany, Ireland, the Netherlands, Poland, Sweden, French- and German-speaking Switzerland, and the United States. In 1996, Australia, Belgium, Great Britain, New Zealand and Northern Ireland were added, followed in 1998 by Chile, the Czech Republic, Denmark, Finland, Hungary, Italy, Norway, Slovenia and Italian-speaking Switzerland, bringing the number of countries participating in the survey in 1998 to 21 in total.

Chart II.3. **Over-qualification rate by level of quantitative literacy and country of birth in Europe and in Australia, Circa 1995**

Percentages

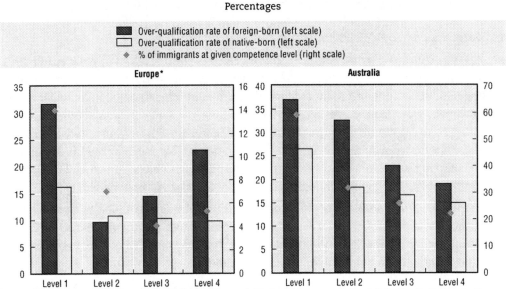

* Sample of European OECD countries: Belgium, Denmark, Finland, Germany, Ireland, Italy, the Netherlands, Norway, Portugal, Sweden, Switzerland and the United Kingdom.

Sources: Europe: International Adult Literacy Survey (IALS) 1994, 1996 or 1998 according to the country (*cf.* Box II.3); Australia: Survey of aspects of Literacy, 1996.

StatLink 🔗 *http://dx.doi.org/10.1787/014300610852*

main socio-demographic variables available (gender, age, level of education) and also indicators of literacy, as well as the other variables mentioned above, namely mother tongue and origin of diploma.[5] The main results are presented in Tables II.6 and II.7.

When gender, age and education level are the only factors taken into account (model 1), people born abroad remain significantly more over-qualified than the native-born. In Australia, for example, a person born abroad would be about 1.8 times more likely to be over-qualified than a native-born. Moreover, young people, and women in Europe, tend to

INTERNATIONAL MIGRATION OUTLOOK: SOPEMI 2007 EDITION – ISBN 978-92-64-03285-9 – © OECD 2007

Table II.6. **Logistic model of the probability of over-qualification (Australia)**

	Model 1	Model 2	Model 3	Model 4	Model 5	Model 6	Model 7	Model 8
Constant	−2.582 ***	−3.308 ***	−3.221 ***	−3.292 ***	−3.414 ***	−3.4119 ***	−3.1053 ***	−3.1634 ***
Birth status								
Native-born	ref.	ref.	ref.	ref.	ref.	ref.	ref.	ref.
Foreign-born	0.589 ***	0.394 ***	0.346 ***	0.377 ***	0.351 ***	0.0146	−0.1063	−0.0987
	1.8	1.5	1.4	1.5	1.4	1.0	0.9	0.9
Gender								
Men	0.168	0.264 **	0.109	0.198 **	0.208 **	0.2205 **	0.2306 **	0.3391 **
	1.2	1.3	1.1	1.2	1.2	1.2	1.3	1.4
Women	ref.	ref.	ref.	ref.	ref.	ref.	ref.	ref.
Age								
15-24	0.691 ***	0.691 ***	0.739 ***	0.753 ***	0.718 ***	0.7573 ***	0.7575 ***	0.749 ***
	2.0	2.0	2.1	2.1	2.0	2.1	2.1	2.1
25-44	ref.	ref.	ref.	ref.	ref.	ref.	ref.	ref.
45-64	−0.073	−0.088	−0.089	−0.099	−0.091	−0.1246	−0.1033	−0.1241
	0.9	0.9	0.9	0.9	0.9	0.9	0.9	0.9
Educational level								
Intermediate	ref.	ref.	ref.	ref.	ref.	ref.	ref.	ref.
High	1.383 ***	1.691 ***	1.691 ***	1.682 ***	1.735 ***	1.7468 ***	1.7327 ***	1.6816 ***
	4.0	5.4	5.4	5.4	5.7	5.7	5.7	5.4
Quantitative literacy proficiency (QUANT)								
Weak		1.613 ***			0.963 ***	1.0803 **	1.1038 ***	0.7455
		5.0			2.6	2.9	3.0	2.1
Average		1.047 ***			0.561 **	0.6215 ***	0.6243 ***	0.6194 **
		2.9			1.8	1.9	1.9	1.9
Average-high		0.523 ***			0.224	0.245	0.2407	0.2558
		1.7			1.3	1.3	1.3	1.3
High		ref.			ref.	ref.	ref.	ref.
Prose literacy proficiency (PROSE)								
Weak			1.490 ***		0.426	0.3178	0.198	0.1056
			4.4		1.5	1.4	1.2	1.1
Average			0.944 ***		0.355	0.3039	0.2471	0.2607
			2.6		1.4	1.4	1.3	1.3
Average-high			0.568 ***		0.291 **	0.2643	0.2439	0.335 **
			1.8		1.3	1.3	1.3	1.4
High			ref.		ref.	ref.	ref.	ref.
Document literacy proficiency (DOC)								
Weak				1.588 ***	0.415	0.2858	0.2684	0.447
				4.9	1.5	1.3	1.3	1.6
Average				1.026 ***	0.283	0.2489	0.2592	0.279
				2.8	1.3	1.3	1.3	1.3
Average-high				0.542 ***	0.165	0.1485	0.1477	0.1264
				1.7	1.2	1.2	1.2	1.1
High				ref.	ref.	ref.	ref.	ref.
"Origin of diploma"								
Country of origin					0.6436 ***	0.6329 ***	0.689 ***
					1.9	1.9	2.0
Receiving country					ref.	ref.	ref.
Mother tongue								
Receiving country language						−0.2995 **	−0.4133 ***
						0.7	0.7
Different from receiving country language						ref.	ref.
Area of residence								
Urban							−0.1124
							0.9
Rural							ref.

Table II.6. **Logistic model of the probability of over-qualification (Australia)** *(Cont.)*

	Model 1	Model 2	Model 3	Model 4	Model 5	Model 6	Model 7	Model 8
Size of enterprise								
< 20 persons								ref.
Between 20 and 200 persons								0.3979 ***
								1.5
Between 200 and 500 persons								−0.1235
								0.9
> 500 persons								0.3722
								1.451
Number of observations	3 638	3 638	3 638	3 638	3 638	3 638	3 638	3 076
% of concordant pairs	66	70.4	70.0	70.4	71.2	71.3	71.3	71.4

Note: *** corresponds to a threshold of 1% and ** to a threshold of 5%. Ref. stands for the category of reference. Figures in italic refer to odds ratios.
Source: Survey of aspects of Literacy, 1996.

StatLink ᛒᛁᛊᛚ *http://dx.doi.org/10.1787/021882380685*

be more over-qualified then older people, or men. These initial results are consistent with those presented earlier.

It is also apparent that having a higher education degree does not specifically protect a person from over-qualification and indeed tends to increase the risk of mismatch between education and job (the risk is at least four times higher in Australia and in the European countries considered).[6] The impact holding a tertiary degree on the relative over-qualification of immigrants *versus* the native-born is *a priori* indeterminate. This would not be the case if the differential observed for immigrants were partially ascribed to differences in the quality of the education system or, more generally, to the transferability of foreign diplomas.[7]

Each literacy variable (models 2 to 5) has a significant effect on both over-qualification, and the "immigrant" variable. If introduced separately, all the literacy variables affect over-qualification significantly, in the sense that, the weaker the indicator the higher the probability of over-qualification. These variables, are however, correlated among themselves and, if introduced simultaneously, the quantitative skills indicator is stronger in Australia, whereas in Europe the prose literacy indicator seems to have a greater impact. It is likely that troubles in reading reflect difficulties in mastering the language of the host country in Europe. This outcome suggests that, beyond the level of education, there are other factors relating to intrinsic skills that affect performance on the labour market. This is consistent with some of the studies on over-qualification previously mentioned (Chevallier, 2003; Bauer, 2002).

It is also noteworthy that, when one controls for the literacy level, the effect associated with the "immigrant" variable diminishes. Even if no causal relationship can be deduced, this result implies that some of the aspects of human capital, which are not included in the level of education, may affect over-qualification. Yet in Australia, as in Europe, the "immigrant" variable remains very significant and exerts a major influence (odds ratio of about 1.5). Ferrer, Green and Riddell (2004) arrive at similar but more pronounced results for Canada, using the Ontario Immigrant Literacy Survey (OILS). They show that immigrants' literacy scores are on average lower than those of native-born workers, and that this explains about two-thirds of the earnings gap.

Table II.7. **Logistic model of the probability of over-qualification (Europe)**

	Model 1	Model 2	Model 3	Model 4	Model 5	Model 6	Model 7	Model 8
Constant	−2.831 ***	−3.177 ***	−3.201 ***	−3.185 ***	−3.248***	−3.2414 ***	−3.3476 ***	−3.682 ***
Birth status								
Native-born	ref.	ref.	ref.	ref.	ref.	ref.	ref.	ref.
Foreign-born	0.518 ***	0.380 ***	0.325 ***	0.404 ***	0.336***	−0.0324	0.0149	0.2642
	1.7	1.5	1.4	1.5	1.4	1.0	1.0	1.3
Gender								
Men	−0.212 ***	−0.163 ***	−0.246 ***	−0.179 ***	−0.219***	−0.2226 ***	−0.2245 ***	−0.3688 ***
	0.8	0.9	0.8	0.8	0.8	0.8	0.8	0.7
Women	ref.	ref.	ref.	ref.	ref.	ref.	ref.	ref.
Age								
15-24	0.974 ***	0.967 ***	0.993 ***	0.990 ***	0.984***	0.9815 ***	0.9837 ***	0.8659 ***
	2.6	2.6	2.7	2.7	2.7	2.7	2.7	2.4
25-44	ref.	ref.	ref.	ref.	ref.	ref.	ref.	ref.
45-64	−0.378 ***	−0.414 ***	−0.455 ***	−0.429 ***	−0.454***	−0.4587 ***	−0.4604 ***	−0.4362 ***
	0.7	0.7	0.6	0.7	0.6	0.6	0.6	0.6
Educational level								
Intermediate	ref.	ref.	ref.	ref.	ref.	ref.	ref.	ref.
High	1.488 ***	1.633 ***	1.656 ***	1.624 ***	1.660***	1.6614 ***	1.6639 ***	1.7691 ***
	4.4	5.1	5.2	5.1	5.3	5.3	5.3	5.9
Quantitative literacy proficiency (QUANT)								
Weak	1.165 ***				0.721***	0.7069 ***	0.7086 ***	0.4611 **
	3.2				2.1	2.0	2.0	1.6
Average	0.465 ***				0.213*	0.209	0.2077	0.0764
	1.6				1.2	1.2	1.2	1.1
Average-high	0.220 ***				0.046	0.032	0.034	−0.0751
	1.2				1.0	1.0	1.0	0.9
High	ref.				ref.	ref.	ref.	ref.
Prose literacy proficiency (PROSE)								
Weak		1.326 ***			1.054***	1.0475 ***	1.0359 ***	1.0355 ***
		3.8			2.9	2.9	2.8	2.8
Average		0.426 ***			0.232*	0.2243 *	0.2231 *	0.316 **
		1.5			1.3	1.3	1.3	1.4
Average-high		0.289 ***			0.191**	0.1888 **	0.1828 **	0.1464
		1.3			1.2	1.2	1.2	1.2
High		ref.			ref.	ref.	ref.	ref.
Document literacy proficiency (DOC)								
Weak				0.868 ***	−0.411**	−0.4085 **	−0.3918 *	−0.1616
				2.4	0.7	0.7	0.7	0.9
Average				0.516 ***	0.076	0.0848	0.0924	0.14
				1.7	1.1	1.1	1.1	1.2
Average-high				0.258 ***	0.101	0.1098	0.1138	0.112
				1.3	1.1	1.1	1.1	1.1
High				ref.	ref.	ref.	ref.	ref.
"Origin of diploma"								
Country of origin						0.6447 ***	0.669 ***	0.4939 **
						1.9	2.0	1.6
Receiving country						ref.	ref.	ref.
Mother tongue								
Receiving country language							0.1043	0.1697
							1.1	1.2
Different from receiving country language							ref.	ref.
Area of residence								
Urban								0.1384 **
								1.1
Rural								ref.

Table II.7. **Logistic model of the probability of over-qualification (Europe)** (*Cont.*)

	Model 1	Model 2	Model 3	Model 4	Model 5	Model 6	Model 7	Model 8
Size of enterprise								
< 20 persons								ref.
Between 20 and 200 persons								0.3845 ***
								1.5
Between 200 and 500 persons								0.5563 ***
								1.7
> 500 persons								0.2625 **
								1.3
Number of observations	15 107	15 107	15 107	15 107	15 107	15 080	15 039	11 626
% of concordant pairs	67.3	71.0	71.4	71.2	72.4	72.3	72.3	73.6

Note: Sample of European OECD countries: Belgium, Denmark, Finland, Germany, Ireland, Italy, the Netherlands, Norway, Portugal, Sweden, Switzerland and the United Kingdom. *** corresponds to a threshold of 1% and ** to a threshold of 5%. Ref. stands for the category of reference. Figures in italic refer to odds ratios.
Source: International Adult Literacy Survey (IALS) 1994, 1996 or 1998 according to the country.

StatLink ᴍᴤᴾ *http://dx.doi.org/10.1787/021886686304*

When the "origin of diploma" variable is introduced (model 6) the results change considerably. This variable is significant in all regressions and alters the effect associated with the "immigrant" variable. The "immigrant" variable is in fact no longer significant, in Australia and in the European countries considered, if one controls for diplomas obtained in the host country. This finding is even more important when one considers that nearly half of immigrants had obtained their diploma in the host country at the time of the survey. This supports the argument that diploma value and intrinsic skills can explain the relatively higher degree of over-qualification among immigrants.

In the case of Canada this argument has been used to explain the fact that immigrants from countries with lower-quality education systems (as measured by international testing results, see Hanushek and Kimko, 2000) have lower returns to education (Sweetman, 2004). Using census data from 1986, 1991 and 1996, the author shows that "a move from the 25th to the 75th percentile of the school quality index is associated with, on average for both sexes, a 10% increase in annual earnings for those with 16 years of school". In another study on Canada, Alboim, Finnie and Meng (2005) show that the effect of the "immigrant" variable in the wage equation disappears when they control for the origin of diploma and for literacy. The gap in the returns to education by origin is in part explained by the level of skills.[8]

However, caution must be used in interpreting the role of the "diploma origin" variable, for it is possible that this betrays labour market selection mechanisms operating, for example, through institutional barriers to diploma recognition, or discriminatory behaviour. This question cannot be entirely dismissed, as the indicators of literacy, which are supposed to measure skills, have a clear effect, but remain supplementary to the origin of the diploma. It is possible, however, that the literacy indicators taken from the IALS are insufficient to explain the unobserved heterogeneity of skills among the most highly qualified, since they aim to identify basic comprehension difficulties.

When the variables explaining the language proficiency indicator are added (model 7), this becomes significant in Australia, with the expected sign (people whose mother tongue is English are less over-qualified). Yet it is not in itself sufficient to cancel the effect of the "immigrant" variable, and it does not change the outcomes obtained with the "diploma origin" variable. Proficiency in the host country language, *ceteris paribus*, thus allows people to capitalise more readily on their skills in the labour market. It may be however, that part of the effect associated with this variable is ascribed to the region of origin, to the extent that, in Australia, a significant portion of English speakers come from OECD member countries (the United Kingdom and New Zealand in particular). The "odds ratio" associated with having a mother tongue different from the host-country language (1.4 times more chance of being over-qualified) is however weaker than that associated with poor or average quantitative literacy (3 and 1.9, respectively). In the European countries considered, the mother-tongue effect is not significant, probably because of the importance of the prose literacy variable.

Finally, if variables relating to labour market conditions are added, in particular firm size (internal labour market size) and urban/rural location (external labour market size), the model's explanatory power increases, although it does not change the previous conclusions. Persons employed in very small firms are more likely to be over-qualified, as are those who live in rural areas where employment opportunities and occupational mobility are limited.

Conclusion

Regardless of the definition used and the country in question, immigrants are more likely than the native-born to hold jobs for which they are over-qualified. Foreign-born women would seem to be at an even greater disadvantage. What is the exact significance of this lesser match between education and employment? Recent literature on over-qualification has shown that much, if not most, of this disadvantage in employment can be explained by intrinsic differences in abilities or human capital not involving education. "Literacy" skills as measured in the IALS may in fact explain a portion (about one-third) of immigrants' relative over-qualification. But these variables are not sufficient, *ceteris paribus*, to explain the entire gap observed between immigrants and the native-born.

The analyses presented in this chapter underline the crucial importance of the place of education. This variable may translate differences in terms of the content and quality of schooling (at a given level of education), but it may also serve to distort employers' interpretation of education levels, given the lack of information available to them. The role of the diploma-origin variable should thus be considered with caution, recognising that it may also reflect differences in terms of social capital or "soft skills".

One might expect that a longer stay in the country would facilitate labour market integration and allow immigrants to capitalise on their qualifications. The fact that a longer period of residence is not always a sufficient condition for closing the over-qualification gap between immigrants and the native-born raises other questions. In any event, deeper analysis, using longitudinal data, is required in order to explain this finding.

More generally, the analysis needs to be sharpened so as to factor in differences between types of diplomas and national particularities, and to get a better grasp on the effects attributable to different waves of migration. One could also further explore the role of over-qualification in the intergenerational transfer of human capital amongst immigrants, *i.e.* the effect of parents' occupational over-qualification in motivating children to pursue higher education.

In any case, the fact that in all of the countries considered, at least 25%, and on average nearly 50%, of skilled immigrants between 15 and 64 years of age are inactive, unemployed or relegated to jobs for which they are over-qualified, poses the question of whether the best use is being made of their skills. This issue is even more relevant, with the aging of populations in OECD countries, particularly in Europe, where the demands for skilled labour are likely to grow. Generally speaking, it is important to find ways to capitalise more effectively on the human resources of skilled immigrants already settled in the host country, and those of new arrivals, whether selected or not.[9] Several OECD countries have already introduced policies in this direction, and their impact should be systematically evaluated.

From this viewpoint, various measures, that could be included in bilateral and multilateral agreements,[10] to grant better recognition to diplomas and qualifications and to give employers access to information on education acquired abroad (such as via Internet platforms, on-the-job skills evaluation, etc.) are very useful. More generally, policies that promote lifelong training (for example refresher programmes, language courses) and occupational mobility (for example reducing the number of regulated professions and jobs closed to foreigners) or anti-discrimination should be part of the range of tools made available to foster labour market integration of immigrants at their level of skills.

Notes

1. In part, this reflects the problems that young people encounter upon first entering the labour market (see Quintini and Martin, 2006) and raises the question of the transition between education and employment. In this context, it may be asked whether the problems encountered by new entrants on the labour market simply reflect the necessary "period of adjustment" in the process of matching jobs and people, or whether they reflect a mismatch between education and the labour market, or perhaps even the fact that employers' recruitment criteria and practices do not focus exclusively on education credentials; see for example Giret, Lopez and Rose (2005) for an in-depth discussion of these issues as they apply to France.

2. This finding is even more compelling in countries where the native-born are highly reluctant to accept jobs beneath their qualifications, and would rather go unemployed (see for instance, Iribarne, 1990, in the case of France).

3. There is no obvious correlation, for the countries examined, between over-qualification rates and participation rates, employment rates or unemployment rates.

4. Controlling for age does not affect over-qualification ratios. While older immigrants have longer average periods of residence (and should therefore be less exposed to over-qualification, see below), in countries where the immigrant over-qualification rate declines with age (Belgium, Spain, France, Ireland, Norway, Portugal and the United Kingdom) this finding applies equally to the native-born.

5. If a portion of people susceptible to over-qualification are assumed to prefer inactivity (while perhaps pursuing studies or supplementary training), or extend their job search in order to find a position better suited to their skills, a selection bias may potentially affect the estimation of a logit model. It could then be argued that this bias affects immigrants and the native-born differently, particularly if the native-born are more averse to accepting a job beneath their qualifications. To take account of this effect, the model has been estimated in two stages, using the marital status variable as an instrument. The results are not significantly changed, but the quality of the instrumentation was disappointing. Further analysis is therefore needed in order to control this potential bias properly.

6. This finding emerges as well from Labour Force Survey data (except for Luxembourg). To some extent, this is due to the definition of over-qualification, in that people with higher education may be over-qualified by one or two levels, while those with only a secondary school diploma would be over-qualified only if they are employed in an elementary occupation (see Annex II.A1). Of course, elementary occupations constitute a very small proportion of total employment in most OECD countries.

7. In this case one might expect that, *ceteris paribus*, having a higher education degree would make immigrants more likely to be over-qualified. The data however contradict this assertion: The cross-

variable "immigrant-higher education degree" is not significant in Australia, and has the reverse sign of that expected for European countries.

8. A number of studies on Canada (Hum and Simpson, 1999; Li, 2001; Reitz, 2000) as well as on the United States (Bratsberg and Ragan, 2002) and Israel (Frieberg, 2000) have analysed the impact of the country where the diploma was obtained on incomes. Overall, these studies confirm that the impact is important and significant. See Alboim, Finnie and Meng (2005) for a summary.

9. See Reitz (2005) or Alboim, Finnie and Meng (2005) for a discussion of policy implications in the Canadian case.

10. UNESCO has established six regional conventions on recognition of academic qualifications (Africa, Arab countries, Asia and Pacific, Latin America and Caribbean, and two European conventions) and an interregional convention (for the Mediterranean). The UNESCO conventions are intended to promote recognition of qualifications for academic purposes, but they sometimes have a role, both *de facto* and *de jure*, of recognising degrees for a vocational purpose (*e.g.* obtaining a job). In this context, there are also agreements on diploma and qualifications recognition within the European Union (*http://europa.eu/scadplus/leg/fr/s19005.htm*) and between Australia and New Zealand (Trans-Tasman Mutual Recognition Arrangement).

Bibliography

ACEMOGLU, D. (1999), "Changes in unemployment and wage inequality: An alternative theory and some evidence", *American Economic Review*, Vol. 89, No. 5, pp. 1259-1278.

ACEMOGLU, D. (2002), "Technical change, inequality and the labor market", *Journal of Economic Literature*, Vol. XL, pp. 7-72.

ALBA-RAMIREZ, A. (1993), "Mismatch in the Spanish labor market: Overeducation?", *The Journal of Human resources*, Vol. 28, No. 2, pp. 259-278.

ALBOIM, N., R. FINNIE and R. MENG (2005), "The discounting of immigrants' skills in Canada. Evidence and Policy recommendations", *IRPP Choices*, Vol. 11, No. 1.

AUTOR D., F. LEVY and R. MURNANE (2003), "The skill content of recent technological change: An empirical exploration", *The Quaterly Journal of Economics*, November 2003, pp. 1279-1333.

BATTU, H. and PJ. SLOANE (2002), "To what extent are ethnic minorities in Britain overeducated ?", *International Journal of Manpower*, Vol. 23, No. 3, pp. 192-208.

BAUER T. (2002), "Educational mismatch and wages: A panel analysis", *Economics of Education Review*, No. 21, pp. 221-229.

BRATSBERG B. and J. RAGAN (2002), "The impact of host-country schooling on earnings: A study of male immigrants in the United States", *Journal of Human Resources*, Vol. 37, No. 1.

BUCHEL, F. and H. BATTUU (2003), "The theory of differential over-qualification: Does it work?", *Scottish Journal of Political Economy*, Vol. 50, No. 1.

CHEVALIER, A. (2003), "Measuring over-education", *Economica*, No. 70, pp. 509-531. *Journal of Political Economy*, No. 86 (October 1978), pp. 897-921.

D'IRIBARNE, P. (1990), *Le chômage paradoxal*, PUF.

DOLTON, P. and A. VIGNOLES (2000), "The incidence and effects of overeducation in the UK, graduate labour market", *Economics of Education Review*, No. 19, pp. 179-198.

DORN, D. and A. SOUSA-POZA (2005), "Over-qualification: Permanent or transitory", mimeographed University of St Gallen, Switzerland.

DUMONT, JC. and T. LIEBIG (2005), "Labour market integration of immigrant women: Overview and recent trends", Conference EU-OECD "Migrant women and the labour market: Diversity and challenges", Brussels, September 2005.

EDIN, PA., LALONDE, R. and O. ASLUND (2000), "Emigration of immigrants and measures of immigrant assimilation: Evidence from Sweden", *Swedish Economic Policy Review*, 7, pp. 163-204.

FERRER, A. and C. RIDDEL (2002), "The Role of Credentials in the Canadian Labour Market", *Revue canadienne d'économie*, Vol. 35, No. 4, pp. 879-905.

FERRER, A., GREEN, D. and C. RIDDEL (2004), "The effect of literacy on immigrant earnings", *Journal of Human Resources*, XLI, 2, pp. 380-410.

FRANK, R. (1978), "Why women earn less: The theory and estimation of differential over-qualification", The *American Economic Review*, Vol. 68, No. 3, pp. 360-373.

FREEMAN, R. (1976), *The overeducated Americans*, NY academic Press.

FRIEBERG, R. (2000), "You can't take it with you? Immigrant assimilation and the portability of human capital", *Journal of Labor Economics* 18, No. 2.

GIRET, J.F., A. LOPEZ and J. ROSE (sous la direction de) (2005), *Des formations pour quels emplois ?*, Edition la Découverte.

GLEWWE, P. and M. KREMER (2005), "Schools, Teachers, and Education Outcomes in Developing Countries", Document de travail, Center for International Development, Harvard University.

GROOT, W. (1996), "The incidence and the return to overeducation in the UK", *Applied Economics*, No. 28, pp. 1345-1350.

GROOT, W. and HM. VAN DER BRINK (2000), "Overeducation in the labor market: A meta-analysis", *Economics of Education Review*, No. 19, pp. 149-158.

HANUSHEK, EA. and DD. KIMKO (2000), "Schooling, labour-force quality and growth of nations", Vol. 90, No. 5, pp.1184-1208.

HARTOG, J. (2000), "Overeducation and earnings: Where we are and where we should go", *Economics of Education Review*, Vol. 19, No. 2, pp. 131-147.

HUM D. ET W. SIMPSON (1999), "Wage opportunities for visible minorities in Canada", *Canadian Public Policy* 25, No. 3.

KRUEGER, A. (1993), "How computers have changed the wage structure: Evidence from microdata", *The Quaterly Journal of Economics*, Vol. 110, pp. 33-60.

LAINÉ, F. and M. OKBA (2004), "L'insertion des jeunes issus de l'immigration : Métiers occupés, trajectoires scolaires et professionnelles", Présenté au Colloque "Le devenir des enfants de familles défavorisées en France", avril 2004.

LI, P. (2001), "Earning disparities between immigrants and native-born Canadians", *Canadian Review of Sociology and Anthropology* 37, No. 3.

MAIER, M., F. PFEIFFER, and W. POHLMEIER (2003), "Overeducation and individual heterogeneity", ZEW Diskussionpapiere No. 03/01.

MC GOLDRICK, KM. and J. ROBST (1996), "Gender differences in overdeducation: A test of the theory of differential over-qualification", *The American Economic Review*, Vol. 86, No. 2, pp. 280-284.

NAUZE-FICHET, E. and E. TOMASINI MAGDA, (2002) "Diplôme et insertion sur le marché du travail : Approches socioprofessionnelle et salariale du déclassement", *Économie et Statistique*, No. 354, 2002.

OECD (2001), *Migration Policies and EU Enlargment. The Case of Central and Eastern Europe*, OECD, Paris.

OECD (2002), "Measures of skill from labour force survey – an assessment", document DEELSA/ELSA/WP7(2002)3, Paris.

OECD (2003), "Upgrading workers' skills and competencies", *OECD Employment Outlook 2003*, OECD, Paris.

OECD (2004a), *Trends in International Migration,* OECD, Paris.

OECD (2004b), *Quality and Recognition in Higher Education: The Cross-border Challenge*, OECD, Paris.

QUINTINI, G. and S. MARTIN (2006), "Starting or losing their way? The position of youth in the labour market in OECD countries", OECD, DELSA/ELSA/WD/SEM(2006)8.

REITZ, J. (2000), "Immigrant success in the knowledge economy: Institutional change and immigrant experience in Canada 1970-1995", miméo cité by Alboim Finnie et Meng (2005).

REITZ, J. (2005), "Tapping Immigrants' Skills. New directions for Canadian Immigration policy in the knowledge economy", *IRPP Choices*, Vol. 11, No. 1.

RUBB, S. (2002), "Overeducation in the labor market: A comment and re-analysis of a meta-analysis", *Economics of Education Review*, No. 22, pp. 621-629.

RUBB, S. (2003), "Overeducation: A short or long run phenomenon for individuals ?", *Economics of Education Review*, No. 22, pp. 389-394.

SICHERMAN, N. (1991), "Overeducation in the labor market", *Journal of Labor Economics*, Vol. 9, No. 2, pp. 101-122.

SLOANE, PJ., H. BATTU and P.T. SEAMAN (1999), "Overeducation, undereducation and the British labour market", *Applied Economics*, No. 31, pp. 1437-1453.

SWEETMAN, A. (2004), "Immigrant Source Country Educational Quality and Canadian Labour Market Outcomes", Statistics Canada, Analytical Studies Branch Research Paper, No. 234, December 2004.

WIRZ, A. and E. ATUKEREN (2005), "An analysis of perceived over-qualification in the Swiss labor market", *Economic Bulletin* Vol. 9, No. 2, pp. 1-10.

ANNEX II.A1

Employment and Unemployment Rates of Native- and Foreign-born Populations by Level of Education, 2003-2004

Table II.A1.1. **Employment and unemployment rates of native- and foreign-born populations by level of education, 2003-2004**

Percentages

	Natives						Foreign-born					
	Employment rate			Unemployment rate			Employment rate			Unemployment rate		
	Low (ISCED 0/1/2)	Medium (ISCED 3/4)	High (ISCED 5/6)	Low (ISCED 0/1/2)	Medium (ISCED 3/4)	High (ISCED 5/6)	Low (ISCED 0/1/2)	Medium (ISCED 3/4)	High (ISCED 5/6)	Low (ISCED 0/1/2)	Medium (ISCED 3/4)	High (ISCED 5/6)
Australia	55.5	78.0	84.0	11.7	4.8	1.6	48.2	64.8	78.7	8.0	5.5	4.2
Austria	43.6	73.1	84.1	8.6	3.8	2.2	54.3	68.5	77.5	12.7	9.4	5.1
Belgium	41.9	66.3	83.9	10.0	6.8	3.0	33.9	53.5	73.7	22.6	16.1	9.6
Canada	54.8	76.2	84.4	11.8	7.7	4.6	55.9	70.5	77.9	8.6	7.7	6.9
Czech Republic	22.9	72.0	85.6	24.0	7.2	2.2	36.9	62.4	86.4	27.1	10.1	1.3
Denmark	59.7	79.7	87.1	7.7	4.3	3.9	46.2	59.7	69.2	15.0	13.2	11.4
Finland	47.7	72.3	85.0	18.7	10.3	4.3	39.1	64.1	69.5	31.5	18.8	15.3
France	47.1	70.6	78.7	12.2	7.9	5.8	47.8	62.1	70.8	18.4	14.4	11.8
Germany	40.2	69.1	84.5	15.6	10.4	4.4	45.1	62.4	68.1	20.3	14.7	12.5
Greece	49.2	59.5	82.1	8.7	12.4	7.0	64.4	64.4	68.7	9.0	12.1	13.2
Hungary	27.9	66.2	82.3	12.5	5.4	1.8	25.8	66.5	82.2	7.0	4.1	2.1
Ireland	48.0	71.5	86.5	7.3	3.7	2.2	44.4	63.8	76.5	10.5	6.4	4.3
Italy	45.6	65.9	81.4	10.2	7.7	5.4	59.5	67.4	78.8	9.6	8.3	5.3
Luxembourg	33.7	61.9	82.8	6.0	2.9	1.9	63.9	64.7	78.4	4.2	6.9	5.9
Netherlands	63.9	80.9	88.1	3.3	1.8	1.5	50.7	69.9	78.3	6.5	7.3	3.3
New Zealand	63.8	76.0	88.2	10.9	6.9	3.3	55.6	62.6	79.5	11.9	9.3	6.1
Norway	52.6	77.9	87.5	8.0	3.6	2.9	43.9	67.9	79.8	15.0	8.9	5.6
Poland	22.8	56.4	80.6	30.4	20.4	7.4	11.0	24.6	51.6	15.4	29.3	3.0
Portugal	66.5	62.3	87.6	6.7	6.4	4.6	67.5	70.0	83.6	11.2	7.5	7.5
Slovak Republic	14.3	66.6	84.3	49.8	16.4	5.2	31.1	53.4	85.0	43.6	23.8	5.7
Spain	53.4	60.2	79.5	12.6	11.1	7.9	61.2	68.9	73.2	15.3	13.0	11.9
Sweden	57.7	80.4	87.4	8.0	5.3	2.9	45.9	66.8	76.0	18.3	11.6	8.8
Switzerland	57.1	80.4	92.4	4.8	3.1	1.9	63.4	74.1	81.9	10.4	8.2	5.7
United Kingdom	52.5	77.5	88.1	8.8	4.7	2.3	39.3	66.9	81.8	12.2	7.9	4.2
United States	35.9	71.0	83.0	15.5	6.7	3.2	58.6	70.0	77.6	9.1	5.7	4.3

Note: 2001 for Canada and New Zealand, 2002 for the Netherlands, 2003 for Australia and 2004 for the United States.
Sources: European countries: European Union Labour Force Survey (data provided by Eurostat); United States: Current Population Survey March Supplement; Australia: Survey of Household, Income and Labour Dynamics; Canada and New Zealand: Population censuses.

StatLink 🔗 *http://dx.doi.org/10.1787/021772210132*

ANNEX II.A2

Measuring Competencies by Educational Level and Job Classification

The analysis presented in this document is based on a correspondence between the level of education and job classification, which makes it possible to formulate a standard for "over-qualification". Underlying this approach is the fact that the ISCO classification system provided by the International Labour Office can be used to distinguish "levels of qualification" that can be linked to the educational levels presumably needed to hold the corresponding jobs (OECD, 2002), and thus to the ISCED categorisation of UNESCO.

As the first step, Table II.A2.1 condenses the ISCO classification into three categories of jobs demanding low, intermediate and high skills. The same is done with the ISCED classification in Table II.A2.2. These categories are used to define an over-qualified individual as one who has "skilled or highly skilled" education level and holds an "intermediate" or "unskilled" job, or one who has an "intermediate" level of education and holds an "unskilled" job. A person who is "under-qualified" can be defined as one who has a lower level of education than that which would correspond to the skills classification of the job he holds.

There are limitations to this approach, which stem first from the categories themselves. The attempt to achieve uniformity through the ISCO and ISCED classification systems can mask certain particularities associated with specific countries or periods of time: The content of diplomas of an apparently similar level in two different countries may differ, and within any given country, the value of a diploma may vary over time. Reporting bias can also affect the findings, and perhaps even more so in respect to the qualifications for a job, which are more readily subject to "over-estimation". The matching of categories of educational levels and categories of qualifications (especially when they are highly aggregated), as noted in ILO recommendations (OECD, 2002), is arbitrary. The exact prerequisites for any given job are not examined (and may vary from one country to another). The existence of widely divergent standards for measuring the correspondence between education and job qualifications attests to the fact that the correspondence cannot be definitively pinned down. Lastly, in many cases the supply of skills as measured by education is not exhaustive: It corresponds to educational attainment at the time individuals complete their schooling, and excludes skills acquired outside the classroom (e.g. ongoing training, etc.).

There is every reason to believe, then, that to calculate an over-qualification rate from a simple correspondence between education and job classification runs the risk of multiple biases. Observing gross rates of over-qualification is certainly not the best approach here. A comparison between over-qualification rates among immigrants and the native-born faces an asymmetric bias from the implicit comparison of two different education systems. Lastly, the comparison of relative degrees of over-qualification requires the assumption that these biases work in the same direction for all countries. The results of this approach to over-qualification must in all cases be interpreted with caution.

Table II.A2.1. **Conversion of ISCO-88 9 categories to 3 categories**

ISCO-88 ↓	Recoding of jobs →	Low-skilled	Intermediate	High-skilled
(0: Armed Forces)				
1: Legislators, senior officials and managers				X
2: Professionals				X
3: Technician and associate professionals				X
4: Clerks			X	
5: Service workers and shop and market sales workers			X	
6: Skilled agricultural and fishery workers			X	
7: Craft and related trades workers			X	
8: Plant and machinery operators and assemblers			X	
9: Elementary occupations		X		

StatLink ᵐˢ⁼ *http://dx.doi.org/10.1787/022003802767*

Table II.A2.2. **Conversion from ISCED 7 categories to 3 categories**

Level of studies ↓	Recoding of level of studies →	Low-skilled	Intermediate	Skills or highly skilled
Pre-primary education or preschool (starting at age 2 or 3)		X		
Primary education (starting at age 5, 6 or 7 and running for four to six years)		X		
Lower secondary education (running 2 to 6 years, with an average of three)		X		
Upper secondary education (running for 2 and 5 years)			X	
Post-secondary non-tertiary education			X	
The first stage of tertiary education (university)				X
Second stage of tertiary education (university)				X

StatLink ᵐˢ⁼ *http://dx.doi.org/10.1787/022003802767*

Table II.A2.3. **Correspondence between ISCED education level and ISCO employment level**

		ISCO employment level		
		Low-skilled	Intermediate	Skilled or highly skilled
ISCED education level	Low-skilled		Under-qualified	Under-qualified
	Intermediate	Over-qualified		Under-qualified
	Skilled or highly skilled	Over-qualified	Over-qualified	

StatLink ᵐˢ⁼ *http://dx.doi.org/10.1787/022003802767*

ANNEX II.A3

Over-qualification Defined by Wages

Over-qualification as defined in main text of this chapter is based on a presumed correspondence between level of education and the qualifications required to carry out the job. This approach has the dual drawbacks of being both subjective and rigid (in the sense that to escape over-qualification one would have to change jobs). Another option for measuring over-qualification is to relate it to wages. Insofar as investment in education – all else being equal – should enhance the productivity of work and thus raise the expected level of wages, it can be considered that individuals, who are paid patently less than the wages corresponding to their level of education, are not valued at their true level of competency. In this connection, "an individual will be considered over-qualified in terms of wage levels if more than a certain percentage of the persons holding a diploma of the next-lowest category earn more than that individual". Here, this measure of over-qualification proposed in the case of France (Nauze-Fichet and Tomasini, 2002) has been extended to a sample of OECD countries. Wage-measured over-qualification rates are calculated at the threshold of the first third; a person is thus over-qualified if two-thirds of the individuals at the level of education immediately lower are better paid (see Chart II.A3.1 below).[1]

Graphical representation of wage-measured over-qualification

Over-qualification rates can be read directly from charts representing cumulative wage curves. The chart below, for example, represents wage profiles in Germany for the

Chart II.A3.1. **Overeducation rates for individuals with higher education in Germany, 2003-2004**

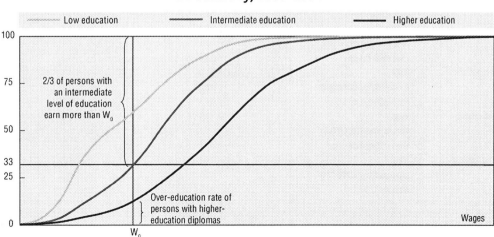

population as a whole. The continuous horizontal line represents the 33.3% cut-off. The abscissa of the intersection of the two straight lines represents the wages earned by more than two-thirds of all individuals with an intermediate education. The intersection of the vertical straight line and the wage curve for persons with higher-education diplomas defines the over-qualification rate for that group, *i.e.* the percentage of higher-education graduates paid less than two-thirds of what those with an intermediate education are paid.

For reasons of statistical availability, the sample of countries is restricted to Belgium, Canada, France, Germany, Greece, Italy, Portugal, Switzerland and the United States. These countries feature highly divergent migration and labour market profiles. This diversity is reflected in widely differing situations with regard to over-qualification. By definition, the study is limited to salaried employees, and to enhance the uniformity of the populations studied, it covers only people who are working full-time.

Wage-measured over-qualification rates calculated in this way are disparate, ranging from 4.5% in Switzerland to 31.7% in Greece (see Table II.A3.1). Given the discrepancy between the two methods, these rates are not very comparable to those calculated with the method used in the chapter. Nevertheless, as in the chapter, immigrants are more over-qualified than the native-born in nearly all countries studied. The over-qualification rate is

Table II.A3.1. **Wage-based over-qualification rate of native- and foreign-born by level of education in some OECD countries, 2003-2004**

	Level of education	Foreign-born	Over-qualification rate foreign-born/native-born
Belgium	Total	**23.5**	**1.2**
	Intermediate (ISCED 3/4)	28.9	1.1
	High (ISCED 5/6)	18.3	1.7
Canada (2003)	Total	**21.4**	**1.1**
	Intermediate (ISCED 3/4)	20.2	1.0
	High (ISCED 5/6)	23.6	1.8
France	Total	**19.8**	**1.0**
	Intermediate (ISCED 3/4)	23.0	0.9
	High (ISCED 5/6)	15.0	1.2
Germany	Total	**10.5**	**1.2**
	Intermediate (ISCED 3/4)	5.6	0.9
	High (ISCED 5/6)	23.3	1.5
Greece	Total	**59.3**	**2.0**
	Intermediate (ISCED 3/4)	62.7	1.6
	High (ISCED 5/6)	51.0	3.6
Italy	Total	**34.9**	**1.7**
	Intermediate (ISCED 3/4)	37.8	1.7
	High (ISCED 5/6)	23.8	1.8
Portugal	Total	**16.5**	**1.8**
	Intermediate (ISCED 3/4)	15.9	1.2
	High (ISCED 5/6)	17.3	3.9
Switzerland	Total	**6.7**	**1.8**
	Intermediate (ISCED 3/4)	2.0	0.7
	High (ISCED 5/6)	14.7	2.3
United States	Total	**13.0**	**1.3**
	Intermediate (ISCED 3/4)	13.4	1.3
	High (ISCED 5/6)	12.7	1.4

Source: European countries: European Union Labour Force Survey (data provided by Eurostat); United States: Current Population Survey March Supplement; Canada: Survey of Labour and Income Dynamics.

StatLink ▒═▶ *http://dx.doi.org/10.1787/021832825511*

relatively high in southern Europe, especially in Greece and Portugal and to a lesser extent in Canada. In France and the United States, immigrant over-qualification remains fairly low. Regardless of the method used, Germany stands in an intermediate position, although wage-measured over-qualification is close to that of France and the United States. The only significant change concerns Switzerland, where occupational over-qualification is low, but wage-measured over-qualification is high. Overall, inter-country differences with respect to the relative over-qualification of immigrants are confirmed.[2]

There is a notable divergence, however, in the fact that the ratio of the wage-measured over-qualification rate for immigrants to that for the native-born in all countries is greater at higher levels than at intermediate levels of education. In Portugal, for example, although amongst persons with a secondary-school education over-qualification rates for the two populations are similar, the chances that a higher-education graduate will be over-qualified are almost four times as great for an immigrant as for a native.

The general literature on over-qualification shows that the occupational over-qualified tend to earn more than people doing the same jobs who are not over-qualified. The above findings would therefore suggest that the wage premium for the occupational over-qualified is greater for higher-education graduates than for those with an intermediate level of education, and that the premium is also higher for the native-born than for immigrants. This is what is suggested by the findings of Battu and Sloane (2002) who show, in the case of the United Kingdom, that white people are paid a higher premium for over-qualification.

Notes

1. Calculations are based on monthly wages net of social security contributions in the case of France, Belgium, Greece, Italy and Portugal, but on gross pay with regard to Germany, the United States and Switzerland. The first and last percentiles of wages are eliminated for all countries.

2. Two supplementary verifications were performed. On the one hand, an analysis taking account of age structures (and thus eliminating the age structure effect within the different levels of qualifications) produced similar results. On the other hand, a logistic regression on the probability of being over-qualified as measured by wages, taking gender, occupational experience, level of education, country of origin, and size of firm as explanatory variables, supported several of the main findings of the study (women are more over-qualified than men, and immigrants are more over-qualified than the native-born).

ISBN 978-92-64-03285-9
International Migration Outlook
Sopemi 2007 Edition
© OECD 2007

PART III

Immigrant Health Workers in OECD Countries in the Broader Context of Highly Skilled Migration*

* This chapter was financed in part by a grant from the European Commission, financed through the Public Health Programme administered by the EC Directorate General for Health and consumer protection, and also through financial support from the Swiss authorities. It has been written by Jean-Christophe Dumont (OECD) and Pascal Zurn (OECD, seconded from WHO). Statistical support was provided by Christine le Thi and Gilles Spielvogel.

Introduction

In recent years, concerns about growing shortages of health professionals, in particular doctors and nurses, have emerged in OECD countries. These shortages are projected to increase over the next 20 years, unless countermeasures are taken, because population ageing and changing technologies are likely to contribute to an increase in the demand for health workers, while workforce ageing will decrease the supply as the "baby-boom" generation of health workers reaches retirement age. One route to partially meeting such shortages is via international migration of health workers, a route which is already being utilised in OECD countries.

In this context, there is increasing competition between OECD countries to attract and retain highly skilled workers in general, and health professionals in particular. This raises concerns in both sending and receiving countries. In the case of developing countries, these concerns were set out in the 2006 World Health Report (WHO, 2006a). Several international initiatives have been set up recently[1] with the aim of formulating policy recommendations to overcome the global health workforce crisis, including through the elaboration of codes of conduct governing the international recruitment of health workers.

Despite this, evidence on the international mobility of health professionals remains scarce and limited, if not anecdotal. This lack of evidence has given rise to much misunderstanding of a complex phenomenon and has hindered the development of effective policy responses. Hence, it is vital to develop reliable and comparable data to identify the role played by international mobility of health workers in shaping the health workforce in OECD countries and its impact on origin countries.

The key objective of this chapter is to present a comprehensive and relevant picture of immigrants in the health sector in OECD countries, in order to better inform the policy dialogue at national and international levels. Section one refers to different sources of data to qualify the nature and the scope of international migration of doctors and nurses in OECD countries and deals with the main issues at stake for origin countries. Section two provides an evaluation of the most recent trends and section three reviews migration policies of OECD member countries related to health professionals. The conclusion summarises the main findings and identifies the opportunities and challenges for origin and receiving countries.[2]

Main findings

- Circa 2000, on average in the OECD 11% of employed nurses and 18% of employed doctors were foreign-born. There are, however, important variations across countries, which partly reflect differences in the characteristics of the health workforce and in the general patterns of migration, notably highly skilled.

- There are significant differences, both in absolute numbers and percentages, between foreign-born and foreign-trained health professionals. These differences are not, however, specific to the health sector and there are uncertainties in terms of the international comparability of the data on the foreign-trained which are based on professional registers.

- About half of foreign-born doctors or nurses working in OECD countries are located in the United States, almost 40% in Europe and the remainder in Australia and Canada. The distribution by country of origin, however, varies significantly across the OECD and intra-OECD movements tend to be important.

- The United States is the only net receiver of doctors and nurses *vis-à-vis* all other countries in the world.

- Filipino-born nurses and Indian-born doctors each represent about 15% of all immigrant nurses and doctors in the OECD. The United Kingdom and Germany are the second and third most important origin countries.

- Caribbean countries and a number of African countries, notably Portuguese and French-speaking, but also Sierra Leone, Tanzania, Liberia and to a lesser extent Malawi, have particularly high emigration rates of doctors. For some of them this is combined with very low density of doctors in the home country, highlighting a very worrying situation for the health sector in these countries. On the other hand, for large origin countries such as India or China, the important number of health professionals working overseas, do not seem to have particularly affected domestic density, at least at an aggregated level.

- Comparison of regional staff shortages estimated by the WHO with total numbers of health professionals emigrated to OECD countries by region of birth reveals that the global health workforce crisis goes far beyond the migration issue. In particular, the needs for health workers in developing countries, as estimated by the WHO, largely outstrip the numbers of immigrant health workers in the OECD. Thus international migration is neither the main cause nor would its reduction be the solution to the worldwide health human resources crisis, although it exacerbates the acuteness of the problems in some countries.

- Long-term trends over the past 25 years or so show that the number and the percentage of foreign-trained doctors has increased significantly in most OECD countries, Canada being a notable exception. This increase has been particularly marked in European countries.

- Over the past 5 years radical upward shifts in the immigration trends have occurred. This is confirmed by both registration and permit data. Nonetheless, this increase has been less marked for nurses than for doctors.

- Recent migration inflows show a trend towards a diversification of origin countries. Main countries of origin, such as India or the Philippines, continue to play the most important role, but this is now accompanied by increased flows originating from small countries, notably African countries and central and eastern European countries.

- In OECD countries, there are very few specific migration programmes to date targeting health professionals. Bilateral agreements do not play an important role so far. Nevertheless, most OECD countries do have special provisions to facilitate the migration of the highly skilled in general, including health professionals.

- Recognition of foreign qualifications remains an important tool to insure high standards and quality in healthcare delivery, but also serves sometimes to control inflows of foreign-trained workers. Despite common features, which include theoretical and practical exams and language tests, OECD countries have different approaches to the recognition of foreign qualifications. Several countries have specific programmes to attract foreign-trained health professionals who do not work in the health sector into the health workforce.

● Immigrants make an important contribution, not only if one considers the sheer numbers involved but also if one takes into account their role in insuring the continuity of service at night or during the week-end, notably in Europe.

1. Foreign-born and foreign-trained health professionals in OECD countries

Discussions on the international mobility of health professionals are severely hampered by data limitations, including ambiguity in data sources and definitions of health worker migrants, or excessive reliance on indirect quotations. These limitations are particularly acute when one seeks to make international comparisons. To a certain extent, this has contributed to confuse the debate on international mobility of health workers. Some recent contributions have acknowledged these difficulties and have made some progress in international comparability of data (e.g. Mullan, 2005; Bourassa et al., 2004; Stilwell et al., 2004; Diallo, 2004; Buchan et al., 2003), although they usually rely on a limited number of receiving countries.

This chapter aims to make a significant step forward on the data comparability front on this politically sensitive topic. This section begins by describing the main characteristics of the immigrant health workforce in OECD countries by using different harmonised data sources to produce the most accurate and relevant snapshot of the situation.

1.A. The size of the immigrant health workforce in OECD countries

Using population censuses and population registers Circa 2000, we assembled information on people employed in health occupations by detailed place of birth for 24 OECD countries.[3, 4] Although these data have some limitations,[5] they provide comparable estimates of the share of foreign-born health professionals in the total health workforce across OECD countries and of the distribution of health workers by country of origin.

This information is synthesized in Table III.1, which shows the total workforce and the percentage of foreign-born by main health occupations. These data are complemented by new statistics on foreign-trained health professionals (see Table III.2) compiled from professional registers and/or certification bodies.

Foreign-born health professionals in OECD: An internationally comparative approach

In 2000, on average in the OECD, 10.7% of employed nurses and 18.2% of employed doctors were foreign-born. However, for both nurses, doctors, and more generally for health professionals, we find large variations in the proportion of foreign-born across countries. For doctors, the percentage of foreign-born ranges from a low of 1.5 to 5% in Mexico, Poland and Finland, to a high of 30 to almost 47% in Luxembourg, the United Kingdom, Canada, Ireland, Australia and New Zealand. In absolute terms the United States has the most important number of foreign-born doctors (almost 200 000), followed by the United Kingdom (50 000) and France (34 000). In the latter case, this includes persons born abroad with French nationality, notably in Algeria before 1962.[6]

In general, the share of foreign-born nurses tends to be lower than for other health professionals. Greece, Switzerland and to a lesser extent Germany are exceptions. Part of the differences in the relative importance of immigrants by health occupation might be explained by the composition of the health workforce in general. According to OECD Health

Table III.1. **Practising health professionals by occupation and place of birth in OECD countries, Circa 2000**

Country of residence	Nurses (ISCO 223 + 323)			Health professionals (except nurses) (ISCO 222)			Doctors (ISCO 2221)			Source	Year
	Total	Foreign-born	% Total (excl. unknown places of birth)	Total	Foreign-born	% Total (excl. unknown places of birth)	Total	Foreign-born	% Total (excl. unknown places of birth)		
AUS Australia	191 105	46 750	24.8	114 184	38 333	33.9	48 211	20 452	42.9	Census	2001
AUT Austria	56 797	8 217	14.5	40 353	5 794	14.4	30 068	4 400	14.6	Census	2001
BEL Belgium	127 384	8 409	6.6	62 101	6 350	10.2	39 133	4 629	11.8	LFS	1998-02
CAN Canada	284 945	48 880	17.2	116 370	37 220	32.0	65 110	22 860	35.1	Census	2001
CHE Switzerland	62 194	17 636	28.6	32 154	8 595	26.7	23 039	6 431	28.1	Census	2000
DEU Germany	781 300	74 990	10.4	445 550	39 097	9.5	282 124	28 494	11.1	LFS	1998-02
DNK Denmark	57 047	2 320	4.1	22 665	2 112	9.3	14 977	1 629	10.9	Register	2002
ESP Spain	167 498	5 638	3.4	201 685	12 937	6.4	126 248	9 433	7.5	Census	2001
FIN Finland	56 365	470	0.8	22 220	755	3.4	14 560	575	4.0	Census	2000
FRA France	421 602	23 308	5.5	331 438	48 823	14.7	200 358	33 879	16.9	Census	1999
GBR United Kingdom	538 647	81 623	15.2	218 369	63 786	29.2	147 677	49 780	33.7	Census	2001
GRC Greece	39 952	3 883	9.7	21 920	1 621	7.4	13 744	1 181	8.6	Census	2001
HUN Hungary	49 738	1 538	3.1	45 411	4 215	9.3	24 671	2 724	11.0	Census	2001
IRL Ireland	43 320	6 204	14.3	13 293	3 735	28.1	8 208	2 895	35.3	Census	2002
LUX Luxembourg	2 551	658	25.8	1 436	438	30.5	882	266	30.2	Census	2001
MEX Mexico	267 537	550	0.2	294 867	3 596	1.2	205 571	3 005	1.5	Census	2000
NLD Netherlands	259 569	17 780	6.9	66 640	9 649	14.5	42 313	7 032	16.7	LFS	1998-02
NOR Norway	70 698	4 281	6.1	20 104	2 906	14.5	12 761	2 117	16.6	LFS	1998-02
NZL New Zeland	33 261	7 698	23.2	15 027	5 790	38.6	9 009	4 215	46.9	Census	2001
POL Poland	243 225	1 074	0.4	163 791	4 389	2.7	99 687	3 144	3.2	Census	2002
PRT Portugal	36 595	5 077	13.9	36 258	6 238	17.2	23 131	4 552	19.7	Census	2001
SWE Sweden	98 505	8 710	8.9	42 065	8 420	20.1	26 983	6 148	22.9	Register	2003
TUR Turkey			..	128 700	6 984	5.4	82 221	5 090	6.2	Census	2000
USA United States	2 818 735	336 183	11.9	1 229 221	256 893	20.9	807 844	196 815	24.4	Census	2000
OECD	6 708 570	711 877	10.7	3 685 822	578 676	15.9	2 348 530	421 746	18.2		

Note: ISCO 222 includes dentists, pharmacists, veterinarians and other health professionals not elsewhere classified. For the United States, the category "nurses" includes registered nurses and licensed practical and licensed vocational nurses (respectively 313 and 350 in the Census 2000 occupation classification). In Belgium, Germany, Spain, Greece, the Netherlands, Portugal, Sweden and Norway, figures for doctors have been estimated based on health professionals (seperately for native-born and foreign-born). For reasons of international comparison, people born in Puerto Rico are considered as foreign-born in the United States (i.e. 5 162 health professionals except nurses; including 3 850 doctors and 6 701 nurses).
LFS: Labour force survey.

StatLink ⟶ http://dx.doi.org/10.1787/022661064856

Data, Greece has the highest ratio of physician per inhabitants (almost 4.5‰) amongst OECD countries but the lowest nurses-to-doctors ratio (less than 1). Conversely, Ireland, Canada and New Zealand have some of the highest nurses-to-doctor ratios in the OECD (above 4), and an higher share of foreign-born doctors (over 13 percentage points difference between foreign-born doctors and nurses).

For nurses, the United States is also the most important receiving country, with about 337 000 foreign-born nurses (although they represent only 12% of the nursing workforce), followed by the United Kingdom (82 000), Canada (49 000) and Australia (47 000).

When population census data are detailed enough to identify other specific health occupations, such as dentists or pharmacists, it appears that the share of foreign-born in these occupations varies widely between countries. Although the share of immigrants is generally higher for doctors than for other health professionals, the share for dentists is higher in Luxembourg, Switzerland or Austria (see Chart III.1). In Australia, about 42% of dentists are foreign-born, the highest figure recorded in the OECD.

Chart III.1. **Share of foreign-born among practicing doctors, dentists and pharmacists in selected OECD countries, Circa 2000**

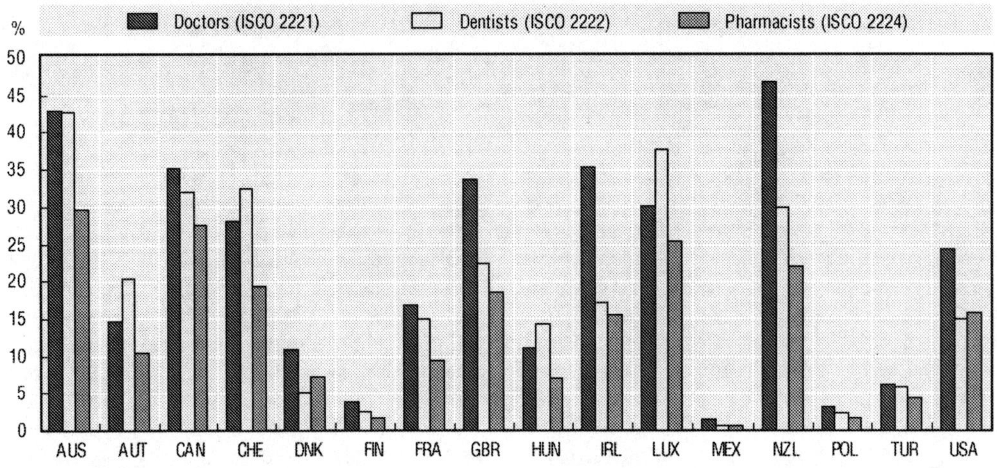

Source: See Table III.1.

StatLink ᔕᔕ http://dx.doi.org/10.1787/015310811861

In all OECD countries for which data are available, the share of foreign-born pharmacists tends to be much lower than for other health professionals. The fact that in addition to the other usual requirements for recognition of foreign qualifications, pharmacists usually need to pass a law exam appears as an additional impediment. This is due to the fact that pharmacists are usually the legal gatekeepers for drug supply. A number of additional explanations could be mentioned here, including: i) the fact that hospitals employ a small share of all pharmacists while it concentrates most of immigrant employment; and ii) application of quite stringent requirements for recognition of foreign qualification, including a quasi systematic period of supervised practice (Chan and Wuliji, 2006).

In total, there are about 50 000 foreign-born dentists and 57 000 foreign-born pharmacists working in the 16 OECD countries for which data are available, corresponding respectively to 10.4% and 12% of all health professionals (except nurses).

Foreign-trained doctors and nurses in OECD: Same issue with a different perspective

The information based on place of birth could give a distorted image of the role of international migration in shaping the health workforce in OECD countries if a significant share of these foreign-born were actually trained in the receiving country and not in their origin country. For that reason, we have also collected data on place of training from professional registers (see Table III.2). Because there is no centralised source, nor harmonized definitions or criteria for registration, the compilation of these data has required a significant amount of work including for analysing and referencing the meta-data. This makes Table III.2 fairly unique but not exempt from data caveats.[7] In particular in some OECD countries, the place of training could not be identified, but the nationality. This is the case for 7 out of 24 countries for doctors and 5 out of 15 for nurses. Furthermore, international comparability of health professionals' registers is also affected by institutional differences in registration processes (see Box III.1). For all these reasons, international comparisons based on the data presented in Table III.2 should be considered with caution.

Box III.1. **International comparability of health professional registration data**

As in all OECD countries, most health professionals, and in particular doctors are supposed to register in order to practice. Therefore, professional registers are an important data source on health professionals. Most registers contain information on the doctor's reference number, name, gender, date of registration, registration status, specialisation. The register is also an important data source to study health worker migration, as it in principle includes information on place of education, therefore allowing one to identify foreign-educated health workers.

Although registers represent probably one of the best data sources on foreign-educated health workers, in particular for doctors, various issues arise when undertaking international comparisons of foreign-educated health workers using these sources. Registration varies across countries: The bodies involved in the registration might differ from one country to another; registration might be at national or regional level; different registration status exist at national level but also across countries; and the availability of data is also dependent on the type of information system.

In some countries registration is carried out by an independent body, such as the Medical Council, in other countries, registration is closely monitored by the Ministry of Health, covering a large range of health professions. For instance, in the Netherlands, the BIG-register is part of an executive agency of the Ministry of Health, Welfare and Sport and deals with the registration of physicians, pharmacists, physiotherapists, health care psychologists, psychotherapists, dentists, midwives and nurses.

In some countries like Finland, New Zealand and the United Kingdom, registration is at national level, whereas it is at regional level in countries like Australia, Switzerland and Spain. In such countries, detailed data are sometimes lacking at national level. For instance, Australia's national agency for health and welfare statistics and information publishes statistics on the country of education of medical doctors, but the figures do not include all States (e.g. detailed information for New South Wales which accounts for about 36% of the medical workforce in 2004 is not included). Collecting registration data for each State would have been very time-consuming and beyond the scope of this study.

The existence of different types of registration status is another source of concern when undertaking international comparisons, as there are variations in the rights and obligations associated with each type of registration. Full, temporary, limited, provisional, conditional, and internship are examples of potential registration status existing in countries. In Ireland, for instance, temporary registration allows non-EU doctors to be employed and to receive further training in the practice of medicine. Temporary registration can be granted for a total aggregate period of seven years. Temporary registrations are not included in our statistics due to lack of harmonised data. In Ireland, it represented about 1 300 doctors in 1999 as compared to 1 200 foreign-trained doctors fully registered (respectively about 1 000 and 4 000 in 2004). In general, the data collected for the purpose of this study refer to full registration only.

Comparisons are also affected by the quality and type of data available. Information systems vary across countries. For instance, although data on place of training are collected by the United Kingdom. Nursing and Midwifery Council, detailed and complete data on the current stock of foreign-educated nurses are not available due to information system constraints. In Canada and the United States, people trained in the United States and in Canada, respectively are not included in the foreign-trained figures (this is also the case for people trained in Puerto Rico with respect to US data).

Box III.1. **International comparability of health professional registration data**
(Cont.)

Finally, a more general concern with registers arises from discrepancies between the number of individuals on the register and those who actually work. While some countries, like New Zealand, issue annual practicing certificates, others do not. About 14 000 doctors were registered in 2005 in New Zealand, but only 11 000 were practicing. In the United Kingdom, there is also a large difference between the number of doctors registered by the General Medical Council (around 210 000 in 2005) and the number of doctors employed by the National Health Service (between 100 000 and 120 000 in 2005). This difference might be explained by the large number of UK-trained doctors who are working overseas but still registered in the United Kingdom, and by all foreign-trained doctors who are registered in the United Kingdom but who are not residing in the United Kingdom or not working in the health sector. It is estimated that more than 60% of foreign-trained doctors who passed the Professional and Linguistic Assessments Board test between June and October 2005 did not find a position as a doctor after one year (GMC, 2007). On the other hand, most of the foreign-trained doctors working in French hospitals were, until recently, not recorded in the professional register as they were considered as medical trainees. As with other registers, deregistration following temporary or permanent inactivity, emigration or death poses specific difficulties.

For all these reasons, international comparisons of foreign-trained health professionals are more difficult and less straightforward than for foreign-born health professionals. Nonetheless, they complement the foreign-born approach and are a key element when assessing the potential impact of the international mobility of doctors and nurses on source countries.

A comparison between foreign-born and foreign-trained health professionals in OECD countries indicates lower percentages for the latter than for the former. This difference is generally explained by the fact that some of the foreign-born were actually trained in the receiving country. Some of them have arrived at younger ages, most probably accompanying their family or in the context of family reunification, while others have entered the receiving country to pursue tertiary education and have stayed after completion of their study. As a result, countries with higher immigration rates, important family migration or significant inflows of international students would tend to have the largest gaps between the two sets of figures.

Despite the recent increase in international mobility of students over the past decade (OECD, 2006), it seems that in most countries, the difference between foreign-born and foreign-trained percentages cannot be explained entirely by international students in tertiary education as they tend to be under-represented in the field of "Health and Welfare" (about 6% for international students in tertiary education as compared to around 10% for all tertiary students). In some OECD European countries, however, the proportion of international students studying in the field of "Health and Welfare" is much higher, particularly in Belgium (about 40% in 2004) and to a lesser extent in Denmark (21%) and the Netherlands (14%).[8]

In Canada, 35% of all employed doctors in 2000 were foreign-born whereas only 23% are foreign-trained. Similar large gaps are recorded in New Zealand and in Australia. The difference between foreign-born and foreign-trained doctors is also

Table III.2. **Immigrants registered in selected OECD countries, doctors and nurses, 2000 and 2005**

Numbers and percentages

Doctors

		2000 Number	2000 %	2005 Number	2005 %
Foreign-trained	Australia	..	..	14 553	25.0
	Austria	461	1.8	964	3.3
	Canada	13 342	23.1	13 715	22.3
	Denmark	1 695	7.7	2 769	11.0
	England	25 360	27.3	38 727	32.7
	Finland	687	3.6	1 816	7.2
	France[1]	7 644	3.9	12 124	5.8
	Ireland	1 359	11.1	3 990	27.2
	Japan	95	–	146	–
	Netherlands[2]	..	..	3 907	6.2
	New Zealand	2 970	34.5	3 203	35.6
	Poland	..	..	734	0.6
	Sweden[1]	3 633	13.1	5 061	16.1
	Switzerland	2 982	11.8	5 302	18.8
	Turkey	33	–	27	–
	United Kingdom[3]	..	..	69 813	33.1
	United States[1]	207 678	25.5	208 733	25.0
Foreigners	Belgium	1 341	3.1	1 633	3.4
	Germany	14 603	4.0	18 582	4.6
	Greece	..	..	897	2.5
	Italy	..	..	12 527	3.4
	Norway	2 327	15.1	2 833	15.6
	Portugal[4]	..	..	1 830	5.3
	Slovak Rep.[1]	130	0.7	139	0.8

Nurses

		2000 Number	2000 %	2005 Number	2005 %
Foreign-trained	Australia[1]	..	..	31 472	12.1
	Canada	14 910	6.4	19 230	7.6
	Denmark	4 618	6.0	5 109	6.2
	Finland	122	0.2	274	0.3
	Ireland[1]	..	..	8 758	14.4
	Netherlands[2]	..	..	3 479	1.4
	New Zealand[1]	6 317	19.3	9 334	24.3
	Sweden[1]	2 517	2.5	2 878	2.7
	United Kingdom[3]	50 564	8.0	..	..
	United States[1]	..	..	101 791	3.5
Foreigners	Belgium	1 009	0.7	1 448	1.0
	France[1]	..	..	7 058	1.6
	Germany	27 427	4.2	25 462	3.8
	Italy	..	..	6 730	2.0
	Turkey	25	–	45	–

Nurses: Australia: AIHW, Medical labour force survey 2004; Canada: CIHI, The Canadian Intituste for Health Information; Denmark: Danish National Board of Health; Finland: National Authority for Medicolegal Affairs; Ireland: An Bord Altranais; the Netherlands: Big Register; New Zealand: New Zealand Health Information Service: New Zealand Health Workforce Statistics 2004; Sweden: National Board of Health and Welfare; the United Kingdom: Aiken and al. (2004); the United States: National Sample Survey of Registered Nurses; Belgium: FODSociale Zekerheid, Dienst Internationale relaties; Germany: Federal Medical Association; France: DREES, ADELI; Italy: IPASVI; Turkey: Ministry of Health, General Directorate of Health Education, Branch Office of Residency.

"–" indicate that percentages are below 0.1%.
1. 2004 instead of 2005.
2. 2007 instead of 2005.
3. 2001 instead of 2000.
4. 2003 instead of 2005.

Doctors: Australia: Productivity Commission, Australia's Health Workforce 2005; Austria: Austrian Medical Chamber; Canada: CIHI, The Canadian Institute for Health Information; Denmark: Danish National Board of Health; Finland: National Authority for Medicolegal Affairs; France: Ordre des Médecins; England: NHS, National Health Service; the United Kingdom: General Medical Council; Ireland: Irish Medical Council; Japan: Ministry of Justice; the Netherlands: Big Register; New Zealand: Ministry of Health of New Zealand; Poland: Polish Chamber of Physicians and Dentists; Turkey: the Ministry of Health, General Directorate of Health Education, Branch Office of Residency; Sweden: National Board of Health and Welfare; Switzerland: Swiss Medical Association FMH; the United States: AMA, American Medical Association; Belgium: FODSociale Zekerheid, Dienst Internationale relaties; Germany: Federal Medical Association; Greece: Medical Associations; Italy: Italian Medical Association; Norway: Den Norske Laegeforening; Portugal: Foreign health professionals working at the Portuguese National Health System Direcção-Geral da Saúde; Slovak Republic: Ministry of Health of Slovak Republic.

StatLink ⬛⬛⬛ http://dx.doi.org/10.1787/022683883013

particularly marked in the cases of France and Portugal, although part of this observation may be explained by the importance of the repatriate community. In the case of the United States, the situation is somewhat different because, while immigrants constitute only a small share of undergraduates, they account for about

26% of postgraduate places.[9] This is due to the fact there are caps on both residency and undergraduate places in the United States, the latter being systematically lower than the former, which induce a quasi-automatic inflow of International Medical Graduates, including US citizens.[10] Because of this situation, the percentages of foreign-born and foreign-trained doctors are very close in the United States.

The distribution of nurses by place of birth and of training is usually closer. Several origin countries, in particular the Philippines, have indeed developed an important nursing education sector for the international market, which is well recognized worldwide. That being said, in Australia, Canada, the United States and to a lesser extent Sweden, the percentage of foreign-born nurses is significantly higher than that for foreign-trained nurses.

One advantage of using professional registers' data as opposed to census data is that they can provide a more up-to-date picture of the relative importance of foreign or foreign-trained health professionals in selected OECD countries. Between 2000 and 2005, in the main receiving OECD countries, mainly located outside Europe, while the share of foreign-trained has remained almost stable for doctors, it has increased slightly for nurses. In Europe there is a rising trend, especially in the Nordic countries and Ireland. It is therefore possible that in the latter countries, recent inflows have contributed to reshape the immigrant health workforce. This issue is addressed in more detail below.

To which extent international migration focuses on health professionals?

The data presented in Table III.1 provide a first glance at the relative importance of immigrants in the health sector. However, these results should be compared to the share of immigrants amongst highly skilled workers in general, to identify potential specificities of international migration of health professionals. Data by place of birth, based on population censuses or population registers, allow one to make such a comparison. Chart III.2a thus compares the share of foreign-born doctors on the one hand and of foreign-born nurses on the other hand, to the share of foreign-born in professional or associate professional occupations (defined as ISCO 1, 2 or 3).

The two sets of estimates are highly clustered along the 45°-line for nurses in most countries, with Switzerland the sole outlier with a relatively higher percentage of foreign-born nurses. The results for doctors are quite different, in that there is a systematic tendency for the share of foreign-born doctors to be higher than the share of foreign-born in professional occupations; Luxembourg is the sole outlier with a relatively low percentage of foreign-born doctors.

The difference observed for doctors could be due to the fact that they have higher degrees than professionals and associate professionals in general. Indeed, if we compare the percentage of foreign-born doctors to that of persons employed and holding a PhD (see Chart III.2b), we find, as for nurses, a much greater clustering around the 45°-line. This is not so surprising taking into account that the average time required to become a medical doctor is generally close to that required to obtain a Ph.D. In this latter chart, Canada, despite the fact that more than a third of its medical workforce is foreign-born, appears to have a relatively low percentage of foreign-born doctors.

These results show that foreign-born health professionals are generally not overrepresented among immigrants when compared to similar professional groups. While international migration tends to be selective towards the highly skilled in general (Dumont

Chart III.2a. **Percentage of foreign-born doctors and nurses compared
to the percentage of foreign-born in highly skilled occupations
in selected OECD countries, Circa 2000**

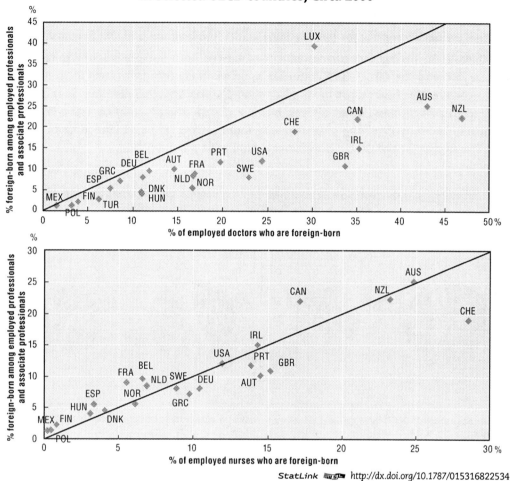

StatLink ⟮⟯ http://dx.doi.org/10.1787/015316822534

Chart III.2b. **Percentage of foreign-born doctors compared to the percentage
of foreign-born among people employed and holding a PhD
in selected OECD countries, Circa 2000**

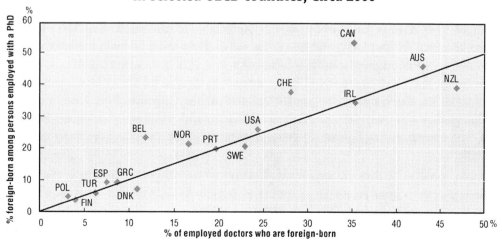

Source: See Table III.1.

StatLink ⟮⟯ http://dx.doi.org/10.1787/015316822534

and Lemaitre, 2005), it is not specifically oriented towards health professionals. This was true in 2000, although, as we will see below, the situation may have changed in more recent years.

Origin-destination matrix for foreign-born health professionals in OECD countries

Overall, the United States received 47% of foreign-born doctors working in the OECD area in 2000 and the OECD-EU25 countries approximately 39% (see Chart III.3). Australia and Canada received each close to 5% of the total. Surprisingly, this distribution is identical for foreign-born nurses. What differs, however, is the distribution between European countries, Germany receiving proportionally more nurses (7%) and France more doctors (8%). The figures for the United Kingdom are similar at around 11%.

Chart III.3. **Distribution of foreign-born doctors and nurses by country of residence in the OECD area, Circa 2000**

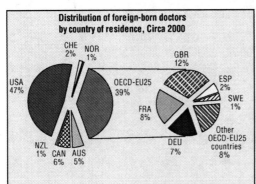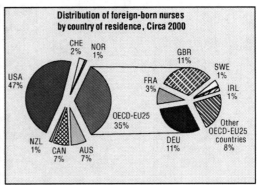

Sources: See Table III.1 OECD-EU25 includes all relevant countries except Italy, the Czech Republic and the Slovak Republic.

StatLink 🔗 http://dx.doi.org/10.1787/015332400840

The data on the share of health professionals received by OECD-EU25 countries should be considered with caution as a significant proportion of the foreign-born originates from within the European Union (about 38% for nurses and 24% for doctors), and notably from the new accession states.

Chart III.4 presents foreign-born health professionals working in the OECD by main regions of origin. Tables III.A1.1 and III.A1.2 in Annex III.A1 show for each receiving country the main regions of origin of immigrant doctors and nurses. Asia is the main source region for health professionals in many OECD countries.[11] In the United States for instance, more than half of the foreign-born doctors (40% of the nurses) originate from Asia. Important percentages are also recorded for Australia (43%), Ireland (48%) and the United Kingdom (55%). The corresponding figures for Asian nurses are much lower (respectively 24%, 29% and 24%).

Latin America is also an important provider of health professionals to the United States as well as to some European countries, especially Spain (55% of foreign-born doctors and 41% of foreign-born nurses). North Africa is a significant source region only for France (about half of foreign-born doctors and nurses).

Chart III.4. **Distribution of foreign-born doctors and nurses by main regions of origin in OECD countries, Circa 2000**

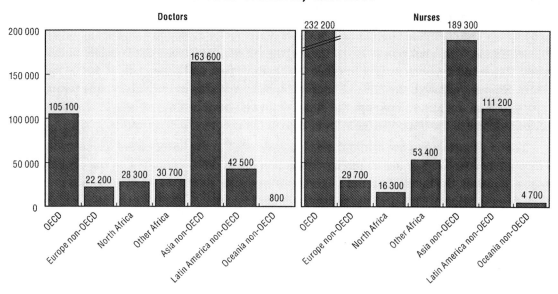

Source: Includes data for all OECD countries identified in Table III.1, except Germany (see Annex III.A1).

StatLink ᴹᴵˢᴾ http://dx.doi.org/10.1787/015372351347

In some OECD countries, intra-OECD movements are predominant. This is the case, for instance, in the Nordic countries, Switzerland and New Zealand for nurses. On average, the share of foreign-born health professionals originating from within the OECD area is lower than for the highly skilled in general (40% of all tertiary-educated immigrants as compared to 27% for doctors and 36% for nurses).

In general, the distribution by region of origin reflects general migration patterns and is determined by language and geographic proximity, cultural and historical ties and bilateral migration policies. All these findings hold for migration flows, in general, and are not specific to the international mobility of health professionals.

Tables III.A1.3 and III.A1.4 in Annex III.A1 present detailed origin-destination matrices for the OECD area. The United Kingdom and Germany are the most important source countries within the OECD area for both doctors and nurses. UK-born immigrants represent about 75% of the immigrant doctors from the OECD in Ireland and New Zealand and more than 50% in Australia. The distribution of German-born doctors is more widespread and represents more than 20% of the immigrant doctors in half of the countries for which data are available. They are predominant for instance in Austria, Switzerland, Poland and Turkey, but more generally represent significant groups in all non-English-speaking OECD countries. Similarly, French-born doctors in Spain, Spanish-born doctors in Portugal, or Canadian-born doctors in the United States represent the main source country from within the OECD area in the three countries.

In an EU context, in 2000, the health professionals originating from the 12 new EU member states (A12) already represented a significant percentage of the immigrant workforce. This was the case for instance in the new accession countries themselves (e.g. Poland and Hungary), but also in Austria for both doctors and nurses (respectively 28% and 33%), as well as in Greece and Sweden for doctors (about 20%) or to a lesser extent in Denmark and Finland (about 14% of foreign-born doctors).

The international migration of health workers is characterized by multiple interactions between OECD countries. Within the OECD international flows of both doctors and nurses can be depicted as a cascade-type model of migration in which the United States appears to be at the bottom of the "fall" (see Chart III.5): it is the only net receiving country *vis-à-vis* all other OECD countries, with a net gain of 79 000 nurses (the difference between OECD nurses in the United States and US-born nurses in other OECD countries), and a net gain of 44 000 for doctors. However, although the United States is the main receiving country in absolute terms for foreign-born doctors and nurses, the share of foreign-born health workers in the total health workforce in the United States is lower than in many other OECD countries.

Canada, Australia and Switzerland are also positioned at the lower end of the cascade as they are net receivers of health professionals from most OECD countries. In the case of Canada, however, the intra-OECD net migration is negative for nurses (–6 000), because of the large emigration of Canadian nurses to the United States.[12]

Chart III.5. **Intra-OECD migration of nurses: A cascade-type pattern, net stocks, Circa 2000**

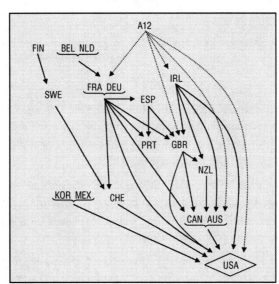

Reading note: Arrows represent a positive difference between the stocks of nurses in origin and receiving countries. Not all possible downward arrows are represented (for instance Finland has a net deficit with Sweden but also with Switzerland and the United States), but there would be no ascending arrows (for instance at the time of the population census, Ireland had only a net gain with regards to new EU member states (A12) and the United States was the only country to have a net gain *vis-à-vis* all other OECD countries).

Sources: See Table III.1. OECD* refers only to origin countries identified in Tables III.A1.4 in Annex III.A1.

1.B. *Impact of international mobility of health professionals on origin countries: Main issues at stake*

One of the key issues in terms of the international mobility of health professionals, on which much of the political attention has been focused in the recent years, relates to its impact on origin countries. Despite important efforts to gather information at the regional level or national level,[13] statistical evidence by origin country remains scarce or difficult to compare. The data presented in Chart III.6 and Annex III.A2 address this shortcoming by presenting data for foreign-born doctors and nurses in OECD countries disaggregated by detailed country of birth.

Chart III.6. **Foreign-born doctors and nurses in the OECD by main countries of origin (top 25), Circa 2000**

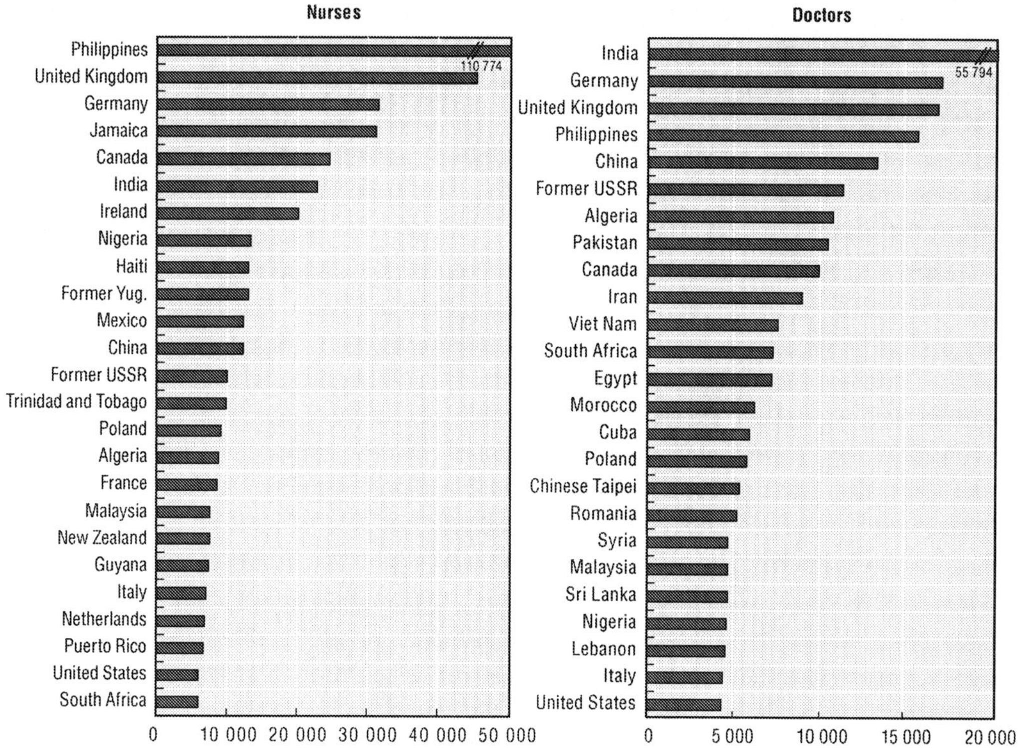

Nurses

Philippines	110 774
United Kingdom	
Germany	
Jamaica	
Canada	
India	
Ireland	
Nigeria	
Haiti	
Former Yug.	
Mexico	
China	
Former USSR	
Trinidad and Tobago	
Poland	
Algeria	
France	
Malaysia	
New Zealand	
Guyana	
Italy	
Netherlands	
Puerto Rico	
United States	
South Africa	

0   10 000   20 000   30 000   40 000   50 000

Doctors

India	55 794
Germany	
United Kingdom	
Philippines	
China	
Former USSR	
Algeria	
Pakistan	
Canada	
Iran	
Viet Nam	
South Africa	
Egypt	
Morocco	
Cuba	
Poland	
Chinese Taipei	
Romania	
Syria	
Malaysia	
Sri Lanka	
Nigeria	
Lebanon	
Italy	
United States	

0   5 000   10 000   15 000   20 000

Source: See Table III.1.

StatLink ᴀᴴᴸ▶ http://dx.doi.org/10.1787/015385521332

What is the size of the "brain drain"?

Nurses born in the Philippines (110 000) and doctors born in India (56 000) account for the bulk of the immigrant health workforce in the OECD. Each represents about 15% of the total stock. More surprisingly, the second and third most important origin countries for doctors or nurses are the United Kingdom and Germany.

For nurses, several other OECD countries, *e.g.* Canada, Ireland and, to a lesser extent, Mexico, rank quite high in the list. Even some Caribbean countries with small populations, notably Jamaica and Haiti, send quite a lot of nurses abroad.

The chart for doctors is dominated by non-OECD countries. China and the former USSR[14] play a striking role with more than 10 000 doctors working in OECD countries. A surprisingly high number of doctors born in the Philippines are working in OECD countries (about 16 000), which contrasts with the general emphasis on emigration of Filipino nurses.[15] South Africa and Cuba are also in the top 25 origin countries for doctors.

The absence of all but two (*i.e.* Nigeria and South Africa) sub-Saharan African countries might be surprising but can be explained by the fact that most African countries have a small population and a small health workforce.[16] In this case, the best way to evaluate the scope of migration is to estimate the percentage of health professionals who have left the country. By taking data on doctors and nurses in countries of origin from the WHO Global Health Atlas, an emigration rate was computed for 160 countries for doctors and 153 countries for nurses (see Annex III.A2).[17]

When comparing the number of expatriated doctors to the number of doctors in the origin country, a quite different picture emerges (see Chart III.7). African and Caribbean countries now stand out as being disproportionably affected by out-migration of health professionals. Most of the countries with expatriation rates above 50% (which means that there are as many doctors born in these countries working in the OECD as there are working in their home country) are from the Caribbean, except Fiji[18] and five African countries: Mozambique, Angola, Sierra Leone, United Republic of Tanzania and Liberia. The latter countries all had major conflicts over the past decades (except Tanzania) and are amongst the poorest countries in the world.[19]

French and Portuguese-speaking African countries also have some of the highest expatriation rates to OECD countries for doctors. Guinea Bissau, Sao Tome and Principe, Senegal, Cape Verde, Congo, Benin and Togo rank between the 17th and the 23rd places just after the Caribbean countries, with expatriation rates above 40%, while English-speaking countries such as Malawi, Kenya or Ghana which are focusing much of the attention in international fora have lower expatriation rates (Malawi ranks 25th, Kenya 28th and Ghana 35th). The cases of Cape Verde and Sao Tome and Principe are easily understood because these countries do not have medical schools but instead have an agreement with Portugal to train doctors. The case of Guinea Bissau may be of a different nature.

Not only do French-speaking countries have high emigration rates but they also tend to have low densities. There are about 2 times less doctors per inhabitant in Senegal than in Kenya, 8 times less than in Cape Verde and 20 times less than in Barbados. Therefore, a greater attention should be paid to the urgency of the situation in these French-speaking

Chart III.7. **Emigration rate and density of doctors by origin country, Circa 2000**

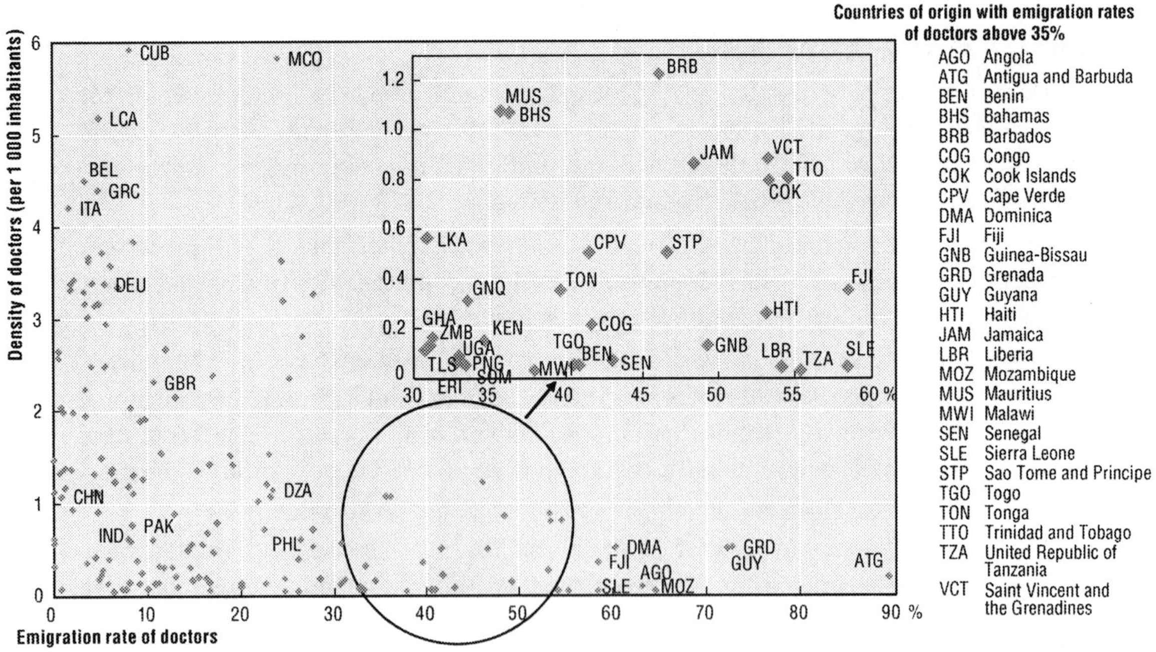

Sources: WHO database for figures by origin countries on density (number of doctors per thousand population). See Annex III.A2 for emigration rates of doctors.

StatLink ▬▬▬ http://dx.doi.org/10.1787/015407728518

African countries. Malawi is another country where, despite a slightly smaller emigration rate, the density of medical doctors is very low.

Some of the countries for which the highest emigration, in absolute or relative terms, has been recorded are in fact less impacted as they still have "not-too-low" density ratios for doctors. Cuba is an obvious example but several Caribbean countries could also be mentioned in this regard (Barbados, Bahamas and to a lesser extent Trinidad and Tobago or Saint Vincent and the Grenadines). The latter countries host a number of medical schools oriented towards supply graduates for the US market, which ultimately may also benefit their population. Furthermore, large countries such as China or Brazil have very low emigration rates (about 1%), and even countries such as India, Pakistan or Indonesia have only about 8% of "their medical workforce" abroad.

In most cases the expatriation rate for nurses is lower than for doctors. This is not the case, however, for a number of countries, notably in the Caribbean (about 90% of the nurses born in Haiti or in Jamaica are working in the OECD), but also for El Salvador or Mexico, for Samoa, Tonga or New Zealand, for Mauritius, Madagascar and the Philippines. In the latter case, by focusing on OECD countries, the impact of migration might have been underestimated. Indeed, according to Philippine Overseas Employment Administration statistics, about 74% of all Filipino nurses deployed between 1992 and 2002 went to non-OECD countries, mainly to Saudi Arabia (ILO, 2005). The same may be true for some other source countries, notably for doctors from Sudan (Badr, 2005). Even if these movements are mainly short term, they should be taken into account when estimating the overall emigration rate and the impact on the origin country.

Emigration rates of doctors can also be compared to that of the highly skilled in general. Chart III.8 shows that both figures are highly correlated. In other words, countries which are most affected by emigration of their professionals in general also face high emigration rates of their health workforce (and inversely). Emigration rates for doctors seem to be above those for the highly skilled in general, and this is mainly due to the fact that doctors hold higher degree than other professionals (see *supra* Chart III.3).

Chart III.8. **Emigration rate of the highly skilled and of doctors, non-OECD countries**

Percentages

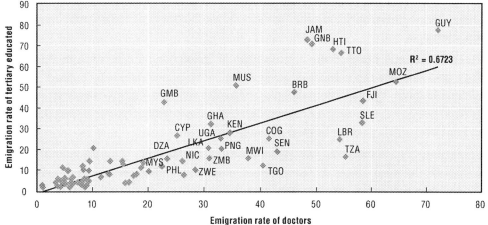

Source: See Dumont and Lemaitre (2005), for emigration rates for the highly skilled (data can be downloaded from *www.oecd.org/els/migration/censusdata*) and Annex III.A2 for the emigration rates of doctors.

StatLink 🔀📈 *http://dx.doi.org/10.1787/015423568330*

However, because of the key role played by health workers in improving the health status of the population, as well as their contribution to economic and social development (e.g. Gyimah-Brempong and Wilson, 2004; WHO, 2001), the impact on origin countries of doctors' and nurses' emigration might be more problematic and challenging than for other categories of skilled professionals. In addition, even limited emigration of certain specialists (e.g. anaesthesiologists, radiologists), associate professionals (e.g. laboratory technicians) or support staff (e.g. hospital managers) may create serious bottlenecks in the health systems with potentially dramatic consequences. Also, over the long-term, migration can have negative effects, as it weakens national capacity to train future cohorts of health professionals.

At the same time, employment opportunities in the home country,[20] as well as the geographic location of migrants in origin countries (most international migrants come from urban areas although the most acute shortages tend to be in rural areas), should be taken into account when evaluating the impact of migration on origin countries. An internal "brain drain" indeed exists in most developing countries (Skeldon, 2005).

Finally, a key question is who pays for the training: The receiving country, the origin country or the migrant herself or himself. While the role of receiving countries was already acknowledged when we discussed the data by place of training, in some countries migrants and/or their families are financing directly or indirectly (if they are required to pay back their training cost if they depart) the training costs. For example, nursing education in the Philippines is mostly provided by private institutions and in India, private medical schools now account for more than 40% of the total number of medical students (Mullan, 2006). The situation is, however, quite different in many other lower income countries, notably in Africa, where the private education sector does not play any role, notably because of severe financial constraints.

International migration and the worldwide health workforce crisis

In the World Health Report (2006a), the WHO estimated a shortage of more than 4 million health workers across the world. In particular, 57 countries were identified as having a critical shortage, including 36 sub-Saharan African countries.[21] To reach the target levels of health worker to close these gaps, about 2.4 million supplementary doctors, nurses and midwives would be required (see Table III.3). It is in the African region and in south East Asia region that the largest increases in the health workforce would be required to meet shortages.

To give a general sense of the contribution of international migration to this global shortage, we estimated the number of foreign-born doctors and nurses by region[22] of birth and compared these figures with the number of health workers shortages estimated by the WHO. This is obviously a purely mechanical exercise but it serves to reveal that the global health workforce crisis goes far beyond the migration issue.

All African-born doctors and nurses working in the OECD represent no more than 12% of the total estimated shortage for the region. The corresponding percentage is even lower (9%) for the region with the greatest need in absolute terms: South East Asia. In the cases of the Americas and the Western Pacific region, the situation is quite different. This is due to the fact that i) a number of immigrants are originating from OECD countries (about a third for the Americas); and ii) some source countries such as the Philippines in the

Table III.3. **Estimated critical shortages of doctors and nurses and midwives, by WHO region**

WHO region	Number of countries		In countries with shortages			Foreign-born doctors and nurses in OECD countries by region of origin	
	Total	With shortages	Total stock	Estimated shortage	Percentage increase required	Number	Percentage of the estimated shortage
Africa	46	36	590 198	817 992	139%	98 329	12%
Americas	35	5	93 603	37 886	40%	199 314	526%
South-East Asia	11	6	2 332 054	1 164 001	50%	101 460	9%
Europe	52	0	–	–	–	. .	. .
Eastern Mediterranean	21	7	312 613	306 031	98%	71 551	23%
Western Pacific	27	3	27 260	32 560	119%	212 280	652%
World	192	57	3 355 728	2 358 470	70%	682 934	

Source: World Health Report -WHO 2006 (see endnote 22 for details on how "critical shortages" are estimated) and authors' calculations for emigration data.

StatLink ⌐⌐⌐ http://dx.doi.org/10.1787/022687473573

Western Pacific region or Caribbean countries in the Americas, are important providers of health workers to the OECD.

When considering individual countries of origin rather than regions of origin, the findings do not change fundamentally. In the case of African countries for instance, with the exception of Cape Verde, immigrant health workers to the OECD represent a maximum of 25% of the estimated shortages.

These calculations show that the needs in human resources in developing countries, as estimated by the WHO, largely outstrip the numbers of immigrant health workers in the OECD, implying that international migration is neither the main cause nor would its reduction be the solution to the worldwide health human resources crisis, even though it exacerbates the acuteness of the problems in some countries. However, even in these latter cases, migration may be more a symptom than a determinant. In this context, global guidelines for the recruitment of foreign health workers could make, to a certain extent, a difference (see Box III.2).

2. Recent trends in migration movements of health professionals

Thanks to the pioneer work of Meija *et al.* in the late 1970s, and based on the new data on foreign-trained that we have collected (see Table III.2), we are able to draw a picture of the evolution of the number and the share of foreign-trained doctors in selected OECD countries over the past 25 years (see Table III.4).

Between 1970 and 2005, the number of foreign-trained doctors has increased at a rapid rate in most OECD countries considered (except Canada), partly because of the very low starting levels in the 1970s. The average annual growth rate is close to 10% in Finland, the Netherlands, Portugal and France. In Denmark and Sweden, the corresponding figures are 6 and 7% a year, respectively. In the United States, Australia and New Zealand, which are amongst the most important receiving countries, the increase has been more moderate although quite sustained (3-4% a year).

As a result, the share of foreign-trained in the medical workforce has increased dramatically. In France and the Netherlands, for instance, it has augmented six-fold, while it has more than tripled in Denmark and Portugal. In Germany, the United States and

Box III.2. **Code of conduct for the recruitment of international health workers**

Growing awareness of the adverse effects of health worker migration on health systems in countries which experience severe shortages of staff has gone hand-in-hand with calls for ethical recruitment strategies. Subsequently, instruments have been developed to guide different health sector stakeholders in the process of international recruitment. This development is quite recent with most of the instruments published from 1999 onwards. All instruments are voluntary, and none is legally binding. However, even a voluntary code of practice carries some moral and political force in those countries that sign up to it.

The United Kingdom has taken the lead in this field. For example, the Department of Health's code of practice for NHS employers involved in the international recruitment of healthcare professionals was first published in October 2001 and subsequently revised in December 2004. The Code identifies the guiding principles to promote high standards in the recruitment and employment of healthcare professionals from overseas. It is also concerned with the provision of health services in developing countries and seeks to prevent targeted recruitment from developing countries who are experiencing shortages of healthcare staff. Some of the principle changes to the 2004 version aimed at including in the Code of Practice the recruitment through agencies of temporary healthcare professionals, as well as permanent staff and at widening the scope of the Code to enable all healthcare organisations, including the independent sector, to sign up to the principles contained within the Code. The NHS also recommended only to use recruitment agencies that comply with the Code of Practice for both domestic and international recruitment.

At international level, the Commonwealth Code of practice for the international recruitment of health workers, adopted in 2003, provides governments with a framework within which international recruitment of health workers should take place. The Code is intended to discourage targeted recruitment of health workers from countries which are experiencing shortages and to safeguard the rights of recruits and the conditions relating to their profession in recruiting countries. The Commonwealth Code is the only policy document with a clause on compensation that was adopted at government level, mainly by developing countries but also by New Zealand.

Martineau and Willets (2004, 2006) review all the existing instruments for ethical international recruitment. This encompasses 8 documents, including 4 codes of practice, 3 guides and one statement from national or international bodies. The authors are relatively sceptical about the efficiency of these instruments due to the lack of support systems, incentives and sanctions as well as monitoring systems. More recently, Mcintosh, Togerson and Klasen (2007) explore the lessons for Canada of the implementation of ethical recruitment of internationally educated health professionals. While they show that there is a consensus on the fact that the ethical issue needs to be confronted, they underline the many practical difficulties, notably in terms of balancing individual rights to migrate and international equity concerns and also as regards the definition of the key concept of active recruitment. The authors strongly emphasise the need to put in place "*a mix of policies to address the broader problem of Canada's supply of health professionals*".

Nonetheless, calls for a more global approach have been made, which have led the 57th World Health Assembly in 2004 to adopt a resolution on migration, urging member states to take actions to address health workers migration issues, and in particular to consider the development of an international Code of Practice on migration.

Table III.4. **Foreign-trained doctors in selected OECD countries, 1970s and 2005**

Country of residence	Number	% of the total workforce	Number	% of the total workforce
Australia	4 385	24%	14 553	25%
Canada	11 244	31%	13 715	22%
Germany*	5 605	5%	18 582	5%
Denmark	235	3%	2 769	11%
Finland	68	1%	1 816	7%
France	600	1%	12 124	6%
United Kingdom	20 923	26%	69 813	33%
Netherlands	102	1%	3 907	6%
New Zealand	934	27%	3 203	36%
Portugal*	79	1%	1 830	5.3%
Sweden	561	5%	5 061	16.1%
United States	70 646	22%	208 733	25%

* Foreign nationals.

Sources: Mejia *et al.* (1979), for the 70s and Table III.2 for 2005.

StatLink ⏤🖳 *http://dx.doi.org/10.1787/022701487571*

Australia, however, the increase in immigrant doctors has matched the upward trend for health workforce in general. Canada is the exception: The share of the foreign-trained doctors has declined sharply over the period.

2.A. Recent flows: Rising figures – rising concerns

To some extent these long-term trends are attributable to the recent increase in migration flows. Chart III.9 presents the recent evolutions for the immigration of doctors and nurses in 12 OECD countries over the past 10 or 5 years.

In general, we observe increasing trends, which responded *inter alia* to i) labour market shortages in OECD countries resulting from increasing demand due to rising spending on health relative to GDP after a period of cost-containment in late 1980s and early 1990s combined with supply constraints (*numerus clausus*); ii) changes in migration policies for the highly skilled in general in receiving countries; and iii) a combination of factors related to easier access to information, decreasing travel cost and deterioration of living and working conditions in the origin countries (Vujicic *et al.*, 2004). In parallel, we also observe emerging trends, alternative to international mobility of health workers, such as patient mobility or e-health (see Box III.3).

The trend for nurses shows a sustained increase in the inflows which started during the 90s and stabilized in 2001/2002. This pattern is particularly clear in the case of temporary migrants in Canada but also in the United States, in the United Kingdom or in Ireland. Only Australia and Finland show a sustained upward trend in inflows of nurses in the most recent years.

The recent reversal of the trend in the United Kingdom is usually explained by indirect effects of an increasing number of UK graduates and policy changes in the NHS which have induced a reduction in the demand for foreign nurses. The introduction of the Overseas Nurses Programme (ONP) in September 2005 also seems to have delayed in the recruitment pipeline many immigrant nurses who are awaiting a place on an ONP course (Buchan and Seccombe, 2006).

For doctors, the most recent data show little or no evidence of moderation in the increasing trend. The evolution for permanent residence permits in Australia is particularly striking, although the number remains quite small, and can be attributed to changes in

Chart III.9. **Inflow of immigrant doctors and nurses in selected OECD countries, 1995-2005**

United States: Nurses (exams)

Source: National Council of State Boards of Nursing passed NCLEX-RN exams.

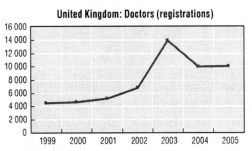

United States: Doctors (exams)

Source: MD Physicians completing USMLE step 3.

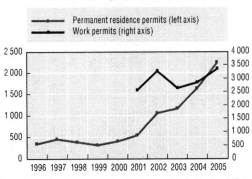

United Kingdom: Nurses (registrations)

Source: Nursing and Midwifery Council – new registrations.

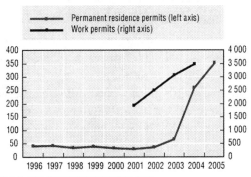

United Kingdom: Doctors (registrations)

Source: General Medical Council – new full registrations.

Australia: Nurses (work and residence permits)

- Permanent residence permits (left axis)
- Work permits (right axis)

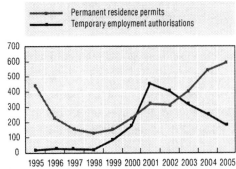

Australia: Doctors (work and residence permits)

- Permanent residence permits (left axis)
- Work permits (right axis)

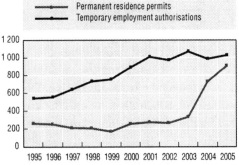

Source: Permanent residence permits: Skill Stream – Principal Applicants Only; Work Permits: Visa subclass 422 and 457, DIMA.

Canada: Nurses (residence permits and temporary employment authorisations)

- Permanent residence permits
- Temporary employment authorisations

Canada: Doctors (residence permits and temporary employment authorisations)

- Permanent residence permits
- Temporary employment authorisations

Source: Citizenship and Immigration Canada, Facts & Figures 2005. Permanent residence permits: Permanent Residents in (Intended) Health Care Occupations (Principal Applicants); Temporary employment authorisations: Annual Flow of Foreign Workers.

StatLink ⟶ http://dx.doi.org/10.1787/015437104614

INTERNATIONAL MIGRATION OUTLOOK: SOPEMI 2007 EDITION – ISBN 978-92-64-03285-9 – © OECD 2007

Chart III.9. **Inflow of immigrant doctors and nurses in selected OECD countries, 1995-2005** *(Cont.)*

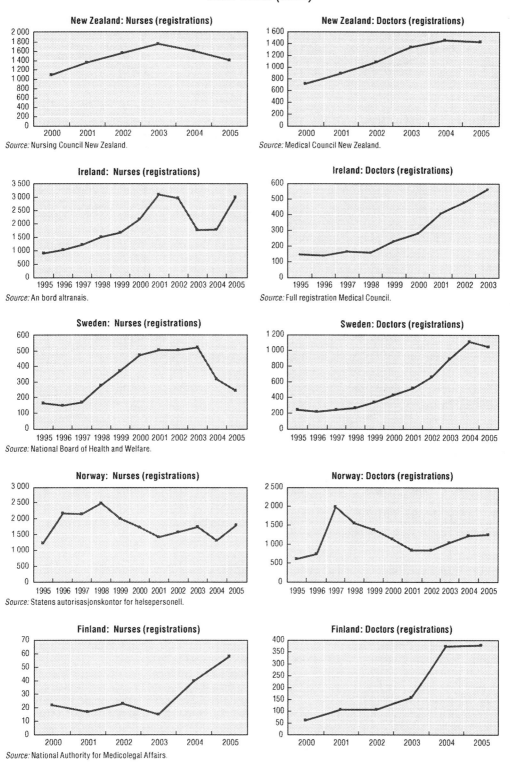

StatLink ⬛▥▤ *http://dx.doi.org/10.1787/015455803325*

Chart III.9. **Inflow of immigrant doctors and nurses in selected OECD countries, 1995-2005** *(Cont.)*

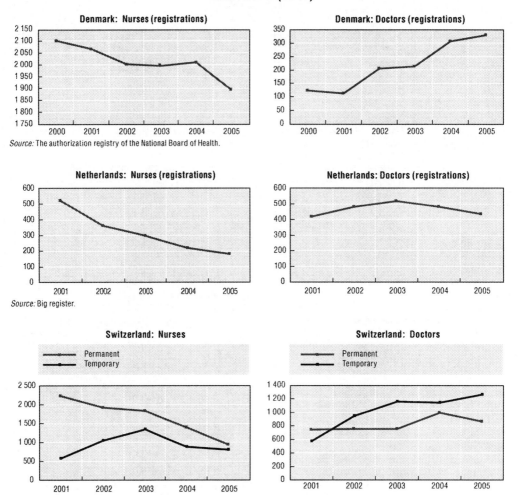

Source: The authorization registry of the National Board of Health.

Source: Big register.

Source: Office fédéral des migrations ODM, Registre central des étrangers RCE.
Permanent: Holders of a permit valid for 12 months or more (settlement and residence permits plus short duration permit longer than 12 months).
Temporary: Holders of a short duration permit (valid for less than 12 months).

Sources:

Nurses: US: National council of state boards of nursing passed NCLEX-RN exams; UK: Nursing and Midwifery Council – new registrations; Australia: Permanent residence permits: Skill Stream – Principal Applicants Only; Work Permits: Visa subclass 422 and 457, DIMA; Canada: Citizenship and Immigration Canada, Facts and Figures 2005. Permanent residence permits: Permanent Residents in (Intended) Health Care Occupations (Principal Applicants); Temporary employment authorisations: Annual Flow of Foreign Workers; New Zealand: Nursing Council New Zealand; Ireland: An bord altranais; Sweden: National Board of Health and Welfare; Norway: Statens autorisasjonskontor for helsepersonell; Finland: National Authority for Medicolegal Affairs; Denmark: The authorization registry of the National Board of Health; the Netherlands: Big register; Switzerland: Office fédéral des migrations ODM, Registre central des étrangers RCE.

Doctors: US: MD Physicians completing USMLE step 3; UK: General Medical Council – new full registrations; Australia: Permanent residence permits: Skill Stream – Principal Applicants Only; Work Permits: Visa subclass 422 and 457, DIMA; Canada: Citizenship and Immigration Canada, Facts and Figures 2005. Permanent residence permits: Permanent Residents in (Intended) Health Care Occupations (Principal Applicants); Temporary employment authorisations: Annual Flow of Foreign Workers; New Zealand: Medical Council New Zealand; Ireland: Full Registration Medical Council; Sweden: National Board of Health and Welfare; Norway: Statens autorisasjonskontor for helsepersonell; Finland: National Authority for Medicolegal Affairs; Denmark: The authorization registry of the National Board of Health; the Netherlands: Big register; Switzerland: Office fédéral des migrations ODM, Registre central des étrangers RCE.

StatLink ⫘ *http://dx.doi.org/10.1787/015455803325*

> ### Box III.3. **Could patient mobility and telemedicine help to alleviate health worker shortage concerns?**
>
> Although patient mobility still remains very modest, as it represents only 1% of overall public health expenditure on health care in the EU, more people are travelling to seek health care, including medically necessary procedures. A combination of factors has led to this recent increase. These include waiting lists and the high cost of healthcare in the home country, the ease and affordability of international travel, and the improvement of technology and standards of care in many countries of the world. Popular medical travel destinations include India, Cuba, Singapore, Mexico, Costa Rica and Thailand. For instance, more than 150 000 Americans travelled abroad for healthcare in 2005, and that number is projected to increase significantly in the future (Woodman, 2007).
>
> Patient mobility is also attracting an increasing interest in the EU. For example, Hungary has become a popular destination for dental care, and English patients travel to France to undergo surgery. Currently, the EU health services are the responsibility of member states. However, in several of its judgments, the European Court of Justice has ruled that EU citizens can seek healthcare in other member states and be reimbursed by their national system if the same service cannot be provided in their country of origin. Given the potential for growth of patient mobility, its complexity and its potential consequences on health systems and financing, the Commission has decided to hold a public consultation with the aim of putting forward a framework proposal in 2007. The issue at stake in this new consultation is the development of a Community framework for safe, high-quality and efficient health services in Europe – with a special emphasis on patient mobility across borders.
>
> Telemedicine is another avenue which some observers argue could help alleviate, to a certain extent, health workforce shortages. It relies on the use of information communication technology (ICT) to improve the delivery of health care at distance. Modern communications technology is particularly appropriate and useful in rural communities, helping to overcome the barriers of distance and isolation. For instance, Australia has developed innovative solutions like telephone call centres operated by health professionals such as registered nurses; tele-health to the home involving internet applications and local monitoring equipment; and teleradiologists using live videoconferencing and stored, digital radiology images. But there are still few evidence on the use of tele-medicine across frontiers, and there remain large barriers, notably in terms of quality concerns.

migration policies. Comparable increases have been recorded in Finland or Sweden. In the United States[23] or the United Kingdom,[24] the rise in the annual inflow is less rapid but not less important in absolute terms. In relative terms, new registrations of foreign-trained doctors represented 68% of all new registrations in the United Kingdom (2005), 82% in New Zealand (2005), 50% in Ireland (2002) or about 35% in the United States (2005).

The registration figures should, however, be considered with caution as they cannot be necessarily equated to the number of doctors or nurses entering the country at a point in time. This is due to the fact that people need to pass the exams and, notably for doctors, to go through a supervision period before being fully registered. It can also happen that people have been out of the health sector during a certain period of time in the host country before they register.

As a result, work permits may provide a more relevant picture of the recent trends. In Chart III.9 work and residence permit data are both presented for Canada, Australia and Switzerland. In most other cases exam or registration figures are presented.

In the United Kingdom, about 3 280 work permits were granted to health professionals (mainly doctors) and 11 110 to associate health professionals (mainly nurses) in 2005. In total, this corresponds to a third of all work permits. These figures more than doubled for doctors since 2000, but actually decreased by about 10% for other health professionals after peaking at 13 700 in 2003. These figures are somewhat lower than those on new registrations presented in Chart III.9 but show similar trends.[25] In Ireland, about 2 700 work permits were issued to medical and nursing occupations in 2005, slightly down compared to previous years but significantly more than in 2000 (1 360). This corresponded to about 10% of all work permits.

In the United States, the H1-B visas are available for most health professionals.[26, 27] In 2005, about 7 200 initial petitions were approved for medicine and health occupations including 2 960 for physicians and surgeons. This corresponded to an increase of about 55% since 2000, although a slight decrease has been observed for non-physicians since 2003. What may be more remarkable in the case of the United States is the increase in the number of petitions approved for continuing employment. For health occupations in general the figures more than doubled between 201 and 2005, from 4 700 to 10 100. This could suggest that immigrant doctors and other health professionals with H1-B visas tend to have longer duration of stay than they used to have.

As a matter of fact the impact of international migration should be evaluated by also taking into account the duration of stay, as permanent settlement and temporary movements have different types of impacts on both sending and receiving countries. Unfortunately this information is generally not available. In the case of New Zealand, however, we have information on the percentage of overseas-trained doctors retained in the New Zealand workforce by duration since registration. The retention of overseas-trained doctors who registered in New Zealand during the previous three years was close to 80% in 2000. For those who registered in the previous 4 to 6 years, it drops to 36% and it is about 20% for those who registered ten years ago (MCNZ, 2000). This would suggest quite high mobility of doctors as such even in a country which is particularly open to settlement migration.

2.B. Diversification of origin countries

Increasing flows and diversification of origin countries are two debated issues regarding the recent immigration trends of health professionals to the OECD. Diversification of origin countries is questioned by the fact that the most significant evolution over the past decade, relates to the increasing inflows from the Philippines and India: Two countries which were already leading in the stock data on the foreign-born which were presented previously. This phenomenon is observed notably in Canada, Ireland, the United Kingdom and in the United States. For the latter two countries, where the most important inflows of health professionals have been recorded recently, Chart III.10 presents the changes in the distribution of region of origin between 1995 and 2005.

In the case of foreign doctors emigrating to the United States, the changes in immigration flows have been quite modest, but the evolution for nurses in the United States and in general for the United Kingdom are much more characteristic of the overall trends. In the United Kingdom for instance, between 1997 and 2004, the share of work permits granted in the health sector to Indians almost tripled to reach 28% at the end of the period. The corresponding trend for the Philippines is even more marked as Filipino health workers received less than 1% of the work permits in 1997, but 33% in 2000 and 24% in 2004. No other origin countries has recorded such a large increase. For the United Kingdom, this is indirectly due to the fact that bilateral agreements were signed with India and the Philippines and that commitments were made not to recruit actively in most other developing countries (the share for South Africa, for instance, decreased from 19% in 1999 to 10% in 2004).

But these trends go far beyond the UK example and are the result of a combination of pull and push factors: The quality of training in the Philippines and India, network effects, the size of the pool of health workers in these origin countries, access to information and to financial resources (including through the diaspora networks). Given these factors there are few reasons to expect a reversal in these trends over the near term, at least in term of share.

China is another country of origin which is playing an increasing role, although flows are still quite small. The number of Chinese nurses registering annually increased, for instance, four-fold in the United States between 1995 and 2005, and Chinese nurses appear for the first time among the top 20 source countries for new registrations in the United Kingdom in 2005/06. It is very likely that this trend will be confirmed, if not amplified, in the coming years.

The situation for African countries is less clear. In particular, there is evidence that the inflows from this region decreased in percentage terms, although the absolute numbers have been increasing. This is what has been observed at least in the United Kingdom for nurses: African nurses accounted for 18% of the new registrations in 1998/99 as compared

Chart III.10. Distribution by region of origin of immigration inflows of health professionals in the United Kingdom and the United States, 1995-97 and 2002-04

Percentages

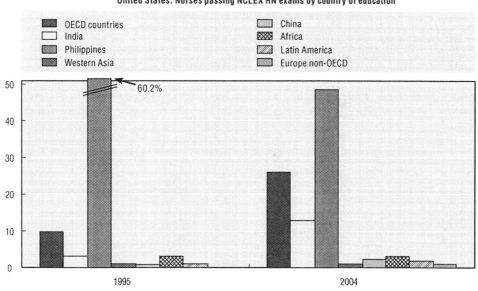

1. South-Asia almost represented totally by India.
2. East-Asia almost represented totally by Philippines.
3. African countries includes the following countries: Botswana, Cameroon, The Democratic Republic of Congo, Eritrea, Ethiopia, Gambia, Ghana, Lesotho, Liberia, Malawi, Mauritius, Nigeria, Sierra Leone, South Africa, Tanzania, Zambia, Zimbabwe.

Source: First-time internationally educated candidates taking the NCLEX RN examination, NCSBN.

StatLink ▄▄▅▆ *http://dx.doi.org/10.1787/015286178415*

Chart III.10. **Distribution by region of origin of immigration inflows of health professionals in the United Kingdom and the United States, 1995-97 and 2002-04**
(Cont.)
Percentages

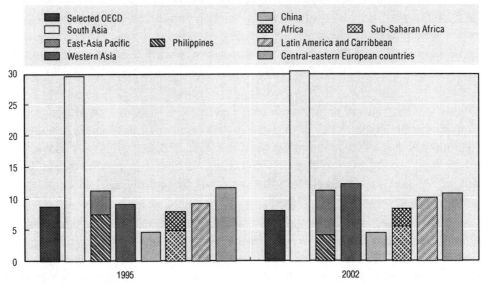

United States: Doctors: IMG residents by citizenship

1. Africa includes North Africa and sub-Saharan Africa.
2. Selected OECD countries include the following countries: Australia, New Zealand, Western Europe, Canada, Japan.
3. South-Asia includes India and Pakistan.

Source: PGY-1 IMG Residents by citizenship at the time of medical school.

StatLink ⟶ http://dx.doi.org/10.1787/015286178415

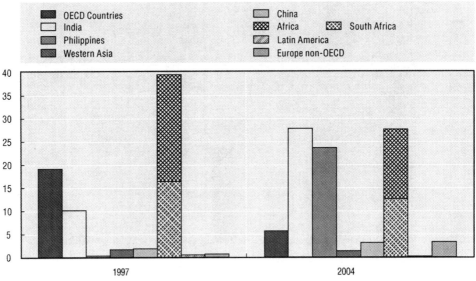

United Kingdom: work permit approvals in the health sector

Note: Figures of work permits in the health sector may include other non-health workers working in a medical environment.
1. South-Asia is almost represented totally by India.
2. East-Asia is almost represented totally by Philippines.
3. Figures for China include Hong Kong, China.

Source: Work permits UK.

StatLink ⟶ http://dx.doi.org/10.1787/015286178415

to 15% in 2005/06, but at the same time the number went from 900 to about 1 600. From a receiving or a sending country perspective, these trends might be interpreted differently. In this context, it should be emphasised, however, that migration of African health workers to the OECD is not driven by a particular country (in fact, flows from South Africa and Nigeria tend to decrease) but is due to a diversification of origin countries within the continent.

Finally, in the European context, the recent enlargement waves have undoubtedly affected the inflows of foreign doctors and nurses from new accession states (see Box III.4), although these changes may be difficult to identify in migration statistics. Poland in absolute numbers and Lithuania in relative terms have been at the forefront of these developments. More recently, immigration from Romania has been showing increasing trends. In Italy, for instance, about half of the recognition of foreign nursing qualification in 2005 were for Romanian nurses (2 400).

Box III.4. **The consequence of recent EU enlargement on health worker migration flows**

As indicated in section I, Circa 2000 and thus prior to the EU enlargements in May 2004 and January 2007, a significant number of doctors and nurses born in the new EU member states were already working abroad. Despite the fact that most EU15 countries applied a transition period for the first two years (except the United Kingdom, Ireland and Sweden), concerns were raised about the potential impact of enlargement on out-migration of health workers, in particular in Poland and the Baltic States.

These concerns were partly motivated by surveys of health professionals' intentions to migrate which were held previously to enlargement (see Chart below). Statistics on intentions generally overstate the expected migration flows but in these surveys the percentages of people with a "definite plan to migrate" were unusually high. A number of factors can explain this situation, including the scope of the needs in some EU15 countries and the large salary disparities (World Bank, 2006).

Share of hearth care professionals who wants to work abroad

%

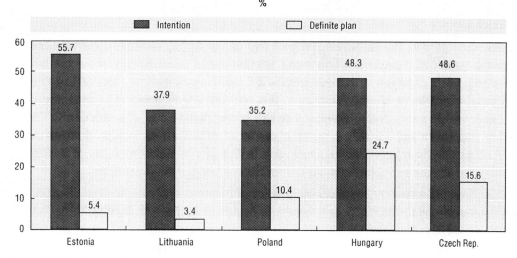

Source: Vörk, Kallaste and Pritinits (2004).

Box III.4. **The consequence of recent EU enlargement on health worker migration flows** (*Cont.*)

To which extent did these flows materialise? Only partial evidences are available so far, but it allows one to draw a first picture of the situation, which both nuances the scope of the outflows and confirms their significance. In the United Kingdom, between May 2004 and December 2006, 530 doctors (hospital), 340 dental practitioners, 950 nurses (including 300 dental nurses) and 410 nursing auxiliaries and assistants were registered in the Worker Registration Scheme (Home Office 2007) as coming from the new member states. In Ireland, the employment of EU8 nationals in the health sector doubled between September 2004 and 2005, from 700 to about 1 300 persons in total (Doyle *et al.*, 2006). In Finland, 432 authorisations were issued to physicians and dentists from EU8 until December 2005 (Dolvik and Fafo, 2006), and in Sweden the number of authorisations granted to EU doctors jumped from 230 in 2003 to 740 in 2004.

Data from the origin countries confirm these trends. In Estonia, by April 2006, 4.4% of all health care professionals had applied for a certificate to leave (61% were physicians). In Latvia, in 2005 more than 200 doctors expressed their intention to leave. In Poland, between May 2004 and June 2006 more than 5000 certificates were issued to doctors (4.3% of the active workforce) and 2 800 to nurses (1.2%) (Kaczmarczyk, 2006). Furthermore, some specialities seem to be more directly affected such as anaesthetists in Poland (about 16% were issued a certificate) or for instance plastic and reconstructive surgeons in Estonia (30% were issued a certificate).

Significant migration flows from new EU members to EU15 have been recorded. Their potential impact on origin countries should, however, be evaluated according to the duration of stay abroad. In this regard, available evidence for Poland suggests that most of the increase in the outflows to EU countries was short-term. That being said, the consequence of temporary outflows of small numbers of highly specialised doctors, such as surgeons or anaesthetists, or more generally dentists, can have in some countries major impacts on health care delivery. A more systematic analysis of the trends and their consequences would be welcome, including for the two countries which have joined recently the EU (Romania and Bulgaria) which face even greater salary disparities with EU25 (Wiskow, 2006).

3. International recruitment of health professionals and migration policies in OECD countries

Since the mid 90s, the international mobility of the highly skilled in general has increased in most OECD countries. This trend has responded to increasing labour market needs along with changes in labour migration policies aimed at facilitating the international recruitment of professionals. In this context, it is interesting to understand better under which conditions migration of health professionals is now possible in OECD countries. Are there any specific programmes aimed at recruiting foreign doctors or nurses? What role do bilateral agreements play in the international mobility of health workers? What are the key conditions for recognition of foreign qualifications?

Table III.5 synthesises the main characteristics of migration policies and qualification recognitions systems for 26 OECD countries (see Annex III.A3 for full details). Table III.5 does not explicitly distinguish between nurses, doctors or other types of health professionals, although specific conditions would generally apply to each of these professions (see Annex III.A3).

Table III.5. Migration programmes and conditions for recognition of qualifications of foreign health professionals (HP)

	Specific migration programmes for HP or specific conditions may apply	HP are included in labour shortage lists	Specific migration programmes for HP in underserved areas or specific conditions in regional migration programmes	Bilateral agreements specific for HP at a national or regional level	Foreign medical students can remain to look for a job or special regulations may apply for status change	Recognition of foreign qualifications for registration*	
AUS							AUS
AUT							AUT
BEL							BEL
CAN							CAN
CHE							CHE
CZE							CZE
DEU							DEU
DNK							DNK
ESP							ESP
FIN							FIN
FRA				Ended			FRA
GBR							GBR
GRC							GRC
IRL							IRL
ITA							ITA
JPN							JPN
LUX							LUX
NLD							NLD
NOR							NOR
NZL							NZL
POL							POL
PRT							PRT
SVK							SVK
SWE							SWE
TUR							TUR
USA							USA

Note: Programmes may concern only nurses or doctors.

(*) Specific conditions generally apply to nurses, doctors and other types of health professionals, specific conditions may also apply for certain countries of training or nationalities.

For detailed information, see Annex III.A3.

1. Yes.
2. Conditional/limited registration may be possible under simplified procedures.
3. Exams and if necessary a supervision period or additional training are required.
4. Condition on nationality, national qualifications required or other types of stringent conditions apply.

StatLink ᘯᔿᔤ *http://dx.doi.org/10.1787/022716122471*

3.A. Special permits and entry conditions

Very few OECD countries have specific migration policies for health professionals. Australia is one major exception. The medical practitioner visa (subclass 422) allows foreign nationals, who are medical practitioners, to work in Australia for a sponsoring employer for a maximum of four years. Since April 2005, however, medical practioners can also apply to the general program for *Temporary Business Long Stay (subclass 457)*.

Australia and New Zealand grant special points for health professionals in most cases in their permanent skilled categories. This facilitates the immigration of health workers but only to a limited extent. In the United Kingdom, since April 2006 all doctors and dentists from outside the European Union require a work permit, but a new category was introduced in September 2006 to the existing Training and Work Experience Scheme called the Medical Training Initiatives (MTI), under which foreign-trained doctors can undertake continuing training in the United Kingdom, normally within the NHS. The individuals are expected to return overseas to put into practice the training they have received in the United Kingdom.[28, 29]

International medical graduates (IMG) completing their graduate medical education in the United States under a J-1 visa are required to return to their home country or country of last residence for at least two years before re-entering the United States. This foreign residence requirement can, however, be waived for instance at the request of a State or Federal agency if the physician agrees to practice in an underserved area for at least 3 years. From 70 doctors in 1990 to more than 1 300 in 1995 and about 1 000 a year since 2002, this programme has became a major channel for placing physicians in underserved areas (GAO, 2006; Hagopian *et al.*, 2003). Initially, states were authorized to request waivers for up to 20 physicians each fiscal year; but in 2002, the limit was increased to 30 waivers per state per year.[30] About 90% of the waivers are requested by the States and about half of them concern physicians working exclusively in primary care. GAO (2006) estimates that "*at the end of fiscal year 2005, there were roughly one and a half times as many waiver physicians practicing in underserved areas (3 128) as US physicians practicing in underserved areas through NHSC programs (2 054)*".

Australia also has specific programmes for attracting foreign health professionals to specific areas (see also Box III.5). The Federal government identifies "Districts of Workforce Shortage" and states define "Areas of need" in which foreign-trained doctors may be recruited, temporarily or permanently, sometimes under conditional registration. Between June 2000 and December 2002, about 5 300 temporary overseas trained doctors were allocated to "Areas of need" visa, including about 2 000 in Queensland (Hawthorne *et al.*, 2006). More generally, there are specific programmes for designated areas (visa 496 or 883) when occupation is included in the relevant shortage list, which will be generally the case for health professionals. In these designated areas overseas students who have completed their studies in Australia but are unable to meet the passmark as an independent migrant may be granted a permanent visa (visa 882). Retention in the rural or remote areas is, however, a matter of concern. Hawthorne *et al.* (2003) note that "*in terms of the Rural Locum Relief Scheme of 276 permanent resident doctors recruited to work in Victorian rural general practice from 1998/99 to 2001/02, just 88 remained in place by 2002 (68% attrition rate)*".

Under the Canadian Constitution, immigration is an area of shared jurisdiction between the federal and the provincial/territorial governments. The latter have progressively developed immigration programmes to serve their specific needs or requirements. In the context of Provincial Nominee Class, health occupations are identified explicitly for instance in British Columbia and Saskatchewan. Furthermore, for occupations included in Regional Lists of Occupations Under Pressure, temporary permits may be granted under simplified procedures. Most health occupations are listed thus in Alberta, Ontario and British Columbia.

In European OECD countries, work permits are generally initially granted for a limited period. These permits may be conditioned on a labour market test (*i.e.*, checks that there are no EU residents available to fill the position). Nonetheless, in most countries there are conditions under which the labour market test may be waived. This is the case, for

---

Box III.5. **Initiatives to recruit foreign medical practitioners in rural areas**

In addition to general programmes, non-governmental organisations sometimes play a key role in trying to address geographical inequalities in terms of availability of healthcare workers through migration. In France, for instance, a non-governmental association organises recruitment campaigns for local authorities or healthcare institutions in Romania to bring in doctors, based on the general incentives offered to recruits who commit to settle for at least five years in underserved areas.

In New Zealand, the Rural General Practice Network is a non-profit organisation which offers recruitment services, mainly targeting foreign doctors, for rural practitioners needing to recruit a locum, or secure a long-term or permanent appointment. This helps medical practitioners to pursue professional training or to take a break and improves retention in rural areas. It also provides a first New Zealand experience to foreign doctors who may choose later on to apply for a permanent residence permit.

In Australia, a Rural Workforce Agency in the State of Victoria (RWAV) was established in 1998 to overcome the shortage of rural doctors and improve access to medical services for rural Victorians. The RWAV is a not-for-profit company funded primarily by the Australian and the State Government and is governed by a Board which includes representatives from key medical and rural stakeholders. The RWAV helps provide individual assistance and expert advice on general practice opportunities in rural and regional Victoria, including to overseas trained doctors.

Outside the OECD, the Rural Doctors' Association and the Academy of Family Practice in South Africa have been developing a recruitment process for doctors, both overseas trained and returnees. To this end, the Rural Health Initiative (RHI) has recently launched a recruitment project to help doctors gain at least a year's experience in South Africa.

---

instance, in the United Kingdom, Belgium, Ireland, Denmark, the Netherlands or Spain for occupations on the shortage list. In all these countries, all or part of health professionals are included in the shortage lists. In some countries, *e.g.* Belgium, Denmark, France, Germany or the Netherlands, there will be no labour market test if the wage is above a certain threshold. If the level is generally too high for nurses, this does not hold for doctors in many cases (generally the threshold annual earnings is about EUR 33 000).

Few OECD countries have bilateral agreements for the international recruitment of health professionals. Switzerland and Canada, for instance, have a small agreement protocol which explicitly mentions health care workers and aims at facilitating the mobility between the two countries. Spain, which is supposed to have a surplus of nurses, has signed bilateral agreements, notably with France and the United Kingdom. Germany has bilateral agreements with several central and eastern European countries for the recruitment of foreign nursing aids. Bilateral agreements are also sometimes organised at the regional level. This is the case for instance in Italy, where several provinces have signed protocols with provinces in Romania to train and recruit nurses.

In Europe, the United Kingdom is the only country which has made intensive use of bilateral agreements and memoranda of understanding with non-OECD countries in the context of the international recruitment of doctors and nurses. It has signed an agreement with South Africa on reciprocal educational exchange of health care concepts and personnel (2003), a memorandum of understanding with India (2002) and a Protocol on Cooperation in Recruiting Health Professionals with China (2005). The Department of

Health committed not to recruit in rural areas in China and in four Indian states that receive DFID aid (Andhra Pradesh, Madhya Pradesh, Orissa and West Bengal). Furthermore, a list of 151 countries from which the NHS should not recruit actively has been established. This is the case for South Africa where the agreement includes international recruitments but with a strong emphasis on training and information exchanges. It also aims at facilitating twining of hospitals to share best practices and strengthen management. This agreement is often quoted as a best-practice example.

Outside Europe, the only relevant example refers to Japan which has signed recently an agreement to recruit Filipino nurses, with at least 3 years experience, to be trained in Japan. This agreement which concerns 450 nurses over a two-year period still needs to be ratified by the Philippines parliament.

In sum, it appears that in most OECD countries, migration programmes do not target specifically health professionals but they can provide simplified procedures to facilitate their recruitment, notably at the local or regional level. Perhaps surprisingly, bilateral agreements, with very few exceptions, do not play an important role so far and usually concern small numbers of professionals. Because much of the migration of health professionals is a part of a wider stream of international migrations of highly skilled people, it cannot be curbed in isolation. Any attempt to do so could simply result in emigrants ceasing to describe themselves as health professionals.

At the same time, the absence of proper migration programmes for health professionals did not prevent some international recruitment agencies, national health services or private healthcare institutions from holding active recruitment campaigns overseas (Dobson and Salt, 2005), which certainly contribute to explain the sharp increase in the inflows that were recorded over the past 5 years or so. In addition, the spread of the Internet has certainly contributed to ease the access to information on vacancies and possibilities for migration worldwide. In the future, policy changes in the context of the on-going GATS negotiations, notably within Mode 4, could also affect in different ways the conditions for the international recruitment of health workers (see Box III.6).

3.B. Recognition of foreign qualifications

As a prerequisite to employment in the receiving country, foreign (and domestic) health professionals have to meet registration or licensing requirements. This process aims at insuring that educational standards and criteria for fitness to practice (e.g. certificate of morality) are met to guarantee patient safety and high quality in healthcare delivery. In this perspective, education curricula are systematically reviewed and it is common for foreign-trained doctors and nurses to be required to pass exams as a condition to registration.

Recognition of foreign qualifications most often requires passing both theoretical and practical exam, as well as a language test. The level required for language proficiency can have a direct impact on inflows of foreign-trained doctors and nurses. The recent tendency, for instance in New Zealand or the United Kingdom, has been to increase the minimum language requirements for nurses.[31] Based on the evaluation of competencies, participation in bridging programmes, retraining in specific area or adaptation periods may be imposed, although in some countries a working period under supervision is systematically required. In the United Kingdom, for instance, foreign-trained doctors need to pass the PLAB test to get a limited registration. After one year of supervised

Box III.6. **Trade and international mobility of health professionals**

The General Agreement on Trade in Services (GATS) came into force in 1995 and constitutes the legal framework through which World Trade Organization (WTO) Members progressively liberalize trade in services, including health-related services. GATS allows WTO Members to choose which service sectors to open up to trade and foreign competition. To date, only 50 WTO Members have made some type of commitment on health services under GATS, much less than in financial services (100 Members). The agreement covers four different modes (Modes 1-4 trade in services) all of which affect health:

Mode 1: Cross-border supply. Health services provided from the territory of one member state in the territory of another member state. This is usually via interactive audio, visual and data communication. Typical examples include Internet consultation, diagnosis, treatment and medical education.

Mode 2: Consumption abroad. This usually covers incidents when patients seek treatment abroad or are abroad when they need treatment. This can generate foreign exchange, but equally can crowd out local patients and act as a drain on resources when their treatment is subsidized by the sending government.

Mode 3: Foreign commercial presence. Health services supplied in one member state through commercial presence in the territory of another member state. This covers the opening up of the health sector to foreign companies, allowing them to invest in hospitals and clinics, health management and health insurance. It is argued that, on the one hand, FDI can make new services available, contribute to driving up quality and create employment opportunities. On the downside, it can create a two-tier health system and an internal "brain drain" – and thus exacerbate inequity of health provision.

Mode 4: Movement of natural persons (individuals rather than companies). The temporary movement of a commercial provider of services (for example, a doctor) from their own country to another country to provide his or her service under contract or as a member of staff transferred to a different country. This is one of the most contentious areas for health, as there is concern that it will increase the "brain drain" of health personnel from poor to rich countries. However, GATS is concerned only with health professionals working in other countries on a temporary basis.

The extent to which GATS will have an impact on public services such as health and education is controversial. GATS comes into the equation when countries decide to allow foreign private suppliers to provide services. Opponents of GATS are concerned that the capacity of states to regulate health-related services will be eroded. The counter-argument stresses that GATS allows WTO Members to decide for themselves which sectors will be liberalized and to define country-specific conditions on the form that liberalization will take. Some WTO Members have already indicated they will not be requesting or offering commitments on health services in the current negotiations. Those states that do proceed are not obliged to respond positively to any particular request. Nor is there any requirement for reciprocity. Moreover, the Doha Declaration specifically reaffirmed the right of Members to regulate or introduce new regulations on the supply of services.

GATS is a complex treaty and it does not lay down minimum standards. Rather, it takes shape through the process of negotiation. Overall, there is a lack of empirical data on the level of international trade in health-related services, as well as on the effects of liberalization in specific countries.

Source: WHO, General Agreement on Trade in Services *www.who.int/trade/glossary/story033/en/index.html.*

training, they can get fully registered. In Ireland, the limited registration can last up to 7 years. In Finland, the licence is granted stepwise: First to work in hospital under supervision, then in health centres and finally in private institutions.

In some countries, the requirements are more restrictive. This is the case, for instance, when people are asked to obtain national qualification. To practice in the United States, all foreign-trained doctors should do or re-do their internship. In Canada, in most cases, graduates of foreign medical schools, who have already completed some or all of their postgraduate training abroad, are required to have two to six years of postgraduate medical training at a Canadian university (Canadian Information Centre of International Medical Graduates). In Italy, Finland, Greece, Turkey and Luxembourg, citizenship of the host country can be required to practice as a medical doctor or as a specialist. In France, despite the fact that the Public Health Code mentions a criteria of nationality (Art. L-4111-1), in practice many foreign doctors are working in public hospitals. Most of them used to be working under precarious contract arrangements as trainees. An important effort has been made recently to regularise their professional status (about 9 500 authorisations have been delivered by the Health Ministry since 1999), and a new procedure has been implemented for recognition of qualifications of foreign-trained doctors (Ordre des Médecins, 2006).

In some OECD countries, conditional or limited registration may be granted under simplified procedures on a temporary basis if qualifications are recognised as being relatively close to the requirements. In the Netherlands, if skills are considered as almost equivalent, registration is made with special stipulations which should be addressed within 2 years. In Australia, people entering through permanent schemes need to have their qualifications recognised prior to arrival. This is not necessarily the case for temporary migrants, in particular those entering through sponsoring schemes. In this context, doctors are granted conditional registration, they can work under supervision and need to take the required exams. It seems that a number of doctors who entered through this route face difficulties in passing the clinical exam, even after several years.[32]

Recognition of qualifications for nurses is usually less problematic, although exams and language tests are often required. Nurses nevertheless may face difficulties in having their specialties recognised or may be downgraded in lower occupational positions (e.g. registered nurses working as license nurses or in care homes as nursing aids…). Allan and Larsen (2003) report that in the United Kingdom many international registered nurses were working in the independent sector as care assistants and felt isolated.[33]

Within free mobility areas, including the Nordic Passport Union, the Trans-Tasman Area or the European Union, specific regulations are in place to facilitate the mutual recognition of qualifications and ease international mobility (see Box III.7). For third-countries nationals, even within the OECD, more or less stringent procedures exist for the recognition of foreign qualifications, which are sometimes considered as impediments to practice.

In many OECD countries, the media have sometimes publicised the case of doctors employed as taxi drivers or in other low-skilled occupations. There is, however, little evidence available on the scope of the brain waste in the medical field, but even so, there is no doubt that foreign doctors and nurses face sometimes difficulties in getting their qualifications fully recognised. The case of refugees who are usually entitled to work but

Box III.7. **Recognition of diplomas within the European Union and in Europe more generally**

The European Union has developed a legal framework in order to encourage more automatic recognition of qualifications, and simplify administrative procedures between its member states. Recently, a new Directive 2005/36/EC has been produced which encompasses twelve sectoral directives – covering the seven professions of doctor, nurse, dental practitioner, veterinary surgeon, midwife, pharmacist and architect – and three directives which have set up a general system for the recognition of professional qualifications and cover most other regulated professions (see *http://europa.eu/scadplus/leg/ en/cha/c11065.htm*). This directive should be implemented by October 2007 by member states.

In this new framework, member states automatically recognize certificates of training giving access to professional activities as a doctor, nurse responsible for general care, dental practitioner, veterinary surgeon, midwife, pharmacist and architect, covered by Annex V to the Directive (no adaptation period, no aptitude test). The Directive also adopts the principle of automatic recognition for medical and dental specialisations common to at least two member states under existing law, but restricts future additions to Directive 2005/36/EC of new medical specialisations – eligible for automatic recognition – to those that are common to at least two fifths of the member states.

For the purposes of equivalence in qualifications, it sets minimum training conditions for **Doctors** (at least six years of study or 5 500 hours of theoretical and practical training and an additional minimum duration of two years for general practitioners and, for instance, 5 years for the specialisation in general surgery); **Nurses responsible for general care** (at least three years of study or 4 600 hours of theoretical and clinical training); **Dental practitioners** (at least five years of theoretical and practical study); **Midwives** (at least three years of theoretical and practical study); and **Pharmacists** (at least four years of theoretical and practical training and a six-month traineeship in a pharmacy).

In addition, member States may that require migrants to have the knowledge of languages necessary for practising the profession. This provision must be applied proportionately, which rules out the systematic imposition of language tests before a professional activity can be practised. Furthermore, evaluation of language skills should be separated from the recognition of professional qualifications and should be organised afterwards.

Two special cases may occur for EEA nationals trained in third countries and for Nationals of third countries trained in the EEA. The former are not covered by the EU legislation but the new Directive on Professional Recognition entitles holders of third-country qualifications to benefit from the Directive if their qualifications have been recognised by a first member state according to its national rules and they have practised the profession for at least three years in that member state.

In October 2005, European countries also signed the **Health Professionals Crossing Border Agreement** which aims at facilitating the exchange of information between competent authorities notably for certificates and fitness to practise.

Finally, within the wider European region, 45 countries are currently participating in the **Bologna process** (started in 1999) which aims at establishing a European Higher Education Area by 2010 and thus to facilitate recognition of qualifications within Europe. Medical education is included in this process, although the World Federation for Medical Education (WFME, 2005) has drawn attention to the lack of specificities of the recommendations.

face particular difficulties in having their qualifications recognised (lack of language proficiency, absence of relevant documents…) may be particularly relevant in this context.

In order to address this issue, several OECD countries have implemented more or less ambitious bridging programmes. Canada is on example which allocated, in 2005, CAD 75 million over a five-year period to the Internationally Educated Health Professional Initiative. This programme aims at assisting the assessment and integration into the workforce of up to 1 000 physicians, 800 nurses and 500 other regulated health care professionals. Additional funds were allocated to this programme in December 2006 (CAD 18 million). On a much smaller scale, an interesting initiative has been launched in Portugal by the Gulbenkian Foundation and developed in cooperation with an NGO supporting immigrants, a Higher Education Nursery School, and a major Portuguese social solidarity institution. Its objective consists in assisting immigrant nurses legally working in Portugal in undifferentiated occupations, to obtain the equivalence of their educational and professional diplomas and skills so that they can work in Portugal as nurses.

The United Kingdom has implemented special programmes to support refugees and overseas qualified health professionals who are settled in the United Kingdom and wish to return to work in the health sector (*www.rose.nhs.uk*). Available estimates count at least 900 refugees and asylum seeker doctors in 2005, with only about 150 currently employed (Butler *et al.*, 2005). These programmes aim at assisting refugee doctors to pass PLAB or Clinical tests or offer bridging courses for nurses. Many similar initiatives exist in other OECD countries, for instance in the United States (*e.g.* the Welcome Back Initiative in California or Chicago Bilingual Nurse Consortium educational programmes for nurses in Chicago)

3.C. *Employment conditions of the immigrant health workforce*

The point has already been made that working conditions of migrant health workers can be, in some cases, less favourable than for their native-trained counterparts. In this perspective, it is often argued that foreign doctors and nurses play a key role in assuring the continuity of service, notably working on night and weekend shifts or in emergency care.

Based on Labour Force Survey data for European countries in 2005, Table III.6 presents data on the working conditions of doctors and nurses by place of birth. For EU15 countries as a whole, it shows that immigrant health professionals work longer hours. This is especially true for foreign nurses: Over 13% work more than 40 hours a week as compared to 7.7% for native born. But it is for nightshift work that the differences are the most striking, with twice as many foreign-born nurses and doctors reporting that they work regularly at night. The differences are also large for Sunday work. The specificity disappears, however, when differentiating the two groups by type of job contract (permanent/temporary).

One possible explanation of these results could be the fact that a number of immigrant doctors are pursuing professional training in host countries and thus have employment conditions which generally are similar to those of (native-born) junior doctors. Another explanation, notably for nurses, could be that foreign-born nurses ask for overtime work or night shifts to earn extra money to remit home to their families. Whatever is the case,

Table III.6. **Employment conditions of health professionals in selected European countries by country of birth, 2005**

Percentages

		Nurses (ISCO 223 + 323)		Health professionals, except nurses (ISCO 222)	
		EU27	EU15	EU27	EU15
Percentage of employees working more than 41 hours a week	**Native-born**	8.5	7.7	40.2	42.9
	Foreign-born	13.6	13.3	48.7	49.8
Percentage of employees working at night regularly	**Native-born**	26.3	26.6	10.8	12.1
	Foreign-born	40.4	41.0	20.9	22.1
Percentage of employees who usually work on Sundays	**Native-born**	35.4	39.4	10.4	11.2
	Foreign-born	47.0	48.1	14.6	15.3
Percentage of salaried employees with a permanent contract	**Native-born**	90.4	90.0	80.1	78.2
	Foreign-born	91.3	90.6	72.6	71.4

Source: European Union Labour Force Survey, 2005, authors' calculations.

StatLink 🔗 *http://dx.doi.org/10.1787/022733271412*

these data provide eloquent testimony to the key role that immigrants now play in health service delivery in a number of OECD countries, including in Europe.

In the context of increasing cultural diversity in host societies, due to rising migration and diversification of origin countries, foreign-born health professionals are more and more considered as an asset to deliver adapted health care services to the migrant community (see *National Standards for Culturally and Linguistically Appropriate Services in Health Care* in the case of the United States or in the European context *The Amsterdam Declaration Towards Migrant-Friendly Hospitals in an ethno-culturally diverse Europe*). This is, however, not always without raising difficulties, notably when immigrant doctors or nurses have to assume tasks for which they are not qualified or paid (*e.g.* translation, mediation with the community...) (Hawthorne *et al.*, 2000).

Conclusion

On average, 11% of employed nurses and 18% of employed doctors in the OECD were foreign-born Circa 2000; there are large variations in the size of the foreign-born health workforce across OECD countries, partly reflecting general migration patterns, notably of the highly skilled. As a result, despite specific concerns related to health worker migration, the latter, as a sub-set of highly skilled migration, can not be looked at in isolation.

While there is a legitimate concern about the consequences of migration on origin countries, especially for lower income countries, the results presented in this chapter show that the global health workforce crisis goes far beyond the migration issue. In particular, the health sector needs for human resources in developing countries, as estimated by the WHO at the regional level, largely exceed the numbers of immigrant health workers in the OECD, implying that international migration is neither the main cause nor would its reduction be the solution to the worldwide health human resources crisis.

However, two key qualifying arguments should be taken into consideration. The first relates to the fact that international migration contributes to exacerbate the acuteness of the problems in some particular countries. This is the case, for instance, in Caribbean countries and a number of African countries, notably Portuguese and French-speaking, but also Sierra Leone, Tanzania and Liberia and to a lesser extent Malawi. Even in these cases, however, international migration of health workers may be more a symptom than a determinant.

Second, since 2000, migration flows of health professionals have increased. If they seem to have mainly affected the main source countries like Philippines and India, they have also involved some African countries as well as central and eastern European countries. Clearly, the rate of growth recorded over the past 5 years or so would not be sustainable for the health systems in some developing countries.

It is important to emphasise that there are very few specific migration programmes targeting health professionals in OECD countries. Furthermore, bilateral agreements seem not to play an important role so far. In this context, because some origin countries nevertheless suffer some depletion of their workforce through migration, the short-term question may become "should receiving countries explicitly exclude health professionals from international recruitments of the highly skilled in order to avoid potential perverse impacts on the health systems of developing countries"? Would it be efficient? Would it be fair?

In the long run, it is probably necessary to pose the question slightly differently and to recognise that active international recruitment is a quick fix and/or a distraction from other home-built solutions to health resources management such as increasing domestic training capacity, improving retention, developing skill mix and co-ordinated care, and increasing productivity.

There is certainly not a unique or unilateral response to the challenges posed by international mobility of health care workers but data are now available to monitor the trends more closely and sound policy proposals to better share the benefits of the international mobility of the health workers, while insuring individual rights to move, have been made (*e.g.* WHO, 2006a; Stilwell *et al.*, 2004; Buchan and Dovlo, 2004; Dumont and Meyer, 2004; JLI, 2004; Martinez and Martineau, 2002). Some of these proposals are already implemented. What is needed now is to scale the best initiatives up and to raise the attention and commitments of all stakeholders, including origin countries, receiving countries and migrants themselves. In this perspective, the increasing trends in Official Development Assistance to health (OECD, 2007) and the current efforts devoted by the WHO to develop a global code of practice for the international recruitment of health workers go in the right direction. However, they would need to be accompanied by measures to reinforce training capacity and to improve the management of health human resources, which is already the case in some of the OECD countries.

Notes

1. The *Joint Learning Initiative on Human Resources for Health and Development* (JLI) was launched in November 2002 in recognition of the centrality of the workforce for global health. As a follow up, the *Global Health Workforce Alliance* (GHWA) has been created recently. GHWA is a partnership hosted and administered by the WHO. Another related initiative was founded by Mary Robinson: *Realizing Rights: The Ethical Globalization Initiative*. It aims at addressing five urgent issues required for greater human development and security, including the international mobility of health workers. Finally, the Commonwealth Secretariat has been very active in this field. It has developed an international code of practice for the international recruitment of health workers.

2. This chapter focuses exclusively on international migration of health workers. It does not address other important aspects of the management of the health workforce, such as education and training policies, skill-mix policies or retention policies. The OECD plans to analyse these additional aspects in further work on the health workforce.

3. When population censuses were not available, either population register data were used (Sweden, Finland, Denmark) or in some cases Labour Force Survey data (Belgium, the Netherlands, Norway and Germany). For Germany, the available dataset does not allow one to identify some specific countries of birth (it also includes a significant number of cases where the place of birth could not be identified). In addition, a number of OECD countries could not be included in the analysis because of lack of data (Iceland, Italy, Japan, Korea, the Czech Republic and the Slovak Republic).

4. A similar approach has been adopted by Clemens and Petterson (2006) focusing on health professionals born in African countries. Their study covers 8 OECD countries (Australia, United Kingdom, United States, Canada, Portugal, Spain, France and Belgium) and South Africa. Lowell and Gerova (2004) also use Population Census data to identify foreign-born health professionals or associate professionals by detailed occupations in the United States.

5. Firstly, data refer to people born abroad and not to people trained overseas but they are completed by additional information based on professional registers by place of training. Secondly, population census data do not allow us to control for nationality at birth in all OECD countries, and thus some people may be incorrectly identified as immigrants based on their place of birth (repatriates or children of expatriates). Finally, data refer to people employed as health professionals and not to people who were trained as health professionals. Difficulties over the recognition of foreign medical qualifications in receiving countries can give rise to a significant gap between the former and the latter.

6. According to the French Employment Survey, 55.6% of the persons born in Algeria with tertiary education and employed in 2005 were repatriates (born in Algeria with French nationality at birth). Applying this ratio to the 10 500 Algerian-born doctors and the 8 200 Algerian-born nurses would reduce the percentage of foreign-born doctors in France by about 3 percentage points – to 14% – and that of nurses by 1 percentage point – to 4.4%.

7. Docquier and Bhargawa (2006) built a database on general practitioners in 16 OECD countries for the period 1991-2004 by place of training to estimate the impact of medical "brain drain" on HIV mortality in sub-Saharan Africa (Barghawa and Docquier, 2006). This pioneer work, after that of Meija in the 70's, is a breakthrough. The database, however, has some severe limitations due to the availability of data and the heterogeneity of sources and definitions. Except for the United States, a significant share of the data has been interpolated casting doubts on the reliability of the figures for origin countries which are not prominent in US immigration.

8. In Belgium, until recently, there were important movements of foreign students from neighbouring countries, notably France, into medical schools and other health education institutions to avoid the numerical caps in their origin country. These possibilities have been reduced recently.

9. Almost all immigrant doctors must go through the US examination system and do their professional training – residency – in the United States

10. In the United States, a significant share (around 15%) of the foreign-trained doctors in fact comprises US citizens trained abroad, mostly in the Caribbean. These off-shore universities are mainly targeting the United States. This temporary migration of US citizens allows them to get round policies aimed at limiting the number of places in medical schools in the United States. Over the past decade, while the number of graduates has remained stable, the number of residency places has increased, and the gap is filled by foreign-trained doctors, increasingly US foreign-trained doctors.

11. On average, Asia is the main region of origin accounting for 42% of foreign-born doctors and 31% of nurses. These percentages are more important than for highly skilled in general (about 30%).

12. The migration of health professionals from Canada to the United States has attracted a lot of attention in the literature. Of the doctors who are leaving Canada, about half choose to go to the United States. The Canada Institute for Health Information, however, reports that over the past 5 years the number of doctors moving abroad has decreased (from 420 doctors in 2000 to 262 in 2004), while the number of returnees has increased. In 2004, Canada experienced a small net positive gain (CIHI, 2005). This is a noticeable change compared to what was observed in the 90s (Barer and Webber, 2000).

13. In the case of Africa, see WHO (2004a), Hagopian et al. (2004), Dolvo and Martineau (2004) and Clemens and Pettersson (2006), Clemens (2007), Connell et al. (2007). For the Pacific region see WHO (2004b). For South-East Asia see Adkoli (2006). For specific country case studies, see for instance Wibulpolprasert et al. (2004) for Thailand, Dumont and Meyer (2004) for South Africa, ILO (2005) or Ronquillo et al. (2005) for the Philippines, Chikanda (2004) for Zimbabwe, Mensah et al. (2005) or Buchan and Dovlo (2004) for Ghana, Badr (2005) for Sudan, Record and Mohiddin (2006) for Malawi.

14. For the former USSR, migration to Germany and to Israel is not taken into account, although large flows have been recorded over the past decades. It is estimated, for instance, that between 1989 and 1995 more than 14 000 physicians from the former Soviet Union emigrated to Israel (Borow, 2007). There are also about 10 000 *Aussiedler* from the former USSR who were employed as a doctors in Germany in 2002 and probably as many persons who entered with a different status (although not identifiable in the German microcensus).

15. It is not clear, however, if the importance of Filipino doctors in OECD countries, mainly in the United States, results from recent or older migration waves. In any case, a recent matter of concern in the Philippines is related to the increase in doctors retraining as nurses to emigrate ("*nursing medics*"). At least 45 Filipino nursing schools offer short courses for doctors to retrain as nurses.

16. For African countries, migration of health workers to South Africa is also supposed to be important, however not accounted for in our figures. According to Clemens and Pettersson (2006) there would be less than 1 500 foreign-born doctors from Africa in South Africa and about 200 nurses. This represents less than 5% of all the sub-Saharan-born doctors in OECD countries.

17. Emigration rates are computed as follows: X_i = number of foreign-born doctors (nurses) working in OECD countries born in country i; Y_i = number of doctors (nurses) working in country i (source WHO Global Health Atlas 1995-2004 average); *emigration rate* = $X_i/(X_i + Y_i)$. Countries with under 50 nurses or with less than 10 nurses abroad have been dropped. (10 and 5 respectively for doctors).

18. Fiji has strong links with two OECD countries, Australia and New Zealand. Emigration as whole is important, and particularly for the highly skilled. Fijians nurses also emigrate, mainly temporarily, to the Middle East and to neighbouring Pacific countries. It seems that Fiji could move towards a situation like the one which prevails in the Philippines where nurses are trained to go overseas. Emigration of doctors seems to be more of a problem, partly compensated by inflows from the Philippines, Burma and China (Connell, 2006).

19. Sierra Leone and Tanzania were the two poorest in 2000, with about 500 dollars per inhabitant (GDP PPP, World Development indicators World Bank). Angola had an higher GDP per capita because of its natural resources (about 1 800 dollars per inhabitant in 2000) but suffered from a civil war for 27 years. To some extent, the result may be inflated for Angola and Mozambique which are overrepresented in Portugal because the repatriates cannot be identified in the population census (in Portugal there are 1 457 doctors born in Angola and 884 born in Mozambique out of 1 512 and 935 foreign-born doctors, respectively).

20. Some countries like South Africa, Kenya, Ghana and Côte d'Ivoire experience a paradoxical situation as they simultaneously have difficulties to fill vacancies and have unemployed health workers. In these countries, a better allocation of resources and targeted incentives could contribute to address, to a certain extent, this situation by making the health sector more attractive particularly in rural areas where poor working conditions, lack of professional perspectives, and safety are often major issues and a serious deterrent for health workers to take a position there. (see Buchan and Dovlo, 2004; Zurn *et al.*, 2002; Dumont and Meyer, 2004)

21. The shortage is calculated on a needs-based approach which sets at 2.28‰ health workers (doctors, nurses and midwifes) per 1 000 population, the threshold under which, on average, countries fail to achieve an 80% coverage rate for deliveries by skilled birth attendants.

22. The WHO regional classification distinguishes: African Region, South-East Asia Region, West Pacific Region, East Mediterranean Region, European Region and the American Region.

23. In 1998, a passing score on ECFMG Clinical Skill Assessment was added to the requirements which induced a significant drop in the number of certificates granted in 1999 (Boulet *et al.*, 2006).

24. The peak in the UK figure for registration of foreign doctors in 2003 can be explained by the fact that the regulation has changed for some origin countries. As a consequence, several thousand doctors secured UK registration even though they had not immediate intention of emigrating to the United Kingdom.

25. To this total, we should add persons entering through the Highly Skilled Migrant Programme (17 631 persons in 2005 of which 33% with a medical occupation mainly doctors – although they are not necessarily employed), as well as the nationals of EU15 and EU10 countries. In total, the figure might be close to or even exceed the number of registrations.

26. H1-B visas are regulated through a quota system. The numerical limit cannot be lower than 65 000. It was raised to 115 000 in 1999 and to 195 000 in 2001. The quota went back to 65 000 as of October 2003, although important exemptions to the quota system have been introduced and still remain.

27. J-1 visas also play a key role for international medical graduates completing their graduate medical education in the United States (see infra).

28. In Italy, nurses are excluded from the annual work permit quota since 2002 (Chaloff, 2006).

29. In the United States, there have been several specific programmes for foreign nurses in the past but they are now terminated. H-1A visa was created through the Nursing Relief Act of 1989 but ended in September 1995. In 1999, the H-1C category was created through the Nursing Relief for Disadvantaged Area Act of 1999. It allowed for an annual quota of 500 registered nurses who could work for up to 3 years in the United States. This programme was terminated in September 2004. Since then, there is no specific programmes for nurses or doctors, except the J1 Waiver programme.

30. Federal agencies are not statutorily limited in the number of waivers that may be granted in response to their requests each year

31. In the United Kingdom, as a result of public consultations for both nursing (November 2003) and midwifery (October 2005) and evidence collected by the British Council, the Nursing and Midwifery Council decided that from the February 2007 a score of IELTS 7 was the lowest level acceptable for language skills (previously 6.5). In New Zealand, the minimum level was also raised recently. The required pass level is a score of not less than 7 in each of the four sections of IELTS. In Australia, the general score should not be less than 7 and each section not less than 6.5.

32. Based on Australian Medical Council (AMC) data, Hawthorne et al. (2006) analyse the pass rate of foreign-trained doctors to the written and clinical exams. It appears that about 80% of those taking the AMC written examination (MCQ) will eventually pass it (51% at first attempt), and that 86% of those taking the clinical exam (CE) passed it, but only 53% of those presenting the first exam took the clinical exam over the period 1978-2005. Length of time between obtaining the medical qualification and sitting the MCQ for the first time and passing the CE were important determinants of passing rates. Region of origin and mother tongue were also key determinants.

33. Bach (2003) reports a set of similar examples in different contexts.

Bibliography

ADKOLI, B.V. (2006), "Migration of health workers: Perspectives from Bangladesh, India, Nepal, Pakistan and Sri Lanka", Regional Health Forum, Vol. 10, No. 1.

ALKEN, L., BUCHAN, J., SOCHALSKI, J., NICHOLS, B. and M. POWEL (2004), "Trends in International Nurse Migration", Health Affairs, Vol. 23, No. 3.

ALLAN, H. and J. LARSEN (2003), "We Need Respect": Experiences of internationally Recruited Nurses in the UK. Presented to the Royal College of Nursing.

AMERICAN MEDICAL ASSOCIATION – AMA (2006), International Medical Graduates in the US Workforce: A Discussion Paper, AMA-IMG Workforce Discussion Paper 2006.

BACH, S. (2003), International Migration of Health Workers: Labour and Social Issues, Working Paper 209, ILO.

BACH, S. (2006), International Mobility of Health Professionals – Brain Drain or Brain Exchange? Research Paper No. 2006/82, UNU-WIDER.

BADR, E. (2005), Brain Drain of Health Professionals in Sudan: Magnitude, Challenges and Prospects for Solution, Mimeo, MA Health Management Planning and Policy.

BARER, M.L. and W. WEBBER (2000), "The great Canadian physician exodus?", Issue Brief, ISUMA, Automn.

BHARGAVA, A. and F. DOCQUIER (2006), HIV Pandemic, Medical Brain Drain and Economic Development in Sub-Saharan Africa. Working Paper, Center for Health Policy, Research in Progress Seminar.

BOROW, M. (2007), The Migration of Physicians: The Israeli Experience, Israeli Medical Association.

BOULET, J., J. NORCINI, G. WHELAN, J. ALLOCK and S. SEELING (2006), "The international medical graduate pipeline: Recent trends in certification and residency training", Health Affairs, Vol. 25, No. 2.

BOURASSA FORCIER, M., S. SIMOENS and A. GIUFFRIDA (2004), "Impact, regulation and health policy implications of physician migration in OECD countries", Human resources for Health, Vol. 2, No. 12.

BOURASSA-FORCIER, M. and A. GUIFFRIDA (2002), International Migration of Physicians and Nurses: Causes, Consequences and Health Policy Implications, Working Paper, DELSA, Health Policy Unit, OECD.

BUCHAN, J. and D. DOVLO (2004), International Recruitment of Health Workers to the UK, A Report for DFID.

BUCHAN, J. and I. SECCOMBE (2006), *Worlds Apart? The UK and International Nurses*. Presented to the Royal College of Nursing.

BUCHAN, J. and L. CALMAN (2004), The Global Shortage of Registered Nurses: An Overview of Issues and Actions, International Council of Nurses.

BUCHAN, J., T. PARKIN and J. SOCHALSKI (2003), *International Nurse Mobility*, Working Paper WHO/EIP/OSD/2003.3, World Health Organization.

BUTLER, C. and J. EVERSLEY (2005), *More Than You Think: Refugee Doctors in London, their Numbers and Success in Getting Jobs*, Refugee Doctor Programme Evaluation Network (UK).

CANADIAN INSTITUTE FOR HEALTH INFORMATION (2005), *Supply, Distribution and Migration of Canadian Physicians 2004*.

CHALOFF, J. (2006), *Mismatches in the Formal Sector, Expansion of the Informal Sector: Immigration of Health Professionals to Italy*, CeSPI, Rome.

CHAN XH. and T. WLIJI (2006), *Global Pharmacy Workforce and Migration Report: A Call for Action*, International Pharmaceutical Federation.

CHANDA, R. (2002), "Trade in Health Services", *Bulletin of the World Health Organization 2002*, Vol. 80, No. 2.

CHIKANDA, A. (2004), *Skilled Health Professionals' Migration and its Impact on Health Delivery in Zimbabwe*, Working Paper 04-04, COMPAS.

CLEMENS, M. (2007), *Do Visas Kill? Health Effects of African Health Professional Emigration*, Working Paper No. 114, Center for Global Development.

CLEMENS, M. and G. PETTERSSON (2006), *A New Database on Health Professional Emigration from Africa*, Working Paper No. 95, Center for Global Development.

CONNELL, J. (2006) "Migration, Dependency and Inequality in the Pacific: Old Wine in Bigger Bottles?" in *Globalisation and Governance in the Pacific Islands*, (Part 1).

CONNELL, J., P. ZURN, B. STILWELL, M. AWASES and J-M. BRAICHET (2007), "Sub-Saharan Africa: Beyond the health worker migration crisis?", *Social Science and Medicine*.

DAL POZ, M., E. QUAIN, M. O'NEIL, J. McCAFFERY, G. ELZINGA and T. MARTINEAU (2006), "Adressing the health workforce crisis: Towards a common approach", *Human Resources for Health 2006*, Vol. 4, No. 21.

DAVENPORT, M., J. BUCHAN, B. KERSHAM and O. MUNJANJA (2005), *A Managed Temporary Migration Scheme for Nurses from Eastern Africa to the European Union*, Draft Report for the Commonwealth and COMSA Secretariats.

DEPARTMENT OF HEALTH (2004), *Code of Practice for NHS Employers*, United Kingdom.

DEPARTMENT OF HEALTH (2004), *Code of Practice for the International Recruitment of Healthcare Professionals*, United Kingdom.

DIALLO, K. (2004), "Data on the migration of health-care workers: Sources, uses, and challenges", *Bulletin of the World Health Organisation*, Vol. 82, No. 8.

DOBSON, J. and SALT, J. (2006), "Foreign recruitment in health and social care: Recent experience reviewed", *International Journal of Migration, Health and Social Leave*.

DOCQUIER, F. and BHARGAVA, A. (2006), *A New Panel Data Set on Physicians' Emigration Rates (1991-2004)* (Preliminary version), Mimeo.

DOLVIK, J.E. and L. ELDRING (2006), *The Nordic Labour Market Two Years after the EU Enlargment*, TemaNord 2006:558.

DOVLO, D. and T. MARTINEAU (2004), *A Review of the Migration of Africa's Health Professionals*, JLI Working Paper 4-4.

DOYLE, N., G. HUGHES and E. WADENSJO (2006), *Freedom of Movement for Workers from Central and Eastern Europe*, SIEPS.

DUMONT, JC. and JB. MEYER (2004), "The international mobility of health professionals: An evaluation and analysis based on the case of South Africa" in *Trends in International Migration*, SOPEMI Edition 2003, OECD Paris.

DUMONT, JC. and G. LEMAITRE (2005), "Counting immigrants and expatriates in OECD countries: A new perspective" in *Trends in International Migration*, SOPEMI Edition 2004, OECD Paris.

EUROPEAN MIGRATION NETWORK (ENM) (2006), *Synthesis Report and National Reports* (Austria, Belgium, Estonia, Germany, Greece, Ireland, Italy, Latvia, Sweden, the Netherlands and the United Kingdom), *www.european-migration-network.org*.

GAO (2006), *Foreign Physicians: Data on Use of J-1 Visa Waivers Needed to Better Address Physician Shortages*, GAO-07-52, United States Government Accountability Office.

GENERAL MEDICAL COUNCIL (2007), *PLAB Survey – A Survey among June-October 2005 PLAB-Pass Doctors*.

GYIMAH-BREMPONG, K. and M. WILSON (2004), "Health human capital and economic growth in Sub-Saharan African and OECD countries", *The Quarterly Review of Economics and Finance*, Vol. 44.

HAGOPIAN, A., M. THOMPSON, E. KALTENBACH and G. HART (2003), "Health Departments' use of international medical graduates in physician shortage areas", *Health Affairs*, Vol. 22, No. 5.

HAGOPIAN, A., M. THOMPSON, M. FORDYCE, K. JOHNSON and G. HART (2004), "The migration of physicians from sub-Saharan Africa to the United States of America: Measures of the African 'brain drain'", *Human Resources for Health*, Vol. 2, No. 17.

HAWTHORNE, L. (2001), "The globalization of the nursing workforce: Barriers confronting overseas qualified nurses in Australia", *Nursing Inquiry 2001*, Vol. 8, No. 4.

HAWTHORNE, L., G. HAWTHORNE and B. CROTTY (2006), *The Registration and Training Status of Overseas Trained Doctors in Australia*, Faculty of Medicine, Dentistry and Health Sciences, The University of Melbourne.

HAWTHORNE, L., J. TOTH and G. HAWTHORNE (2000), "Patient demand for bilingual bicultural nurses in Australia", *Journal of Intercultural Studies*, Vol. 21, No. 2.

HAWTHORNE, L., with B. BIRRELL and D. YOUNG (2003), *The Retention of Overseas Trained Doctors in General Practices in Regional Victoria*, Rural Workforce Agency Victoria, Melbourne.

HOME OFFICE (2007), *Accession Monitoring Report*, May 2004-December 2006.

ILO (2005), *Migration of Health Workers: Country Case Study Philippines*, Working Paper No. 236.

IOM (2006), "Migration and Human Resources for Health: From Awareness to Action", *International Dialogue on Migration*, No. 9.

JOINT LEARNING INITIATIVE – JLI (2004), *Human Resources for Health: Overcoming the Crisis*, Harvard University Press.

KACZMARCZYK, P. (2006), *Highly Skilled Migration from Poland and Other OECD Countries – Myths and Reality*, Reports and Analyses 17/06, Center for International Relations.

KANGASNIEMI, M., A. WINTERS and S. COMMANDER (2004), *Is the Medical Brain Drain Beneficial? Evidence from Overseas Doctors in the UK*, London School of Economics and Political Science, Centre for Economic Performance.

LABONTE, R., C. PACKER and N. KLASSEN (2006), "Managing health professional migration from sub-Saharan Africa to Canada: A stakeholder inquiry into policy options", *Human Resources for Health 2006*, Vol. 4, No. 22.

LEBOLD, M. and C. WALSH (2006), "Innovations in health care delivery: Response to global nurse migration – An education example", *Policy, Politics and Nursing Practice*, Supplement to Vol. 7, No. 3.

LEVINE, L. (2003), *Education and Training Funded by the H-1B Visa Fee and the Demand for Information Technology and Other Professional Specialty Workers*, Congressional Research Service, The Library of Congress.

LOWELL, L. and S. GEROVA (2004), "Immigrants and the health workforce", *Work and Occupations*, Vol. 34.

MARTINEAU, T. and A. WILLETTS (2006), "The health workforce: Managing the crisis ethical international recruitment of health professionals: Will codes of practice protect developing country health systems?", *Health Policy*, Vol. 75.

MARTINEZ, J. and T. MARTINEAU (2002), *Human Resources in the Health Sector: An International Perspective*, DFID Health Systems Resource Centre.

McINTOSH, T., R. TORGESON and N. KLASSEN (2007), *The Ethical Recruitment of Internationally Educated Health Professionals: Lessons from Abroad and Options for Canada*, Research Report H/11, Health Network.

MEDICAL COUNCIL OF NEW ZEALAND -MCNZ (2000), *The New Zealand Medical Workforce in 2000*.

MEIJA A., PIZURKI and E. ROYSTON (1979), *Physician and nurse migration: Analysis and policy implications*, World Health Organization, Geneva.

MENSAH, K., M. MACKINTOSH and H. LEROI (2005), The "Skills Drain" of Health Professionals from the Developing World: A Framework for Policy Formulation, Working Paper, MEDACT, London, United Kingdom.

MERÇAY, C. (2006), *L'immigration des infirmières en Suisse – Le recrutement dans le milieu hospitalier de 1970 à nos jours*, Mémoire de Licence, Université de Neuchatel.

MULLAN, F. (2004), *Filling the Gaps: International Medical Graduates in the United States, the United Kingdom, Canada and Australia*, Working Paper prepared for The 8th International Medical Workforce Conference, Washington DC, 6-9 October 2004.

MULLAN, F. (2005), "The metrics of the physician 'brain drain'", *The New England Journal of Medicine*, Massachusetts Medical Society.

MULLAN, F. (2006), "Doctors for the World: Indian physician emigration", *Health Affairs*, Vol. 25, No. 2.

OECD (2003), *Factors Shaping the Medical Workforce*, SG/ADHOC/HEA(2003)6, Ad Hoc Group on the OECD Health Project.

OECD (2007), *Recent Trends in Official Development Assistance to Health*, OECD Development Assistance Committee.

ORDRE NATIONAL DES MÉDECINS (2006), *Étude de la problématique des PADHUE*, 28 avril.

PANG, T., M.A. LANSANG and A. HAINES (2002), "Brain drain and health professionals", *BMJ*, Vol. 324, March.

RAGHURAM, P. and E. KOFMAN (2002), "The state, skilled labour markets, and immigration: The case of doctors in England", *Environment and Planning A*, Vol. 34.

RECORD, R. and A. MOHIDDIN (2006), "An economic perspective on Malawi's medical 'brain drain'", *Globalization and Health*, Vol. 2, No. 12.

RONQUILLO, K, F.M. ELEGADO-LORENZO and R. NODORA (2005), Human Resources for Health, Working Paper for Asian Learning Network for Human Resources for Health, Bangkok, Thailand.

ROWE, A. and M. GARCIA-BARBERO (2005), *Regulation and Licensing of Physicians in the WHO European Region*, WHO Regional Office for Europe.

SACHS, J. (chaired by) (2001), *Macroeconomics and Health, Investing in Health for Economic Development*, World Health Organization.

SHELDON, G. (2006), "Globalization and the health workforce shortage", *Surgery*, Vol. 140, No. 3, September.

SIMOENS, S. and J. HURST (2006), *The Supply of Physician Services in OECD Countries*, OECD Health Working Papers, DELSA/HEA/WD/HWP(2006)1.

SIMOENS, S., M. VILLENEUVE and J. HURST (2005), *Tackling Nurse Shortages in OECD Countries*, OECD Health Working Papers, DELSA/ELSA/WD/HEA(2005)1.

SKELDON, R. (2005), *Globalisation, Skilled Migration and Poverty Alleviation: Brain Drains in Context*. Issued by the Development Research centre on Migration, Globalisation and Poverty.

STILWELL, B., K. DIALLO, P. ZURN, M. DAL POZ, O. ADAM and J. BUCHAN (2003), "Developing evidence-based ethical policies on the migration of health workers: Conceptual and practical challenges", *Human Resources for Health*, Vol. 1, No. 8.

US DEPARTMENT OF HEALTH AND HUMAN SERVICES (2001), *National Standards for Culurally and Linguistically – Appropriate Services in Health Care*, Office of Minority Health, Washington D.C.

US DEPARTMENT OF HEALTH AND HUMAN SERVICES (2001), National Standards for Culturally and Linguistically Appropriate Services in Health Care, *http://omhrc.gov/omh/programs/2pgprograms/finalreport.pdf*.

US IMMIGRATION AND NATURALIZATION SERVICE (2002, 2004, 2006), *Report on Characteristics of Specialty Occupation Workers – H1B*.

VORK, A., PRIINITS, M. and E. KALLASTE (2004), *Migration of Healthcare Workers from Estonia*, PRAXIS Centre for Policy Studies.

VUJICIC, M., P. ZURN, K. DIALLO, O. ADAMS and M. DAL POZ (2004), "The role of wages in the migration of health care professionals from developing countries", Human Resources for Health, Vol. 2, No. 3.

WHELAN, G., N. GARY, J. KOSTIS, J. BOULET and J. HALLOCK (2002), "The changing pool of international medical graduates seeking certification training in US graduate medical education programs", *The Journal of the Medical Association (JAMA)*, September 4, Vol. 288, No. 9.

WIBULPOLPRASERT, S., C. PACHANEE, S. PITAYARANGSARIT and P. HEMPISUT (2004), "International service trade and its implications for human resources for health: A case study of Thailand", *Human Resources for Health*, Vol. 2, No. 10.

WISKOW, C. (2006), *Health Worker Migration Flows in Europe: Overview and Case Studies in Selected CEE Countries (Romania, the Czech Republic, Serbia and Croatia)*, Working Paper No. 45, ILO.

WOODMAN, J. (2007), *Patients Beyond Borders*, Healthy Travel Media.

WORLD BANK (2006), *Quarterly Economic Report, Part II: Special Topic*, World Bank EU8.

WORLD FEDERATION FOR MEDICAL EDUCATION – WFME (2005), *Statement on the Bologna Process and Medical Education*, WFME.

WORLD HEALTH ORGANIZATION (2004a), *Migration of Health Professionals in Six Countries: A Synthesis Report*, WHO Regional Office for Africa.

WORLD HEALTH ORGANIZATION (2004b), *The Migration of Skilled Health Personnel in the Pacific Region: A Summary Report*.

WORLD HEALTH ORGANIZATION (2006), *Human Resources for Health in the WHO European Region*, WHO Regional Office for Europe.

WORLD HEALTH ORGANIZATION (2006), *Working Together for Health*, The World Health Report 2006.

ZURN, P., M. DAL POZ, B. STILWELL and O. ADAMS (2002), *Imbalances in the Health Workforce*, Briefing Paper, World Health Organization.

ANNEX III.A1

Origin-destination of Immigrant Health Professionals in OECD Countries, Circa 2000

Table III.A1.1. **Distribution of foreign-born doctors by countries of origin in selected OECD countries**

Percentages

	OECD	Europe non-OECD	North Africa	Other Africa	Asia non-OECD	Latin America non-OECD	Oceania non-OECD	Total**	EU15	EU12 (A10, BUL, ROM)
AUS	41.2	3.0	2.7	8.1	42.5	0.7	1.7	100	29.6	4.4
AUT	65.1	15.0	2.1	0.7	16.6	0.6	–	100	37.4	27.8
CAN	40.5	4.2	4.1	12.1	32.5	6.5	0.1	100	25.5	7.8
CHE	72.4	11.0	2.8	2.3	7.3	4.2	–	100	55.6	14.0
DNK	55.3	14.3	2.0	2.8	23.3	2.3	–	100	30.0	14.6
ESP	23.8	2.4	8.5	1.7	8.7	55.0	–	100	16.7	1.2
FIN	38.3	43.5	3.5	2.6	10.4	1.7	–	100	26.1	13.9
FRA	14.1	1.7	53.8	11.3	16.7	2.4	–	100	11.4	1.9
GBR	20.0	2.3	3.6	16.9	54.9	2.2	0.1	100	13.6	2.6
GRC	37.4	36.2	9.1	4.8	11.4	0.9	–	100	17.8	20.1
HUN	10.4	75.4	0.3	2.9	10.2	0.8	–	100	3.7	58.4
IRL	45.1	0.4	–	6.5	48.1	–	–	100	38.1	0.4
LUX	79.7	2.3	2.6	5.6	8.6	1.1	–	100	74.8	3.4
MEX	27.1	0.8	0.2	0.4	1.8	69.6	–	100	8.9	0.9
NZL	50.4	1.7	0.9	15.9	27.3	0.6	3.3	100	40.2	0.3
POL	8.0	74.9	1.2	2.8	12.6	0.5	0.1	100	5.8	18.9
PRT	15.3	1.1	0.2	61.4	3.8	18.3	–	100	13.2	0.5
SWE	55.7	15.5	1.0	2.9	21.0	3.9	–	100	31.5	19.9
TUR	46.9	32.1	0.3	–	20.7	–	–	100	41.5	25.9
USA	21.7	4.3	2.3	4.6	51.8	15.2	0.1	100	9.7	4.0
OECD*	**26.7**	**5.6**	**7.2**	**7.8**	**41.6**	**10.8**	**0.2**	100	**16.0**	**5.3**

* Weighted average for the above countries plus Belgium, the Netherlands and Norway for which detailed figures are not significant.
** Excluding unknown and unclassified countries of birth.
– Negligeable.
Source: See Table III.1.

StatLink ⊞⤳ *http://dx.doi.org/10.1787/022583014365*

Table III.A1.2. **Distribution of foreign-born nurses by countries of origin in selected OECD countries**

Percentages

	OECD	Europe non-OECD	North Africa	Other Africa	Asia non-OECD	Latin America non-OECD	Oceania non-OECD	Total**	EU15	EU12 (A10, BUL, ROM)
AUS	63.2	2.6	0.3	4.4	23.6	1.9	4.0	100	47.2	2.5
AUT	48.7	26.9	0.8	0.4	22.6	0.6	–	100	18.7	32.7
CAN	38.4	2.8	0.4	3.9	29.8	24.2	0.4	100	26.0	5.1
CHE	68.1	17.1	1.2	2.6	7.7	3.2	–	100	60.1	4.1
DNK	78.8	3.8	0.6	4.4	10.3	2.0	–	100	39.7	5.7
ESP	39.5	2.7	10.5	3.1	3.3	40.9	–	100	30.9	1.9
FIN	69.1	25.5	–	3.2	1.1	1.1	–	100	62.8	7.4
FRA	22.7	0.8	52.9	15.8	6.5	1.3	–	100	21.0	0.6
GBR	33.4	2.0	0.3	25.4	24.5	14.3	0.1	100	25.4	2.1
GRC	50.6	39.0	1.0	1.8	7.2	0.4	–	100	35.4	16.2
HUN	11.1	87.8	0.1	0.1	0.7	0.1	–	100	3.4	77.7
IRL	66.7	0.4	–	3.6	29.3	–	–	100	58.9	0.3
LUX	88.5	2.9	1.8	4.0	2.1	0.6	–	100	85.3	2.1
MEX	68.1	0.4	–	0.2	2.2	28.8	0.4	100	14.4	–
NZL	64.3	0.7	0.1	7.7	13.3	0.9	13.0	100	51.7	0.7
POL	17.7	79.3	–	0.3	2.7	–	–	100	14.4	21.3
PRT	33.1	0.5	0.1	57.6	1.7	7.0	–	100	31.3	0.2
SWE	69.8	9.2	0.3	2.6	13.5	4.5	–	100	52.1	9.1
USA	26.0	2.2	0.4	6.1	39.8	25.1	0.5	100	11.7	1.7
OECD*	**36.5**	**4.7**	**2.6**	**8.4**	**29.7**	**17.5**	**0.7**	**100**	**15.0**	**53.9**

* Weighted average for the above countries plus Belgium, the Netherlands and Norway for which detailed figures are not significant.
** Excluding unknown and unclassified countries of birth.
– Negligeable.
Source: See Table III.1.

StatLink ⧉ *http://dx.doi.org/10.1787/022583014365*

Table III.A1.3. Foreign-born doctors by country of birth and country of residence in selected OECD countries

Numbers

Country of residence ↓ / Country of birth →	AUS	AUT	BEL	CAN	CHE	CZE	SVK	DEU	DNK	ESP	FIN	FRA	GBR	GRC	HUN	IRL	ISL	ITA	JPN	KOR	LUX	MEX	NLD	NOR	NZL	POL	PRT	SWE	TUR	USA	Total
Australia		74	27	143	45	59	22	409	26	22	17	58	4 587	120	183	329		202	46	96		9	139	4	1 086	378	218	25	55	232	8 409
Austria	4		8	17	70	292	135	1 195	5	12	10	33	19	50	227	2	2		11	8	34	5	20	11		245	1	22	106	63	2 809
Canada	150	110	125		110	135	120	430	45	75	30	410	3 630	105	345	380		180	70	200		65	210	20	115	645	50	55	35	1 350	9 195
Switzerland	17	178	104	51		207	78	2 050	10	107	32	383	85	61	170	4	4	317	10	9	16	21	77	12	4	169	22	42	62	240	4 538
Denmark	2	7	5	20	16	3		190		22	22	14	37	8	13	1	24	12	1	14		3	12	117		105	4	154	16	65	887
Spain	15	14	76	36	142	5	2	459	18		12	496	213	8	3	10	1	99	7	21	3	222	76	15	1	24	61	30	6	168	2 243
Finland		5		5				50	5	5		10	10		10				5					5		20	5	60	10	10	215
France	21	97	646	114	184	47	12	1 611	36	297	16		125	114	40	36	4	562	40	29	92	24	64	4		134	164	9	102	133	4 757
United Kingdom	858	76	166	388	69	126	18	1 775	96	571	44	217		477	89	2 332	16	364	104	29	3	16	442	44	398	282	49	82	103	642	9 876
Greece	39	6	7	15	4	9	1	141	1	2	1	7	6		1			28				1	3		1	19	1	8	98	44	442
Hungary	1	20	1	1	4	15	143	57		1	3	3	2	9				2	2				1			11	1	1	1	8	284
Ireland	24	3	6	33	4			42		9	3	9	780	3				3	3				15	1	6	3		3		96	1 041
Luxembourg	1	1	61	1	3	2		62		7	1	47	4	1	3			9					5			4	2		1	2	212
Mexico	1	5	1	20	7	4		27	4	141		39	6		3			32	25				8			12		1		472	811
New Zealand	186			66				57					1 512	1		51				6			42			12				93	2 025
Poland	3	9		3	39	1	1	99				51	9	12	6				3				17				3	4		9	249
Portugal	3	1	15	24	9	1		85	1	276		166	23	1	1	3		7	3		4	4	17	2		3		4	2	40	696
Sweden	7	44	11	11	22	7	11	532	463	69	547	36	69	77	171	7	128	40	11	29		4	26	266	4	678	15		51	87	3 423
Turkey	9	65	52	13	28	9		1 130	22	33	8	67	98	217	5	4		67	8	3	1		109			39		38		112	2 158
United States	665	475	320	8 985	315			5 270	185	895	90	1 010	4 715	1 150	1 175	870	165	2 090	2 330		10	3 860	505	135	245	2 715	200	440	1 080		39 895
Grand Total*	**2 067**	**1 210**	**2 223**	**9 946**	**1 062**	**987**	**549**	**17 214**	**1 426**	**2 632**	**879**	**3 940**	**16 181**	**2 547**	**2 456**	**4 029**	**4 146**	**2 674**	**444**	**435**	**178**	**4 234**	**2 042**	**712**	**1 904**	**5 742**	**792**	**1 254**	**2 076**	**4 049**	**39 895**

StatLink ᵃᵐˢ http://dx.doi.org/10.1787/02258260324

Note: 973 doctors born in former Czechoslovakia who could not be attributed have been omitted. 8 014 doctors born in the Korean peninsula for whom the distinction between North and Korea was not possible are also omitted. In both cases the figures mainly concern the United States as a receiving country. For Belgium, the Netherlands and Norway as receiving countries, the detailed figures are not reported because they are not significant but are included in the column totals. Data for Germany are not available by detailed countries of birth.
Source: See Table III.1.

INTERNATIONAL MIGRATION OUTLOOK: SOPEMI 2007 EDITION – ISBN 978-92-64-03285-9 – © OECD 2007

Table III.A1.4. Foreign-born nurses by country of birth and country of residence in selected OECD countries

Numbers

Country of birth →

Country of residence ↓	AUS	AUT	BEL	CAN	CHE	CZE	SVK	DEU	DNK	ESP	FIN	FRA	GBR	GRC	HUN	IRL	ISL	ITA	JPN	KOR	LUX	MEX	NLD	NOR	NZL	POL	PRT	SWE	TUR	USA	Total
Australia		156	59	491	95	83	34	1 126	132	96	147	119	16 686	118	97	1 717	10	339	64		4	8	1 102	32	5 443	561	67	97	51	478	29 412
Austria	21		16	14	108	583	512	1 112	4	13	26	39	26	7	220	3	1	136	3	53	5	2	93	8	3	841	3	33	53	18	3 956
Canada	350	125	190		155	145	85	1 275	145	60	205	570	7 010	75	200	460		725	50	320		105	1 340	30	295	1 530	470	75	15	2 695	18 700
Switzerland	34	567	394	454		150	56	4 236	56	331	299	2 331	274	14	79	35		692	10	100	37	18	735	18	12	187	283	115	164	112	11 793
Denmark	16	8	10	43	27	1		240		15	95	29	122	2	6	13	72	5	6	92		5	54	433	5	93	1	327	16	81	1 817
Spain	21	8	101	19	232	6	1	494	17		7	690	203	5	1	12	1	47	5	9	1	72	83	14	1	27	49	26	1	75	2 228
Finland	5			5	5			20	5			5	5												5	5		260		10	325
France	14	93	1 316	103	61	21	8	2 175	65	123	20		61	17	28	62		799	9	58	41	21	17	3	24	24	108	4	9	4	5 261
United Kingdom	2 227	123	154	898	130	92	39	2 776	278	539	588	403		94	65	14 238	12	315	78	50	3	11	519	159	1 283	263	118	276	70	975	26 776
Greece	155	9	33	63	20	100	1	1 199	4	3	3	19	22		18			10				1	24	3	3	133	50	50	38	53	1 964
Hungary	2	8	6	2	2	9	88	33		1	3	3	2										2	1	1	13		1		1	171
Ireland	108	3	188	51	6	2		51	6	30	15	117	3 408		1			6					21	60		6		6		246	4 035
Luxembourg	1	4	2	2	6			128	5	3			5		1	1		23	2	1		1	19			3	58	6	2	2	578
Mexico	1	2	2	8	1			9		44		9	3					9					1							282	373
New Zealand	615	9	6	135	21	6		111	21		6	9	3 291	3	6	186		3	24				309	6		12		12		105	4 929
Poland						12	3	111				15	34	3	6									3	3					6	177
Portugal	5	9	12	31	18	1		177	2	616	1	702	115	2	1			3		130	13	3	15	2	1			7		35	1 681
Sweden	20	50	20	20	15			340	430	35	3 340	30	115	40	100	25	55	25	10		6	10	65	565	5	475	20		55	85	6 080
United States	937	482	248	22 110	285	83	176	12 960	371	722	381	1 370	13 143	424	500	3 128	135	2 245	4 450	1 721	29	12 100	1 246	399	405	2 721	710	646	400		84 363
Grand Total*	4 620	2 041	3 813	24 620	1 315	1 329	1 139	33 983	2 257	3 205	5 596	8 975	45 168	804	1 372	20 166	287	5 866	4 711	2 567	133	12 357	6 092	1 700	7 564	6 999	1 951	3 028	1 260	5 663	84 363

Note: 367 nurses born in former Czechoslovakia who could not be attributed have been omitted. 7 572 nurses born in the Korean peninsula for whom the distinction between North and Korea was not possible are also omitted. In both cases the figures mainly concern the United States as a receiving country. For Belgium, the Netherlands and Norway as receiving countries, the detailed figures are not reported because they are not significant but are included in the column totals. Data for Germany are not available by detailed countries of birth.

Source: See Table III.1.

StatLink ᴍᴬᴾ http://dx.doi.org/10.1787/022582603240

ANNEX III.A2

Expatriation Rates for Doctors and Nurses, Circa 2000

Table III.A2.1. **Expatriation rates for doctors and nurses, Circa 2000**

Country of birth		Nurses		Country of birth		Doctors	
		Number of persons working in OECD countries	Expatriation rate			Number of persons working in OECD countries	Expatriation rate
Albania	ALB	415	3.5	Afghanistan	AFG	613	13.0
Algeria	DZA	8 796	12.4	Albania	ALB	271	6.2
Angola	AGO	1 703	11.5	Algeria	DZA	10 793	23.4
Antigua and Barbuda	ATG	678	74.4	Angola	AGO	1 512	63.2
Argentina	ARG	1 288	4.3	Antigua and Barbuda	ATG	100	89.3
Australia	AUS	4 620	2.6	Argentina	ARG	4 143	3.7
Austria	AUT	2 914	3.7	Australia	AUS	2 067	4.1
Bahamas	BHS	560	29.7	Austria	AUT	1 599	5.5
Bahrain	BHR	77	2.5	Bahamas	BHS	178	36.3
Bangladesh	BGD	651	3.1	Bahrain	BHR	74	8.4
Barbados	BRB	3 496	78.0	Bangladesh	BGD	2 127	5.2
Belgium	BEL	4 125	6.4	Barbados	BRB	275	46.1
Belize	BLZ	1 365	81.8	Belgium	BEL	2 438	5.0
Benin	BEN	166	3.2	Belize	BLZ	76	23.2
Bolivia	BOL	358	1.3	Benin	BEN	215	40.9
Botswana	BWA	47	1.0	Bolivia	BOL	717	6.5
Brazil	BRA	2 258	0.3	Botswana	BWA	33	4.4
Brunei Darussalam	BRN	129	12.6	Brazil	BRA	2 288	1.1
Bulgaria	BGR	789	2.6	Brunei Darussalam	BRN	94	21.9
Burkina Faso	BFA	16	0.3	Bulgaria	BGR	1 856	6.2
Burundi	BDI	57	4.1	Burkina Faso	BFA	65	7.6
Cambodia	KHM	1 119	12.2	Burundi	BDI	71	26.2
Cameroon	CMR	1 338	4.9	Cambodia	KHM	669	24.6
Canada	CAN	24 620	7.4	Cameroon	CMR	572	15.5
Cape Verde	CPV	261	38.9	Canada	CAN	9 946	13.0
Central African Republic	CAF	92	8.4	Cape Verde	CPV	165	41.7
Chad	TCD	117	5.2	Central African Republic	CAF	83	20.0
Chile	CHL	1 965	16.4	Chad	TCD	69	16.7
China	CHN	12 249	0.9	Chile	CHL	863	4.8
Colombia	COL	2 625	9.9	China	CHN	13 391	1.0
Comoros	COM	64	11.7	Colombia	COL	3 885	6.2
Congo	COG	452	12.3	Comoros	COM	20	14.8
Congo, Dem. Rep. Of	COD	404	1.4	Congo	COG	539	41.6
Costa Rica	CRI	562	13.4	Congo, Dem. Rep. Of	COD	350	5.7
Côte d'Ivoire	CIV	337	4.2	Cook Islands	COK	16	53.3

Table III.A2.1. **Expatriation rates for doctors and nurses, Circa 2000** (*Cont.*)

Country of birth		Nurses Number of persons working in OECD countries	Expatriation rate	Country of birth		Doctors Number of persons working in OECD countries	Expatriation rate
Cuba	CUB	4 209	4.8	Costa Rica	CRI	340	6.1
Cyprus	CYP	706	19.1	Côte d'Ivoire	CIV	261	11.1
Denmark	DNK	2 641	4.5	Cuba	CUB	5 911	8.2
Dominica	DMA	620	66.2	Cyprus	CYP	627	25.2
Dominican Republic	DOM	1 857	10.8	Denmark	DNK	1 629	9.4
Ecuador	ECU	1 126	5.4	Djibouti	DJI	25	16.2
Egypt	EGY	1 128	0.8	Dominica	DMA	58	60.4
El Salvador	SLV	2 398	32.0	Dominican Republic	DOM	1 602	9.3
Equatorial Guinea	GNQ	98	31.0	Ecuador	ECU	970	5.0
Eritrea	ERI	548	18.8	Egypt	EGY	7 243	15.8
Ethiopia	ETH	1 421	9.1	El Salvador	SLV	833	9.5
Fiji	FJI	2 025	56.2	Equatorial Guinea	GNQ	78	33.8
Finland	FIN	5 870	7.3	Eritrea	ERI	104	32.6
Former Czechoslovakia	CSFR	2 835		Ethiopia	ETH	633	24.6
Former USSR	F_USSR	10 034		Fiji	FJI	382	58.5
Former Yugoslavia	F_YUG	12 948		Finland	FIN	1 018	5.8
France	FRA	8 589	1.9	Former Czechoslovakia	CSFR	2 509	
Gabon	GAB	106	1.6	Former USSR	F_USSR	11 360	
Gambia	GMB	62	3.7	Former Yugoslavia	F_YUG	3 772	
Germany	DEU	31 623	3.8	France	FRA	4 131	2.0
Ghana	GHA	5 230	24.9	Gabon	GAB	57	12.6
Greece	GRC	1 367	3.1	Gambia	GMB	46	22.8
Grenada	GRD	2 131	87.6	Germany	DEU	17 214	5.8
Guatemala	GTM	1 204	2.6	Ghana	GHA	1 469	31.2
Guinea	GIN	94	2.1	Greece	GRC	2 830	5.6
Guinea-Bissau	GNB	227	18.0	Grenada	GRD	109	72.7
Guyana	GUY	7 450	81.1	Guatemala	GTM	486	4.7
Haiti	HTI	13 001	94.0	Guinea	GIN	99	9.1
Honduras	HND	917	9.9	Guinea-Bissau	GNB	182	49.2
Hungary	HUN	2 117	2.4	Guyana	GUY	949	72.2
Iceland	ISL	287	6.8	Haiti	HTI	2 209	53.1
India	IND	22 786	2.6	Honduras	HND	329	8.2
Indonesia	IDN	3 449	2.7	Hungary	HUN	2 538	7.2
Iran	IRN	4 234	4.8	Iceland	ISL	435	29.2
Iraq	IRQ	415	1.3	India	IND	55 794	8.0
Ireland	IRL	20 166	24.9	Indonesia	IDN	2 773	8.6
Israel	ISR	980	2.4	Iran	IRN	8 991	12.9
Italy	ITA	6 945	2.2	Iraq	IRQ	3 730	18.0
Jamaica	JAM	31 186	87.7	Ireland	IRL	4 029	26.6
Japan	JPN	4 711	0.5	Israel	ISR	2 436	9.0
Jordan	JOR	363	2.0	Italy	ITA	4 386	1.8
Kenya	KEN	2 523	6.4	Jamaica	JAM	2 114	48.4
Kiribati	KIR	19	9.0	Japan	JPN	2 674	1.1
Kuwait	KWT	152	1.6	Jordan	JOR	1 014	8.2
Laos	LAO	867	15.0	Kenya	KEN	2 385	34.6
Lebanon	LBN	1 400	25.2	Kuwait	KWT	465	11.5
Liberia	LBR	1 240	66.9	Laos	LAO	331	10.5
Libya	LBY	100	0.6	Lebanon	LBN	4 552	28.3
Luxembourg	LUX	104	2.4	Lesotho	LSO	7	7.3
Madagascar	MDG	1 157	24.4	Liberia	LBR	122	54.2
Malawi	MWI	200	2.7	Libya	LBY	592	8.5

Table III.A2.1. **Expatriation rates for doctors and nurses, Circa 2000** *(Cont.)*

Country of birth		Nurses		Country of birth		Doctors	
		Number of persons working in OECD countries	Expatriation rate			Number of persons working in OECD countries	Expatriation rate
Malaysia	MYS	7 569	19.6	Luxembourg	LUX	549	31.3
Mali	MLI	227	3.7	Madagascar	MDG	889	14.6
Malta	MLT	649	22.0	Malawi	MWI	162	37.9
Mauritania	MRT	96	5.5	Malaysia	MYS	4 679	22.5
Mauritius	MUS	4 502	50.4	Maldives	MDV	6	1.9
Mexico	MEX	12 357	12.2	Mali	MLI	160	13.2
Morocco	MAR	5 730	20.5	Malta	MLT	458	26.8
Mozambique	MOZ	779	16.5	Mauritania	MRT	38	10.8
Myanmar	MMR	418	4.1	Mauritius	MUS	725	35.7
Namibia	NAM	30	0.5	Mexico	MEX	4 234	2.1
Nepal	NPL	205	3.5	Mongolia	MNG	39	0.6
Netherlands	NLD	6 798	3.0	Morocco	MAR	6 221	28.0
New Zealand	NZL	7 564	19.5	Mozambique	MOZ	935	64.5
Nicaragua	NIC	1 155	16.5	Myanmar	MMR	1 725	8.8
Niger	NER	19	0.8	Namibia	NAM	75	11.1
Nigeria	NGA	13 398	9.5	Nepal	NPL	288	5.1
Norway	NOR	1 700	2.5	Netherlands	NLD	2 412	4.5
Oman	OMN	18	0.2	New Zealand	NZL	1 904	17.4
Pakistan	PAK	1 803	3.6	Nicaragua	NIC	722	26.1
Panama	PAN	1 902	29.5	Niger	NER	26	6.5
Papua New Guinea	PNG	455	13.8	Nigeria	NGA	4 611	11.7
Paraguay	PRY	130	1.3	Norway	NOR	712	4.8
Peru	PER	2 807	14.1	Oman	OMN	23	0.6
Philippines	PHL	110 774	46.5	Pakistan	PAK	10 505	8.3
Poland	POL	9 153	4.6	Panama	PAN	1 026	18.8
Portugal	PRT	2 655	5.7	Papua New Guinea	PNG	136	33.1
Romania	ROU	4 440	4.9	Paraguay	PRY	283	4.3
Rwanda	RWA	54	1.5	Peru	PER	2 546	7.9
Saint Kitts and Nevis	KNA	711	76.7	Philippines	PHL	15 859	26.4
Saint Lucia	LCA	369	52.7	Poland	POL	5 821	5.8
Saint Vincent and the Grenadines	VCT	1 228	81.6	Portugal	PRT	792	2.2
Samoa	WSM	566	62.1	Qatar	QAT	45	3.3
Sao Tome and Principe	STP	138	35.0	Romania	ROU	5 182	10.9
Saudi Arabia	SAU	151	0.2	Rwanda	RWA	45	10.1
Senegal	SEN	256	8.9	Saint Kitts and Nevis	KNA	15	22.7
Seychelles	SYC	151	19.2	Saint Lucia	LCA	39	4.9
Sierra Leone	SLE	2 057	56.3	Saint Vincent and the Grenadines	VCT	115	53.2
Singapore	SGP	1 913	9.9	Samoa	WSM	46	27.7
Solomon Islands	SLB	38	10.1	Sao Tome and Principe	STP	71	46.7
Somalia	SOM	250	14.4	Saudi Arabia	SAU	421	1.2
South Africa	ZAF	6 016	3.2	Senegal	SEN	449	43.0
Spain	ESP	3 527	1.1	Seychelles	SYC	36	22.9
Sri Lanka	LKA	2 032	8.1	Sierra Leone	SLE	236	58.4
Sudan	SDN	183	1.0	Singapore	SGP	1 356	19.1
Suriname	SUR	18	2.5	Solomon Islands	SLB	11	16.9
Swaziland	SWZ	37	0.8	Somalia	SOM	155	33.3
Sweden	SWE	3 028	3.2	South Africa	ZAF	7 355	17.4
Switzerland	CHE	1 839	2.3	Spain	ESP	2 687	1.9
Syria	SYR	319	1.0	Sri Lanka	LKA	4 668	30.8
Thailand	THA	3 050	1.7	Sudan	SDN	778	9.3
Timor-Leste	TLS	61	4.0	Suriname	SUR	39	17.0

Table III.A2.1. **Expatriation rates for doctors and nurses, Circa 2000** (*Cont.*)

Country of birth		Nurses Number of persons working in OECD countries	Nurses Expatriation rate	Country of birth		Doctors Number of persons working in OECD countries	Doctors Expatriation rate
Togo	TGO	78	4.0	Swaziland	SWZ	9	5.0
Tonga	TON	449	58.2	Sweden	SWE	1 532	5.0
Trinidad and Tobago	TTO	9 808	72.9	Switzerland	CHE	1 125	4.2
Tunisia	TUN	410	1.6	Syria	SYR	4 721	16.6
Turkey	TUR	3 565	2.9	Thailand	THA	1 390	5.8
United Arab Emirates	ARE	11	0.1	Timor-Leste	TLS	35	30.7
United Kingdom	GBR	45 638	6.1	Togo	TGO	153	40.5
United Republic of Tanzania	TZA	970	6.8	Tonga	TON	23	39.7
United States	USA	6 022	0.2	Trinidad and Tobago	TTO	1 206	54.6
Unganda	UGA	1 210	7.4	Tunisia	TUN	2 415	15.3
Uruguay	URY	506	14.9	Turkey	TUR	2 311	2.4
Vanuatu	VUT	20	4.5	United Arab Emirates	ARE	44	0.7
Viet Nam	VNM	5 778	11.5	United Kingdom	GBR	17 006	11.3
Yemen	YEM	231	1.7	United Republic of Tanzania	TZA	1 018	55.3
Zambia	ZMB	820	4.6	United States	USA	4 354	0.6
Zimbabwe	ZWE	3 619	27.9	Uganda	UGA	1 084	32.9
				Uruguay	URY	493	3.8
				Vanuatu	VUT	5	20.0
				Venezuela	VEN	1 710	3.4
				Viet Nam	VNM	7 591	15.2
				Yemen	YEM	248	3.5
				Zambia	ZMB	567	31.0
				Zimbabwe	ZWE	828	28.4

Note: Countries for which expatriates are under 10 for nurses (5 for doctors) or resident in the origin country are below 50 for nurses (10 for doctors) are not reported.

StatLink ⧉ *http://dx.doi.org/10.1787/022648658554*

ANNEX III.A3

Migration Policies and Recognition of Foreign Qualifications for Health Professionals

			AUSTRALIA	**AUSTRIA**
Main characteristics of migration policy and specificities for health professionals	**Permanent migration**	Permanent migration programmes relevant for health professionals	❊ **General Skilled Migration** Programme (GSM). ❊ **Employer Nomination** Scheme (EN). ❊ **Regional Sponsored Migration** Scheme (RSM).	❊ **Permanent residence permit and unrestricted work permit** (generally after 5 years of residence and fulfilment of the integration agreement). EU8 nationals after 1 year and third country nationals with a key worker permit after 18 months can get an unlimited residence permit.
		Specific conditions for health professionals (*e.g.* point system)	Most medical occupations are included in the Skilled Occupation List (needed for GSM), in ENSOL (needed for EN), and in the Migration Occupation List in Demand (15 extra points).	**No**
	Temporary migration	Temporary migration programmes relevant for health professionals #Y: Maximum duration ®: Renewable LMT: Labour market test	❊ **Temporary business long stay** (457) 4Y®. ❊ **Temporary medical practitioner** (422) 4Y®. ❊ **Occupational trainee** (medical) (442) 2Y®. ❊ **Working holidays** 1Y (work period ≤ 6 months).	❊ **Key workers permits**. ❊ **Restricted work permit** 1Y® LMT. ❊ **Work permit** 2Y® LMT (52 weeks in employment over the last 14 months). ❊ Issuance of **work permits** to EU8 nationals working in the health and caretaking occupations (mainly qualified nurses) has been eased since 2004 (wage ≥ 1 500 € instead of 2 250 €).
		Quota	**No**	**Yes,** but no specific quota for health professionals.
	Shortage occupation list, specific mention of health professionals		❊ **Yes,** in SOL, ENSOL, MOLD and SSASSL. ❊ **Yes,** in most regional occupation in demand lists: New South Wales (except nurses), Western Australia, Australian Capital Territory, Victoria (except medical practitioner), Tasmania.	Work permits for EU8 nationals working in health and caretaking occupations are exempted from the Federal quota (*Bundeshöchstzahl*).
	Specific programmes for health professionals in underserved areas or particular regions		District of Workforce Shortage (Federal definition) or Area of need (State definition) enable to recruit under Region or Employer sponsored schemes. Medical practitioners in District of Workforce Shortage, even under conditional registration, are authorized to cash on Medicare (bulk bill).	**No,** but employment of non-EEA nationals is limited to Area of need of doctors.
	Bilateral agreements relevant for the recruitment of health professionals.		**No,** except with New-Zealand (Trans-Tasman Mutual Recognition Arrangement).	**No,** except with the EU.
Recognition of foreign qualifications	Conditions on citizenship		**No**	**No**
	Language proficiency test		**Yes**	**Yes** (5 years of practice in a German speaking country or a language test).
	Professional examination		It is necessary to pass Australian Medical Council (AMC) or Australian Nursing Council (ANC) exams to be registered, but State and Territory Medical Boards can proceed to conditional registration of doctors without examination.	**For EEA and Swiss nationals (and non-EEA in some cases),** qualifications from Switzerland or EEA are recognised in accordance to EU Directive. **Doctors:**
	Probation period Training programmes		**Doctors:** 1 year supervised training is needed after passing the AMC exam to obtain general registration. **Nurses:** It may be required to complete a 7 weeks competency based assessment programme when educational requirements for registration are not met.	❊ Special rules apply notably to qualification from former Yougoslavian countries. ❊ Third countries nationals or qualification need to be assessed. The Medical Doctors' Act mentions additional criteria (except for refugees) including a limitation to practice to 3 years (renewable) and a labor market test. **Nurses:** conditions are more or less similar than for Doctors. If third country diploma is not conform to EU standards additional board exams and/or practical training are required.
International recruitment agencies operating for health professionals are contracted or regulated			**Yes,** 16 recruitment agencies have been contracted by the Federal government to place foreign trained doctors in medical vacancies (no fee for employers). Some States also have contracted recruitment agencies.	**No,** but in general private employment agencies need a trade licence issued by the district authorities which are under supervision of the Ministry for Economics and Labour.
Foreign medical students can change status after the completion of their studies to obtain a work permit			**Yes,** Skill Independent (880), Australian Sponsored (881) and Designated Area Overseas Student (882). ❊ Overseas students in Australia who have completed a medical degree, can undertake their internship in Australia but places are capped.	**Possible,** but no specific programme. No permit is needed for "vocational training".
Code of conduct for international recruitment of health professionals			**No,** but supports the principles outlined in the *Commonwealth Code of Practice for the International Recruitment of Health Workers.*	**No**
Competent authorities for registration/ certification or other relevant links			*www.doctorconnect.gov.au* *www.amc.org.au* *www.anmc.org.au*	*www.aerztekammer.at*

BELGIUM	CANADA	CZECH REPUBLIC
❀ **A Permit** (generally after 4 years of continuous residence with a B permit over the last 10 years).	❀ **Skilled Worker Class** (R 75). ❀ **Provincial Nominee Class** (R 87).	❀ **Permanent residence** (after 5 years of continuous residence with a Long-term Residence Permit).
No	No	No
❀ **B Permit** 1Y®LMT and limited to bilateral agreements (wage ≥ €33k no labour market test and no condition on nationality). ❀ **"Professional Card"** for Independent practice delivered by *SPF Economie*, 5 Y®.	❀ **Temporary Foreign Worker** (R200) limited to the duration of employment, LMT except if included in Regional Lists of Occupations under Pressure (Alberta, Ontario, BC: Most health prof. included). ❀ **Medical students visa** (R186(p)) may work up to 4 months as a trainee (interns need a work permit). ❀ **TN visa** 1Y® (NAFTA).	❀ **Long-term residence permit** for the purpose of employment >1Y® LMT. ❀ **Work Permit** 1Y® LMT. ❀ **Project of Active Selection of Qualified Foreign Labour:** For young qualified foreigners (from selected nationalities) already legally resident in the Czech Rep. (it gives a quicker access to a permanent resident status).
No	No	No
Yes, since June 2006 nurses are included in regional shortage occupation lists (as well as pharmacist in some regions). UE8 nationals with a job offer can get a Permit B without a labour market test.	Lists of occupations under pressure.	No
No, but shortage occupation lists are defined at the regional level.	Provinces and territories have the jurisdictional responsibility for Health Human Resource planning within their respective regions, recruiting domestically as well as supporting the integration of internationally educated health care providers into the Canadian health care system. This recruitment can be unique to the provincial or territorial jurisdiction of origin.	No
No, except within the EU.	❀ North American Free Trade Agreement (NAFTA).	**No,** except with the EU.
No	No	No
No, systematic exam.	**Yes**	**Yes**
The following are for all health professionals. **For EEA and Swiss nationals (and non-EEA in some cases),** qualifications from Switzerland or EEA are recognised in accordance to EU Directive. **EEA nationals/non-EEA qualification.** Need to have their qualification recognized by SPF Santé. **Non-EEA nationals/non-Belgium qualification.** Need to have: their qualification recognized, a work permit or a professional card but also an authorization to practice. In practice the latter is almost never delivered to doctors, dentists or pharmacists but may be to nurses (because of shortages).	**Foreign-trained doctors** must pass the Medical Council of Canada Evaluating Exam and after completing supervised clinical training they need to pass the Certification Exam of the relevant college. In addition, for independent license to practice (LMCC) doctors need to pass the *MCC Qualifying Examination* I&II. **Foreign trained nurses** who lack a component of the education, (*e.g.* some internationally educated nurses do not study psychiatric nursing), may be asked to study or do clinical practice under supervision. Each province/territory is responsible for the regulation of the practice of medicine in their respective jurisdiction.	**For EEA and Swiss nationals (and non-EEA in some cases),** qualifications from Switzerland or EEA are recognised in accordance to EU Directive. **Non-EEE nationals** need to pass a professional accreditation exam (IPVZ) and a language test.
No	No	**No,** but private recruitment agency need to have a licence.
Possible, but no specific programme.	**Possible,** but no specific programme except within Provincial Nominee Class.	**Possible,** but no specific programme. ❀ Foreign students may be allowed to work in health services only under the supervision of a professional for specific period of time (legally specified by occupation).
No	**No,** but supports the principles outlined in the *Commonwealth Code of Practice for the International Recruitment of Health Workers.*	No
www.ordomedic.be	*www.cic.gc.ca* *www.img-canada.ca*	*www.lkcr.cz*

			DENMARK	FINLAND
Main characteristics of migration policy and specificities for health professionals	*Permanent migration*	Permanent migration programmes relevant for health professionals	◈ **Permanent Residence permit** (after 7 years).	◈ **Permanent permit P** (after 4 years with an A-permit).
		Specific conditions for health professionals (*e.g.* point system)	No	No
	Temporary migration	Temporary migration programmes relevant for health professionals #Y: Maximum duration ®: Renewable LMT: Labour market test	◈ **Work Permit** 1Y® Danish Immigration Service requests a statement from a relevant branch organisation about the need for labour. ◈ **Job Card Scheme** 3Y® for occupations in the "positive list" and a job offer ≥ DKK 450k.	◈ **A-Permit** 3Y® LMT. ◈ **B-Permit** 1Y® LMT. Local labour market authorities also check the skill level and that the job offer satisfies collective agreements.
		Quota	No	No
	Shortage occupation list, specific mention of health professionals		Doctors and nurses are included in the "positive list".	No
	Specific programmes for health professionals in underserved areas or particular regions		No	No
	Bilateral agreements relevant for the recruitment of health professionals.		**No,** except with the EU and the Agreement on a Common Nordic Labour Market.	**No,** except with the EU and the Agreement on a Common Nordic Labour Market.
Recognition of foreign qualifications	Conditions on citizenship		No	**Yes,** in general but exemptions can be granted on an individual basis by the NAMA.
	Language proficiency test		**Yes,** for people trained outside EU/Nordic countries.	**Yes**
	Professional examination		**For EEA and Swiss nationals (and non-EEA in some cases),** qualifications from Switzerland or EEA are recognised in accordance to EU Directive. Doctors and nurses must possess an authorisation from the National Board of Health.	**For EEA and Swiss nationals (and non-EEA in some cases),** qualifications from Switzerland or EEA are recognised in accordance to EU Directive. To register, a **doctor trained outside EEA** has to receive practical training (6 months), pass a 3 part examination and a language test. Licenses are granted stage wise. The initial license is valid only for hospital work. It can be extended to cover health-centre work, then work in other institutions and finally private practice. If a holder of an extended license is granted Finnish citizenship, the National Authority for Medicolegal Affairs (NAMA) can authorize to practice medicine independently. Other non EEA health professionals trained outside the EEA must have their qualification recognized and get a special authorization from NAMA.
	Probation period Training programmes		**People trained outside EU/Nordic countries** must have their qualification assessed (including language proficiency). If the training is not fully equivalent to the Danish training, the doctor/midwife/nurse must complete probationary appointments and- for doctors/midwives – professional tests.	
International recruitment agencies operating for health professionals are contracted or regulated			**No,** but some regions ("amter") have an agreement with private recruitment agencies to recruit health professionals mainly from eastern European countries.	
Foreign medical students can change status after the completion of their studies to obtain a work permit			Graduate Doctors, Doctor of Pharmacy, Midwife and nurses with a Bachelor Degree, Dental hygienist and clinical dental technician can extend for 3 months their residence permits after completion of their study to search work in Denmark.	Foreign students who earn a degree in Finland can apply for a work permit for a maximum of six months.
Code of conduct for international recruitment of health professionals			No	No
Competent authorities for registration/ certification or other relevant links			*www.nyidanmark.dk* *www.sst.dk*	*www.laakariliitto.fi/e/* *www.teo.fi* *www.mol.fi/finnwork* *www.uvi.fi*

FRANCE	GERMANY	GREECE
● **Residence permit** (after 3 years for people with a permanent worker permit).	● **Settlement permit** (generally after 5 years of residence or immediately for highly qualified – for instance with a job offer over 7 000 €).	● **Residence permit-employment** (1Y® but may be indefinite after 10 years).
No	No	No
● **Permanent worker permit** 1Y® LMT: A job contract for unlimited duration is needed (Carte de Séjour Temporaire salarié). ● **Temporary work permit** <1Y® LMT (*Autorisation Provisoire de Travail*). ● Card "*Compétences et Talents*" 3Y®.	● **Temporarily restricted residence permit** for the purpose of employment (1Y® LMT) for people with a post-secondary qualifying education (incl. medical doctors and medical personnel with at least 3 years of vocational training). It is subject to a local labour market test and to Federal Employment Agency agreement.	● **A-permit** 1Y® LMT.
No	No	No
Since 2006, there is a shortage occupation list for nationals of new EU member states (No labour market test to obtain a work permit). No Health occupation are included.	No	The Law 2910/01 introduced the possibility to respond to local needs in labour force by specialty but in practice this has not been implemented.
No, but labour market tests are implemented at the local level.	**No,** but labour market tests are implemented at the local level.	No
Bilateral agreement to recruit Spanish nurses started in 2002 was ended in December 2004 (1 364 have been recruited in this framework).	Recruitment of foreign nursing aids is organised within bilateral agreements (no labour market test). In 2005, such agreement were signed with Croatia, Ukraine as well as Poland, Slovenia, the Czech and the Slovak Rep., Bulgaria and Romania.	**No,** specific bilateral agreement for health professionals, except with the EU.
Yes in general, but exemptions can be granted on an individual basis by the Health Minister.	No	No
Yes	**Yes**	**No,** but should produce a certificate of attendance in School of Foreign Language; Interview is in Greek.
For EEA and Swiss nationals (and non-EEA in some cases), qualifications from Switzerland or EEA are recognised in accordance to EU Directive. **Doctors:** In theory one needs to be French, trained in France, registered and to hold a work permit. In practice, despite the recent efforts to regularise the situation (about 9 500 since 1999), many foreigner or foreign trained doctors work in public hospitals positions (about 6 700) with a student status (AFS or AFSA) or in precarious positions (DIS as associate). **Nurses:** Non-EU or Swiss trained nurses need to pass the selection exam in nursing schools and to do the training in France (on an individual basis they may avoid the 1st or 2nd years). People trained as doctors may be allowed to work as nurses for maximum 3 years on a case by case basis.	**For EEA and Swiss nationals (and non-EEA in some cases),** qualifications from Switzerland or EEA are recognised in accordance to EU Directive. **Foreign-trained health professionals** need to have their qualification recognised as fully equivalent to a German degree. If this is not the case they need to pass an exam. Licence to practice should also be delivered by responsible local authorities according to "public interest". Doctors who fail to obtain this licence can apply for the permission to practice at the local health authorities. The permit is then issued for the purpose of "vocational training and further education" for a maximum of 4 years.	**For EEA and Swiss nationals (and non-EEA in some cases),** qualifications from Switzerland or EEA are recognised in accordance to EU Directive. **Non EEA nationals/people trained outside EEA** 1- *Academic recognition* by the Inter-scientific Organisation for Academic Titles Recognition and Information (DOATAP). 2- Submit to DOATAP a *residence and work permit*. 3- *Professional experience recognition* by the Council of Recognition of Professional Equivalence of Higher Education Diplomas (SAEI). Third country nationals with EU qualification must have 3 years of professional experience in the EU. 4- *License to practice* by the Health Directorate of the relevant Prefecture. 5- *Registration* by the professional association.
No	No	No
Student with a French master degree, with the perspective to return in their origin country, can ask for 6 months permit to seek work in France. Other foreign students can change status under general rules.	Students are entitled to remain in Germany for up to one year after successfully completing their studies for the purpose of seeking employment.	**Possible,** but no specific programme.
No	No	No
www.ordmed.org	*www.baek.de*	*www.pis.gr*

			IRELAND	ITALY
Main characteristics of migration policy and specificities for health professionals	Permanent migration	Permanent migration programmes relevant for health professionals	● **Long-term residency permit** (validity 5 years after 5 years of residence and unlimited duration after 10 years).	● **Residence permit** (generally after 5 years of legal stay).
		Specific conditions for health professionals (*e.g.* point system)	**No**	**No**
	Temporary migration	Temporary migration programmes relevant for health professionals #Y: Maximum duration ®: Renewable LMT: Labour market test	● **Green card permit** 2Y® (€30k < salary < €60k and shortage occupation list or all occupations with salary > €60k). ● **Work permit** 1Y® LMT (salary < €30k, occupation should not be included in the ineligible occupation list).	● **Work permit** 1Y® LMT (fix-term contract). ● **Work permit** 2Y® LMT (open-end contract).
		Quota	**No**	**Yes,** but except for nurses since 2002.
	Shortage occupation list, specific mention of health professionals		Shortage occupation list includes most health occupations (since 2000 for nurses, and 2003 for others). Ineligible occupation list does not include health occupations. Furthermore, no labour market test is needed for work permit applications in respect of nurses or doctors.	**No**
	Specific programmes for health professionals in underserved areas or particular regions		**No**	**No,** but work permit quotas are defined by sector and region.
	Bilateral agreements relevant for the recruitment of health professionals.		**No,** formal agreement but close links have been established with the Philippines for nurses.	**Yes,** some Italian regions have signed bilateral agreements notably with Romanian provinces (*e.g.* Parma with that of Cluj-Napoca or Veneto with Timis County). There are also semi-formal links with Spain to recruit Spanish nurses.
Recognition of foreign qualifications	Conditions on citizenship		**No**	**Yes,** for specialists and there are legal restrictions for non-EU nurses in the public sector.
	Language proficiency test		**Yes**	**Yes**
	Professional examination		**For EEA and Swiss nationals (and non-EEA in some cases),** qualifications from Switzerland or EEA are recognised in accordance to EU Directive. **Doctors** Most people trained in old Commonwealth States or South Africa can be granted full registration. Other people can apply for a temporary registration (up to 7 years) which implies to pass the Temporary Registration Assessment Scheme (TRAS). **Nurses** An Bord Altranais determines the adequacy of the education and training. It has introduced a competency based assessment which includes an adaptation period under supervision (at least 6 weeks 12 on average) if necessary.	**For EEA and Swiss nationals (and non-EEA in some cases),** qualifications from Switzerland or EEA are recognised in accordance to EU Directive. **Foreign-trained doctors** need to have their qualification recognized by the Health Ministry (before 2002 a presidential Decree in the Official Gazette of the Italia Rep. was needed). The process takes about 5 years. Alternatively they can enrol in the 6th year of medicine to pass an Italian degree. **Foreign-trained nurses** are required to pass both language and nursing qualification exam organised by IPASVI (in 2004-06 about 60 evaluation commissions were organised in the main origin countries). Limited deficiencies can be compensated with work experience abroad or further formation in Italy.
	Probation period Training programmes			
International recruitment agencies operating for health professionals are contracted or regulated			**No**	Some temporary work agencies have been licensed to organise abroad evaluation commissions. Both private and public institutions used recruitment agencies to recruit foreign nurses.
Foreign medical students can change status after the completion of their studies to obtain a work permit			Students who completed a primary, master or doctorate degree may be permitted to remain in Ireland for 6 months to seek employment.	**Yes,** annual quota sets a maximum number of conversion of study permit to work permits.
Code of conduct for international recruitment of health professionals			**No**	**No**
Competent authorities for registration/ certification or other relevant links			*www.entemp.ie/labour/workpermits/index.htm* *www.medicalcouncil.ie* *www.nursingboard.ie*	*www.ministerosalute.it/professioniSanitarie/ paginaInterna.jsp?id=92&menu=strumentieservizi* *www.fnomceo.it*

JAPAN	LUXEMBOURG	NETHERLANDS
No	❋ **Permit type C** (after 5 years of residence).	❋ **Permanent residence permit** (after 5 years of residence).
No	No	No
❋ **"Medical Services"** residence permit 1-3Y® (maximum 4 years for midwifes and 7 years for registered nurses).	❋ **Permit type A** 1Y® LMT (can not change employer or occupation). ❋ **Permit type B** 4Y® LMT (can not change occupation).	❋ **Labour migrant work permit** 3Y LMT non renewable. In general people are required to take a civil immigration test in their home country (Applicants must be between the ages of 18-45). ❋ **Highly skilled migrant** 5Y (wage ≥ €33.3k for people under 30 or wage ≥ €45.5k. No labour market test and spouse can work).
No, except within the Japan-Philippines Economic Partnership Agreement. A quota will be 400 nurses for the first 2 years (starting in 2008).	No	**No,** except for nationals from Bulgaria and Romania.
No	No	**No,** but in some cases the labour market test can be lifted for specific occupations or sectors. This was the case for instance for several occupations in the health sector for nationals of new EU countries between January and May 2004.
For doctors previous limitation on workplace to remote areas, where Japanese doctors cannot be recruited, have been lifted (they still apply to dentists for instance).	No	No
Japan-Philippines Economic Partnership Agreement (JPEPA): nurses with 3 years exp. and a contract with a hospital can stay for 3 years to obtain a Japanese qualification, including to pursue a language course and follow a supervised training.	**No,** except with the EU.	**No,** except with the EU. In 2003-05, "Pilot project for polish nurses in the Netherlands; development of competencies".
No	**Yes,** in general but derogations can be given by the Minister on exceptional cases.	No
Yes	Yes	Yes
Need to obtain Japanese legal qualification.	**For EEA and Swiss nationals (and non-EEA in some cases),** qualifications from Switzerland or EEA are recognised in accordance to EU Directive.	**For EEA and Swiss nationals (and non-EEA in some cases),** qualifications from Switzerland or EEA are recognised in accordance to EU Directive. **Foreign-trained doctors** have to pass a knowledge and skills test (including in Dutch). If the skills are almost equivalent, registration is made with special stipulations which should be addressed within 2 years (full equivalence with no Dutch experience = 6 months supervision). If the skills are not equivalent (but not too low) and the applicant has professional experience he may be allowed in a Dutch training institute. This procedure started in December 2005 for doctors. It should be progressively applied to other health professionals (as of now they do not always have to take an exam but may be interviewed).
No	**EU and Swiss nationals non EU trained** need to have their qualification recognized. In some cases complementary courses or training may be required (maximum 1 year for doctors). Foreign doctors need to be proficient in 2 (out of 3) official languages.	
No	No	Recruitment agencies play an important role in both public and private sectors.
Yes, but overseas students have to obtain a "Medical Services" residence permit under general regulation.	Luxembourg does not have its own medical school.	**Yes,** international students after graduating can stay for up to 3 months to seek a job.
No	No	No
	www.etat.lu/MS/	*www.bigregister.nl* *www.minvws.nl (Working in the Dutch health sector with a foreign certificate)*

			NEW ZEALAND	NORWAY
Main characteristics of migration policy and specificities for health professionals	*Permanent migration*	Permanent migration programmes relevant for health professionals	✱ **Skilled Migrant Category** (SMC).	✱ **Permanent residence permit** (after 3 years with temporary permit).
		Specific conditions for health professionals (*e.g.* point system)	**Yes,** most health occupations are listed in the Long-Term Skill Shortage List and get 10 extra points.	**No**
	Temporary migration	Temporary migration programmes relevant for health professionals #Y: Maximum duration ®: Renewable LMT: Labour market test	**Work to Residence policy:** ✱ Accredited employer (talent programme). ✱ Long-term Skill Shortage List. **Work permits:** Fast track if occupation in ISSL. **Working holidays** 1Y (work period ≤ 6 months).	✱ **Skilled worker/specialist** (SWS) 1Y®. ✱ **Job seeker visa** (generally 3 months).
		Quota	**No**	**Yes,** for skilled worker specialists, but if the quota is full, it is still possible to grant a permit but under stricter conditions (labour market test).
		Shortage occupation list, specific mention of health professionals	**Yes,** for medical doctors, dentists and other health occupation (except nursing), in the 6 regional Immediate Skill Shortage Lists (ISSL). **Yes,** for most health occupations, in Long-Term Skill Shortage List.	**No**
		Specific programmes for health professionals in underserved areas or particular regions	**No,** but people with a job offer outside Auckland get extra points.	**No**
		Bilateral agreements relevant for the recruitment of health professionals.	**No,** except with Australia (Trans-Tasman Mutual Recognition Arrangement).	**No,** except with the EU and the Agreement on a Common Nordic Labour Market.
Recognition of foreign qualifications		Conditions on citizenship	**No**	**No**
		Language proficiency test	**Yes**	**Yes,** course and examination for doctors with a first language other than Norwegian, Swedish or Danish.
		Professional examination	**Doctors:** IMG generally need to pass the New Zealand Registration Exam (NZREX) and to do 2 years of post graduate training (1 year for UK and Irish graduates) **but** people who worked in so called "comparable health system" (18 countries are recorded) for at least 3 years can practice with a 2 years supervision period.	**For EEA and Swiss nationals (and non-EEA in some cases),** qualifications from Switzerland or EEA are recognised in accordance to EU Directive. The Norwegian Registration Authority for Health Personnel gives the authorisations and licenses. **Authorisation** is granted to applicants who have successfully completed "turnus" (residency). **Licence** is a permission to practise as medical practitioner, but on certain conditions (may be restricted in terms of time, locality, etc., and may only be granted following an assessment). If qualification is not fully equivalent it is possible to take bridging courses. When the foreign qualification has been approved the applicant start "turnus". Prior work experience cannot be subtracted from the length of the turnus period.
		Probation period Training programmes	**Nurses:** Need to go through a competence assessment programme when educational requirements for registration are not met.	
		International recruitment agencies operating for health professionals are contracted or regulated	**No,** but the Department of Labour's Immigration New Zealand has a Relationship Management Team aiming at organising expos and recruitment campaigns abroad.	**No**
		Foreign medical students can change status after the completion of their studies to obtain a work permit	**Yes,** people who have completed in New Zealand a 3 year course or a qualification that would qualify under Skill Migration Category, may be granted a work permit for a maximum of 6 months to enable them to look for work.	**Possible,** foreign students *with a job offer* as health professional after completion of their education, may be granted a work permit for up to 1 year. Norway offers scholarship grants (1 100) to students from developing countries = return or repay.
		Code of conduct for international recruitment of health professionals	**Yes,** signatory of the *Commonwealth Code of Practice for the International Recruitment of Health Workers.*	**No**
		Competent authorities for registration/ certification or other relevant links	*www.immigration.govt.nz* *www.mcnz.org.nz/* *www.nursingcouncil.org.nz/*	*www.safh.no* *www.udi.no*

POLAND	PORTUGAL	SLOVAK REPUBLIC
❋ **Settlement permit** (after 5 years of residence).	❋ **Permanent residence permit** (after 5 or 8 years of residence depending whether the person is from PALOPS country – country with Portuguese as official language – or not).	❋ **Permanent residence permit** (after 3 years of residence).
No	No	No
❋ **Work Permit**1Y® LMT	❋ **Work permit type II** 1Y® (to carry out a scientific research activity or an activity that requires highly qualified technical skills – including doctors and nurses). ❋ **Work permit type IV** 1Y® LMT (IEFP list).	❋ **Work Permit** 1Y® LMT.
No	**Yes,** but in practice health occupations are not covered by the quota system.	No
Health professionals (doctors and dentists) who are trained according to the Polish law can obtain work permit without taking in consideration the local labour market situation.	No	No
No, but labour market test is organised at the regional level.	No	No
No, except with the EU	**No,** except with the EU.	**No,** except with the EU.
No	No	No
Yes for third country nationals (declaration of Polish language proficiency for EU/Swiss nationals).	**Yes** (All doctors, including Portuguese nationals, are required to take a medical communication test).	**Yes**
For EEA and Swiss nationals (and non-EEA in some cases), qualifications from Switzerland or EEA are recognised in accordance to EU Directive. **Third countries nationals** must have their qualification recognised and pass a test in Polish language.	**For EEA and Swiss nationals (and non-EEA in some cases),** qualifications from Switzerland or EEA are recognised in accordance to EU Directive. **Foreign trained** health professionals must have their qualifications recognized and be registered in their professional associations ("Ordens"). Qualifications are certified by the Education Ministry and the Health Ministry. Doctors, need at least 2 years of professional experience within the last 5 years to be allowed to autonomous practice. A Project developed by Calouste Gulbenkian Foundation with other partners is directed at immigrant nurses legally working in undifferentiated occupations. It helps them to obtain the equivalence of their educational and professional diplomas so that they can work as nurses.	**For EEA and Swiss nationals (and non-EEA in some cases),** qualifications from Switzerland or EEA are recognised in accordance to EU Directive.
Recruitment agencies should possess special certificate issued by regional self-government authorities attesting their entry in the employment agency register.	No	No
Yes, no labour market test for medical students with a polish diploma. Doctors and nurses graduated in Poland do not need a work permit for post graduate training.	**Possible,** but no specific programme.	**Possible,** but no specific programme.
No	No	No
www.nil.org.pl	*www.ordemdosmedicos.pt* *www.ordemenfermeiros.pt*	*http://www.lekom.sk/*

			SPAIN	SWEDEN
Main characteristics of migration policy and specificities for health professionals	*Permanent migration*	Permanent migration programmes relevant for health professionals	❂ **Permanent residence permit** (after 5 years of legal residence).	❂ **Permanent Residence Permit** (PUT).
		Specific conditions for health professionals (*e.g.* point system)	**No**	**No**
	Temporary migration	Temporary migration programmes relevant for health professionals #Y: Maximum duration ®: Renewable LMT: Labour market test	❂ **Work permit B** type 1Y® LMT (limited to specific activities and area; can be renewed for 2 years). ❂ **Work permit C** type 3Y LMT (after B type permits; no restriction). ❂ **Permits D and E** for self employed.	❂ **Work Permit** 5Y LMT7.
		Quota	**Yes**	**No**
		Shortage occupation list, specific mention of health professionals	**Yes,** when occupations are included in the shortage list (*Catalogo de occupations de dificil cobertura*) no labour market test is needed but the number of permits is capped.	**No**
		Specific programmes for health professionals in underserved areas or particular regions	**No,** but shortage occupation list are defined at the regional level. Health occupation are included in a limited number of areas (mainly nursing aids and General Practitioners in Barcelona, Girona, Lleida, Tarragona Zamora, Ourense, Las Palmas and Tenerife).	**No,** but labour market test is organised by County Labour Board and some County Councils or Regions have been active in recruiting abroad (mainly within EU – Germany, Poland and Spain).
		Bilateral agreements relevant for the recruitment of health professionals.	Spain and the Philippines have agreed to develop a pilot project to recruit personnel for nursing homes (no nurses or doctors). Spain has also signed agreements with other EU countries (UK, FRA…) to send Spanish nurses abroad.	**No,** except with the EU and the Agreement on a Common Nordic Labour Market.
Recognition of foreign qualifications		Conditions on citizenship	**No**	**No**
		Language proficiency test	**No,** but exams and interviews are in Spanish.	**Yes**
		Professional examination	**For EEA and Swiss nationals (and non-EEA in some cases),** qualifications from Switzerland or EEA are recognised in accordance to EU Directive.	**For EEA and Swiss nationals (and non-EEA in some cases),** qualifications from Switzerland or EEA are recognised in accordance to EU Directive. People must present evidence of sufficient knowledge of the Swedish language.
		Probation period Training programmes	**Foreign medical graduates qualified outside the EU/EEA/ Switzerland** need to have their qualification recognised as fully equivalent to the Spanish one or need to take a two stages exam (multi choice exam and oral exam on clinical cases). This exam can not be taken more than twice.	**Foreign medical graduates qualified outside the EU/EEA/ Switzerland** are unable to work – temporarily or permanently – in the medical profession without passing a complementary training programme in Sweden. This programme involves courses and tests in the Swedish language, a medical exam as well as supervised practice and introductory courses in the medical legislation of this country.
		International recruitment agencies operating for health professionals are contracted or regulated	**No**	**No,** but some private agencies play an active role in recruiting internationally health professionals, including for the public sector.
		Foreign medical students can change status after the completion of their studies to obtain a work permit	**Yes,** foreign students can have a residence and a work permit after graduation if they have been in Spain for at least 3 years and did not benefit from a grant from their origin country or a co-operation programme.	**No,** as a general rule, a foreign student from outside the EU/ EEA/Switzerland must leave after completing his/her studies.
		Code of conduct for international recruitment of health professionals	**No**	**No**
		Competent authorities for registration/ certification or other relevant links	*http://extranjeros.mtas.es/* *www.msc.es/profesionales/formacion/home.htm* *wwwn.mec.es mecd/titulos/convalidacion.html*	*www.migrationsverket.se* *www.socialstyrelsen.se*

SWITZERLAND	TURKEY	UNITED KINGDOM
❋ **Settlement permit** can be delivered after 5 years of residence for EFTA, USA and Canadian nationals or 10 years for other countries.	❋ **Indefinite work and residence permit** (after 8 years of legal residence and 6 years of legal employment).	❋ **Permanent residence** – indefinite leave to remain (after 5 years of legal residence with a work permit or a HSM permit).
No	**No**	**No**
❋ **Residence permit** 1Y® (5Y® for EEA nationals). ❋ **Short-term permit** 1Y ® once. ❋ **Trainee exchange schemes** with about 30 countries 18 months maximum (may include a non negligible number of health professionals, notably nurses).	❋ **Work permit** 1Y® LMT (can be renewed for up to 3 years after one year and for up to six years the following times).	❋ **Work permit** 5Y LMT (no labour market test if occupation in included the skill shortage list). ❋ **Highly Skilled Migrant Programme** 5Y (no job offer needed, points test and language requirement). ❋ **Training and work experience** 3Y non renewable no leave to remain (incl. Medical Training Initiative). ❋ **Student internship work permit** 3 months.
No	**No**	**No**
No	**No**	**Skill shortage occupation list** includes almost all health occupation except general nurses since July 2006.
No	**No**	**Fresh Talent: Working in Scotland scheme:** Allow graduates from Scottish universities (Master or PhD) to stay in Scotland for up to 2 years without a job offer or any professional experience.
❋ **Bilateral agreement with the EU** ❋ **Agreement Protocol with Canada** to facilitate migration notably of Canadians in the health sector.	**No,** however, within the context of EU Accession (free movement of workers, recognition of qualifications and diplomas) preparatory work has been started.	Recruitment agreements with China, Spain and India. Memorandum of understanding with the Philippines. Agreement with South Africa for reciprocal education exchange of health workers.
No	**Yes**	**No**
Yes (reintroduced for EEA nurses in 2006).	**Yes**	**Yes**
For EEA and Swiss nationals (and non-EEA in some cases), qualifications from Switzerland or EEA are recognised in accordance to EU Directive. **Doctors:** *Recognition of diploma* is a Federal responsibility. *Authorisation to practice* is a cantonal responsibility. **Nurses:** Diplomas are recognised by the Swiss Red Cross. If educational requirements are not met people will have to do an adaptation period for at least 6 months which could include a training component or an assessment test. Cantonal responsibilities are very limited.	Only Turkish citizens are allowed to work in health occupations.	**For EEA and Swiss nationals (and non-EEA in some cases),** qualifications from Switzerland or EEA are recognised in accordance to EU Directive. **Foreign graduates qualified outside the EU/EEA/ Switzerland.** A language test is requested. *Doctors* with acceptable primary medical education and who pass the Professional and Linguistic Assessment Board (PLAB) test get limited registration (1 year supervision). Special regulations may apply for Australia, New Zealand, Hong Kong (China), Singapore, South Africa, West Indies. *Nurses* (people trained as a doctor are not eligible) need equivalent training, 12 months of practice after qualifying (or 450h in the last 3 years) and to go through Overseas Nurses programme. ONP includes a compulsory 20-day period of protected learning and when appropriate a period of supervised practice.
No	**No** such agencies.	**Yes,** Employment agencies must comply with the Employment Agencies Act 1973. Private Recruitment Agencies wishing to supply to the NHS should comply with the Code of Practice for the international recruitment of healthcare professionals.
Possible, but no specific programme.	**Possible,** but there is no specific programme.	Non-EEA student who has obtained a degree level qualification may apply to switch into work permit employment without leaving the UK. Since April 2006, doctors and dentists in post-graduate training are considered in employment.
No	**No**	**Yes,** recruitment for the NHS is subject to Code of Practice for the international recruitment of healthcare professionals.
www.bfm.admin.ch *www.bag.admin.ch* *www.srk.ch* *www.fmh.ch*		*www.gmc-uk.org/* *www.nmc-uk.org* *www.workingintheuk.gov.uk/*

			UNITED STATES
Main characteristics of migration policy and specificities for health professionals	**Permanent migration**	Permanent migration programmes relevant for health professionals	⊛ **Employment based immigrant visa EB2 or EB3 – Green card** (H1B visa holders can ask for a **green card** after 6 years).
		Specific conditions for health professionals (*e.g.* point system)	**No**
	Temporary migration	Temporary migration programmes relevant for health professionals #Y: Maximum duration ®: Renewable LMT: Labour market test	⊛ **H1B** visa 2Y® maximum 6Y *(specialty professional workers – bachelor degree or more: Includes doctors and registered nurses). H-1B1 for nationals of Chile and Singapore (special quota). ⊛ **TN visa** 1Y® (NAFTA), NAFTA occupation list includes most health professionals but physicians only for research and teaching activities. ⊛ J1 visa 3Y® maximum 6Y (exchange visitor skill) generally must return for 2 years to its former country of permanent residence (except if eligible to J1 waiver programme see below). ** **H1A** Registered nurses (ended in 1995).
		Quota	**Yes** for H1B but not by occupation, not for TN or J1 visa.
		Shortage occupation list, specific mention of health professionals	**No**
		Specific programmes for health professionals in underserved areas or particular regions	**J1 waiver programme** allow someone who has been in the US for 2 years under a J1 visa and are medical graduate who has an offer of full-time employment at a health care facility in a designated health care professional shortage area or at a health care facility which serves patients from such a designated area, can remain in the US (each state is allowed to recommend 30 waivers per year to the US department of State and Bureau of Citizenship and Immigration services). ** **H1C** Nurses in shortage areas (ended in 2004).
		Bilateral agreements relevant for the recruitment of health professionals.	**No,** except with Canada and Mexico with the North American Free Trade Agreement (NAFTA).
Recognition of foreign qualifications		Conditions on citizenship	**No**
		Language proficiency test	**Yes**
		Professional examination	**Doctors:** It is almost always required that physicians complete residency in the United-States. All International Medical Graduates (IMG) must hold a certificate from the Educational Commission for Foreign Medical Graduates (ECFMG). To obtain this certification they have to pass an exam which covers USMLE Step 1 and Step 2 (*i.e.* Medical Science Examination and Clinical Skills Requirement) and a language test. They must also prove that they have attended at least 4 years and graduated from a medical school in IMED. IMGs can then take the USMLE Step 3 but States may impose additional requirements (16 state boards allow IMGs to take USMLE Step 3 before they have had GME in a US or Canadian hospital). All states, however, require at least 1 year of GME for licensure, and 29 states require 3 years (39 states endorse for licensure the Licentiate of the Medical Council of Canada). Special conditions apply in some cases for Americans wishing to return to the US after attending a foreign medical school (Fifth Pathway Programme). ECFMG is authorized by the US Department of State to sponsor foreign national physicians as Exchange Visitors in accredited programmes of graduate medical education. **Nurses:** In order to be licensed for nursing in the US, one must usually pass the CGFNS Qualifying Exam (including a language test) in order to be able to take the NCLEX-RN or NCLEX-PN (National Council Licensure Examination) which is required in order to be able to practice as a nurse in the US.
		Probation period Training programmes	
		International recruitment agencies operating for health professionals are contracted or regulated	**No**
		Foreign medical students can change status after the completion of their studies to obtain a work permit	**Yes,** F1 visas allow graduates to stay for up to 12 months to pursue professional training (6 months for M1 visa holders). Within the H1B programme there is special quota (20 000) reserved for foreign students with a Master or PhD from US academic institutions.
		Code of conduct for international recruitment of health professionals	**No**
		Competent authorities for registration/certification or other relevant links	*www.ecfmg.org* *www.ncsbn.org* *http://travel.state.gov/visa*

ISBN 978-92-64-03285-9
International Migration Outlook
Sopemi 2007 Edition
© OECD 2007

PART IV

Recent Changes in Migration Movements and Policies

(COUNTRY NOTES)

Australia

The number of permanent migrants accepted to Australia under the Migration Programme in 2005-06 was almost 143 000, the largest in over a decade. With more than two thirds of these admitted in the skilled migrant stream, the programme was the most highly skilled ever. The points-tested skilled independent category had the largest increase in absolute terms, now reaching almost 50 000 (including dependents of primary applicants). The number of admissions sponsored by the States and Territories increased almost twofold, from about 4 100 in 2004-05 to about 8 000 in 2005-06. This seems to be linked with several measures taken to enhance the attractiveness of some of the visa classes under this title, including the introduction of "sponsorship" points in July 2005.

Admission of family members of Australian residents was also the highest in a decade, amounting to more than 45 000. Humanitarian immigration has also continued to grow. More than 14 000 visas for permanent immigration on humanitarian grounds were granted in 2005-06. Australia provides pre-departure orientation to all refugee and humanitarian entrants over the age of twelve years. In 2006-07, this orientation will be extended from three to five days, and special children programmes are made available in all relevant locations.

Like permanent immigration, temporary migration has also shown significant increases in all major categories. In 2005-06, the number of temporary entrants on Business (long stay) visas increased by more than 20 000 to about 71 000. A record number of more than 190 000 visas were granted for foreign students.

The Working Holiday Maker (WHM) programme continued to grow, with more than 130 000 arrivals in 2005-06. There have been a variety of changes to expand the Working Holiday Maker Scheme and to enhance its benefits for both students and Australian employers. From 1 July 2006, persons under this programme are able to study or train for up to four months (previously three months), and work for up to six months (previously three months) with any one employer. Since 1 November 2005, WHMs who have done at least three months of seasonal work in regional Australia are able to apply for a second Working Holiday visa. In July 2006, the range of industries in which seasonal work may be undertaken has been expanded from agriculture to other primary industries, such as butchery, shearing, fishing and pearling, and tree farming and forestry. This initiative is intended to help address seasonal labour shortages in regional Australia, and to further boost tourism industries by enabling backpackers to stay longer in the country.

Changes in citizenship legislation have been proposed by the government in late 2006 and are currently being debated in parliament. The most important change concerns the residence requirements. Currently, access to citizenship is possible for persons who have been permanent residents in Australia for a period of two years. Under the new legislation, it is planned to increase this period to four years. Furthermore, the Australian government has launched a consultation process to examine the merits of introducing a formal citizenship test for people who wish to become Australian citizens, which would replace the current interview.

New business processes and systems will be phased in over the next four years to improve the processing of visa applications. This includes, in particular, the introduction of a comprehensive health information system for applicants. In this context, further expansion of the electronic processing of visa health requirements is also being considered.

The Australian government has also enhanced its efforts against irregular migration. In 2006, the government introduced the Migration Amendment (Employer Sanctions) Bill 2006 which would make it a criminal offence to knowingly or recklessly allow an illegal worker to work or to refer an illegal worker for work with another business.

For further information...

www.immi.gov.au/

Flow data on foreigners

Migration flows (foreigners) National definition	1995	2000	2004	2005	Average		Level ('000)
					1995-2000	2001-2005	2005
Per 1 000 inhabitants							
Inflows	..	6.0	7.5	8.2	5.6	7.1	*167.3*
Outflows	0.9	1.1	1.5	1.6	1.0	1.3	*31.6*

Migration inflows (foreigners) by type Permit based statistics (standardised)	Thousands		% distribution	
	2004	2005	2004	2005
Work	53.8	59.0	*32.2*	*32.8*
Family (incl. accompanying family)	94.2	102.3	*56.3*	*56.9*
Humanitarian	17.5	17.0	*10.5*	*9.4*
Others	1.8	1.6	*1.1*	*0.9*
Total	167.3	179.8		

Inflows of top 10 nationalities as a % of total inflows of foreigners

Legend: 1990-2004 annual average / 2005

United Kingdom, New Zealand, China, India, South Africa, Philippines, Malaysia, Sri Lanka, United States, Hong Kong (China) — scale 0 5 10 15 20 25 — 54.2 / 55.1

Temporary migration	2000	2004	2005	Annual average
				2000-2005
Thousands				
International students	74.4	115.2	116.7	100.0
Trainees	7.1	7.0	7.0	6.8
Working holiday makers	71.5	93.8	104.4	86.7
Seasonal workers	..	..	..	..
Intra-company transfers	..	..	..	..
Other temporary workers	54.5	58.6	71.6	59.2

Inflows of asylum seekers	1995	2000	2004	2005	Average		Level ('000)
					1995-2000	2001-2005	2005
Per 1 000 inhabitants	0.4	0.7	0.2	0.2	0.5	0.3	*3.2*

Macroeconomic, demographic and labour market indicators

Macroeconomic indicators	1995	2000	2004	2005	Average		Level
					1995-2000	2001-2005	2005
Real GDP (growth, %)	4.1	1.9	2.7	2.8	3.9	3.2	
GDP/capita (growth, %) – level in US dollars	2.7	0.7	1.5	1.5	2.7	2.0	*30 123*
Employment (growth, %) – level in thousands	4.3	2.7	1.9	3.3	1.6	2.3	*10 014*
Unemployment (% of labour force)	8.2	6.3	5.5	5.1	7.6	6.0	

Components of population growth	1995	2000	2004	2005	Average	
					1995-2000	2001-2005
Per 1 000 inhabitants						
Total	13.1	12.1	11.3	..	11.8	11.8
Natural increase	7.2	6.3	6.1	..	6.6	6.0
Net migration	5.9	5.8	5.2	..	5.2	5.8

Total population	1995	2000	2004	2005	Average		Level ('000)
					1995-2000	2001-2005	2005
(Annual growth %)							
Native-born	1.0	1.3	0.9	0.9	1.2	0.9	*15 500*
Foreign-born	1.9	1.0	2.1	1.7	1.2	1.9	*4 830*
National	..	..	..	..	..	..	..
Foreign	..	..	..	..	..	..	..

Naturalisations	1995	2000	2004	2005	Average		Level
					1995-2000	2001-2005	2005
As a percentage of foreign population	..	..	..	..	..	..	*93 095*

Labour market outcomes	1995	2000	2004	2005	Average	
					1995-2000	2001-2005
Employment/population ratio						
Native-born men	78.0	78.7	80.6	80.5	78.1	79.1
Foreign-born men	73.4	73.8	76.2	74.3	72.9	74.3
Native-born women	61.7	64.0	65.9	68.3	62.3	65.9
Foreign-born women	53.1	54.4	57.6	58.6	52.7	56.2
Unemployment rate						
Native-born men	8.4	6.6	5.6	4.7	7.8	6.1
Foreign-born men	10.7	6.6	5.5	5.0	9.0	6.2
Native-born women	7.3	6.2	5.7	5.0	7.1	5.8
Foreign-born women	9.2	7.6	5.6	5.2	8.7	6.4

Notes and sources are at the end of the Chapter.

StatLink ᔕᓫ *http://dx.doi.org/10.1787/015827886753*

Austria

The inflow of permanent immigrants in 2005 has remained at the high levels observed in 2003 and 2004. The number of third country nationals (*i.e.* non-EEA citizens) admitted for residence on permanent grounds reached 32 200 in 2005, roughly the same as in 2004. In addition, according to national statistics, some 27 700 persons from the EEA settled in Austria. The vast majority of third country nationals immigrate under the heading of family migration (more than 90% of permanent immigrants from these countries in 2005).

Since 1 January 2006, a new immigration law is in force, which brought several changes in the permit system, mainly with a view to incorporating EU directives on the admission and stay of third country nationals. There is now a special entry category for third country nationals residing in other EU country, but entries under this category have been negligible. In addition, EEA nationals benefiting from the free movement provisions now have the obligation to register after three months. As a result, the inflow of EEA citizens is now better documented.

The most fundamental change in the new law concerns the introduction of the requirement that in the case of family reunification (including family formation), the sponsoring family member in Austria needs to have the financial means to provide for the partner (*i.e.*, regular income at or above the minimum wage). This is an important entry barrier of unskilled third country spouses of welfare recipients who are natives or permanent residents in Austria, although dependent children continue to have the right to join their parents even if the latter are living on welfare. In turn, labour market access of family reunification migrants is now facilitated. Preliminary data for 2006 show that the inflow of third country citizens for settlement declined as a result of the reformed immigration law (NAG 2005).

A further change relates to international students, who are now required to provide proof of a certain income level to cover their expenses while studying in Austria. While in 2004 and 2005 some 5 000 third country students received a temporary resident permit for study purposes, this number is thus expected to decline somewhat in 2006.

Under the new immigration act, the scale and scope of the integration courses has been expanded. The new government, in power since January 2006, announced a variety of further measures to foster integration, including more language training offers for immigrants and measures to promote participation in kindergarten and language acquisition of immigrant children.

With about 22 500 requests in 2005, asylum seeking has continued its decline since the 2002 peak of more than 39 000. However, relative to the population, Austria remains the OECD country with the highest number of asylum requests. Parallel to the new immigration act, new legislation with respect to asylum took effect on 1 January 2006. This included a variety of measures aimed at strengthening the asylum procedure and at preventing abuse.

The number of foreigners taking Austrian nationality reached 35 400 in 2005. It thus continued its decline compared to the all time high in 2003 with 45 100. The main origin groups of former nationalities are from the successor states of the former Yugoslavia (48%), followed by Turkish nationals (27%). Legislation introduced in 2005 brought changes regarding naturalisation which made the acquisition of Austrian citizenship more restrictive.

For further information...

www.bmi.gv.at/publikationen/

Flow data on foreigners

Migration flows (foreigners) *National definitions*	1995	2000	2004	2005	Average		Level ('000)
					1995-2000	2001-2005	2005
Per 1 000 inhabitants							
Inflows	..	8.1	13.3	12.3	8.1	11.7	*101.5*
Outflows	..	5.5	5.9	5.8	5.6	5.7	*47.5*

Long-term migration inflows (foreigners) by type *Permit based statistics (standardised)*	Thousands		% distribution	
	2004	2005	2004	2005
Work	11.1	17.9	*20.5*	*31.5*
Family (incl. accompanying family)	34.4	32.3	*63.5*	*56.9*
Humanitarian (incl. accompanying family)	7.4	5.9	*13.6*	*10.4*
Others	1.3	0.7	*2.4*	*1.2*
Total	54.2	56.8		

Inflows of top 10 nationalities as a % of total inflows of foreigners

Temporary migration	2000	2004	2005	Annual average
				2000-2005
Thousands				
International students	3.2	5.4	–	4.6
Trainees	0.9	0.8	–	1.1
Working holiday makers	..	..	..	..
Seasonal workers	9.1	15.7	–	14.1
Intra-company transfers	0.2	0.2	–	0.2
Other temporary workers	6.0	9.8	–	8.8

Inflows of asylum seekers	1995	2000	2004	2005	Average		Level ('000)
					1995-2000	2001-2005	2005
Per 1 000 inhabitants	0.7	2.3	3.0	2.7	1.5	3.7	*22.5*

Macroeconomic, demographic and labour market indicators

Macroeconomic indicators	1995	2000	2004	2005	Average		Level
					1995-2000	2001-2005	2005
Real GDP (growth, %)	1.9	3.4	2.4	2.0	2.9	1.6	
GDP/capita (growth, %) – level in US dollars	1.8	3.1	1.7	1.3	2.8	1.0	*30 036*
Employment (growth, %) – level in thousands	−0.1	1.0	−0.4	0.3	1.0	−0.1	*4 118*
Unemployment (% of labour force)	5.3	4.6	5.7	5.8	5.3	5.4	

Components of population growth	1995	2000	2004	2005	Average	
					1995-2000	2001-2005
Per 1 000 inhabitants						
Total	1.2	2.3	6.9	6.3	1.6	4.9
Natural increase	0.9	0.2	0.6	0.4	0.5	0.3
Net migration	0.3	2.2	6.2	5.9	1.1	4.6

Total population	1995	2000	2004	2005	Average		Level ('000)
					1995-2000	2001-2005	2005
(Annual growth %)							
Native-born	..	0.7	−1.1	0.2	..	−0.4	*7 133*
Foreign-born	..	−3.3	14.7	3.9	..	5.3	*1 100*
National	..	0.1	0.5	0.4	0.1	0.1	*7 431*
Foreign	..	1.1	2.2	3.3	0.7	2.8	*802*

Naturalisations	1995	2000	2004	2005	Average		Level
					1995-2000	2001-2005	2005
As a percentage of foreign population	..	3.5	5.5	4.5	3.3	5.1	*34 876*

Labour market outcomes	1995	2000	2004	2005	Average	
					1995-2000	2001-2005
Employment/population ratio						
Native-born men	77.5	76.2	73.4	74.5	76.4	74.9
Foreign-born men	78.5	76.1	61.3	67.9	76.3	70.5
Native-born women	59.4	59.9	61.4	62.9	59.5	61.4
Foreign-born women	57.5	58.3	45.0	55.9	56.2	55.0
Unemployment rate						
Native-born men	3.6	4.3	4.3	4.1	4.3	4.1
Foreign-born men	6.2	8.7	12.7	11.6	9.2	10.3
Native-born women	4.6	4.2	4.3	4.4	4.6	4.1
Foreign-born women	7.0	7.2	12.7	9.7	8.0	8.7

Notes and sources are at the end of the Chapter.

StatLink ⟶ *http://dx.doi.org/10.1787/015875368764*

Belgium

In 2005, migration continued to rise: According to national statistics, over 77 000 foreigners immigrated into Belgium (7% more than in 2004). Around half were from other EU Member States. France and the Netherlands were the two most common sending countries, between them accounting for a quarter of new entries. However, there was a sharp increase in immigrants from Poland (almost 5 000, up 40% on 2004).

With regard to short-term labour migration, over 6 000 new temporary work permits were issued to wage-earners (not including the self-employed), an increase of 30% on 2004. Almost one-third of those permits went to Polish nationals. Such permits are confined to industries with labour shortages, as established in regional lists. They can thus be granted to nationals from the new EU Member States, even though Belgium extended its restrictions during the second phase of the transition period. At the same time, 6 000 temporary work permits were granted to highly skilled workers, half of whom were Indian, Japanese or US nationals.

Over 31 000 people acquired Belgian nationality in 2005. The number of naturalisations was very much the same as in previous years, remaining high compared with other OECD countries. The brisk pace of naturalisations since the latest amendment to the Code of Nationality in 2000 has given rise to a debate in Belgium about the usefulness of "ethnic statistics" to measure the integration of, and discrimination against, people with immigrant backgrounds on the labour market.

In late 2006, several laws were adopted on the entry, residence and removal of foreigners, as well as on asylum, and these will come into force in April 2007. The new legislation is tighter with regard to family reunion: Foreigners living in Belgium and wishing to marry a non-European Union national (EU27) will now have to be 21 years of age rather than 18. Once family reunion has been authorised, checks may be carried out over a three-year period to ensure that family members are actually living together. Victims of human trafficking may now be granted right of abode.

2006 was also the first year in which non-EU foreigners became eligible to vote in local elections (on 13 October). 17 000 foreigners had registered to vote in these municipal elections, i.e. 17% of the 100 000 potential voters. The low participation rate may stem from the fact that many of the immigrants most likely to show an interest in local politics (those who are both better integrated and have spent a long time in the country) have become Belgian citizens. But other factors which appear to have had an impact include red tape (Belgian nationals do not have to register, as voting is compulsory) and the absence of a nationwide information campaign. The participation rate among non-EU nationals also needs to be set against that of EU nationals, only 7% of whom actually registered to vote in Belgium when entitled to do so under the new legislation.

For further information...

http://ecodata.mineco.fgov.be/
www.statbel.fgov.be/

Flow data on foreigners

Migration flows (foreigners) National definition	1995	2000	2004	2005	Average		Level ('000)
					1995-2000	2001-2005	2005
Per 1 000 inhabitants							
Inflows	5.2	5.6	7.0	7.4	5.2	6.8	77.4
Outflows	3.3	3.5	3.6	3.7	3.4	3.3	38.5

Long-term migration inflows (foreigners) by type Permit based statistics (standardised)	Thousands		% distribution	
	2004	2005	2004	2005
Work	..	14.0	..	39.0
Family (incl. accompanying family)	..	18.8	..	52.5
Humanitarian (incl. accompanying family)	..	3.1	..	8.5
Others	..	..	..	..
Total	..	35.9		

Inflows of top 10 nationalities as a % of total inflows of foreigners

Temporary migration	2000	2004	2005	Annual average
				2000-2005
Thousands				
International students	..	..	..	..
Trainees	..	..	..	..
Working holiday makers	..	..	..	..
Seasonal workers	..	1.0	2.7	1.4
Intra-company transfers	..	..	..	..
Other temporary workers	..	0.5	2.8	1.5

Inflows of asylum seekers	1995	2000	2004	2005	Average		Level ('000)
					1995-2000	2001-2005	2005
Per 1 000 inhabitants	1.1	4.2	1.5	1.5	2.2	1.8	16.0

Macroeconomic, demographic and labour market indicators

Macroeconomic indicators	1995	2000	2004	2005	Average		Level
					1995-2000	2001-2005	2005
Real GDP (growth, %)	2.4	3.9	2.6	1.2	2.7	1.6	
GDP/capita (growth, %) – level in US dollars	2.2	3.6	2.2	0.7	2.4	1.1	28 038
Employment (growth, %) – level in thousands	0.7	2.0	0.6	0.8	1.1	0.3	4 251
Unemployment (% of labour force)	9.7	6.9	8.4	8.4	8.9	7.8	

Components of population growth	1995	2000	2004	2005	Average	
					1995-2000	2001-2005
Per 1 000 inhabitants						
Total	2.4	2.4	..	..	2.2	..
Natural increase	1.0	1.0	..	..	1.0	..
Net migration	1.3	1.4	..	..	1.1	..

Total population	1995	2000	2004	2005	Average		Level ('000)
					1995-2000	2001-2005	2005
(Annual growth %)							
Native-born	0.2	0.1	−0.1	0.3	0.1	0.1	9 210
Foreign-born	0.2	1.6	2.9	4.0	1.5	3.4	1 269
National	0.4	0.6	0.1	0.5	0.3	0.4	9 578
Foreign	−1.4	−3.9	1.2	3.4	−1.1	1.6	900

Naturalisations	1995	2000	2004	2005	Average		Level
					1995-2000	2001-2005	2005
As a percentage of foreign population	2.8	6.9	4.0	3.6	3.7	4.9	31 512

Labour market outcomes	1995	2000	2004	2005	Average	
					1995-2000	2001-2005
Employment/population ratio						
Native-born men	67.8	70.8	68.9	68.7	68.3	69.0
Foreign-born men	59.1	62.2	60.3	61.1	60.7	59.9
Native-born women	46.9	53.8	54.8	56.7	49.5	54.2
Foreign-born women	31.7	37.3	40.1	38.9	34.9	37.9
Unemployment rate						
Native-born men	6.3	4.2	5.6	6.3	6.0	5.5
Foreign-born men	16.8	14.7	14.9	14.8	16.1	15.6
Native-born women	11.2	7.4	7.5	7.5	10.2	7.0
Foreign-born women	23.8	17.5	15.0	20.3	20.1	17.2

Notes and sources are at the end of the Chapter.

StatLink ⇨ http://dx.doi.org/10.1787/021211587725

Bulgaria

Although exact migration data for Bulgaria is difficult to obtain, it appears that migration from and to Bulgaria has remained broadly constant in 2005 and 2006, with emigration still dominating the picture. According to the National Statistical Institute, annual emigration is currently at about 10 000-12 000 persons, and is expected to decline to around 6 000-8 000 persons after 2010.

The key policy development was the ongoing preparation in the area of migration legislation prior to Bulgaria's accession to the European Union on 1 January 2007, which required significant changes in several major areas of migration policy. The government opted for full implementation of the Community law in the area of free movement of workers and provided for a freedom of all EU citizens to work without limitations in Bulgaria. In order to implement this policy, among other legislative changes, a new "law on entry into, residence in and departure from the Republic of Bulgaria of EU citizens and members of their families" was introduced.

With the strong and sustained economic growth and ongoing emigration, the declining labour supply is a matter of growing policy concern in Bulgaria. Two options are being considered. The first is to open all areas of the labour market for migrant workers. The alternative option is to open access only for some professional groups. As part of the growing orientation towards labour migration, a more flexible regime was established for the secondment of foreign workers by foreign companies providing services in Bulgaria.

Further changes concerned the functioning of labour recruitment agencies. In the past, recruitment agencies have been mainly active in the area of construction and ocean transport. If recruitment agencies are EU based, they are no longer required to be registered by the Bulgarian Ministry of Labour and Social Policy. In addition, since early 2006, private recruitment agencies have no longer the right to receive commissions from workers for their services. Prior to this, such agencies had the right to charge up to 25% of the first salary.

With the prospect of EU membership, the number of naturalisation demands has more than tripled since 2002, reaching 23 200 in 2005. A large part of these have been granted to former Macedonian nationals.

In spite of the growing economy and the improving labour market situation, the policy of encouraging labour migration of Bulgarian citizens continued, mainly by implementing bilateral labour agreements with EU countries. Recent legislative changes enlarged the scope of cross-border employment services provided by the National Employment Agencies to both local and foreign employers, as well as to local and foreign nationals.

To estimate the emigration potential of Bulgarian nationals after EU accession, a large poll on migration intentions was conducted in 2006, which had the same basic setup as a prior 2001 survey. The results indicated that migration intentions had remained broadly stable since 2001, with a growth in intentions to emigrate temporarily compensating for a decline in intentions for permanent emigration. Spain was the intended destination that was mentioned most often, followed by Germany.

A number of changes in border control and visa policy were implemented in 2005 to meet the obligations of the Schengen *acquis*. In particular, several new initiatives were introduced to prevent illegal migration and to assure a more stringent border and entry control. At the end of 2005, the Integrated Border Management Strategy was approved, and border facilities have been upgraded subsequently. Enforcement mechanisms, better internal co-ordination and institutional capacity building in the area of migration remain the main migration policy targets.

Officially recorded remittance inflows reached almost EUR 1 billion in 2005. This represented an increase of more than 12% compared to 2004, which was above expectations.

For further information...

www.nsi.bg
www.aref.government.bg
www.mlsp.government.bg

Flow data on foreigners

Migration flows (foreigners) *National definition*	1995	2000	2004	2005	Average		Level ('000)
					1995-2000	2001-2005	2005
Per 1 000 inhabitants							
Inflows	0.3	0.5	2.1	2.0	0.4	1.5	*15.6*
Outflows	..	..	..	..	..	..	..

Long-term migration inflows (foreigners) by type *Permit based statistics (standardised)*	Thousands		% distribution	
	2004	2005	2004	2005
Work	..	..	..	..
Family (incl. accompanying family)	..	..	..	..
Humanitarian (incl. accompanying family)	..	..	..	..
Others	..	..	..	..
Total	..	..		

Temporary migration	2000	2004	2005	Annual average
				2000-2005
Thousands				
International students	1.5	1.8	1.5	1.6
Trainees	..	..	..	..
Working holiday makers	..	..	..	..
Seasonal workers	..	..	..	..
Intra-company transfers	..	..	..	..
Other temporary workers	0.3	1.0	0.6	0.5

Inflows of asylum seekers	1995	2000	2004	2005	Average		Level ('000)
					1995-2000	2001-2005	2005
Per 1 000 inhabitants	0.1	0.2	0.1	0.1	0.1	0.2	*0.8*

Macroeconomic, demographic and labour market indicators

Macroeconomic indicators	1995	2000	2004	2005	Average		Level
					1995-2000	2001-2005	2005
Real GDP (growth, %)	37.7	−2.7	21.5	9.4	−0.7	18.1	
GDP/capita (growth, %) – level in US dollars	38.3	−2.2	22.2	9.5	−0.1	18.8	*9 223*
Employment (growth, %) – level in thousands	..	−2.7	3.1	2.1	−3.3	3.2	*2 982*
Unemployment (% of labour force)	..	17.9	12.0	10.1	15.4	13.9	

Components of population growth	1995	2000	2004	2005	Average		
					1995-2000	2001-2005	
Per 1 000 inhabitants							
Total	..	..	..	−8.9	..	..	
Natural increase	..	..	..	−4.6	..	..	
Net migration	..	..	..	−4.3	..	..	

Total population	1995	2000	2004	2005	Average		Level ('000)
					1995-2000	2001-2005	2005
(Annual growth %)							
Native-born	..	..	..	..	..	..	..
Foreign-born	..	..	..	..	..	..	..
National	..	..	−0.6	−0.5	..	..	*7 675*
Foreign	..	..	12.4	−2.3	..	..	*65*

Naturalisations	1995	2000	2004	2005	Average		Level
					1995-2000	2001-2005	2005
As a percentage of foreign population	..	..	9.6	8.8	..	11.4	*5 848*

Notes and sources are at the end of the Chapter.

StatLink 🔗 *http://dx.doi.org/10.1787/021217454010*

Canada

Immigration to Canada reached its highest level in more than a decade. In 2005, more than 260 000 people were admitted to Canada as permanent residents, an increase of 11% over the 2004 total. The increase was observed across all categories, though the growth was most marked with respect to work related migration, which now accounts for 60% of permanent immigration.

Canada operates with target ranges in its immigration programme, and the 2005 admissions surpassed the original target range of 220 000 to 245 000. There are a variety of factors that explain this spike in the level of admissions in 2005. Firstly, the number of skilled workers exceeded the original targets by almost 18 000 in response to favourable labour market conditions. Provincial and territorial governments also increased their involvement in the immigration process by identifying and designating immigrants that meet their local economic needs. As a result, the number of Provincial Nominees has increased more than five-fold in the past five years although it still remains limited, accounting for about 8 000 immigrants. Since 2003, Canada has also placed particular priority on ensuring prompt and efficient processing to facilitate family reunification in certain cases (including sponsored spouses, partners and dependent children). In addition, new funding was committed in April 2005 – for two years – to increase processing of parent and grandparent applications. For 2005, this resulted in about 7 000 parents and grandparents being admitted above the original target level. Finally, immigrants used their visas faster in 2005 than in 2004, with the standard time between visa issuance and immigrant arrival in Canada declining by 30 days. This resulted in one "extra" month of admissions. The year 2005 also witnessed a substantial drop in the number of immigrant visa holders who chose not to immigrate. China and India remained the leading source countries, representing 29% of new permanent residents.

Temporary labour migration grew to reach about 100 000. At the same time, the trend decline in asylum seeking continued. Fewer than 20 000 persons demanded asylum, the lowest figure since the late 1980s.

At a meeting of Federal, provincial and territorial ministers in November 2005, a number of priorities for immigration and integration policy were identified. These included efforts to improve selection of migrants, measures to improve outcomes to ensure that immigrants' skills are used to full potential, an increased regionalisation to share the benefits of immigration more widely across the country; and an improved client service.

The government of Canada has introduced a number of initiatives to facilitate integration of immigrants. Continued focus was put on enhanced language training for newcomers to Canada in order to assist them with their integration into the Canadian workforce. The Enhanced Language Training initiative provides for the delivery of labour market levels of language training and job-specific language training for skilled immigrants. In addition, in concert with other authorities and external stakeholders, progress has been made in the establishment of an agency for the recognition of foreign credentials.

A comprehensive Immigration Agreement has been signed on November 21, 2005, between Canada and Ontario. This marks the first agreement between the federal government and Canada's largest immigrant-receiving province and addresses, among other issues, a range of integration needs such as pre-arrival orientation, basic settlement services and language training.

In 2005-06, a number of service improvements were introduced progressively to improve information, application management, processing times and client service. The government of Canada has invested in a number of initiatives to improve service delivery and to reduce inventories of applications.

Also in 2005, in collaboration with provincial and territorial authorities, the government of Canada expanded key initiatives aimed at increasing Canada's attractiveness for foreign students. Foreign students at Canadian post-secondary institutions, who can work for a year after graduation outside of Montreal, Toronto and Vancouver, can now prolong their stay for a second year. Since April 2006, foreign students are also allowed to seek off-campus employment during their studies.

For further information...

www.cic.gc.ca/english/index.html

Flow data on foreigners

Migration flows (foreigners) National definition	1995	2000	2004	2005	Average 1995-2000	Average 2001-2005	Level ('000) 2005
Per 1 000 inhabitants							
Inflows	7.3	7.4	7.4	8.1	6.9	7.6	*262.2*
Outflows	..	..	..	..	..	..	..

Migration inflows (foreigners) by type Permit based statistics (standardised)	Thousands 2004	Thousands 2005	% distribution 2004	% distribution 2005
Work	55.2	61.6	23.4	23.5
Family (incl. accompanying family)	140.8	158.0	59.7	60.3
Humanitarian (incl. accompanying family)	39.7	42.4	16.8	16.2
Others	0.1	0.1	0.1	–
Total	235.8	262.2		

Inflows of top 10 nationalities as a % of total inflows of foreigners

Temporary migration	2000	2004	2005	Annual average 2000-2005
Thousands				
International students	60.0	55.6	57.5	61.0
Trainees	..	..	..	..
Working holiday makers	..	..	..	..
Seasonal workers	16.6	19.0	20.3	18.6
Intra-company transfers	1.6	4.2	4.5	3.2
Other temporary workers	75.2	55.8	..	62.3

Inflows of asylum seekers	1995	2000	2004	2005	Average 1995-2000	Average 2001-2005	Level ('000) 2005
Per 1 000 inhabitants	0.9	1.1	0.8	0.6	0.9	1.0	*20.8*

Macroeconomic, demographic and labour market indicators

Macroeconomic indicators	1995	2000	2004	2005	Average 1995-2000	Average 2001-2005	Level 2005
Real GDP (growth, %)	2.8	5.2	3.3	2.9	4.1	2.7	
GDP/capita (growth, %) – level in US dollars	1.7	4.3	2.3	2.0	3.2	1.7	*30 692*
Employment (growth, %) – level in thousands	1.8	2.5	1.8	1.4	2.1	2.0	*16 169*
Unemployment (% of labour force)	9.5	6.8	7.2	6.8	8.5	7.3	

Components of population growth	1995	2000	2004	2005	Average 1995-2000	Average 2001-2005
Per 1 000 inhabitants						
Total	11.2	10.1	9.5	..	9.8	10.2
Natural increase	5.7	3.6	3.3	..	4.5	3.4
Net migration	5.5	6.5	6.2	..	5.3	6.8

Total population	1995	2000	2004	2005	Average 1995-2000	Average 2001-2005	Level ('000) 2005
(Annual growth %)							
Native-born	0.8	0.8	0.7	0.8	0.7	0.8	*26 375*
Foreign-born	2.2	1.8	1.8	2.1	1.8	2.0	*5 896*
National	..	..	..	..	..	..	..
Foreign	..	..	..	..	..	..	..

Naturalisations	1995	2000	2004	2005	Average 1995-2000	Average 2001-2005	Level 2005
As a percentage of foreign population	..	..	..	..	..	..	*196 291*

Labour market outcomes	1995	2000	2004	2005	Average 1995-2000	Average 2001-2005
Employment/population ratio						
Native-born men	75.9	77.4	..	..	75.8	77.6
Foreign-born men	75.6	77.0	..	..	75.3	75.6
Native-born women	62.0	66.0	..	..	63.3	67.5
Foreign-born women	55.0	59.6	..	..	56.8	58.7
Unemployment rate						
Native-born men	8.6	5.7	..	..	7.5	6.3
Foreign-born men	10.4	6.1	..	..	8.3	7.7
Native-born women	9.8	6.2	..	..	8.3	6.1
Foreign-born women	13.3	8.7	..	..	10.3	9.5

Notes and sources are at the end of the Chapter.

StatLink *http://dx.doi.org/10.1787/021217652304*

Czech Republic

Immigration to the Czech Republic increased in 2005, reaching 60 3000 according to national statistics. The increase was mainly driven by a strong increase in immigration of Ukrainians, who account for more than a third of total immigration. However, many of these are short-term, and due to a parallel increase in emigration, net migration of Ukrainians remained broadly constant. The situation for Slovak nationals is the reverse of this, with a slight decline in immigration coinciding with a strong decrease in outflows. Over the whole, emigration declined by about 10 000, leading to a substantial increase in net migration to over 36 000, the highest level registered over the past decade.

With about 4 000 applications, asylum seeking continued its downward trend, reaching the lowest level since 1998. Ukrainians, followed by Slovak nationals, Indians, Chinese and Russians were the most numerous nationalities of asylum seekers entering the Czech Republic in 2005.

Illegal migration also appears to have continued its decline. About 5 700 persons were detected attempting to cross the border illegally, the lowest number since 1993. The fight against illegal migration remains a priority of the security policy of the Czech Republic.

In 2005/2006, there were two significant amendments to the Act on Residence of Aliens. The first one, which entered in force on 24 November 2005, aimed, among other objectives, at implementing the EU directive on family reunification. An important change, which represents a simplified entry procedure for foreigners from the third countries, was the introduction of the possibility to apply for a residence permit and a work permit in a single procedure. Previously, two separate applications were necessary.

The principal aim of the second amendment, which came into effect on 27 April 2006, has been the implementation of a number of EU directives: i) on the status of third country nationals who are long-term residents; ii) on the right of citizens of the European Union and their family members to move and reside freely within the territory of the Member States; iii) on residence permits issued to third country nationals who are victims of trafficking in human beings or who otherwise participated in illegal immigration and who co-operate with the competent authorities; iv) on the conditions of admission of third country nationals for the purposes of study, student exchange, unremunerated training or voluntary service. One important change concerns the duration of residence until a permanent residence permit can be granted, which was shortened from 10 to 5 years. In addition, entrepreneurs from non-EU countries can now apply for a residence permit and a business licence in a single procedure.

Further legislative changes concerned the Act on Asylum, which also incorporated EU legislation in this field.

An important step in launching an active migration policy by the Czech Republic has been a pilot project of the selection of qualified foreign workers. The project aims at attracting young, qualified immigrants. These persons (and their family members) are offered a possibility to obtain permanent residence in the Czech Republic already after 2 years and 6 months. In October 2006, the first 30 participants of the project and their family members obtained their permanent residence permit in the Czech Republic. The countries of origin of these have been Bulgaria, Croatia and Kazakhstan. The pilot project has been expanded further. In the fourth year (July 2006 to July 2007) of the five-year pilot phase, the number of available places has augmented to 1 000.

Along with the growing focus on permanent labour immigration, increasing attention is also being paid to integration, in particular with regard to Czech language courses, advisory services for foreigners, and the removal of legislative obstacles which could hamper integration of foreigners.

For further information...

http://mvcr.cz/english/index.html
www.imigracecz.org
www.cizinci.cz

Flow data on foreigners

Migration flows (foreigners) *National definition*	1995	2000	2004	2005	Average		Level ('000)
					1995-2000	2001-2005	2005
Per 1 000 inhabitants							
Inflows	0.6	0.4	5.0	5.7	0.7	4.3	*58.6*
Outflows	–	–	3.3	2.1	–	2.8	*21.8*

Long-term migration inflows (foreigners) by type *Permit based statistics (standardised)*	Thousands		% distribution	
	2004	2005	2004	2005
Work	..	..	..	..
Family (incl. accompanying family)	..	..	..	..
Humanitarian (incl. accompanying family)	..	..	..	..
Others	..	..	..	..
Total	..	..		

Temporary migration	2000	2004	2005	Annual average
				2000-2005
Thousands				
International students	..	..	..	..
Trainees	..	..	..	..
Working holiday makers	..	..	..	..
Seasonal workers	..	..	..	..
Intra-company transfers	..	..	..	..
Other temporary workers	..	..	..	..

Inflows of top 10 nationalities as a % of total inflows of foreigners

1990-2004 annual average   2005

(Ukraine, Slovak Republic, Viet Nam, Russian Federation, Moldova, Germany, United States, Poland, Mongolia, Bulgaria)

≈84.8 ▭85.6

Inflows of asylum seekers	1995	2000	2004	2005	Average		Level ('000)
					1995-2000	2001-2005	2005
Per 1 000 inhabitants	0.1	0.9	0.5	0.4	0.4	0.9	*4.2*

Macroeconomic, demographic and labour market indicators

Macroeconomic indicators	1995	2000	2004	2005	Average		Level
					1995-2000	2001-2005	2005
Real GDP (growth, %)	5.9	3.6	4.2	6.1	1.5	3.9	
GDP/capita (growth, %) – level in US dollars	6.0	3.8	4.2	5.8	1.6	3.9	*17 802*
Employment (growth, %) – level in thousands	0.9	−0.7	−0.3	1.4	−1.0	0.3	*4 749*
Unemployment (% of labour force)	4.1	8.8	8.3	8.0	6.2	7.9	

Components of population growth	1995	2000	2004	2005	Average		
					1995-2000	2001-2005	
Per 1 000 inhabitants							
Total	−1.1	−1.1	1.5	3.0	−1.1	0.5	
Natural increase	−2.1	−1.8	−0.3	−0.6	−2.0	−1.2	
Net migration	1.0	0.6	1.8	3.5	0.9	1.7	

Total population	1995	2000	2004	2005	Average		Level ('000)
					1995-2000	2001-2005	2005
(Annual growth %)							
Native-born	..	0.1	−0.1	−0.2	..	−0.2	*9 697*
Foreign-born	..	−4.7	3.5	4.9	..	3.9	*523*
National	..	0.2	–	−0.1	..	−0.2	*9 942*
Foreign	53.0	−12.2	5.8	9.4	4.8	7.2	*278*

Naturalisations	1995	2000	2004	2005	Average		Level
					1995-2000	2001-2005	2005
As a percentage of foreign population	–	3.6	2.1	1.0	1.5	1.9	*2 626*

Labour market outcomes	1995	2000	2004	2005	Average		
					1995-2000	2001-2005	
Employment/population ratio							
Native-born men	..	..	72.3	73.3	..	73.2	
Foreign-born men	..	..	64.5	70.3	..	67.1	
Native-born women	..	..	56.3	56.1	..	56.6	
Foreign-born women	..	..	49.9	50.7	..	50.9	
Unemployment rate							
Native-born men	..	..	7.0	6.2	..	6.2	
Foreign-born men	..	..	12.2	10.3	..	10.7	
Native-born women	..	..	9.6	9.7	..	9.4	
Foreign-born women	..	..	13.6	17.1	..	14.3	

Notes and sources are at the end of the Chapter.

StatLink ᵐˢᵇ *http://dx.doi.org/10.1787/021270007333*

Denmark

Immigration of foreign nationals has remained broadly constant in 2004 and stood at about 19 000. 2005 figures are not yet available, as national statistics define immigrants *ex post* as persons who entered in 2005 and stayed in Denmark for at least one year. The number of residence permits granted in 2005 has increased, particularly in work-related migration. In contrast, permits for family reunification and humanitarian immigration continued to decline. Asylum seeking also dropped, by about 30% in 2005.

A number of significant changes in legislation took place in 2006. The key political event was the June 2006 Welfare Agreement between the government and various parties aimed at securing the Danish welfare system for the future. The agreement touches on several areas, including employment, retirement, education, research and integration of immigrants.

In the area of integration, the agreement concerns a variety of initiatives to improve the employment of immigrants and their children, including more job advisors to improve the match between companies and jobseekers, a new wage subsidy targeted at persons who have been unemployed for a long period, and activation offers such as job training for persons who do not receive social benefits (such as family reunification migrants). The corresponding bill was adopted by the parliament in February 2007.

The second major event was an agreement between the government and the Danish People's Party concerning future immigration to Denmark. As a result, the government put forward a bill in November 2006 which, among other measures, proposes that foreigners with a specific job offer earning at least EUR 60 000 (DKK 450 000) can obtain a residence permit, even for employment in sectors where there is no shortage of labour. The bill also envisages the introduction of a points system ("green card-scheme") by which high-qualified foreigners may be granted a residence permit for up to 6 months in order to seek employment in Denmark. Points are given according to a set of criteria including education, language, work experience and age. Furthermore, foreigners who have concluded a post-secondary educational programme in Denmark shall have the possibility to seek a job for a period for up to 6 months.

The bill also includes measures to further tighten conditions for obtaining a permanent residence permit. An "integration exam" is planned according to which, among other restrictions, an applicant must have been at least 2½ years in full-time employment in order to obtain a permanent residence permit. In addition, the bill contains proposals on further restrictions on family reunification and on the issuance of residence permits for religious preachers. Applicants must have passed a test in Danish language and Danish society in order to obtain a residence permit.

Already in March 2006, conditions for obtaining a permanent residence permit had been tightened. Applicants must, among other obligations, have signed an "integration contract" and declare that they will involve themselves actively in integration into Danish society.

New rules concerning education and activation of adult asylum seekers were introduced in April 2006. The new rules imply, among other measures, more education and activation offers to rejected asylum seekers with a view of better preparing them for return to their home countries. In May 2006, rules on expulsion were tightened, including a broader definition of offences which will normally lead to expulsion.

In January 2007, a bill was adopted which simplified rules for family reunification. It is no longer decisive how much the family earns, but whether or not the family is self-supporting. Families who do not receive public assistance under the Act of Active Social Policy or the Integration Act will be considered self-supportive. The bill also contained new rules regarding residence permits for students.

The Danish government also issued new guidelines regarding naturalisation. Applicants are tested on their knowledge of Danish society, history and culture. The conditions concerning language mastery were also tightened. The first tests in Danish society, history and culture will take place in May and June 2007.

A number of measures were taken in the area of integration, including initiatives to diversify recruitment channels and the initiation of a major evaluation of Danish Language Education for foreigners.

For further information...

www.nyidanmark.dk/en-us/

Flow data on foreigners

Migration flows (foreigners) *National definition*	1995	2000	2004	2005	Average		Level ('000)
					1995-2000	2001-2005	2004
Per 1 000 inhabitants							
Inflows	6.3	4.3	3.5	–	4.5	3.9	18.8
Outflows	1.0	1.6	1.7	–	1.3	1.7	9.4

Long-term migration inflows (foreigners) by type *Permit based statistics (standardised)*	Thousands		% distribution	
	2004	2005	2004	2005
Work	6.7	7.6	40.7	42.1
Family (incl. accompanying family)	6.9	8.0	42.1	44.5
Humanitarian (incl. accompanying family)	1.6	1.1	9.7	6.4
Others	1.2	1.3	7.5	7.0
Total	16.4	18.0		

Inflows of top 10 nationalities as a % of total inflows of foreigners

Temporary migration	2000	2004	2005	Annual average
				2000-2005
Thousands				
International students	4.2	6.2	6.9	5.4
Trainees	1.4	1.5	1.9	1.6
Working holiday makers	..	..	..	..
Seasonal workers	..	..	..	..
Intra-company transfers	..	..	..	..
Other temporary workers	1.4	3.4	2.6	2.4

Inflows of asylum seekers	1995	2000	2004	2005	Average		Level ('000)
					1995-2000	2001-2005	2005
Per 1 000 inhabitants	1.0	2.3	0.6	0.4	1.6	1.1	2.3

Macroeconomic, demographic and labour market indicators

Macroeconomic indicators	1995	2000	2004	2005	Average		Level
					1995-2000	2001-2005	2005
Real GDP (growth, %)	3.1	3.5	2.1	3.1	2.9	1.5	
GDP/capita (growth, %) – level in US dollars	2.6	3.2	1.9	2.8	2.4	1.2	30 351
Employment (growth, %) – level in thousands	0.9	0.4	–0.1	0.7	1.0	–0.2	2 761
Unemployment (% of labour force)	6.7	4.3	5.5	4.8	5.4	4.9	

Components of population growth	1995	2000	2004	2005	Average		
					1995-2000	2001-2005	
Per 1 000 inhabitants							
Total	6.9	3.4	2.4	2.9	4.2	2.8	
Natural increase	1.3	1.7	1.5	1.7	1.4	1.3	
Net migration	5.5	1.7	0.9	1.2	2.7	1.4	

Total population	1995	2000	2004	2005	Average		Level ('000)
					1995-2000	2001-2005	2005
(Annual growth %)							
Native-born	–	0.1	0.2	0.2	0.2	0.1	5 066
Foreign-born	11.1	4.0	1.6	2.1	4.3	2.2	350
National	0.0	0.4	0.3	0.2	0.3	0.3	5 146
Foreign	13.2	–0.3	–1.3	0.9	3.0	0.3	270

Naturalisations	1995	2000	2004	2005	Average		Level
					1995-2000	2001-2005	2005
As a percentage of foreign population	2.7	7.3	5.5	3.8	4.2	4.6	10 197

Labour market outcomes	1995	2000	2004	2005	Average		
					1995-2000	2001-2005	
Employment/population ratio							
Native-born men	78.9	80.9	79.1	80.8	..	..	
Foreign-born men	51.2	59.0	55.8	69.4	..	..	
Native-born women	69.5	73.9	73.5	72.6	..	..	
Foreign-born women	41.5	48.3	44.8	52.7	..	..	
Unemployment rate							
Native-born men	6.4	3.4	4.6	4.0	..	..	
Foreign-born men	20.5	9.5	11.8	7.2	..	..	
Native-born women	8.4	4.3	5.2	5.0	..	..	
Foreign-born women	20.7	9.6	12.7	12.4	..	..	

Notes and sources are at the end of the Chapter. Data on labour market outcomes refer to population register till 2004 and to labour force survey since 2005.

StatLink http://dx.doi.org/10.1787/021273136401

Finland

According to national statistics, immigration of foreign nationals to Finland has continued its upward trend in 2005 and reached a new high with almost 13 000 (2004: About 11 500). However, immigration remains relatively limited compared to other OECD countries, with long-term migration mainly consisting of family formation and reunification with Finnish citizens, refugees and persons of former Finnish nationality – in particular Swedes – or of Finnish descent from Russia and Estonia.

The number of decisions for residence permits submitted by foreign students increased in 2005 and was over 3 000. Most foreign students came from Russia and China. The Aliens Act was amended in 2006 in order to promote the entry of students from non-EU/EFTA countries into the Finnish labour market. Foreign graduates of Finnish universities can now apply for a work permit for job search for a maximum of six months.

The Finnish government adopted a Migration Policy Programme in October 2006 which seeks to provide a new comprehensive framework for migration to Finland with regard to immigration from non-EU/EFTA countries. The main emphasis of the programme is on the promotion of labour migration. In this context, the entry of foreign graduates from Finnish universities into the Finnish labour market will be facilitated by a series of measures, including teaching in Finnish and Swedish, training placements and an expansion of the residence permit for job search to ten months. Other central themes include the promotion of integration, a more flexible allocation of the refugee quota, changes in the selection of quota refugees and a simplification of the permit system. The special regime for the immigration of Ingrians (ethnic Finns, mainly from Russia) will be phased out. However, applications which have already been placed (about 12 000 to 13 000, including family members) will still be treated according to the previous regime.

As a complement to the Migration Policy Programme, the government passed a resolution on the Expatriation Policy Programme for the period from 2006 to 2011. This programme aims at creating stronger links between Finland and persons of Finnish origin living abroad, among other measures by information about life and career opportunities in Finland, as well as by teaching the Finnish (and Swedish) language and Finnish culture abroad.

The Integration Act was amended in 2006 to improve the integration of immigrants and to enhance the efficiency of integration services. The division of work and the responsibilities between the different authorities were clarified at all levels of the administration. Provincial state offices now take part in the promotion of integration. As mentioned above, further measures are planned to foster integration under the new Migration Policy Programme. These include the creation of a so-called "guidance system" for all immigrants including the possibility of pre-departure orientation and training.

With the exception of Estonians – who are the second most important origin country group after Russians – immigration from the new EU member countries has been very limited. The two-year transition period, which concerned citizens of these countries, ended on 30 April 2006. Work restrictions no longer apply and the requirement of a work permit has been abandoned. To enable better monitoring of labour immigration from the new EU member countries, a new reporting procedure was launched in June 2006.

In August 2005, the government adopted an action plan against human trafficking, which specifies the measures against human trafficking to be implemented in the various sectors of the administration. Victims of trafficking are now allowed to request a residence permit. The corresponding amendment to the Aliens Act entered into force in July 2006. A further proposal to amend the Integration Act to provide services and aid for victims of human trafficking is expected to be passed in 2007. International co-operation is also in place to prevent human trafficking to or via Finland.

For further information...

www.mol.fi/mol/en/index.jsp

Flow data on foreigners

Migration flows (foreigners) _National definition_	1995	2000	2004	2005	Average		Level ('000)
					1995-2000	2001-2005	2005
Per 1 000 inhabitants							
Inflows	1.4	1.8	2.2	2.4	1.6	2.1	_12.7_
Outflows	0.3	0.8	0.8	0.5	0.5	0.5	_2.6_

Long-term migration inflows (foreigners) by type _Permit based statistics (standardised)_	Thousands		% distribution	
	2004	2005	2004	2005
Work	..	..	..	..
Family (incl. accompanying family)	..	..	..	..
Humanitarian (incl. accompanying family)	..	..	..	..
Others	..	..	..	..
Total	11.5	12.7		

Inflows of top 10 nationalities as a % of total inflows of foreigners

Temporary migration	2000	2004	2005	Annual average
				2000-2005
Thousands				
International students	..	..	..	..
Trainees	..	..	..	..
Working holiday makers	..	..	..	..
Seasonal workers	..	..	..	..
Intra-company transfers	..	..	..	..
Other temporary workers	..	..	..	..

Inflows of asylum seekers	1995	2000	2004	2005	Average		Level ('000)
					1995-2000	2001-2005	2005
Per 1 000 inhabitants	0.2	0.6	0.7	0.7	0.3	0.6	_3.6_

Macroeconomic, demographic and labour market indicators

Macroeconomic indicators	1995	2000	2004	2005	Average		Level
					1995-2000	2001-2005	2005
Real GDP (growth, %)	3.9	5.0	3.7	2.9	4.8	2.5	
GDP/capita (growth, %) – level in US dollars	3.5	4.8	3.4	2.6	4.5	2.2	_29 191_
Employment (growth, %) – level in thousands	2.2	1.7	0.0	1.5	2.5	0.3	_2 392_
Unemployment (% of labour force)	16.7	9.8	8.9	8.4	12.8	8.9	

Components of population growth	1995	2000	2004	2005	Average		
					1995-2000	2001-2005	
Per 1 000 inhabitants							
Total	3.3	1.9	3.3	3.4	2.6	2.8	
Natural increase	2.7	1.5	2.1	1.9	2.0	1.6	
Net migration	0.6	0.4	1.1	1.5	0.6	1.1	

Total population	1995	2000	2004	2005	Average		Level ('000)
					1995-2000	2001-2005	2005
(Annual growth %)							
Native-born	..	0.1	0.1	0.2	..	0.1	_5 069_
Foreign-born	..	3.9	4.7	6.2	..	5.0	_177_
National	0.3	0.1	0.3	0.2	0.2	0.2	_5 132_
Foreign	10.6	3.9	1.3	5.1	5.8	3.7	_114_

Naturalisations	1995	2000	2004	2005	Average		Level
					1995-2000	2001-2005	2005
As a percentage of foreign population	1.1	3.4	6.4	5.2	3.2	4.5	_5 683_

Labour market outcomes	1995	2000	2004	2005	Average		
					1995-2000	2001-2005	
Employment/population ratio							
Native-born men	61.8	71.2	70.5	71.3	66.2	71.0	
Foreign-born men	..	..	65.5	62.5	..	65.0	
Native-born women	58.4	65.3	66.8	68.0	61.3	67.4	
Foreign-born women	..	..	46.8	49.1	..	50.3	
Unemployment rate							
Native-born men	17.7	10.3	9.9	9.3	13.6	10.0	
Foreign-born men	..	..	21.4	23.1	..	21.0	
Native-born women	16.1	12.0	10.2	9.3	14.0	9.9	
Foreign-born women	..	..	25.1	23.5	..	22.6	

Notes and sources are at the end of the Chapter.

StatLink http://dx.doi.org/10.1787/021284637268

France

After ten years of regular and sustained growth, the number of permanent entries in 2005 was similar to that of 2004, roughly 135 000 according to national figures. This stability covers contradictory trends. On one hand, there was a fall in permanent entries for family reasons (95 000 in 2005 compared to 103 000 in 2004), in part due to the fact that nationals of the new Member States who do not require visas to work in certain sectors, disappeared from the statistics. Family reunion, however, remains the main source of permanent entries. On the other hand, direct entries onto the labour market and the number of refugees increased although the numbers involved are much smaller; fewer than 9 000 permanent workers in 2005, and approximately 14 000 refugees (twice as many as in 2000, partly because of the high numbers of asylum seekers). Countries of origin are also changing rapidly: Nearly two-thirds (compared to little over half five years ago) come from Africa, in particular Algeria and Morocco.

Despite a 16% drop in asylum applications in 2005 (42 000 new applications), France remains the OECD country in which most such applications are recorded.

During the summer of 2006, a regularisation procedure for certain illegal immigrants with close ties to France was introduced. The purpose was to allow parents whose children had attended school in France since at least September 2005 to obtain residence permits for one year, which could be renewed. Of the applications submitted to *préfectures* – estimated at a little under 30 000 – the situation of some 7 000 persons was finally regularised.

On 24 July 2006, a new Immigration and Integration Act entered into force. It comprises first of all a series of provisions on employment conditions in order to attract more skilled labour and facilitate temporary migration. The Act creates three new three-year residence permits for highly qualified workers, for staff who have been seconded in France by their enterprise and for seasonal workers. It also provides that the employment market situation is no longer an argument that can be used as an objection in a number of occupations experiencing a shortage of labour. A list of such occupations is published annually by each region. Lastly, foreign students wishing to work now enjoy more flexible conditions: During their studies, they are allowed to work up to 60% of annual work time. Those with a Master's degree are allowed to stay after their studies for six months to find a job related to their training. If successful, they may obtain a renewable residence permit of one year duration.

The Act also includes provisions regarding welcome and integration. It makes the Welcome and Integration Contract (*Contrat d'accueil et d'intégration – CAI*) mandatory for all persons aged over 16 years. A trial had been carried out in 2003 before the measure was adopted generally. The CAI offers a number of individualised services intended to facilitate the welcome and integration of new entrants. In 2005, a CAI was signed by more than nine out of ten new arrivals to whom it was proposed. Since the great majority of CAI signatories were French-speaking, they did not need a language course: Only 25% of contracts made provision for language training. Signing a CAI is now one of the criteria used to assess the level of integration of persons applying for a ten-year residence card. Such cards are no longer available as of right except to refugees, other applicants having to prove their personal commitment to the integration process. The year 2005 was also characterised by the creation of a new Agency for welcoming foreigners and migrants (ANAEM), bringing together different services (including the International Migration Office) and entrusted with the task of facilitating the welcome and integration of foreigners in France. Since January 2005, this Agency's monopoly, dating from 1945, over economic immigration has been withdrawn. From now on, foreigners wishing to come to work in France may contact other bodies. However, the numbers affected by this measure remain low.

For further information...

www.social.gouv.fr/
www.anaem.social.fr/
www.halde.fr/
www.lasce.fr/

Flow data on foreigners

Migration flows (foreigners) National definition	1995	2000	2004	2005	Average		Level ('000)
					1995-2000	2001-2005	2005
Per 1 000 inhabitants							
Inflows	0.9	1.6	2.3	2.2	1.3	2.1	*134.8*
Outflows	..	..	..	..	..	..	..

Long-term migration inflows (foreigners) by type Permit based statistics (standardised)	Thousands		% distribution	
	2004	2005	2004	2005
Work	20.9	22.8	*12.0*	*13.5*
Family (incl. accompanying family)	109.8	102.5	*63.1*	*60.8*
Humanitarian (incl. accompanying family)	12.9	15.4	*7.4*	*9.1*
Others	30.3	28.0	*17.4*	*16.6*
Total	173.9	168.6		

Inflows of top 10 nationalities as a % of total inflows of foreigners

Temporary migration	2000	2004	2005	Annual average
				2000-2005
Thousands				
International students	36.1	55.0	46.2	47.5
Trainees	0.9	0.5	0.4	0.8
Working holiday makers	..	..	..	..
Seasonal workers	7.9	15.7	16.2	13.1
Intra-company transfers	..	..	..	..
Other temporary workers	7.6	10.0	10.5	9.6

Inflows of asylum seekers	1995	2000	2004	2005	Average		Level ('000)
					1995-2000	2001-2005	2005
Per 1 000 inhabitants	0.4	0.7	1.0	0.8	0.4	0.9	*49.7*

Macroeconomic, demographic and labour market indicators

Macroeconomic indicators	1995	2000	2004	2005	Average		Level
					1995-2000	2001-2005	2005
Real GDP (growth, %)	2.2	4.0	2.3	1.2	2.8	1.4	
GDP/capita (growth, %) – level in US dollars	1.8	3.4	1.7	0.6	2.4	0.8	*27 048*
Employment (growth, %) – level in thousands	1.0	2.8	0.0	0.3	1.6	0.2	*24 763*
Unemployment (% of labour force)	11.5	9.4	10.0	9.9	11.2	9.5	

Components of population growth	1995	2000	2004	2005	Average	
					1995-2000	2001-2005
Per 1 000 inhabitants						
Total	4.1	5.3	6.0	5.6	4.4	5.5
Natural increase	3.4	4.1	4.3	4.1	3.6	3.9
Net migration	0.7	1.2	1.7	1.6	0.8	1.6

Total population	1995	2000	2004	2005	Average		Level ('000)
					1995-2000	2001-2005	2005
(Annual growth %)							
Native-born	..	..	..	..	..	..	*55 947*
Foreign-born	..	..	..	..	..	..	*4 926*
National	..	..	..	..	..	..	..
Foreign	..	..	..	..	..	..	..

Naturalisations	1995	2000	2004	2005	Average		Level
					1995-2000	2001-2005	2005
As a percentage of foreign population	..	4.6	..	..	..	..	*154 827*

Labour market outcomes	1995	2000	2004	2005	Average	
					1995-2000	2001-2005
Employment/population ratio						
Native-born men	68.3	69.8	69.2	68.6	68.5	69.8
Foreign-born men	65.6	66.7	66.3	66.1	65.4	66.2
Native-born women	53.6	56.6	58.1	58.7	54.7	58.2
Foreign-born women	44.2	45.6	47.9	48.0	44.3	47.4
Unemployment rate						
Native-born men	9.1	7.7	8.0	8.1	9.2	7.3
Foreign-born men	16.5	14.5	13.8	13.3	16.8	13.7
Native-born women	13.5	11.3	10.0	9.2	13.1	9.5
Foreign-born women	19.0	19.7	17.4	16.5	20.3	16.4

Notes and sources are at the end of the Chapter.

StatLink *http://dx.doi.org/10.1787/021318604457*

Germany

Migration to Germany continued to decline in 2005. The new immigration law entered into force in 2005. This brought about comprehensive changes in the permit system and the registering of permits. Due to the change in the system, reliable data for work-related permanent migration are not yet available. With respect to permanent migration on other grounds, a significant decrease in migration levels was observed across all categories. The decline was most marked with respect to immigration of persons of German origin from the successor countries of the former Soviet Union, in particular from Russia. Their number has more than halved since 2003, and now stands at about 35 000, the lowest number since the fall of the Iron Curtain. Family reunification also continued its recent decline, with the 2005 figure of about 53 000 being almost 40% lower than in 2002. Immigration of Jewish resettlers also decreased further and is now at below 6 000, only about half of the 2004 inflow.

Asylum seeking also continued its downward trend. About 29 000 persons requested asylum in 2005, a decline of almost 20% compared to 2004. The main origin country was Serbia and Montenegro, accounting for about 5 500 asylum seekers. Preliminary figures for 2006 show a further significant decline in overall asylum seeking by more than 25%.

Temporary labour migration also declined. There was a modest decline of seasonal labour migration to about 330 000 in 2005. Poland remains the main origin country of seasonal labour migration, accounting for more than 80% of the migrants in this category. In 2006, a new regulation was introduced which concerns the admission of seasonal workers. 10% of the seasonal workers, *i.e.* about 32 500, are now expected to be recruited from the German labour market instead of from central and eastern Europe. As a result, preliminary figures show a decline in immigration of seasonal workers by more than 15% in 2006. Immigration of contract workers decreased to about 22 000 in 2005, down from about 34 000 in 2005. As in the previous years, Poland was the main origin country, accounting for about half of contract worker migration.

The 2005 German Microcensus obtained a special module on migration which provided, among other information, for the first time data on the place of birth of the parents, thereby allowing for an identification of the second generation (i.e. native-born children of foreign-born parents). The Microcensus showed that almost 20% of the German population consists of either immigrants or persons who have foreign-born parents. It is planned to expand identification of persons with a migration background on the basis of place of birth (instead of nationality) to other data sources.

A number of initiatives have been taken to foster integration. Vocationally oriented language courses are now available for recipients of social assistance under certain circumstances. Under the new integration act, so-called integration courses are offered since 2005 for most new immigrants. More than 115 000 persons participated in these courses in 2005. In July 2006, for the first time, an "integration summit" was conducted reuniting all major actors. It is planned to establish a comprehensive "national integration plan" by mid-2007. Finally, co-operation with origin countries has been enhanced, in particular with Turkey.

For further information...

www.bmas.bund.de

www.bmi.bund.de

www.bamf.de

www.destatis.de

Flow data on foreigners

Migration flows (foreigners) National definition	1995	2000	2004	2005	Average		Level ('000)
					1995-2000	2001-2005	2005
Per 1 000 inhabitants							
Inflows	9.7	7.9	7.3	7.0	8.2	7.6	*579.3*
Outflows	6.9	6.8	6.6	5.9	7.1	6.1	*483.6*

Long-term migration inflows (foreigners) by type Permit based statistics (standardised)	Thousands		% distribution	
	2004	2005	2004	2005
Work	48.5	64.9	*22.8*	*32.7*
Family (incl. accompanying family)	90.5	89.1	*42.6*	*44.9*
Humanitarian (incl. accompanying family)	14.2	9.1	*6.7*	*4.6*
Others	59.1	35.5	*27.8*	*17.9*
Total	212.4	198.6		

Inflows of top 10 nationalities as a % of total inflows of foreigners

1990-2004 annual average   2005

Temporary migration	2000	2004	2005	Annual average
				2000-2005
Thousands				
International students	..	58.2	..	59.2
Trainees	3.6	2.3	..	2.8
Working holiday makers	..	..	..	..
Seasonal workers	255.5	324.0	320.4	297.6
Intra-company transfers	1.3	2.3	..	1.9
Other temporary workers	99.8	77.5	..	91.3

Inflows of asylum seekers	1995	2000	2004	2005	Average		Level ('000)
					1995-2000	2001-2005	2005
Per 1 000 inhabitants	1.6	1.0	0.4	0.4	1.3	0.7	*28.9*

Macroeconomic, demographic and labour market indicators

Macroeconomic indicators	1995	2000	2004	2005	Average		Level
					1995-2000	2001-2005	2005
Real GDP (growth, %)	1.9	3.2	1.2	0.9	2.0	0.5	
GDP/capita (growth, %) – level in US dollars	1.6	3.1	1.3	1.0	1.9	0.5	*26 308*
Employment (growth, %) – level in thousands	0.2	1.9	0.4	−0.1	0.8	−0.3	*38 820*
Unemployment (% of labour force)	7.1	6.8	9.2	9.1	7.6	8.3	

Components of population growth	1995	2000	2004	2005	Average	
					1995-2000	2001-2005
Per 1 000 inhabitants						
Total	3.4	1.2	−0.4	..	1.5	0.7
Natural increase	−1.5	−0.9	−1.4	..	−1.0	−1.4
Net migration	4.9	2.0	1.0	..	2.4	2.2

Total population	1995	2000	2004	2005	Average		Level ('000)
					1995-2000	2001-2005	2005
(Annual growth %)							
Native-born	−0.2	0.1	..	..	−0.1	..	..
Foreign-born	4.4	0.8	..	..	1.8	..	..
National	0.1	0.2	0.8	−0.1	0.1	0.2	*75 710*
Foreign	2.6	−0.6	−8.1	0.3	0.3	−2.0	*6 756*

Naturalisations	1995	2000	2004	2005	Average		Level
					1995-2000	2001-2005	2005
As a percentage of foreign population	1.0	2.5	1.7	1.7	1.6	2.0	*117 241*

Labour market outcomes	1995	2000	2004	2005	Average	
					1995-2000	2001-2005
Employment/population ratio						
Native-born men	..	73.8	71.0	72.2	73.6	72.2
Foreign-born men	..	66.3	63.5	66.0	65.7	65.5
Native-born women	..	59.6	60.5	61.8	59.3	60.8
Foreign-born women	..	46.6	46.6	48.0	45.7	47.7
Unemployment rate						
Native-born men	..	6.9	10.3	10.6	7.3	9.1
Foreign-born men	..	12.9	18.3	17.5	14.1	15.7
Native-born women	..	8.0	9.6	10.1	8.3	8.8
Foreign-born women	..	12.1	15.2	16.3	13.8	13.9

Notes and sources are at the end of the Chapter.

StatLink http://dx.doi.org/10.1787/021272746306

Greece

Data on migration flows does not exist in Greece, and much of the flows are of an irregular nature. Estimates regarding the changes in the stock of the foreign population indicate that the immigrant population has continued to grow in recent years, with a large part of the new flows once again being attributable to Albanians, who already account for about 60% of all foreign nationals.

In contrast to the downward trend observed in most other OECD countries, asylum seeking in Greece has more than doubled in 2005 compared to 2004, with more than 9 000 requests. This is the highest figure on records for Greece. The increase was the largest in among OECD countries, both in absolute and relative terms, except for Korea, where inflows are negligible. Much of the growth is attributable to large increases in asylum seekers from Georgia (1 900 in 2005 *versus* 350 in 2004) and Pakistan (1 150 in 2005 compared to 250 in 2004), which have replaced Iraq and Afghanistan as the most important origin countries. Recognition rates, however, remained low.

In 2005, Greece conducted the third major regularisation programme in a decade. With the 2005 regularisation, two categories of irregular migrants residing in the country were regularised. The first category concerned migrants who had lost their legal status because of the expiry of their residence permit before 23 August 2005 and who did not have it renewed, the second concerned those who had never stayed legally in the country, provided they could prove their presence in Greece before 1 January 2005. Workers also had to prove 150 days of employment (200 days if employment was with several employers) in the year preceding the regularisation. Spouses had to submit a separate application and were granted an individual residence permit, as were children above the age of 14.

In the framework of the 2005 regularisation program, about 142 000 applications have been submitted. This was less than expected, and the objective of the programme has apparently only been partially achieved. This seems to be attributable to the restrictions imposed, both concerning the number of days employed and the documents required. As a result, a new law has been implemented in early 2007 to enlarge access to the regularisation programme. Additional documents, such as birth certificates of children born in Greece, are now accepted. In addition, migrants who are unable to provide proof of the full number of 200 or 150 days employed were given the opportunity to "buy" up to 20% of the required number of days by a payment into the social security system. For a range of occupations, the required number of days has been halved. Finally, third country nationals who attended public primary or secondary schools or universities may now also benefit from the regularisation.

Greece has taken a variety of measures to combat irregular migration. This included reinforced co-operation with Albania, one of the main origin countries of migrants, in particular of irregular migration. Greece provides assistance to the Albanian government to implement the readmission agreement that has been concluded between the Republic of Albania and the European Union.

A further major development concerned Greece's opening of its labour market for the eight new EU member states from central and eastern Europe on 1 May 2006.

For further information...

www.imepo.gr

www.inegsee.gr/equal/equal2/para_body.htm

www.esye.gr

Flow data on foreigners

Migration flows (foreigners) *National definition*	1995	2000	2004	2005	Average		Level ('000)
					1995-2000	2001-2005	2005
Per 1 000 inhabitants							
Inflows	..	..	..	..	3.5	..	..
Outflows					..	..	..

Long-term migration inflows (foreigners) by type *Permit based statistics (standardised)*	Thousands		% distribution	
	2004	2005	2004	2005
Work	..	..	..	..
Family (incl. accompanying family)	..	..	..	..
Humanitarian (incl. accompanying family)	..	..	..	..
Others	..	..	..	..
Total	..	..		

Temporary migration	2000	2004	2005	Annual average
				2000-2005
Thousands				
International students	..	..	..	..
Trainees	..	..	..	..
Working holiday makers	..	..	..	..
Seasonal workers	..	..	..	..
Intra-company transfers	..	..	..	..
Other temporary workers	..	..	..	..

Inflows of asylum seekers	1995	2000	2004	2005	Average		Level ('000)
					1995-2000	2001-2005	2005
Per 1 000 inhabitants	0.1	0.3	0.4	0.8	0.2	0.6	*9.1*

Macroeconomic, demographic and labour market indicators

Macroeconomic indicators	1995	2000	2004	2005	Average		Level
					1995-2000	2001-2005	2005
Real GDP (growth, %)	2.1	4.5	4.7	3.7	3.4	4.3	
GDP/capita (growth, %) – level in US dollars	1.8	4.1	4.4	3.3	2.9	3.9	*25 452*
Employment (growth, %) – level in thousands	0.9	–0.2	2.9	1.3	0.6	1.4	*4 148*
Unemployment (% of labour force)	9.1	11.7	11.0	10.4	10.7	10.8	

Components of population growth	1995	2000	2004	2005	Average	
					1995-2000	2001-2005
Per 1 000 inhabitants						
Total	7.5	2.5	..	..	5.2	3.4
Natural increase	0.1	–0.2	..	..	0.0	–0.1
Net migration	7.3	2.7	..	..	5.2	3.4

Total population	1995	2000	2004	2005	Average		Level ('000)
					1995-2000	2001-2005	2005
(Annual growth %)							
Native-born	..	..	..	..	..	..	..
Foreign-born	..	..	..	..	..	..	..
National	..	–	–0.2	–4.1	..	–1.2	*10 098*
Foreign	..	11.2	12.8	3.7	..	11.7	*553*

Naturalisations	1995	2000	2004	2005	Average		Level
					1995-2000	2001-2005	2005
As a percentage of foreign population	..	..	..	..	..	..	..

Labour market outcomes	1995	2000	2004	2005	Average	
					1995-2000	2001-2005
Employment/population ratio						
Native-born men	72.3	71.3	73.3	73.8	71.7	72.6
Foreign-born men	70.6	78.1	81.5	82.6	75.7	81.9
Native-born women	37.8	41.6	45.3	45.9	39.6	43.9
Foreign-born women	42.2	45.0	47.2	49.3	44.8	47.7
Unemployment rate						
Native-born men	6.1	7.5	6.5	5.9	6.7	6.4
Foreign-born men	14.3	9.5	6.4	6.4	11.5	7.2
Native-born women	13.7	17.0	15.7	15.2	16.0	15.2
Foreign-born women	20.6	21.4	18.8	15.8	22.0	18.1

Notes and sources are at the end of the Chapter.

StatLink http://dx.doi.org/10.1787/021357831088

Hungary

Migration from and to Hungary is still relatively limited. According to national statistics, immigration to Hungary has declined somewhat in 2005, although the level is still in the same range as that observed in the past few years. Immigration is still largely from Romania, accounting for more than half of all immigrants, followed by Ukraine and former Yugoslavia.

Officially registered emigration was also broadly stable. However, it is difficult to ascertain the exact scope of emigration. The duration of actual emigration is not known as there is no system in place to record returns. Notwithstanding these limitations, in contrast to most of the other new EU member countries, it is apparent that the extent of emigration from Hungary has been substantial overall. However, certain sectors (healthcare, research and development, etc.) and certain regions (*e.g.* Western Trans-danubia) suffered significant losses, leading to labour shortages in these areas and sectors. Survey data suggest that the emigration intentions of Hungarian men have declined in recent years, whereas women are now more willing to emigrate.

In 2005, about 9 800 people were granted Hungarian citizenship, almost twice the 2004 number. The large increase is attributable to legislative changes introduced in 2005 in the framework of a major governmental programme which, among other objectives, aimed at facilitating naturalisation for the ethnic Hungarian minorities from the neighbouring countries who have emigrated to Hungary. The majority of immigrants in Hungary is made up of persons from these groups. The procedural rules for naturalisation were also simplified. Almost 70% of the naturalisations in 2005 concerned former Romanian citizens, a further 10% were citizens of Serbia-Montenegro, and 9% were Ukrainians. A large majority of the new citizens speak Hungarian as their native language.

In the context of the new programme, the government also introduced measures to simplify stay in Hungary by Hungarian minorities abroad. A new visa type, the so-called "national visa" was introduced. It authorises multiple entries and stays in Hungary for up to five years without the need to obtain any further authorisation. However, holders of a "national visa" are not allowed to engage in employment or any gainful activity, in studies or any other scientific training in the Republic of Hungary. A further change in the Aliens Act concerned the employment of foreign students, who are no longer required to obtain an employment visa to undertake employment during their studies.

Although a general integration policy for immigrants is still lacking, the topic has moved up the policy agenda in recent years. A project aimed at facilitating refugee integration in Hungary was launched in August 2005. The overall objective of the project was to lay the groundwork for integration policy and to provide training for officials in charge of the implementation of such policy and integration programs. In this context, a White Paper has been put forward which outlines the political, legal and administrative framework as well as the contents for a comprehensive national strategy for refugee and migrant integration in Hungary. In addition, an Inter-ministerial Committee has been set up in 2005 to coordinate efforts in different ministries. This Committee is also responsible for drawing up a national integration policy for migrants.

For further information...

www.magyarorszag.hu/english

www.htmh.hu/en/

http://portal.ksh.hu/

Flow data on foreigners

Migration flows (foreigners) *National definition*	1995	2000	2004	2005	Average		Level ('000)
					1995-2000	2001-2005	2005
Per 1 000 inhabitants							
Inflows	1.4	2.0	2.2	1.9	1.6	1.9	*18.8*
Outflows	0.2	0.2	0.3	0.4	0.2	0.3	*3.8*

Long-term migration inflows (foreigners) by type *Permit based statistics (standardised)*	Thousands		% distribution	
	2004	2005	2004	2005
Work	..	..	..	..
Family (incl. accompanying family)	..	..	..	..
Humanitarian (incl. accompanying family)	..	..	..	..
Others	..	..	..	..
Total	..	..		

Inflows of top 10 nationalities as a % of total inflows of foreigners

Temporary migration	2000	2004	2005	Annual average
				2000-2005
Thousands				
International students	..	..	..	..
Trainees	..	..	..	..
Working holiday makers	..	..	..	..
Seasonal workers	..	..	..	..
Intra-company transfers	..	..	..	..
Other temporary workers	..	..	..	..

Inflows of asylum seekers	1995	2000	2004	2005	Average		Level ('000)
					1995-2000	2001-2005	2005
Per 1 000 inhabitants	–	0.8	0.2	0.2	0.4	0.4	*1.6*

Macroeconomic, demographic and labour market indicators

Macroeconomic indicators	1995	2000	2004	2005	Average		Level
					1995-2000	2001-2005	2005
Real GDP (growth, %)	1.5	5.2	4.9	4.2	4.0	4.4	
GDP/capita (growth, %) – level in US dollars	0.8	5.5	5.1	4.4	4.3	4.7	*15 447*
Employment (growth, %) – level in thousands	−1.8	1.6	−0.6	0.0	1.3	0.2	*3 856*
Unemployment (% of labour force)	10.4	6.5	6.2	7.3	8.5	6.2	

Components of population growth	1995	2000	2004	2005	Average	
					1995-2000	2001-2005
Per 1 000 inhabitants						
Total	−1.5	−2.1	−1.9	−2.1	−2.2	−2.4
Natural increase	−3.2	−3.7	−3.7	−3.8	−3.9	−3.7
Net migration	1.7	1.7	1.8	1.7	1.7	1.3

Total population	1995	2000	2004	2005	Average		Level ('000)
					1995-2000	2001-2005	2005
(Annual growth %)							
Native-born	−0.1	−0.3	−0.3	−0.3	−0.3	−0.3	*9 756*
Foreign-born	–	1.8	3.6	3.9	0.8	2.5	*331*
National	−0.2	0.2	−0.4	−0.3	−0.2	−0.3	*9 933*
Foreign	1.4	−28.1	9.3	8.6	−4.7	7.3	*154*

Naturalisations	1995	2000	2004	2005	Average		Level
					1995-2000	2001-2005	2005
As a percentage of foreign population	7.3	4.9	4.2	6.9	5.8	5.3	*9 822*

Labour market outcomes	1995	2000	2004	2005	Average	
					1995-2000	2001-2005
Employment/population ratio						
Native-born men	..	62.6	62.9	62.8	61.1	62.9
Foreign-born men	..	69.4	74.6	71.9	68.5	72.2
Native-born women	..	49.4	50.4	50.9	47.4	50.3
Foreign-born women	..	49.8	50.7	53.7	48.8	50.2
Unemployment rate						
Native-born men	..	7.3	5.9	7.0	8.6	6.3
Foreign-born men	..	3.5	2.0	2.4	5.2	2.3
Native-born women	..	5.8	5.9	7.4	7.0	5.7
Foreign-born women	..	4.8	6.4	7.7	5.7	6.6

Notes and sources are at the end of the Chapter.

StatLink ⋙ http://dx.doi.org/10.1787/021365714255

Ireland

Immigration to Ireland continued its strong growth path in 2005 and 2006. According to national population statistics almost 87 000 immigrants entered Ireland in the year ending April 2006. This represents an increase of almost 25% over 2004, which was also the highest immigration on record.

Together with Sweden and the United Kingdom, Ireland was the only EU15 member country which had fully opened its labour market for immigrants from all ten new EU member countries at the time of accession, and an estimated 40% of the recent inflows were from these countries. There is some ambiguity concerning the actual impact of EU enlargement on the labour market in Ireland, as the amount of Personal Public Service (PPS) numbers – a necessary requirement for employment – issued to citizens from the new EU member countries was almost three times higher than the number of immigrant inflows in the population statistics. Measures are now being taken to identify the reasons for this and to address shortcomings of the PPS system. In contrast to the 2004 EU enlargement, the Irish government decided not to give free access to nationals of Romania and Bulgaria following accession of these countries in January 2007.

There are indications that the recent immigrant inflow has been more oriented towards low-skilled occupations than in the past. Over half of the new immigrants were in such occupations, compared to about one third in the mid-1990s.

A new Employment Permit Act entered into force in January 2007, with a view to favouring skilled labour immigration from non-EU/EFTA countries. Among the key changes are the introduction of a so-called "Green Card" for highly skilled employees in most occupations with an annual salary above EUR 60 000, and in a restricted number of occupations in sectors with skills shortages in a salary range between EUR 30 000 and EUR 60 000. Applicants do not need to pass a labour market test and are entitled to bring their family with them. Green Card holders can already apply for permanent residence after two years.

Under the regular work permit system, on the other hand, a labour market test is required, and the testing procedure has recently been strengthened. Immigrants with a regular work permit must have been legally in the country for at least one year before their family can join them, and may only apply for permanent residence after five years.

With the new act, a new Intra-Company transfer scheme has also been established to facilitate the transfer of key personnel and trainees. In addition, new arrangements have been introduced to allow spouses and dependants of employment permit holders to apply for work permits without labour market testing. Finally, graduates of tertiary education institutions in Ireland may now remain in Ireland for six months after termination of their studies to search for employment.

A proposal for a new Immigration, Residence and Protection Bill was published in September 2006 with a view to providing a new and comprehensive framework for migration policy. Among the envisaged changes are the introduction of a long-term residence permit which would initially be valid for five years, designed to attract highly skilled labour migrants. Changes are also planned with respect to the asylum application process, including the introduction of a single procedure for all protection claims and a replacement of the current Refugee Appeals Tribunal by a Protection Review Tribunal.

In January 2007, Ireland's largest immigration research programme ever was launched by Trinity College, aimed at addressing the key challenges of immigration in Ireland and at helping to develop policies in relation to immigration and integration.

For further information...

www.entemp.ie/labour/workpermits/

www.justice.ie/

www.ria.gov.ie/

Flow data on foreigners

Migration flows (foreigners) *National definition*	1995	2000	2004	2005	Average		Level ('000)
					1995-2000	2001-2005	2005
Per 1 000 inhabitants							
Inflows	3.8	7.3	8.2	12.3	5.9	9.5	*51.0*
Outflows	..	..	..	..	..	..	..

Long-term migration inflows (foreigners) by type *Permit based statistics (standardised)*	Thousands		% distribution	
	2004	2005	2004	2005
Work	..	..	..	..
Family (incl. accompanying family)	..	..	..	..
Humanitarian (incl. accompanying family)	..	..	..	..
Others	..	..	..	..
Total	..	..		

Temporary migration	2000	2004	2005	Annual average
				2000-2005
Thousands				
International students	..	..	..	..
Trainees	..	..	..	..
Working holiday makers	..	..	..	..
Seasonal workers	..	..	..	..
Intra-company transfers	..	..	..	..
Other temporary workers	..	..	..	..

Inflows of asylum seekers	1995	2000	2004	2005	Average		Level ('000)
					1995-2000	2001-2005	2005
Per 1 000 inhabitants	0.1	2.9	1.2	1.0	1.3	2.0	*4.3*

Macroeconomic, demographic and labour market indicators

Macroeconomic indicators	1995	2000	2004	2005	Average		Level
					1995-2000	2001-2005	2005
Real GDP (growth, %)	9.6	9.4	4.3	5.5	9.7	5.0	
GDP/capita (growth, %) – level in US dollars	9.2	8.0	2.6	3.2	8.5	3.2	*34 047*
Employment (growth, %) – level in thousands	4.9	4.8	3.0	4.7	5.4	2.8	*1 952*
Unemployment (% of labour force)	12.5	4.3	4.4	4.4	8.8	4.3	

Components of population growth	1995	2000	2004	2005	Average	
					1995-2000	2001-2005
Per 1 000 inhabitants						
Total	6.4	14.5	19.9	..	10.6	17.4
Natural increase	4.7	6.1	8.4	..	5.5	8.0
Net migration	1.6	8.4	11.6	..	5.1	9.4

Total population	1995	2000	2004	2005	Average		Level ('000)
					1995-2000	2001-2005	2005
(Annual growth %)							
Native-born	..	0.7	1.1	1.2	..	1.1	*3 644*
Foreign-born	..	7.4	6.3	9.9	..	8.1	*487*
National	..	1.1	1.7	1.3	..	1.2	*3 871*
Foreign	..	7.2	0.3	16.4	..	13.7	*259*

Naturalisations	1995	2000	2004	2005	Average		Level
					1995-2000	2001-2005	2005
As a percentage of foreign population	..	..	..	..	..	..	..

Labour market outcomes	1995	2000	2004	2005	Average	
					1995-2000	2001-2005
Employment/population ratio						
Native-born men	66.9	75.8	75.3	75.8	70.5	75.4
Foreign-born men	65.0	74.5	74.1	78.8	69.6	75.7
Native-born women	41.3	53.1	56.0	58.0	46.9	55.7
Foreign-born women	42.0	55.6	54.3	57.5	49.0	55.6
Unemployment rate						
Native-born men	12.0	4.4	4.9	4.5	8.6	4.5
Foreign-born men	16.5	5.3	6.5	5.8	10.6	5.8
Native-born women	11.9	4.1	3.7	3.6	8.1	3.6
Foreign-born women	15.0	5.9	5.0	6.4	10.2	5.4

Notes and sources are at the end of the Chapter.

StatLink 🔗 http://dx.doi.org/10.1787/021412333334

Italy

Although only limited data for 2005 are available for Italy, there are a number of indications that permanent immigration to Italy has remained at relatively high levels. Family reunification, which is the largest component of permanent immigration, increased slightly to about 90 000 in 2005. The stock in the registered foreign population increased by more than 10% in 2005 to reach about 2.7 million. This is less than in 2004, which was, however, marked by the effects of the 2002 regularisation.

Labour immigration to Italy is governed by a system of numerical limits ("quotas"). In past years, supply of available permits has repeatedly been well below actual labour market demands. To better align the system with labour market needs, total quotas for 2006 were almost doubled compared to 2005, from 99 500 to 170 000. This still proved to be insufficient, as witnessed by almost 490 000 applications for permits in 2006 and the fact that the quotas were already fully exhausted in the course of the first day of their release. Indeed, the ongoing disparity between the numerical limits and the number of applications became much more visible in 2006, as applications were now filed at the post offices instead of the provincial labour offices. It seems that in many cases, the persons queuing to file applications were immigrants (often undocumented overstayers) and not the employers – as originally intended by the system. Those whose applications were postmarked too late to count among the first 170 000 later benefited from the change of government in May 2006. The new government decided to accept all the applications filed. A major reform of the system is expected to be discussed in parliament in 2007.

The 2006 quotas expanded the number of permits available for home care and domestic workers, from 15 000 to 45 000. A new category for fishermen was added, as well as the possibility to convert study and training permits into work permits.

In contrast to the excess demand for the quotas for non-EU nationals, the special entry quotas for the new EU member states were not fully reached. A little over 50 000 applications from nationals of the new EU member countries were filed in 2005, well below the quota level of 79 500. Nevertheless, this constituted a significant increase over 2004, when about 26 000 authorisations were granted (the 2004 quota was 36 000). About 70% of the applications in 2005 were for seasonal work. 57% were from Polish nationals, and a further 27% concerned Slovak nationals.

Asylum seeking in Italy remained unchanged. 9 500 asylum seekers were registered in 2005, one of the smallest per capita figures among European OECD countries. A new asylum application system which decentralised the asylum procedures, in place since April 2005, has led to significant changes in the refugee system in Italy. Recognition rates remained low – as in the past – but the new system appears to have reduced the number of no-shows in the asylum hearings (from more than 40% to below 5%) and to have increased the number of humanitarian permits issued. Under the new system, decisions are made much quicker – generally within two weeks – and, as a consequence, the number of asylum seekers awaiting a decision dropped sharply. At the same time, the number of rejected asylum seekers who have not left Italy has also risen.

Unauthorised migration remained significant in 2005. More than 22 000 unauthorised migrants were intercepted along the southern Italian coasts, the vast majority near the small island of Lampedusa, which is located close to Tunisia. However, these captured sealandings only account for about 14% of all apprehended immigrants. Most apprehended migrants – more than 60% – are overstayers, and a further 25% were apprehended within Italy with false documents. These consist largely of illegal entries via the other countries of the Schengen area.

For further information...

www.interno.it/
www.caritasitaliana.it/
www.istat.it/
www.lavoro.gov.it/lavoro/

Flow data on foreigners

Migration flows (foreigners) _National definition_	1995	2000	2004	2005	Average		Level ('000)
					1995-2000	2001-2005	2004
Per 1 000 inhabitants							
Inflows	..	4.7	5.5	..	3.8	5.5	319.3
Outflows	..	..	..	..	..	..	..

Long-term migration inflows (foreigners) by type _Permit based statistics (standardised)_	Thousands		% distribution	
	2004	2005	2004	2005
Work	49.4	68.9	_32.3_	_37.4_
Family (incl. accompanying family)	97.0	106.4	_63.3_	_57.7_
Humanitarian (incl. accompanying family)	3.1	5.3	_2.0_	_2.9_
Others	3.6	3.8	_2.3_	_2.0_
Total	153.1	184.3		

Inflows of top 10 nationalities as a % of total inflows of foreigners

Temporary migration	2000	2004	2005	Annual average
				2000-2005
Thousands				
International students	..	44.6	32.7	40.4
Trainees	..	..	..	..
Working holiday makers	..	0.3	0.4	0.2
Seasonal workers	..	77.0	70.2	71.7
Intra-company transfers	..	..	..	..
Other temporary workers	..	..	..	..

Inflows of asylum seekers	1995	2000	2004	2005	Average		Level ('000)
					1995-2000	2001-2005	2005
Per 1 000 inhabitants	–	0.3	0.2	0.2	0.2	0.2	_9.5_

Macroeconomic, demographic and labour market indicators

Macroeconomic indicators	1995	2000	2004	2005	Average		Level
					1995-2000	2001-2005	2005
Real GDP (growth, %)	2.8	3.6	1.1	–	1.9	0.4	
GDP/capita (growth, %) – level in US dollars	2.8	3.5	0.1	–0.6	1.9	–0.3	_25 998_
Employment (growth, %) – level in thousands	–0.6	1.9	1.5	0.7	1.0	1.2	_22 306_
Unemployment (% of labour force)	11.3	10.2	8.1	7.8	11.2	8.5	

Components of population growth	1995	2000	2004	2005	Average	
					1995-2000	2001-2005
Per 1 000 inhabitants						
Total	1.1	2.8	9.9	..	1.7	6.9
Natural increase	–0.5	–0.3	0.3	..	–0.5	–0.3
Net migration	1.6	3.1	9.6	..	2.2	7.1

Total population	1995	2000	2004	2005	Average		Level ('000)
					1995-2000	2001-2005	2005
(Annual growth %)							
Native-born	..	..	..	..	..	..	..
Foreign-born	..	..	..	..	..	..	..
National	0.1	0.1	–0.2	0.6	–0.1	–0.2	_55 464_
Foreign	7.6	2.9	7.8	11.2	13.6	16.5	_2 671_

Naturalisations	1995	2000	2004	2005	Average		Level
					1995-2000	2001-2005	2005
As a percentage of foreign population	1.1	0.7	0.5	–	1.0	0.5	–

Labour market outcomes	1995	2000	2004	2005	Average	
					1995-2000	2001-2005
Employment/population ratio						
Native-born men	66.4	67.4	69.8	69.4	66.6	69.0
Foreign-born men	80.5	82.4	83.1	81.6	82.1	82.6
Native-born women	35.5	39.3	45.0	45.3	37.1	43.1
Foreign-born women	40.1	40.5	51.1	46.7	42.2	47.2
Unemployment rate						
Native-born men	9.2	8.4	6.4	6.2	9.2	6.9
Foreign-born men	7.0	6.5	5.7	6.0	6.4	5.7
Native-born women	16.1	14.9	10.1	9.2	16.1	11.4
Foreign-born women	24.5	21.2	15.6	14.6	18.9	15.0

Notes and sources are at the end of the Chapter.

StatLink 〓〓 http://dx.doi.org/10.1787/021432212476

Japan

Government policy in Japan is to more actively promote migration of high-skilled labour, while remaining cautious with respect to the admission of less qualified migrants. In this context, immigration to Japan has slightly grown in 2005, but still remains limited compared to other OECD countries. National statistics show a significant increase in immigration of Chinese nationals (105 000 in 2005 compared to 90 000 in 2004). At the same time, there was a large decline in immigration of Philippinos by more than a third, to 63 000.

In quantitative terms, the role of foreign labour in tackling the challenges of the ongoing ageing of the Japanese population is negligible, Japan having one of the smallest immigrant populations in the OECD in relative terms. The total number of legal foreign workers in Japan, including various groups of temporary migrants, such as foreign students who are engaged in part-time jobs as well as temporary labour migrants under the Technical Trainee and Working-Holiday Scheme, was estimated to be only about 605 000 at the end of 2005, i.e. less than 1% of the workforce.

Naturalisations are still limited and amounted to a little over 15 000 in 2005. Almost two-thirds of all naturalisations concerned Korean nationals.

As with labour migration, humanitarian migration is also still negligible, and Japan has by far the lowest per capita figure of asylum seekers in the OECD. Nevertheless, in 2005 there was a slight increase in permanent immigration on humanitarian grounds to 231 (compared to 168 in 2004). This increase may be linked with the introduction of a new refugee recognition system in 2005, which permitted for stabilisation of the legal status of irregular migrants if they are recognised as refugees.

The number of overstayers stood at about 193 000 in January 2006, a decline of more than 13 500 compared to the previous year. The numbers have been falling for several years, which appears to be linked with several measures taken to combat irregular migration, including more stringent enforcement and public relation activities targeting the prevention of illegal employment.

The government has taken a variety of measures to further reduce irregular migration. In 2005, enhanced information and airport examination systems were introduced. In the two main origin countries of irregular migrants – Korea and China – pre-clearance system were implemented. The Immigration Control and Refugee Recognition Act was amended in May 2006 to further enhance control over migration movements. A key change related to a simplification and facilitation of landing examination procedures by means of a new automated gate system. The new legislation also included provisions to facilitate expulsion. Further measures were introduced which aimed at preventing terrorist attacks.

The amendment of the Immigration Control and Refugee Recognition Act also enhanced the possibilities for high-skilled immigration. Special programmes promoting immigration of foreign researchers and information processing engineers which were previously mainly limited to Special Zones for Structural Reforms have been made available nation-wide. In addition, the maximum term of residence for immigrants under these titles has been extended from three to five years.

For further information...

www.immi-moj.go.jp/english/

Flow data on foreigners

Migration flows (foreigners) National definition	1995	2000	2004	2005	Average		Level ('000)
					1995-2000	2001-2005	2005
Per 1 000 inhabitants							
Inflows	1.7	2.7	2.9	2.9	2.1	2.8	*372.3*
Outflows	1.6	1.7	2.2	2.3	1.5	2.1	*292.0*

Long-term migration inflows (foreigners) by type *Permit based statistics (standardised)*	Thousands		% distribution	
	2004	2005	2004	2005
Work	18.3	20.6	*24.3*	*25.4*
Family (incl. accompanying family)	25.7	26.9	*34.2*	*33.1*
Humanitarian (incl. accompanying family)	0.2	0.2	*0.2*	*0.3*
Others	31.1	33.5	*41.3*	*41.2*
Total	75.3	81.3		

Inflows of top 10 nationalities as a % of total inflows of foreigners

1990-2004 annual average   2005

China, Philippines, Brazil, Korea, United States, Indonesia, Thailand, Viet Nam, United Kingdom, Russian Federation

※77.9 ☐ 78.5

Temporary migration	2000	2004	2005	Annual average
				2000-2005
Thousands				
International students	41.9	37.0	41.5	45.2
Trainees	54.0	75.4	83.3	65.9
Working holiday makers	..	..	..	..
Seasonal workers	..	..	..	..
Intra-company transfers	3.9	3.6	4.2	3.6
Other temporary workers	114.3	146.6	110.2	129.6

Inflows of asylum seekers	1995	2000	2004	2005	Average		Level ('000)
					1995-2000	2001-2005	2005
Per 1 000 inhabitants	–	–	–	–	–	–	*0.4*

Macroeconomic, demographic and labour market indicators

Macroeconomic indicators	1995	2000	2004	2005	Average		Level
					1995-2000	2001-2005	2005
Real GDP (growth, %)	2.0	2.9	2.7	1.9	1.0	1.6	
GDP/capita (growth, %) – level in US dollars	1.7	2.7	2.7	1.9	0.8	1.5	*27 101*
Employment (growth, %) – level in thousands	0.1	–0.2	0.2	0.4	0.0	–0.2	*63 560*
Unemployment (% of labour force)	3.1	4.7	4.7	4.4	3.9	5.0	

Components of population growth	1995	2000	2004	2005	Average	
					1995-2000	2001-2005
Per 1 000 inhabitants						
Total	1.7	2.1	..	..	2.1	..
Natural increase	2.1	1.8	..	..	2.1	..
Net migration	–0.4	0.3	..	..	0.0	..

Total population	1995	2000	2004	2005	Average		Level ('000)
					1995-2000	2001-2005	2005
(Annual growth %)							
Native-born	..	..	..	..	..	..	..
Foreign-born	..	..	..	..	..	..	..
National	0.4	0.1	0.0	0.0	0.2	0.0	*125 745*
Foreign	0.6	8.4	3.1	1.9	4.4	3.1	*2 012*

Naturalisations	1995	2000	2004	2005	Average		Level
					1995-2000	2001-2005	2005
As a percentage of foreign population	1.0	1.0	0.9	0.8	1.0	0.9	*15 251*

Notes and sources are at the end of the Chapter.

StatLink ⟪⟫ http://dx.doi.org/10.1787/021453568388

Korea

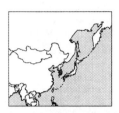

Immigration to Korea has continued to grow in 2005. Increases in the number of immigrants were observed in all major visa categories, and – according to population register data – the number of resident foreigners surpassed one per cent of the total population for the first time.

Family formation accounts for a significant and rapidly growing part of immigration to Korea. The number of Korean citizens getting married with foreigners increased from less than 16 000 in 2002 to more than 43 000 in 2005. International marriages accounted for almost 14% of all marriages in 2005, with even higher percentages in farmland areas. The government is preparing a bill to regulate the activities of the agencies and brokers which are often involved in the organisation of such international marriages, with a view to preventing potential offences to human rights for the spouses concerned. The government has also increased its efforts to counter discrimination against foreigners, which is perceived as an emerging source of potential social conflict. Among other measures, a Foreigner Policy Commission has been launched in May 2006, which is discussing measures to combat discrimination and to safeguard the human rights of immigrants, to promote social integration, and to attract skilled foreign labour by relaxing some of the restrictive elements in immigration policy and further reform of the framework for immigration.

The Korean immigration framework is currently undergoing a significant change. The employment permit scheme, in place since 2004, has been expanded in January 2007 to replace the industrial trainee system which has been phased out. Introduced in 1994, the industrial trainee system used to be Korea's main framework for the admission of low-skilled labour migrants. Targeted at menial occupations, migrants under this scheme were formally considered as trainee and did not enjoy the legal status of workers. Among other things, this practice meant also payment of below-minimum wages. In contrast, the new employment permit system, while still focusing on low-skilled occupations provides these migrants the same basic rights and treatment on the labour market as Korean nationals. Employers must pay into the social security system for these workers. There are also several changes concerning procedures for admission to Korea, previously administered by private agencies who often charged excessive recruitment fees. Under the new system, the government plays a stronger role in the admission of labour migrants. This is expected to increase transparency of the process. Migrant workers can now change jobs up to three times in three years if the original contract is either cancelled or not renewed.

Recruitment under the employment permit scheme is limited to sending countries with whom Korea has bilateral agreements. The government has signed a series of such agreements with labour-exporting countries in Asia, covering various aspects of the selection process. Recently, China, Pakistan, Uzbekistan and Cambodia have been added to the sending countries under the scheme, but as yet, Memorandums of Understanding have been signed only with the latter three countries. In 2005, more than 60 000 foreign workers immigrated to Korea under the employment permit scheme, and 31 700 under the industrial trainee scheme, which will no longer exist as of 2007. For 2006, 105 000 entries were scheduled under the employment permit scheme.

In addition, the introduction of a so-called "visitors' employment system" for foreigners who do simple manual labour is planned. While the new system applies to all foreigners in Korea, special attention is paid to three groups: i) Chinese of Korean origin; ii) family formation migrants; and iii) migrant workers and refugees in precarious situations. Under this new system, foreigners of ethnic Korean origin will be able to immigrate and work in Korea on 5-year visas allowing 3 years of continuous stay per entry. However, annual numerical limits on admissions and a preference list, based on a Korean language exam, are being considered to maintain a degree of control of migration to Korea. The government is also looking into granting a special visa to the parents of foreign students of Korean heritage (including ethnic Koreans from China and Russia), allowing them to stay in the country for up to five years and have jobs. However, only one parent per student will be allowed to benefit from the measure.

Irregular migration – mainly overstayers – continues to be significant, despite various measures aimed at tackling the problem. However, the numbers seem to be stabilising. By mid-2006 about 190 000 individuals, *i.e.* about half of all migrant workers, lived and worked illegally in Korea.

For further information...
http://english.molab.go.kr

Flow data on foreigners

Migration flows (foreigners) *National definition*	1995	2000	2004	2005	Average		Level ('000)
					1995-2000	2001-2005	2005
Per 1 000 inhabitants							
Inflows	..	3.9	3.9	5.5	3.9	4.1	266.3
Outflows	..	1.9	3.1	5.5	..	..	266.7

Long-term migration inflows (foreigners) by type *Permit based statistics (standardised)*	Thousands		% distribution	
	2004	2005	2004	2005
Work	..	..	..	..
Family (incl. accompanying family)	..	..	..	..
Humanitarian (incl. accompanying family)	..	..	..	..
Others	..	..	..	..
Total	..	..		

Inflows of top 10 nationalities as a % of total inflows of foreigners

Temporary migration	2000	2004	2005	Annual average
				2000-2005
Thousands				
International students	..	18.9	25.6	19.0
Trainees	..	46.7	51.6	52.4
Working holiday makers	..	..	..	..
Seasonal workers	..	..	..	..
Intra-company transfers	..	8.5	8.4	8.2
Other temporary workers	..	8.3	11.9	9.1

Inflows of asylum seekers	1995	2000	2004	2005	Average		Level ('000)
					1995-2000	2001-2005	2005
Per 1 000 inhabitants	–	–	–	–	–	–	0.4

Macroeconomic, demographic and labour market indicators

Macroeconomic indicators	1995	2000	2004	2005	Average		Level
					1995-2000	2001-2005	2005
Real GDP (growth, %)	9.2	8.5	4.7	4.0	4.4	4.7	
GDP/capita (growth, %) – level in US dollars	8.1	7.6	4.2	3.5	3.5	4.2	19 835
Employment (growth, %) – level in thousands	2.9	4.3	1.9	1.3	0.7	1.5	22 856
Unemployment (% of labour force)	2.1	4.4	3.7	3.7	4.1	3.6	

Components of population growth	1995	2000	2004	2005	Average		
					1995-2000	2001-2005	
Per 1 000 inhabitants							
Total	..	..	..	..	..	..	
Natural increase	..	..	..	..	..	..	
Net migration	..	..	..	..	..	..	

Total population	1995	2000	2004	2005	Average		Level ('000)
					1995-2000	2001-2005	2005
(Annual growth %)							
Native-born	..	..	..	..	..	..	..
Foreign-born	..	..	..	..	..	..	..
National	1.0	0.8	0.4	0.4	0.8	0.4	47 809
Foreign	29.6	24.4	7.1	3.5	13.8	20.6	485

Naturalisations	1995	2000	2004	2005	Average		Level
					1995-2000	2001-2005	2005
As a percentage of foreign population	..	..	..	..	..	..	..

Notes and sources are at the end of the Chapter.

StatLink http://dx.doi.org/10.1787/021456475267

Lithuania

Migration movements with respect to Lithuania continue to be largely dominated by emigration. Lithuania has the highest emigration rates among all EU countries, exceeding by a factor of five the emigration rates of, for example, Estonia, Latvia and Poland. Officially recorded emigration figures of Lithuanian nationals after accession to the EU in 2004 and 2005 show an outflow of about 15 000 both in 2004 and 2005, which amounted to about 1% of the population. A survey carried out by the Lithuanian statistical office in 2006 revealed that real figures are much higher, and recorded emigration accounts for only 40% of the total outflows. Both officially recorded emigration and estimated undeclared emigration remained broadly stable in 2005 compared to 2004. The United Kingdom was the main destination country (accounting for about one third of total emigration), followed by Ireland.

Most emigration for work reasons takes place without the assistance of recruiters or other agents. In 2005, only 2 300 Lithuanian nationals migrated through some kind of formal mediation service, the vast majority of these via private recruitment agencies.

In spite of ongoing economic growth and emerging labour shortages, immigration to Lithuania remains small. According to national definitions, immigration of foreign nationals has even continued to decrease in 2005, with a little more than 2 000 immigrants of foreign nationality recorded in 2005. In contrast, return migration of Lithuanian citizens continued to increase, now composing almost 70% of total immigration, compared to only about 15% in 2001/2002.

Employment of non-EU nationals in Lithuania remains insignificant and rather strictly regulated. In 2005, only about 1 600 work permits were issued to citizens from third countries, about 30% of which for nationals from Ukraine and Belarus, respectively. This modest number nevertheless constitutes an increase of about 80% compared to the 2004 figure. More than 40% of the work permits were issued for secondments. A new economic migration management strategy, aimed at promoting labour immigration, reducing emigration and fostering return migration of Lithuanians abroad, is currently under development.

The phenomenon of illegal migration to and illegal transit migration via Lithuania appears to have been gradually decreasing over the past two years due to strengthened border control in the framework of EU membership. Illegal migration is now more focused on false passports than on crossing green (land) borders. In recent years, the Lithuanian government reinforced its efforts to combat irregular migration. Several readmission agreements were signed, including agreements with Romania, Armenia and Moldova. However, Lithuania has not yet signed such an agreement with Belarus, the most important origin country of unauthorised migration. In May 2005, the government adopted a new programme for prevention and control of trafficking. Carriers are now responsible for assuring that the foreigners travelling in them have proper documents.

Further key policy developments in 2005 included the implementation of an action plan to adopt the Schengen *acquis* and new regulations regarding asylum procedures, including provisions for the accommodation of unaccompanied minor asylum seekers in refugee reception centres.

For further information...

www.migracija.lt/MDEN/defaulte.htm
www.pasienis.lt/english/index.html
www.socmin.lt/index.php?-846611483
www.ldb.lt/LDB_Site/index.htm

Flow data on foreigners

Migration flows (foreigners) National definition	1995	2000	2004	2005	Average		Level ('000)
					1995-2000	2001-2005	2005
Per 1 000 inhabitants							
Inflows	0.6	0.4	1.6	2.0	0.7	1.6	6.8
Outflows	7.0	6.2	4.4	4.5	6.9	3.3	15.6

Long-term migration inflows (foreigners) by type Permit based statistics (standardised)	Thousands		% distribution	
	2004	2005	2004	2005
Work	..	..	..	..
Family (incl. accompanying family)	..	..	..	..
Humanitarian (incl. accompanying family)	..	..	..	..
Others	..	..	..	..
Total	..	..		

Temporary migration	2000	2004	2005	Annual average
				2000-2005
Thousands				
International students	..	..	..	..
Trainees	..	..	..	..
Working holiday makers	..	..	..	..
Seasonal workers	..	..	..	..
Intra-company transfers	..	..	..	..
Other temporary workers	..	..	..	..

Inflows of asylum seekers	1995	2000	2004	2005	Average		Level ('000)
					1995-2000	2001-2005	2005
Per 1 000 inhabitants	–	0.1	–	–	–	0.1	0.1

Macroeconomic, demographic and labour market indicators

Macroeconomic indicators	1995	2000	2004	2005	Average		Level
					1995-2000	2001-2005	2005
Real GDP (growth, %)	..	..	..	..	..	..	
GDP/capita (growth, %) – level in US dollars	..	..	..	..	..	..	..
Employment (growth, %) – level in thousands	..	–4.0	–0.1	2.6	–3.1	2.2	1 474
Unemployment (% of labour force)	..	16.4	11.4	8.3	14.7	12.7	

Components of population growth	1995	2000	2004	2005	Average		
					1995-2000	2001-2005	
Per 1 000 inhabitants							
Total	–7.6	–7.2	–6.0	–6.5	–7.3	–4.8	
Natural increase	–1.1	–1.4	–3.2	–3.9	–1.1	–3.2	
Net migration	–6.5	–5.8	–2.8	–2.6	–6.2	–1.7	

Total population	1995	2000	2004	2005	Average		Level ('000)
					1995-2000	2001-2005	2005
(Annual growth %)							
Native-born	..	..	..	..	..	..	..
Foreign-born	..	..	..	..	..	..	..
National	..	..	–0.6	–0.7	..	–0.5	3 390
Foreign	..	..	–1.0	7.9	..	1.9	35

Naturalisations	1995	2000	2004	2005	Average		Level
					1995-2000	2001-2005	2005
As a percentage of foreign population	–	–	2.0	1.4	..	2.1	435

Notes and sources are at the end of the Chapter.

StatLink 🔗 http://dx.doi.org/10.1787/021514488628

Luxembourg

In Luxembourg, the number of foreigners continues to grow as does their proportion of the population: In 2006, nearly 40% of the 460 000 inhabitants of the Grand Duchy were foreigners. This is the highest proportion of all OECD countries, the main reason being that the migration balance continues to be higher than natural change: Net immigration accounts for over 60% of demographic growth. There were more entries than in previous years (+13 500) while the number of departures remained stable (10 800). Immigrants into Luxembourg tend to be young and female; two-thirds of arrivals are aged between 20 and 40 years, with women making up 60% of the net balance. Portuguese (47% of the migratory balance), French (11%) and nationals from east European countries account for most of the new entrants.

The other marked feature of Luxembourg is the large number of trans-frontier workers in the labour market, namely 40% of the labour force, with 70% of new jobs being held by nationals of its neighbouring countries: France, Belgium and Germany. Luxembourg is one of the rare OECD countries in which the employment rate for foreigners is higher than that for nationals, and this applies to both men and women.

The trend towards an increase in naturalisations was confirmed with a jump in acquisitions of nationality between 2004 and 2005: 954 persons acquired nationality in 2005 (up 13% on 2004). However, given the number of foreigners, and despite the fact that naturalisation procedures were eased in 2002, this is a low figure.

Some 800 new applications for asylum were recorded in 2005, nearly two times fewer than in 2004. Compared to the number of inhabitants, this figure nevertheless remains one of the highest in the OECD area. The law on asylum changed in 2005, in line with a new European Directive in this sphere. Measures were taken to accelerate the processing of applications and allow applicants to accede temporarily to the labour market if no reply is given within nine months of the application being submitted.

Given the large immigrant population, the education of the children of foreign residents is a constant concern in Luxembourg. More than a third of pupils at school are foreign, of whom 50% Portuguese. The results of the latest PISA survey show very considerable differences in scores between Luxemburgish and foreign pupils, even when the socio-economic level of the family concerned is taken into account.

New measures have therefore been taken to improve the school results of these pupils, in particular to promote the learning of foreign languages. Now that pre-school education based on multilingualism has been introduced in nearly all communes, this should facilitate the integration at school of children who arrived in Luxembourg at a young age. Emphasis is placed not only on learning the three official languages (Luxemburgish, German and French) but also on the respect of children's mother tongues. This last point is particularly important given the large number of Portuguese pupils and the efforts of the Portuguese government to promote such learning. In secondary education, welcoming and integration classes have been introduced as well as a welcome unit for new arrivals. Since 2005, the possibility of preparing the international *baccalauréat* has also been offered in certain classes. Similarly, the same year, the Ministry for National Education and Vocational Training set up a new service for the recognition of diplomas and equivalences.

For further information...

www.statistiques.public.lu
www.mae.lu/
www.cge.etat.lu/

Flow data on foreigners

Migration flows (foreigners) *National definition*	1995	2000	2004	2005	Average		Level ('000)
					1995-2000	2001-2005	2005
Per 1 000 inhabitants							
Inflows	23.2	24.7	27.6	29.7	24.1	26.5	13.5
Outflows	12.0	16.3	24.1	23.8	14.5	21.0	10.8

Long-term migration inflows (foreigners) by type *Permit based statistics (standardised)*	Thousands		% distribution	
	2004	2005	2004	2005
Work	..	..	..	..
Family (incl. accompanying family)	..	..	..	..
Humanitarian (incl. accompanying family)	..	..	..	..
Others	..	..	..	..
Total	..	..		

Inflows of top 10 nationalities as a % of total inflows of foreigners

Temporary migration	2000	2004	2005	Annual average
				2000-2005
Thousands				
International students	..	..	..	..
Trainees	..	..	..	..
Working holiday makers	..	..	..	..
Seasonal workers	..	..	..	..
Intra-company transfers	..	..	..	..
Other temporary workers	..	..	..	..

Inflows of asylum seekers	1995	2000	2004	2005	Average		Level ('000)
					1995-2000	2001-2005	2005
Per 1 000 inhabitants	1.0	1.4	3.5	1.8	2.5	2.5	0.8

Macroeconomic, demographic and labour market indicators

Macroeconomic indicators	1995	2000	2004	2005	Average		Level
					1995-2000	2001-2005	2005
Real GDP (growth, %)	1.4	8.4	3.6	4.0	6.1	3.2	
GDP/capita (growth, %) – level in US dollars	0.0	7.0	2.9	3.1	4.7	2.3	56 588
Employment (growth, %) – level in thousands	0.9	4.2	1.3	1.8	2.2	1.4	202
Unemployment (% of labour force)	3.0	2.6	4.2	4.6	3.1	3.6	

Components of population growth	1995	2000	2004	2005	Average	
					1995-2000	2001-2005
Per 1 000 inhabitants						
Total	15.1	12.8	7.5	9.7	13.7	8.1
Natural increase	3.9	4.5	4.0	3.8	4.0	3.6
Net migration	11.2	8.3	3.5	5.8	9.6	4.5

Total population	1995	2000	2004	2005	Average		Level ('000)
					1995-2000	2001-2005	2005
(Annual growth %)							
Native-born	0.7	0.2	0.3	0.2	0.4	0.5	303
Foreign-born	3.3	2.2	0.8	1.6	2.6	1.2	152
National	0.2	−0.5	−0.4	−0.5	−0.2	−0.1	273
Foreign	4.2	3.3	1.8	2.5	3.6	2.2	182

Naturalisations	1995	2000	2004	2005	Average		Level
					1995-2000	2001-2005	2005
As a percentage of foreign population	0.6	0.4	0.5	0.5	0.5	0.5	966

Labour market outcomes	1995	2000	2004	2005	Average	
					1995-2000	2001-2005
Employment/population ratio						
Native-born men	70.7	73.2	68.8	68.8	71.4	69.9
Foreign-born men	81.3	78.1	77.6	80.1	80.0	80.0
Native-born women	38.8	46.5	47.6	50.5	42.6	48.4
Foreign-born women	48.9	55.3	54.8	58.3	51.9	56.8
Unemployment rate						
Native-born men	2.1	1.4	2.5	3.0	1.7	2.2
Foreign-born men	2.1	2.5	4.4	4.2	2.5	3.4
Native-born women	3.7	3.0	4.5	4.5	3.2	3.3
Foreign-born women	5.5	3.3	9.6	7.5	4.8	6.4

Notes and sources are at the end of the Chapter.

StatLink ᴬᴵˢᴾ *http://dx.doi.org/10.1787/021514683840*

Mexico

Migration from and to Mexico is still largely dominated by emigration to the United States. With much of the emigration flows being of irregular nature, it is difficult to assess their magnitude. The unauthorized Mexican population in the United States is estimated to be growing at about 260 000 per year, reaching a total number of about 6 million in 2005.

In light of the ongoing irregular migration movements between the two countries, US President George W. Bush continued his calls on Congress in 2006 and early 2007 to pass comprehensive immigration reform that would tighten border enforcement while at the same time creating a temporary worker programme and resolving the status of undocumented immigrants, albeit without general amnesty. The United States' "Secure Fence Act of 2006" was signed into law in December 2006. It envisages the construction of a 700-mile security fence along the border between the United States and Mexico. The United States' Congress also passed a bill which included additional border patrol agents and detention beds. That funding bill also provided USD 1.2 billion for border fencing, vehicle barriers, technology, and tactical infrastructure. These legislative actions followed an initiative launched by the US government in May 2006 to enhance border enforcement, including the transfer of 6 000 National Guard members to help secure the border with Mexico.

Notwithstanding the predominance of emigration in migration movements, long-term immigration appears to be growing. Between September 2005 and August 2006, more than 47 000 persons legally immigrated to Mexico, an increase of more than 34% over the previous period.

In contrast to this increase in long-term migration, the number of seasonal agricultural workers from Guatemala is declining somewhat and seems to be stabilising at around 45 000 annually. Official figures also show a decline in transit migrants, from more than 210 000 in 2004 to less than 150 000 in 2005.

However, as with emigration, a large part of migration to Mexico – which is predominantly transit migration – continues to be of irregular nature, as witnessed by almost 140 000 expulsions from Mexico between January and September 2006. Almost half of these concerned Guatemalan citizens, followed by nationals from Honduras (almost a third) and El Salvador (about 15%).

In 2005 and 2006, the Mexican government has signed a series of bilateral agreements on orderly and safe repatriation with the main origin countries of irregular migration to Mexico. In December 2005, the National Institute for Migration published a proposal for a comprehensive migration policy on Mexico's southern border. The proposal included several measurements aimed at a better management of migration flows, including the facilitation of legal migration and enhancing the human rights of migrants, while at the same time fostering border security. Preparations for its implementation were put forward in the course of 2006.

On 15 June 2006, the Mexican government decided to prolong the ongoing regularisation programme, in place since September 2005 and originally scheduled to end 30 June 2006, until 31 October of that year. At the same time, its scope was expanded to all employed immigrants who had entered Mexico before 1 January 2005. Prior to this, the programme was limited to employed migrants who had immigrated before 1 January 2006. As was also the case with regularisation programmes in the past, the number of applications has been relatively minor. A little over 4 100 applications were received in the course of the programme. By the end of 2006, almost two thirds of these had been accepted, and a further 30% were still being considered.

For further information...

www.migracion.gob.mx/

Flow data on foreigners

Migration flows (foreigners) National definition	1995	2000	2004	2005	Average		Level ('000)
					1995-2000	2001-2005	2005
Per 1 000 inhabitants							
Inflows	0.3	0.2	0.3	0.4	0.3	0.3	_39.5_
Outflows	0.4	0.2	0.2	0.3	0.3	0.3	_31.4_

Long-term migration inflows (foreigners) by type _Permit based statistics (standardised)_	Thousands		% distribution	
	2004	2005	2004	2005
Work	..	..	..	..
Family (incl. accompanying family)	..	..	..	..
Humanitarian (incl. accompanying family)	..	..	..	..
Others	..	..	..	..
Total	..	..		

Temporary migration	2000	2004	2005	Annual average
				2000-2005
Thousands				
International students	6.3	4.9	5.1	6.3
Trainees	..	..	..	..
Working holiday makers	..	..	..	..
Seasonal workers	69.0	41.9	45.5	47.2
Intra-company transfers	..	..	..	..
Other temporary workers	..	..	..	..

Inflows of asylum seekers	1995	2000	2004	2005	Average		Level ('000)
					1995-2000	2001-2005	2005
Per 1 000 inhabitants	..	..	..	..	..	..	..

Macroeconomic, demographic and labour market indicators

Macroeconomic indicators	1995	2000	2004	2005	Average		Level
					1995-2000	2001-2005	2005
Real GDP (growth, %)	−6.2	6.6	4.2	3.0	5.5	2.3	
GDP/capita (growth, %) – level in US dollars	−7.0	5.0	2.9	1.7	3.6	1.0	_9 332_
Employment (growth, %) – level in thousands	1.5	1.8	3.9	−0.7	3.0	1.7	_40 978_
Unemployment (% of labour force)	5.8	2.2	3.0	3.5	3.4	2.7	

Components of population growth	1995	2000	2004	2005	Average	
					1995-2000	2001-2005
Per 1 000 inhabitants						
Total	..	..	..	..	..	..
Natural increase	..	..	..	..	..	..
Net migration	..	..	..	..	..	..

Total population	1995	2000	2004	2005	Average		Level ('000)
					1995-2000	2001-2005	2005
(Annual growth %)							
Native-born	..	..	..	..	..	..	_104 865_
Foreign-born	..	..	..	..	..	..	_435_
National	..	..	..	..	..	..	..
Foreign	..	..	..	..	..	..	..

Naturalisations	1995	2000	2004	2005	Average		Level
					1995-2000	2001-2005	2005
As a percentage of foreign population	..	..	..	..	..	..	_8 527_

Notes and sources are at the end of the Chapter.

StatLink http://dx.doi.org/10.1787/021585010441

Netherlands

According to national statistics, immigration to the Netherlands continued to decline in 2005, albeit more slowly than in the previous years. With about 92 000 immigrants (including Dutch nationals), the lowest inflow since the late 1980s was observed. In parallel, emigration from the Netherlands continued to increase, reaching 83 000 in 2005 – the highest figure since 1980, leading to a significant drop in net migration from 19 000 in 2004 to 9 000 in 2005. If unreported emigration ("administrative corrections") is also considered, there was even net emigration, amounting to about 27 000. Preliminary data for 2006 show a further significant increase in emigration, which has raised concerns about the impact on population trends in the Netherlands.

The decline in immigration was particularly evident among Turkish and Moroccan nationals, which suggests that the observed decline in family reunification, following the introduction of more restrictive family reunification measures, has continued. However, 2005 data on family reunification are not yet available.

In contrast to the decline in asylum seeking observed in most other OECD countries, the number of asylum requests increased in the Netherlands in 2005 to about 12 400 (2004: About 9 800). This is still lower than in any other year since 1989.

The number of temporary work permits issued to foreign workers continued to grow and reached 46 000. More than half of these temporary work permits were given to immigrants from Poland, predominantly in agriculture and horticulture. Indeed, most of the rapid growth in temporary labour since 2000 – it has almost doubled – is attributable to Polish temporary migrants working in these sectors. As of January 2007, citizens of the ten member states who joined the EU in 2004 have the right to free movement of workers to the Netherlands. Their movements up to 2007 were subject to a numerical limit of 22 000 per year.

In a 2006 position paper, the Dutch government proposed a new migration policy to promote highly skilled immigration, including a point system for self-employed immigrants. Improvements in residence opportunities for international students who complete their studies in the Netherlands are also envisaged. The Dutch government plans to extend the period of job search during which a graduate is allowed to stay in the country and to lower the current income thresholds for jobs.

Since March 2006, immigrants wishing to settle in the Netherlands for a prolonged period, including family reunification migrants, must pass a civic integration examination on Dutch language and society at a Dutch embassy or consulate in the country of origin prior to entry. The examination abroad is to be followed by further civic integration after entry. In January 2007, a new Integration Act entered into force, providing for compulsory measures and a results-oriented integration system. Although immigrants are no longer obliged to take specific courses, they are obliged to pass a so-called "civic integration exam" to obtain an unlimited residence permit. Preparatory courses are now provided on the free market, and immigrants taking these courses have to pay for the cost. The obligation to pass an exam also holds for some categories of established migrants, in particular for those living on social benefits.

Beginning in 2006, persons wishing to acquire Dutch citizenship are obliged to participate in a naturalisation ceremony. The first so-called "naturalisation day" was held on 1 October 2006.

Following general elections, a new government took office in February 2007. It has announced a regularisation programme for persons who filed their asylum request before 2001 but are still in the country. It is estimated that this concerns 24 000 to 30 000 persons. This regularisation concerns a population that did not benefit from improvements in the asylum procedure for people who entered 2001 and thereafter.

In January 2007, a "repatriation service" under the Ministry of Justice for refused asylum seekers to facilitate their return was introduced. In addition, the Dutch government now provides financial aid for travel and to assist in building a new life in the country of origin for repatriated migrants.

For further information...

www.cbs.nl/en-GB

www.ind.nl/EN/

INTERNATIONAL MIGRATION OUTLOOK: SOPEMI 2007 EDITION – ISBN 978-92-64-03285-9 – © OECD 2007

Flow data on foreigners

Migration flows (foreigners) *National definition*	1995	2000	2004	2005	Average		Level ('000)
					1995-2000	2001-2005	2005
Per 1 000 inhabitants							
Inflows	4.3	5.7	4.0	3.9	5.0	4.7	*63.4*
Outflows	1.4	1.3	1.4	1.5	1.4	1.4	*24.0*

Long-term migration inflows (foreigners) by type *Permit based statistics (standardised)*	Thousands		% distribution	
	2004	2005	2004	2005
Work	15.6	15.2	*27.5*	*25.1*
Family (incl. accompanying family)	28.4	27.6	*49.8*	*45.5*
Humanitarian (incl. accompanying family)	13.0	17.9	*22.8*	*29.5*
Others	–	–	–	–
Total	57.0	60.7		

Inflows of top 10 nationalities as a % of total inflows of foreigners

Temporary migration	2000	2004	2005	Annual average
				2000-2005
Thousands				
International students	6.4	10.2	..	8.4
Trainees	..	..	..	..
Working holiday makers	..	..	..	..
Seasonal workers	..	..	..	..
Intra-company transfers	..	..	..	..
Other temporary workers	27.7	44.1	46.1	36.8

Inflows of asylum seekers	1995	2000	2004	2005	Average		Level ('000)
					1995-2000	2001-2005	2005
Per 1 000 inhabitants	1.9	2.8	0.6	0.8	2.3	1.1	*12.3*

Macroeconomic, demographic and labour market indicators

Macroeconomic indicators	1995	2000	2004	2005	Average		Level
					1995-2000	2001-2005	2005
Real GDP (growth, %)	3.0	3.9	2.0	1.5	4.0	1.0	
GDP/capita (growth, %) – level in US dollars	2.5	3.2	1.6	1.3	3.4	0.5	*29 344*
Employment (growth, %) – level in thousands	2.3	2.3	−0.9	0.0	2.6	−0.2	*8 191*
Unemployment (% of labour force)	6.8	3.0	4.9	5.0	4.9	3.9	

Components of population growth	1995	2000	2004	2005	Average	
					1995-2000	2001-2005
Per 1 000 inhabitants						
Total	5.7	7.5	4.7	3.7	6.9	5.4
Natural increase	3.6	4.2	3.5	3.1	3.7	3.6
Net migration	2.1	3.4	1.2	0.6	3.2	1.9

Total population	1995	2000	2004	2005	Average		Level ('000)
					1995-2000	2001-2005	2005
(Annual growth %)							
Native-born	0.4	0.4	0.3	0.3	0.4	0.4	*14 585*
Foreign-born	1.4	3.8	0.2	−0.1	2.8	0.9	*1 735*
National	0.7	0.6	0.3	0.3	0.7	0.4	*15 629*
Foreign	−4.2	2.5	−0.4	−1.1	−1.6	0.0	*691*

Naturalisations	1995	2000	2004	2005	Average		Level
					1995-2000	2001-2005	2005
As a percentage of foreign population	9.4	7.7	3.7	4.1	9.3	5.1	*28 488*

Labour market outcomes	1995	2000	2004	2005	Average	
					1995-2000	2001-2005
Employment/population ratio						
Native-born men	77.0	84.0	81.9	81.6	80.3	83.1
Foreign-born men	56.2	69.9	68.4	69.0	63.0	70.0
Native-born women	54.9	65.6	68.1	68.5	59.7	67.9
Foreign-born women	38.4	48.8	50.0	52.6	44.8	52.2
Unemployment rate						
Native-born men	4.9	1.8	3.6	3.6	3.2	2.7
Foreign-born men	19.6	5.4	10.4	11.9	11.9	8.2
Native-born women	7.7	3.0	4.3	4.5	5.8	3.4
Foreign-born women	19.5	7.6	10.5	9.6	11.6	7.8

Notes and sources are at the end of the Chapter.

StatLink *http://dx.doi.org/10.1787/021602817255*

New Zealand

Immigration to New Zealand has grown in 2005/2006. More than 51 000 people were approved for residence, an increase of about 2 400 compared to the previous year. The largest source countries were the United Kingdom (29%), China (13%), South Africa (8%) and India (7%).

Temporary labour migration has also grown significantly. Almost 100 000 work permits were granted in 2005/2006, which is an increase of more than 20%. The largest increase was observed among Chinese (+5 000) and Indian (+1 700) nationals.

In contrast to the increase in temporary labour immigration, the number of student permits declined strongly, from almost 78 000 in 2004/2005 to about 69 000. Most of the decline was attributable to a decrease of the number of students from China, the main origin country of foreign students. Their number declined from more than 34 000 to less than 27 000 in 2005/2006. In light of the decline in foreign students, which has been ongoing since the 2002/2003 peak in student permits, a number of policy changes were introduced in July 2005 to ease work restrictions for students and their partners.

A comprehensive Immigration Change Programme has been put in place in 2006. A key element of the programme is a new Immigration Act, which is expected to be introduced in parliament in the first half of 2007. One of the key proposed changes is a simplified visa system designed to provide more clarity and flexibility in managing travel and stay of foreigners in New Zealand. A variety of measures are also planned with respect to strengthening compliance and enforcement, including a streamlined deportation process and a new appeals system.

A further element of the Immigration Change Programme is a new service delivery model consisting of a comprehensive and integrated IT system to manage risk assessment and to facilitate decision making. A third element in the programme concerns preparatory work for repositioning policy in the light of future needs and to better manage the impact of migration.

In August 2006, two key changes were made with respect to family-sponsored immigration. Firstly, an age limit of 55 years was introduced for principal applicants in the adult child and sibling categories of the Family Sponsored Stream. Parallel to this, a new uncapped Family Sponsored Stream of the New Zealand Residence Programme for partners and dependent children of New Zealand citizens and permanent residents has been created, based on the view that it is not appropriate to place numerical controls on such residents who wish to live in New Zealand with their partners and dependent children. The new stream comes into affect in July 2007.

To meet labour shortages in the New Zealand horticulture and viticulture industry, a so-called "Recognised Seasonal Employer policy" is planned to be introduced in April 2007. Under this policy, if New Zealanders are not available for jobs in these seasonal sectors, recruitment of Pacific nationals will be possible, and, following this, recruitment from the rest of the world. The Pacific has been given priority over other regions to contribute to regional development and stability. The policy includes a return worker element and good employer provisions.

In March 2006, New Zealand joined Australia and the United States in a pilot project for a Regional Movement Alert System, a passport-checking scheme initiated by the Asia-Pacific Economic Co-operation group (APEC) which allows participating countries to detect the use of invalid travel documents either at airport check-in counters before departure or before their arrival in the destination country.

New Zealand is currently engaged in bilateral free trade agreement negotiations with Malaysia and China. In addition, New Zealand is also negotiating a regional free trade agreement with the ten countries of the Association of Southeast Asian Nations (ASEAN) and Australia. It is envisaged that the negotiations include provisions on temporary entry, encompassing both Mode 4 (movement of natural persons for service provisions under the General Agreement on Trades and Services) and facilitation of business travel.

For further information...

www.immigration.govt.nz/

Flow data on foreigners

Migration flows (foreigners) *National definition*	1995	2000	2004	2005	Average		Level ('000)
					1995-2000	2001-2005	2005
Per 1 000 inhabitants							
Inflows	15.2	9.8	8.9	13.2	10.1	11.8	*54.1*
Outflows	2.9	4.0	7.1	7.5	3.8	6.8	*30.6*

Long-term migration inflows (foreigners) by type *Permit based statistics (standardised)*	Thousands		% distribution	
	2004	2005	2004	2005
Work	10.6	17.4	*25.5*	*29.4*
Family (incl. accompanying family)	27.3	37.1	*65.5*	*62.4*
Humanitarian (incl. accompanying family)	3.7	4.9	*8.9*	*8.2*
Others	–	–	–	–
Total	41.6	59.4		

Inflows of top 10 nationalities as a % of total inflows of foreigners

Temporary migration	2000	2004	2005	Annual average
				2000-2005
Thousands				
International students	45.8	77.6	69.2	73.5
Trainees	0.8	2.4	1.8	1.5
Working holiday makers	13.0	21.4	29.0	20.3
Seasonal workers	..	..	2.9	..
Intra-company transfers	..	..	..	..
Other temporary workers	24.1	43.7	44.3	36.5

Inflows of asylum seekers	1995	2000	2004	2005	Average		Level ('000)
					1995-2000	2001-2005	2005
Per 1 000 inhabitants	0.2	0.4	0.1	0.1	0.4	0.2	*0.3*

Macroeconomic, demographic and labour market indicators

Macroeconomic indicators	1995	2000	2004	2005	Average		Level
					1995-2000	2001-2005	2005
Real GDP (growth, %)	4.2	2.1	3.7	1.9	2.6	3.4	
GDP/capita (growth, %) – level in US dollars	2.6	1.5	2.3	1.0	1.6	2.1	*23 275*
Employment (growth, %) – level in thousands	4.5	1.7	3.4	2.8	1.3	2.8	*2 073*
Unemployment (% of labour force)	6.2	6.0	3.9	3.7	6.5	4.5	

Components of population growth	1995	2000	2004	2005	Average		
					1995-2000	2001-2005	
Per 1 000 inhabitants							
Total	15.9	4.8	11.1	9.3	9.4	12.4	
Natural increase	8.1	7.7	7.4	7.6	7.8	7.1	
Net migration	7.7	−2.9	3.7	1.7	1.6	5.3	

Total population	1995	2000	2004	2005	Average		Level ('000)
					1995-2000	2001-2005	2005
(Annual growth %)							
Native-born	..	0.1	1.1	0.2	..	0.9	*3 303*
Foreign-born	..	3.0	2.0	4.3	..	3.3	*796*
National	..	..	..	..	..	..	..
Foreign	..	..	..	..	..	..	..

Naturalisations	1995	2000	2004	2005	Average		Level
					1995-2000	2001-2005	2005
As a percentage of foreign population	..	..	..	..	..	..	*24 341*

Notes and sources are at the end of the Chapter.

StatLink 🔗 http://dx.doi.org/10.1787/021666365727

Norway

According to national statistics, net immigration of foreigners in 2005 was almost 19 000 persons, an increase of more than 5 000 compared to 2004. This was the second highest level ever recorded. The increase was mainly a result of the rising number of labour migrants, especially from Poland.

Norway decided to prolong the transitional rules for labour migrants from the eight new EU member countries from central and eastern Europe beyond May 2006. As of January 2007, Norway had not reached an agreement with the European Union regarding the migration of Romanian and Bulgarian citizens. As a result, they will receive the same treatment as third country nationals.

Family ties remained the most important source of long-term immigration from non-Nordic countries. The number of permits for this reason increased slightly in 2005 to about 13 000 permits. There was a large increase, in particular, in family-related migration from Poland.

Some new measures have been implemented in 2006 to prevent negative effects of family-based immigration. These are first of all aimed at preventing forced or pro forma marriages, as well as marriages with abusive men. Further measures in this respect are envisaged in the context of a new Immigration Act, which will be submitted to parliament in the first half of 2007. Among the most controversial issues are whether or not the act should attempt to prevent forced marriages by increasing the minimum age for family reunification migrants and by requiring candidates to have established links to Norway prior to marriage.

The number of new employment-related permits issued decreased in 2005, compared to 2004, but there was a significant increase in the number of renewals. Overall, there was an increase of more than 10 000 permits, mainly due to the high number of permits granted to nationals from Poland and Lithuania. The number of work permits issued for skilled work almost doubled to 1 200, which is nevertheless still far below the limit of 5 000 for which no labour market needs test is required.

In February 2006, new measures were implemented which aimed at preventing employers from hiring labour migrants below standard wages and working conditions.

A new nationality act entered into force in September 2006. Among the most important changes is a requirement to document language skills in Norwegian or Sami to obtain Norwegian nationality. There are also a variety of measures with respect to naturalisation of children, who now automatically obtain the nationality of both parents at birth and may maintain dual nationality even in adulthood. As a general rule, however, dual citizenship remains to be avoided.

The number of asylum seekers continued its significant decline. 5 400 persons sought asylum in Norway in 2005, which is about a third of the number registered in 2003. In February 2006, the Immigration Act was amended, regulating the right of asylum seekers to accommodation in reception centres. Persons with a final negative decision in their asylum case are, with some exceptions, not permitted to reside in the regular reception centres. They are offered housing in a special centre until they leave Norway.

Since September 2005, it is compulsory for newly arrived adult migrants to participate in 300 hours of training in Norwegian language and social studies. Depending on the needs of the individual, migrants have the opportunity to take up to 3 000 hours of lessons. Together with the state budget for 2007, a comprehensive Plan of action for integration and social inclusion of the immigrant population has been presented. The objectives of the Plan are to prevent lower participation and poorer living conditions among immigrants compared to the population in general; to ensure that immigrants can contribute to the Norwegian labour market and society as quickly as possible; and to ensure equal opportunities for migrants and their offspring. More labour market measures and targeted assistance for immigrants are central proposals in the plan.

More comprehensive anti-discrimination legislation was implemented in January 2006, which prohibits both direct and indirect discrimination based on ethnicity, national origin, descent, colour, language, religion or belief. At the same time, an Equality and Anti-Discrimination Ombudsman and an Equality and Anti-Discrimination Tribunal were established to enforce and monitor the law.

For further information...

www.ssb.no/english/subjects/00/00/10/ innvandring_en/
www.udi.no/default.aspx?id=2112

Flow data on foreigners

Migration flows (foreigners) *National definition*	1995	2000	2004	2005	Average		Level ('000)
					1995-2000	2001-2005	2005
Per 1 000 inhabitants							
Inflows	3.8	6.2	6.1	6.8	5.4	6.2	*31.4*
Outflows	2.1	3.3	2.0	2.7	2.6	2.8	*12.6*

Long-term migration inflows (foreigners) by type *Permit based statistics (standardised)*	Thousands		% distribution	
	2004	2005	2004	2005
Work	6.2	7.4	*24.9*	*29.1*
Family (incl. accompanying family)	13.7	14.0	*55.2*	*55.1*
Humanitarian (incl. accompanying family)	4.9	4.0	*19.9*	*15.8*
Others	–	–	–	–
Total	24.7	25.4		

Inflows of top 10 nationalities as a % of total inflows of foreigners

Temporary migration	2000	2004	2005	Annual average
				2000-2005
Thousands				
International students	2.3	3.9	4.3	3.2
Trainees	..	0.5	0.3	0.5
Working holiday makers	..	..	..	..
Seasonal workers	9.9	25.4	20.9	17.0
Intra-company transfers	..	..	..	..
Other temporary workers	2.5	2.1	1.1	2.3

Inflows of asylum seekers	1995	2000	2004	2005	Average		Level ('000)
					1995-2000	2001-2005	2005
Per 1 000 inhabitants	0.3	2.4	1.7	1.2	1.3	2.7	*5.4*

Macroeconomic, demographic and labour market indicators

Macroeconomic indicators	1995	2000	2004	2005	Average		Level
					1995-2000	2001-2005	2005
Real GDP (growth, %)	4.4	2.8	3.1	2.3	3.6	1.9	
GDP/capita (growth, %) – level in US dollars	3.9	2.2	2.5	1.6	3.0	1.3	*39 043*
Employment (growth, %) – level in thousands	2.2	0.4	0.3	0.6	1.8	0.1	*2 289*
Unemployment (% of labour force)	4.9	3.4	4.5	4.6	3.9	4.2	

Components of population growth	1995	2000	2004	2005	Average	
					1995-2000	2001-2005
Per 1 000 inhabitants						
Total	4.8	5.3	6.1	7.4	5.9	5.9
Natural increase	3.4	3.3	3.3	3.5	3.4	3.0
Net migration	1.4	2.0	2.8	3.9	2.4	2.9

Total population	1995	2000	2004	2005	Average		Level ('000)
					1995-2000	2001-2005	2005
(Annual growth %)							
Native-born	0.4	0.4	0.3	0.3	0.3	0.3	*4 243*
Foreign-born	3.0	4.3	4.0	5.3	4.9	4.8	*380*
National	0.6	0.5	0.4	0.5	0.5	0.4	*4 401*
Foreign	−1.9	3.2	4.2	4.2	2.8	4.6	*222*

Naturalisations	1995	2000	2004	2005	Average		Level
					1995-2000	2001-2005	2005
As a percentage of foreign population	7.2	5.3	4.0	5.9	6.4	4.9	*12 655*

Labour market outcomes	1995	2000	2004	2005	Average	
					1995-2000	2001-2005
Employment/population ratio						
Native-born men	76.7	82.3	78.6	78.6	80.9	79.7
Foreign-born men	63.6	75.3	70.9	67.2	72.6	71.8
Native-born women	68.4	74.6	73.4	72.4	72.5	73.7
Foreign-born women	55.6	63.3	62.0	60.2	61.2	62.6
Unemployment rate						
Native-born men	6.1	3.4	4.3	4.2	4.1	4.0
Foreign-born men	11.0	6.8	8.9	12.4	7.5	9.8
Native-born women	6.1	3.2	3.7	4.3	4.4	3.8
Foreign-born women	11.9	..	7.3	8.6	5.3	6.4

Notes and sources are at the end of the Chapter.

StatLink http://dx.doi.org/10.1787/021640781345

Poland

Despite some growth in immigration in recent years, migration movements with respect to Poland are still largely dominated by emigration. Migration from Poland has increased continuously since the end of the nineties. The upward trend accelerated with Poland's accession to the EU on 1 May 2004. Labour Force Survey data reveal that in the second quarter of 2006, approximately 389 000 Poles normally residing in the interviewed household were residing abroad for a period more than two months, about 125 000 more than in the corresponding quarter of 2005. The vast majority of these individuals migrated for work, and they tended to be younger and better educated than the pre-accession migrants. Short-term movements continue to predominate, but recent data suggest that long-term migration is slowly gaining in importance. Migration to the United Kingdom and to Ireland recorded the largest increases. Despite labour market restrictions placed upon citizens of the new accession countries, Germany is still a major destination for Polish migrants.

Migration to Poland remains low. The overall number of residence permits granted in 2005 was 38 500, a slight increase over 2004. Germany contributed considerably to this growth, with the number of permits almost tripling between 2004 and 2005. To a large extent, however, this increase appears to be a merely statistical one, and attributable to certain administrative advantages for Germans if they happen to hold Polish residence permits (notably, passing a Polish drivers' license). Other major nationalities reported declines, however. The share of permits granted to EU nationals increased from 24% in 2004 to 31% in 2005.

The general downward trend in the admission of asylum seekers in most of the industrialised countries was also observed in Poland. The number of asylum seekers in the country decreased in 2005 by 15%, and preliminary figures for 2006 show a further decline. Refugee status was granted to approximately 330 applicants in 2005. Nationals of the Russian Federation (particularly Chechens) continued to be the main source of both applicants and recognised refugees. At the same time, the population of foreigners with a so-called "tolerated" status increased: Between 2003 and October of 2006, approximately 3 800 such statuses were granted – three quarters of these in 2005 and 2006. Again, the main recipients were Russians.

There have been a number of significant policy developments in Poland. The first concerns the alignment of Polish laws with EU legislation, which continued in 2006. In August, new legislation governing entry, stay, and exit of EU citizens and their family members came into force. The new law introduced and defined conditions for the right to short and permanent residence of EU citizens and their family members, following EU regulations.

The second major development concerns the facilitation of access to the Polish labour market for various categories of workers. To address labour shortages in agriculture, since September 2006, farmers are authorized to employ seasonal workers from Ukraine, Belarus and the Russian Federation without work permits. The duration of the work spell must not exceed 3 months in any given 6-month period. To facilitate the issuance of special visas for these seasonal workers, employers must provide the potential worker with formal documentation regarding their employment. Certification from the local authorities that the employer is a genuine farmer is also required.

In 2006, permit-fee employment was made legal in several cases. They concern citizens of EU/EEA/Switzerland who perform statutory functions on executive boards of enterprises; teachers of foreign languages in their linguistic domain; and graduates of Polish medical and nursing schools who are engaged in their post-graduate internships. Furthermore, the labour market situation is not taken into account when granting work permits to medical doctors and dentists who take up work in Poland in order to pursue their specialisation. In spite of these facilitating measures, employers are still generally not allowed to employ a foreigner if they have not employed at least two workers who do not require work permits in the course of the year prior to lodging an application.

For further information...

www.uric.gov.pl
www.stat.gov.pl

Flow data on foreigners

Migration flows (foreigners)	1995	2000	2004	2005	Average		Level ('000)
National definition					1995-2000	2001-2005	2005
Per 1 000 inhabitants							
Inflows	..	0.4	1.0	1.0	0.3	0.8	*38.5*
Outflows	..	..	..	..	..	..	..

Long-term migration inflows	Thousands		% distribution		
(foreigners) by type	2004	2005	2004	2005
Permit based statistics (standardised)				
Work	..	..	..	..
Family (incl. accompanying family)	..	..	..	..
Humanitarian (incl. accompanying family)	..	..	..	..
Others	..	..	..	..
Total	..	..		

Inflows of top 10 nationalities
as a % of total inflows of foreigners

Temporary migration	2000	2004	2005	Annual average
				2000-2005
Thousands				
International students	..	..	..	..
Trainees	..	..	..	..
Working holiday makers	..	..	..	..
Seasonal workers	..	..	..	..
Intra-company transfers	..	..	..	..
Other temporary workers	..	..	..	..

Inflows of asylum seekers	1995	2000	2004	2005	Average		Level ('000)
					1995-2000	2001-2005	2005
Per 1 000 inhabitants	–	0.1	0.2	0.2	0.1	0.2	*6.9*

Macroeconomic, demographic and labour market indicators

Macroeconomic indicators	1995	2000	2004	2005	Average		Level
					1995-2000	2001-2005	2005
Real GDP (growth, %)	7.0	4.2	5.3	3.2	5.4	3.4	
GDP/capita (growth, %) – level in US dollars	6.8	5.3	5.3	3.3	5.6	3.5	*12 404*
Employment (growth, %) – level in thousands	0.9	−1.5	1.3	2.3	−0.4	−0.2	*14 116*
Unemployment (% of labour force)	13.3	16.1	19.0	17.7	12.9	18.9	

Components of population growth	1995	2000	2004	2005	Average	
					1995-2000	2001-2005
Per 1 000 inhabitants						
Total	0.8	−0.3	−0.4	−0.4	0.3	−0.5
Natural increase	1.2	0.3	−0.2	−0.1	0.7	−0.1
Net migration	−0.5	−0.5	−0.2	−0.3	−0.4	−0.4

Total population	1995	2000	2004	2005	Average		Level ('000)
					1995-2000	2001-2005	2005
(Annual growth %)							
Native-born	..	..	..	..	..	..	..
Foreign-born	..	..	..	..	..	..	..
National	..	..	..	..	..	..	..
Foreign	..	..	..	..	..	..	..

Naturalisations	1995	2000	2004	2005	Average		Level
					1995-2000	2001-2005	2005
As a percentage of foreign population	..	..	..	..	..	..	*2 866*

Labour market outcomes	1995	2000	2004	2005	Average	
					1995-2000	2001-2005
Employment/population ratio						
Native-born men	..	..	56.9	58.3	..	57.6
Foreign-born men	..	..	36.9	31.1	..	33.9
Native-born women	..	..	46.3	46.6	..	46.4
Foreign-born women	..	..	19.0	24.4	..	21.6
Unemployment rate						
Native-born men	..	..	18.8	17.4	..	18.1
Foreign-born men	..	..	–	–	..	–
Native-born women	..	..	20.0	19.4	..	19.7
Foreign-born women	..	..	29.3	19.2	..	24.2

Notes and sources are at the end of the Chapter.

StatLink ᴍᴵᴸᴵ *http://dx.doi.org/10.1787/022288141143*

Portugal

Because of the successive regularisations in 2001 (for foreigners in employment) and in 2004-05 (for foreign workers paying into the social security system and especially for Brazilians following a special bilateral regularisation agreement), it is difficult to provide a precise picture of migration flows to Portugal. In recent years, there has been an apparent decline in immigration, which continued in 2005. According to national statistics, there were about 28 000 new immigrants in 2005, 6 000 less than in 2004.

The decline in immigration appears to be linked to the low growth of the Portuguese economy. This is particularly evident from the fact that almost half of the residence permits subject to extension were not renewed in 2005. There was also a significant decrease in the number of work visas, which declined from 12 800 in 2004 to 7 800 in 2005. This decline, however, was almost entirely attributable to a massive decline in the number of work visas given to Brazilians (a drop of 5 500), who had benefited from the 2004 regularisation and who account for the vast majority of all work permits.

In contrast to the overall decline in immigration, the numbers of both student visas and of temporary stay visas – which are family members in the process of family reunification – have increased in 2005 to 8 350, the highest level ever registered in Portugal. This could indicate a process of consolidation among the migrant communities in Portugal, with family reunification gaining importance following the substantial inflows immigrants and the successive regularisations.

The trend towards the feminization of migration flows registered in previous years seems to be continuing. According to new residence permits issued yearly, the percentage of women among new immigrants has increased from below 50% in the late 1990s to 55% in 2004 and to 58% in 2005.

After the predominance of eastern Europe among the origin countries of immigration to Portugal around the turn of the millennium, current immigration is mainly from Portuguese speaking countries, mainly from Brazil (around one third of the new entries registered in 2005) and Cape Verde (about 12%). However, immigration from eastern Europe remains sizable, although a shift in the composition is observed here as well. In 2005, Moldavians have replaced Ukrainians as the third most important origin group of new immigrants.

In order to implement EU directives and to streamline national immigration legislation, the Portuguese government presented a proposal for a new Immigration Law (Law on the conditions of entry, stay, duration and expulsion of foreigners residing in Portugal) in May 2006. The proposal envisages a simplification of the visa system through a reduction of the number of visa types and more transparency relating the visa content. It is also proposed that the current system of numerical limits be abandoned. Family reunion procedures will be simplified and facilitated. Finally, the EU status of "Long-Term Resident" will be transposed into the law and measures to combat human trafficking and exploitation of immigrants will be enhanced.

A new nationality law has been approved in April 2006, which introduced mechanisms to facilitate acquisition of Portuguese nationality for the native-born children of foreign parents. If one parent is native-born in Portugal, the child gets Portuguese citizenship at birth. If both parents are foreign-born, the child born in Portugal can obtain Portuguese nationality once one of the ancestors has had 5 years continuous legal residence in Portugal. Other dispositions included in the law facilitate naturalisation for persons who have attended basic schooling in Portugal and for persons who passed part of their childhood in the country (10 years of continuous residence in Portugal by the age of 18).

The issue of immigration remains high on the government agenda, as witnessed by the relevance given to the topic in the priorities for the Portuguese EU presidency in the second semester of 2007.

For further information...

www.acime.gov.pt/

Flow data on foreigners

Migration flows (foreigners) _National definition_	1995	2000	2004	2005	Average		Level ('000)
					1995-2000	2001-2005	2005
Per 1 000 inhabitants							
Inflows	0.5	1.6	3.2	2.7	0.7	6.1	_28.1_
Outflows	0.1	–	–	–	0.1	–	_0.2_

Long-term migration inflows (foreigners) by type _Permit based statistics (standardised)_	Thousands		% distribution	
	2004	2005	2004	2005
Work	7.7	5.5	_48.2_	_41.1_
Family (incl. accompanying family)	4.7	5.3	_29.3_	_39.6_
Humanitarian (incl. accompanying family)	–	–	–	–
Others	3.6	2.6	_22.5_	_19.4_
Total	15.9	13.3		

Inflows of top 10 nationalities as a % of total inflows of foreigners

Temporary migration	2000	2004	2005	Annual average
				2000-2005
Thousands				
International students	3.9	3.3	4.1	3.9
Trainees	..	..	..	..
Working holiday makers	..	..	..	..
Seasonal workers	..	..	..	..
Intra-company transfers	..	..	..	..
Other temporary workers	..	..	..	..

Inflows of asylum seekers	1995	2000	2004	2005	Average		Level ('000)
					1995-2000	2001-2005	2005
Per 1 000 inhabitants	–	–	–	–	–	–	_0.1_

Macroeconomic, demographic and labour market indicators

Macroeconomic indicators	1995	2000	2004	2005	Average		Level
					1995-2000	2001-2005	2005
Real GDP (growth, %)	4.3	3.9	1.2	0.4	4.1	0.3	
GDP/capita (growth, %) – level in US dollars	3.9	3.4	0.6	–0.1	3.7	–0.3	_18 396_
Employment (growth, %) – level in thousands	–0.6	2.3	0.1	0.1	1.7	0.1	_5 094_
Unemployment (% of labour force)	7.2	4.0	6.7	7.7	5.8	5.9	

Components of population growth	1995	2000	2004	2005	Average		
					1995-2000	2001-2005	
Per 1 000 inhabitants							
Total	2.6	6.1	5.1	..	3.9	6.6	
Natural increase	0.4	1.5	0.7	..	0.7	0.6	
Net migration	2.2	4.6	4.5	..	3.2	5.9	

Total population	1995	2000	2004	2005	Average		Level ('000)
					1995-2000	2001-2005	2005
(Annual growth %)							
Native-born	..	0.6	0.5	1.1	..	0.6	_9 902_
Foreign-born	..	0.7	1.3	–7.4	..	0.4	_661_
National	–	0.4	0.3	0.9	0.7	0.5	_10 131_
Foreign	7.2	8.8	5.5	–7.9	4.3	4.6	_432_

Naturalisations	1995	2000	2004	2005	Average		Level
					1995-2000	2001-2005	2005
As a percentage of foreign population	0.9	0.4	0.3	0.2	0.6	0.3	_939_

Labour market outcomes	1995	2000	2004	2005	Average		
					1995-2000	2001-2005	
Employment/population ratio							
Native-born men	71.5	76.2	74.2	73.1	76.3	75.1	
Foreign-born men	65.5	75.5	77.1	78.4	70.2	78.7	
Native-born women	54.5	60.2	61.5	61.4	59.5	61.3	
Foreign-born women	49.7	65.2	64.0	67.5	56.8	66.3	
Unemployment rate							
Native-born men	6.6	3.1	5.7	6.8	3.7	5.0	
Foreign-born men	10.8	6.0	9.8	8.3	8.2	7.4	
Native-born women	7.8	4.9	7.4	8.4	5.0	6.8	
Foreign-born women	13.6	6.9	9.6	9.5	11.2	8.9	

Notes and sources are at the end of the Chapter.   StatLink ▓█▊ _http://dx.doi.org/10.1787/022543751708_

Romania

Migration movements in Romania still largely concern emigration. National statistics show some decline in permanent emigration in 2005, to 11 000 persons. However, it is difficult to relate this statistical decline to a decrease in actual emigration, since officially recorded emigration covers only a fraction of actual movements. Data from a number of main receiving countries suggest that emigration has not decreased, but rather stagnated or has even grown slightly.

In contrast to the decline in officially recorded permanent emigration, temporary emigration of Romanian workers negotiated through bilateral agreements and other intermediation of Romanian authorities increased significantly in 2005, by more than 20%. More than 52 000 persons migrated under such schemes, mainly to Germany (about 60%) and Spain (about 25%), predominantly for work in agriculture. In addition to these official channels, there is also a large number of legal employment abroad arranged by private employment agencies. This covered about 100 000 contracts in 2004. Data for 2005 are not yet available.

The significant emigration of Romanian nationals in recent years is mirrored in an increase in remittances. In 2005, more than EUR 4.3 billion (almost 5% of GDP, an increase of almost 50% over 2004) were officially remitted, the highest amount ever.

The number of Romanian citizens detected in an illegal situation in other countries and repatriated in accordance with readmission agreements decreased slightly to 24 400 in 2005 (2004: 26 600). More than a third of the returns were from Italy (about 9 300), a further 15% from France (about 3 500) and slightly more than 10% from Spain (about 3 200). To combat irregular emigration of Romanians, requirements for travel abroad were tightened in July 2005. Candidates must now present documents justifying the reason for the travel and demonstrate a minimum level of resources for the specified period of stay in the country of destination.

The stock of foreign residents in Romania in 2005 remained at about the same level as in previous years (about 50 000), which represents only 0.2% of the total population. More than 90% of these are temporary residents.

In light of Romania's accession to the European Union on 1 January 2007, harmonisation with the European Union's legal immigration framework has been the driving factor behind rather comprehensive changes in legislation in 2005 and 2006. An ordinance of July 2006 changed the legal provisions concerning entry and stay of EU and EEA citizens and their family members, who are now entitled to an initial 3-months right of residence. After this period they can obtain the right of residence if they have a job and the means to support their family. Romania has given EU/EEA nationals unlimited access to its labour market.

A 2005 ordinance granted the Office for Labour Force Migration the mandate to monitor the impact of immigration on the labour market. At the same time, different types of work permits have been introduced for permanent workers, seconded workers, seasonal workers, trainees, sportsmen and cross-border workers. In October 2006, the Romanian government approved a draft of a law amending current legislation with respect to foreigners. The draft envisages changes with respect to the entry and stay of migrants arriving for family reunification, to measures concerning withdrawal of migrants who do not have a residence permit, and to the admission and stay of asylum seekers.

In May 2006, the National Office for Refugees introduced a draft law on asylum in Romania to harmonise Romanian legislation with the *acquis communautaire*, including the Dublin agreements and Eurodac (the database of asylum seekers and illegal migrants). Several procedural changes, including the provisions on removal, are also planned. In addition, legal differences between refugees and migrants with so-called "conditioned humanitarian protection" will be removed. Various measures were also taken with respect to the reception and housing of asylum seekers.

For further information...

www.insse.ro/index_eng.htm
www.mmssf.ro/website/en/dms.jsp
www.omfm.ro/w3c/index.php

Flow data on foreigners

Migration flows (foreigners) National definition	1995	2000	2004	2005	Average		Level ('000)
					1995-2000	2001-2005	2005
Per 1 000 inhabitants							
Inflows	..	0.5	0.1	..	0.5	0.3	..
Outflows	..	0.7	0.6	0.5	..	..	10.9

Long-term migration inflows (foreigners) by type Permit based statistics (standardised)	Thousands		% distribution	
	2004	2005	2004	2005
Work	..	..	..	..
Family (incl. accompanying family)	..	..	..	..
Humanitarian (incl. accompanying family)	..	..	..	..
Others	..	..	..	..
Total	..	..		

Temporary migration	2000	2004	2005	Annual average
				2000-2005
Thousands				
International students	..	..	..	..
Trainees	..	..	..	..
Working holiday makers	..	..	..	..
Seasonal workers	..	..	..	..
Intra-company transfers	..	..	..	..
Other temporary workers	..	..	..	..

Inflows of asylum seekers	1995	2000	2004	2005	Average		Level ('000)
					1995-2000	2001-2005	2005
Per 1 000 inhabitants	–	0.1	–	–	0.1	0.1	0.6

Macroeconomic, demographic and labour market indicators

Macroeconomic indicators	1995	2000	2004	2005	Average		Level
					1995-2000	2001-2005	2005
Real GDP (growth, %)	..	..	..	..	..	..	
GDP/capita (growth, %) – level in US dollars	..	..	..	..	..	..	..
Employment (growth, %) – level in thousands	..	–0.1	–0.7	..	–0.4	–5.0	9 158
Unemployment (% of labour force)	..	7.1	8.0	9.0	6.6	7.8	

Components of population growth	1995	2000	2004	2005	Average	
					1995-2000	2001-2005
Per 1 000 inhabitants						
Total	..	..	..	..	..	..
Natural increase	–1.6	–0.9	–1.9	..	–1.6	–2.2
Net migration	..	..	..	..	..	..

Total population	1995	2000	2004	2005	Average		Level ('000)
					1995-2000	2001-2005	2005
(Annual growth %)							
Native-born (2002 Census data)	..	..	..	..	..	..	21 547
Foreign-born (2002 Census data)	..	..	..	..	..	..	134
National	..	–0.1	–0.1	–0.2	..	–0.8	21 609
Foreign	..	11.7	15.4	0.2	..	–7.5	49

Naturalisations	1995	2000	2004	2005	Average		Level
					1995-2000	2001-2005	2005
As a percentage of foreign population	..	0.6	0.7	–	0.9	0.3	15

Notes and sources are at the end of the Chapter.

StatLink ⟨⟩ http://dx.doi.org/10.1787/022546507283

Slovak Republic

Immigration to the Slovak Republic continued growing in 2005, albeit at very modest levels. Along with the sustained growth path of the Slovak economy in recent years, immigration had more than doubled since 2003, and reached about 5 300 in 2005, according to national statistics.

In contrast to some of the other new EU member countries, accession to the EU did not have a large impact on emigration. Less than 2 000 persons left the country in 2005, only slightly more than in previous years.

The Czech Republic remains to be the main origin and destination country of migration, accounting for about 40% of the outflows and 20% of the inflows. The second most important country with respect to migration flows was Germany, accounting for 22% of emigration and 16% of immigration.

Irregular migration seems to have continued its recent downward trend but remains significant when compared to the low overall level of migration flows. The number of apprehensions at the border was about 5 200 in 2005, which is a third of the apprehensions in 2002. Illegal migrants come mainly from the Commonwealth of Independent States (the Russian Federation, Moldova, Georgia, Ukraine), South Asia (India, Pakistan, Bangladesh) as well as from China and Viet Nam. Border controls with the EU neighbouring countries are still in place and will be abolished only once the Slovak Republic joins the Schengen area. This was envisaged for 2007, but the exact date still depends on developments in several areas related to border control.

The number of asylum seekers dropped sharply, from about 11 400 in 2004 to 3 500 in 2005, the largest decline in relative terms of all OECD countries. Preliminary data for 2006 indicate a further significant decline. Over the past years, most applicants for asylum came from India, followed by the Russian Federation and China.

In the course of 2005, a new migration policy concept has been adopted as a reaction to the EU accession and related changes in migration policy. Further elaboration has been ongoing by the responsible government agencies.

The Act on the stay of foreigners was amended in 2005. Among the noteworthy changes is the relaxation of regulations on the granting of residence permits to spouses and dependent children below the age of 21 of nationals of OECD member states. These family members of nationals of OECD countries who reside in the Slovak Republic and work in foreign companies or who are foreign investors can now apply for residence permits immediately. Previously, residence permits for the family were only granted after one year of residence.

A further easing of restrictions is being prepared. Among other measures, foreigners who are relatives of a national of an EEA country or Switzerland will be exempted from visa requirements, providing that they hold a residence permit of one of these countries. In addition, the rights of family members of EU nationals will be enhanced, and what constitutes a family member of an EU national will be defined more broadly. In accordance with the EU provisions relating to the free movement of persons, the obligation to apply for a residence permit will be lifted for several groups of migrants.

Improvements in the recognition of foreign degrees and qualifications are also being discussed.

For further information...

www.minv.sk/en/index.htm

www.employment.gov.sk/en/index.htm

Flow data on foreigners

Migration flows (foreigners) *National definition*	1995	2000	2004	2005	Average 1995-2000	Average 2001-2005	Level ('000) 2005
Per 1 000 inhabitants							
Inflows	1.3	0.9	1.5	1.4	1.1	1.1	7.7
Outflows	..	..	0.9	0.5	..	..	2.8

Long-term migration inflows (foreigners) by type *Permit based statistics (standardised)*	Thousands 2004	Thousands 2005	% distribution 2004	% distribution 2005
Work	..	..	..	..
Family (incl. accompanying family)	..	..	..	..
Humanitarian (incl. accompanying family)	..	..	..	..
Others	..	..	..	..
Total	..	..		

Temporary migration	2000	2004	2005	Annual average 2000-2005
Thousands				
International students	..	..	..	..
Trainees	..	..	..	..
Working holiday makers	..	..	..	..
Seasonal workers	..	..	..	..
Intra-company transfers	..	..	..	..
Other temporary workers	..	..	..	..

Inflows of top 10 nationalities as a % of total inflows of foreigners

Legend: 2003-2004 annual average | 2005

Czech Republic, Germany, Ukraine, Poland, Austria, Hungary, Korea, France, United States, Russian Federation

(axis 0 to 20) ⊞ 66.5 ▭ 62.8

Inflows of asylum seekers	1995	2000	2004	2005	Average 1995-2000	Average 2001-2005	Level ('000) 2005
Per 1 000 inhabitants	0.1	0.3	2.1	0.7	0.1	1.6	3.5

Macroeconomic, demographic and labour market indicators

Macroeconomic indicators	1995	2000	2004	2005	Average 1995-2000	Average 2001-2005	Level 2005
Real GDP (growth, %)	5.8	2.0	5.4	6.1	3.7	4.9	
GDP/capita (growth, %) – level in US dollars	5.5	1.9	5.4	6.0	3.5	5.0	13 617
Employment (growth, %) – level in thousands	1.7	−1.4	0.3	2.1	−0.4	1.1	2 216
Unemployment (% of labour force)	13.1	18.8	18.1	16.2	14.0	17.9	

Components of population growth	1995	2000	2004	2005	Average 1995-2000	Average 2001-2005
Per 1 000 inhabitants						
Total	2.2	0.7	0.9	0.8	1.4	0.4
Natural increase	1.6	0.4	0.4	0.2	1.1	0.0
Net migration	0.5	0.3	0.5	0.6	0.3	0.4

Total population	1995	2000	2004	2005	Average 1995-2000	Average 2001-2005	Level ('000) 2005
(Annual growth %)							
Native-born	..	..	..	..	..	..	..
Foreign-born	..	..	..	..	..	..	..
National	0.2	0.1	0.2	–	0.1	0.1	5 362
Foreign	29.7	−2.4	−23.8	14.9	5.7	−3.5	26

Naturalisations	1995	2000	2004	2005	Average 1995-2000	Average 2001-2005	Level 2005
As a percentage of foreign population	..	..	13.8	6.3	–	6.4	1 393

Labour market outcomes	1995	2000	2004	2005	Average 1995-2000	Average 2001-2005
Employment/population ratio						
Native-born men	..	..	62.9	64.1	..	63.5
Foreign-born men	..	..	66.7	66.7	..	66.0
Native-born women	..	..	50.7	50.9	..	51.3
Foreign-born women	..	..	42.6	42.1	..	44.5
Unemployment rate						
Native-born men	..	..	17.8	15.7	..	16.8
Foreign-born men	..	..	..	..	..	8.9
Native-born women	..	..	19.5	17.0	..	17.9
Foreign-born women	..	..	30.5	27.3	..	26.5

Notes and sources are at the end of the Chapter.

StatLink ⫘ http://dx.doi.org/10.1787/022576825003

Spain

According to statistics obtained from the municipal registers, entries in 2005 amounted to more than 680 000 foreigners, a further increase compared to the record high inflow of 640 000 registered in 2004. For the second consecutive year, Romanians were the most important origin group, accounting for 94 000 entries, slightly more than in the previous year. With almost 70 000 new immigrants – an increase of more than 10 000 compared to 2004 – Moroccans were the second most important origin group.

Irregular immigration of Africans by boats to the Canary Islands became a matter of key concern in 2006, with about 19 000 illegal migrants arriving between June and October 2006 alone. Although this was only a minor part of total migration movements to Spain, deaths during the ocean passage and the unique destination point attracted much attention to the issue. This lead to the most extensive operation ever of the joint European frontier agency FRONTEX. An action plan for security in the Canary Islands has been approved by the Spanish government in July 2006 to increase, among other measures, controls around these islands.

In contrast to the increase in irregular migration to the Canary Islands, illegal entries into the Spanish enclaves of Ceuta and Melilla declined significantly in 2006.

In light of the growing irregular immigration by sea, Spain expanded co-operation with the key origin countries in Africa. A programme providing 4 000 temporary jobs to Senegalese – one of the main origin counties of irregular migration to the Canary Islands is planned for 2008. Development co-operation with Senegal and other origin countries in Africa was also enhanced.

In January 2007, cabinet passed a bilateral agreement with Ukraine to better control and manage migration movements, including the selection and pre-departure training of labour migrants.

As the most important destination country for Bulgarian and Romanian emigrants in recent years, Spain decided to apply a transition period with respect to the access of the citizens of these two countries following their accession to the European Union in January 2007.

Parliament passed legislation in November 2006 to provide Spanish emigrants residing abroad the same constitutional rights and duties as Spanish nationals residing in Spain.

A government report released in December 2006 indicated that immigration accounted for 50% of GDP growth over the past five years. It is estimated that immigration has raised income per capita by increasing both the working-age population and the aggregate employment rate in the economy over the last decade.

In light of the rapid growth of the immigrant population in Spain in recent years, integration has moved up the policy agenda. In 2006, EUR 182 million were dedicated to assist regions and municipalities in integration, an increase of more than 60 million. A number of further programmes and initiatives to promote integration have been established in 2006, including the creation of a Forum for Social Integration of Immigrants, a consultative and information body.

For further information...

http://extranjeros.mtas.es/

Flow data on foreigners

Migration flows (foreigners) National definition	1995	2000	2004	2005	Average		Level ('000)
					1995-2000	2001-2005	2005
Per 1 000 inhabitants							
Inflows	..	8.2	15.1	15.7	4.0	12.3	682.7
Outflows	..	..	..	..	..	..	..

Long-term migration inflows (foreigners) by type Permit based statistics (standardised)	Thousands		% distribution	
	2004	2005	2004	2005
Work	..	..	..	..
Family (incl. accompanying family)	..	..	..	..
Humanitarian (incl. accompanying family)	..	..	..	..
Others	..	..	..	..
Total	..	..		

Temporary migration	2000	2004	2005	Annual average
				2000-2005
Thousands				
International students	28.8	35.8	30.7	29.8
Trainees	..	..	..	..
Working holiday makers	..	..	..	..
Seasonal workers	..	..	..	..
Intra-company transfers	..	..	..	..
Other temporary workers	..	..	..	..

Inflows of top 10 nationalities as a % of total inflows of foreigners

Inflows of asylum seekers	1995	2000	2004	2005	Average		Level ('000)
					1995-2000	2001-2005	2005
Per 1 000 inhabitants	0.1	0.2	0.1	0.1	0.2	0.2	5.3

Macroeconomic, demographic and labour market indicators

Macroeconomic indicators	1995	2000	2004	2005	Average		Level
					1995-2000	2001-2005	2005
Real GDP (growth, %)	2.8	5.0	3.2	3.5	4.1	3.1	
GDP/capita (growth, %) – level in US dollars	2.6	4.2	1.6	1.8	3.6	1.5	22 938
Employment (growth, %) – level in thousands	2.5	5.6	3.9	4.8	4.4	3.9	18 973
Unemployment (% of labour force)	18.7	10.8	10.5	9.2	15.0	10.4	

Components of population growth	1995	2000	2004	2005	Average	
					1995-2000	2001-2005
Per 1 000 inhabitants						
Total	1.3	9.9	..	..	3.9	14.6
Natural increase	0.4	0.9	..	..	0.4	1.2
Net migration	0.9	8.9	..	..	3.5	13.4

Total population	1995	2000	2004	2005	Average		Level ('000)
					1995-2000	2001-2005	2005
(Annual growth %)							
Native-born	..	..	..	..	..	..	..
Foreign-born	..	..	..	..	..	..	..
National	0.1	0.6	0.9	–0.1	0.2	0.7	40 659
Foreign	8.3	11.8	20.1	38.5	12.4	25.4	2 739

Naturalisations	1995	2000	2004	2005	Average		Level
					1995-2000	2001-2005	2005
As a percentage of foreign population	1.5	1.5	2.3	2.2	1.8	2.1	42 830

Labour market outcomes	1995	2000	2004	2005	Average	
					1995-2000	2001-2005
Employment/population ratio						
Native-born men	62.0	70.8	73.0	74.4	65.8	72.9
Foreign-born men	61.1	75.4	78.8	79.5	70.1	78.8
Native-born women	31.6	41.0	47.2	50.0	35.5	45.7
Foreign-born women	36.7	45.7	54.6	60.4	41.8	55.2
Unemployment rate						
Native-born men	17.8	9.4	7.8	7.0	14.2	7.5
Foreign-born men	24.2	11.8	11.7	9.5	15.8	10.7
Native-born women	30.8	20.4	15.1	12.0	26.3	14.8
Foreign-born women	30.4	20.0	16.8	13.5	25.4	15.9

Notes and sources are at the end of the Chapter.

StatLink 〓〓 http://dx.doi.org/10.1787/021280286464

Sweden

Immigration to Sweden continued to grow in 2005, with much of the increase being attributable to immigration from the new EU member countries, for whom Sweden has opened its labour market. More than two thirds of the about 8 100 residence permits to nationals from the EU10 were granted to Polish citizens. However, the overall impact of EU enlargement on the labour market has thus far been limited.

Immigration from non-EU countries consists largely of family reunification and humanitarian migration. In 2005, Sweden accepted more than 8 000 refugees. Asylum seeking declined by almost 25% in 2005 to 17 530, although Sweden continues to be one of the destinations where asylum seeking is highest in per capita terms. Serbia-Montenegro, Iraq and the Russian Federation remained the main origin countries of new asylum seekers to Sweden.

A non-negligible part of asylum seekers are unaccompanied minors, about 400 in 2005. On July 2005, new legislation entered into force which strengthened protection of unaccompanied children who come to Sweden and apply for a residence permit. This law implies that these children will be provided with a special legal guardian during the asylum procedure. In July 2006, responsibility for providing accommodation for unaccompanied minor asylum seekers was transferred to the municipalities.

A new Aliens Act entered into force on 31 March 2006, which aimed at making the asylum process more transparent and at introducing more oral proceedings. A new system for appeals has been introduced, and so-called "migration courts" (regular courts in three counties which are now also in charge of dealing with appeals) have replaced the former Aliens Appeals Board. Appeals are thus no longer an administrative process but a judicial one. In the new Act, the different grounds for residence permits have also been more clearly defined, and the grounds for protection are given more prominence. The new Aliens Act also foresees the granting of residence permits for witnesses before international courts and tribunals. Sweden has conducted agreements with international courts and tribunals regarding the transfer to Sweden of witnesses in need of protection, including their family where necessary.

Between 15 November 2005 and the entry into force of the new Act, a temporary amendment to the Alien's Act was introduced which gave aliens whose expulsion was pending the right to a new assessment of their situation. This allowed the Migration Board to grant residence permits in certain cases such as urgent humanitarian interest. Almost 2 400 persons benefited from this temporary measure and were granted a residence permit on humanitarian grounds.

Student migration continued to grow in 2005. More than 6 800 residence permits were given to students from non-EEA countries.

Following general elections in September 2006, a new government has been formed which presented a number of measures targeted at improving integration of immigrants. Among other measures, a review and reform of the present language instruction is planned as well as a system of anonymous job applications in the public sector on a trial basis. Measures relating to skills assessment on the job and to the verification of foreign qualifications and work experience have now been fully integrated into the "trial opportunity" programme which provides on-the-job training for persons lacking work experience in Sweden. A number of administrative changes are also envisaged, including the closure of the Swedish integration board. Finally, the government is considering comprehensive legislation against discrimination.

For further information...

www.migrationsverket.se/english.html

Flow data on foreigners

Migration flows (foreigners) National definition	1995	2000	2004	2005	Average		Level ('000)
					1995-2000	2001-2005	2005
Per 1 000 inhabitants							
Inflows	4.1	4.8	5.3	5.7	4.0	5.3	*51.3*
Outflows	1.7	1.4	1.8	1.8	1.6	1.7	*15.9*

Long-term migration inflows (foreigners) by type Permit based statistics (standardised)	Thousands		% distribution	
	2004	2005	2004	2005
Work	11.8	13.7	*24.0*	*25.5*
Family (incl. accompanying family)	30.2	30.9	*61.5*	*57.4*
Humanitarian (incl. accompanying family)	6.1	8.1	*12.5*	*15.0*
Others	1.0	1.1	*2.0*	*2.1*
Total	49.1	53.8		

Inflows of top 10 nationalities as a % of total inflows of foreigners

Temporary migration	2000	2004	2005	Annual average
				2000-2005
Thousands				
International students	5.2	9.8	10.8	7.9
Trainees	..	..	..	..
Working holiday makers	..	..	..	..
Seasonal workers	..	4.9	5.9	6.0
Intra-company transfers	..	..	..	..
Other temporary workers	..	3.4	2.2	2.7

Inflows of asylum seekers	1995	2000	2004	2005	Average		Level ('000)
					1995-2000	2001-2005	2005
Per 1 000 inhabitants	1.0	1.8	2.6	1.9	1.2	2.9	*17.5*

Macroeconomic, demographic and labour market indicators

Macroeconomic indicators	1995	2000	2004	2005	Average		Level
					1995-2000	2001-2005	2005
Real GDP (growth, %)	3.9	4.3	4.1	2.9	3.2	2.7	
GDP/capita (growth, %) – level in US dollars	3.4	4.2	3.7	2.5	3.1	2.3	*30 002*
Employment (growth, %) – level in thousands	1.6	2.2	-0.4	1.0	0.8	0.1	*4 254*
Unemployment (% of labour force)	7.7	4.7	5.5	5.8	6.8	4.8	

Components of population growth	1995	2000	2004	2005	Average	
					1995-2000	2001-2005
Per 1 000 inhabitants						
Total	2.3	2.5	3.9	4.0	1.3	3.7
Natural increase	1.0	-0.3	1.1	1.0	-0.1	0.5
Net migration	1.2	2.8	2.8	3.0	1.4	3.1

Total population	1995	2000	2004	2005	Average		Level ('000)
					1995-2000	2001-2005	2005
(Annual growth %)							
Native-born	0.4	-0.1	0.2	0.1	-0.1	0.1	*7 904*
Foreign-born	1.5	2.3	2.1	2.3	1.4	2.3	*1 126*
National	0.6	0.3	0.4	0.4	0.2	0.4	*8 550*
Foreign	-1.0	-2.0	1.1	-0.3	-2.1	0.2	*480*

Naturalisations	1995	2000	2004	2005	Average		Level
					1995-2000	2001-2005	2005
As a percentage of foreign population	6.0	8.9	5.6	8.2	6.9	7.3	*39 573*

Labour market outcomes	1995	2000	2004	2005	Average	
					1995-2000	2001-2005
Employment/population ratio						
Native-born men	73.2	75.8	75.7	76.3	73.8	76.6
Foreign-born men	51.7	59.6	63.6	64.1	56.1	64.7
Native-born women	71.7	73.2	72.9	72.9	71.4	73.9
Foreign-born women	50.0	54.7	59.2	57.5	50.6	58.6
Unemployment rate						
Native-born men	8.8	5.1	6.2	7.9	8.2	5.7
Foreign-born men	28.1	13.5	14.1	15.6	22.0	13.0
Native-born women	7.0	4.3	5.2	7.8	6.8	5.1
Foreign-born women	19.9	11.2	12.5	14.1	17.7	11.0

Notes and sources are at the end of the Chapter.

StatLink ⟪ᵐᔆᔆ⟫ *http://dx.doi.org/10.1787/022577755384*

Switzerland

The growth in work-related permanent immigration which Switzerland has experienced since the gradual implementation of the free-movement regime with the EU15/EFTA countries continued in 2005. The shift in the composition of the origin countries towards EU nationals since the start of the implementation in 2002 also continued, although it was somewhat less pronounced than in 2002-04. German and Portuguese remain the main nationalities involved, accounting for 21% and 13%, respectively, of new arrivals. The current numerical limits on migration for the EU15/EFTA nationals will be lifted on 1 June 2007. In total, based on standardised statistics, about 33 000 persons immigrated to Switzerland for work – about 42% of all permanent migration. Immigration on family reunification and humanitarian grounds continued its downward trend. On the whole, total permanent immigration declined somewhat.

Asylum seeking continued its downward trend and dropped by a further 30% in 2005. The 10 000 requests received was the lowest figure since the late 1980s. Preliminary figures for 2006 show, however, a slight increase to about 10 500.

The number of naturalisations has grown slightly to about 38 500 persons, but the naturalisation rate remains low in international comparison. Nationals from Serbia and Montenegro accounted for more than 20% of all naturalizations. Following the rejection of more ambitious changes in naturalisation policy in a popular vote in September 2004, some changes in the naturalisation procedures were applied in January 2006. The fees which can be charged for naturalisation demands are now restricted to procedural costs. Prior to this, fees varied widely across the country. Some further changes concerned facilitated naturalisation for some groups of persons of Swiss origin.

In April 2006, the treaty on the free movement of persons with the EU15/EFTA was extended to the ten new EU member states, with a transition regime operating until 2011 for nationals from these countries, with the exception of Cyprus and Malta. The transition regime includes numerical limits, priority of residents on the labour market, and control of salaries and work conditions).

In September 2006, the new foreigners' law was approved in a referendum. For the first time, the main objectives of labour market admission and integration policy are incorporated in a law. Among other provisions, the new law restricts work-related immigration of non-EEA nationals to qualified labour, abolishes some obstacles for professional and geographical mobility within Switzerland and reinforces measures against irregular migration. It will come into force in January 2008.

A new law on asylum was also approved in a referendum in September 2006. A first set of key elements entered into force in January 2007. Among the changes are tightened access to asylum and more stringent enforcement policies. Requests without identification papers are generally no longer treated unless exceptional circumstances apply. It is now also possible to resort to imprisonment for persons resisting to their expulsion. In addition, a person whose asylum request has been denied and who is required to leave the country may now only receive financial emergency aid. At the same time, the new law facilitates family reunification and labour market access of provisionally admitted persons, although their access to social assistance will now generally be limited to seven years. Furthermore, closer co-operation with origin and transit countries is envisaged. In this context, Switzerland is enhancing its efforts to negotiate readmission agreements for persons in an irregular situation. In 2005, such agreements have been signed with the Benelux countries, Nigeria, Slovak Republic, Algeria, Greece and Afghanistan.

There have also been several changes in integration policy, in force since February 2006. The degree of integration is now to be considered upon the issuance or prolongation of residence permits. Successful integration may shorten the time required for obtaining a permanent residence permit from ten to five years. Furthermore, co-ordination in integration policy between the three layers of government (federal, cantonal and local) is reinforced.

For further information...

www.bfm.admin.ch

Flow data on foreigners

Migration flows (foreigners) National definition	1995	2000	2004	2005	Average		Level ('000)
					1995-2000	2001-2005	2005
Per 1 000 inhabitants							
Inflows	12.5	11.9	13.0	12.7	11.1	13.0	*94.4*
Outflows	9.6	7.8	6.5	6.7	8.7	6.7	*49.7*

Long-term migration inflows (foreigners) by type Permit based statistics (standardised)	Thousands		% distribution	
	2004	2005	2004	2005
Work	31.6	32.8	*39.1*	*41.6*
Family (incl. accompanying family)	38.8	37.0	*48.1*	*46.9*
Humanitarian (incl. accompanying family)	4.4	3.3	*5.4*	*4.2*
Others	6.0	5.7	*7.4*	*7.3*
Total	80.7	78.8		

Inflows of top 10 nationalities as a % of total inflows of foreigners

Temporary migration	2000	2004	2005	Annual average
				2000-2005
Thousands				
International students	..	..	..	..
Trainees	..	0.4	0.3	0.4
Working holiday makers	..	..	..	..
Seasonal workers	49.3	–	–	–
Intra-company transfers	..	7.5	1.8	7.9
Other temporary workers	..	..	..	..

Inflows of asylum seekers	1995	2000	2004	2005	Average		Level ('000)
					1995-2000	2001-2005	2005
Per 1 000 inhabitants	2.4	2.5	1.9	1.3	3.8	2.5	*10.1*

Macroeconomic, demographic and labour market indicators

Macroeconomic indicators	1995	2000	2004	2005	Average		Level
					1995-2000	2001-2005	2005
Real GDP (growth, %)	0.4	3.6	2.3	1.9	2.0	1.1	
GDP/capita (growth, %) – level in US dollars	–0.2	3.0	1.6	1.3	1.7	0.3	*30 796*
Employment (growth, %) – level in thousands	0.0	1.0	0.3	0.1	0.7	0.2	*4 183*
Unemployment (% of labour force)	3.3	2.5	4.2	4.3	3.3	3.6	

Components of population growth	1995	2000	2004	2005	Average	
					1995-2000	2001-2005
Per 1 000 inhabitants						
Total	4.7	5.0	7.1	6.2	3.4	7.2
Natural increase	2.7	2.2	1.7	1.6	2.5	1.5
Net migration	2.1	2.8	5.4	4.6	0.9	5.7

Total population	1995	2000	2004	2005	Average		Level ('000)
					1995-2000	2001-2005	2005
(Annual growth %)							
Native-born	0.3	0.3	0.2	0.6	0.3	0.3	*5 686*
Foreign-born	1.9	1.7	2.3	2.0	0.9	2.4	*1 773*
National	0.3	0.4	0.5	0.9	0.3	0.6	*5 947*
Foreign	2.3	1.1	1.6	1.1	0.8	1.6	*1 512*

Naturalisations	1995	2000	2004	2005	Average		Level
					1995-2000	2001-2005	2005
As a percentage of foreign population	1.3	2.1	2.4	2.6	1.6	2.4	*38 437*

Labour market outcomes	1995	2000	2004	2005	Average	
					1995-2000	2001-2005
Employment/population ratio						
Native-born men	..	..	85.6	85.1	..	85.6
Foreign-born men	..	..	81.2	80.7	..	81.2
Native-born women	..	..	72.6	73.1	..	73.0
Foreign-born women	..	..	63.8	63.0	..	63.5
Unemployment rate						
Native-born men	..	..	2.9	2.7	..	2.8
Foreign-born men	..	..	7.5	7.8	..	7.5
Native-born women	..	..	3.4	3.7	..	3.4
Foreign-born women	..	..	9.2	9.7	..	9.4

Notes and sources are at the end of the Chapter.

StatLink 🔗 *http://dx.doi.org/10.1787/021218486647*

Turkey

With migration statistics for Turkey being based on estimates derived from several separate sources, a reliable description of migration from and to Turkey remains difficult. Notwithstanding this caveat, there are several indications that emigration from Turkey continued to weaken in 2005. Entry data in a number of OECD countries with significant Turkish population showed a decline. In particular, visas for family reunification have declined in a number of major host countries, and the registered number of asylum seekers with Turkish nationality declined by a further 30% in 2005, totalling about 11 200.

In contrast to the general decline in emigration, contract-dependent temporary labour migration via the intermediary of the Turkish Employment Office recovered from a temporary but sharp fall in the late 1990s to reach 66 355 in 2005 (+50% from 2004). Most of this temporary migration is towards the Commonwealth of Independent States and Arab countries, which account for 50% and 40%, respectively, of the flows.

Emigration also seems to play an ever decreasing role economically, as witnesses by the continuing strong decline in remittances. In 2005, workers' remittances by the Turkish expatriate community stood at only $ 851 million or 0.2% of GNP, the lowest level since the 1970s and a strong decrease compared to 2003 ($ 1.7 billion or 0.7% of GNP). Part of the decline observed in the figures appears to be due to changes in the calculation of remittances in the national accounts.

Several key institutions have made independent attempts to improve the collection and compilation of data on international migration in Turkey. There has also been a proposal on integrating international migration statistics into the recently established computer-based population registration system, the Central Population Administration System (CPAS). To date these attempts have not advanced far enough to result in significant progress in producing international migration statistics.

Irregular migration remains a significant element in international migration to Turkey. The number of apprehensions, however, has declined significantly. There are three main groups of undocumented immigrants in Turkey: Foreign nationals from eastern European countries in search for employment in Turkey who either arrived illegally or overstayed their visas; transit migrants (mainly from the Middle East); and rejected asylum seekers. Turkey's signature to the 1951 Geneva Convention is subject to a geographic reservation: Only requests from persons from eastern Europe and the Commonwealth of Independent States are accepted. With the recent fall in asylum seeking by persons from Afghanistan, Iran and Iraq, the role of Turkey as a country of transit to Europe may have diminished in importance.

In the domain of legislation, a significant change took place in March 2005 with the national action plan for asylum and migration. The action plan envisages completely reformed immigration legislation by 2012 with a view to gradually harmonising the Turkish immigration framework to the EU *acquis* in the light of accession negotiations. It is also expected that the above-mentioned geographical reservation on the Geneva Convention is to be dropped in this context. Likewise, the draft of a new *Settlement Law*, which has been presented to the Turkish parliament in the early 2000s, is still waiting for parliamentary debate. This law, which is to replace the current settlement law of 1934, is central to the whole immigration legislation debate as it still generally restricts immigration to Turkey to persons of "Turkish descent and culture".

For further information...

www.die.gov.tr/ENGLISH/index.html

www.egm.gov.tr/hizmet.yabancilar.asp

www.iskur.gov.tr

Flow data on foreigners

Migration flows (foreigners) *National definition*	1995	2000	2004	2005	Average		Level ('000)
					1995-2000	2001-2005	2005
Per 1 000 inhabitants							
Inflows	..	2.5	2.2	1.8	2.5	2.2	131.6
Outflows	..	..	..	..	..	..	..

Long-term migration inflows (foreigners) by type *Permit based statistics (standardised)*	Thousands		% distribution	
	2004	2005	2004	2005
Work	..	..	..	..
Family (incl. accompanying family)	..	..	..	..
Humanitarian (incl. accompanying family)	..	..	..	..
Others	..	..	..	..
Total	..	..		

Inflows of top 10 nationalities as a % of total inflows of foreigners

Temporary migration	2000	2004	2005	Annual average
				2000-2005
Thousands				
International students	..	..	..	..
Trainees	..	..	..	..
Working holiday makers	..	..	..	..
Seasonal workers	..	..	..	..
Intra-company transfers	..	..	..	..
Other temporary workers	..	..	..	..

Inflows of asylum seekers	1995	2000	2004	2005	Average		Level ('000)
					1995-2000	2001-2005	2005
Per 1 000 inhabitants	0.1	0.1	0.1	0.1	0.1	0.1	3.9

Macroeconomic, demographic and labour market indicators

Macroeconomic indicators	1995	2000	2004	2005	Average		Level
					1995-2000	2001-2005	2005
Real GDP (growth, %)	7.2	7.4	8.9	7.4	3.9	7.5	
GDP/capita (growth, %) – level in US dollars	5.3	2.4	7.3	7.0	2.1	6.2	7 882
Employment (growth, %) – level in thousands	2.8	−2.1	3.0	1.1	0.9	0.6	22 546
Unemployment (% of labour force)	7.5	6.3	10.1	10.0	6.9	9.8	

Components of population growth	1995	2000	2004	2005	Average	
					1995-2000	2001-2005
Per 1 000 inhabitants						
Total	..	..	..	..	..	..
Natural increase	..	..	..	..	..	..
Net migration	..	..	..	..	..	..

Total population	1995	2000	2004	2005	Average		Level ('000)
					1995-2000	2001-2005	2005
(Annual growth %)							
Native-born	..	..	..	..	..	..	..
Foreign-born	..	..	..	..	..	..	..
National	..	..	..	..	..	..	..
Foreign	..	..	..	..	..	..	..

Naturalisations	1995	2000	2004	2005	Average		Level
					1995-2000	2001-2005	2005
As a percentage of foreign population	..	..	..	..	..	..	..

Notes and sources are at the end of the Chapter.

StatLink http://dx.doi.org/10.1787/022761082774

United Kingdom

According to national statistics, immigration to the United Kingdom in 2005 declined somewhat compared to 2004, but nevertheless remained at significantly higher levels than in the previous decade. A significant proportion of the inflows is attributable to labour migration from the new EU member countries. In contrast to most other EU15 countries, the United Kingdom had opened its labour market for citizens of the new EU member countries since May 2004. By June 2006, 427 000 registrations for workers from these countries had taken place. Labour migration from non-EU countries also remained strong. About 17 600 migrants from Non-EU countries were accepted under the Highly Skilled Migrant Programme (HSMP), more than twice the 2004 number, whereas work permits for third country nationals remained broadly unchanged (about 86 000 in 2005 compared to about 89 500 in 2004).

Asylum seeking continued its strong decline. In 2005, there were about 30 000 applications (–25% less than in 2004).

The key policy developments were related to the planned introduction of the new five-tier immigration system that aims to "rationalise" the existing complex of more than 80 routes of entry for work and study. Plans for a strategic shift towards a points-based system (PBS) to manage labour migration into the United Kingdom have advanced in 2006. Among the major changes from the existing system are that the current two-stage application process for a work permit and entry clearance/leave to remain will be replaced by a single-step application that can be self-assessed in advance by the applicant. In addition, employers will have less influence than at present over their chosen candidates' applications and checks for integrity will be decentralised to entry clearance officers and caseworkers in the country where the application is made.

The PBS will be phased in gradually over 2007 to 2009, beginning with Tier 1 (similar to the existing HSMP) in the third quarter of 2007. As a first step, enhanced points criteria for entry via the HSMP were introduced in December 2006 to reduce discrepancies between the existing system and the PBS. Points are no longer granted, for example, for work experience, significant achievements or for having a skilled partner. These are replaced by new tests that reflect academic qualifications, previous earnings and age. Bonus points are available for those who have previously worked or studied in the United Kingdom.

With respect to the second points-based tier (skilled workers with a job offer who meet certain requirements), companies will need to register to become approved sponsors. Such approved sponsors are expected to anticipate their demand for foreign workers to fill non-specific jobs in a particular year and to request a corresponding number of certificates of sponsorship. It is assumed that, for non-shortage jobs where no local or EEA candidates are suitable, employers will be able to hire a migrant worker who self-assesses against the points-based system. The employer will send the candidate foreign worker a certificate of sponsorship reference number and the candidate will make a formal (online) application for entry clearance.

The government decided not to grant Bulgarian and Romanian citizens automatic access to the UK labour market. Admission for low-skilled occupations (tier 3 under the new system) will thus be restricted to Romanians and Bulgarians who, under the current system, enter to fill low-skilled jobs via the Sectors Based Scheme (food-processing) and Seasonal Agricultural Workers Scheme. This reflects the government's expectation that employers should look exclusively to the EU to meet low-skilled labour shortages. All existing low-skilled migration schemes for workers from outside the EU are phased out from January 2007. Recruitment through this low-skilled channel will be operator-led, time limited and quota based.

On 1 November 2005, a new requirement for acquiring British citizenship was introduced. Applicants now have to demonstrate some knowledge about life in Great Britain and their English language ability. This new requirement has led to an increase in naturalisation demands just prior to the introduction, with the number of citizenship demands in 2005 being 60% higher than in 2004.

Other new developments include a comprehensive organisational reform of the Immigration and Nationality Directorate. In addition, it is planned to introduce a new charging system for processing visas and applications.

For further information...

www.ind.homeoffice.gov.uk/

Flow data on foreigners

Migration flows (foreigners) *National definition*	1995	2000	2004	2005	Average		Level ('000)
					1995-2000	2001-2005	2005
Per 1 000 inhabitants							
Inflows	3.9	6.4	8.3	7.9	4.8	7.3	*473.8*
Outflows	1.7	2.7	2.5	3.0	2.2	2.8	*181.5*

Long-term migration inflows (foreigners) by type *Permit based statistics (standardised)*	Thousands		% distribution	
	2004	2005	2004	2005
Work	136.1	161.6	*44.3*	*44.6*
Family (incl. accompanying family)	99.9	113.8	*32.5*	*31.4*
Humanitarian (incl. accompanying family)	52.6	67.8	*17.1*	*18.7*
Others	18.9	19.2	*6.1*	*5.3*
Total	307.3	362.4		

Inflows of top 10 nationalities as a % of total inflows of foreigners

Temporary migration	2000	2004	2005	Annual average
				2000-2005
Thousands				
International students	102.8	152.6	..	131.6
Trainees	..	..	..	..
Working holiday makers	38.4	62.4	56.6	46.9
Seasonal workers	10.1	19.8	15.7	16.0
Intra-company transfers	..	..	..	..
Other temporary workers	64.6	113.4	111.2	93.7

Inflows of asylum seekers	1995	2000	2004	2005	Average		Level ('000)
					1995-2000	2001-2005	2005
Per 1 000 inhabitants	0.9	1.7	0.7	0.5	1.1	1.1	*30.8*

Macroeconomic, demographic and labour market indicators

Macroeconomic indicators	1995	2000	2004	2005	Average		Level
					1995-2000	2001-2005	2005
Real GDP (growth, %)	2.9	3.8	3.3	1.9	3.2	2.5	
GDP/capita (growth, %) – level in US dollars	2.6	3.5	2.8	1.2	2.9	2.0	*28 223*
Employment (growth, %) – level in thousands	1.2	1.2	1.0	0.9	1.3	0.9	*28 730*
Unemployment (% of labour force)	8.6	5.5	4.7	4.8	6.9	5.0	

Components of population growth	1995	2000	2004	2005	Average	
					1995-2000	2001-2005
Per 1 000 inhabitants						
Total	2.6	3.7	..	..	3.0	3.6
Natural increase	1.6	1.2	..	..	1.5	1.2
Net migration	1.0	2.5	..	..	1.6	2.5

Total population	1995	2000	2004	2005	Average		Level ('000)
					1995-2000	2001-2005	2005
(Annual growth %)							
Native-born	..	..	..	..	..	..	..
Foreign-born	..	..	..	..	..	..	..
National	0.4	0.1	0.3	0.3	0.2	0.3	*57 175*
Foreign	–4.1	6.1	4.2	6.2	3.8	4.1	*3 035*

Naturalisations	1995	2000	2004	2005	Average		Level
					1995-2000	2001-2005	2005
As a percentage of foreign population	2.0	3.7	5.1	5.7	2.5	4.9	*161 780*

Labour market outcomes	1995	2000	2004	2005	Average	
					1995-2000	2001-2005
Employment/population ratio						
Native-born men	75.4	78.3	78.1	77.9	76.9	78.1
Foreign-born men	67.3	71.1	72.7	72.4	69.8	72.3
Native-born women	62.3	65.7	66.9	67.0	64.1	66.6
Foreign-born women	51.3	53.1	55.0	56.1	53.0	54.9
Unemployment rate						
Native-born men	9.9	5.9	4.7	4.7	7.8	5.0
Foreign-born men	14.2	9.6	7.3	7.5	11.3	7.7
Native-born women	6.7	4.6	3.9	3.7	5.5	3.9
Foreign-born women	11.0	7.8	7.3	7.1	8.8	6.9

Notes and sources are at the end of the Chapter.

StatLink *http://dx.doi.org/10.1787/021347804631*

United States

During the Fiscal Year 2005, the United States registered its highest level of permanent immigration since 1991. More than 1.1 million persons were granted legal permanent resident status (green cards), an increase of 17% over the approximately 960 000 persons admitted during the previous fiscal year. The largest increases were in the employment-based preference group (almost 250 000 admissions, an increase of more than 90 000 compared to 2004) and in the category of refugees and asylees, whose number doubled from about 70 000 to more than 140 000. The upward trend was also observed in most major categories of legal temporary migration.

In August 2006, the Department of Homeland Security's Office of Immigration Statistics released its latest estimates of the size and characteristics of the unauthorized US population. An estimated 10.5 million unauthorized migrants are believed to have been residing in the United States in January 2005, up from 8.5 million in January 2000. It is estimated that during this five-year period the unauthorized population grew by about 408 000 (net) per year.

In 2006, President George W. Bush continued his call on Congress to pass comprehensive immigration reform that would tighten border enforcement, enhance interior and worksite enforcement, create a temporary worker programme, resolve – without amnesty – the status of undocumented immigrants, and promote assimilation into the United States. The President repeatedly expressed his belief that all elements must be addressed together through a comprehensive approach.

During 2006, the US House of Representatives sought a legislative solution that focused on securing the nation's borders. The House passed such a bill, which had no provision for a temporary worker programme. The Senate passed a broader immigration bill that combined tighter enforcement with a new temporary worker programme.

The 109th Congress ended without enactment of a comprehensive immigration bill, but it did pass the "The Secure Fence Act of 2006," which was signed into law in December 2006. It mandated construction of a 700-mile security fence along the southern border. Congress also passed the Fiscal Year 2007 Homeland Security Appropriations bill, which included unprecedented funding for the Secure Border Initiative, including additional border patrol agents and detention beds. That funding bill also provided USD 1.2 billion for border fencing, vehicle barriers, technology and tactical infrastructure. These legislative actions followed a White House initiative launched in May of 2006 to promote greater border enforcement. "Operation Jumpstart" deployed 6 000 National Guard members to help secure the southern border.

With regard to the existing "non-immigrant" (i.e. temporary) worker programmes, the 65 000 numerical limit for H-1B visas (for workers in specialty occupations) for 2007 was exhausted by late May 2006 – four months before the beginning of the applicable fiscal year. While Congress set aside another 20 000 visas for 2007, the availability of H-1B visas still falls far short of the annual demand for such workers by US employers.

The US Citizenship and Immigration Services premium processing programme, already in use for several non-immigrant visas, was extended to applications for the employment-based green card, a change or extension of non-immigrant status, and employment authorisation. Eligible applicants can now pay USD 1 000 to receive a 15-day turnaround.

The newly established Refugee Corps greatly improved processing by stationing USCIS officers on-site in more than 50 countries to interview refugee applicants from nearly 60 nations.

A new passport rule went into effect on 23 January 2007, requiring nearly all travellers to the United States to show a passport for entry.

For further information...

www.dhs.gov/ximgtn/
www.dol.gov/compliance/laws/comp-ina.htm

Flow data on foreigners

Migration flows (foreigners) *National definition*	1995	2000	2004	2005	Average		Level ('000)
					1995-2000	2001-2005	2005
Per 1 000 inhabitants							
Inflows	2.7	3.0	3.3	3.8	2.8	3.4	1 122.4
Outflows	..	..	..	..	..	..	..

Long-term migration inflows (foreigners) by type *Permit based statistics (standardised)*	Thousands		% distribution	
	2004	2005	2004	2005
Work	72.6	114.0	7.6	10.2
Family (incl. accompanying family)	714.9	782.1	74.6	69.7
Humanitarian (incl. accompanying family)	71.2	143.0	7.4	12.7
Others	99.2	83.3	10.4	7.4
Total	957.9	1 122.4		

Inflows of top 10 nationalities as a % of total inflows of foreigners

1990-2004 annual average   2005

Mexico, India, China, Philippines, Cuba, Viet Nam, Dominican Republic, Korea, Colombia, Ukraine

0 5 10 15 20 25 30

✳48.9 ☐ 54.6

Temporary migration	2000	2004	2005	Annual average
				2000-2005
Thousands				
International students	284.1	218.9	237.9	247.4
Trainees	1.5	1.4	1.8	1.5
Working holiday makers	..	..	..	..
Seasonal workers	30.2	31.8	31.9	31.1
Intra-company transfers	55.0	62.7	65.5	59.6
Other temporary workers	184.8	221.8	218.6	205.2

Inflows of asylum seekers	1995	2000	2004	2005	Average		Level ('000)
					1995-2000	2001-2005	2005
Per 1 000 inhabitants	0.6	0.1	0.1	0.1	0.3	0.1	24.2

Macroeconomic, demographic and labour market indicators

Macroeconomic indicators	1995	2000	2004	2005	Average		Level
					1995-2000	2001-2005	2005
Real GDP (growth, %)	2.5	3.7	3.9	3.2	4.1	2.8	
GDP/capita (growth, %) – level in US dollars	1.3	2.6	2.9	2.3	2.9	1.8	37 063
Employment (growth, %) – level in thousands	1.5	2.5	1.1	1.8	1.9	0.9	141 719
Unemployment (% of labour force)	5.6	4.0	5.5	5.1	4.8	5.4	

Components of population growth	1995	2000	2004	2005	Average		
					1995-2000	2001-2005	
Per 1 000 inhabitants							
Total	10.3	10.3	9.5	9.2	10.3	9.7	
Natural increase	6.0	5.7	5.9	5.6	5.8	5.7	
Net migration	4.4	4.6	3.7	3.5	4.5	4.0	

Total population	1995	2000	2004	2005	Average		Level ('000)
					1995-2000	2001-2005	2005
(Annual growth %)							
Native-born	..	0.7	0.7	0.8	..	0.5	258 067
Foreign-born	..	5.1	2.9	2.0	..	4.3	38 343
National	..	..	..	..	..	..	..
Foreign	..	..	..	..	..	..	..

Naturalisations	1995	2000	2004	2005	Average		Level
					1995-2000	2001-2005	2005
As a percentage of foreign population	..	..	..	..	..	..	604 280

Labour market outcomes	1995	2000	2004	2005	Average		
					1995-2000	2001-2005	
Employment/population ratio							
Native-born men	76.0	76.7	73.0	73.3	76.2	74.0	
Foreign-born men	76.9	81.6	80.2	81.7	79.3	81.0	
Native-born women	65.2	67.8	65.4	65.3	66.6	66.1	
Foreign-born women	53.3	57.3	56.2	56.4	56.2	57.0	
Unemployment rate							
Native-born men	6.2	4.5	6.9	6.3	5.6	6.3	
Foreign-born men	7.9	4.5	5.8	5.1	6.1	5.5	
Native-born women	5.3	4.2	5.5	5.2	4.7	5.1	
Foreign-born women	8.2	5.5	6.8	5.2	6.5	6.2	

Notes and sources are at the end of the Chapter.

StatLink ⫘⫘⫘ *http://dx.doi.org/10.1787/022817488177*

HOW TO READ THE TABLES OF PART IV

Annual averages have been calculated for most of the series presented. The averages cover the periods 1995-2000 and 2001-2005. In some cases, depending on the availabilty of data, they may be calculated for shorter periods.

Sources and notes

Migration flows of foreigners

Sources and notes are available in the Statistical Annex (metadata related to Tables A.1.1. and B.1.1.)

Long-term migration inflows of foreigners by type

The statistics are based largely on residence and work permit data and have been standardised, to the extent possible (cf. www.oecd.org/els/migration/imo2007).

Temporary migration

Based on residence or work permit data. Data on temporary workers generally do not cover workers who benefit from a free circulation agreement.

Inflows of asylum seekers

United Nations High Commission for Refugees.

Macroeconomic and labour market indicators

Real GDP and GDP per capita

Annual National Accounts – Comparative tables at the price levels and PPPs of 2000.

Employment and unemployment

Employment Outlook, OECD, 2006. Some series appearing in the latter have been revised since they were published.

Components of population growth

Labour Force Statistics, OECD, 2006.

Total population

Foreign-born population

National sources and Secretariat estimates (cf.: www.oecd.org/els/migration/imo2007 for more information on methods of estimation). Sources and notes of national sources are provided in the Statistical Annex (see metadata for Tables A.1.4. and B.1.4.).

Foreign population

National sources. Exact sources and notes are given in the Statistical Annex (metadata related to Tables A.1.5. and B.1.5.).

Naturalisations

National sources. Exact sources and notes are given in the Statistical Annex (metadata related to Tables A.1.6. and B.1.6.).

Labour market outcomes

European countries: European Union Labour Force Survey (data provided by Eurostat) except for Denmark (Population Register data except for 2005 where data refer to the European Union Labour Force Survey); Australia: Labour Force Survey; Canada: Survey of Labour and Income Dynamics; United States: Current Population Survey, March supplement.

HOW TO READ THE CHART

Inflows of top 10 nationalities as a % of total inflows of foreigners

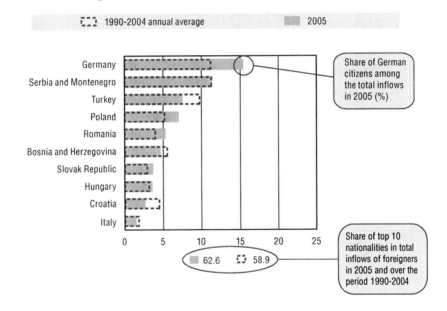

ISBN 978-92-64-03285-9
International Migration Outlook
SOPEMI 2007 Edition
© OECD 2007

STATISTICAL ANNEX

Introduction

Most of the data published in this annex are taken from the individual contributions of national correspondents appointed by the OECD Secretariat with the approval of the authorities of member countries. Consequently, these data have not necessarily been harmonised at international level. This network of correspondents, constituting the Continuous Reporting System on Migration (SOPEMI), covers most OECD member countries as well as the Baltic States, Bulgaria and Romania. SOPEMI has no authority to impose changes in data collection procedures. It has an observatory role which, by its very nature, has to use existing statistics. However, it does play an active role in suggesting what it considers to be essential improvements in data collection and makes every effort to present consistent and well-documented statistics.

No data are presented on the native population, since the purpose of this annex is to describe the "immigrant" population as defined in the specific host country (i.e. the foreign or foreign-born population, as the case may be). The information gathered concerns the flows and stocks of the total immigrant population and immigrant labour force, together with acquisition of nationality. The presentation of the tables in a relatively standard format should not lead users to think that the data have been fully standardised and are comparable at an international level, since few sources are specifically designed to record migration trends. Because of the great variety of sources used, different populations may be measured. In addition, the criteria for registering population and the conditions for granting residence permits, for example, vary across countries, which means that measurements may differ greatly even if a theoretically identical source is being used.

In addition to the problem of the comparability of statistics, there is the difficulty of the very partial coverage of illegal migrants. Part of this population can be counted through censuses. The number of immigrants who entered legally but then stay on after their residence permits (or visas) have expired can be calculated from permit statistics, but without it being possible to determine what the number of these immigrants that have left the country. Regularisation programmes, when they exist, make it possible to account for a far from negligible fraction of illegal immigrants after the fact. In terms of measurement, this makes it possible better to evaluate the volume of the foreign population at a given time, although it is not always possible to classify these immigrants by the year when they entered the country.

The rationale used to arrange the series has been to present first the tables covering the total population (series 1.1 to 1.6: Inflows and outflows of foreign population, inflows of asylum seekers, stocks of foreign-born and foreign population, acquisition of nationality), and then focus on the labour force (series 2.1 to 2.4): Inflows of foreign workers, inflows of seasonal workers, stocks of foreign-born and foreign labour force).

Since the nature of the sources used differs considerably across countries, each series is preceded by an explanatory note aimed at making it easier to understand and use the data produced. A summary table then follows (series A, giving the total for each host country), which introduces the tables by nationality or country of birth as the case may be (series B). At the end of each series, a table provides for each country the sources and notes of the data presented in the tables.

General comments on tables

a) The tables provide annual series for the ten most recent years (in general 1996-2005).

b) The series A tables are presented in alphabetical order by the name of the country in English. In the other tables, nationalities or countries are ranked by decreasing order of the stocks for the last year available.

c) In the tables by country of origin (series B) only the 15 main countries are shown and only when this information is available. "Other countries" is a residual calculated as the difference between the total foreign population and the sum of the nationalities indicated in the table. For some nationalities, data are not available for all years and this is reflected in the residual entry of "Other countries". This must be borne in mind when interpreting changes in this category.

d) Tables on inflows of asylum seekers by nationality (series B.1.3) are presented for the top ten host countries in 2005. The data on outflows of foreign population (series 1.2), inflows of workers (series 2.1) and seasonal workers (series 2.2) are not broken down by nationality. Only totals are presented, in Tables A.1.2, A.2.1 and A.2.2, respectively.

e) The rounding of entries may cause totals to differ slightly from the sum of the component entries.

f) The symbols used in the tables are the following:

　.. Data not available.

　− Nil, or negligible.

Inflows and Outflows of Foreign Population

OECD countries seldom have specific tools for measuring inflows and outflows of foreign population, and national estimates are generally based either on population registers or residence permit data. This note is aimed at describing more systematically what is measured by each of the sources used.

Flows derived from population registers

Population registers can usually produce inflow and outflow data for both nationals and foreigners. To register, foreigners may have to indicate possession of an appropriate residence and/or work permit valid for at least as long as minimum registration period. Emigrants are usually identified by a stated intention to leave the country, although the period of (intended) absence is not always specified.

When population registers are used, departures tend to be less well recorded than arrivals. Indeed, the emigrant who plans to return in the host country in the more or less long-term can hesitate to inform about his departure to avoid losing the rights related to the affiliation to the register. Registration criteria vary considerably across countries (as the minimum duration of stay for individuals to be defined as immigrants ranges from three months to one year), which poses major problems of international comparison. For example, in some countries, register data cover a portion of temporary migrants, in some cases including asylum seekers when they live in private households (as opposed to reception centres or hostels for immigrants).

Flows derived from residence and/or work permits

Statistics on permits are generally based on the number of permits issued during a given period and depend on the types of permits used. The so-called "settlement countries" (Australia, Canada, New Zealand and the United States) consider as immigrants persons who have been issued "acceptances for settlement". Statistics on temporary immigrants are also published in this annex for these countries since the legal duration of their residence is often similar to long-term migration (over a year). In the case of France, the permits covered are valid for at least one year (only students are not included). Data for Italy and Portugal include temporary migrants.

Another characteristic of permit data is that flows of nationals are not recorded. Some flows of foreigners may also not be recorded, either because the type of permit they hold is not used for statistics or because they are not required to have a permit (freedom of movement agreements). In addition, permit data do not necessarily reflect physical flows or actual lengths of stay since: i) permits may be issued overseas but individuals may decide not to use them, or delay their arrival; ii) permits may be issued to persons who have in fact been resident in the country for some time, the permit indicating a change of status, or a renewal of the same permit. The data for Australia do not include those who have been accepted for permanent settlement whilst resident in Australia, whereas data for Canada and the United States include all issues of permanent settlement permits.

Permit data may be influenced by the processing capacity of government agencies. In some instances a large backlog of applications may build up and therefore the true demand for permits may only emerge once backlogs are cleared.

Flows estimated from specific surveys

Ireland provides estimates based on the results of Quarterly National Household Surveys and other sources such as permit data and asylum applications. These estimates are revised periodically on the basis of census data. Data for the United Kingdom are based on a survey of passengers entering or exiting the country by plane, train or boat (International Passenger Survey). One of the aims of this survey is to estimate the number and characteristics of migrants. The survey is based on a random sample of approximately one out of every 500 passengers. The figures were revised significantly following the latest census in each of these two countries, which seems to indicate that these estimates do not constitute an "ideal" source either. Australia and New Zealand also conduct passenger surveys which enable them to establish the length of stay on the basis of migrants' stated intentions when they enter or exit the country.

Table A.1.1. Inflows of foreign population into selected OECD countries

Thousands

	1996	1997	1998	1999	2000	2001	2002	2003	2004	2005
Inflow data based on population registers:										
Austria	..	..	59.2	72.4	66.0	74.8	92.6	97.2	108.9	101.5
Belgium	51.9	49.2	50.7	57.8	57.3	66.0	70.2	68.8	72.4	77.4
Czech Republic	7.4	9.9	7.9	6.8	4.2	11.3	43.6	57.4	50.8	58.6
Denmark	24.7	20.4	21.3	20.3	22.9	25.2	22.0	18.7	18.8	..
Finland	7.5	8.1	8.3	7.9	9.1	11.0	10.0	9.4	11.5	12.7
Germany	708.0	615.3	605.5	673.9	648.8	685.3	658.3	601.8	602.2	579.3
Hungary	13.7	13.3	16.1	20.2	20.2	20.3	18.0	19.4	22.2	18.8
Japan	225.4	274.8	265.5	281.9	345.8	351.2	343.8	373.9	372.0	372.3
Luxembourg	9.2	9.4	10.6	11.8	10.8	11.1	11.0	11.5	12.5	13.5
Netherlands	77.2	76.7	81.7	78.4	91.4	94.5	86.6	73.6	65.1	63.4
Norway	17.2	22.0	26.7	32.2	27.8	25.4	30.8	26.8	27.9	31.4
Slovak Republic	5.4	6.1	6.4	5.9	4.6	4.7	4.8	4.6	7.9	7.7
Spain	..	..	57.2	99.1	330.9	394.0	443.1	429.5	645.8	682.7
Sweden	29.3	33.4	35.7	34.6	42.6	44.1	47.6	48.0	47.6	51.3
Switzerland	74.3	70.1	72.4	83.4	85.6	99.5	97.6	90.6	96.3	94.4
Inflow data based on residence permits or on other sources:										
Australia										
Permanent inflows	115.7	101.0	92.4	101.6	114.6	138.3	119.8	130.2	150.7	167.3
Temporary inflows	130.2	147.1	173.2	194.1	224.0	245.1	240.5	244.7	261.6	289.4
Canada	..	..	..	..	..	..	..			
Permanent inflows	226.1	216.0	174.2	190.0	227.5	250.6	229.0	221.4	235.8	262.2
Temporary inflows	186.9	194.5	198.6	233.0	261.4	282.4	262.3	243.7	244.7	247.1
France	48.4	74.5	110.7	82.9	92.2	106.8	124.0	135.1	140.0	134.8
Greece	..	..	38.2	..	..	..	..	..	..	..
Ireland	21.5	23.7	21.7	22.2	27.8	32.7	39.9	33.0	33.2	51.0
Italy	..	..	111.0	268.0	271.5	232.8	388.1	..	319.3	..
Korea	..	..	..	..	185.4	172.5	170.9	178.3	188.8	266.3
Mexico	29.2	27.1	25.3	22.7	24.2	26.1	24.6	29.1	34.0	39.5
New Zealand	42.7	32.9	27.4	31.0	37.6	54.4	47.5	43.0	36.2	54.1
Poland	..	..	5.2	17.3	15.9	21.5	30.2	30.3	36.9	38.5
Portugal	3.6	3.3	6.5	10.5	15.9	151.4	72.0	31.8	34.1	28.1
Turkey	..	..	..	..	168.1	161.2	157.6	152.2	155.5	131.6
United Kingdom	224.2	237.2	287.3	337.4	379.3	373.3	418.2	406.8	494.1	473.8
United States	..	..	..	..	..	..	..			
Permanent inflows	915.6	797.8	653.2	644.8	841.0	1 058.9	1 059.4	703.5	957.9	1 122.4
Temporary inflows	..	999.6	997.3	1 106.6	1 249.4	1 375.1	1 282.6	1 233.4	1 299.3	1 323.5
EU25 (among above countries) + Norway and Switzerland	..	..	**1 602.2**	**1 943.0**	**2 224.9**	**2 485.8**	**2 708.6**	**2 194.2**	**2 847.6**	**2 518.8**
North America (permanent)	**1 141.6**	**1 013.9**	**827.4**	**834.7**	**1 068.5**	**1 309.5**	**1 288.4**	**924.9**	**1 193.7**	**1 384.6**

Note: For details on definitions and sources, refer to the metadata at the end of Tables B.1.1.

StatLink 🔗 http://dx.doi.org/10.1787/015518260417

Table A.1.2. **Outflows of foreign population from selected OECD countries**

Thousands

	1996	1997	1998	1999	2000	2001	2002	2003	2004	2005
Outflow data based on population registers:										
Austria	..	..	44.9	47.3	44.4	51.0	38.8	46.1	48.3	47.5
Belgium	32.4	34.6	36.3	36.4	35.6	31.4	31.0	33.9	37.7	38.5
Czech Republic	0.2	0.1	0.2	0.1	0.2	20.6	31.1	33.2	33.8	21.8
Denmark	6.0	6.7	7.7	8.2	8.3	8.9	8.7	8.7	9.4	..
Finland	3.0	1.6	1.7	2.0	4.1	2.2	2.8	2.3	4.2	2.6
Germany	559.1	637.1	639.0	555.6	562.4	497.0	505.6	499.1	547.0	483.6
Hungary	2.8	1.9	2.3	2.5	2.2	1.9	2.4	2.6	3.5	3.8
Japan	161.1	177.8	188.1	199.7	210.9	232.8	248.4	259.4	278.5	292.0
Luxembourg	5.6	5.8	6.7	6.9	7.1	7.8	8.3	9.4	10.9	10.8
Netherlands	22.4	21.9	21.3	20.7	20.7	20.4	21.2	21.9	23.5	24.0
Norway	10.0	10.0	12.0	12.7	14.9	15.2	12.3	14.3	9.0	12.6
Sweden	14.5	15.3	14.1	13.6	12.6	12.7	14.3	15.1	16.0	15.9
Switzerland	67.7	63.4	59.0	58.1	55.8	52.7	49.7	46.3	47.9	49.7
Outflow data based on residence permits or on other sources:										
Australia										
Permanent departures	17.7	18.2	19.2	17.9	20.8	23.4	24.1	24.9	29.9	31.6
Long-term departures	27.7	28.6	30.3	29.4	30.0	42.2	31.9	29.5	29.6	31.8
Korea	..	..	..	..	89.1	107.2	114.0	152.3	148.8	266.7
Mexico	30.7	27.0	25.0	21.5	22.6	25.7	26.8	24.4	24.1	31.4
New Zealand	12.6	14.7	16.2	15.9	15.6	28.6	22.4	25.4	29.0	30.6
United Kingdom	108.0	130.6	125.7	151.6	159.6	148.5	173.7	170.6	151.9	181.5

Note: For details on definitions and sources, refer to the metadata at the end of Tables B.1.1.

StatLink ⟶ http://dx.doi.org/10.1787/015524217811

INTERNATIONAL MIGRATION OUTLOOK: SOPEMI 2007 EDITION – ISBN 978-92-64-03285-9 – © OECD 2007

Table B.1.1. **Inflows of foreign population by nationality**

Thousands

AUSTRALIA

	1996	1997	1998	1999	2000	2001	2002	2003	2004	2005
United Kingdom	14.4	12.7	12.1	11.7	13.3	14.3	13.8	18.2	18.1	19.8
New Zealand	12.3	13.1	14.7	18.7	21.9	25.2	15.7	12.4	14.4	17.4
China	13.2	8.8	5.5	8.9	9.5	11.9	10.0	11.1	13.6	16.0
India	4.1	3.1	3.2	3.0	5.4	9.0	7.6	9.0	11.6	12.9
South Africa	3.6	3.8	5.2	6.0	7.4	7.6	7.4	6.3	7.6	6.3
Philippines	4.0	3.4	3.4	4.0	4.0	3.9	3.5	3.8	4.9	5.0
Malaysia	1.3	1.4	1.2	1.6	2.3	2.9	3.2	4.1	5.6	4.8
Sri Lanka	2.1	1.6	1.4	1.2	1.6	2.4	2.4	2.5	2.3	3.1
United States	2.4	2.4	2.0	1.8	2.1	2.6	2.3	2.8	2.6	2.8
Hong Kong, China	4.7	4.1	3.5	2.2	1.8	2.1	1.6	2.0	2.4	2.5
Viet Nam	3.9	3.2	2.6	2.6	2.0	2.4	2.5	3.1	2.5	2.5
Fiji	2.3	2.1	1.4	1.8	2.1	2.5	2.0	2.0	1.8	2.0
Lebanon	1.6	1.3	1.2	1.1	1.4	1.7	1.3	1.8	1.4	1.6
Germany	1.2	1.2	1.0	1.1	1.2	1.3	1.2	1.3	1.5	1.5
Chinese Taipei	1.8	2.4	1.7	1.7	2.0	3.0	2.1	1.6	1.4	1.3
Other countries	42.7	36.5	32.1	34.1	36.5	45.4	43.2	48.4	59.1	67.8
Total	**115.7**	**101.0**	**92.4**	**101.6**	**114.6**	**138.3**	**119.8**	**130.2**	**150.7**	**167.3**

Note: For details on definitions and sources, please refer to the metadata at the end of the tables.

StatLink ⬛ http://dx.doi.org/10.1787/016056318225

Table B.1.1. **Inflows of foreign population by nationality**

Thousands

AUSTRIA

	1998	1999	2000	2001	2002	2003	2004	2005
Germany	6.6	7.5	7.7	10.4	8.3	10.9	13.3	15.6
Serbia and Montenegro	9.4	13.5	6.4	6.2	8.8	9.3	10.8	11.5
Turkey	5.9	7.2	7.0	7.7	10.4	9.7	7.8	7.7
Poland	5.0	5.1	3.5	3.5	2.5	2.9	7.0	7.2
Romania	1.5	1.8	1.9	2.4	4.2	5.1	5.3	5.3
Bosnia and Herzegovina	2.6	3.9	4.1	6.5	4.0	4.8	5.0	4.7
Slovak Republic	1.7	1.8	1.9	2.4	2.2	2.3	3.5	3.7
Hungary	2.1	2.3	2.5	3.1	2.2	2.5	3.1	3.6
Croatia	3.3	3.8	4.4	5.4	3.1	2.9	2.9	2.7
Italy	1.2	1.4	1.4	1.7	1.3	1.3	1.4	1.5
FYROM	0.8	1.0	0.9	1.4	1.7	1.5	1.5	1.4
Czech Republic	1.4	1.5	1.4	1.5	1.0	1.1	1.4	1.4
Slovenia	0.6	0.6	0.5	0.7	0.4	0.4	0.6	0.6
Other countries	17.2	20.9	22.4	21.9	42.7	42.5	45.3	34.6
Total	**59.2**	**72.4**	**66.0**	**74.8**	**92.6**	**97.2**	**108.9**	**101.5**

Note: For details on definitions and sources, please refer to the metadata at the end of the tables.

StatLink ⬛ http://dx.doi.org/10.1787/016117761640

Table B.1.1. **Inflows of foreign population by nationality**

Thousands

BELGIUM

	1996	1997	1998	1999	2000	2001	2002	2003	2004	2005
France	6.6	7.0	7.4	7.9	8.1	8.0	8.1	8.2	9.5	10.4
Netherlands	7.8	6.3	6.2	6.2	7.2	8.2	8.4	8.5	8.8	10.1
Morocco	4.0	3.9	4.3	4.9	5.7	7.1	8.5	8.4	8.0	7.1
Poland	0.9	1.1	1.1	1.2	1.1	2.9	2.4	2.1	3.5	4.8
Turkey	2.5	1.4	2.4	2.2	2.8	3.0	3.9	3.8	3.2	3.4
Germany	3.2	3.1	3.2	3.1	3.0	2.9	3.0	2.9	3.3	3.3
Italy	2.7	2.8	2.5	2.6	2.6	2.4	2.3	2.3	2.3	2.5
United States	3.0	3.1	2.8	2.9	2.8	2.9	2.7	2.5	2.6	2.4
Romania	0.3	0.4	..	0.6	0.7	1.0	1.0	1.0	1.4	2.3
United Kingdom	2.8	2.7	2.7	3.0	3.2	2.7	2.5	2.5	2.4	2.2
Portugal	1.8	1.6	1.4	1.3	1.3	1.3	1.6	1.8	1.9	1.9
Spain	1.0	1.2	1.1	1.2	1.4	1.5	1.5	1.5	1.6	1.8
India	0.5	0.4	..	0.6	0.7	0.9	1.0	1.1	1.2	1.3
China	0.6	0.6	0.7	0.7	0.8	1.3	2.1	1.6	1.4	1.2
Democratic Republic of the Congo	0.8	0.6	0.7	0.8	0.8	1.4	1.3	1.1	1.1	1.1
Other countries	13.3	13.0	14.0	18.6	15.1	18.5	19.9	19.3	20.2	21.5
Total	**51.9**	**49.2**	**50.7**	**57.8**	**57.3**	**66.0**	**70.2**	**68.8**	**72.4**	**77.4**

Note: For details on definitions and sources, please refer to the metadata at the end of the tables.

StatLink ᵐˢ▬ http://dx.doi.org/10.1787/016145867164

Table B.1.1. **Inflows of foreign population by nationality**

Thousands

CANADA

	1996	1997	1998	1999	2000	2001	2002	2003	2004	2005
China	17.5	18.5	19.8	29.2	36.8	40.4	33.3	36.3	36.4	42.3
India	21.3	19.6	15.4	17.5	26.1	27.9	28.8	24.6	25.6	33.1
Philippines	13.2	10.9	8.2	9.2	10.1	12.9	11.0	12.0	13.3	17.5
Pakistan	7.8	11.2	8.1	9.3	14.2	15.4	14.2	12.4	12.8	13.6
United States	5.9	5.0	4.8	5.5	5.8	5.9	5.3	6.0	7.5	9.3
Colombia	0.4	0.6	0.9	1.3	2.2	3.0	3.2	4.3	4.4	6.0
United Kingdom	5.6	4.7	3.9	4.5	4.6	5.4	4.7	5.2	6.1	5.9
Korea	3.2	4.0	4.9	7.2	7.6	9.6	7.3	7.1	5.3	5.8
Iran	5.8	7.5	6.8	5.9	5.6	5.7	7.9	5.7	6.1	5.5
France	3.4	2.9	3.9	3.9	4.3	4.4	4.0	4.1	5.0	5.4
Romania	3.7	3.9	3.0	3.5	4.4	5.6	5.7	5.5	5.7	5.0
Sri Lanka	6.2	5.1	3.3	4.7	5.8	5.5	5.0	4.4	4.1	4.7
Bangladesh	2.4	2.9	1.9	1.8	2.7	3.4	2.6	1.9	2.4	3.9
Russian Federation	2.5	3.7	4.3	3.8	3.5	4.1	3.7	3.5	3.7	3.6
Chinese Taipei	13.2	13.3	7.2	5.5	3.5	3.1	2.9	2.1	2.0	3.1
Other countries	114.2	102.2	77.9	77.2	89.9	98.4	89.4	86.4	95.4	97.5
Total	**226.1**	**216.0**	**174.2**	**190.0**	**227.5**	**250.6**	**229.0**	**221.4**	**235.8**	**262.2**

Note: For details on definitions and sources, please refer to the metadata at the end of the tables.

StatLink ᵐˢ▬ http://dx.doi.org/10.1787/016172323575

INTERNATIONAL MIGRATION OUTLOOK: SOPEMI 2007 EDITION – ISBN 978-92-64-03285-9 – © OECD 2007

Table B.1.1. **Inflows of foreign population by nationality**

Thousands

CZECH REPUBLIC

	1996	1997	1998	1999	2000	2001	2002	2003	2004	2005
Ukraine	1.1	1.4	1.5	1.6	1.1	2.8	10.7	15.5	16.3	23.9
Slovak Republic	2.6	2.4	2.0	1.7	1.0	2.4	13.0	23.7	15.0	10.1
Viet Nam	0.7	1.7	1.2	0.8	0.3	2.2	5.7	3.6	4.5	4.9
Russian Federation	0.4	0.7	0.5	0.6	0.4	0.7	2.4	1.8	2.0	3.3
Moldova	0.0	0.1	0.0	0.1	0.0	0.2	0.8	1.2	1.0	1.7
Germany	0.3	0.3	0.3	0.2	0.1	0.2	0.8	0.8	1.3	1.4
United States	0.2	0.2	0.2	0.1	0.1	0.1	0.7	0.9	0.7	1.4
Poland	0.2	0.1	0.1	0.1	0.1	0.4	1.7	1.6	1.8	1.3
Mongolia	..	..	..	..	..	..	..	0.5	0.6	0.9
Bulgaria	0.1	0.2	0.2	0.1	0.1	0.2	0.7	0.6	0.7	0.8
China	..	..	..	..	..	..	..	0.5	0.5	0.8
Belarus	0.0	0.4	0.1	0.1	0.1	0.3	0.6	0.6	0.6	0.7
Japan	..	..	..	..	..	..	..	0.4	0.3	0.5
Romania	0.2	0.2	0.2	0.1	0.0	0.2	0.3	0.4	0.3	0.4
United Kingdom	..	..	..	..	..	..	..	0.4	0.6	0.4
Other countries	1.5	2.3	1.8	1.3	0.9	1.6	6.2	4.9	4.9	6.0
Total	**7.4**	**9.9**	**7.9**	**6.8**	**4.2 |**	**11.3**	**43.6**	**57.4**	**50.8**	**58.6**

Note: For details on definitions and sources, please refer to the metadata at the end of the tables.

StatLink ⫘ http://dx.doi.org/10.1787/016243241022

Table B.1.1. **Inflows of foreign population by nationality**

Thousands

DENMARK

	1996	1997	1998	1999	2000	2001	2002	2003	2004
China	..	..	0.4	0.5	0.6	0.7	1.1	1.5	1.3
Norway	1.0	1.1	1.1	1.2	1.3	1.2	1.3	1.3	1.3
Iceland	1.2	0.9	0.7	0.8	0.8	0.8	1.1	1.0	1.1
Germany	1.2	1.1	1.2	1.0	0.9	1.0	0.9	0.9	1.0
Sweden	0.9	1.0	1.0	1.0	0.9	0.8	0.7	0.8	0.8
Poland	0.4	0.3	0.4	0.4	0.3	0.4	0.4	0.4	0.7
United Kingdom	1.0	0.9	1.0	0.7	0.8	0.9	0.7	0.8	0.7
United States	0.6	0.5	0.6	0.6	0.5	0.6	0.6	0.5	0.6
Ukraine	..	..	0.1	0.2	0.3	0.3	0.4	0.5	0.6
Lithuania	..	..	0.3	0.3	0.4	0.4	0.4	0.3	0.5
Thailand	0.4	0.4	0.5	0.6	0.6	0.7	0.5	0.4	0.5
Afghanistan	0.3	0.3	0.4	0.6	1.5	3.0	1.3	0.7	0.5
India	..	..	0.2	0.3	0.3	0.3	0.3	0.4	0.5
Philippines	..	..	0.2	0.2	0.2	0.2	0.2	0.2	0.4
Iraq	1.1	1.3	2.3	1.9	2.9	3.2	2.1	1.2	0.4
Other countries	16.7	12.5	10.9	10.2	10.7	10.7	10.1	7.8	7.8
Total	**24.7**	**20.4**	**21.3**	**20.3**	**22.9**	**25.2**	**22.0**	**18.7**	**18.8**

Note: For details on definitions and sources, please refer to the metadata at the end of the tables.

StatLink ⫘ http://dx.doi.org/10.1787/016278502720

Table B.1.1. **Inflows of foreign population by nationality**

Thousands

FINLAND

	1996	1997	1998	1999	2000	2001	2002	2003	2004	2005
Russian Federation	2.0	2.4	2.5	2.2	2.5	2.5	2.0	1.7	1.9	2.1
Estonia	0.7	0.6	0.7	0.6	0.7	1.1	1.2	1.1	1.7	1.9
Sweden	0.6	0.7	0.8	0.7	0.7	0.7	0.6	0.7	0.7	0.7
China	0.1	0.1	0.2	0.2	0.2	0.3	0.4	0.4	0.4	0.6
Thailand	0.1	0.1	0.2	0.1	0.2	0.3	0.3	0.4	0.4	0.4
Somalia	0.3	0.5	0.4	0.1	0.2	0.3	0.3	0.2	0.2	0.4
Turkey	0.1	0.2	0.1	0.1	0.1	0.2	0.3	0.3	0.2	0.3
Germany	0.2	0.1	0.2	0.2	0.2	0.2	0.2	0.2	0.3	0.3
United Kingdom	0.2	0.2	0.2	0.2	0.2	0.3	0.3	0.3	0.3	0.3
United States	0.2	0.2	0.2	0.2	0.2	0.2	0.2	0.2	0.2	0.3
Iran	0.2	0.3	0.2	0.3	0.2	0.3	0.2	0.3	0.2	0.2
Serbia and Montenegro	0.1	0.2	0.1	0.4	0.3	0.0	0.2	..	0.3	0.2
Bosnia and Herzegovina	0.4	0.1	0.0	0.1	0.0	0.0	0.0	0.0	0.1	0.2
Ukraine	0.2	0.1	0.1	0.1	0.1	0.2	0.1	0.1	0.1	0.1
Iraq	0.5	0.5	0.3	0.3	0.2	0.3	0.3	0.1	0.3	0.1
Other countries	1.6	1.8	2.2	2.1	2.9	4.1	3.2	3.4	4.0	4.7
Total	**7.5**	**8.1**	**8.3**	**7.9**	**9.1**	**11.0**	**10.0**	**9.4**	**11.5**	**12.7**

Note: For details on definitions and sources, please refer to the metadata at the end of the tables.

StatLink ▒▒▒ http://dx.doi.org/10.1787/016325274616

Table B.1.1. **Inflows of foreign population by nationality**

Thousands

FRANCE

	1996	1997	1998	1999	2000	2001	2002	2003	2004	2005
Algeria	7.8	12.2	16.7	11.4	12.4	15.1	23.3	28.3	27.6	24.6
Morocco	6.6	10.3	16.1	14.3	17.4	19.1	21.7	22.5	22.2	20.0
Turkey	3.4	5.1	6.8	5.8	6.6	6.9	8.5	8.6	9.0	8.8
Tunisia	2.2	3.6	5.3	4.0	5.6	6.6	7.7	9.4	8.8	7.9
Cameroon	0.7	1.3	2.4	1.4	1.8	2.4	2.8	3.3	4.0	4.2
Congo	0.4	1.0	2.1	1.6	1.8	2.3	3.2	3.7	4.1	4.0
Côte d'Ivoire	1.0	1.5	2.5	1.4	1.8	2.2	2.7	3.3	3.9	3.7
Russian Federation	0.6	0.7	0.9	1.0	1.2	1.4	1.9	2.4	2.9	3.0
Haiti	0.8	1.9	1.9	1.4	1.8	2.1	2.1	2.6	3.0	3.0
China	0.7	2.8	5.7	1.7	1.8	2.3	1.8	2.4	2.9	2.8
Senegal	0.9	1.6	3.0	1.9	2.0	2.2	2.4	2.6	2.5	2.5
Mali	0.5	1.5	4.2	2.5	1.5	1.7	1.8	2.5	2.5	2.5
United States	2.7	2.8	2.5	2.7	2.6	2.6	2.4	2.3	2.6	2.4
Democratic Republic of the Congo	0.9	2.9	4.6	1.6	1.1	1.4	1.7	1.7	1.7	2.3
Serbia and Montenegro	0.7	1.0	1.8	1.3	1.2	1.4	1.6	1.7	2.0	2.0
Other countries	18.4	24.3	34.2	28.8	31.7	37.2	38.3	37.8	40.2	41.2
Total	**48.4**	**74.5**	**110.7**	**82.9**	**92.2**	**106.8**	**124.0**	**135.1**	**140.0**	**134.8**

Note: For details on definitions and sources, please refer to the metadata at the end of the tables.

StatLink ▒▒▒ http://dx.doi.org/10.1787/016333475528

INTERNATIONAL MIGRATION OUTLOOK: SOPEMI 2007 EDITION – ISBN 978-92-64-03285-9 – © OECD 2007

Table B.1.1. **Inflows of foreign population by nationality**

Thousands

GERMANY

	1996	1997	1998	1999	2000	2001	2002	2003	2004	2005
Poland	77.4	71.2	66.1	72.2	74.1	79.7	81.6	88.2	125.0	147.7
Turkey	73.2	56.0	48.0	47.1	49.1	54.6	58.1	49.8	42.6	36.0
Romania	17.1	14.2	17.0	18.8	24.2	20.3	24.0	23.8	23.5	23.3
Russian Federation	31.9	24.8	21.3	27.8	32.1	36.6	36.5	31.8	28.5	23.1
Hungary	16.6	11.2	13.3	14.9	16.0	17.4	20.6	14.3	17.4	18.6
Italy	45.8	39.0	35.6	34.9	32.8	29.0	25.0	21.6	19.6	18.3
Serbia and Montenegro	42.9	31.2	59.9	87.8	33.0	28.3	26.4	22.8	21.7	17.5
United States	16.3	15.1	17.0	16.8	17.5	17.4	15.5	14.7	15.3	15.2
France	14.9	14.4	14.3	15.3	15.9	14.5	12.7	12.3	12.5	12.3
Ukraine	13.7	12.5	14.1	15.3	18.2	20.5	20.6	17.7	15.0	10.9
Croatia	12.3	10.0	10.1	12.6	14.1	13.9	13.1	11.6	10.5	9.3
Bulgaria	6.3	6.3	5.3	8.1	10.3	..	13.2	13.4	11.6	9.1
Greece	18.8	16.4	16.1	17.6	17.4	16.5	15.0	12.1	10.2	9.0
Czech Republic	8.9	7.7	7.7	9.3	11.3	11.3	10.2	8.4	8.9	8.5
Spain	7.8	7.8	7.5	8.3	9.1	9.4	8.5	7.7	7.6	7.1
Other countries	304.0	277.4	252.2	267.1	273.7	315.8	277.5	251.6	232.2	213.5
Total	**708.0**	**615.3**	**605.5**	**673.9**	**648.8**	**685.3**	**658.3**	**601.8**	**602.2**	**579.3**

Note: For details on definitions and sources, please refer to the metadata at the end of the tables.

StatLink 🔗 http://dx.doi.org/10.1787/016275146804

Table B.1.1. **Inflows of foreign population by nationality**

Thousands

GREECE

	1998
Russian Federation	4.8
Bulgaria	2.9
Albania	2.7
Egypt	2.2
Romania	2.1
Ukraine	1.7
Former Yugoslavia	1.4
United States	1.4
Poland	1.3
Germany	1.3
United Kingdom	1.2
Philippines	1.0
Turkey	0.8
Syria	0.7
Lebanon	0.7
Other countries	12.0
Total	**38.2**

Note: For details on definitions and sources, please refer to the metadata at the end of the tables.

StatLink 🔗 http://dx.doi.org/10.1787/016354685677

Table B.1.1. **Inflows of foreign population by nationality**

Thousands

HUNGARY

	1996	1997	1998	1999	2000	2001	2002	2003	2004	2005
Romania	4.2	4.0	5.5	7.8	8.9	10.6	10.3	9.6	12.1	10.3
Ukraine	1.4	1.4	1.8	2.4	2.4	2.5	2.1	2.6	3.6	2.0
Serbia and Montenegro	0.9	0.8	1.5	2.5	1.8	1.0	0.4	0.7	1.6	1.3
China	1.8	1.7	1.3	1.2	1.1	0.4	0.1	0.7	0.8	0.7
Germany	0.6	0.6	0.7	0.8	0.8	0.8	0.3	0.4	0.1	0.6
Slovak Republic	0.3	0.3	0.4	0.6	1.0	0.5	0.5	0.4	0.1	0.4
United States	0.5	0.4	0.4	0.4	0.4	0.5	0.4	0.5	0.4	0.3
Viet Nam	0.3	0.4	0.5	0.4	0.2	0.1	0.1	0.2	0.4	0.2
United Kingdom	0.2	0.2	0.2	0.2	0.1	0.2	0.3	0.4	0.1	0.2
France	0.2	0.2	0.2	0.2	0.2	0.2	0.2	0.2	0.0	0.2
Israel	0.2	0.2	0.2	0.2	0.2	0.2	0.2	0.3	0.3	0.2
Japan	0.1	0.1	0.1	0.1	0.2	0.2	0.2	0.2	0.2	0.2
Russian Federation	0.5	0.4	0.5	0.4	0.3	0.3	0.3	0.3	0.3	0.2
Austria	0.1	0.2	0.1	0.2	0.2	0.1	0.1	0.1	0.0	0.1
Turkey	0.1	0.1	0.1	0.1	0.1	0.1	0.1	0.1	0.2	0.1
Other countries	2.4	2.4	2.6	2.6	2.4	2.5	2.3	2.5	2.1	1.8
Total	**13.7**	**13.3**	**16.1**	**20.2**	**20.2**	**20.3**	**18.0**	**19.4**	**22.2**	**18.8**

Note: For details on definitions and sources, please refer to the metadata at the end of the tables.

StatLink ᴀ᷆ɪꜱ▸ *http://dx.doi.org/10.1787/016366311080*

Table B.1.1. **Inflows of foreign population by nationality**

Thousands

IRELAND

	1996	1997	1998	1999	2000	2001	2002	2003	2004	2005
United Kingdom	8.3	8.4	8.6	8.2	8.4	9.0	7.4	6.9	5.9	6.9
United States	4.0	4.2	2.3	2.5	2.5	3.7	2.7	1.6	1.8	1.6
Other countries	9.2	11.1	10.8	11.5	16.9	20.0	29.8	24.5	25.5	42.5
Total	**21.5**	**23.7**	**21.7**	**22.2**	**27.8**	**32.7**	**39.9**	**33.0**	**33.2**	**51.0**

Note: For details on definitions and sources, please refer to the metadata at the end of the tables.

StatLink ᴀ᷆ɪꜱ▸ *http://dx.doi.org/10.1787/016383783482*

INTERNATIONAL MIGRATION OUTLOOK: SOPEMI 2007 EDITION – ISBN 978-92-64-03285-9 – © OECD 2007

Table B.1.1. **Inflows of foreign population by nationality**

Thousands

ITALY

	1998	1999	2000	2001	2002	2003	2004
Romania	5.9	20.9	20.7	18.7	50.2	..	62.3
Albania	11.2	37.2	31.2	27.9	39.1	..	29.6
Morocco	7.3	24.9	24.7	17.8	26.1	..	24.6
Poland	3.9	6.7	7.1	8.7	15.3	..	14.3
Ukraine	1.0	2.6	4.1	5.1	8.1	..	11.2
China	3.4	11.0	15.4	8.8	15.4	..	10.6
United States	4.7	5.7	7.2	7.3	11.2	..	8.0
Brazil	2.4	3.5	3.7	4.3	6.9	..	8.0
Serbia and Montenegro	5.7	24.5	5.3	6.0	8.2	..	6.3
Tunisia	1.5	5.8	6.8	6.5	8.0	..	6.0
Russian Federation	3.2	3.8	3.3	5.3	6.4	..	5.9
India	2.6	5.4	7.0	4.8	7.2	..	5.7
Philippines	2.6	5.7	12.2	4.6	10.4	..	5.2
Moldova	..	..	1.9	..	..	..	5.1
Ecuador	..	4.3	3.0	..	5.3	..	5.0
Other countries	55.6	106.3	118.0	106.6	170.5	..	111.6
Total	**111.0**	**268.0**	**271.5**	**232.8**	**388.1**	**..**	**319.3**

Note: For details on definitions and sources, please refer to the metadata at the end of the tables.

StatLink http://dx.doi.org/10.1787/016426022328

Table B.1.1. **Inflows of foreign population by nationality**

Thousands

JAPAN

	1996	1997	1998	1999	2000	2001	2002	2003	2004	2005
China	45.6	52.3	55.7	59.1	75.3	86.4	88.6	92.2	90.3	105.8
Philippines	30.3	43.2	47.6	57.3	74.2	84.9	87.2	93.4	96.2	63.5
Brazil	16.4	39.6	21.9	26.1	45.5	29.7	22.7	33.4	32.2	33.9
Korea	17.1	17.9	17.1	23.1	24.3	24.7	22.9	21.9	22.8	22.7
United States	27.9	27.7	27.7	24.7	24.0	20.6	21.5	21.5	21.3	22.1
Indonesia	8.3	10.2	8.6	8.8	9.9	10.6	9.7	11.1	10.7	12.9
Thailand	6.6	6.4	7.5	6.4	6.6	6.8	5.9	6.6	7.1	9.0
Viet Nam	2.1	2.7	3.0	3.2	3.8	4.7	5.3	6.6	6.5	7.7
United Kingdom	6.4	6.9	6.8	7.0	7.0	6.7	6.6	6.6	6.3	6.3
Russian Federation	6.0	5.1	4.6	4.3	6.4	6.3	6.6	7.7	7.1	6.2
Other countries	58.8	62.8	65.0	62.0	68.7	69.7	66.9	73.1	71.4	82.2
Total	**225.4**	**274.8**	**265.5**	**281.9**	**345.8**	**351.2**	**343.8**	**373.9**	**372.0**	**372.3**

Note: For details on definitions and sources, please refer to the metadata at the end of the tables.

StatLink http://dx.doi.org/10.1787/016477432618

Table B.1.1. **Inflows of foreign population by nationality**

Thousands

LUXEMBOURG

	1996	1997	1998	1999	2000	2001	2002	2003	2004	2005
Portugal	2.0	1.9	2.0	2.1	2.2	2.3	2.8	3.3	3.1	3.3
France	1.5	1.7	2.0	2.2	2.3	2.1	1.9	1.8	1.8	2.1
Belgium	1.1	1.2	1.2	1.3	1.3	1.5	1.3	1.1	1.0	1.0
Germany	0.7	0.7	0.8	0.7	0.6	0.7	0.6	0.7	0.7	0.7
Italy	0.5	0.5	0.6	0.6	0.6	0.6	0.5	0.5	0.5	0.5
United States	0.3	0.2	0.3	0.2	0.3	0.2	0.1	0.2	0.2	0.2
Netherlands	0.2	0.3	0.2	0.2	0.2	0.2	0.2	0.2	0.1	0.2
Spain	0.1	0.1	0.1	0.1	0.2	0.2	0.2	0.1	0.1	0.2
Other countries	2.8	2.7	3.4	4.4	3.1	3.4	3.4	3.8	5.0	5.2
Total	**9.2**	**9.4**	**10.6**	**11.8**	**10.8**	**11.1**	**11.0**	**11.5**	**12.5**	**13.5**

Note: For details on definitions and sources, please refer to the metadata at the end of the tables.

StatLink http://dx.doi.org/10.1787/016482855775

Table B.1.1. **Inflows of foreign population by nationality**

Thousands

NETHERLANDS

	1996	1997	1998	1999	2000	2001	2002	2003	2004	2005
Germany	5.7	5.7	4.7	4.5	4.9	5.1	5.1	4.8	5.3	5.9
Poland	1.4	1.4	1.5	0.9	1.3	1.4	1.6	1.5	4.5	5.7
United Kingdom	4.3	4.3	4.7	5.0	5.9	5.9	4.8	4.1	3.6	3.2
Turkey	6.4	6.5	5.1	4.2	4.5	4.8	5.4	6.2	4.1	3.1
China	1.3	1.6	1.4	1.3	1.8	2.8	3.4	3.8	3.0	3.0
United States	3.1	3.1	3.3	3.3	3.4	3.1	3.0	2.5	2.3	2.5
Morocco	4.3	4.5	5.3	4.4	4.2	4.9	4.9	4.5	3.3	2.1
France	1.7	2.1	2.1	2.0	2.2	2.2	2.0	1.9	1.8	1.8
Belgium	1.9	2.2	1.9	2.0	2.0	1.8	1.8	1.7	1.5	1.4
Italy	1.2	1.2	1.4	1.5	1.5	1.5	1.4	1.3	1.2	1.4
Suriname	2.8	2.6	3.2	1.8	2.1	2.2	2.2	2.4	2.0	1.3
Spain	1.0	1.3	1.2	1.2	1.3	1.4	1.4	1.3	1.3	1.3
India	..	..	..	..	0.7	0.7	0.6	0.6	0.6	1.2
Japan	1.3	1.2	1.2	1.3	1.3	1.3	1.3	1.3	1.2	1.2
Indonesia	..	..	..	..	1.4	1.6	1.6	1.4	1.2	1.1
Other countries	40.8	39.0	44.7	44.9	53.1	53.9	45.9	34.3	28.4	27.3
Total	**77.2**	**76.7**	**81.7**	**78.4**	**91.4**	**94.5**	**86.6**	**73.6**	**65.1**	**63.4**

Note: For details on definitions and sources, please refer to the metadata at the end of the tables.

StatLink http://dx.doi.org/10.1787/016552134778

INTERNATIONAL MIGRATION OUTLOOK: SOPEMI 2007 EDITION – ISBN 978-92-64-03285-9 – © OECD 2007

Table B.1.1. **Inflows of foreign population by nationality**

Thousands

NEW ZEALAND

	1996	1997	1998	1999	2000	2001	2002	2003	2004	2005
United Kingdom	5.4	5.5	4.4	4.4	5.0	6.8	6.6	8.2	8.7	17.1
China	5.3	4.5	3.5	3.1	4.3	7.9	7.6	5.9	4.0	5.6
South Africa	2.8	4.1	3.4	3.5	3.5	4.8	3.3	2.4	2.4	4.5
India	3.2	2.2	2.2	2.7	4.3	7.4	8.2	4.8	3.1	3.5
Samoa	2.1	2.2	1.5	1.8	2.5	2.0	1.2	2.2	1.6	2.6
Fiji	1.3	1.6	1.6	1.8	2.2	3.6	2.3	2.5	2.3	2.6
United States	0.9	0.7	0.7	0.8	0.8	1.0	1.0	1.1	1.0	2.1
Korea	2.0	0.7	0.5	0.7	1.1	2.4	2.4	1.6	1.5	2.1
Tonga	0.9	0.9	1.0	1.0	0.9	0.8	0.7	2.4	1.2	1.1
Philippines	1.2	0.9	0.6	0.8	1.0	1.3	1.6	0.9	0.8	1.1
Germany	0.5	0.3	0.4	0.4	0.4	0.4	0.3	0.4	0.4	0.8
Japan	0.3	0.3	0.3	0.4	0.4	0.6	0.4	0.5	0.4	0.8
Malaysia	0.4	0.3	0.3	0.6	1.0	2.1	1.2	1.0	0.5	0.6
Netherlands	0.2	0.3	0.3	0.2	0.3	0.3	0.3	0.3	0.3	0.6
Canada	0.4	0.4	0.3	0.4	0.3	0.4	0.3	0.3	0.3	0.5
Other countries	15.9	8.3	6.4	8.4	9.5	12.5	10.0	8.5	7.5	8.6
Total	**42.7**	**32.9**	**27.4**	**31.0**	**37.6**	**54.4**	**47.5**	**43.0**	**36.2**	**54.1**

Note: For details on definitions and sources, please refer to the metadata at the end of the tables.

StatLink 🔗 http://dx.doi.org/10.1787/016631837721

Table B.1.1. **Inflows of foreign population by nationality**

Thousands

NORWAY

	1996	1997	1998	1999	2000	2001	2002	2003	2004	2005
Poland	0.2	0.2	0.2	0.3	0.2	0.4	0.7	0.6	1.6	3.3
Sweden	2.9	4.9	6.0	4.5	3.5	3.1	2.9	2.7	2.4	2.7
Germany	0.6	0.8	1.1	1.1	1.0	1.1	1.2	1.2	1.4	1.7
Denmark	1.6	1.8	2.1	1.8	1.9	2.0	2.1	1.7	1.6	1.5
Iraq	0.4	0.7	1.1	2.1	4.5	1.2	2.7	1.1	1.0	1.4
Russian Federation	0.5	0.6	0.6	0.8	0.9	0.9	1.4	1.8	1.7	1.4
Thailand	0.3	0.3	0.3	0.4	0.5	0.6	0.9	0.9	1.1	1.1
Somalia	0.4	0.5	1.1	1.2	1.5	1.1	2.2	1.7	1.2	1.1
United Kingdom	0.9	1.0	1.3	1.0	0.8	0.9	0.8	0.6	0.9	0.8
Philippines	0.2	0.3	0.4	0.3	0.4	0.5	0.6	0.6	0.6	0.8
Afghanistan	0.0	0.0	0.0	0.2	0.5	0.9	1.1	1.4	0.7	0.8
United States	0.9	1.0	1.0	0.7	0.7	0.7	0.7	0.6	0.6	0.7
China	0.3	0.3	0.4	0.3	0.3	0.3	0.5	0.6	0.5	0.6
Pakistan	0.5	0.5	0.6	0.5	0.5	0.6	0.6	0.6	0.5	0.5
Serbia and Montenegro	0.2	0.2	0.3	6.5	0.7	0.6	0.7	0.5	0.6	0.5
Other countries	7.4	8.8	10.2	10.6	9.9	10.6	11.7	10.4	11.4	12.2
Total	**17.2**	**22.0**	**26.7**	**32.2**	**27.8**	**25.4**	**30.8**	**26.8**	**27.9**	**31.4**

Note: For details on definitions and sources, please refer to the metadata at the end of the tables.

StatLink 🔗 http://dx.doi.org/10.1787/016565048571

Table B.1.1. **Inflows of foreign population by nationality**

Thousands

POLAND

	1998	1999	2000	2001	2002	2003	2004	2005
Ukraine	0.9	2.6	3.4	4.8	6.9	8.4	10.2	9.8
Germany	0.2	0.8	0.7	1.1	1.6	1.5	2.2	6.1
Belarus	0.2	0.7	0.8	1.3	2.7	2.5	2.4	2.4
Viet Nam	0.8	1.5	1.2	1.1	1.2	1.3	2.2	1.9
Russian Federation	0.4	1.1	1.1	1.6	2.0	2.1	2.1	1.9
Armenia	0.4	0.6	0.7	0.6	0.7	1.0	2.0	1.5
France	0.0	0.6	0.9	1.0	1.5	1.0	1.5	1.1
United Kingdom	0.1	0.5	0.4	0.8	1.2	0.9	1.0	0.9
United States	0.2	0.8	0.5	0.7	1.2	1.0	1.0	0.8
India	0.1	0.4	0.3	0.4	0.5	0.6	0.7	0.7
Italy	0.0	0.2	0.2	0.3	0.5	0.5	0.7	0.7
China	0.1	0.4	0.4	0.4	0.5	0.4	0.5	0.6
Turkey	0.0	0.2	0.2	0.3	0.6	0.6	0.5	0.6
Kazakhstan	0.1	0.3	0.2	0.4	0.6	0.4	0.5	0.5
Netherlands	0.0	0.2	0.2	0.3	0.4	0.3	0.5	0.5
Other countries	1.5	6.5	4.6	6.3	8.2	7.8	8.9	8.5
Total	**5.2**	**17.3**	**15.9**	**21.5**	**30.2**	**30.3**	**36.9**	**38.5**

Note: For details on definitions and sources, please refer to the metadata at the end of the tables.

StatLink http://dx.doi.org/10.1787/016635268260

Table B.1.1. **Inflows of foreign population by nationality**

Thousands

PORTUGAL

	1996	1997	1998	1999	2000	2001	2002	2003	2004	2005
Brazil	0.3	0.3	0.7	1.2	1.7	26.6	14.7	6.7	14.4	9.5
Cape Verde	0.3	0.2	0.8	1.0	2.1	9.1	5.9	3.4	3.1	3.5
Moldova	..	..	..	..	..	10.1	4.0	1.4	1.7	1.8
Ukraine	..	..	..	..	..	45.5	17.5	4.1	1.9	1.6
Angola	0.1	0.0	0.4	0.9	2.5	7.6	4.7	2.1	1.1	1.2
Guinea-Bissau	0.1	0.1	0.2	1.0	1.6	5.1	2.6	1.3	1.0	1.1
United Kingdom	0.5	0.4	0.5	0.7	0.8	0.9	1.0	0.9	1.2	1.0
Romania	..	..	..	..	..	7.8	3.2	0.9	0.8	0.8
Sao Tome and Principe	0.0	0.0	0.1	0.3	0.6	2.6	1.6	0.8	0.9	0.7
Russian Federation	..	..	..	..	..	5.6	2.0	0.4	0.5	0.6
Spain	0.3	0.3	0.5	1.0	1.1	1.4	0.9	0.7	0.6	0.6
Germany	0.5	0.4	0.6	0.8	0.8	0.7	0.7	0.6	0.6	0.5
Mozambique	0.0	0.0	0.1	0.1	0.1	0.9	0.7	0.5	0.4	0.5
France	0.3	0.2	0.5	0.7	0.7	0.6	0.6	0.5	0.5	0.4
India	..	..	..	..	..	2.9	0.8	0.3	0.2	0.3
Other countries	1.3	1.2	2.1	2.9	3.9	24.0	11.0	7.1	5.3	4.2
Total	**3.6**	**3.3**	**6.5**	**10.5**	**15.9**|	**151.4**	**72.0**	**31.8**	**34.1**	**28.1**

Note: For details on definitions and sources, please refer to the metadata at the end of the tables.

StatLink http://dx.doi.org/10.1787/016645342546

INTERNATIONAL MIGRATION OUTLOOK: SOPEMI 2007 EDITION – ISBN 978-92-64-03285-9 – © OECD 2007

Table B.1.1. **Inflows of foreign population by nationality**
Thousands
SLOVAK REPUBLIC

	2003	2004	2005
Czech Republic	0.6	1.6	1.1
Germany	0.3	0.6	0.9
Ukraine	0.7	0.7	0.6
Poland	0.1	0.9	0.5
Austria	0.1	0.4	0.4
Hungary	0.1	0.3	0.4
Korea	0.0	0.1	0.3
France	0.1	0.3	0.3
United States	0.3	0.2	0.3
Russian Federation	0.2	0.2	0.2
Viet Nam	0.3	0.2	0.2
China	0.2	0.2	0.2
United Kingdom	0.2	0.3	0.2
Italy	0.1	0.2	0.2
Serbia and Montenegro	0.1	0.1	0.1
Other countries	1.2	1.6	1.6
Total	**4.6**	**7.9**	**7.7**

Note: For details on definitions and sources, please refer to the metadata at the end of the tables.

StatLink 🔗 http://dx.doi.org/10.1787/016650827808

Table B.1.1. **Inflows of foreign population by nationality**
Thousands
SPAIN

	1998	1999	2000	2001	2002	2003	2004	2005
Romania	0.5	1.8	17.5	23.3	48.3	55.0	89.5	94.0
Morocco	10.6	14.9	38.3	39.5	40.2	40.9	58.8	69.3
United Kingdom	4.5	7.9	10.9	16.0	25.3	32.1	44.3	41.6
Bolivia	0.2	0.5	3.3	4.9	10.6	18.1	35.3	38.3
Argentina	1.2	1.9	6.7	16.0	35.4	24.8	23.2	23.7
Brazil	0.9	1.6	4.1	4.3	4.7	7.3	13.0	20.8
Colombia	2.3	7.5	46.1	71.2	34.2	10.9	16.6	20.5
Peru	2.1	2.9	6.0	7.1	8.0	13.3	13.0	17.1
Bulgaria	0.2	0.7	6.5	11.8	15.9	13.6	17.9	15.5
China	1.0	1.6	4.8	5.2	5.7	7.3	14.4	14.7
Germany	7.1	9.3	10.2	10.7	11.2	11.1	11.8	13.5
Portugal	1.4	2.1	3.0	3.1	3.5	5.1	8.0	12.0
Ecuador	2.0	9.0	91.1	82.6	89.0	72.6	11.9	11.6
Paraguay	0.0	0.1	0.2	0.3	..	..	..	11.1
Venezuela	0.9	1.6	3.4	4.1	5.4	10.4	10.2	11.1
Other countries	22.4	35.8	78.8	94.0	105.7	107.0	277.8	267.9
Total	**57.2**	**99.1**	**330.9**	**394.0**	**443.1**	**429.5**	**645.8**	**682.7**

Note: For details on definitions and sources, please refer to the metadata at the end of the tables.

StatLink 🔗 http://dx.doi.org/10.1787/016304302781

Table B.1.1. **Inflows of foreign population by nationality**
Thousands
SWEDEN

	1996	1997	1998	1999	2000	2001	2002	2003	2004	2005
Denmark	1.4	1.0	1.1	1.3	2.0	2.5	3.2	3.6	3.8	4.0
Poland	0.7	0.6	0.6	0.7	0.6	0.8	1.1	1.0	2.5	3.4
Iraq	2.1	3.7	5.4	5.5	6.6	6.5	7.4	5.4	2.8	2.9
Finland	2.6	2.8	3.0	3.4	3.6	3.4	3.3	3.2	2.8	2.9
Norway	1.5	1.5	1.6	2.0	2.9	3.0	3.5	3.2	2.6	2.4
Thailand	0.4	0.4	0.5	0.7	0.8	0.9	1.2	2.0	2.1	2.1
Germany	1.0	0.9	1.1	1.1	1.5	1.6	1.7	1.8	1.8	2.0
China	0.6	0.6	0.7	0.8	0.9	1.0	1.2	1.4	1.5	1.7
Somalia	0.4	1.1	0.8	0.4	0.6	0.7	0.9	1.3	1.1	1.3
Turkey	1.1	0.8	0.8	0.8	0.7	0.7	0.8	1.2	1.1	1.1
India	0.2	0.2	0.3	0.3	0.4	0.4	0.6	0.8	0.8	1.1
Iran	0.8	1.7	1.5	1.0	1.1	1.3	1.4	1.0	1.5	1.1
United Kingdom	0.9	0.8	1.0	1.0	1.3	1.4	1.4	1.2	1.2	1.1
Russian Federation	0.8	0.7	0.8	1.0	1.0	1.0	1.0	1.0	1.3	1.0
United States	1.1	0.9	1.0	1.0	1.1	1.1	1.0	0.9	0.9	0.9
Other countries	13.7	15.5	15.5	13.6	17.5	17.6	18.1	19.1	19.8	22.3
Total	**29.3**	**33.4**	**35.7**	**34.6**	**42.6**	**44.1**	**47.6**	**48.0**	**47.6**	**51.3**

Note: For details on definitions and sources, please refer to the metadata at the end of the tables.

StatLink 🔗 *http://dx.doi.org/10.1787/016656410636*

Table B.1.1. **Inflows of foreign population by nationality**
Thousands
SWITZERLAND

	1996	1997	1998	1999	2000	2001	2002	2003	2004	2005
Germany	8.7	8.5	9.2	10.9	12.4	14.5	15.0	14.6	18.1	20.4
Portugal	5.5	4.0	3.5	3.7	3.6	3.7	6.6	10.1	13.6	12.2
France	5.0	4.8	5.2	6.1	6.5	6.5	6.6	6.4	6.7	6.9
Italy	5.4	5.0	5.0	5.8	5.2	5.4	5.6	5.3	5.7	5.4
Serbia and Montenegro	. .	8.0	7.5	8.4	6.7	7.5	7.7	6.3	5.7	4.9
United Kingdom	2.4	2.4	2.7	3.3	3.7	3.9	3.1	2.7	2.9	3.0
United States	2.9	2.7	2.8	3.2	3.3	3.3	2.9	2.5	2.7	2.9
Turkey	3.4	2.9	2.6	3.0	2.8	3.1	3.2	2.7	2.4	2.1
Austria	1.3	1.3	1.2	1.4	2.0	2.4	2.4	1.9	2.3	1.9
Spain	2.0	1.6	1.5	1.5	1.6	1.6	1.7	1.7	1.7	1.5
Netherlands	1.4	1.1	1.0	1.1	1.2	1.3	1.1	1.0	1.1	1.2
Canada	0.8	0.8	0.9	1.1	1.3	1.3	1.0	0.8	0.8	0.9
Other countries	35.7	27.0	29.3	33.9	35.3	45.0	40.7	34.6	32.6	31.1
Total	**74.3**	**70.1**	**72.4**	**83.4**	**85.6**	**99.5**	**97.6**	**90.6**	**96.3**	**94.4**

Note: For details on definitions and sources, please refer to the metadata at the end of the tables.

StatLink 🔗 *http://dx.doi.org/10.1787/016220472878*

Table B.1.1. **Inflows of foreign population by nationality**

Thousands

TURKEY

	2000	2001	2002	2003	2004	2005
Bulgaria	61.0	58.0	59.0	55.0	52.0	49.7
Azerbaijan	11.0	10.0	10.0	12.5	11.0	7.5
Iran	6.0	7.0	7.0	5.5	6.5	4.3
Russian Federation	7.0	6.0	6.0	8.9	11.5	4.2
United States	6.0	5.5	6.0	6.5	7.0	3.7
Greece	7.0	7.0	7.0	5.0	7.5	3.4
Other countries	70.1	67.7	62.6	58.8	60.0	58.8
Total	**168.1**	**161.2**	**157.6**	**152.2**	**155.5**	**131.6**

Note: For details on definitions and sources, please refer to the metadata at the end of the tables.

StatLink 🔗 http://dx.doi.org/10.1787/016674705668

Table B.1.1. **Inflows of foreign population by nationality**

Thousands

UNITED KINGDOM

	1992	1993	1994	1995	1996	1997	1998	1999	2000	2001
Australia	10.0	11.0	9.0	12.0	13.0	14.0	27.2	26.4	23.8	33.5
China	1.0	1.0	2.0	5.0	3.0	1.0	5.8	15.1	18.6	18.5
France	9.0	4.0	3.0	12.0	11.0	21.0	15.0	13.6	14.7	16.2
Germany	6.0	4.0	8.0	5.0	8.0	8.0	9.1	9.2	11.4	16.1
India	4.0	6.0	6.0	6.0	6.0	10.0	6.2	10.3	17.2	16.0
South Africa	1.0	2.0	1.0	3.0	4.0	6.0	11.7	12.0	14.2	13.1
United States	11.0	14.0	15.0	11.0	15.0	11.0	21.1	16.9	14.0	13.1
Philippines	1.0	1.0	..	1.0	2.0	1.0	0.1	5.4	6.1	11.6
New Zealand	6.0	6.0	7.0	8.0	9.0	7.0	14.5	13.4	12.4	11.6
Pakistan	6.0	4.0	4.0	4.0	8.0	5.0	4.2	6.6	9.5	9.6
Greece	3.0	8.0	3.0	3.0	6.0	9.0	12.5	10.3	5.5	5.6
Malaysia	5.0	5.0	8.0	10.0	5.0	10.0	5.1	4.1	5.5	5.4
Korea	2.0	1.0	1.0	3.0	4.0	..	1.7	1.4	4.3	5.3
Japan	4.0	5.0	5.0	5.0	5.0	8.0	7.1	7.9	7.3	4.8
Bangladesh	2.0	4.0	2.0	2.0	1.0	5.0	1.7	3.2	3.1	4.5
Other countries	42.0	42.0	58.0	60.0	64.0	66.0	71.1	81.0	93.1	81.5
Total	**113.0**	**118.0**	**132.0**	**150.0**	**164.0**	**182.0**	**214.0**	**237.0**	**260.5**	**266.2**
Total (adjusted figures)	**175.0**	**179.2**	**206.2**	**228.0**	**224.2**	**237.2**	**287.3**	**337.4**	**379.3**	**373.3**

Note: For details on definitions and sources, please refer to the metadata at the end of the tables.

StatLink 🔗 http://dx.doi.org/10.1787/016343510105

Table B.1.1. **Inflows of foreign population by nationality**

Thousands

UNITED STATES

	1996	1997	1998	1999	2000	2001	2002	2003	2004	2005
Mexico	163.6	146.8	131.4	147.4	173.5	205.6	218.8	115.6	175.4	161.4
India	44.8	38.0	36.4	30.2	41.9	70.0	70.8	50.2	70.2	84.7
China	41.7	41.1	36.9	32.2	45.6	56.3	61.1	40.6	55.5	70.0
Philippines	55.9	49.1	34.4	30.9	42.3	52.9	51.0	45.3	57.8	60.7
Cuba	26.4	33.5	17.3	14.0	19.0	27.5	28.2	9.3	20.5	36.3
Viet Nam	42.1	38.5	17.6	20.3	26.6	35.4	33.6	22.1	31.5	32.8
Dominican Republic	39.6	27.0	20.4	17.8	17.5	21.2	22.5	26.2	30.5	27.5
Korea	18.2	14.2	14.2	12.8	15.7	20.5	20.7	12.4	19.8	26.6
Colombia	14.3	13.0	11.8	9.9	14.4	16.6	18.8	14.7	18.8	25.6
Ukraine	21.1	15.7	7.4	10.1	15.5	20.9	21.2	11.6	14.2	22.8
Canada	15.8	11.6	10.1	8.8	16.1	21.8	19.4	11.4	15.6	21.9
El Salvador	17.9	18.0	14.6	14.6	22.5	31.1	31.1	28.2	29.8	21.4
United Kingdom	13.6	10.7	9.0	7.6	13.3	18.3	16.3	9.5	14.9	19.8
Jamaica	19.1	17.8	15.1	14.7	15.9	15.3	14.8	13.3	14.4	18.3
Russian Federation	19.7	16.6	11.5	12.3	16.9	20.3	20.8	13.9	17.4	18.1
Other countries	361.9	306.1	265.1	261.1	344.3	425.2	410.3	279.3	371.6	474.6
Total	**915.6**	**797.8**	**653.2**	**644.8**	**841.0**	**1 058.9**	**1 059.4**	**703.5**	**957.9**	**1 122.4**

Note: For details on definitions and sources, please refer to the metadata at the end of the tables.

StatLink 🔗 *http://dx.doi.org/10.1787/016841353467*

Metadata related to Tables A.1.1, A.1.2. and B.1.1. **Migration flows in selected OECD countries**

Flow data based on Population Registers

Country	Types of migrant recorded in the data	Other comments	Source
Austria	*Criteria for registering foreigners:* Holding a residence permit and intending to stay in the country for at least 6 weeks.	Until 2001, data are from local population registers. Starting in 2002, they are from the central population register, where the nationality field is optional. The "other countries" line includes persons whose nationality is unknown.	Statistics Austria.
Belgium	*Criteria for registering foreigners:* Holding a residence permit and intending to stay in the country for at least 3 months. Outflows include administrative corrections.	Figures do not include asylum seekers who are recorded in a separate register.	Population Register, National Statistical Office.
Czech Republic	*Criteria for registering foreigners:* Holding a permanent or a long-term residence permit.	Until 2000, data include only holders of a permanent residence permit. From 2001 on, data also include refugees and long-term residence permit holders (valid for 90 days or more) whose stay exceeds a year.	Czech Statistical Office.
Denmark	*Criteria for registering foreigners:* Holding a residence permit and intending to stay in the country for at least 3 months. However, the data on immigrants only count those who have lived in the country for at least one year. Outflows include administrative corrections.	Asylum seekers and all those with temporary residence permits are excluded from the data.	Central population register, Statistics Denmark.
Finland	*Criteria for registering foreigners:* Holding a residence permit, intending to stay in the country for at least 1 year.	Foreign persons of Finnish origin are included.	Central population register, Statistics Finland.
Germany	*Criteria for registering foreigners:* Holding a residence permit and intending to stay in the country for at least 1 week. Data refer to the 24 member countries of the EU in 2004.	Includes asylum seekers living in private households. Excludes inflows of ethnic Germans.	Central Population register, Federal Statistical Office.
Hungary	*Criteria for registering foreigners:* Holding a long-term residence permit (valid for up to 1 year).	Data include foreigners who have been residing in the country for at least a year and who currently hold a long-term permit. Data are presented by actual year of entry (whatever the type of permit when entering the country). Outflow data do not include people whose permit has expired.	Register of long-term residence permits, Ministry of the Interior and Central Statistical Office.
Japan	*Criteria for registering foreigners:* Holding a valid visa and intending to remain in the country for more than 90 days.	Excluding temporary visitors and re-entries.	Register of foreigners, Ministry of Justice, Immigration Bureau.
Luxembourg	*Criteria for registering foreigners:* Holding a residence permit and intending to stay in the country for at least 3 months.		Central population register, Central Office of Statistics and Economic Studies (Statec).
Netherlands	*Criteria for registering foreigners:* Holding a residence permit and intending to stay in the country for at least 4 of the next 6 months. Outflows include administrative corrections.	Inflows include some asylum seekers (except those staying in reception centres).	Population register, Central Bureau of Statistics.
Norway	*Criteria for registering foreigners:* Holding a residence permit and intending to stay in the country for at least 6 months.	Includes asylum seekers awaiting decisions on their application for refugee status. In 1999, inflow data include refugees from Kosovo who received temporary protection in Norway.	Central population register, Statistics Norway.
Slovak Republic	Data from 1993 to 2002 refer to newly granted long-term and permanent residence permits. In accordance with the 2002 law, data include permanent residence, temporary residence, and tolerated residence.		Register of foreigners, Statistical Office of the Slovak Republic.
Spain	*Criteria for registering foreigners:* Residing in the municipality. Data refer to country of origin and not to country of birth.	Statistics on changes of residence (EVR).	Local register (Padron municipal de habitantes), National Statistical Institute (INE).
Sweden	*Criteria for registering foreigners:* Holding a residence permit and intending to stay in the country for at least 1 year.	Asylum seekers and temporary workers are not included in inflows.	Population register, Statistics Sweden.
Switzerland	*Criteria for registering foreigners:* Holding a permanent or an annual residence permit. Holders of an L-permit (short duration) are also included if their stay in the country is longer than 12 months.		Register of foreigners, Federal Office of Immigration, Integration and Emigration.

Metadata related to Tables A.1.1, A.1.2, and B.1.1. **Migration flows in selected OECD countries**
(cont.)

Flow data based on residence permits or other sources

Country	Types of migrant recorded in the data	Other comments	Source
Australia	A. Permanent migrants: Permanent arrivals are travellers who hold migrant visas, New Zealand citizens who indicate an intention to settle and those who are otherwise eligible to settle. Permanent departures are persons who on departure state that they do not intend to return to Australia.	Data refer to the fiscal year (July to June of the year indicated) from 1992 on. From 1996 on, inflow data include those persons granted permanent residence while already temporary residents in Australia.	Department of Immigration and Multicultural and Indigenous Affairs, Population Research.
	B. Temporary residents: Entries of temporary residents (*i.e.* excluding students). Includes short and long-term temporary entrants, *e.g.*, top managers, executives, specialist and technical workers, diplomats and other personnel of foreign governments, temporary business entry, working holiday makers and entertainers. Long-term departures include persons departing for a temporary stay of more than twelve months.	Data refer to the fiscal year (July to June of the year indicated).	
Canada	*Permanent:* Issues of permanent residence permits. *Temporary:* Inflows of foreign workers entering Canada to work temporarily (excluding seasonal workers) provided by reason for initial entry.	Data include those already present in Canada, and also those granted residence as part of a programme to eliminate a backlog of applications.	Statistics Canada.
France	Data consist of those entering as permanent workers plus those entering under family reunification. Persons entering as self-employed and persons entering under other permits relating to family reunification are also included.		ANAEM (Agence nationale de l'accueil des étrangers et des migrations).
Greece	Issues of residence permits.	Excluding ethnic Greeks.	Ministry of Public Order.
Ireland	Figures are derived from the CSO series of Annual Labour Force Surveys over the period from 1987 to 1996 and the QNHS series from 1997 on. The estimates relate to those persons resident in the country at the time of the survey and who were living abroad at a point in time twelve months earlier. Data for EU refer to EU25.		Central Statistical Office.
Italy	Issues of residence permits, including short-term ones (excluding renewals) which are still valid at the end of the year. In principle, this excludes seasonal workers.	New entries were 130 745 in 1999 and 155 264 in 2000. Other permits are first-time permits issued to foreigners who had applied for regularisation in 1998.	Ministry of the Interior.
Korea	Data refer to long-term inflows/outflows (more than 90 days).		Ministry of Justice.
Mexico	*Inflows:* Entries of *inmigrantes* (retirees, highly skilled workers, family members, artists, sportsmen...), including re-entries. *Outflows:* Data refer to *inmigrantes.*	Data are not available by country of origin.	National Statistical Office *(INM).* Instituto Nacional de Migracion.
New Zealand	*Inflows:* Residence approvals. *Outflows:* Permanent and long-term departures (foreign-born persons departing permanently or intending to be away for a period of 12 months or more).	Data refer to calendar years.	New Zealand. Immigration Service and New Zealand Statistics.
Poland	Number of permanent and "fixed-time" residence permits issued.		Office for repatriation and Aliens.
Portugal	Data based on residence permits. 2001, 2002 and 2003 figures include respectively 126 901, 47 657 and 9 097 permits which were delivered under the 2001 programme of regularisation.		SEF and National Statistical Office (INE).

Metadata related to Tables A.1.1, A.1.2, and B.1.1. **Migration flows in selected OECD countries**
(cont.)
Flow data based on residence permits or other sources

Country	Types of migrant recorded in the data	Other comments	Source
Turkey	Residence permits issued for a duration of residence longer than one month.		Directorate of General Security, Ministry of Interior.
United Kingdom	*Inflows:* Non-British citizens admitted to the United Kingdom. Data in Table A.1.1 have been adjusted to include short-term migrants (including asylum seekers) who actually stayed longer than one year. Data by nationality (Table B.1.1.) on inflows are not adjusted.		*International Passenger Survey,* Office for National Statistics. Data by nationality are provided by Eurostat.
	Outflows: Non-British citizens leaving the territory of the United Kingdom.		
United States	*Permanent inflows:* Issues of permanent residence permits.	The figures include those persons already present in the United States, that is, those who changed status and those benefiting from the 1986 legalisation programme. Data cover the fiscal year (October to September of the year indicated).	US Department of Justice.
	Temporary inflows: Data refer to non-immigrant visas issued, excluding visitors and transit passengers (B and C visas) and crew members (D visas). Includes family members.		United States Department of State. Bureau of Consular Affairs.

Inflows of Asylum Seekers

The statistics on asylum seekers published in this annex are based on data provided by the United Nations High Commission for Refugees. Since 1950, the UNHCR, which has a mission of conducting and co-ordinating international initiatives on behalf of refugees, has regularly produced complete statistics on refugees and asylum seekers in OECD countries and other countries of the world (*www.unhcr.org/cgi-bin/texis/vtx/statistics*).

These statistics are most often derived from administrative sources, but there are differences depending on the nature of the data provided. In some countries, asylum seekers are registered when the application is accepted. Consequently, they are shown in the statistics at that time rather than at the date when they arrived in the country (it should be pointed out that acceptance of the application means that the administrative authorities are going to review the applicants' files and grant them certain rights during this review procedure). In other countries, the data do not include the applicants' family members, who are admitted under different provisions (France), while other countries register the entire family (Switzerland).

The figures presented in the summary table (Table A.1.3) generally concern initial applications (primary processing stage) and sometimes differ significantly from the totals presented in Tables B.1.3, which give data by country of origin. This is because the data that the UNHCR receives by country of origin combine initial applications and appeals, and it is sometimes difficult to separate these two categories retrospectively. The reference for total asylum applications remains the figures shown in summary table A.1.3. The data by nationality for the United States refer to the number of applications registered rather than the total number of persons concerned. For further details by host country, refer to Chapter VI of the 2003 statistical yearbook of the UNHCR.

Table A.1.3. **Inflows of asylum seekers into OECD countries**

	1996	1997	1998	1999	2000	2001	2002	2003	2004	2005
Australia	9 758	9 312	8 156	9 451	13 065	12 366	5 863	4 295	3 201	3 204
Austria	6 991	6 719	13 805	20 096	18 284	30 135	39 354	32 359	24 634	22 461
Belgium	12 433	11 788	21 965	35 780	42 691	24 549	18 805	16 940	15 357	15 957
Bulgaria	302	429	833	1 331	1 755	2 428	2 888	1 549	1 127	822
Canada	26 120	22 584	23 838	29 393	34 252	44 038	39 498	31 937	25 750	20 786
Czech Republic	2 211	2 109	4 085	7 220	8 788	18 094	8 484	11 396	5 459	4 160
Denmark	5 893	5 092	9 370	12 331	12 200	12 512	6 068	4 593	3 235	2 260
Estonia	..	..	23	21	3	12	9	14	14	11
Finland	711	973	1 272	3 106	3 170	1 651	3 443	3 221	3 861	3 574
France	17 405	21 416	22 375	30 907	38 747	54 291	58 971	59 768	58 545	49 733
Germany	116 367	104 353	98 644	95 113	78 564	88 287	71 127	50 563	35 607	28 914
Greece	1 643	4 376	2 953	1 528	3 083	5 499	5 664	8 178	4 469	9 050
Hungary	152	209	7 097	11 499	7 801	9 554	6 412	2 401	1 600	1 609
Iceland	4	6	19	17	24	52	117	80	76	88
Ireland	1 179	3 883	4 626	7 724	10 938	10 325	11 634	7 900	4 769	4 324
Italy	675	1 858	11 122	33 364	15 564	9 620	16 015	13 455	9 722	9 548
Japan	147	242	133	223	216	353	250	336	426	384
Korea	1	44	17	4	43	39	37	86	145	412
Latvia	..	..	58	19	4	14	30	5	7	20
Lithuania	..	320	163	133	199	256	294	183	167	118
Luxembourg	263	431	1 709	2 921	621	687	1 043	1 549	1 577	802
Netherlands	22 170	34 443	45 217	42 733	43 895	32 579	18 667	13 402	9 782	12 347
New Zealand	1 317	1 495	1 972	1 528	1 551	1 601	997	841	580	348
Norway	1 778	2 271	8 373	10 160	10 842	14 782	17 480	15 959	7 945	5 402
Poland	3 211	3 533	3 373	2 955	4 589	4 529	5 170	6 909	8 079	6 860
Portugal	270	297	365	307	224	234	245	88	113	114
Romania	588	1 425	1 236	1 670	1 366	2 431	1 151	1 077	662	594
Slovak Republic	415	645	506	1 320	1 556	8 151	9 700	10 358	11 391	3 549
Spain	4 730	4 975	6 654	8 405	7 926	9 489	6 309	5 918	5 535	5 254
Sweden	5 753	9 662	12 844	11 231	16 303	23 515	33 016	31 348	23 161	17 530
Switzerland	18 001	23 982	41 302	46 068	17 611	20 633	26 125	20 806	14 248	10 061
Turkey	4 183	5 053	6 838	6 606	5 685	5 041	3 795	3 952	3 908	3 921
United Kingdom	37 000	41 500	58 500	91 200	98 900	91 600	103 080	60 050	40 620	30 840
United States	107 130	52 200	35 903	32 711	40 867	59 432	58 439	43 338	27 907	24 247
EU25, Norway and Switzerland	**259 251**	**284 835**	**376 401**	**476 141**	**442 503**	**470 998**	**467 145**	**377 363**	**289 897**	**244 498**
North America	**133 250**	**74 784**	**59 741**	**62 104**	**75 119**	**103 470**	**97 937**	**75 275**	**53 657**	**45 033**
OECD	**407 911**	**375 451**	**453 033**	**555 901**	**538 000**	**593 638**	**575 808**	**462 026**	**351 702**	**297 739**

Note: For details on definitions and sources, refer to the metadata at the end of Tables B.1.3.
The symbol ("..") indicates that the value is zero or not available.

StatLink ⚙ http://dx.doi.org/10.1787/015571456220

Table B.1.3. **Inflows of asylum seekers by nationality**
AUSTRIA

	1996	1997	1998	1999	2000	2001	2002	2003	2004	2005
Serbia and Montenegro	1 025	1 084	6 647	6 834	1 486	1 637	4 723	2 526	2 835	4 403
Russian Federation	102	37	59	120	291	366	2 221	6 709	6 172	4 355
India	201	253	472	874	2 441	1 802	3 366	2 822	1 839	1 530
Moldova	0	7	22	43	106	166	819	1 178	1 346	1 210
Turkey	477	340	210	335	592	1 868	3 561	2 854	1 114	1 064
Georgia	0	0	25	33	34	597	1 921	1 525	1 731	954
Afghanistan	766	723	467	2 206	4 205	12 955	6 651	2 357	757	923
Nigeria	157	202	189	270	390	1 047	1 432	1 849	1 828	880
Mongolia	0	1	0	2	23	43	143	140	511	640
Bangladesh	141	110	167	305	305	949	1 104	887	330	548
Armenia	0	11	76	180	165	1 235	2 038	1 098	414	516
Pakistan	270	221	242	316	624	486	359	508	575	498
China	0	14	32	64	91	154	779	661	663	492
FYROM	0	10	19	51	21	947	786	415	323	452
Iran	656	502	950	3 343	2 559	734	760	979	343	306
Other countries	3 196	3 204	4 228	5 120	4 951	5 141	8 691	5 851	3 853	3 690
Total	**6 991**	**6 719**	**13 805**	**20 096**	**18 284**	**30 127**	**39 354**	**32 359**	**24 634**	**22 461**

Note: For details on definitions and sources, please refer to the metadata at the end of the tables.

StatLink 🖼️ http://dx.doi.org/10.1787/016845634606

Table B.1.3. **Inflows of asylum seekers by nationality**
BELGIUM

	1996	1997	1998	1999	2000	2001	2002	2003	2004	2005
Russian Federation	274	213	277	1 376	3 604	2 424	1 156	1 680	1 361	1 438
Democratic Republic of the Congo	860	1 230	1 714	1 402	1 421	1 371	1 789	1 778	1 471	1 272
Serbia and Montenegro	1 822	1 290	6 057	13 067	4 921	1 932	1 523	1 280	1 294	1 203
Iraq	223	243	231	293	569	368	461	282	388	903
Slovak Republic	233	284	985	1 175	1 392	898	635	390	730	773
Armenia	991	604	697	1 472	1 331	571	340	316	477	706
Guinea	250	165	336	342	488	494	515	354	565	643
Rwanda	405	565	1 049	1 007	866	617	487	450	427	565
Nepal	12	12	53	146	366	550	210	100	373	557
Cameroon	60	99	166	267	417	324	435	625	506	530
Iran	118	97	101	165	3 183	1 164	743	1 153	512	497
Turkey	713	436	403	518	838	900	970	618	561	453
Bulgaria	605	243	471	887	1 693	508	347	168	259	434
Togo	54	82	128	108	184	153	364	365	331	409
Romania	758	641	1 572	1 703	948	697	631	282	154	385
Other countries	5 405	5 584	7 724	11 850	20 470	11 578	8 199	7 099	5 949	5 189
Total	**12 783**	**11 788**	**21 964**	**35 778**	**42 691**	**24 549**	**18 805**	**16 940**	**15 358**	**15 957**

Note: For details on definitions and sources, please refer to the metadata at the end of the tables.

StatLink 🖼️ http://dx.doi.org/10.1787/016857857754

INTERNATIONAL MIGRATION OUTLOOK: SOPEMI 2007 EDITION – ISBN 978-92-64-03285-9 – © OECD 2007

Table B.1.3. **Inflows of asylum seekers by nationality**

CANADA

	1996	1997	1998	1999	2000	2001	2002	2003	2004	2005
Mexico	951	926	1 158	1 172	1 310	1 669	2 397	2 560	2 918	3 541
China	929	900	1 420	2 443	1 855	2 413	2 862	1 848	1 982	1 821
Colombia	87	71	270	622	1 063	1 831	2 718	2 131	3 664	1 487
Sri Lanka	2 946	2 665	2 634	2 915	2 822	3 001	1 801	1 270	1 141	934
India	1 367	1 166	1 157	1 346	1 360	1 300	1 313	1 125	1 083	844
Pakistan	1 105	1 047	1 607	2 335	3 088	3 192	3 884	4 257	1 006	746
Zimbabwe	4	11	9	27	178	2 653	257	70	95	683
Nigeria	410	482	580	583	800	790	828	637	589	591
Saint Vincent and the Grenadines	59	0	68	63	96	178	459	402	322	418
Haiti	210	212	174	295	354	237	256	195	175	378
Albania	145	288	349	476	665	782	569	419	349	358
Iran	1 728	1 210	880	794	767	768	381	329	352	357
Democratic Republic of the Congo	1 127	767	744	880	985	1 245	649	435	394	330
Israel	1 270	416	360	302	254	443	632	533	447	300
Turkey	161	172	298	419	869	1 755	1 144	425	276	291
Other countries	13 621	12 251	12 130	14 721	17 786	21 781	19 348	15 301	10 957	7 707
Total	**26 120**	**22 584**	**23 838**	**29 393**	**34 252**	**44 038**	**39 498**	**31 937**	**25 750**	**20 786**

Note: For details on definitions and sources, please refer to the metadata at the end of the tables.

StatLink ᴹˢ▬ *http://dx.doi.org/10.1787/016860222183*

Table B.1.3. **Inflows of asylum seekers by nationality**

FRANCE

	1996	1997	1998	1999	2000	2001	2002	2003	2004	2005
Haiti	138	134	357	503	1 886	2 713	1 904	1 488	3 133	5 060
Serbia and Montenegro	699	717	1 283	2 480	2 053	1 591	1 629	2 704	3 812	3 997
Turkey	1 205	1 548	1 621	2 219	3 735	5 347	6 582	7 192	4 741	3 867
Russian Federation	..	..	..	..	..	..	..	3 347	3 331	3 080
Democratic Republic of the Congo	1 064	1 348	1 778	2 272	2 950	3 781	5 260	5 093	3 848	3 022
China	1 435	1 754	2 076	5 174	4 968	2 948	2 869	5 330	4 196	2 590
Bosnia and Herzegovina	..	..	..	..	..	..	..	1 179	2 915	2 306
Moldova	..	..	..	..	..	..	..	1 901	2 227	2 090
Sri Lanka	1 169	1 831	1 832	2 001	2 117	2 000	1 992	2 129	2 246	2 071
Algeria	643	895	920	1 306	1 818	2 933	2 865	2 794	4 209	2 018
Armenia	..	..	..	..	..	..	..	1 106	1 292	1 642
Congo	153	304	387	1 158	1 592	1 943	2 266	1 952	1 489	1 172
Côte d'Ivoire	25	13	44	101	350	727	600	1 420	1 106	1 147
Guinea	150	139	205	313	544	745	753	808	1 020	1 147
Azerbaijan	..	..	..	..	..	..	..	532	773	1 112
Other countries	10 724	13 954	11 872	13 380	17 762	22 563	24 367	20 793	18 239	13 412
Total	**17 405**	**22 637**	**22 375**	**30 907**	**39 775**	**47 291**	**51 087**	**59 768**	**58 577**	**49 733**

Note: For details on definitions and sources, please refer to the metadata at the end of the tables.

StatLink ᴹˢ▬ *http://dx.doi.org/10.1787/016883171373*

Table B.1.3. **Inflows of asylum seekers by nationality**
GERMANY

	1996	1997	1998	1999	2000	2001	2002	2003	2004	2005
Serbia and Montenegro	24 773	30 962	34 979	31 451	11 121	7 758	6 679	4 909	3 855	5 522
Turkey	31 732	25 937	11 754	9 065	8 968	10 869	9 575	6 301	4 148	2 958
Iraq	10 934	14 189	7 435	8 662	11 601	17 167	10 242	3 850	1 293	1 983
Russian Federation	1 647	1 592	867	2 094	2 763	4 523	4 058	3 383	2 757	1 719
Viet Nam	1 907	2 855	2 991	2 425	2 332	3 721	2 340	2 096	1 668	1 222
Syria	2 196	2 025	1 753	2 156	2 641	2 232	1 829	1 192	768	933
Iran	5 264	4 490	2 955	3 407	4 878	3 455	2 642	2 049	1 369	929
Azerbaijan	866	1 245	1 566	2 628	1 418	1 645	1 689	1 291	1 363	848
Afghanistan	6 217	6 033	3 768	4 458	5 380	5 837	2 772	1 473	918	711
China	1 370	1 843	869	1 236	2 072	1 532	1 738	2 387	1 186	633
Nigeria	2 178	1 568	664	305	420	526	987	1 051	1 130	608
Lebanon	1 734	1 456	604	598	757	671	779	637	344	588
India	4 128	3 027	1 491	1 499	1 826	2 651	2 246	1 736	1 118	557
Armenia	4 598	3 800	1 655	2 386	903	913	894	762	567	555
Pakistan	3 800	3 774	1 520	1 727	1 506	1 180	1 084	1 122	1 062	551
Other countries	45 813	46 904	23 773	21 016	19 978	23 607	21 573	16 324	12 067	8 597
Total	**149 157**	**151 700**	**98 644**	**95 113**	**78 564**	**88 287**	**71 127**	**50 563**	**35 613**	**28 914**

Note: For details on definitions and sources, please refer to the metadata at the end of the tables.

StatLink http://dx.doi.org/10.1787/016880801166

Table B.1.3. **Inflows of asylum seekers by nationality**
NETHERLANDS

	1996	1997	1998	1999	2000	2001	2002	2003	2004	2005
Iraq	4 378	9 641	8 300	3 703	2 773	1 329	1 020	3 473	1 043	1 620
Somalia	1 461	1 280	2 775	2 731	2 110	1 098	533	451	792	1 315
Afghanistan	3 019	5 920	7 118	4 400	5 055	3 614	1 067	492	688	902
Iran	1 521	1 253	1 679	1 527	2 543	1 519	663	555	450	557
Burundi	51	64	147	204	335	427	448	402	405	419
China	468	1 161	919	1 246	1 406	706	534	298	285	356
Colombia	2	14	28	39	24	48	26	34	170	342
Sudan	658	678	1 875	1 694	1 426	869	512	293	255	339
Serbia and Montenegro	797	1 652	4 289	7 126	3 851	908	514	393	395	336
Turkey	692	1 135	1 222	1 491	2 277	1 400	629	414	338	289
Azerbaijan	185	315	1 268	2 450	1 163	634	326	265	253	287
Russian Federation	551	459	519	960	1 021	918	426	245	206	285
Syria	306	458	828	850	1 077	522	325	234	180	278
Angola	422	373	608	1 585	2 193	4 111	1 880	370	177	222
Georgia	188	291	290	321	291	298	216	116	73	213
Other countries	8 158	9 749	13 352	12 406	16 350	14 178	9 548	5 367	4 072	4 587
Total	**22 857**	**34 443**	**45 217**	**42 733**	**43 895**	**32 579**	**18 667**	**13 402**	**9 782**	**12 347**

Note: For details on definitions and sources, please refer to the metadata at the end of the tables.

StatLink http://dx.doi.org/10.1787/017065072584

Table B.1.3. **Inflows of asylum seekers by nationality**
SWEDEN

	1996	1997	1998	1999	2000	2001	2002	2003	2004	2005
Serbia and Montenegro	636	2 115	3 446	1 812	2 055	3 102	5 852	5 305	4 022	2 944
Iraq	1 557	3 057	3 843	3 576	3 499	6 206	5 446	2 700	1 456	2 330
Russian Federation	203	232	229	449	590	841	1 496	1 361	1 288	1 057
Bulgaria	15	31	17	11	18	461	767	688	567	751
Iran	401	356	613	854	739	780	762	787	660	582
Libya	12	10	6	15	26	114	456	435	419	451
Afghanistan	148	176	330	351	374	593	527	811	903	435
Azerbaijan	14	2	27	46	60	158	778	1 032	1 041	431
Burundi	7	17	1	3	11	61	135	237	393	427
Eritrea	33	21	27	73	127	151	266	641	395	425
Turkey	186	208	280	220	229	458	696	733	445	423
Somalia	434	364	228	289	260	525	1 107	3 069	905	422
Syria	102	131	226	307	335	441	541	666	411	392
Bosnia and Herzegovina	262	742	1 331	486	4 244	2 775	2 885	1 397	785	387
Belarus	24	33	35	84	231	327	722	901	519	372
Other countries	1 719	2 167	2 205	2 655	3 505	6 522	10 580	10 585	8 952	5 701
Total	**5 753**	**9 662**	**12 844**	**11 231**	**16 303**	**23 515**	**33 016**	**31 348**	**23 161**	**17 530**

Note: For details on definitions and sources, please refer to the metadata at the end of the tables.

StatLink ᴍᴍ☐▬ *http://dx.doi.org/10.1787/017065252476*

Table B.1.3. **Inflows of asylum seekers by nationality**
SWITZERLAND

	1996	1997	1998	1999	2000	2001	2002	2003	2004	2005
Serbia and Montenegro	6 228	6 913	20 396	28 913	3 613	3 425	3 692	2 921	1 777	1 506
Turkey	1 317	1 395	1 565	1 453	1 431	1 960	1 940	1 652	1 154	723
Somalia	700	884	610	517	470	369	387	471	592	485
Iraq	413	522	2 041	1 658	908	1 201	1 182	1 444	631	468
Bulgaria	25	118	155	66	58	229	785	281	624	461
Georgia	57	300	813	323	179	273	687	756	731	397
Russian Federation	144	192	193	263	254	456	507	534	505	375
Bosnia and Herzegovina	1 269	1 987	1 891	1 513	1 304	1 230	1 548	729	301	301
Iran	134	129	168	206	728	336	286	262	200	291
Democratic Republic of the Congo	695	605	536	523	540	602	746	521	345	262
Afghanistan	198	215	245	363	433	530	237	218	207	238
Sri Lanka	1 965	2 137	1 901	1 487	898	684	459	340	251	233
Nigeria	253	210	239	116	226	289	1 062	480	418	219
Guinea	148	193	335	388	455	679	751	652	412	211
Côte d'Ivoire	18	40	74	67	87	130	203	255	187	206
Other countries	4 437	8 142	10 140	8 212	6 027	8 240	11 653	9 290	5 913	3 685
Total	**18 001**	**23 982**	**41 302**	**46 068**	**17 611**	**20 633**	**26 125**	**20 806**	**14 248**	**10 061**

Note: For details on definitions and sources, please refer to the metadata at the end of the tables.

StatLink ᴍᴍ☐▬ *http://dx.doi.org/10.1787/016871180103*

Table B.1.3. **Inflows of asylum seekers by nationality**
UNITED KINGDOM

	1996	1997	1998	1999	2000	2001	2002	2003	2004	2005
Iran	585	585	745	1 320	5 610	3 415	2 630	3 495	3 990	3 505
Pakistan	1 640	1 615	1 975	2 615	3 165	2 860	2 405	3 145	3 030	2 290
Somalia	1 780	2 730	4 685	7 495	5 020	6 465	6 540	7 195	3 295	2 105
Eritrea	0	0	0	0	0	620	1 180	1 070	1 265	1 900
China	820	1 945	1 925	2 625	4 000	2 390	3 675	3 495	2 410	1 775
Afghanistan	675	1 085	2 395	3 975	5 555	9 000	7 205	2 590	1 605	1 775
Iraq	965	1 075	1 295	1 800	7 475	6 705	14 570	4 290	1 880	1 595
Zimbabwe	115	60	80	230	1 010	2 115	7 655	4 020	2 520	1 390
Democratic Republic of the Congo	650	690	660	1 240	1 030	1 395	2 215	1 920	1 825	1 390
Nigeria	2 540	1 480	1 380	945	835	870	1 125	1 110	1 210	1 230
India	1 795	1 285	1 030	1 365	2 120	1 850	1 865	2 410	1 485	1 000
Sudan	280	230	250	280	415	390	655	1 050	1 445	990
Turkey	1 420	1 445	2 015	2 850	3 990	3 700	2 835	2 990	1 590	950
Sri Lanka	1 260	1 830	3 505	5 130	6 395	5 510	3 130	810	400	480
Bangladesh	560	545	460	530	795	500	720	820	550	465
Other countries	14 555	15 900	23 615	38 745	32 900	23 585	25 730	19 637	12 123	8 000
Total	**29 640**	**32 500**	**46 015**	**71 145**	**80 315**	**71 370**	**84 135**	**60 047**	**40 623**	**30 840**

Note: For details on definitions and sources, please refer to the metadata at the end of the tables.

StatLink ⚏ http://dx.doi.org/10.1787/017062748725

Table B.1.3. **Inflows of asylum seekers by nationality**
UNITED STATES

	1996	1997	1998	1999	2000	2001	2002	2003	2004	2005
Haiti	3 792	4 310	2 676	2 492	4 257	4 938	3 643	3 316	3 543	4 121
China	1 976	2 377	3 074	4 210	5 541	8 008	10 237	4 906	2 860	3 684
Colombia	250	251	200	334	2 631	7 144	7 950	4 661	2 452	1 570
Mexico	7 820	13 663	4 460	2 251	3 669	8 747	8 775	3 955	1 454	1 247
Venezuela	0	0	33	18	0	96	259	899	1 408	1 146
Ethiopia	948	961	868	1 101	1 445	1 467	1 287	890	976	707
Cameroon	107	219	229	349	528	560	1 307	1 626	1 189	651
Guinea	0	105	130	109	268	619	808	664	660	602
Russian Federation	512	554	1 073	770	856	844	837	761	668	588
Guatemala	8 857	2 386	2 526	1 107	890	1 131	1 193	2 236	785	559
Armenia	351	420	446	803	1 758	2 147	1 347	919	606	484
Togo	0	0	70	77	105	198	425	638	477	409
Nepal	0	0	92	51	28	53	172	314	298	387
Indonesia	0	0	154	2 330	867	1 671	1 577	2 833	484	372
Côte d'Ivoire	99	41	21	15	25	86	85	480	334	326
Other countries	82 418	26 930	18 986	16 694	17 999	21 723	18 502	14 240	9 713	7 394
Total	**107 130**	**52 217**	**35 038**	**32 711**	**40 867**	**59 432**	**58 404**	**43 338**	**27 907**	**24 247**

Note: For details on definitions and sources, please refer to the metadata at the end of the tables.

StatLink ⚏ http://dx.doi.org/10.1787/017082814885

INTERNATIONAL MIGRATION OUTLOOK: SOPEMI 2007 EDITION – ISBN 978-92-64-03285-9 – © OECD 2007

Metadata related to Tables A.1.3. and B.1.3. **Inflows of asylum seekers**

Sources for all countries: Governments, compiled by UNHCR, Population Data Unit.
www.unhcr.org/statistics

General comments:

All data are based on annual submissions.

Data by nationality for the United States refer to number of cases and not persons.

Data for the United States refer to fiscal year and not calendar year.

From 2003 on, data for France include unaccompanied minors.

Data for Table A.1.3. generally refer to first instance/new applications only and exclude repeat/review/appeal applications while data by origin (Tables B.1.3) may include some repeat/review/appeal applications. This explains why totals in Tables A.1.3. and B.1.3. may be slightly different for some countries.

Stocks of Foreign and Foreign-born Population

Two questions must be asked before examining stocks of immigrants in OECD countries: 1) Who is considered as an "immigrant" in OECD countries (the answer is clearest for inflows), and 2) what is the nature of the problems of international comparison?

Who is an immigrant?

There are major differences in how immigrants are defined. Some countries have traditionally focused on producing data on foreign residents (European countries, Japan and Korea) whilst others refer to the foreign-born (settlement countries, i.e. Australia, Canada, New Zealand and the United States). This difference in focus relates in part to the nature and history of immigration systems and legislation on citizenship and naturalisation.

The foreign-born population can be viewed as representing first-generation migrants, and may consist of both foreign and national citizens. The size and composition of the foreign-born population is influenced by the history of migration flows and mortality amongst the foreign-born. For example, where inflows have been declining over time, the stock of the foreign-born will tend to age and represent an increasingly established community.

The concept of foreign population may also include immigrants having retained the nationality of their country of origin as of the second and third generations born in the host country. The characteristics of the population of foreign nationals depend on a number of factors: The history of migration flows, natural increase in the foreign population and naturalisations. It is possible to find people having always the statute of immigrant even if they born in the host country. The nature of legislation on citizenship and the incentives foreigners have to naturalise both play a role in determining the extent to which this occurs in practice.

Sources and problems of measuring the immigrant population

Four types of sources are used: Population registers, residence permits, labour force surveys and censuses. In countries that have a population register and in those that use residence permit data effectively, stocks and flows of immigrants are most often calculated using the same source. There are exceptions, however, as some countries instead use census or labour force survey data to evaluate the stock of the immigrant population. The same problems for studying stocks and flows are encountered whether registers or permit data are used (in particular, the risk of underestimation when minors are registered on the permit of one of the parents or if the migrants are not required to have permits because of a free movement agreement). To this must be added the difficulty of "clearing" series regularly to eliminate permits that have expired.

Census data enable comprehensive, albeit infrequent analysis of the stock of immigrants (censuses are generally conducted every five to ten years). In addition, many labour force surveys now include questions about nationality and place of birth, thus providing a source of annual stock data. However, some care has to be taken with detailed breakdowns of the immigrant population from survey data as sample sizes can be very small. Inevitably, both census and survey data may underestimate the number of immigrants, especially where they tend not to be registered for census purposes, or where they do not live in private households (labour force surveys generally do not cover those living in institutions such as reception centres and hostels for immigrants). Both these sources can detect a portion of the illegal population, which is by definition excluded from population registers and residence permit systems.

Table A.1.4. **Stocks of foreign-born population in selected OECD countries**
Thousands

	1996	1997	1998	1999	2000	2001	2002	2003	2004	2005
Australia	4 258.6	4 315.8	4 334.8	4 373.3	4 417.5	4 482.0	4 565.8	4 655.3	4 751.1	4 829.5
% of total population	23.3	23.3	23.2	23.1	23.0	23.1	23.2	22.8	23.6	23.8
Austria	..	..	895.7	872.0	843.0	893.9	873.3	923.4	1 059.1	1 100.5
% of total population	..	..	11.2	10.9	10.5	11.1	10.8	11.4	13.0	13.5
Belgium	999.2	1011.0	1023.4	1042.3	1 058.8	1 112.2	1 151.8	1 185.5	1 220.1	1 268.9
% of total population	9.8	9.9	10.0	10.2	10.3	10.8	11.1	11.4	11.7	12.1
Canada	4 971.1	5082.5	5165.6	5233.8	5327.0	5 448.5	5568.2	5670.6	5774.2	5895.9
% of total population	17.4	17.7	17.8	18.0	18.1	18.4	18.6	18.7	18.9	19.1
Czech Republic	..	..	440.1	455.5	434.0	448.5	471.9	482.2	499.0	523.4
% of total population	..	..	4.3	4.4	4.2	4.4	4.6	4.7	4.9	5.1
Denmark	265.8	276.8	287.7	296.9	308.7	321.8	331.5	337.8	343.4	350.4
% of total population	5.1	5.2	5.4	5.6	5.8	6.0	6.2	6.3	6.3	6.5
Finland	111.1	118.1	125.1	131.1	136.2	145.1	152.1	158.9	166.4	176.6
% of total population	2.1	2.3	2.4	2.5	2.6	2.7	2.8	2.9	3.2	3.4
France	..	..	..	4 306.0	4380.8	4469.8	4575.6	4691.3	4811.6	4 926.0
% of total population	..	..	..	7.3	..	..	..	..	..	8.1
Germany	9708.5	9918.7	10002.3	10172.7	10 256.1	10404.9	10527.7	10620.8	..	..
% of total population	11.9	12.1	12.2	12.4	12.5	12.6	12.8	12.9	..	..
Greece	..	..	..	..	..	1 122.9	..	..	..	..
% of total population	..	..	..	..	..	10.3	..	..	..	..
Hungary	283.9	284.2	286.2	289.3	294.6	300.1	302.8	307.8	319.0	331.5
% of total population	2.8	2.8	2.8	2.9	2.9	3.0	3.0	3.0	3.2	3.3
Ireland	251.6	271.2	288.4	305.9	328.7	356.0	390.0	416.6	443.0	486.7
% of total population	6.9	7.4	7.8	8.2	8.7	9.3	10.0	10.5	11.0	11.0
Italy	..	..	..	..	..	1 446.7	..	..	..	..
% of total population	..	..	..	..	..	2.5	..	..	..	..
Luxembourg	130.9	134.1	137.5	141.9	145.0	144.8	147.0	148.5	149.6	152.1
% of total population	31.5	31.9	32.2	32.8	33.2	32.8	32.9	33.0	33.1	33.4
Mexico	..	..	..	..	406.0	..	..	..	..	434.6
% of total population	..	..	..	..	0.5	..	..	..	..	0.4
Netherlands	1 433.6	1 469.0	1 513.9	1 556.3	1 615.4	1 674.6	1 714.2	1 731.8	1 736.1	1 734.7
% of total population	9.2	9.4	9.6	9.8	10.1	10.4	10.6	10.7	10.6	10.6
New Zealand	605.0	620.8	630.5	643.6	663.0	698.6	726.3	748.6	763.6	796.1
% of total population	16.2	16.4	16.5	16.8	17.2	18.0	18.4	18.7	18.8	19.4
Norway	246.9	257.7	273.2	292.4	305.0	315.2	333.9	347.3	361.1	380.4
% of total population	5.6	5.8	6.1	6.5	6.8	6.9	7.3	7.6	7.8	8.2
Poland	..	..	..	..	..	..	776.2	..	..	..
% of total population	..	..	..	..	..	..	1.6	..	..	..
Portugal	529.2	523.4	516.5	518.8	522.6	651.5	699.1	705.0	714.0	661.0
% of total population	5.4	5.3	5.1	5.1	5.1	6.3	6.7	6.7	6.8	6.3
Slovak Republic	..	..	..	..	..	119.1	143.4	171.5	207.6	249.4
% of total population	..	..	..	..	..	2.5	..	..	3.9	..
Spain	..	..	..	..	..	2 172.2	..	..	..	..
% of total population	..	..	..	..	..	5.3	..	..	..	..
Sweden	943.8	954.2	968.7	981.6	1 003.8	1 028.0	1 053.5	1 078.1	1 100.3	1 125.8
% of total population	10.7	10.8	11.0	11.8	11.3	11.5	11.8	12.0	12.2	12.4
Switzerland	1509.5	1512.8	1522.8	1544.8	1 570.8	1613.8	1658.7	1697.8	1737.7	1772.8
% of total population	21.3	21.3	21.4	21.6	21.9	22.3	22.8	23.1	23.5	23.8
Turkey	..	..	..	..	1 278.7	..	..	..	..	..
% of total population	..	..	..	..	1.9	..	..	..	..	..
United Kingdom	4131.9	4222.4	4335.1	4486.9	4666.9	4 865.6	5075.6	5290.2	5552.7	5841.8
% of total population	7.1	7.2	7.4	7.6	7.9	8.2	8.6	8.9	9.3	9.7
United States (revised)	27721.5	29272.2	29892.7	29592.4	31 107.9	32341.2	35312.0	36520.9	37591.8	38343.0
% of total population	10.3	10.7	10.8	10.6	11.0	11.3	12.3	12.6	12.8	12.9

Note: Estimated figures are in italic. Data for Canada, France, Ireland, New Zealand, the Slovak Republic, the United Kingdom and the United States are estimated with the parametric method (PM). Data for Belgium (1995-1999), the Czech Republic, Germany, Luxembourg, Portugal and Switzerland are estimated with the component method (CM).

Note: For details on estimation methods, please refer to *www.oecd.org/els/migration/foreignborn*.

Note: For details on definitions and sources, refer to the metadata at the end of Tables B.1.4.

StatLink ☜☞ http://dx.doi.org/10.1787/015587767146

INTERNATIONAL MIGRATION OUTLOOK: SOPEMI 2007 EDITION – ISBN 978-92-64-03285-9 – © OECD 2007

Table B.1.4. **Stock of foreign-born population by country of birth**

Thousands

AUSTRALIA

	1996	1997	1998	1999	2000	2001	2002	2003	2004	2005
United Kingdom	1 164.1	1 156.8	1 149.2	1 141.0	1 134.0	1 126.9	1 123.9	1 126.2	1 134.2	1 137.4
New Zealand	315.1	323.8	331.7	349.6	369.5	394.1	413.7	428.0	442.2	455.1
Italy	259.1	255.2	251.3	247.2	243.0	238.5	235.2	231.6	227.9	224.3
China	121.1	131.6	135.1	141.5	148.2	157.0	164.9	173.1	182.0	191.2
Viet Nam	164.2	167.6	168.8	169.8	169.8	169.5	171.6	174.6	176.6	177.7
India	84.8	87.8	89.4	91.2	95.8	103.6	110.6	118.3	128.6	138.7
Philippines	102.7	104.4	105.6	108.2	110.2	112.2	115.8	120.0	125.1	129.4
Greece	141.8	140.6	138.8	136.7	134.7	132.5	131.2	130.0	128.7	127.2
Germany	120.8	120.5	119.8	119.0	118.3	117.5	117.1	116.6	116.1	115.2
South Africa	61.7	66.1	69.4	74.9	80.8	86.9	95.3	101.6	109.2	113.8
Malaysia	83.0	83.8	84.1	84.6	85.4	87.2	89.6	93.2	97.8	100.3
Netherlands	95.3	94.8	94.0	93.0	92.1	91.2	90.4	89.6	88.7	87.8
Lebanon	77.6	78.3	78.7	78.8	79.2	80.0	81.2	83.1	84.3	85.3
Hong Kong, China	77.1	79.2	79.2	78.3	76.7	75.2	75.6	76.3	76.5	76.2
Serbia and Montenegro	61.9	62.3	62.0	63.7	64.0	64.0	66.5	68.3	68.9	68.8
Other countries	1 328.3	1 363.0	1 377.7	1 395.8	1 415.8	1 445.7	1 483.2	1 524.8	1 564.3	1 601.1
Total	**4 258.6**	**4 315.8**	**4 334.8**	**4 373.3**	**4 417.5**	**4 482.0**	**4 565.8**	**4 655.3**	**4 751.1**	**4 829.5**

Note: For details on definitions and sources, please refer to the metadata at the end of the tables.

StatLink 🔗 http://dx.doi.org/10.1787/017107300416

Table B.1.4. **Stock of foreign-born population by country of birth**

Thousands

AUSTRIA

	1998	1999	2000	2001	2002	2003	2004	2005	Of which: Women		
									2003	2004	2005
Former Yugoslavia	129.9	123.8	111.0	114.4	124.2	131.2	158.3	152.4	66.1	80.7	75.8
Bosnia and Herzegovina	113.1	125.1	115.4	132.3	130.1	132.3	139.7	151.4	63.2	68.1	73.7
Turkey	118.8	124.5	110.1	128.0	121.2	127.6	141.9	143.1	59.5	66.6	69.3
Germany	122.8	122.2	126.0	125.3	114.2	126.7	140.4	138.1	71.7	86.1	82.3
Former Czechoslovakia	52.5	47.4	45.6	41.1	47.1	33.7	60.6	64.5	22.4	36.4	41.2
Poland	41.2	41.0	42.3	44.1	34.8	35.4	51.4	49.6	19.7	28.9	30.8
Romania	40.5	34.0	31.2	36.9	38.0	41.0	42.6	49.4	23.1	23.7	28.7
Croatia	50.8	50.5	54.7	53.4	42.4	33.8	42.8	43.1	17.3	21.9	20.9
Hungary	24.2	22.3	18.0	23.3	28.8	27.6	26.3	35.5	16.8	15.0	19.0
Italy	24.8	18.8	23.2	19.5	21.8	23.6	23.4	21.0	11.6	11.9	10.4
Slovenia	29.1	17.9	15.9	17.7	14.0	16.8	14.9	16.8	10.1	8.5	9.9
Other countries	148.0	144.5	149.6	157.8	156.6	193.7	216.8	235.6	104.9	114.3	126.4
Total	**895.7**	**872.0**	**843.0**	**893.9**	**873.3**	**923.4**	**1059.1**	**1100.5**	**486.4**	**562.0**	**588.4**

Note: For details on definitions and sources, please refer to the metadata at the end of the tables.

StatLink 🔗 http://dx.doi.org/10.1787/017128736502

Table B.1.4. **Stock of foreign-born population by country of birth**

Thousands

BELGIUM

	2000	2001	2002	2003	2004	2005	Of which: Women		
							2003	2004	2005
France	150.3	151.9	152.5	153.0	154.2	156.2	86.6	87.2	88.2
Morocco	107.3	118.8	126.5	134.2	141.3	147.9	61.1	65.2	68.8
Italy	135.2	132.2	130.5	128.7	126.7	125.1	62.2	61.3	60.7
Netherlands	92.3	97.8	101.3	104.4	107.7	111.6	53.4	54.8	56.6
Turkey	66.5	71.6	78.6	78.6	81.0	83.8	38.0	39.2	40.7
Germany	83.7	83.4	80.1	83.3	83.5	83.6	46.7	46.6	46.6
Democratic Republic of the Congo	46.8	50.8	52.7	53.8	66.8	68.5	27.9	37.8	35.8
Spain	37.3	37.0	36.6	36.2	35.7	35.5	19.6	19.4	19.4
Former Yugoslavia	21.9	21.1	23.6	25.8	27.9	30.3	12.5	13.5	14.8
Poland	18.4	20.4	21.9	23.0	25.2	29.0	15.1	16.2	17.9
United Kingdom	26.1	26.1	25.9	25.6	25.3	24.9	12.7	12.5	12.2
Portugal	21.2	21.3	21.7	22.3	22.8	23.3	11.3	11.6	11.9
Algeria	14.0	15.1	16.0	17.0	17.7	18.5	7.4	7.8	8.2
Former Soviet Union	10.7	11.0	12.9	14.6	25.1	17.6	9.6	15.4	11.4
Greece	15.4	15.1	15.1	15.1	14.8	14.7	7.3	7.2	7.2
Other countries	211.7	238.4	255.9	269.6	264.2	298.6	142.3	137.1	158.3
Total	**1 058.8**	**1 112.2**	**1 151.8**	**1 185.5**	**1 220.1**	**1 268.9**	**613.7**	**632.8**	**658.5**

Note: For details on definitions and sources, please refer to the metadata at the end of the tables.

StatLink http://dx.doi.org/10.1787/017163457376

Table B.1.4. **Stock of foreign-born population by country of birth**

Thousands

CANADA

	1996	2001	Of which: Women	
			1996	2001
United Kingdom	655.5	606.0	352.2	323.1
China	231.1	332.8	122.2	177.6
Italy	332.1	315.5	158.0	152.2
India	235.9	314.7	117.0	156.6
United States	244.7	237.9	139.8	136.6
Hong Kong, China	241.1	235.6	124.3	122.3
Philippines	184.6	232.7	111.7	139.3
Poland	193.4	180.4	100.1	95.7
Germany	181.7	174.1	95.2	90.9
Portugal	158.8	153.5	79.3	77.5
Viet Nam	139.3	148.4	69.7	75.7
Former Yugoslavia	122.0	145.4	59.3	71.1
Former Soviet Union	108.4	133.2	57.1	76.3
Jamaica	115.8	120.2	67.3	69.6
Netherlands	124.5	117.7	60.9	56.9
Other countries	1 702.2	2 000.4	851.4	1 004.5
Total	**4 971.1**	**5 448.5**	**2 565.7**	**2 825.9**

Note: For details on definitions and sources, please refer to the metadata at the end of the tables.

StatLink http://dx.doi.org/10.1787/017207323750

INTERNATIONAL MIGRATION OUTLOOK: SOPEMI 2007 EDITION – ISBN 978-92-64-03285-9 – © OECD 2007

Table B.1.4. **Stock of foreign-born population by country of birth**

Thousands

DENMARK

	1996	1997	1998	1999	2000	2001	2002	2003	2004	2005
Turkey	26.5	27.3	28.2	29.0	29.7	30.4	30.8	30.9	30.9	31.0
Germany	22.5	22.6	22.9	22.9	22.7	22.6	22.5	22.5	22.6	23.0
Iraq	7.6	8.7	10.8	12.5	15.1	18.0	19.7	20.7	20.8	20.7
Bosnia and Herzegovina	16.9	17.9	18.0	18.0	18.0	18.1	18.1	18.2	17.9	17.7
Norway	12.4	12.6	12.9	13.1	13.4	13.4	13.6	13.9	14.0	14.1
Sweden	11.9	12.3	12.5	12.6	12.6	12.5	12.3	12.2	12.3	12.5
Poland	9.9	10.1	10.2	10.3	10.4	10.6	10.7	10.9	11.3	12.4
Lebanon	11.3	11.5	11.6	11.7	11.9	12.0	12.1	12.1	12.1	12.0
Former Yugoslavia	12.3	12.3	12.5	12.5	12.5	12.5	12.4	12.3	11.9	11.7
Iran	10.5	10.7	11.0	11.1	11.3	11.4	11.6	11.7	11.7	11.7
United Kingdom	10.3	10.5	10.7	10.5	10.5	10.6	10.6	10.7	10.7	10.8
Somalia	8.4	9.9	10.7	11.3	11.8	12.2	12.3	11.8	11.2	10.7
Pakistan	9.2	9.4	9.7	9.9	10.3	10.5	10.6	10.7	10.6	10.6
Afghanistan	1.6	1.9	2.3	2.9	4.3	7.2	8.4	9.0	9.4	9.5
Viet Nam	7.8	7.9	8.1	8.2	8.3	8.5	8.6	8.6	8.7	8.7
Other countries	86.8	91.2	95.7	100.3	105.7	111.4	117.1	121.8	127.3	133.4
Total	**265.8**	**276.8**	**287.7**	**296.9**	**308.7**	**321.8**	**331.5**	**337.8**	**343.4**	**350.4**

Note: For details on definitions and sources, please refer to the metadata at the end of the tables.

StatLink ᴍꜱ▤ http://dx.doi.org/10.1787/017228734251

Table B.1.4. **Stock of foreign-born population by country of birth**

Thousands

FINLAND

	1996	1997	1998	1999	2000	2001	2002	2003	2004	2005
Former Soviet Union	26.4	28.8	31.4	33.5	32.9	34.4	36.3	37.3	38.5	40.2
Sweden	27.0	27.4	27.8	27.9	28.0	28.3	28.6	28.9	29.2	29.5
Estonia	6.0	6.5	7.0	7.4	7.8	8.7	9.5	10.3	11.2	12.6
Somalia	3.5	3.8	4.1	4.2	4.4	4.3	4.6	4.7	4.8	5.1
Former Yugoslavia	3.6	3.7	3.8	5.9	4.2	4.5	4.6	4.7	4.9	5.0
Germany	3.0	3.3	3.3	3.5	3.6	3.8	3.9	4.1	4.3	4.6
Iraq	1.8	2.3	2.6	3.0	3.2	3.5	3.8	4.0	4.3	4.4
China	1.5	1.7	1.9	2.0	2.1	2.4	2.7	3.1	3.6	4.1
Thailand	1.2	1.3	1.5	1.6	1.8	2.1	2.4	2.8	3.1	3.6
United Kingdom	2.2	2.4	2.5	2.6	2.7	2.9	3.1	3.2	3.4	3.5
Turkey	1.6	1.8	1.9	2.0	2.2	2.4	2.6	2.9	3.1	3.4
Viet Nam	2.5	2.6	2.8	2.8	2.9	2.9	3.0	3.0	3.1	3.3
United States	2.7	2.8	2.9	3.0	2.9	3.0	3.1	3.1	3.1	3.2
Iran	1.4	1.6	1.7	1.9	2.1	2.3	2.5	2.7	3.0	3.2
India	0.8	0.9	0.9	1.1	1.2	1.3	1.5	1.6	1.8	2.1
Other countries	26.0	27.2	28.9	28.6	34.3	38.3	40.0	42.5	45.1	48.9
Total	**111.1**	**118.1**	**125.1**	**131.1**	**136.2**	**145.1**	**152.1**	**158.9**	**166.4**	**176.6**

Note: For details on definitions and sources, please refer to the metadata at the end of the tables.

StatLink ᴍꜱ▤ http://dx.doi.org/10.1787/017255285366

Table B.1.4. **Stock of foreign-born population by country of birth**

Thousands

FRANCE

	1999	2005
Algeria	574	677
Morocco	523	619
Portugal	572	565
Italy	379	342
Spain	316	280
Turkey	174	225
Tunisia	202	220
Cambodia	160	163
Other countries	1 406	1 835
Total	**4 306**	**4 926**

Note: For details on definitions and sources, please refer to the metadata at the end of the tables.

StatLink http://dx.doi.org/10.1787/017353750802

Table B.1.4. **Stock of foreign-born population by country of birth**

Thousands

GREECE

	2001	Of which: Women
		2001
Albania	403.9	166.6
Germany	101.4	54.5
Turkey	76.6	45.1
Russian Federation	72.7	42.1
Georgia	71.7	38.6
Bulgaria	38.9	23.8
Egypt	32.7	15.6
Romania	26.5	12.7
Kazakhstan	24.4	12.9
United States	23.1	12.9
Cyprus	22.5	13.0
Australia	20.4	11.0
Ukraine	16.7	12.5
Poland	15.5	8.7
United Kingdom	13.3	8.5
Other countries	162.7	78.9
Total	**1 122.9**	**557.4**

Note: For details on definitions and sources, please refer to the metadata at the end of the tables.

StatLink http://dx.doi.org/10.1787/017365876261

INTERNATIONAL MIGRATION OUTLOOK: SOPEMI 2007 EDITION – ISBN 978-92-64-03285-9 – © OECD 2007

Table B.1.4. **Stock of foreign-born population by country of birth**

Thousands

HUNGARY

	1996	1997	1998	1999	2000	2001	2002	2003	2004	2005
Romania	141.5	141.7	142.0	142.3	144.2	145.2	146.5	148.5	152.7	155.4
Former Czechoslovakia	41.8	40.3	38.9	37.5	36.0	34.6	33.3	33.4	31.4	32.6
Former Soviet Union	27.8	28.3	29.2	30.2	31.5	30.4	31.0	31.4	32.2	31.9
Former Yugoslavia	33.6	33.3	33.5	34.4	35.1	33.4	30.3	30.7	29.9	29.6
Germany	13.4	13.6	13.8	14.1	14.4	15.3	15.9	16.3	18.8	21.9
Austria	3.8	3.8	3.8	3.8	3.9	4.0	4.2	4.3	4.7	5.4
China	0.7	1.0	1.7	2.6	3.5	3.6	3.8	3.9	4.2	4.5
United States	2.2	2.2	2.2	2.2	2.3	2.1	2.4	2.7	3.0	3.4
Poland	2.7	2.7	2.7	2.7	2.7	2.7	2.7	2.7	2.9	3.2
France	1.3	1.3	1.3	1.4	1.4	1.4	1.5	1.6	2.2	2.7
Viet Nam	0.5	0.6	0.8	1.0	1.2	1.5	1.6	1.6	1.6	1.7
Greece	1.2	1.2	1.1	1.1	1.1	1.5	1.4	1.5	1.5	1.5
Bulgaria	1.4	1.4	1.4	1.4	1.4	1.4	1.4	1.4	1.4	1.4
Other countries	12.2	12.8	13.7	14.6	16.1	23.0	26.8	27.8	32.5	36.3
Total	**283.9**	**284.2**	**286.2**	**289.3**	**294.6**	**300.1**	**302.8**	**307.8**	**319.0**	**331.5**

Note: For details on definitions and sources, please refer to the metadata at the end of the tables.

StatLink ᴍᴤ▰ http://dx.doi.org/10.1787/017437517777

Table B.1.4. **Stock of foreign-born population by country of birth**

Thousands

IRELAND

	2002
United Kingdom	242.2
United States	21.0
Nigeria	8.9
Germany	8.5
France	6.7
South Africa	6.1
Australia	5.9
Romania	5.8
China	5.6
Spain	4.5
Philippines	3.9
Canada	3.9
Italy	3.6
Netherlands	3.4
Pakistan	3.3
Other countries	56.6
Total	**390.0**

Note: For details on definitions and sources, please refer to the metadata at the end of the tables.

StatLink ᴍᴤ▰ http://dx.doi.org/10.1787/017516343566

Table B.1.4. **Stock of foreign-born population by country of birth**

Thousands

LUXEMBOURG

	2001	Of which: Women
		2001
Portugal	41.7	20.0
France	18.8	9.9
Belgium	14.8	7.2
Germany	12.8	7.6
Italy	12.3	5.4
Serbia and Montenegro	6.5	3.0
Netherlands	3.3	1.6
United Kingdom	3.2	1.4
Spain	2.1	1.1
Denmark	1.5	0.8
United States	1.1	0.5
Poland	1.0	0.6
Sweden	1.0	0.5
Greece	0.9	0.4
Switzerland	0.8	0.4
Other countries	23.2	12.6
Total	**144.8**	**73.1**

Note: For details on definitions and sources, please refer to the metadata at the end of the tables.

StatLink ⬛ꜚ *http://dx.doi.org/10.1787/017517588625*

Table B.1.4. **Stock of foreign-born population by country of birth**

Thousands

NETHERLANDS

	1996	1997	1998	1999	2000	2001	2002	2003	2004	2005
Turkey	169.3	172.7	175.5	178.0	181.9	186.2	190.5	194.6	195.9	196.0
Suriname	181.6	182.2	184.2	185.0	186.5	188.0	189.0	189.7	190.1	189.2
Morocco	142.7	145.8	149.6	152.7	155.8	159.8	163.4	166.6	168.5	168.6
Indonesia	174.8	172.1	170.3	168.0	165.8	163.9	161.4	158.8	156.0	152.8
Germany	128.0	126.8	125.5	124.2	123.1	122.1	120.6	119.0	117.7	116.9
Former Yugoslavia	46.1	46.7	47.5	50.5	53.9	55.9	56.2	55.5	54.5	53.7
Belgium	43.3	44.0	44.6	45.3	46.0	46.5	46.8	47.1	47.1	47.1
United Kingdom	41.7	42.3	42.7	43.6	45.7	47.9	48.5	48.3	47.5	46.6
Former Soviet Union	10.1	11.7	13.7	16.1	21.6	27.1	30.8	32.8	34.5	35.3
Iraq	14.4	20.4	27.3	29.9	33.7	36.0	35.8	36.0	35.9	35.3
China	16.9	18.0	19.4	20.6	22.7	25.8	28.7	31.5	33.5	34.8
Afghanistan	7.2	10.8	14.6	19.8	24.3	28.5	31.0	32.1	32.4	32.0
Poland	14.3	15.1	15.9	16.3	17.4	18.6	20.1	21.2	25.0	30.0
Iran	17.3	18.5	19.3	20.1	21.5	23.2	24.2	24.2	24.1	23.8
United States	17.9	18.6	19.5	20.3	21.4	22.1	22.5	22.6	22.6	22.8
Other countries	407.9	423.5	444.3	465.6	494.3	523.2	544.7	551.9	550.9	549.9
Total	**1 433.6**	**1 469.0**	**1 513.9**	**1 556.3**	**1 615.4**	**1 674.6**	**1 714.2**	**1 731.8**	**1 736.1**	**1 734.7**

Note: For details on definitions and sources, please refer to the metadata at the end of the tables.

StatLink ⬛ꜚ *http://dx.doi.org/10.1787/017545811634*

Table B.1.4. **Stock of foreign-born population by country of birth**

Thousands

NEW ZEALAND

	2001	Of which: Women
		2001
United Kingdom	218.4	109.7
Australia	56.3	30.1
Samoa	47.1	24.7
China	38.9	20.5
South Africa	26.1	13.4
Fiji	25.7	13.5
Netherlands	22.2	10.2
India	20.9	10.2
Tonga	18.1	9.1
Korea	17.9	9.4
Cook Islands	15.2	7.9
United States	13.3	6.8
Chinese Taipei	12.5	6.8
Malaysia	11.5	6.0
Hong Kong, China	11.3	6.0
Other countries	143.2	75.6
Total	**698.6**	**359.7**

Note: For details on definitions and sources, please refer to the metadata at the end of the tables.

StatLink ⫘ http://dx.doi.org/10.1787/017626070252

Table B.1.4. **Stock of foreign-born population by country of birth**

Thousands

NORWAY

	1996	1997	1998	1999	2000	2001	2002	2003	2004	2005
Sweden	26.0	29.3	32.6	33.4	33.2	33.0	33.0	33.1	33.1	33.9
Denmark	20.9	21.1	21.7	21.7	22.0	22.1	22.3	22.3	22.2	22.3
Pakistan	12.1	12.4	12.9	13.3	13.6	14.1	14.6	14.9	15.2	15.6
Germany	9.7	10.1	10.8	11.4	11.8	12.2	12.9	13.5	14.1	15.2
United Kingdom	13.5	13.6	14.1	14.3	14.2	14.1	14.3	14.3	14.6	14.7
United States	15.0	15.0	15.1	15.0	14.7	14.6	14.6	14.6	14.5	14.6
Bosnia and Herzegovina	11.1	11.1	11.2	11.6	11.7	11.8	13.5	13.2	12.6	12.6
Viet Nam	10.8	10.9	11.0	11.2	11.3	11.5	11.7	11.9	12.1	12.3
Iran	7.3	7.7	8.3	8.9	9.3	10.1	10.7	11.3	11.6	11.8
Poland	5.4	5.5	5.6	5.7	5.9	6.2	6.7	7.0	8.3	11.2
Serbia and Montenegro	7.3	7.2	7.5	13.3	12.9	11.7	8.1	8.7	9.7	9.9
Turkey	6.3	6.6	6.9	7.3	7.6	7.9	8.4	8.8	9.1	9.4
Philippines	5.0	5.1	5.4	5.7	6.0	6.4	7.0	7.5	8.0	8.7
Sri Lanka	6.5	6.7	7.0	7.3	7.5	7.7	8.0	8.1	8.2	8.3
Korea	5.6	5.7	5.8	6.0	6.1	6.2	6.4	6.4	6.6	6.7
Other countries	84.3	89.7	97.2	106.4	117.4	125.6	141.8	151.7	161.1	173.3
Total	**246.9**	**257.7**	**273.2**	**292.4**	**305.0**	**315.2**	**333.9**	**347.3**	**361.1**	**380.4**

Note: For details on definitions and sources, please refer to the metadata at the end of the tables.

StatLink ⫘ http://dx.doi.org/10.1787/017571248851

Table B.1.4. **Stock of foreign-born population by country of birth**

Thousands

POLAND

	2002	Of which: Women
		2002
Ukraine	312.3	191.0
Belarus	105.2	63.2
Germany	98.2	56.8
Lithuania	79.8	48.6
Russian Federation	55.2	35.7
France	33.9	18.9
United States	8.4	5.0
Czech Republic	6.3	3.7
Austria	3.9	2.0
Kazakhstan	3.8	2.1
Serbia and Montenegro	3.6	1.9
Romania	3.4	2.0
Italy	3.3	1.5
Bosnia and Herzegovina	3.3	1.9
United Kingdom	2.8	1.1
Other countries	52.8	25.0
Total	**776.2**	**460.3**

Note: For details on definitions and sources, please refer to the metadata at the end of the tables.

StatLink ⬛ http://dx.doi.org/10.1787/017628810640

Table B.1.4. **Stock of foreign-born population by country of birth**

Thousands

PORTUGAL

	2001	Of which: Women
		2001
Angola	174.2	91.7
France	95.3	50.7
Mozambique	76.0	40.1
Brazil	49.9	25.4
Cape Verde	45.0	22.0
Germany	24.3	12.4
Venezuela	22.4	11.7
Guinea-Bissau	21.4	8.6
Spain	14.0	8.3
Switzerland	12.9	6.4
Sao Tome and Principe	12.5	6.7
South Africa	11.2	5.9
United Kingdom	10.1	5.1
Canada	7.3	3.8
United States	7.3	3.7
Other countries	67.8	28.0
Total	**651.5**	**330.5**

Note: For details on definitions and sources, please refer to the metadata at the end of the tables.

StatLink ⬛ http://dx.doi.org/10.1787/017712321287

INTERNATIONAL MIGRATION OUTLOOK: SOPEMI 2007 EDITION – ISBN 978-92-64-03285-9 – © OECD 2007

Table B.1.4. **Stock of foreign-born population by country of birth**

Thousands

SLOVAK REPUBLIC

	2001	2004
Czech Republic	71.5	107.7
Hungary	17.2	22.5
Ukraine	7.1	13.3
Poland	3.4	7.2
Russian Federation	1.6	5.8
Germany	0.6	4.7
FYROM	0.1	4.6
Romania	3.0	4.4
Austria	0.7	3.9
United States	0.7	3.5
France	1.3	3.4
Viet Nam	0.6	2.4
Bulgaria	1.0	1.7
Belgium	0.2	0.9
Serbia and Montenegro	1.4	0.8
Other countries	8.4	21.0
Total	**119.1**	**207.6**

Note: For details on definitions and sources, please refer to the metadata at the end of the tables.

StatLink ⟪ᵐˢᴸ⟫ http://dx.doi.org/10.1787/017748242685

Table B.1.4. **Stock of foreign-born population by country of birth**

Thousands

SWEDEN

	1996	1997	1998	1999	2000	2001	2002	2003	2004	2005
Finland	203.4	201.0	198.8	197.0	195.4	193.5	191.5	189.3	186.6	183.7
Former Yugoslavia	72.8	70.9	70.9	70.4	72.0	73.3	74.4	75.1	74.6	74.0
Iraq	29.0	32.7	37.9	43.1	49.4	55.7	62.8	67.6	70.1	72.6
Bosnia and Herzegovina	46.8	48.3	50.0	50.7	51.5	52.2	52.9	53.9	54.5	54.8
Iran	49.2	49.8	50.3	50.5	51.1	51.8	52.7	53.2	54.0	54.5
Poland	39.5	39.6	39.7	39.9	40.1	40.5	41.1	41.6	43.5	46.2
Norway	43.8	42.7	41.9	41.8	42.5	43.4	44.5	45.1	45.0	44.8
Denmark	39.8	38.9	38.2	37.9	38.2	38.9	39.9	40.9	41.7	42.6
Germany	36.5	36.8	37.2	37.4	38.2	38.9	39.4	40.2	40.8	41.6
Turkey	30.2	. .	31.0	31.4	31.9	32.5	33.1	34.1	35.0	35.9
Chile	26.9	26.7	26.6	26.6	26.8	27.2	27.3	27.5	27.7	27.8
Lebanon	21.6	21.4	20.2	20.0	20.0	20.2	20.5	20.8	21.1	21.4
Thailand	8.2	. .	9.0	9.6	10.4	11.2	12.4	14.3	16.3	18.3
United Kingdom	13.1	13.3	13.7	14.0	14.6	15.5	16.1	16.4	16.8	17.2
Syria	. .	. .	12.8	13.6	14.2	14.6	15.2	15.7	16.2	16.8
Other countries	283.0	332.0	290.5	297.5	307.6	318.7	329.7	342.1	356.5	373.8
Total	**943.8**	**954.2**	**968.7**	**981.6**	**1 003.8**	**1 028.0**	**1 053.5**	**1 078.1**	**1 100.3**	**1 125.8**

Note: For details on definitions and sources, please refer to the metadata at the end of the tables.

StatLink ⟪ᵐˢᴸ⟫ http://dx.doi.org/10.1787/017753472541

Table B.1.4. **Stock of foreign-born population by country of birth**

Thousands

TURKEY

	1990	2000	Of which: Women	
			1990	2000
Bulgaria	462.8	480.8	237.9	252.5
Germany	176.8	273.5	88.3	140.6
Greece	101.8	59.2	54.0	32.3
Netherlands	9.9	21.8	5.0	11.1
Russian Federation	11.4	19.9	5.1	12.1
United Kingdom	6.5	18.9	3.3	10.1
France	10.3	16.8	5.0	8.2
Austria	7.0	14.3	3.5	7.2
United States	12.9	13.6	5.2	6.1
Iran	10.5	13.0	3.9	4.9
Cyprus	9.2	10.4	4.8	5.6
Switzerland	8.1	10.4	4.1	5.4
Other countries	310.1	326.1	154.4	167.6
Total	**1 137.2**	**1 278.7**	**574.5**	**663.6**

Note: For details on definitions and sources, please refer to the metadata at the end of the tables.

StatLink ᵐˢ🖳 *http://dx.doi.org/10.1787/017788713818*

Table B.1.4. **Stock of foreign-born population by country of birth**

Thousands

UNITED KINGDOM

	2006	Of which: Women
		2006
India	570.0	280.0
Ireland	417.0	236.0
Pakistan	274.0	139.0
Germany	269.0	155.0
Poland	229.0	109.0
Bangladesh	221.0	101.0
South Africa	198.0	104.0
United States	169.0	90.0
Kenya	138.0	71.0
Jamaica	135.0	70.0
Nigeria	117.0	60.0
Australia	116.0	60.0
France	111.0	64.0
Zimbabwe	111.0	59.0
Ghana	106.0	53.0
Other countries	310.1	154.4
Total	**5 757.0**	**2 984.0**

Note: For details on definitions and sources, please refer to the metadata at the end of the tables.

StatLink ᵐˢ🖳 *http://dx.doi.org/10.1787/017356141066*

INTERNATIONAL MIGRATION OUTLOOK: SOPEMI 2007 EDITION – ISBN 978-92-64-03285-9 – © OECD 2007

Table B.1.4. **Stock of foreign-born population by country of birth**

Thousands

UNITED STATES

	1996	1997	1998	1999	2000	2001	2002	2003	2004	2005	Of which: Women		
											2003	2004	2005
Mexico	6 894.8	7 298.2	7 382.4	7 429.1	8 072.3	8 494.0	9 900.4	10 237.2	10 739.7	11 053.0	4 599.1	4 807.2	4 922.4
Philippines	1 239.0	1 205.6	1 324.6	1 549.4	1 313.8	1 333.1	1 488.1	1 457.5	1 449.0	1 621.3	857.1	827.1	930.2
India	772.2	770.0	747.7	849.2	1 010.1	1 028.8	1 322.4	1 183.6	1 296.7	1 438.3	542.5	630.2	688.8
China	825.0	961.4	865.9	890.6	898.0	968.2	986.9	1 167.6	1 463.0	1 398.0	634.9	773.3	736.3
El Salvador	728.6	645.4	791.6	811.3	787.7	840.9	882.8	1 025.3	958.4	1 130.1	450.4	465.2	511.8
Viet Nam	800.9	805.9	1 013.8	988.1	872.7	768.2	831.5	946.7	985.7	1 037.7	510.4	515.1	534.3
Germany	1 096.1	1 204.2	1 200.8	986.9	1 147.4	1 128.2	1 161.8	1 091.5	1 093.0	1 036.1	627.2	632.4	589.2
Cuba	790.6	927.3	930.6	960.9	957.3	859.6	935.7	1 005.2	1 075.0	965.9	514.3	527.3	478.1
Canada	867.0	739.9	787.3	825.1	879.3	957.4	921.2	852.6	831.9	833.2	431.9	451.9	445.3
Korea	595.5	659.0	657.6	660.7	801.8	889.2	811.2	916.2	854.1	770.6	530.0	486.6	424.8
United Kingdom	693.6	713.4	761.9	796.2	758.2	715.3	745.1	700.7	730.9	724.6	387.6	409.6	367.2
Dominican Republic	526.6	643.4	646.8	692.1	699.2	640.1	668.6	725.9	641.4	713.5	431.8	388.8	445.2
Jamaica	510.5	400.1	355.6	405.2	422.5	488.4	537.8	671.1	660.0	615.3	371.4	377.5	365.0
Haiti	396.5	439.7	481.6	402.2	384.7	522.6	571.2	496.8	567.4	565.9	258.7	290.7	280.4
Guatemala	349.5	454.8	474.3	407.2	328.7	315.6	408.1	448.5	526.7	556.6	179.1	217.0	225.9
Other countries	9 192.5	9 880.5	9 914.5	9 398.1	10 155.3	10 708.5	11 301.6	11 693.8	11 762.7	11 887.6	5 962.5	6 001.0	6 076.9
Total	**26 278.9**	**27 748.8**	**28 337.1**	**28 052.4**	**29 489.0**	**30 658.1**	**33 474.4**	**34 620.3**	**35 635.5**	**36 347.6**	**17 288.9**	**17 800.9**	**18 021.9**

Note: For details on definitions and sources, please refer to the metadata at the end of the tables.

StatLink ⬛⬛ http://dx.doi.org/10.1787/017801536111

Metadata related to Tables A.1.4. and B.1.4. **Foreign-born population**

Data in italic in Table A.1.4. are estimated. Estimates by country of birth are not available. Therefore all data presented in Tables B.1.4. are observed numbers.
For details on sources for observed figures, refer to ® below.

Legend: ® Observed figures.

ε Estimates with the component method (CM) or with the parametric method (PM).

For more details on the method of estimation, please refer to *www.oecd.org/els/migration/foreignborn*.

Country	Comments	Source
Australia	® Estimated resident population (ERP) based on Population Censuses. In between Censuses, the ERP is updated by data on births, deaths and net overseas migration. *Reference date*: 30 June.	Australian Bureau of Statistics.
Austria	® *Reference date:* March of the given year.	Labour Force Survey, Statistics Austria.
Belgium	® Stock of foreign-born citizens recorded in the population register. Asylum seekers are recorded in a separate register.	Population register, National Statistical Office.
Canada	® for 2001: Total immigrants (excluding non-permanent residents). "Other countries" include "not stated". ε PM for other years.	Censuses of Population, Statistics Canada.
Denmark	® Immigrants are defined as persons born abroad by parents that are both foreign citizens or born abroad. When no information is available on the country of birth, the person is classified as an immigrant.	Statistics Denmark.
Finland	® Stock of foreign-born citizens recorded in population register. Includes foreign-born persons of Finnish origin.	Central population register, Statistics Finland.
France	® 1999 Census and 2005 (2004-2005 average from the continuous Labour force surveys). ε PM for other years.	National Institute for Statistics and Economic Studies (INSEE).
Germany	® 2000. ε CM for other years.	OECD database on immigrants and expatriates, (*www.oecd.org/els/migration/censusdatabase*).
Greece	® Stock of foreign-born citizens recorded in the census (usual resident population).	National Statistical Service of Greece.
Hungary	® Holders of a permanent or a long-term residence permit. *Reference date:* 31 December.	Register of foreigners, Ministry of the Interior.
Ireland	® for 1996 and 2002: Persons usually resident and present in their usual residence on census night. ε PM for other years.	Census, Central Statistics Office.
Italy	® *Reference date:2001.*	Census, ISTAT.
Luxembourg	® for 2001. ε CM for other years.	Census 2001, Central Office of Statistics and Economic Studies (Statec).
Mexico	® Population aged 5 and over.	2000 Census, National Council on Population (CONAPO).
Netherlands	® *Reference date:* 31 December.	Register of Population, Central Bureau of Statistics (CBS).
New Zealand	® for 1996 and 2001. ε PM for other years.	Census of population, Statistics New Zealand.
Norway	® *Reference date:* 31 December.	Central Population Register, Statistics Norway.
Poland	® Excluding foreign temporary residents who at the time of the census had been staying at a given address in Poland for less than 12 months. Country of birth in accordance with political (administrative) boundaries at the time of the census.	Census, Central Statistical Office.
Portugal	® 2001 Census data. ε CM for other years.	Census of population, National Statistical Office (INE).
Slovak Republic	® Census of population who had permanent residence at the date of the Census, 1996 and 2004. ε PM for other years.	Ministry of the Interior.
Spain	® for 2001.	OECD database on immigrants and expatriates, (*www.oecd.org/els/migration/censusdatabase*).
Sweden	® *Reference date:* 31 December.	Population register, Statistics Sweden.
Switzerland	® for 2000. ε CM for other years.	OECD database on immigrants and expatriates, (*www.oecd.org/els/migration/censusdatabase*).
Turkey		Census of Population, State Institute of Statistics (SIS).
United Kingdom	® for 2001 (Table A.1.4.). ε PM for other years. Table B.1.4. Foreign-born residents in 2006. Figures are rounded and not published if less than 10 000.	Census, Office for National Statistics. Labour Force Survey, Office for National Statistics.
United States	In Table A.1.4, the statistic for the year 2000 is from the population census. Starting with this level the series is estimated using the trend in foreign-born levels from the CPS. On the other hand, the statistics by country of birth (Table B.1.4) are taken directly from CPS estimates.	Current Population Survey March Supplement and Census, US Department of Commerce, Bureau of the Census.

Table A.1.5. **Stocks of foreign population in selected OECD countries**
Thousands

	1996	1997	1998	1999	2000	2001	2002	2003	2004	2005
Austria	681.7	683.4	686.5	694.0	701.8	718.3	743.3	759.6	776.1	801.6
% of total population	8.6	8.6	8.6	8.7	8.8	8.9	9.2	9.4	9.5	9.7
Belgium	911.9	903.1	892.0	897.1	861.7	846.7	850.1	860.3	870.9	900.5
% of total population	9.0	8.9	8.7	8.8	8.4	8.2	8.2	8.3	8.4	8.6
Czech Republic	198.6	209.8	219.8	228.9	201.0	210.8	231.6	240.4	254.3	278.3
% of total population	1.9	2.0	2.1	2.2	1.9	2.0	2.3	2.4	2.5	2.7
Denmark	237.7	249.6	256.3	259.4	258.6	266.7	265.4	271.2	267.6	270.1
% of total population	4.7	4.7	4.8	4.9	4.8	5.0	4.9	5.0	4.9	5.0
Finland	73.8	80.6	85.1	87.7	91.1	98.6	103.7	107.0	108.3	113.9
% of total population	1.4	1.6	1.6	1.7	1.8	1.8	1.9	2.0	2.1	2.2
France	..	..	..	3 263.2	..	..	..	..	..	..
% of total population	..	..	..	5.6	..	..	..	..	..	..
Germany	7 314.0	7 365.8	7 319.6	7 343.6	7 296.8	7 318.6	7 335.6	7 334.8 |	6 738.7	6 755.8
% of total population	8.9	9.0	8.9	8.9	8.9	8.9	8.9	8.9 |	8.9	8.8
Greece	..	..	292.0	273.9	304.6	355.8	436.8	472.8	533.4	553.1
% of total population	..	..	2.8	2.6	2.9	3.4	4.1	4.5	5.0	5.2
Hungary	142.5	148.3	150.2	153.1	110.0	116.4	115.9	130.1	142.2	154.4
% of total population	1.4	1.4	1.4	1.5	1.1	1.1	1.1	1.3	1.4	1.5
Ireland	118.0	114.4	110.8	117.8	126.3	155.0	187.7	222.2	222.8	259.4
% of total population	3.2	3.1	3.0	3.1	3.3	4.0	4.8	5.6	5.5	6.3
Italy	986.0	1 022.9	1 090.8	1 340.7	1 379.7	1 448.4	1 503.3	2 227.6	2 402.2	2 670.5
% of total population	2.0	2.1	2.1	2.2	2.4	2.5	2.6	3.9	4.2	4.6
Japan	1 415.1	1 482.7	1 510.0	1 556.1	1 686.4	1 778.5	1 851.8	1 915.0	1 973.7	2 011.6
% of total population	1.1	1.2	1.2	1.2	1.3	1.4	1.5	1.5	1.5	1.6
Korea	148.7	176.9	147.9	169.0	210.2	229.6	252.5	438.0	468.9	485.1
% of total population	0.3	0.3	0.3	0.4	0.4	0.5	0.5	0.9	0.9	1.0
Luxembourg	142.9	147.7	152.9	159.4	164.7	166.7	170.7	174.2	177.4	181.8
% of total population	34.1	34.9	35.6	36.0	37.3	37.5	38.1	38.6	39.0	39.6
Netherlands	679.9	678.1	662.4	651.5	667.8	690.4	700.0	702.2	699.4	691.4
% of total population	4.4	4.3	4.2	4.1	4.2	4.3	4.3	4.3	4.3	4.2
Norway	157.5	158.0	165.1	178.7	184.3	185.9	197.7	204.7	213.3	222.3
% of total population	3.7	3.6	3.6	3.7	4.0	4.1	4.1	4.3	4.6	4.8
Poland	..	..	..	..	..	..	49.2	..	..	..
% of total population	..	..	..	..	..	..	0.1	..	..	..
Portugal	172.9	175.3	177.8	190.9	207.6	360.8	423.8	444.6	469.1	432.0
% of total population	1.7	1.8	1.8	1.9	2.1	3.5	4.1	4.3	4.5	4.1
Slovak Republic	24.1	24.8	28.4	29.5	28.8	29.4	29.5	29.2	22.3	25.6
% of total population	0.5	0.5	0.5	0.5	0.5	0.5	0.5	0.5	0.4	0.5
Spain	539.0	609.8	719.6	801.3	895.7	1 109.1	1 324.0	1 647.0	1 977.3	2 738.9
% of total population	1.4	1.6	1.8	2.0	2.2	2.7	3.1	3.9	4.6	6.2
Sweden	526.6	522.0	499.9	487.2	477.3	476.0	474.1	476.1	481.1	479.9
% of total population	6.0	5.9	5.6	5.5	5.4	5.3	5.3	5.3	5.3	5.3
Switzerland	1 337.6	1 340.8	1 347.9	1 368.7	1 384.4	1 419.1	1 447.3	1 471.0	1 495.0	1 511.9
% of total population	18.9	19.0	19.0	19.2	19.3	19.7	19.9	20.0	20.2	20.3
United Kingdom	1 934.0	2 066.0	2 207.0	2 208.0	2 342.0	2 587.0	2 584.0	2 742.0	2 857.0	3 035.0
% of total population	3.4	3.6	3.8	3.8	4.0	4.4	4.5	4.7	4.9	5.2

Note: For details on definitions and sources, refer to the metadata at the end of Tables B.1.5.

StatLink ᛜᛁᛚ *http://dx.doi.org/10.1787/015600186665*

Table B.1.5. **Stock of foreign population by nationality**

Thousands

AUSTRIA

	1996	1997	1998	1999	2000	2001	2002	2003	2004	2005
Former Yugoslavia	314.2	314.4	315.8	319.9	322.2	316.9	314.1	313.9	311.1	310.2
Turkey	135.0	133.0	132.2	129.6	127.3	126.9	126.8	124.8	120.0	115.5
Other countries	232.5	235.9	238.4	244.4	252.3	274.5	302.3	320.8	345.1	376.0
Total	**681.7**	**683.4**	**686.5**	**694.0**	**701.8**	**718.3**	**743.3**	**759.6**	**776.1**	**801.6**

Note: For details on definitions and sources, please refer to the metadata at the end of the tables.

StatLink ᴍᴣ￫ http://dx.doi.org/10.1787/017805831788

Table B.1.5. **Stock of foreign population by nationality**

Thousands

BELGIUM

	1996	1997	1998	1999	2000	2001	2002	2003	2004	2005	Of which: Women		
											2003	2004	2005
Italy	208.2	205.8	202.6	200.3	195.6	190.8	187.0	183.0	179.0	175.5	83.1	81.5	80.1
France	101.7	103.6	105.1	107.2	109.3	111.1	113.0	114.9	117.3	120.6	59.5	60.9	62.7
Netherlands	80.6	82.3	84.2	85.8	88.8	92.6	96.6	100.7	105.0	110.5	45.8	47.8	50.6
Morocco	138.3	132.8	125.1	122.0	106.8	90.6	83.6	81.8	81.3	80.6	38.1	38.7	38.8
Spain	47.9	47.4	46.6	45.9	43.4	45.0	44.5	43.8	43.2	42.9	21.8	21.6	21.5
Turkey	78.5	73.8	70.7	69.2	56.2	45.9	42.6	41.3	39.9	39.7	20.8	20.1	20.0
Germany	32.7	33.3	34.0	34.3	34.6	34.7	35.1	35.5	36.3	37.0	17.7	18.2	18.6
Portugal	24.9	25.3	25.5	25.6	25.6	25.8	26.0	26.8	27.4	28.0	13.2	13.6	13.9
United Kingdom	26.2	26.1	25.9	26.2	26.6	26.4	26.2	26.2	26.0	25.7	11.7	11.6	11.5
Poland	5.7	6.0	6.3	6.7	6.9	8.9	10.4	11.6	14.0	18.0	7.0	8.1	9.9
Greece	19.5	19.2	18.8	18.4	18.0	17.6	17.3	17.1	16.6	16.3	8.1	7.9	7.9
Democratic Republic of the Congo	12.0	12.1	12.4	12.5	11.3	13.0	13.6	13.8	13.2	13.5	6.8	6.5	6.8
Former Yugoslavia	1.1	1.3	6.0	14.4	9.8	10.3	10.4	8.1	11.1	12.4	3.3	5.4	6.0
United States	12.3	12.6	12.4	12.2	11.9	11.8	11.7	11.6	11.5	11.2	5.8	5.8	5.7
Romania	2.2	2.2	2.1	2.3	2.4	3.3	4.0	4.6	5.6	7.5	2.7	3.2	4.2
Other countries	120.1	119.3	114.1	114.1	114.6	119.1	128.0	139.4	143.5	161.1	72.0	74.3	83.4
Total	**911.9**	**903.1**	**892.0**	**897.1**	**861.7**	**846.7**	**850.1**	**860.3**	**870.9**	**900.5**	**417.6**	**425.2**	**441.4**

Note: For details on definitions and sources, please refer to the metadata at the end of the tables.

StatLink ᴍᴣ￫ http://dx.doi.org/10.1787/017852873431

INTERNATIONAL MIGRATION OUTLOOK: SOPEMI 2007 EDITION – ISBN 978-92-64-03285-9 – © OECD 2007

Table B.1.5. **Stock of foreign population by nationality**
Thousands
CZECH REPUBLIC

	1996	1997	1998	1999	2000	2001	2002	2003	2004	2005
Ukraine	46.3	43.4	52.7	65.9	50.2	51.8	59.1	62.3	78.3	87.8
Slovak Republic	50.3	52.2	49.6	40.4	44.3	53.2	61.1	64.9	47.4	49.4
Viet Nam	17.6	21.0	22.9	24.8	23.6	23.9	27.1	29.0	34.2	36.8
Poland	24.5	25.0	22.2	18.3	17.1	16.5	16.0	15.8	16.3	17.8
Russian Federation	6.7	8.9	10.0	16.9	13.0	12.4	12.8	12.6	14.7	16.3
Germany	5.9	5.9	5.1	6.1	5.0	4.9	5.2	5.2	5.8	7.2
Bulgaria	4.3	6.6	6.0	5.0	4.0	4.1	4.2	4.0	4.4	4.6
United States	4.1	3.8	3.9	3.8	3.2	3.2	3.4	3.3	3.8	4.0
China	4.8	4.5	4.2	4.3	3.6	3.3	3.2	4.0	3.4	3.6
Serbia and Montenegro	5.0	3.8	3.9	4.1	3.7	3.3	3.2	3.1	3.4	3.6
Romania	1.8	2.4	2.7	2.6	2.4	2.3	2.3	2.3	2.6	2.7
Austria	2.2	2.3	2.3	2.3	1.9	1.9	1.9	1.9	2.1	2.4
United Kingdom	1.5	2.1	1.6	1.7	1.5	1.6	1.8	1.7	1.8	2.2
Other countries	23.6	27.9	32.8	32.7	27.7	28.3	30.2	30.3	36.2	40.0
Total	**198.6**	**209.8**	**219.8**	**228.9**	**201.0**	**210.8**	**231.6**	**240.4**	**254.3**	**278.3**

Note: For details on definitions and sources, please refer to the metadata at the end of the tables.

StatLink 🔗 http://dx.doi.org/10.1787/018017150171

Table B.1.5. **Stock of foreign population by nationality**
Thousands
DENMARK

	1996	1997	1998	1999	2000	2001	2002	2003	2004	2005	Of which: Women		
											2003	2004	2005
Turkey	36.8	37.5	38.1	36.6	35.2	33.4	31.9	30.3	30.0	29.5	14.8	14.6	14.4
Iraq	8.1	9.4	11.3	12.7	13.8	16.5	18.0	19.4	19.2	18.7	9.0	9.0	8.8
Germany	11.4	11.9	12.4	12.7	12.7	12.9	13.0	13.3	13.6	14.2	6.3	6.4	6.7
Norway	11.5	11.9	12.2	12.6	13.0	13.2	13.4	13.8	13.9	13.9	8.0	8.1	8.2
United Kingdom	12.5	12.8	12.9	12.7	12.6	12.8	12.7	12.8	12.8	12.9	4.5	4.5	4.5
Bosnia and Herzegovina	..	..	..	..	..	..	17.8	17.2	14.0	12.7	8.5	6.8	6.2
Sweden	9.4	10.0	10.4	10.8	10.8	10.8	10.7	10.8	10.9	11.2	6.2	6.3	6.5
Somalia	9.7	11.9	13.1	14.3	14.4	14.6	13.3	13.1	11.3	9.8	6.5	5.5	4.8
Afghanistan	1.6	2.0	2.4	2.9	4.2	7.1	8.2	9.1	9.3	9.4	4.2	4.4	4.5
Former Yugoslavia	32.2	33.9	34.5	35.1	35.0	34.8	10.8	10.7	9.8	9.4	5.2	4.8	4.6
Iceland	5.6	5.9	5.9	5.8	5.9	6.0	6.6	7.1	7.4	7.7	3.6	3.8	3.9
Poland	5.3	5.5	5.5	5.6	5.5	5.7	5.7	5.9	6.2	7.4	4.0	4.2	4.6
Pakistan	6.7	6.9	7.1	7.1	7.1	7.2	6.9	7.0	6.9	6.7	3.7	3.6	3.5
China	1.9	2.1	2.3	2.5	2.7	3.2	3.9	5.2	5.9	6.2	2.7	3.1	3.2
Thailand	3.0	3.4	3.7	4.1	4.4	4.9	5.2	5.4	5.6	5.9	4.5	4.6	4.9
Other countries	81.9	84.6	84.5	84.1	81.2	83.7	87.2	90.2	90.9	94.6	46.7	46.9	48.7
Total	**237.7**	**249.6**	**256.3**	**259.4**	**258.6**	**266.7**	**265.4**	**271.2**	**267.6**	**270.1**	**138.4**	**136.5**	**137.9**

Note: For details on definitions and sources, please refer to the metadata at the end of the tables.

StatLink 🔗 http://dx.doi.org/10.1787/018042162481

Table B.1.5. **Stock of foreign population by nationality**
Thousands
FINLAND

| | 1996 | 1997 | 1998 | 1999 | 2000 | 2001 | 2002 | 2003 | 2004 | 2005 | Of which: Women | | |
											2003	2004	2005
Russian Federation	11.8	14.3	16.9	18.6	20.6	22.7	24.3	25.0	24.6	24.6	15.5	15.2	15.1
Estonia	9.0	9.7	10.3	10.7	10.8	11.7	12.4	13.4	14.0	15.5	7.6	7.8	8.6
Sweden	7.3	7.5	7.8	7.8	7.9	8.0	8.0	8.1	8.3	8.2	3.5	3.6	3.5
Somalia	4.6	5.2	5.4	4.4	4.2	4.4	4.5	4.6	4.7	4.7	2.3	2.4	2.3
Serbia and Montenegro	2.6	2.8	2.9	3.4	3.6	4.2	2.2	2.8	3.3	3.3	1.4	1.6	1.6
Iraq	1.9	2.4	2.7	3.0	3.1	3.2	3.4	3.5	3.4	3.3	1.6	1.5	1.4
China	1.5	1.6	1.7	1.7	1.7	1.9	2.1	2.4	2.6	3.0	1.2	1.4	1.6
United Kingdom	1.8	1.9	2.1	2.2	2.2	2.4	2.5	2.7	2.7	2.8	0.6	0.6	0.6
Germany	1.8	2.0	2.1	2.2	2.2	2.3	2.5	2.6	2.6	2.8	0.9	1.0	1.0
Thailand	0.9	1.0	1.1	1.2	1.3	1.5	1.8	2.1	2.3	2.6	1.7	1.9	2.2
Turkey	1.5	1.7	1.7	1.7	1.8	2.0	2.1	2.3	2.4	2.6	0.6	0.7	0.8
Iran	1.4	1.7	1.7	1.9	1.9	2.2	2.4	2.5	2.6	2.6	1.1	1.1	1.1
United States	1.8	1.9	2.0	2.1	2.0	2.1	2.1	2.1	2.0	2.1	0.9	0.8	0.8
Viet Nam	2.1	2.2	2.0	1.8	1.8	1.8	1.7	1.7	1.5	1.7	0.8	0.8	0.8
Bosnia and Herzegovina	1.3	1.4	1.5	1.6	1.6	1.7	1.7	1.7	1.6	1.6	0.8	0.8	0.8
Other countries	22.4	23.4	23.3	23.6	24.4	26.5	29.8	29.6	29.7	32.6	12.8	12.8	13.9
Total	**73.8**	**80.6**	**85.1**	**87.7**	**91.1**	**98.6**	**103.7**	**107.0**	**108.3**	**113.9**	**53.5**	**53.9**	**56.1**

Note: For details on definitions and sources, please refer to the metadata at the end of the tables.

StatLink 📊 http://dx.doi.org/10.1787/018078232150

Table B.1.5. **Stock of foreign population by nationality**
Thousands
FRANCE

| | 1982 | 1990 | 1999 | Of which: Women | | |
				1982	1990	1999
Portugal	767.3	649.7	553.7	361.6	304.2	258.9
Morocco	441.3	572.7	504.1	172.4	250.7	229.2
Algeria	805.1	614.2	477.5	310.5	253.9	204.6
Turkey	122.3	197.7	208.0	51.8	87.5	98.3
Italy	340.3	252.8	201.7	147.3	108.0	87.3
Spain	327.2	216.0	161.8	154.5	103.7	80.6
Tunisia	190.8	206.3	154.4	72.0	84.8	63.8
Senegal	32.3	43.7	39.0	9.7	17.0	16.5
Poland	64.8	47.1	33.8	37.9	28.9	20.9
Cambodia	37.9	47.4	26.0	17.6	22.6	13.0
Viet Nam	33.8	33.7	21.2	16.0	15.3	10.9
Laos	32.5	31.8	16.2	15.4	15.0	7.8
Other countries	518.6	683.4	866.0	228.0	322.6	439.1
Total	**3 714.2**	**3 596.6**	**3 263.2**	**1 594.6**	**1 614.3**	**1 530.9**

Note: For details on definitions and sources, please refer to the metadata at the end of the tables.

StatLink 📊 http://dx.doi.org/10.1787/018082767781

Table B.1.5. **Stock of foreign population by nationality**

Thousands

GERMANY

	1996	1997	1998	1999	2000	2001	2002	2003	2004	2005	Of which: Women		
											2003	2004	2005
Turkey	2 049.1	2 107.4	2 110.2	2 053.6	1 998.5	1 947.9	1 912.2	1 877.7	1 764.3	1 764.0	866.8	820.3	826.5
Italy	599.4	607.9	612.0	615.9	619.1	616.3	609.8	601.3	548.2	540.8	244.9	224.3	221.7
Poland	283.4	283.3	283.6	291.7	301.4	310.4	317.6	326.9	292.1	326.6	169.5	160.0	173.9
Greece	362.5	363.2	363.5	364.4	365.4	362.7	359.4	354.6	316.0	309.8	160.9	143.8	141.1
Serbia and Montenegro	754.3	721.0	719.5	737.2	662.5	627.5	591.5	568.2	125.8	297.0	259.1	58.6	139.7
Croatia	201.9	206.6	208.9	214.0	216.8	223.8	231.0	236.6	229.2	228.9	117.8	115.7	116.3
Former Yugoslavia	..	..	..	..	..	..	..	..	381.6	196.9	..	176.8	92.0
Russian Federation	..	69.1	81.1	98.4	115.9	136.1	155.6	173.5	178.6	185.9	101.0	105.0	110.2
Austria	184.9	185.1	185.2	186.1	187.7	189.0	189.3	189.5	174.0	174.8	87.0	81.4	81.9
Bosnia and Herzegovina	340.5	281.4	190.1	167.7	156.3	159.0	163.8	167.1	156.0	156.9	80.4	75.2	75.8
Ukraine	..	51.4	63.8	76.8	89.3	103.5	116.0	126.0	128.1	130.7	74.1	76.4	78.8
Netherlands	113.3	112.8	112.1	110.5	110.8	112.4	115.2	118.7	114.1	118.6	53.8	51.9	53.9
Portugal	130.8	132.3	132.6	132.6	133.7	132.6	131.4	130.6	116.7	115.6	57.9	52.9	52.7
Spain	132.5	131.6	131.1	129.9	129.4	128.7	127.5	126.0	108.3	107.8	60.9	53.7	53.7
France	101.8	103.9	105.8	107.2	110.2	111.3	112.4	113.0	100.5	102.2	60.5	54.3	55.2
Other countries	2 059.6	2 008.9	2 020.1	2 057.8	2 099.8	2 157.3	2 203.0	2 225.2	2 005.3	1 999.3	1 045.4	967.1	987.3
Total	**7 314.0**	**7 365.8**	**7 319.6**	**7 343.6**	**7 296.8**	**7 318.6**	**7 335.6**	**7 334.8**	**6 738.7**	**6 755.8**	**3 440.1**	**3 217.5**	**3 260.5**

Note: For details on definitions and sources, please refer to the metadata at the end of the tables.

StatLink ⟨⟩ http://dx.doi.org/10.1787/018042023048

Table B.1.5. **Stock of foreign population by nationality**

Thousands

GREECE

	1998	1999	2000	2001	2002	2003	2004	2005	Of which: Women		
									2003	2004	2005
Albania	169.4	153.3	185.7	209.5	262.1	294.7	325.6	341.0	139.8	148.3	154.0
Bulgaria	6.7	7.0	8.1	12.6	18.6	17.3	25.3	27.9	10.1	16.4	18.8
Romania	4.3	6.0	5.2	7.2	13.8	14.6	16.2	18.9	7.7	7.6	10.9
Russian Federation	21.1	10.5	15.6	19.9	22.0	17.8	16.8	17.6	11.5	10.8	10.5
Georgia	5.9	6.3	4.4	10.2	12.0	9.5	14.1	16.9	6.2	8.4	10.5
Poland	6.7	10.4	11.2	13.5	14.1	15.9	17.0	16.1	7.4	9.9	9.0
Ukraine	3.8	6.1	2.5	6.4	11.3	10.2	13.1	12.2	7.5	9.0	10.4
Cyprus	6.1	9.5	6.8	5.2	7.7	8.1	12.2	11.0	4.2	6.3	5.2
Philippines	2.9	2.4	2.7	2.9	3.8	3.2	7.2	8.9	2.5	5.5	6.0
United Kingdom	2.9	5.2	4.0	5.3	3.6	6.2	7.1	7.7	4.6	4.9	4.8
Armenia	5.9	3.5	2.9	5.1	4.0	4.7	7.3	6.1	2.3	3.8	3.1
Germany	4.5	1.1	4.8	3.5	2.3	4.3	3.8	5.6	3.0	3.1	4.1
Pakistan	4.6	2.1	3.7	2.9	4.8	6.2	4.2	5.5	0.0	0.1	0.1
Iraq	4.6	2.5	3.1	4.6	4.2	5.7	4.3	5.4	1.1	1.1	1.8
Turkey	3.0	3.2	3.8	3.3	4.3	3.3	2.5	2.8	1.6	1.3	1.5
Other countries	39.5	44.8	40.1	43.7	48.1	51.3	56.5	49.2	24.4	27.2	23.8
Total	**292.0**	**273.9**	**304.6**	**355.8**	**436.8**	**472.8**	**533.4**	**553.1**	**233.8**	**263.8**	**274.7**

Note: For details on definitions and sources, please refer to the metadata at the end of the tables.

StatLink ⟨⟩ http://dx.doi.org/10.1787/018127652205

Table B.1.5. **Stock of foreign population by nationality**
Thousands
HUNGARY

	1996	1997	1998	1999	2000	2001	2002	2003	2004	2005	Of which: Women		
											2003	2004	2005
Romania	61.6	62.1	57.4	57.3	41.6	45.0	47.3	55.7	67.5	66.2	28.6	34.8	33.4
Ukraine	12.0	7.2	9.9	11.0	8.9	9.8	9.9	13.1	13.9	15.3	7.1	7.3	8.0
Germany	8.3	9.0	9.4	9.6	7.5	7.7	7.1	7.4	6.9	10.5	4.5	4.5	5.8
China	6.7	7.8	8.3	8.9	5.8	6.8	6.4	6.8	6.9	8.6	3.1	3.1	3.8
Serbia and Montenegro	..	7.1	9.9	10.9	8.6	8.4	7.9	8.3	13.6	8.4	4.1	6.3	3.9
Former Yugoslavia	14.9	..	..	..	..	..	..	4.1	..	3.7	1.7	..	1.6
Slovak Republic	3.7	1.0	1.6	1.7	1.6	2.2	1.5	2.5	1.2	3.6	1.8	0.8	2.1
Viet Nam	1.6	1.8	2.2	2.4	1.9	2.2	2.1	2.4	2.5	3.1	1.1	1.1	1.5
Former Soviet Union	..	7.9	7.1	6.3	5.6	5.1	5.7	4.0	5.1	3.0	2.8	3.5	2.1
Russian Federation	4.1	2.5	2.8	3.0	1.9	2.0	1.8	2.2	2.6	2.8	1.3	1.6	1.7
Poland	4.3	4.5	4.4	4.1	2.3	2.2	1.9	2.2	2.2	2.4	1.4	1.4	1.5
Former Czechoslovakia	..	3.2	3.0	2.8	2.4	2.2	2.4	2.1	2.2	1.8	1.6	1.8	1.4
Austria	0.9	1.0	1.0	1.1	0.7	0.8	0.8	0.8	0.5	1.5	0.3	0.2	0.5
United Kingdom	1.0	1.1	1.3	1.4	0.6	0.7	0.9	1.0	0.4	1.5	0.3	0.2	0.5
France	0.6	0.8	1.0	1.0	0.5	0.6	0.7	0.8	0.3	1.3	0.3	0.1	0.5
Other countries	22.9	31.2	31.1	31.4	20.2	20.6	19.5	17.0	16.1	20.8	7.1	6.6	8.7
Total	**142.5**	**148.3**	**150.2**	**153.1**	**110.0**	**116.4**	**115.9**	**130.1**	**142.2**	**154.4**	**67.0**	**73.5**	**77.1**

Note: For details on definitions and sources, please refer to the metadata at the end of the tables.

StatLink ⬛⬛⬛ http://dx.doi.org/10.1787/018135472163

Table B.1.5. **Stock of foreign population by nationality**
Thousands
IRELAND

	2002	Of which: Women
		2002
United Kingdom	101.257	51.764
United States	11.135	6.049
Nigeria	8.65	4.523
Germany	7.033	3.913
France	6.231	3.238
China	5.766	2.386
Romania	4.91	2.114
Spain	4.347	2.648
South Africa	4.113	1.986
Philippines	3.742	2.425
Italy	3.691	1.592
Australia	3.61	1.907
Netherlands	3.039	1.432
Pakistan	2.881	1.038
Russian Federation	2.647	1.275
Other countries	46.2	21.0
Total	**219.3**	**109.3**

Note: For details on definitions and sources, please refer to the metadata at the end of the tables.

StatLink ⬛⬛⬛ http://dx.doi.org/10.1787/018147408300

INTERNATIONAL MIGRATION OUTLOOK: SOPEMI 2007 EDITION – ISBN 978-92-64-03285-9 – © OECD 2007

Table B.1.5. **Stock of foreign population by nationality**

Thousands

ITALY

	1996	1997	1998	1999	2000	2001	2002	2003	2004	2005
Albania	66.6	72.6	87.6	133.0	146.3	159.3	171.6	240.4	316.7	348.8
Morocco	115.0	122.2	128.3	155.9	162.3	167.9	170.7	231.0	294.9	319.5
Romania	26.9	28.8	33.8	61.2	70.0	83.0	94.8	244.4	248.8	297.6
China	31.6	35.3	41.2	56.7	60.1	62.1	64.0	105.0	111.7	127.8
Ukraine	1.3	1.9	3.1	6.5	9.1	12.6	14.8	117.2	93.4	107.1
Philippines	56.2	57.3	59.1	67.4	65.1	67.7	65.6	76.1	82.6	89.7
Tunisia	40.0	41.4	41.1	46.8	46.0	53.4	51.1	62.7	78.2	83.6
Serbia and Montenegro	33.0	31.7	36.1	41.2	40.2	39.3	40.2	46.8	58.2	64.1
Ecuador	4.3	4.7	4.9	10.5	11.2	12.3	12.3	48.3	53.2	62.0
India	19.1	20.5	22.0	27.6	30.0	32.5	34.3	49.2	54.3	61.8
Poland	23.2	22.9	23.3	29.5	30.4	32.9	35.0	64.9	50.8	60.8
Peru	21.9	23.0	23.6	29.1	30.1	31.7	31.3	48.8	53.4	59.3
Egypt	23.5	23.6	23.8	34.0	32.4	31.8	31.1	47.1	52.9	58.9
Senegal	31.5	32.0	31.4	40.9	39.2	37.8	37.0	49.7	53.9	57.1
Sri Lanka	23.7	24.8	27.4	32.0	33.8	38.8	35.7	43.0	45.6	50.5
Other countries	468.1	480.1	504.1	568.4	573.7	585.2	613.8	753.0	753.5	822.0
Total	**986.0**	**1 022.9**	**1 090.8**	**1 340.7**	**1 379.7**	**1 448.4**	**1 503.3**	**2 227.6**	**2 402.2**	**2 670.5**

Note: For details on definitions and sources, please refer to the metadata at the end of the tables.

StatLink ⟨⟨⟩⟩ http://dx.doi.org/10.1787/018153440167

Table B.1.5. **Stock of foreign population by nationality**

Thousands

JAPAN

	1996	1997	1998	1999	2000	2001	2002	2003	2004	2005
Korea	657.2	645.4	638.8	636.5	635.3	632.4	625.4	613.8	607.4	598.7
China	234.3	252.2	272.2	294.2	335.6	381.2	424.3	462.4	487.6	519.6
Brazil	201.8	233.3	222.2	224.3	254.4	266.0	268.3	274.7	286.6	302.1
Philippines	84.5	93.3	105.3	115.7	144.9	156.7	169.4	185.2	199.4	187.3
Peru	37.1	40.4	41.3	42.8	46.2	50.1	51.8	53.6	55.8	57.7
United States	44.2	43.7	42.8	42.8	44.9	46.2	48.0	47.8	48.8	49.4
Thailand	18.2	20.7	23.6	25.3	29.3	31.7	33.7	34.8	36.3	37.7
Viet Nam	10.2	11.9	13.5	14.9	16.9	19.1	21.1	23.9	26.0	28.9
Indonesia	8.7	11.9	15.0	16.4	19.3	20.8	21.7	22.9	23.9	25.1
United Kingdom	13.3	14.4	14.8	15.4	16.5	17.5	18.5	18.2	18.1	17.5
India	6.3	7.5	8.7	9.1	10.1	11.7	13.3	14.2	15.5	17.0
Canada	8.0	8.8	9.0	9.2	10.1	11.0	11.9	12.0	12.1	12.0
Australia	6.3	6.9	7.6	8.2	9.2	10.6	11.4	11.6	11.7	11.3
Bangladesh	5.9	6.1	6.4	6.6	7.2	7.9	8.7	9.7	10.7	11.0
Sri Lanka	3.2	3.9	4.7	5.1	5.7	6.5	7.3	8.0	8.8	9.0
Other countries	75.9	82.4	84.2	89.8	101.1	109.1	117.0	122.2	125.1	127.3
Total	**1 415.1**	**1 482.7**	**1 510.0**	**1 556.1**	**1 686.4**	**1 778.5**	**1 851.8**	**1 915.0**	**1 973.7**	**2 011.6**

Note: For details on definitions and sources, please refer to the metadata at the end of the tables.

StatLink ⟨⟨⟩⟩ http://dx.doi.org/10.1787/018201530425

Table B.1.5. **Stock of foreign population by nationality**

Thousands

KOREA

| | 1996 | 1997 | 1998 | 1999 | 2000 | 2001 | 2002 | 2003 | 2004 | 2005 | Of which: Women | | |
											2003	2004	2005
China	26.7	35.4	30.9	39.7	59.0	73.6	84.6	77.2	80.0	70.7	32.8	33.9	33.1
Viet Nam	10.3	13.5	8.1	10.0	15.6	16.0	16.9	23.3	26.1	35.5	8.3	9.4	12.4
Philippines	10.8	13.1	8.0	10.8	16.0	16.4	17.3	27.6	27.9	30.6	12.2	11.7	11.9
United States	26.4	27.9	26.1	25.8	22.8	22.0	22.8	23.2	22.6	23.5	9.9	9.5	9.7
Indonesia	9.6	13.6	9.7	13.6	16.7	15.6	17.1	28.3	26.1	22.6	5.3	4.4	3.0
Chinese Taipei	23.3	23.2	22.9	23.0	23.0	22.8	22.7	22.6	22.3	22.2	10.4	10.3	10.2
Thailand	1.2	1.9	1.6	1.8	3.2	3.6	4.8	2.0	21.9	21.4	7.3	7.1	5.2
Japan	12.4	13.7	13.0	13.2	14.0	14.7	12.1	16.0	16.4	17.2	10.9	11.2	11.7
Uzbekistan	1.0	2.2	2.0	2.3	3.7	4.0	4.2	10.7	11.5	10.8	2.1	2.1	1.9
Bangladesh	6.3	7.9	5.7	6.7	7.9	9.1	9.0	13.6	13.1	9.1	0.5	0.4	0.3
Pakistan	1.1	1.7	1.3	1.8	3.2	3.3	3.7	7.1	9.2	8.7	0.2	0.2	0.2
Sri Lanka	2.9	3.7	2.4	2.2	2.5	2.5	2.7	4.9	5.5	8.5	0.7	0.7	0.7
Canada	3.7	4.2	3.0	3.0	3.3	4.0	5.0	5.4	5.8	6.4	2.1	2.3	2.5
Nepal	1.0	1.2	1.0	1.2	2.0	2.1	2.3	4.2	5.3	4.9	0.6	0.7	0.6
Russian Federation	0.8	1.0	1.0	1.5	2.6	3.3	4.0	6.1	4.6	3.7	4.0	2.8	2.4
Other countries	11.3	12.7	11.2	12.1	14.7	16.7	23.2	165.7	170.7	189.5	71.6	83.9	95.3
Total	**148.7**	**176.9**	**147.9**	**169.0**	**210.2**	**229.6**	**252.5**	**438.0**	**468.9**	**485.1**	**179.0**	**190.6**	**201.2**

Note: For details on definitions and sources, please refer to the metadata at the end of the tables.

StatLink ⟡⟡⟡ http://dx.doi.org/10.1787/018241216630

Table B.1.5. **Stock of foreign population by nationality**

Thousands

LUXEMBOURG

	1996	1997	1998	1999	2000	2001	2002	2003	2004	2005
Portugal	53.1	54.5	55.9	57.0	58.5	59.8	61.4	63.8	65.7	67.8
France	15.7	16.5	17.5	18.8	20.1	20.9	21.6	21.9	22.4	22.9
Italy	19.8	19.9	20.0	20.1	20.3	19.1	19.0	18.9	18.8	18.8
Belgium	12.5	13.2	13.8	14.5	15.1	15.4	15.9	16.0	16.1	16.1
Germany	9.9	10.0	10.3	10.5	10.6	10.1	10.2	10.3	10.4	10.4
United Kingdom	4.4	4.4	4.4	4.6	4.9	4.5	4.7	4.6	4.5	4.5
Netherlands	3.8	3.8	3.8	3.8	3.9	3.6	3.6	3.6	3.6	3.5
Spain	2.8	2.9	2.9	3.0	3.0	2.8	2.9	2.9	2.9	3.0
Denmark	2.0	2.0	2.0	2.0	2.2	2.0	2.0	2.0	1.9	1.9
Sweden	0.8	0.9	1.0	1.1	1.2	1.2	1.2	1.2	1.2	1.2
Greece	1.2	1.3	1.3	1.3	1.4	1.2	1.2	1.2	1.2	1.2
Ireland	0.9	0.9	1.0	1.0	1.1	1.0	1.0	1.0	1.0	1.0
Finland	0.6	0.6	0.6	0.7	0.7	0.8	0.8	0.8	0.8	0.9
Austria	0.5	0.5	0.5	0.6	0.6	0.6	0.6	0.6	0.6	0.6
Other countries	15.0	16.3	17.9	20.5	21.4	23.5	24.6	25.4	26.4	28.0
Total	**142.9**	**147.7**	**152.9**	**159.4**	**164.7**	**166.7**	**170.7**	**174.2**	**177.4**	**181.8**

Note: For details on definitions and sources, please refer to the metadata at the end of the tables.

StatLink ⟡⟡⟡ http://dx.doi.org/10.1787/018316351003

INTERNATIONAL MIGRATION OUTLOOK: SOPEMI 2007 EDITION – ISBN 978-92-64-03285-9 – © OECD 2007

Table B.1.5. **Stock of foreign population by nationality**

Thousands

NETHERLANDS

| | 1996 | 1997 | 1998 | 1999 | 2000 | 2001 | 2002 | 2003 | 2004 | 2005 | Of which: Women | | |
											2003	2004	2005
Turkey	127.0	114.7	102.0	100.7	100.8	100.3	100.3	101.8	100.6	98.9	51.5	51.1	50.4
Morocco	138.7	135.7	128.6	119.7	111.4	104.3	97.8	94.4	91.6	86.2	46.3	45.1	42.7
Germany	53.5	53.9	54.1	54.3	54.8	55.6	56.1	56.5	57.1	58.5	28.9	29.6	30.6
United Kingdom	39.3	39.2	38.8	39.5	41.4	43.6	44.1	43.7	42.5	41.5	17.4	17.1	16.7
Belgium	24.0	24.4	24.8	25.4	25.9	26.1	26.3	26.2	26.1	26.0	14.0	14.0	14.0
Italy	17.3	17.4	17.6	17.9	18.2	18.6	18.7	18.5	18.4	18.5	6.5	6.5	6.6
Spain	16.6	16.6	16.8	16.9	17.2	17.4	17.5	17.4	17.1	16.9	8.6	8.5	8.4
Poland	5.6	5.7	5.9	5.6	5.9	6.3	6.9	7.4	11.0	15.2	5.4	7.4	9.3
China	7.3	7.3	7.5	7.5	8.0	9.4	11.2	13.3	14.7	15.0	7.5	8.4	8.5
France	10.6	11.2	11.9	12.5	13.3	14.1	14.5	14.5	14.5	14.7	7.3	7.3	7.5
United States	12.6	13.0	13.4	14.1	14.8	15.2	15.4	15.1	14.8	14.6	7.5	7.4	7.3
Portugal	8.8	8.7	8.8	9.2	9.8	10.6	11.3	11.8	12.0	12.1	5.3	5.5	5.5
Indonesia	7.9	8.0	8.4	8.7	9.3	10.1	10.8	11.2	11.4	11.5	7.4	7.6	7.7
Suriname	12.0	11.8	10.5	8.7	8.5	8.5	8.6	9.4	9.6	8.5	5.2	5.3	4.7
Greece	5.2	5.3	5.3	5.5	5.7	6.0	6.2	6.3	6.4	6.5	2.3	2.3	2.4
Other countries	193.4	205.4	208.1	205.3	222.9	244.2	254.3	254.6	251.5	246.6	125.1	126.6	126.5
Total	**679.9**	**678.1**	**662.4**	**651.5**	**667.8**	**690.4**	**700.0**	**702.2**	**699.4**	**691.4**	**346.2**	**349.6**	**348.7**

Note: For details on definitions and sources, please refer to the metadata at the end of the tables.

StatLink ⫘ http://dx.doi.org/10.1787/018361375715

Table B.1.5. **Stock of foreign population by nationality**

Thousands

NORWAY

| | 1996 | 1997 | 1998 | 1999 | 2000 | 2001 | 2002 | 2003 | 2004 | 2005 | Of which: Women | | |
											2003	2004	2005
Sweden	17.3	20.6	24.0	25.1	25.2	25.1	25.2	25.4	25.8	26.6	12.8	12.9	13.3
Denmark	18.1	18.4	19.1	19.2	19.4	19.7	20.0	20.0	20.1	20.2	9.5	9.5	9.6
Iraq	2.8	3.3	4.2	5.8	9.9	10.8	13.0	13.4	13.7	13.1	5.4	5.8	5.6
United Kingdom	10.9	10.8	11.2	11.4	11.1	11.0	11.2	11.0	11.2	11.2	4.2	4.3	4.3
Germany	5.1	5.4	6.0	6.7	7.1	7.5	8.2	8.8	9.6	10.6	4.3	4.6	5.0
Somalia	3.6	3.7	4.1	4.8	6.2	6.6	8.4	9.9	10.5	10.6	4.4	4.8	4.9
United States	8.7	8.6	8.6	8.3	8.0	7.9	8.0	7.7	7.6	7.6	4.0	4.0	3.9
Poland	2.3	2.1	2.1	2.0	2.0	2.2	2.6	2.7	3.9	6.8	1.8	2.0	2.6
Pakistan	8.6	7.5	6.9	7.4	6.7	6.9	6.7	6.6	6.4	6.1	3.5	3.4	3.3
Finland	3.9	4.5	5.3	5.7	6.0	6.1	6.4	6.3	6.0	5.8	3.6	3.5	3.4
Serbia and Montenegro	6.0	5.7	5.5	10.2	8.8	6.5	6.0	5.7	5.8	5.4	2.7	2.8	2.7
Netherlands	3.1	3.2	3.4	3.5	3.6	3.7	3.8	4.0	4.2	4.6	1.8	1.9	2.1
Bosnia and Herzegovina	11.5	11.6	11.8	12.2	11.6	8.8	7.9	6.0	5.2	4.6	3.0	2.6	2.3
Iran	3.8	3.5	3.6	3.7	3.8	4.2	4.7	5.1	5.0	4.4	2.5	2.4	2.2
Iceland	3.2	3.7	4.1	4.0	3.9	4.0	4.2	4.1	3.9	3.8	2.0	2.0	1.9
Other countries	48.7	45.2	45.2	48.5	51.0	54.8	61.4	68.1	74.4	80.7	38.2	42.0	45.7
Total	**157.5**	**158.0**	**165.1**	**178.7**	**184.3**	**185.9**	**197.7**	**204.7**	**213.3**	**222.3**	**103.9**	**108.5**	**112.7**

Note: For details on definitions and sources, please refer to the metadata at the end of the tables.

StatLink ⫘ http://dx.doi.org/10.1787/018365452075

Table B.1.5. **Stock of foreign population by nationality**

Thousands

POLAND

	2002	Of which: Women 2002
Ukraine	9.9	6.8
Russian Federation	4.3	3.1
Germany	3.7	1.5
Belarus	2.9	2.0
Viet Nam	2.1	0.8
Armenia	1.6	0.7
United States	1.3	0.5
Bulgaria	1.1	0.4
United Kingdom	1.0	0.3
France	1.0	0.3
Lithuania	0.9	0.6
Czech Republic	0.8	0.5
Italy	0.7	0.2
Greece	0.5	0.1
Kazakhstan	0.5	0.3
Other countries	16.9	6.7
Total	**49.2**	**24.7**

Note: For details on definitions and sources, please refer to the metadata at the end of the tables.

StatLink ⧉ http://dx.doi.org/10.1787/018421364653

Table B.1.5. **Stock of foreign population by nationality**

Thousands

PORTUGAL

	1996	1997	1998	1999	2000	2001	2002	2003	2004	2005	Of which: Women		
											2003	2004	2005
Brazil	20.0	20.0	19.9	20.9	22.2	48.7	61.6	66.3	78.6	70.4	27.1	28.7	31.4
Cape Verde	39.6	39.8	40.1	43.8	47.1	57.3	62.1	63.6	65.6	69.6	27.6	28.8	30.7
Ukraine	..	..	..	..	..	45.7	63.0	66.4	67.0	44.9	12.0	12.6	14.2
Angola	16.3	16.3	16.5	17.7	20.4	28.4	32.7	34.4	35.4	34.6	15.4	16.0	15.9
Guinea-Bissau	12.6	12.8	12.9	14.1	15.9	21.3	23.8	24.8	25.6	25.2	7.7	8.2	8.2
United Kingdom	12.0	12.3	12.7	13.3	14.1	15.0	15.9	16.9	18.0	19.0	7.5	8.4	8.9
Spain	9.3	8.8	10.2	11.2	12.2	13.6	14.6	15.3	15.9	16.4	7.7	8.1	8.3
Moldova	..	..	..	..	..	10.1	13.1	13.7	14.8	15.5	1.7	2.0	4.5
Germany	7.9	8.3	8.8	8.0	10.4	11.1	11.9	12.5	13.1	13.6	5.7	6.0	6.2
Sao Tome and Principe	4.2	4.3	4.4	4.8	5.4	8.3	9.6	10.1	10.9	11.9	4.9	5.3	6.0
Romania	0.1	0.1	0.2	0.2	0.4	8.4	11.3	12.0	12.5	11.1	2.3	2.5	3.8
France	5.1	5.4	5.8	6.5	7.2	7.8	8.4	8.9	9.3	9.6	4.2	4.5	4.6
China	2.4	2.4	2.5	2.7	3.3	7.3	8.5	9.1	9.7	9.4	3.3	3.5	3.9
United States	8.5	8.4	8.1	9.6	8.0	8.4	8.3	8.4	8.3	8.5	3.5	3.5	3.6
Mozambique	4.4	4.4	4.4	4.5	4.6	5.6	5.7	5.8	5.8	6.3	2.3	2.4	2.8
Other countries	30.5	31.8	31.4	33.5	36.3	63.9	73.2	76.5	78.6	66.2	25.9	27.0	26.6
Total	**172.9**	**175.3**	**177.8**	**190.9**	**207.6**	**360.8**	**423.8**	**444.6**	**469.1**	**432.0**	**158.9**	**167.3**	**179.6**

Note: For details on definitions and sources, please refer to the metadata at the end of the tables.

StatLink ⧉ http://dx.doi.org/10.1787/018424138307

INTERNATIONAL MIGRATION OUTLOOK: SOPEMI 2007 EDITION – ISBN 978-92-64-03285-9 – © OECD 2007

Table B.1.5. **Stock of foreign population by nationality**

Thousands

SLOVAK REPUBLIC

	1996	1997	1998	1999	2000	2001	2002	2003	2004	2005
Czech Republic	5.1	5.8	6.6	7.0	6.3	5.9	5.4	4.9	3.6	4.4
Ukraine	3.0	3.5	3.8	3.9	4.3	4.6	4.7	4.9	4.0	3.7
Poland	2.5	2.8	2.9	2.6	2.4	2.4	2.4	2.4	2.5	2.8
Former Yugoslavia	2.0	2.0	2.3	2.7	2.6	2.7	1.6	1.5	0.4	0.2
Other countries	11.6	10.7	12.8	13.4	13.2	13.8	15.5	15.5	11.7	14.5
Total	**24.1**	**24.8**	**28.4**	**29.5**	**28.8**	**29.4**	**29.5**	**29.2**	**22.3**	**25.6**

Note: For details on definitions and sources, please refer to the metadata at the end of the tables.

StatLink ⟪⟫ http://dx.doi.org/10.1787/018437063511

Table B.1.5. **Stock of foreign population by nationality**

Thousands

SPAIN

	1996	1997	1998	1999	2000	2001	2002	2003	2004	2005	Of which: Women		
											2003	2004	2005
Morocco	77.2	111.1	140.9	161.9	199.8	234.9	282.4	333.8	387.0	493.1	113.7	139.8	170.6
Ecuador	2.9	4.1	7.0	12.9	30.9	84.7	115.3	174.3	221.5	357.1	85.0	110.3	182.9
Colombia	7.9	8.4	10.4	13.6	24.7	48.7	71.2	107.5	137.4	204.3	63.2	81.0	118.1
Romania	1.4	2.4	3.5	5.1	11.0	24.9	33.7	54.7	83.4	192.1	20.8	34.3	84.4
United Kingdom	68.4	68.7	74.4	76.4	74.0	80.2	90.1	105.5	128.3	149.1	52.7	63.9	74.4
China	10.8	15.8	20.7	24.7	28.7	36.1	45.8	56.1	71.9	85.7	24.7	32.4	38.2
Italy	21.4	22.6	26.5	29.9	30.9	35.6	45.2	59.7	72.0	84.9	23.0	28.3	33.6
Peru	18.0	21.2	24.9	27.3	27.9	33.8	39.0	57.6	71.2	82.5	31.2	38.0	43.1
Argentina	18.2	17.2	17.0	9.4	16.6	20.4	27.9	43.3	56.2	82.4	21.2	28.2	40.5
Germany	45.9	49.9	58.1	60.8	60.6	62.5	65.8	68.0	69.7	71.5	34.0	34.9	36.0
Portugal	38.3	38.2	42.3	44.0	42.0	42.6	43.3	45.6	51.0	59.8	19.1	20.6	22.8
France	33.1	34.3	39.5	43.3	42.3	44.8	47.0	49.2	49.9	52.3	24.8	25.1	26.3
Dominican Republic	17.8	20.4	24.3	26.9	26.5	29.3	32.4	36.7	42.9	50.8	23.6	27.0	31.2
Cuba	7.8	10.5	13.2	16.6	19.2	21.5	24.2	27.3	30.7	36.1	15.7	17.6	19.9
Algeria	3.7	5.8	7.0	9.9	13.8	15.2	20.1	23.8	27.5	35.4	5.2	6.9	8.5
Other countries	166.1	179.2	209.8	238.7	247.0	293.8	340.4	404.0	476.6	701.8	181.1	218.7	320.5
Total	**539.0**	**609.8**	**719.6**	**801.3**	**895.7**	**1 109.1**	**1 324.0**	**1 647.0**	**1 977.3**	**2 738.9**	**739.2**	**907.1**	**1 250.9**

Note: For details on definitions and sources, please refer to the metadata at the end of the tables.

StatLink ⟪⟫ http://dx.doi.org/10.1787/018050645170

Table B.1.5. **Stock of foreign population by nationality**

Thousands

SWEDEN

	1996	1997	1998	1999	2000	2001	2002	2003	2004	2005	Of which: Women		
											2003	2004	2005
Finland	103.1	101.3	99.9	99.0	98.6	97.5	96.3	93.5	90.3	87.1	53.1	51.5	49.8
Norway	31.7	31.0	30.6	30.9	32.0	33.3	34.7	35.5	35.6	35.4	18.1	18.2	18.0
Denmark	26.0	25.4	25.0	25.0	25.6	26.6	28.1	29.7	31.2	32.9	12.4	12.9	13.6
Iraq	22.8	24.8	26.6	30.2	33.1	36.2	40.1	41.5	39.8	31.9	19.4	18.9	15.3
Germany	13.9	14.5	15.1	15.5	16.4	17.3	18.1	19.1	19.9	21.0	9.0	9.4	9.9
Poland	15.9	15.8	15.9	16.3	16.7	15.5	13.9	13.4	14.7	17.2	8.9	9.4	10.4
Serbia and Montenegro	0.0	0.0	0.0	0.0	0.0	0.0	0.0	18.6	18.2	17.1	8.9	8.7	8.1
United Kingdom	11.5	11.7	12.1	12.4	13.1	13.8	14.2	14.4	14.6	14.7	4.5	4.5	4.5
Bosnia and Herzegovina	55.4	54.8	44.5	34.2	22.8	19.7	17.0	15.5	14.8	13.7	7.8	7.5	6.9
Turkey	18.9	18.4	17.4	16.4	15.8	13.9	12.6	12.4	12.3	11.7	6.0	5.8	5.4
Iran	27.2	26.2	19.8	16.1	14.3	13.5	12.9	12.5	12.4	11.5	6.4	6.4	5.8
Thailand	4.9	5.1	5.3	5.5	5.8	6.3	6.8	8.3	9.8	11.2	6.6	7.9	9.0
Somalia	12.2	13.1	13.5	13.5	11.5	9.6	8.7	8.8	9.0	9.6	4.5	4.5	4.8
United States	9.4	9.4	9.5	9.6	10.0	10.0	9.6	9.4	9.3	9.2	4.2	4.1	4.0
Chile	12.4	11.9	11.4	10.8	10.3	9.9	9.4	9.1	8.9	8.6	4.0	3.9	3.7
Other countries	161.4	158.6	153.5	151.7	151.4	152.8	151.6	134.5	140.4	147.2	57.5	60.6	63.6
Total	**526.6**	**522.0**	**499.9**	**487.2**	**477.3**	**476.0**	**474.1**	**476.1**	**481.1**	**479.9**	**231.2**	**234.1**	**233.0**

Note: For details on definitions and sources, please refer to the metadata at the end of the tables.

StatLink 🔗 http://dx.doi.org/10.1787/018458886021

Table B.1.5. **Stock of foreign population by nationality**

Thousands

SWITZERLAND

	1996	1997	1998	1999	2000	2001	2002	2003	2004	2005	Of which: Women		
											2003	2004	2005
Italy	350.3	342.3	335.4	327.7	321.6	314.0	308.3	303.8	300.2	296.4	128.6	127.0	125.3
Serbia and Montenegro	..	..	..	189.4	190.7	194.7	198.1	199.8	199.2	196.2	..	..	..
Portugal	137.1	136.3	135.8	135.0	140.2	135.5	141.1	149.8	159.7	167.3	70.5	74.4	77.3
Germany	92.7	94.7	97.9	102.7	110.7	116.6	125.0	133.6	144.9	157.6	61.7	66.7	71.9
Turkey	79.4	79.6	79.5	79.9	79.5	79.5	78.8	77.7	76.6	75.4	36.0	35.4	34.8
Spain	97.7	94.0	90.4	86.8	83.8	81.0	78.9	76.8	74.3	71.4	34.7	33.6	32.3
France	54.2	55.0	56.1	58.0	61.1	61.5	63.2	65.0	67.0	69.0	30.6	31.5	32.4
FYROM	..	..	..	..	55.9	58.4	59.8	60.5	60.8	60.7	28.5	28.7	28.8
Bosnia and Herzegovina	..	..	..	..	44.3	45.7	46.0	45.4	44.8	43.2	22.3	21.9	21.2
Croatia	..	..	..	..	43.6	43.9	43.4	42.7	41.8	40.6	21.4	20.9	20.4
Austria	28.1	28.0	28.6	28.2	29.6	29.9	31.1	31.6	32.5	32.8	14.3	14.6	14.8
United Kingdom	18.3	18.3	18.7	19.6	20.8	22.2	22.8	23.4	24.1	24.9	9.9	10.2	10.5
Netherlands	13.9	13.9	13.8	13.9	14.4	14.6	15.0	15.2	15.4	15.8	7.1	7.1	7.3
United States	11.6	11.6	11.1	12.2	16.9	13.4	18.1	13.2	13.2	13.7	6.3	6.3	6.5
Belgium	6.5	6.6	6.9	7.1	7.5	7.9	8.0	8.2	8.5	8.8	4.0	4.1	4.2
Other countries	447.8	460.6	473.6	308.1	163.7	200.2	209.8	224.3	232.1	238.2	216.3	221.5	224.7
Total	**1 337.6**	**1 340.8**	**1 347.9**	**1 368.7**	**1 384.4**	**1 419.1**	**1 447.3**	**1 471.0**	**1 495.0**	**1 511.9**	**692.0**	**704.1**	**712.5**

Note: For details on definitions and sources, please refer to the metadata at the end of the tables.

StatLink 🔗 http://dx.doi.org/10.1787/018014872401

Table B.1.5. **Stock of foreign population by nationality**

Thousands

UNITED KINGDOM

	1996	1997	1998	1999	2000	2001	2002	2003	2004	2005	Of which: Women		
											2003	2004	2005
Ireland	441.0	446.0	448.0	442.0	404.0	436.0	403.0	367.0	368.0	369.0	197.0	206.0	204.0
India	128.0	110.0	139.0	149.0	153.0	132.0	145.0	154.0	171.0	190.0	83.0	92.0	97.0
Poland	..	..	..	..	..	34.0	24.0	34.0	48.0	110.0	19.0	26.0	56.0
United States	105.0	104.0	120.0	123.0	114.0	148.0	100.0	120.0	133.0	106.0	68.0	68.0	61.0
France	53.0	54.0	74.0	68.0	85.0	82.0	92.0	102.0	95.0	100.0	64.0	51.0	56.0
South Africa	22.0	24.0	39.0	50.0	..	68.0	64.0	95.0	92.0	100.0	49.0	49.0	54.0
Australia	50.0	62.0	50.0	55.0	75.0	67.0	75.0	73.0	80.0	79.0	42.0	41.0	42.0
Pakistan	78.0	68.0	69.0	73.0	94.0	82.0	97.0	83.0	86.0	95.0	43.0	38.0	43.0
Germany	53.0	59.0	75.0	85.0	64.0	59.0	68.0	70.0	96.0	100.0	40.0	59.0	61.0
Portugal	28.0	27.0	38.0	44.0	29.0	58.0	85.0	88.0	83.0	85.0	45.0	44.0	45.0
Italy	85.0	77.0	89.0	80.0	95.0	102.0	98.0	91.0	121.0	88.0	49.0	61.0	44.0
Zimbabwe	..	..	..	..	..	20.0	35.0	51.0	73.0	68.0	30.0	40.0	34.0
Bangladesh	43.0	63.0	69.0	78.0	55.0	70.0	61.0	48.0	69.0	64.0	28.0	27.0	30.0
Philippines	12.0	15.0	12.0	..	20.0	27.0	32.0	54.0	52.0	51.0	31.0	34.0	36.0
Ghana	..	..	..	..	..	31.0	27.0	35.0	30.0	38.0	17.0	18.0	20.0
Other countries	836.0	957.0	985.0	961.0	1 154.0	1 171.0	1 178.0	1 277.0	1 260.0	1 392.0	671.0	663.0	721.0
Total	**1 934.0**	**2 066.0**	**2 207.0**	**2 208.0**	**2 342.0**	**2 587.0**	**2 584.0**	**2 742.0**	**2 857.0**	**3 035.0**	**1 476.0**	**1 517.0**	**1 604.0**

Note: For details on definitions and sources, please refer to the metadata at the end of the tables.

StatLink ⟨⟩ http://dx.doi.org/10.1787/018121361606

Metadata related to Tables A.1.5. and B.1.5. **Foreign population**

Country	Comments	Source
Austria	Stock of foreign citizens recorded in the population register. *Reference date:* Annual average.	Population Register, Central Office of Statistics.
Belgium	Stock of foreign citizens recorded in the population register. Asylum seekers are recorded in a separate register. *Reference date:* 31 December.	Population register, National Statistical Office.
Czech Republic	Holders of a permanent residence permit (mainly for family reasons) or a long-term residence permit (1-year permit, renewable). *Reference date:* 31 December, except for 2004 where data are for 30 June.	Register of foreigners, Ministry of the Interior.
Denmark	Stock of foreign citizens recorded in the population register. Excludes asylum seekers and all persons with temporary residence permits. *Reference date:* 31 December.	Central population register, Statistics Denmark.
Finland	Stock of foreign citizens recorded in population register. Includes foreign persons of Finnish origin. *Reference date:* 30 September.	Central population register, Statistics Finland.
France	Foreigners with permanent residence in France. Includes permanent workers, trainees, students and their dependent families. Seasonal and cross-border workers are not included. *Reference dates:* 8 March 1999.	Census, National Institute for Statistics and Economic Studies (INSEE).
Germany	Stock of foreign citizens recorded in the population register. Includes asylum seekers living in private households. Excludes foreign-born persons of German origin *(Aussiedler)*. Decrease in 2004 is due to cross checking of residence register and central alien register. *Reference date:* 31 December. *Other comments:* Disaggregation by sex and nationality covers only those aged 16 and over.	Central population register, Federal Office of Statistics.
Greece	Labour Force Survey.	National Statistical Service of Greece.
Hungary	Holders of a permanent or a long-term residence permit. From 2000 on, registers have been purged of expired permits. *Reference date:* 31 December.	Register of foreigners, Ministry of the Interior.
Ireland	Estimates in Table A.1.5. are from the Labour Force Survey. Data by nationality (Table B.1.5.) are from the 2002 Census and refer to persons aged 15 years and over. *Reference date:* 28 April 2002 (2002 Census) and 2nd quarter of each year (Labour Force survey).	Central Statistics Office (CSO).
Italy	Holders of a residence permit. Children under 18 who are registered on their parents' permit are not counted. Data include foreigners who were regularised following the 1987-1988, 1990, 1995-1996, 1998 and 2002 programmes. In 1999 and 2000, figures include 139 601 and 116 253 regularised persons, respectively. Data for "Former Yugoslavia" refer to persons entering with a Yugoslav passeport (with no other specification). *Reference date:* 31 December.	Ministry of the Interior.
Japan	Foreigners staying in Japan more than 90 days and registered in population registers. *Reference date:* 31 December.	Register of foreigners, Ministry of Justice, Immigration Bureau.
Korea	Foreigners staying in Korea more than 90 days and registered in population registers. The large increase in 2003 is mainly due to a regularisation program introduced in mid 2003.	Ministry of Justice.
Luxembourg	Stock of foreign citizens recorded in population register. Does not include visitors (less than three months) and cross-border workers. *Reference date:* 31 December.	Population register, Central Office of Statistics and Economic Studies (Statec).
Netherlands	Stock of foreign citizens recorded in the population register. Figures include administrative corrections and asylum seekers (except those staying in reception centres). *Reference date:* 31 December.	Population register, Central Bureau of Statistics (CBS).

Metadata related to Tables A.1.5. and B.1.5. **Foreign population** (*cont.*)

Country	Comments	Source
Norway	Stock of foreign citizens recorded in population register, including asylum seekers waiting decisions on their application for refugee status. *Reference date*: 31 December.	CPR, Statistics Norway.
Poland	Excluding foreign permanent residents who had been staying abroad for more than 12 months and foreign temporary residents who had been staying in Poland for less than 12 months. *Reference date:* May 2002.	Census, Central Statistical Office.
Portugal	Holders of a valid residence permit. Data for 1996 include 21 800 permits delivered following the regularisation programmes. Data for 2001 and 2002 include permanent permits delivered following the 2001 regularisation programme, 126 901 and 47 657, respectively. Data for 2004 and 2005 include work visas issued under a specific regularisation procedure and under the specific regularisation programme of Brazilian workers.	Ministry of the Interior; National Statistical Office (INE).
Slovak Republic	Holders of a long-term or a permanent residence permit.	Register of foreigners, Ministry of the Interior.
Spain	Holders of a residence permit, excluding those with temporary permits (less that six months duration) and students. In 1996 and 2001, data include 21 300 and 234 600 permits respectively delivered following the 1996 and 2001 regularisation programme. *Reference date*: 31 December.	Ministry of the Interior.
Sweden	Stock of foreign citizens recorded in the population register. *Reference date*: 31 December.	Population register, Statistics Sweden.
Switzerland	Stock of all those with residence or settlement permits (permits B and C respectively). Holders of an L-permit (short duration) are also included if their stay in the country is longer than 12 months. Does not include seasonal or cross-border workers. *Reference date*: 31 December	Register of foreigners, Federal Office of Immigration, Integration and Emigration.
United Kingdom	Foreign residents. Those with unknown nationality from the New Commonwealth are not included (around 10 000 to 15 000 persons). There is a break in the series as 2004 data are calculated using a new weighting system. *Reference date*: 31 December. *Other comments*: Figures are rounded and not published if less than 10 000.	Labour Force Survey, Home Office.

Acquisition of Nationality

Naturalisations must be taken into account in the analysis of the population of foreigners and nationals. Also, differing national approaches to naturalisation between countries must be considered when making international comparisons. In France and Belgium, for example, where foreigners can fairly easily acquire nationality, increases in the foreign population through immigration and births can eventually contribute to a significant rise in the native population. However, in countries where naturalisation is more difficult, increases in immigration and births amongst foreigners manifest themselves almost exclusively as rises in the foreign population. In addition, changes in rules regarding naturalisation can have significant numerical effects. For example, during the 1980s, a number of OECD countries made naturalisation easier and this resulted in noticeable falls in the foreign population (and rises in the population of nationals).

However, host-country legislation is not the only factor affecting naturalisation. For example, where naturalisation involves forfeiting citizenship of the country of origin, there may be incentives to remain as a foreign citizen. Where the difference between remaining a foreign citizen or becoming a national is marginal, naturalisation may largely be influenced by the time and effort required to make the application, and the symbolic and political value individuals attach to being citizens of one country or another.

Data on naturalisations are usually readily available from administrative sources. As with other administrative data, resource constraints in processing applications may result in a backlog of unprocessed applications which are not reflected in the figures. The statistics generally cover all means of acquiring the nationality of a country. These include standard naturalisation procedures subject to criteria such as age or residency, etc. as well as situations where nationality is acquired through a declaration or by option (following marriage, adoption or other situations related to residency or descent), recovery of former nationality and other special means of acquiring the nationality of the country).

Table A.1.6. **Acquisition of nationality in selected OECD countries**
Numbers and percentages

	1996	1997	1998	1999	2000	2001	2002	2003	2004	2005
Countries where the national/foreigner distinction is prevalent										
Austria	15 627	15 792	17 786	24 678	24 320	31 731	36 011	44 694	41 645	34 876
% of foreign population	2.3	2.3	2.6	3.6	3.5	4.4	4.8	5.9	5.4	4.4
Belgium	24 581	31 687	34 034	24 273	62 082	62 982	46 417	33 709	34 754	31 512
% of foreign population	2.7	3.5	3.8	2.7	6.9	7.3	5.5	4.0	4.0	3.5
Czech Republic	..	..	..	8 107	8 335	6 321	4 532	3 410	5 020	2 626
% of foreign population	..	..	..	3.7	3.6	3.1	2.1	1.5	2.1	0.9
Denmark	7 283	5 482	10 262	12 416	18 811	11 902	17 300	6 583	14 976	10 197
% of foreign population	3.3	2.3	4.1	4.8	7.3	4.6	6.5	2.5	5.5	3.8
Finland	981	1 439	4 017	4 730	2 977	2 720	3 049	4 526	6 880	5 683
% of foreign population	1.3	1.8	4.7	5.4	3.3	2.8	2.9	4.3	6.5	5.1
France	..	..	..	147 522	150 026	127 548	128 092	144 640	168 826	154 827
% of foreign population	..	..	..	..	4.6	..	..	..	..	..
Germany	86 356	82 913	106 790	142 670	186 688	178 098	154 547	140 731	127 153	117 241
% of foreign population	1.2	1.1	1.4	2.0	2.5	2.4	2.1	1.9	1.9	1.6
Hungary	12 266	8 658	6 435	6 066	7 538	8 590	3 369	5 261	5 432	9 822
% of foreign population	8.8	6.1	4.3	4.0	4.9	7.8	2.7	4.5	4.2	6.9
Italy	8 823	9 789	12 016	11 335	9 563	10 382	10 685	13 406	11 934	..
% of foreign population	1.2	1.0	1.2	1.0	0.7	0.8	0.7	0.9	0.5	..
Japan	14 495	15 061	14 779	16 120	15 812	15 291	14 339	17 633	16 336	15 251
% of foreign population	1.1	1.1	1.0	1.1	1.0	0.9	0.8	1.0	1.0	0.8
Luxembourg	779	749	631	549	684	496	754	785	841	966
% of foreign population	0.6	0.5	0.4	0.4	0.4	0.3	0.5	0.5	0.5	0.5
Netherlands	82 700	59 830	59 170	62 090	49 968	46 667	45 321	28 799	26 173	28 488
% of foreign population	11.4	8.8	8.7	9.4	7.7	7.0	6.6	4.1	3.7	4.1
Norway	12 237	12 037	9 244	7 988	9 517	10 838	9 041	7 867	8 154	12 655
% of foreign population	7.6	7.6	5.8	4.8	5.3	5.9	4.9	4.0	4.0	5.7
Poland	..	..	871	1 000	975	766	1 186	1 634	1 937	2 866
% of foreign population	..	..	..	..	..	..	..	3.3	..	..
Portugal	1 154	1 364	519	946	721	1 082	1 369	1 747	1 346	939
% of foreign population	0.7	0.8	0.3	0.5	0.4	0.5	0.4	0.4	0.3	0.2
Slovak Republic	..	..	..	..	..	..	..	3 492	4 016	1 393
% of foreign population	..	..	..	..	..	..	..	11.8	13.8	6.3
Spain	8 433	10 311	13 177	16 394	11 999	16 743	21 810	26 556	38 335	42 830
% of foreign population	1.7	1.9	2.2	2.3	1.5	1.9	2.0	2.0	2.3	2.2
Sweden	25 552	28 867	46 502	37 777	43 474	36 397	37 792	33 006	26 769	39 573
% of foreign population	4.8	5.5	8.9	7.6	8.9	7.6	7.9	7.0	5.9	8.2
Switzerland	19 375	19 170	21 280	20 363	28 700	27 586	36 515	35 424	35 685	38 437
% of foreign population	1.5	1.4	1.6	1.5	2.1	2.0	2.6	2.4	2.4	2.6
United Kingdom	43 069	37 010	53 525	54 902	82 210	90 295	120 125	125 535	140 705	161 780
% of foreign population	2.2	1.9	2.6	2.5	3.7	3.9	4.6	4.9	5.1	5.7
Countries where native-born / foreign-born distinction is prevalent										
Australia	111 637	108 266	112 343	76 474	70 836	72 070	86 289	79 164	87 049	93 095
Canada	155 645	154 624	134 485	158 753	214 568	167 353	141 588	155 117	192 590	196 291
Mexico	655	1 061	1 795	1 625	3 227	1 094	4 737	4 245	5 554	8 527
New Zealand	..	15 757	20 173	34 470	29 609	23 535	19 469	18 296	22 142	24 341
United States	1 044 689	598 225	463 060	839 944	888 788	608 205	573 708	463 204	537 151	604 280
EU25, Norway and Switzerland	..	..	..	**582 806**	**697 613**	**670 378**	**676 729**	**660 171**	**689 491**	**687 035**
North America	**1 200 989**	**753 910**	**599 340**	**1 000 322**	**1 106 583**	**776 652**	**720 033**	**622 566**	**735 295**	**809 098**

Note: Statistics cover all means of acquiring the nationality of a country, except where otherwise indicated. These include standard naturalisation procedures subject to criteria such as age, residency, etc., as well as situations where nationality is acquired through a declaration or by option (following marriage, adoption, or other situations related to residency or descent), recovery of former nationality and other special means of acquiring the nationality of a country. For details on definitions and sources, refer to the metadata at the end of Tables B.1.6. The naturalisation rate ("% of foreign population") gives the number of persons acquiring the nationality of the country as a percentage of the stock of the foreign population at the beginning of the year.

StatLink http://dx.doi.org/10.1787/015626402766

Table B.1.6. **Acquisition of nationality by country of former nationality**
AUSTRALIA

	1996	1997	1998	1999	2000	2001	2002	2003	2004	2005
United Kingdom	35 431	27 294	23 080	13 529	14 592	12 474	16 411	14 854	17 201	20 127
India	2 638	2 563	3 358	2 695	2 381	2 335	2 510	3 051	3 638	5 027
New Zealand	11 724	9 982	8 764	6 320	6 676	11 007	17 334	13 994	13 052	9 363
China	4 250	16 173	21 053	10 947	7 664	6 890	6 416	7 126	7 072	7 798
South Africa	1 262	1 578	1 880	1 606	2 253	2 992	3 922	3 998	4 908	5 085
Philippines	4 021	3 815	3 688	2 606	2 349	2 211	2 849	2 885	3 019	3 653
Iraq	..	1 591	2 877	1 698	1 853	1 862	2 182	1 502	1 271	2 115
Viet Nam	7 741	5 083	4 685	3 083	3 441	1 953	2 090	1 676	2 215	2 056
Malaysia	..	764	719	1 002	1 154	1 057	1 504	1 619	1 846	1 798
Sri Lanka	1 644	1 620	2 049	1 707	1 832	1 672	1 362	1 328	1 582	1 711
United States	2 272	1 701	1 565	1 083	989	1 004	1 318	1 194	1 409	1 648
Fiji	1 815	1 721	1 934	1 665	1 379	1 398	1 567	1 509	1 582	1 548
Ireland	1 688	1 278	1 167	724	698	682	852	734	905	941
Iran	870	891	1 143	876	755	827	864	928	644	877
Bosnia and Herzegovina	..	1 637	2 728	1 841	1 531	2 661	2 194	1 475	1 490	822
Other countries	36 281	30 575	31 653	25 092	21 289	21 045	22 914	21 291	25 215	28 526
Total	**111 637**	**108 266**	**112 343**	**76 474**	**70 836**	**72 070**	**86 289**	**79 164**	**87 049**	**93 095**

Note: For details on definitions and sources, please refer to the metadata at the end of the tables.

StatLink ⬛⬛ http://dx.doi.org/10.1787/018461487015

Table B.1.6. **Acquisition of nationality by country of former nationality**
AUSTRIA

	1996	1997	1998	1999	2000	2001	2002	2003	2004	2005
Turkey	7 492	5 064	5 664	10 324	6 720	10 046	12 623	13 665	13 004	9 545
Bosnia and Herzegovina	645	734	993	1 536	2 761	3 856	5 913	8 268	8 657	7 026
Serbia and Montenegro	847	1 854	1 640	3 853	2 810	4 296	4 806	9 836	7 245	6 681
Croatia	769	741	1 102	1 008	1 642	1 986	2 537	2 588	2 212	2 276
Romania	691	1 096	1 500	1 635	2 682	2 813	1 774	2 096	1 373	1 128
FYROM	105	206	320	257	241	471	574	786	803	991
Poland	496	660	749	531	545	606	930	768	768	443
Russian Federation	89	112	181	137	168	166	161	83	194	235
Bulgaria	159	185	318	302	385	386	321	364	274	221
Ukraine	37	31	73	38	49	71	104	146	230	182
Slovak Republic	141	198	283	186	267	304	318	196	174	171
Germany	135	156	151	89	102	106	85	106	135	135
Hungary	297	332	412	407	351	315	246	262	174	120
Czech Republic	98	182	256	193	273	223	149	124	96	79
Slovenia	163	99	87	74	103	128	160	96	128	63
Other countries	3 463	4 142	4 057	4 108	5 221	5 958	5 310	5 310	6 178	5 580
Total	**15 627**	**15 792**	**17 786**	**24 678**	**24 320**	**31 731**	**36 011**	**44 694**	**41 645**	**34 876**

Note: For details on definitions and sources, please refer to the metadata at the end of the tables.

StatLink ⬛⬛ http://dx.doi.org/10.1787/018468403672

INTERNATIONAL MIGRATION OUTLOOK: SOPEMI 2007 EDITION – ISBN 978-92-64-03285-9 – © OECD 2007

Table B.1.6. **Acquisition of nationality by country of former nationality**
BELGIUM

	1996	1997	1998	1999	2000	2001	2002	2003	2004	2005
Morocco	7 912	11 076	13 484	9 133	21 917	24 018	15 832	10 565	8 704	7 977
Turkey	6 609	6 884	6 177	4 402	17 282	14 401	7 805	5 186	4 467	3 602
Italy	1 940	1 726	1 536	1 187	3 650	3 451	2 341	2 646	2 271	2 086
Democratic Republic of the Congo	442	756	1 202	1 890	2 993	2 991	2 809	1 796	2 585	1 876
Former Yugoslavia	0	438	499	756	2 187	2 487	2 678	1 593	2 155	1 823
France	539	530	491	363	948	1 025	856	698	780	772
Algeria	556	608	672	520	1 071	1 281	926	826	830	739
Rwanda	..	..	..	..	..	794	1 012	557	571	700
Netherlands	259	292	249	234	492	601	646	522	665	672
Poland	175	220	277	253	551	677	630	460	465	470
Philippines	115	147	162	190	315	323	388	283	442	370
Romania	115	358	387	267	403	321	294	277	314	332
Pakistan	91	133	155	131	75	474	404	270	298	306
Tunisia	406	566	585	301	859	729	521	383	406	297
Russian Federation	..	..	..	..	..	265	301	237	339	297
Other countries	5 422	7 953	8 158	4 646	9 339	9 144	8 974	7 410	9 462	9 193
Total	**24 581**	**31 687**	**34 034**	**24 273**	**62 082**	**62 982**	**46 417**	**33 709**	**34 754**	**31 512**

Note: For details on definitions and sources, please refer to the metadata at the end of the tables.

StatLink ⋙ *http://dx.doi.org/10.1787/018481856665*

Table B.1.6. **Acquisition of nationality by country of former nationality**
CANADA

	1996	1997	1998	1999	2000	2001	2002	2003	2004	2005
China	10 563	11 535	14 110	17 991	24 310	18 555	16 973	20 558	25 189	25 501
India	10 756	10 766	8 804	11 446	19 402	14 788	13 136	14 530	21 622	21 743
Pakistan	2 598	2 867	2 394	3 226	8 478	8 904	7 654	6 622	10 454	12 237
Philippines	9 771	12 703	11 069	11 565	14 134	9 560	7 705	8 289	9 031	10 851
United Kingdom	8 944	11 484	6 177	4 741	5 278	3 586	3 003	4 399	7 784	6 916
Korea	1 679	1 205	1 395	2 129	3 724	3 129	3 503	4 357	5 884	5 382
United States	3 120	2 760	2 143	2 429	3 180	2 443	2 362	3 309	5 273	5 014
Iran	3 226	2 602	2 631	3 645	6 637	6 449	5 823	5 249	4 637	4 950
Sri Lanka	6 288	4 925	6 114	6 302	6 692	4 448	3 555	3 312	5 091	4 451
Romania	2 294	3 297	2 856	3 824	4 571	3 404	2 694	3 128	3 296	4 433
Jamaica	3 039	2 245	2 010	2 390	2 944	2 678	2 218	2 942	4 468	3 896
Chinese Taipei	3 774	4 751	4 351	4 818	8 945	6 750	4 745	4 062	3 272	2 798
Hong Kong, China	15 110	9 751	13 096	15 050	17 886	11 200	6 188	4 794	3 996	2 045
Viet Nam	4 579	5 528	4 150	3 967	4 128	2 750	2 192	1 814	1 885	1 851
Portugal	2 547	1 998	1 498	1 416	2 394	2 920	1 428	1 252	2 179	1 687
Other countries	67 357	66 207	51 687	63 814	81 865	65 789	58 409	66 500	78 529	82 536
Total	**155 645**	**154 624**	**134 485**	**158 753**	**214 568**	**167 353**	**141 588**	**155 117**	**192 590**	**196 291**

Note: For details on definitions and sources, please refer to the metadata at the end of the tables.

StatLink ⋙ *http://dx.doi.org/10.1787/018503441385*

Table B.1.6. **Acquisition of nationality by country of former nationality**
CZECH REPUBLIC

	1999	2000	2001	2002	2003	2004	2005
Slovak Republic	6 278	5 377	3 593	2 109	989	1 741	1 259
Ukraine	263	373	173	251	419	446	239
Former Czechoslovakia	798	1 899	1 607	1 273	1 154	1 784	190
Poland	23	8	163	304	170	298	167
Romania	38	58	140	109	116	101	143
Russian Federation	100	71	87	65	7	86	134
Bosnia and Herzegovina	10	11	13	20	47	62	63
Viet Nam	87	101	76	29	46	47	62
Bulgaria	84	105	132	95	54	62	48
Kazakhstan	3	17	25	43	156	89	43
Belarus	7	13	19	13	14	21	35
Armenia	11	8	11	8	18	23	32
Serbia and Montenegro	50	12	35	16	14	42	26
FYROM	16	18	28	18	21	19	13
Moldova	. .	. .	. .	. .	. .	. .	11
Other countries	339	264	219	179	185	199	161
Total	**8 107**	**8 335**	**6 321**	**4 532**	**3 410**	**5 020**	**2 626**

Note: For details on definitions and sources, please refer to the metadata at the end of the tables.

StatLink http://dx.doi.org/10.1787/018522586184

Table B.1.6. **Acquisition of nationality by country of former nationality**
DENMARK

	1996	1997	1998	1999	2000	2001	2002	2003	2004	2005
Somalia	32	17	159	215	1 189	1 074	2 263	324	2 022	1 709
Former Yugoslavia	629	291	695	709	1 523	1 134	3 399	1 245	4 349	1 699
Iraq	339	244	718	918	2 210	871	1 161	153	1 015	961
Turkey	917	1 036	1 243	3 154	2 787	3 130	2 418	2 158	732	878
China	42	32	117	169	228	195	289	203	339	382
Sri Lanka	765	376	613	523	819	365	594	119	678	332
Iran	829	553	969	914	1 105	437	519	120	505	317
Pakistan	220	149	284	463	545	297	573	94	332	305
Afghanistan	29	15	101	98	276	215	301	40	367	282
Viet Nam	200	126	365	439	647	318	508	280	318	232
Morocco	201	110	248	322	485	213	313	69	244	147
Germany	126	138	173	197	240	129	174	82	178	144
Lebanon	314	160	811	601	1 099	309	376	69	219	140
Thailand	65	44	85	137	214	124	172	62	180	114
Poland	237	130	241	173	201	126	309	130	186	103
Other countries	2 338	2 061	3 440	3 384	5 243	2 965	3 931	1 435	3 312	2 452
Total	**7 283**	**5 482**	**10 262**	**12 416**	**18 811**	**11 902**	**17 300**	**6 583**	**14 976**	**10 197**

Note: For details on definitions and sources, please refer to the metadata at the end of the tables.

StatLink http://dx.doi.org/10.1787/018608614507

Table B.1.6. **Acquisition of nationality by country of former nationality**
FINLAND

	1996	1997	1998	1999	2000	2001	2002	2003	2004	2005
Former Soviet Union	52	44	138	135	48	51	56	85	138	. .
Other countries	929	1 395	3 879	4 595	2 929	2 669	2 993	4 441	6 742	5 683
Total	**981**	**1 439**	**4 017**	**4 730**	**2 977**	**2 720**	**3 049**	**4 526**	**6 880**	**5 683**

Note: For details on definitions and sources, please refer to the metadata at the end of the tables.

StatLink http://dx.doi.org/10.1787/018660324333

INTERNATIONAL MIGRATION OUTLOOK: SOPEMI 2007 EDITION – ISBN 978-92-64-03285-9 – © OECD 2007

Table B.1.6. **Acquisition of nationality by country of former nationality**
FRANCE

	1999	2000	2001	2002	2003	2004	2005
Morocco	38 298	37 795	34 922	33 967	36 875	32 878	37 848
Algeria	15 743	17 627	15 498	15 711	20 245	25 474	25 435
Turkey	11 380	12 137	10 755	10 468	10 492	9 464	13 618
Tunisia	12 467	12 763	10 251	9 956	11 412	9 472	12 012
Portugal	13 151	11 201	9 182	8 844	9 576	3 753	8 888
Haiti	1 711	1 920	1 571	2 082	2 734	2 367	2 744
Serbia and Montenegro	2 249	2 358	1 880	1 902	2 129	2 459	2 737
Democratic Republic of the Congo	1 495	1 765	1 401	1 572	2 012	2 647	2 631
Congo	932	1 083	1 100	1 475	1 769	2 005	2 390
Senegal	1 530	1 595	1 463	1 858	2 185	2 491	2 345
Cameroon	1 400	1 556	1 381	1 770	2 196	2 267	2 081
Sri Lanka	1 439	1 819	1 345	1 377	1 748	1 992	2 011
Côte d'Ivoire	1 113	1 409	1 194	1 495	1 869	2 143	1 987
Cambodia	2 843	2 958	2 241	1 861	1 734	1 515	1 818
Madagascar	1 288	1 406	1 281	1 352	1 628	1 728	1 440
Other countries	29 396	32 064	26 166	27 144	31 325	32 594	31 876
Total	**136 435**	**141 456**	**121 631**	**122 834**	**139 930**	**135 249**	**151 861**

Note: For details on definitions and sources, please refer to the metadata at the end of the tables.
StatLink http://dx.doi.org/10.1787/018682422320

Table B.1.6. **Acquisition of nationality by country of former nationality**
GERMANY

	1996	1997	1998	1999	2000	2001	2002	2003	2004	2005
Turkey	46 294	42 420	59 664	103 900	82 861	76 573	64 631	56 244	44 465	32 661
Serbia and Montenegro	2 733	1 989	2 404	3 120	9 776	12 000	8 375	5 504	3 539	8 824
Iran	649	919	1 171	1 529	14 410	12 020	13 026	9 440	6 362	4 482
Morocco	2 918	4 010	4 981	4 312	5 008	4 425	3 800	4 118	3 820	3 684
Afghanistan	1 819	1 475	1 200	1 355	4 773	5 111	4 750	4 948	4 077	3 133
Lebanon	784	1 159	1 782	2 491	5 673	4 486	3 300	2 651	2 265	1 969
Bosnia and Herzegovina	1 847	995	3 469	3 745	4 002	3 791	2 357	1 770	2 103	1 907
Croatia	2 268	1 789	2 198	1 536	3 316	3 931	2 974	2 048	1 689	1 287
Viet Nam	3 464	3 129	3 452	2 270	4 489	3 014	1 482	1 423	1 371	1 278
Other countries	23 580	25 028	26 469	18 412	52 380	52 747	49 852	52 585	57 462	58 016
Total	**86 356**	**82 913**	**106 790**	**142 670**	**186 688**	**178 098**	**154 547**	**140 731**	**127 153**	**117 241**

Note: For details on definitions and sources, please refer to the metadata at the end of the tables.
StatLink http://dx.doi.org/10.1787/018547506865

Table B.1.6. **Acquisition of nationality by country of former nationality**
HUNGARY

	1996	1997	1998	1999	2000	2001	2002	2003	2004	2005
Romania	8 549	5 229	3 842	3 463	4 231	5 644	2 238	3 415	3 605	6 869
Former Soviet Union	1 227	788	713	874	1 015	1 143	434	721	884	1 323
Former Yugoslavia	1 999	1 610	1 082	1 135	1 655	1 302	487	794	557	996
Other countries	491	1 030	799	594	637	501	210	331	386	634
Total	**12 266**	**8 658**	**6 435**	**6 066**	**7 538**	**8 590**	**3 369**	**5 261**	**5 432**	**9 822**

Note: For details on definitions and sources, please refer to the metadata at the end of the tables.
StatLink http://dx.doi.org/10.1787/018723752021

Table B.1.6. **Acquisition of nationality by country of former nationality**
ITALY

	1996	1997	1998	1999	2000	2001	2002	2003	2004
Morocco	549	570	634	638	573	579	624	1 132	1 046
Albania	259	438	535	748	521	687	703	830	882
Romania	821	796	1 086	936	665	855	968	977	847
Poland	378	422	469	502	448	475	519	677	619
Brazil	268	339	537	461	512	619	604	726	579
Cuba	70	140	357	379	377	512	542	646	539
Argentina	321	335	345	255	240	316	411	541	515
Switzerland	608	1 005	952	836	724	533	514	546	506
Russian Federation	0	0	0	452	347	384	439	463	436
Colombia	152	214	292	245	240	322	300	453	360
Dominican Republic	548	580	694	423	377	354	393	409	317
Egypt	287	220	287	270	266	235	195	264	283
Tunisia	243	205	256	237	208	215	175	271	258
Venezuela	57	94	107	113	121	121	215	252	255
Peru	167	196	326	252	228	263	305	383	253
Other countries	4 095	4 235	5 139	4 588	3 716	3 912	3 778	4 836	4 239
Total	**8 823**	**9 789**	**12 016**	**11 335**	**9 563**	**10 382**	**10 685**	**13 406**	**11 934**

Note: For details on definitions and sources, please refer to the metadata at the end of the tables.

StatLink ᴍᴎ𝒔ᴾ *http://dx.doi.org/10.1787/018744748707*

Table B.1.6. **Acquisition of nationality by country of former nationality**
JAPAN

	1996	1997	1998	1999	2000	2001	2002	2003	2004	2005
Korea	9 898	9 678	9 561	10 059	9 842	10 295	9 188	11 778	11 031	9 689
China	3 976	4 729	4 637	5 335	5 245	4 377	4 442	4 722	4 122	4 427
Other countries	621	654	581	726	725	619	709	1 133	1 183	1 135
Total	**14 495**	**15 061**	**14 779**	**16 120**	**15 812**	**15 291**	**14 339**	**17 633**	**16 336**	**15 251**

Note: For details on definitions and sources, please refer to the metadata at the end of the tables.

StatLink ᴍᴎ𝒔ᴾ *http://dx.doi.org/10.1787/018745304524*

Table B.1.6. **Acquisition of nationality by country of former nationality**
LUXEMBOURG

	1996	1997	1998	1999	2000	2001	2002	2003	2004	2005
Belgium	65	64	48	53	72	39	87	73	83	101
Italy	193	192	149	94	157	105	119	120	111	97
Germany	55	60	44	41	50	45	47	50	62	79
France	85	79	53	43	52	33	65	57	44	51
Netherlands	20	17	15	11	14	13	11	17	6	7
Other countries	361	337	322	307	339	261	425	468	535	631
Total	**779**	**749**	**631**	**549**	**684**	**496**	**754**	**785**	**841**	**966**

Note: For details on definitions and sources, please refer to the metadata at the end of the tables.

StatLink ᴍᴎ𝒔ᴾ *http://dx.doi.org/10.1787/018762530785*

INTERNATIONAL MIGRATION OUTLOOK: SOPEMI 2007 EDITION – ISBN 978-92-64-03285-9 – © OECD 2007

Table B.1.6. **Acquisition of nationality by country of former nationality**

NETHERLANDS

	1996	1997	1998	1999	2000	2001	2002	2003	2004	2005
Morocco	15 600	10 480	11 250	14 220	13 471	12 721	12 033	7 126	5 873	7 086
Turkey	30 700	21 190	13 480	5 210	4 708	5 513	5 391	3 726	4 026	3 493
Suriname	4 450	3 020	2 990	3 190	2 008	2 025	1 957	1 242	1 421	2 031
China	1 394	975	800	977	1 002	1 111	908	722	739	1 291
Former Soviet Union	289	298	537	1 021	681	544	411	296	296	660
Afghanistan	360	217	905	1 847	945	803	1 118	982	801	550
Russian Federation	302	288	289	489	422	335	347	207	242	521
Former Yugoslavia	2 156	3 356	2 795	2 577	1 163	764	538	323	378	424
Germany	780	560	560	580	508	573	608	445	297	349
Poland	1 129	827	677	688	587	597	530	318	212	347
Iraq	854	798	2 721	3 834	2 403	2 315	2 367	832	489	333
Indonesia	436	314	368	514	456	416	380	291	203	293
Romania	519	203	179	157	161	162	164	106	109	287
United States	489	410	261	161	160	168	225	181	181	267
Egypt	1 080	550	390	500	443	528	437	190	97	238
Other countries	22 162	16 344	20 968	26 125	20 850	18 092	17 907	11 812	10 809	10 318
Total	**82 700**	**59 830**	**59 170**	**62 090**	**49 968**	**46 667**	**45 321**	**28 799**	**26 173**	**28 488**

Note: For details on definitions and sources, please refer to the metadata at the end of the tables.

StatLink ☜ http://dx.doi.org/10.1787/018771181836

Table B.1.6. **Acquisition of nationality by country of former nationality**

NEW ZEALAND

	1997	1998	1999	2000	2001	2002	2003	2004	2005
China	1 346	2 232	4 687	3 752	2 579	1 896	2 032	2 849	3 323
India	520	895	1 779	1 847	1 376	1 350	1 255	2 127	2 905
South Africa	937	1 181	1 645	2 010	2 028	1 973	1 992	2 407	2 425
United Kingdom	2 744	3 031	4 212	3 670	3 019	2 187	2 266	2 377	2 423
Fiji	808	739	1 104	1 253	1 273	1 139	1 047	1 452	1 543
Korea	1 238	1 072	2 314	1 982	1 053	685	642	1 099	1 523
Samoa	1 495	1 663	1 649	1 702	1 590	1 307	1 189	1 065	1 153
Philippines	329	403	1 007	949	829	652	555	702	844
Former Soviet Union	162	338	879	695	508	392	365	489	554
Iraq	261	473	1 699	1 047	528	434	509	516	477
Sri Lanka	213	363	836	774	738	568	472	511	436
Chinese Taipei	1 010	1 365	3 213	1 970	1 619	1 069	546	355	414
United States	282	288	427	363	281	335	348	335	268
Hong Kong, China	1 251	1 416	1 600	1 270	740	539	255	259	223
Former Yugoslavia	513	1 223	1 507	945	404	315	372	262	185
Other countries	2 648	3 491	5 912	5 380	4 970	4 628	4 451	5 337	5 645
Total	**15 757**	**20 173**	**34 470**	**29 609**	**23 535**	**19 469**	**18 296**	**22 142**	**24 341**

Note: For details on definitions and sources, please refer to the metadata at the end of the tables.

StatLink ☜ http://dx.doi.org/10.1787/018806862518

Table B.1.6. **Acquisition of nationality by country of former nationality**
NORWAY

	1996	1997	1998	1999	2000	2001	2002	2003	2004	2005
Former Yugoslavia	554	520	560	1 176	1 322	1 199	614	310	303	852
Pakistan	1 530	1 583	1 097	106	1 077	409	829	497	568	694
Turkey	836	837	705	170	523	356	412	398	393	385
Philippines	315	360	155	199	157	261	299	265	249	322
Sweden	112	167	154	241	246	249	216	211	221	276
Morocco	318	294	154	90	131	154	160	86	235	225
India	313	274	157	232	188	235	230	196	207	223
Viet Nam	1 446	1 276	781	651	738	594	292	210	222	216
Denmark	91	143	149	158	170	162	108	129	167	166
Germany	41	63	55	73	74	68	95	75	74	129
Poland	267	282	192	209	196	159	165	167	171	126
Chile	531	416	240	252	156	172	234	138	141	121
China	383	348	279	315	156	113	135	84	82	109
United Kingdom	162	142	129	94	104	57	83	68	78	92
Korea	122	109	146	144	113	143	106	74	93	82
Other countries	5 216	5 223	4 291	3 878	4 166	6 507	5 063	4 959	4 950	8 637
Total	**12 237**	**12 037**	**9 244**	**7 988**	**9 517**	**10 838**	**9 041**	**7 867**	**8 154**	**12 655**

Note: For details on definitions and sources, please refer to the metadata at the end of the tables.

StatLink ‌ http://dx.doi.org/10.1787/018785126640

Table B.1.6. **Acquisition of nationality by country of former nationality**
POLAND

	1998	1999	2000	2001	2002	2003	2004	2005
Ukraine	14	15	46	62	214	431	538	759
Belarus	13	15	25	31	54	108	129	316
Russian Federation	16	24	23	14	22	52	145	257
Germany	66	85	101	47	49	60	62	156
Israel	114	138	112	84	91	101	162	113
Sweden	10	8	10	13	30	107	81	90
Canada	64	74	44	23	22	46	36	73
Kazakhstan	39	49	54	43	53	68	38	62
United States	30	30	26	11	9	32	41	59
Syria	20	30	22	18	27	9	37	57
Bulgaria	61	47	50	29	30	41	32	54
Algeria	11	6	11	11	17	6	12	47
Serbia and Montenegro	15	25	18	25	19	11	12	37
Lithuania	39	52	95	64	93	126	85	36
Viet Nam	13	14	7	13	17	11	11	36
Other countries	346	388	331	278	439	425	516	714
Total	**871**	**1 000**	**975**	**766**	**1 186**	**1 634**	**1 937**	**2 866**

Note: For details on definitions and sources, please refer to the metadata at the end of the tables.

StatLink ‌ http://dx.doi.org/10.1787/018818624146

Table B.1.6. **Acquisition of nationality by country of former nationality**
PORTUGAL

	1996	1997	1998	1999	2000	2001	2002	2003	2004	2005
Venezuela	411	431	1	219	186	162	221	311	301	314
Brazil	241	296	46	186	175	283	345	345	307	162
Cape Verde	80	93	159	117	69	228	271	370	274	132
United States	120	203	7	91	64	90	108	94	72	49
Canada	69	92	4	70	55	54	65	68	38	46
Angola	57	56	56	62	42	65	82	144	63	38
Guinea-Bissau	27	16	67	37	27	55	73	38	95	36
United Kingdom	14	9	0	17	8	5	12	28	21	20
Sao Tome and Principe	10	12	28	15	7	20	34	58	22	7
Spain	12	9	3	3	4	4	9	6	4	6
India	..	..	6	4	10	6	9	11	3	6
Russian Federation	..	..	1	..	..	..	..	..	9	6
Romania	..	..	..	..	..	..	..	..	4	5
France	11	18	3	8	6	8	9	12	8	5
Mozambique	19	26	56	37	10	24	27	56	17	4
Other countries	83	103	82	80	58	78	104	206	108	103
Total	**1 154**	**1 364**	**519**	**946**	**721**	**1 082**	**1 369**	**1 747**	**1 346**	**939**

Note: For details on definitions and sources, please refer to the metadata at the end of the tables.

StatLink ⫘ http://dx.doi.org/10.1787/018871327254

Table B.1.6. **Acquisition of nationality by country of former nationality**
SLOVAK REPUBLIC

	2003	2004	2005
Ukraine	251	549	450
Romania	450	442	220
Serbia and Montenegro	438	506	183
Czech Republic	597	775	167
United States	97	136	64
Viet Nam	405	619	40
Russian Federation	65	96	37
Bulgaria	66	42	24
Croatia	35	50	22
Poland	43	26	14
FYROM	175	143	12
Israel	8	3	11
Germany	19	30	10
Kazakhstan	5	18	8
Iran	15	20	8
Other countries	823	561	123
Total	**3 492**	**4 016**	**1 393**

Note: For details on definitions and sources, please refer to the metadata at the end of the tables.

StatLink ⫘ http://dx.doi.org/10.1787/020052121111

Table B.1.6. **Acquisition of nationality by country of former nationality**
SPAIN

	1996	1997	1998	1999	2000	2001	2002	2003	2004	2005
Colombia	457	478	624	818	302	848	1 267	1 802	4 194	7 334
Morocco	687	1 056	1 542	2 053	1 921	2 822	3 111	6 827	8 036	5 556
Peru	1 150	1 159	1 863	2 374	1 488	2 322	3 117	2 932	3 958	3 645
Cuba	250	442	773	1 109	893	1 191	2 088	1 601	1 889	2 506
Dominican Republic	833	1 257	1 860	2 652	1 755	2 126	2 876	2 639	2 834	2 322
Argentina	1 387	1 368	1 126	1 027	661	791	997	1 015	1 746	2 293
Venezuela	133	153	203	290	197	326	439	529	703	752
Brazil	128	217	299	308	273	411	477	500	683	695
Philippines	455	583	499	551	365	554	831	670	800	680
Chile	425	428	473	432	594	359	353	349	484	621
China	109	180	238	302	240	263	308	396	318	492
Portugal	452	524	677	683	452	568	627	536	634	478
Equatorial Guinea	. .	140	200	278	206	321	338	342	479	455
Uruguay	260	279	310	309	177	239	219	234	327	409
India	128	172	206	270	232	287	271	291	295	248
Other countries	1 579	1 875	2 284	2 938	2 243	3 315	4 491	5 893	10 955	14 344
Total	**8 433**	**10 311**	**13 177**	**16 394**	**11 999**	**16 743**	**21 810**	**26 556**	**38 335**	**42 830**

Note: For details on definitions and sources, please refer to the metadata at the end of the tables.

StatLink http://dx.doi.org/10.1787/018618608850

Table B.1.6. **Acquisition of nationality by country of former nationality**
SWEDEN

	1996	1997	1998	1999	2000	2001	2002	2003	2004	2005
Iraq	1 851	2 328	3 719	2 328	4 181	4 043	4 160	4 678	5 298	11 544
Serbia and Montenegro	2 416	6 052	8 991	4 000	5 134	1 642	2 747	2 061	2 124	3 254
Finland	2 009	1 882	1 668	1 632	1 389	1 512	1 561	2 816	2 703	2 588
Iran	2 696	2 423	7 480	4 476	2 798	2 031	1 737	1 350	1 296	1 889
Bosnia and Herzegovina	98	2 550	10 860	11 348	12 591	4 241	4 064	3 090	1 469	1 788
Turkey	2 030	1 402	1 694	1 833	1 398	2 796	2 127	1 375	1 269	1 702
Syria	616	567	653	438	693	588	1 063	1 218	1 117	1 208
China	363	302	334	300	434	460	563	675	654	920
Russian Federation	. .	. .	. .	. .	. .	. .	626	642	535	886
Poland	636	523	454	159	264	1 906	2 604	1 325	990	793
Somalia	491	491	737	739	2 843	2 802	1 789	1 121	840	688
Afghanistan	. .	. .	. .	. .	. .	. .	285	278	361	623
Thailand	264	343	336	492	525	454	606	443	500	585
Chile	707	545	426	693	687	727	689	548	464	543
Croatia	. .	. .	. .	. .	. .	. .	1 569	1 531	780	504
Other countries	11 375	9 459	9 150	9 339	10 537	13 195	11 602	9 855	6 369	10 058
Total	**25 552**	**28 867**	**46 502**	**37 777**	**43 474**	**36 397**	**37 792**	**33 006**	**26 769**	**39 573**

Note: For details on definitions and sources, please refer to the metadata at the end of the tables.

StatLink http://dx.doi.org/10.1787/020061562153

INTERNATIONAL MIGRATION OUTLOOK: SOPEMI 2007 EDITION – ISBN 978-92-64-03285-9 – © OECD 2007

Table B.1.6. **Acquisition of nationality by country of former nationality**
SWITZERLAND

	1996	1997	1998	1999	2000	2001	2002	2003	2004	2005
Serbia and Montenegro	..	..	2 085	2 365	3 285	3 686	5 803	6 332	7 854	9 503
Italy	5 167	4 982	5 613	5 510	6 652	5 386	6 633	5 085	4 196	4 032
Turkey	1 432	1 814	2 093	2 260	3 127	3 116	4 128	4 216	3 565	3 467
Bosnia and Herzegovina	..	..	205	409	999	1 128	1 865	2 268	2 371	2 790
FYROM	..	..	308	410	857	1 022	1 639	1 802	1 981	2 171
Croatia	..	..	634	671	970	1 045	1 638	1 565	1 616	1 681
Portugal	262	291	421	481	765	779	920	1 165	1 199	1 505
France	1 045	985	1 152	848	1 360	1 307	1 367	1 215	1 181	1 021
Spain	453	481	619	507	851	699	691	800	823	975
Germany	675	644	605	461	646	586	817	670	639	773
United Kingdom	299	269	285	228	339	310	350	306	289	287
Netherlands	55	71	76	45	74	90	90	155	254	178
Austria	248	223	186	140	240	233	227	194	150	167
Slovak Republic	..	..	78	75	69	78	105	105	73	88
Czech Republic	..	..	153	109	132	130	104	68	63	78
Other countries	9 739	9 410	6 767	5 844	8 334	7 991	10 138	9 478	9 431	9 721
Total	**19 375**	**19 170**	**21 280**	**20 363**	**28 700**	**27 586**	**36 515**	**35 424**	**35 685**	**38 437**

Note: For details on definitions and sources, please refer to the metadata at the end of the tables.

StatLink ▄▇▆ http://dx.doi.org/10.1787/018510455778

Table B.1.6. **Acquisition of nationality by country of former nationality**
UNITED STATES

	1996	1997	1998	1999	2000	2001	2002	2003	2004	2005
Mexico	254 988	142 569	112 442	207 750	189 705	103 234	76 531	56 093	63 840	77 089
Philippines	51 346	30 898	24 872	38 944	46 563	35 431	30 487	29 081	31 448	36 673
India	33 113	21 206	17 060	30 710	42 198	34 311	33 774	29 790	37 975	35 962
Viet Nam	51 910	36 178	30 185	53 316	55 934	41 596	36 835	25 995	27 480	32 926
China	34 320	20 947	16 145	38 409	54 534	34 423	32 018	24 014	27 309	31 708
Dominican Republic	29 459	21 092	11 916	23 089	25 176	15 010	15 591	12 627	15 464	20 831
Korea	27 969	16 056	10 305	17 738	23 858	18 053	17 307	15 968	17 184	19 223
Jamaica	25 458	20 253	15 040	28 604	22 567	13 978	13 973	11 232	12 271	13 674
El Salvador	35 478	18 273	12 267	22 991	24 073	13 663	10 716	8 738	9 602	12 174
Colombia	27 483	11 645	7 024	13 168	14 018	10 872	10 634	7 962	9 819	11 396
Cuba	63 234	13 155	15 331	25 467	15 661	11 393	10 889	7 727	11 236	11 227
Iran	19 278	11 434	10 739	18 268	19 251	13 881	11 796	10 807	11 781	11 031
Poland	14 047	8 037	5 911	13 127	16 405	11 661	12 823	9 140	10 335	9 801
Haiti	25 012	16 477	10 416	19 550	14 428	10 408	9 280	7 263	8 215	9 740
Pakistan	11 251	7 266	3 572	6 572	8 726	8 375	8 658	7 431	8 744	9 699
Other countries	340 343	202 739	159 835	282 241	315 691	231 916	242 396	199 336	234 448	261 126
Total	**1044 689**	**598 225**	**463 060**	**839 944**	**888 788**	**608 205**	**573 708**	**463 204**	**537 151**	**604 280**

Note: For details on definitions and sources, please refer to the metadata at the end of the tables.

StatLink ▄▇▆ http://dx.doi.org/10.1787/020063853012

Metadata related to Tables A.1.6. and B.1.6. **Acquisition of nationality**

Country	Comments	Source
Australia		Department of Immigration and Multicultural and Indigenous Affairs.
Austria		Central Office of Statistics.
Belgium		National Statistical Office and Ministry of Justice.
Canada	Citizenship data provided for 2004 and 2005 are preliminary figures based on country of birth rather than country of previous nationality.	Statistics Canada.
Czech Republic		Ministry of the Interior.
Denmark		Statistics Denmark.
Finland	Includes naturalisations of persons of Finnish origin.	Statistics Finland.
France	The data by former nationality include induced acquisitions (by minors) when a parent acquires French nationality by decree or as a result of marriage. The total in Table A.1.6 includes estimates of the number of acquisitions due to entitlement (without formal procedures) as a result of birth and residence in France. In 2004, the breakdown by former nationality of acquisitions of nationality by advance declaration is not available. This explains the high number of estimates for 2004 (29 872 advance declarations).	Ministry of Social Affairs, Labour and Solidarity.
Germany	Figures do not include ethnic Germans.	Federal Office of Statistics.
Hungary	Including grants of nationality to ethnic Hungarians mainly from former Yugoslavia and Ukraine.	Ministry of the Interior.
Italy		Ministry of the Interior.
Japan		Ministry of Justice, Civil Affairs Bureau.
Luxembourg	Excludes children acquiring nationality as a consequence of the naturalisation of their parents.	Ministry of Justice.
Mexico		Ministry of Foreign Affairs.
Netherlands		Central Bureau of Statistics (CBS).
New Zealand	The country of origin of persons granted New Zealand citizenship is the country of birth if birth documentation is available. If not, the country of origin is the country of citizenship as shown on the person's passport.	Department of Internal Affairs.
Norway		Statistics Norway.
Poland	Until 2001, data include naturalisations in conferment procedure. Starting in 2002, they include conferment procedure, acknowledgment procedure and marriage procedure.	Office for Repatriation and Aliens.
Portugal	Data do not include the acquisition of nationality through marriage and adoption.	National Statistical Office (INE).
Slovak Republic		Ministry of the Interior.
Spain	Excludes individuals recovering their former (Spanish) nationality.	Ministry of Justice and Ministry of the Interior.
Sweden		Statistics Sweden.
Switzerland		Federal Office of Immigration, Integration and Emigration.
United Kingdom		Home Office.
United States	Data refer to fiscal years (October to September of the year indicated).	US Department of Justice.

Inflows of Foreign Workers

Inflows of foreign workers

Most of the statistics published herein are based on the number of work permits issued during the year. As was the case for overall immigration flows, the settlement countries (Australia, Canada, New Zealand and the United States) consider as immigrant workers persons who have received a permanent immigration permit for employment purposes. In each of these four countries, it is also possible to work on a temporary basis under various programmes (these data are also available in this annex). Data by country of origin are not published in this annex.

The data on European countries are based on initial work permits granted, which sometimes include temporary and seasonal workers. Major flows of workers are not covered, either because the type of permit that they hold is not covered in these statistics, or because they do not need permits in order to work (free circulation agreements, beneficiaries of family reunification, refugees). Some data also include renewals of permits. The administrative backlog in the processing of work permit applications is sometimes large (as in the United States, for example) and affects the flows observed, The data may also cover initial entries into the labour market and include young foreigners born in the country who are entering the labour market.

Table A.2.1. **Inflows of foreign workers into selected OECD countries**

Thousands

	1996	1997	1998	1999	2000	2001	2002	2003	2004	2005
Australia										
Permanent settlers	20.0	19.7	26.0	27.9	32.4	35.7	36.0	38.5	51.5	53.1
Temporary workers	15.4	31.7	37.3	37.0	39.2	36.9	33.5	36.8	39.5	48.6
Austria	16.3	15.2	15.4	18.3	25.4	27.0	24.6	24.1	24.5	23.2
Belgium	2.2	2.5	7.3	8.7	7.5	7.0	6.7	4.6	4.3	6.3
Canada	71.2	75.5	79.9	86.9	96.9	99.8	94.1	87.1	93.5	99.1
Denmark	2.8	3.1	3.2	3.1	3.6	5.1	4.8 |	2.3	4.3	7.4
Finland	..	..	..	..	10.4	14.1	13.3	13.8	14.2	17.4
France										
Permanents	4.8	5.2	5.4	6.3	6.4	9.2	8.0	6.9	7.0	8.9
APT	4.8	4.7	4.3	5.8	7.5	9.6	9.8	10.1	10.0	10.4
Germany	262.5	285.4	275.5	304.9	333.8	373.8	374.0	372.2	380.3	..
Hungary	14.5	19.7	22.6	29.6	40.2	47.3	49.8	57.4	79.2	72.6
Ireland	3.8	4.5	5.7	6.3	18.0	36.4	40.3	47.6	34.1	27.1
Italy	..	..	21.6	21.4	58.0	92.4	139.1	..	..	..
Japan	78.5	93.9	101.9	108.0	129.9	142.0	145.1	155.8	158.9	125.4
Luxembourg	18.3	18.6	22.0	24.2	26.5	25.8	22.4	22.6	22.9	24.8
Mexico	72.4	73.2	73.9	64.9	65.3	61.9	57.0	60.1	68.8	75.3
Netherlands	9.2	11.1	15.2	20.8	27.7	30.2	34.6	38.0	44.1	46.1
New Zealand										
Permanent settlers	..	..	4.8	5.6	7.8	13.3	13.4	9.2	7.7	14.5
Temporary workers	..	..	28.4	32.1	35.2	48.3	59.6	64.5	77.2	88.1
Norway	..	..	..	15.3	15.9	19.0	24.2	25.7	33.0	28.4
Poland	11.9	15.3	16.9	17.1	17.8	17.0	22.8	18.8	12.4	10.3
Portugal	1.5	1.3	2.6	4.2	7.8 |	136.0	55.3	16.4	19.3	13.1
Spain	36.6	25.9	48.1	49.7 |	172.6	154.9 |	101.6	74.6	158.9	643.1
Sweden	..	..	..	..	..	..	..	10.2	8.5	13.3
Switzerland	24.5	25.4	26.8	31.5	34.0	41.9	40.1	35.4	40.0	40.3
United Kingdom	26.4	31.7	37.5	42.0	64.6	85.1	88.6	85.8	89.5	86.2
United States										
Permanent settlers	117.5	90.5	77.4	56.7	106.6	178.7	173.8	81.7	155.3	246.9
Temporary workers	..	208.1	242.0	303.7	355.1	413.6	357.9	352.1	396.7	388.3

Note: For details on definitions and sources, refer to the metadata which follow.

StatLink http://dx.doi.org/10.1787/015676185207

Metadata related to Table A.2.1. **Inflows of foreign workers**

Country	Types of workers covered in the data	Source
Australia	*Permanent settlers:* Skilled workers including the following categories of visas: Employer nominations, Business skills, *Occupational Shares System*, special talents, Independent. Including accompanying dependents. *Period of reference:* Fiscal years (July to June of the given year). *Temporary workers:* Skilled temporary resident programme (including accompanying dependents). Including Long Stay Temporary Business Programme from 1996/1997 on. *Period of reference:* Fiscal years (July to June of the given year).	Department of Immigration and Multicultural and Indigenous Affairs.
Austria	Data for all years cover initial work permits for both direct inflows from abroad and for first participation in the Austrian labour market of foreigners already present in the country. Seasonal workers are included. EU citizens are excluded.	Ministry of Labour, Health and Social Affairs.
Belgium	Work permits issued to first-time immigrants in wage and salary employment. Citizens of European Union (EU) member states are not included.	Ministry of Employment and Labour.
Canada	Persons issued employment authorisations to work temporarily in Canada (excluding people granted a permit on humanitarian grounds, foreign students and their spouses). From 1997 on, persons are shown in the year in which they received their first temporary permit except for seasonal workers who are counted each time they enter the country. Country of origin refers to country of last residence.	Citizenship and Immigration Canada.
Denmark	Residence permits issued for employment. Nordic and EU citizens are not included. From 2003 on, data only cover the categories Wage earners, Work permits to persons from the new EU member states and Specialists included by the jobcard scheme. Persons granted a residence permit on basis of employment who previously obtained an educational residence permit are no longer included.	Statistics Denmark.
Finland	Work and residence permits for foreign workers entering Finland are granted from abroad through Finnish Embassies and Consulates.	Directorate of Immigration, Ministry of Foreign Affairs.
France	*Permanent workers:* "Permanents" are foreign workers subject to control by the *ANAEM*. Data only include non-EEA permanent workers (including self-employed). Resident family members of workers who enter the labour market for the first time and the self-employed are not included. *Provisional work permits (APT):* Provisional work permits (APT) cannot exceed 9 months, are renewable and apply to trainees, students and other holders of non-permanent jobs.	ANAEM (Agence nationale de l'accueil des étrangers et des migrations).
Germany	New work permits issued. Data include essentially newly entered foreign workers, contract workers and seasonal workers. Citizens of EU member states are not included.	Federal Labour Office.
Hungary	Grants of work permits (including renewals).	Ministry of Labour.
Ireland	Work permits issued (including renewals). EU citizens do not need a work permit.	Ministry of Labour, Department of Enterprise, Trade and Employment.
Italy	New work permits issued to non-EU foreigners (excl. self-employed).	Ministry of Labour and National Institute of Statistics (ISTAT).
Japan	Residents with restricted permission to work. Excluding temporary visitors and re-entries. Including renewals of permits.	Ministry of Justice.
Luxembourg	Data cover both arrivals of foreign workers and residents admitted for the first time to the labour market.	Social Security Inspection Bureau.
Mexico	Immigrants and residents with permission to work.	National Migration Institute.
Netherlands	Holders of a temporary work permit (regulated since 1995 under the Dutch Foreign nationals labour act, WAV).	Center for work and income.
New Zealand	Permanent settlers refer to principal applicants 16 and over in the business and skill streams. Temporary workers refer to work applications approved for persons entering New Zealand for the purpose of employment.	Statistics New Zealand.
Norway	Data include granted work permits on the grounds of Norway's need for workers. This includes permanent, long-term and short-term work permits.	Directorate of Immigration.
Poland	Data refer to work permits granted.	Ministry of Economy, Labour, and Social Policy.

Metadata related to Table A.2.1. **Inflows of foreign workers** (*cont.*)

Country	Types of workers covered in the data	Source
Portugal	Persons who obtained a residence permit for the first time and who declared that they have a job or are seeking a job. Data for 2001 and 2002 include permits delivered following the 2001 regularisation programme.	National Statistical Office.
Spain	Data include both initial "B" work permits, delivered for 1 year maximum (renewable) for a specific salaried activity and "D" work permits (same type of permit for the self-employed).	Ministry of Labour and Social Security.
	From 1997 on, data also include permanent permits. Since 1992, EU citizens do not need a work permit.	
	The large increase in 2000 is due to the regularisation programme which affected statistics for 2000 and 2001. The results for 2002 and 2003 are from Social Security statistics ("Anuario de Estadísticas Laborales y de Asuntos Sociales").	
Sweden	Data include seasonal workers and other temporary workers (fitters, specialists, artists and athletes).	Population register (Statistics Sweden) and Migration Board.
Switzerland	Data cover foreigners who enter Switzerland to work and who obtain an annual residence permit, whether the permit is renewable or not (*e.g.* trainees).	Federal Office of Immigration, Integration and Emigration.
	The data also include holders of a settlement permit returning to Switzerland after a short stay abroad. Issues of an annual permit to persons holding a seasonal one are not included.	
United Kingdom	Grants of work permits and first permissions.	Overseas Labour Service.
	Data exclude dependents and EEA nationals.	
United States	*Permanent workers:*	US Department of Justice.
	Data include immigrants issued employment-based preference visas.	
	Period of reference: fiscal years (October to September of the given year).	
	Temporary workers:	United States Department of State, Bureau of Consular Affairs.
	Data refer to non-immigrant visas issued (categories H, O, P, Q, R, NATO, and NAFTA). Family members are included.	
	Period of reference: Fiscal years (October to September of the given year).	

INTERNATIONAL MIGRATION OUTLOOK: SOPEMI 2007 EDITION – ISBN 978-92-64-03285-9 – © OECD 2007

Stocks of Foreign and Foreign-Born Labour

The international comparison of "immigrant" workers faces the difficulties already mentioned earlier regarding measuring the overall stock of immigrants and taking into account different concepts of employment and unemployment.

For the European countries, the main difficulty consists of covering EU nationals, who have free labour market access in EU member states. They are sometimes issued work permits, but this information is not always as readily available as for third-country nationals. Switzerland recently revised the sampling of its labour-force survey in order to compensate for the information that was no longer available on EU workers in registers of foreign nationals following the signature of free movement agreements with the European Union. These bilateral agreements enable employees who are holders of "EU/EFTA" permits to change their job or profession (professional mobility), and this change is not registered in the Central Register for Foreign Nationals, the usual source for statistics on the stock of foreign workers.

The use of work permit statistics can result in counting the same person more than once if the data include temporary workers and this person has successively been granted two permits during the same reference period. On the other hand, holders of "permanent" residence permits allowing access to the labour market are not systematically covered, especially since it is not always possible to determine the proportion of those who are actually working.

Another difficulty concerns determining the number of unemployed, self-employed and cross-border workers. The unemployed are generally included, except when the source is work permit records and when permits are granted subject to a definite job offer. Self-employed and cross-border workers are much less well covered by statistics. The reference periods of data are highly variable, as they are generally the end of December for register data, and the end of the first quarter of the reference year for employment survey data.

The management of population registers (when the population in the labour force can be identified) and work permits results in numerous breaks in series when expired work permits are eliminated, when this is not done automatically, or when regularisation programmes are implemented, which often give priority to foreigners who can show that they are employed or have a job offer. When these breaks occur, the analysis of the growth of the stock of foreign workers is significantly biased.

Table A.2.2. **Stocks of foreign-born labour force in selected OECD countries**

Thousands and percentages

	1996	1997	1998	1999	2000	2001	2002	2003	2004	2005
Australia	2 249.3	2 270.1	2 313.7	2 318.1	2 372.8	2 367.3	2 438.0	2 486.8	2 524.1	2 604.1
% of total labour force	24.9	24.7	24.8	24.6	24.7	24.6	24.6	24.9	24.4	24.9
Austria	..	..	..	..	..	..	..	..	601.7	633.2
% of total labour force	..	..	..	..	..	..	..	..	15.3	14.8
Canada	2 839.1	..	..	..	..	3 150.8	..	..	..	..
% of total labour force	19.2	..	..	..	..	19.9	..	..	..	..
Denmark	..	..	..	..	..	..	..	154.4	161.0	167.1
% of total labour force	..	..	..	..	..	..	..	5.4	5.9	6.1
Finland	..	..	..	..	..	..	..	81.3	87.6	..
% of total labour force	..	..	..	..	..	..	..	3.1	3.4	..
Mexico	..	..	..	..	120.5	..	..	..	..	..
% of total labour force	..	..	..	..	0.4	..	..	..	..	..
New Zealand	..	..	..	..	..	372.3	..	..	..	..
% of total labour force	..	..	..	..	..	19.9	..	..	..	..
Sweden	..	..	..	428.3	445.5	448.7	442.5	452.8	461.4	..
% of total labour force	..	..	..	10.2	10.5	10.5	10.3	10.5	10.6	..
United States	15 288.6	16 677.1	17 345.1	17 054.7	18 028.5	18 994.1	20 917.6	21 563.6	21 985.2	22 421.6
% of total labour force	11.6	12.3	12.7	12.3	12.9	13.4	14.6	14.8	15.1	15.2

Note: For details on definitions and sources, refer to the metadata at the end of Tables B.2.1.

StatLink http://dx.doi.org/10.1787/015723132537

Table B.2.1. **Stock of foreign-born labour by country of birth**

Thousands

AUSTRALIA

	1996	2001	2002	2003	2004	2005	*Of which:* Women		
							2003	2004	2005
United Kingdom	661.3	630.0	637.6	662.7	635.6	672.4	274.9	255.9	293.3
New Zealand	208.7	251.1	245.2	257.4	274.2	279.0	111.7	127.3	121.4
China	56.3	80.0	93.5	90.2	96.8	113.1	40.1	44.8	53.6
India	49.0	75.0	71.1	75.7	93.8	107.4	28.6	38.5	35.6
Former Yugoslavia	110.8	92.9	96.1	98.6	91.1	100.9	41.8	35.3	41.4
Viet Nam	83.6	90.8	101.3	105.6	103.3	91.2	43.8	44.1	39.4
Philippines	56.4	64.8	79.1	81.6	84.5	79.5	50.9	49.3	49.7
Italy	95.8	86.2	75.8	83.7	77.6	66.2	27.0	24.0	21.5
Malaysia	51.1	47.1	58.0	55.9	56.6	70.2	27.1	29.2	32.1
Germany	59.8	62.3	64.7	57.6	55.7	54.4	25.9	26.0	22.3
Netherlands	45.0	40.7	40.8	46.8	44.9	36.6	18.0	18.4	15.3
Greece	60.1	45.3	37.3	44.2	43.5	33.9	15.7	17.5	13.4
Lebanon	35.8	39.3	34.7	33.7	35.6	33.0	9.5	11.3	8.7
Poland	31.2	32.7	32.5	28.9	24.4	..	14.1	11.8	..
Malta	30.1	20.3	24.1	21.6	21.6	..	7.2	7.9	..
Other countries	614.3	708.8	746.2	742.6	784.9	866.3	323.7	350.1	392.9
Total	**2 249.3**	**2 367.3**	**2 438.0**	**2 486.8**	**2 524.1**	**2 604.1**	**1 060.0**	**1 091.4**	**1 140.6**

Note: For details on definitions and sources, please refer to the metadata at the end of the tables.

StatLink http://dx.doi.org/10.1787/020087213202

INTERNATIONAL MIGRATION OUTLOOK: SOPEMI 2007 EDITION – ISBN 978-92-64-03285-9 – © OECD 2007

Table B.2.1. **Stock of foreign-born labour by country of birth**

Thousands

AUSTRIA

	2004	2005
Bosnia and Herzegovina	100.8	106.7
Turkey	79.3	82.3
Serbia and Montenegro	82.5	80.0
Germany	65.3	70.5
Poland	35.0	33.1
Romania	24.2	29.0
Croatia	26.5	25.8
Hungary	13.8	20.1
Czech Republic	12.2	13.2
Slovak Republic	8.5	11.5
FYROM	11.3	9.1
Italy	9.3	9.1
Switzerland	8.1	7.6
Philippines	9.6	7.6
Iran	6.5	7.6
Other countries	108.8	119.8
Total	**601.7**	**633.2**

Note: For details on definitions and sources, please refer to the metadata at the end of the tables.

StatLink http://dx.doi.org/10.1787/020143458281

Table B.2.1. **Stock of foreign-born labour by country of birth**

Thousands

CANADA

	1996	2001	Of which: Women	
			1996	2001
United Kingdom	372.5	335.4	180.6	154.9
India	158.3	209.4	68.2	91.8
Philippines	126.7	166.1	76.4	97.8
China	113.8	162.8	51.8	76.7
Hong Kong, China	129.4	140.9	62.5	68.9
Italy	166.2	140.1	62.7	54.3
United States	142.0	137.1	74.2	73.2
Poland	98.0	104.1	45.1	50.3
Viet Nam	85.8	103.5	37.7	47.6
Portugal	101.0	95.6	43.4	41.4
Germany	100.7	87.0	45.3	39.6
Jamaica	79.5	85.4	44.1	47.8
Netherlands	70.5	60.2	28.2	23.9
Other countries	1 094.7	1 323.3	468.7	590.1
Total	**2 839.1**	**3 150.8**	**1 288.9**	**1 458.3**

Note: For details on definitions and sources, please refer to the metadata at the end of the tables.

StatLink http://dx.doi.org/10.1787/020171380446

Table B.2.1. **Stock of foreign-born labour by country of birth**

Thousands

DENMARK

	2003	2004	2005	Of which: Women	
				2004	2005
Turkey	17.6	18.1	18.0	7.1	7.1
Germany	10.6	10.4	10.3	4.6	4.5
Bosnia and Herzegovina	8.1	8.4	8.5	3.7	3.8
Sweden	7.2	7.1	7.2	4.2	4.2
Norway	6.7	6.7	6.8	4.2	4.2
United Kingdom	6.8	6.7	6.8	2.0	1.9
Poland	6.0	6.2	6.4	4.1	4.2
Former Yugoslavia	6.2	6.1	6.0	2.6	2.6
Iraq	3.9	5.2	5.9	1.4	1.7
Iran	5.6	5.9	5.8	2.0	2.0
Pakistan	5.0	5.2	5.2	1.6	1.6
Viet Nam	4.9	5.1	5.1	2.3	2.4
Lebanon	3.8	4.1	4.2	1.2	1.3
Sri Lanka	4.2	4.2	4.1	1.8	1.8
Thailand	3.3	3.6	3.9	3.2	3.4
Other countries	54.5	57.9	62.6	26.5	28.8
Total	**154.4**	**161.0**	**167.1**	**72.4**	**75.4**

Note: For details on definitions and sources, please refer to the metadata at the end of the tables.

StatLink http://dx.doi.org/10.1787/020238436542

Table B.2.1. **Stock of foreign-born labour by country of birth**

Thousands

FINLAND

	2003	2004
Former Soviet Union	19.0	20.6
Sweden	18.4	19.1
Estonia	5.8	6.6
Former Yugoslavia	2.4	2.6
Germany	2.1	2.2
United Kingdom	1.8	1.9
Viet Nam	1.9	1.9
Turkey	1.7	1.9
Somalia	1.7	1.8
Iraq	1.4	1.6
China	1.3	1.4
Iran	1.2	1.4
Thailand	1.1	1.3
United States	1.1	1.1
India	0.8	1.0
Other countries	19.5	21.1
Total	**81.3**	**87.6**

Note: For details on definitions and sources, please refer to the metadata at the end of the tables.

StatLink http://dx.doi.org/10.1787/020248826584

INTERNATIONAL MIGRATION OUTLOOK: SOPEMI 2007 EDITION – ISBN 978-92-64-03285-9 – © OECD 2007

Table B.2.1. **Stock of foreign-born labour by country of birth**

Thousands

MEXICO

	2000
United States	46.3
Guatemala	12.2
Spain	10.0
Argentina	3.8
Cuba	3.5
Colombia	3.1
El Salvador	3.0
France	3.0
Germany	2.9
Italy	2.3
Peru	2.1
Chile	2.1
Canada	1.9
Honduras	1.8
Japan	1.5
Other countries	21.0
Total	**120.5**

Note: For details on definitions and sources, please refer to the metadata at the end of the tables.

StatLink http://dx.doi.org/10.1787/020316678278

Table B.2.1. **Stock of foreign-born labour by country of birth**

Thousands

NEW ZEALAND

	2001	Of which: Women 2001
United Kingdom	115.2	51.5
Australia	29.2	14.8
Samoa	26.8	12.7
Fiji	16.3	7.7
South Africa	15.2	7.2
China	15.2	7.2
India	12.2	5.1
Netherlands	11.3	4.7
Tonga	10.0	4.3
Cook Islands	8.2	3.8
United States	7.4	3.5
Malaysia	6.9	3.4
Philippines	6.5	4.4
Korea	6.0	2.7
Germany	5.0	2.4
Other countries	80.6	37.0
Total	**372.3**	**172.2**

Note: For details on definitions and sources, please refer to the metadata at the end of the tables.

StatLink http://dx.doi.org/10.1787/020317132840

Table B.2.1. **Stock of foreign-born labour by country of birth**

Thousands

SWEDEN

| | 1999 | 2000 | 2001 | 2002 | 2003 | 2004 | Of which: Women | | |
							2002	2003	2004
Finland	103.2	101.7	96.7	98.4	94.4	90.7	52.7	51.3	50.2
Former Yugoslavia	51.2	61.4	64.9	62.4	64.6	65.8	27.1	28.7	29.2
Bosnia and Herzegovina	21.2	29.2	28.8	26.0	27.0	27.8	10.8	12.2	12.8
Iran	24.0	23.5	23.0	22.7	25.2	24.3	8.2	10.4	9.6
Iraq	12.1	13.3	16.3	17.6	21.3	23.4	5.8	6.5	6.3
Turkey	13.5	14.2	14.0	14.6	16.1	17.1	5.5	6.2	6.5
Poland	20.3	23.1	21.1	20.5	20.2	17.0	13.4	13.5	11.5
Denmark	16.0	17.3	16.0	14.5	13.0	15.8	6.5	5.6	7.2
Norway	17.9	17.2	15.6	15.1	14.6	15.5	9.5	8.8	9.5
Other countries	148.9	144.6	152.3	150.7	156.4	164.0	73.7	76.0	80.5
Total	**428.3**	**445.5**	**448.7**	**442.5**	**452.8**	**461.4**	**213.2**	**219.2**	**223.3**

Note: For details on definitions and sources, please refer to the metadata at the end of the tables.

StatLink ⟪⟫ http://dx.doi.org/10.1787/020423014223

Table B.2.1. **Stock of foreign-born labour by country of birth**

Thousands

UNITED KINGDOM

| | 2006 | Of which: Women |
		2006
India	329.0	128.0
Ireland	178.0	94.0
Germany	160.0	78.0
Poland	157.0	66.0
South Africa	131.0	61.0
Pakistan	101.0	17.0
Kenya	91.0	40.0
United States	90.0	44.0
Bangladesh	86.0	13.0
Australia	84.0	41.0
Ghana	76.0	34.0
Nigeria	73.0	34.0
Zimbabwe	72.0	39.0
France	63.0	32.0
Jamaica	63.0	32.0
Other countries	1 327.0	601.0
Total	**3 081.0**	**1 354.0**

Note: For details on definitions and sources, please refer to the metadata at the end of the tables.

StatLink ⟪⟫ http://dx.doi.org/10.1787/020300842880

Table B.2.1. **Stock of foreign-born labour by country of birth**

Thousands

UNITED STATES

	1996	1997	1998	1999	2000	2001	2002	2003	2004	2005	Of which: Women		
											2003	2004	2005
Mexico	4 033.8	4 414.8	4 578.1	4 618.6	5 005.2	5 334.6	6 348.7	6 458.4	6 726.3	6 952.4	2 059.2	2 049.0	2 063.0
Philippines	840.8	873.5	922.1	1 016.8	938.7	941.1	1 016.0	1 010.9	977.4	1 059.4	590.9	538.5	599.3
India	536.5	514.5	510.4	584.7	681.3	670.1	890.5	787.7	909.6	941.0	270.9	344.0	334.6
El Salvador	479.9	463.0	566.9	574.3	557.4	614.0	667.6	788.6	688.2	829.5	285.6	280.0	313.6
China	498.6	531.0	537.7	548.2	565.7	597.9	590.6	657.6	825.1	826.5	306.6	368.4	383.2
Viet Nam	484.1	551.8	682.4	629.9	485.8	488.2	544.9	579.7	659.2	688.8	272.0	312.2	317.9
Germany	514.9	595.7	629.7	517.1	625.2	617.7	632.8	585.8	629.8	567.8	300.7	325.1	293.1
Cuba	448.9	513.7	502.9	545.0	520.0	458.2	452.4	492.2	558.6	505.7	212.2	217.3	204.4
Canada	475.4	424.0	419.8	462.9	495.1	536.0	519.3	519.5	459.9	447.5	241.1	232.7	205.8
United Kingdom	394.8	441.0	440.3	473.3	438.9	401.4	443.7	399.0	436.0	443.6	187.6	204.0	180.1
Dominican Republic	272.0	330.0	363.2	370.1	369.5	362.8	384.2	432.3	374.1	434.5	242.1	210.5	249.6
Korea	283.2	407.0	411.1	340.1	441.0	511.5	461.3	543.9	460.2	428.9	278.6	242.3	219.5
Jamaica	336.7	273.1	262.8	282.3	311.5	362.9	378.0	460.9	449.3	416.8	253.2	258.3	228.5
Guatemala	244.8	319.5	295.4	273.9	241.2	224.6	301.5	310.8	371.4	389.8	97.2	105.6	112.5
Haiti	255.6	289.8	316.2	254.4	268.6	395.5	412.9	324.7	365.5	347.4	148.1	187.0	152.1
Other countries	5 188.8	5 734.8	5 906.1	5 563.1	6 083.3	6 477.8	6 873.1	7 211.5	7 094.6	7 142.0	3 148.1	3 017.5	3 014.2
Total	**15 288.6**	**16 677.1**	**17 345.1**	**17 054.7**	**18 028.5**	**18 994.1**	**20 917.6**	**21 563.6**	**21 985.2**	**22 421.6**	**8 894.1**	**8 892.4**	**8 871.4**

Note: For details on definitions and sources, please refer to the metadata at the end of the tables.

StatLink ⟨ﾐﾖ⟩ http://dx.doi.org/10.1787/020445741754

Metadata related to Tables A.2.2. and B.2.1. **Foreign-born labour force**

Country	Comments	Source
Australia	Labour force aged 15 and over. *Reference date*: August. Data for China exclude Hong Kong, China and Chinese Taipei. Data in Table A.2.2. are annual averages whereas data in Table B.2.1. refer to August.	Labour Force Survey (ABS).
Austria		Labour Force Survey.
Canada	Labour force aged 15 and over.	Censuses of Population, Statistics Canada.
Denmark		Ministry of Refugee, Immigration and Integration Affairs.
Finland		Statistics Finland.
Mexico	Data refer to the foreign-born labour force population aged 12 and over.	Census of Population, CONAPO.
New Zealand	Labour force aged 15 and over.	2001 Census, Statistics New Zealand.
Sweden		Statistics Sweden.
United Kingdom	Estimates are from the 2006 Labour Force Survey. The unemployed are not included. Figures are rounded and not published if less than 10 000.	Labour Force Survey, Office for National Statistics.
United States	Labour force aged 15 and over (including those born abroad with US citizenship at birth). Data by nationality are not statistically relevant. *Reference date:* March.	Current Population Survey, US Department of Commerce, Bureau of the Census.

INTERNATIONAL MIGRATION OUTLOOK: SOPEMI 2007 EDITION – ISBN 978-92-64-03285-9 – © OECD 2007

Table A.2.3. **Stocks of foreign labour force in selected OECD countries**

Thousands and percentages

	1996	1997	1998	1999	2000	2001	2002	2003	2004	2005
Austria	328.0	326.3	327.1	333.6	345.6	359.9	370.6	388.6	402.7	418.0
% of total labour force	10.0	9.9	9.9	10.0	10.5	11.0	10.9	11.8	11.9	12.0
Belgium	370.9	380.5	394.9	382.7	387.9	392.5	393.9	396.0	427.7	435.3
% of total labour force	8.4	8.6	8.9	8.5	8.6	8.6	8.6	8.5	9.1	9.1
Czech Republic	143.2	130.8	111.2	93.5	103.6	103.7	101.2	105.7	108.0	151.7
% of total labour force	2.8	2.5	2.1	1.8	2.0	2.0	1.9	2.1	2.1	2.9
Denmark	88.0	93.9	98.3	96.3	96.8	100.6	101.9	101.5	106.9	109.3
% of total labour force	3.1	3.3	3.4	3.4	3.4	3.5	3.6	3.6	3.9	4.0
Finland	..	..	..	..	41.4	45.4	46.3	47.6	50.0	53.0
% of total labour force	..	..	..	..	1.6	1.7	1.8	1.8	1.9	2.1
France	1 604.7	1 569.8	1 586.7	1 593.8	1 577.6	1 617.6	1 623.8	1 526.8	1 541.1	1 456.4
% of total labour force	6.3	6.1	6.1	5.8	6.0	6.2	6.2	5.6	5.6	5.3
Germany	..	3 575.0	3 501.0	3 545.0	3 546.0	3 616.0	3 634.0	3 703.0	3 701.0	3 823.0
% of total labour force	..	8.9	8.7	8.8	8.8	9.1	9.2	9.4	9.1	9.3
Greece	..	..	169.8	157.3	169.1	204.8	258.9	274.5	309.6	324.6
% of total labour force	..	..	3.7	3.4	3.7	4.5	5.5	5.8	6.4	6.7
Hungary	18.8	20.4	22.4	28.5	35.0	38.6	42.7	48.7	66.1	62.9
% of total labour force	0.5	0.5	0.6	0.7	0.8	0.9	1.0	1.2	1.6	1.5
Ireland	52.4	51.7	53.7	57.5	63.9	84.2	101.7	..	..	..
% of total labour force	3.5	3.4	3.3	3.4	3.7	4.7	5.5	..	..	..
Italy	656.6	660.3	660.6	827.6	837.9	841.0	829.8	1 479.4	..	..
% of total labour force	2.9	2.9	2.9	4.0	3.9	3.9	3.8	6.0	..	..
Japan	98.3	107.3	119.0	125.7	154.7	168.8	179.6	185.6	192.1	180.5
% of total labour force	0.1	0.2	0.2	0.2	0.2	0.2	0.3	0.3	0.3	0.3
Korea	82.9	106.8	76.8	93.0	122.5	128.5	137.3	415.0	297.8	198.5
% of total labour force	0.4	0.5	0.4	0.4	0.6	0.6	0.6	1.8	1.3	0.8
Luxembourg	117.8	124.8	134.6	145.7	152.7	169.3	175.1	180.4	187.5	196.2
% of total labour force	53.8	55.1	57.7	57.3	57.3	61.2	61.3	65.5	62.0	62.6
Netherlands	280.5	275.2	269.5	267.5	300.1	302.6	295.9	317.2	299.4	287.5
% of total labour force	3.9	3.8	3.6	3.5	3.9	3.8	3.7	3.9	3.8	3.4
Norway	54.8	59.9	66.9	104.6	111.2	133.7	138.4	140.6	149.3	159.3
% of total labour force	2.6	2.8	3.0	4.7	4.9	5.7	5.8	6.3	6.6	6.9
Portugal	86.8	87.9	88.6	91.6	99.8	236.6	288.3	300.8	315.8	271.4
% of total labour force	1.8	1.8	1.8	1.8	2.0	4.4	5.3	5.5	5.5	4.9
Slovak Republic	4.8	5.5	5.9	4.5	4.7	4.4	4.7	5.0	2.8	6.2
% of total labour force	0.2	0.2	0.2	0.2	0.2	0.2	0.2	0.2	0.1	0.2
Spain	166.5	178.7	197.1	199.8	454.6	607.1	831.7	982.4	1 076.7	1 688.6
% of total labour force	1.0	1.1	1.2	1.1	2.5	3.4	4.5	5.1	5.4	8.1
Sweden	218	220	219	222	222	227	218	221	216	..
% of total labour force	5.1	5.2	5.1	5.1	5.0	5.1	4.9	4.9	4.8	..
Switzerland	709.1	692.8	691.1	701.2	717.3	738.8	829.6	814.3	817.3	830.1
% of total labour force	20.9	20.5	20.7	20.1	20.1	21.1	20.9	20.6	20.6	20.9
United Kingdom	865	949	1 039	1 005	1 107	1 229	1 251	1 322	1 445	1 504
% of total labour force	3.3	3.6	3.9	3.7	4.0	4.4	4.6	4.8	5.2	5.4

Note: For details on definitions and sources, refer to the metadata at the end of Tables B.2.2.

StatLink 🔗 *http://dx.doi.org/10.1787/015813414431*

Table B.2.2. **Stock of foreign labour by nationality**

Thousands

AUSTRIA

	1996	1997	1998	1999	2000	2001	2002	2003	2004	2005
Former Yugoslavia	126.1	123.3	122.3	122.9	124.2	122.8	119.8	117.1	113.4	108.8
Turkey	53.6	52.8	54.2	55.6	57.1	56.8	56.3	55.7	54.6	53.5
Germany	14.6	15.7	16.9	18.8	20.9	23.5	26.5	31.5	39.0	46.7
Bosnia and Herzegovina	13.6	15.1	16.5	18.5	21.3	24.1	25.4	26.7	27.5	28.2
Hungary	9.3	9.2	9.2	9.7	10.4	11.3	12.0	12.7	13.6	14.7
Croatia	5.3	5.3	6.2	7.0	8.4	9.8	10.6	11.4	12.1	12.7
Poland	11.0	10.9	10.7	10.9	11.2	11.2	11.3	11.5	12.0	12.6
Romania	9.3	9.1	9.1	9.3	9.7	9.9	10.1	10.7	11.0	11.3
Slovak Republic	1.0	1.2	1.4	1.6	1.9	2.4	2.9	3.5	4.4	5.5
Slovenia	3.0	2.9	3.2	3.4	3.6	3.8	3.9	4.0	4.3	4.7
Former Czechoslovakia	8.1	7.5	7.1	6.9	6.7	6.3	5.5	5.2	4.9	4.6
Czech Republic	0.9	0.9	1.1	1.2	1.4	1.7	2.4	2.7	3.1	3.6
Serbia and Montenegro	..	..	..	..	..	..	..	..	1.3	3.2
Philippines	2.4	2.4	2.4	2.5	2.6	2.6	2.7	2.9	3.1	3.2
FYROM	..	..	0.5	0.7	1.1	1.3	1.6	2.0	2.2	2.5
Other countries	42.3	42.5	37.7	37.3	39.5	41.7	43.4	52.8	55.7	57.9
Total	**300.4**	**298.8**	**298.6**	**306.4**	**319.9**	**329.3**	**334.4**	**350.4**	**362.3**	**373.7**

Note: For details on definitions and sources, please refer to the metadata at the end of the tables.

StatLink ⟪≣⟫ http://dx.doi.org/10.1787/020450442365

Table B.2.2. **Stock of foreign labour by nationality**

Thousands

BELGIUM

	1996	1997	1998	1999	2000	2001	2002	2003	2004	2005
Italy	101.6	104.0	104.5	97.1	94.4	91.4	88.9	86.1	86.3	83.6
France	54.3	57.3	60.8	63.3	68.8	71.2	71.7	73.0	77.7	79.7
Netherlands	32.2	33.6	34.4	33.6	34.0	34.2	34.4	35.1	38.0	39.6
Morocco	44.6	44.5	46.1	43.4	41.3	40.2	38.6	36.8	39.9	37.9
Spain	22.9	23.3	23.6	23.0	22.6	22.2	22.0	21.4	21.7	21.3
Turkey	30.5	30.1	31.6	26.6	24.0	21.9	21.0	20.2	21.1	19.1
Portugal	11.3	11.9	12.2	12.3	12.3	12.4	12.7	13.3	14.2	14.7
Germany	8.6	9.1	9.4	9.2	9.2	9.2	9.6	9.8	10.9	11.5
United Kingdom	8.4	8.7	8.8	8.9	9.2	9.2	9.3	9.1	9.6	9.6
Democratic Republic of the Congo	4.0	4.2	4.6	4.9	5.4	6.3	7.0	7.0	8.7	9.4
Poland	..	..	..	2.8	3.2	4.0	4.8	5.6	7.7	9.1
Greece	7.1	7.1	7.2	7.1	7.0	6.8	6.6	6.4	6.5	6.3
Algeria	3.2	3.4	3.4	3.4	3.3	3.6	3.8	4.1	4.3	4.7
Tunisia	2.3	2.2	2.2	2.0	2.0	1.9	1.9	1.9	2.2	2.3
Luxembourg	1.5	1.5	1.6	1.5	1.5	1.4	1.4	1.4	1.4	1.4
Other countries	38.5	39.7	44.6	43.6	49.7	56.2	60.3	64.7	77.5	85.1
Total	**370.9**	**380.5**	**394.9**	**382.7**	**387.9**	**392.5**	**393.9**	**396.0**	**427.7**	**435.3**

Note: For details on definitions and sources, please refer to the metadata at the end of the tables.

StatLink ⟪≣⟫ http://dx.doi.org/10.1787/020475127538

INTERNATIONAL MIGRATION OUTLOOK: SOPEMI 2007 EDITION – ISBN 978-92-64-03285-9 – © OECD 2007

Table B.2.2. **Stock of foreign labour by nationality**

Thousands

CZECH REPUBLIC

	1996	1997	1998	1999	2000	2001	2002	2003	2004	2005
Slovak Republic	72.2	69.7	61.3	53.2	63.6	63.6	56.6	58.0	59.8	75.3
Ukraine	42.1	25.2	19.3	16.6	15.8	17.5	20.0	22.5	22.4	40.1
Poland	12.8	13.7	9.9	6.9	7.7	6.7	7.3	7.4	8.9	12.6
Moldova	0.3	2.0	2.1	1.4	1.4	1.4	1.4	1.5	1.5	2.7
Russian Federation	0.9	1.1	1.1	1.2	1.0	0.9	0.9	0.9	1.1	2.4
Mongolia	0.6	0.8	0.9	0.6	0.7	1.0	1.2	1.4	1.6	1.8
Germany	1.5	1.5	1.5	1.5	1.5	1.2	1.3	1.4	1.3	1.7
Bulgaria	1.4	3.3	2.7	1.7	1.5	1.9	2.0	1.8	1.7	1.7
United States	1.6	1.5	1.4	1.4	1.4	1.3	1.4	1.4	1.2	1.2
United Kingdom	1.2	1.3	1.2	1.1	1.1	1.0	1.0	1.0	0.7	1.1
Belarus	0.9	2.5	2.0	1.3	1.1	1.0	1.2	1.0	0.8	1.0
China	0.1	0.1	0.1	0.1	0.2	0.3	0.2	0.3	0.3	0.9
Romania	0.9	1.2	1.1	0.7	0.9	0.8	0.7	0.7	0.6	0.9
France	0.5	0.5	0.5	0.6	0.6	0.6	0.7	0.7	0.5	0.7
Austria	0.4	0.5	0.5	0.4	0.4	0.4	0.4	0.5	0.4	0.5
Other countries	5.8	6.0	5.5	4.7	4.8	4.2	4.8	5.3	5.3	7.0
Total	**143.2**	**130.8**	**111.2**	**93.5**	**103.6**	**103.7**	**101.2**	**105.7**	**108.0**	**151.7**

Note: For details on definitions and sources, please refer to the metadata at the end of the tables.

StatLink ⟨⟩ *http://dx.doi.org/10.1787/020518323050*

Table B.2.2. **Stock of foreign labour by nationality**

Thousands

DENMARK

	1996	1997	1998	1999	2000	2001	2002	2003	2004	2005
Turkey	13.6	14.0	14.1	13.8	13.0	13.0	12.5	11.9	11.8	11.9
United Kingdom	7.5	7.6	7.6	7.5	7.6	7.7	7.8	7.6	7.6	7.7
Germany	6.2	6.5	6.8	6.7	6.9	7.1	7.1	7.0	7.0	7.1
Norway	6.2	6.2	6.3	6.2	6.5	6.7	6.8	6.8	6.9	7.0
Sweden	5.2	5.5	5.7	5.6	5.8	5.9	5.9	5.8	5.7	5.9
Former Yugoslavia	7.3	9.3	11.3	10.8	11.5	12.7	12.5	3.7	3.7	3.3
Iceland	2.7	2.9	2.8	2.8	2.7	2.8	2.8	2.9	3.1	3.1
Pakistan	2.4	2.5	2.4	2.4	2.3	2.3	2.3	2.2	2.4	2.3
Finland	1.0	1.1	1.0	1.0	1.0	1.1	1.0	1.0	1.0	1.0
Other countries	35.9	38.3	40.1	39.3	39.5	41.4	43.2	52.7	57.8	59.8
Total	**88.0**	**93.9**	**98.3**	**96.3**	**96.8**	**100.6**	**101.9**	**101.5**	**106.9**	**109.3**

Note: For details on definitions and sources, please refer to the metadata at the end of the tables.

StatLink ⟨⟩ *http://dx.doi.org/10.1787/020536885150*

Table B.2.2. **Stock of foreign labour by nationality**

Thousands

FINLAND

	2000	2001	2002	2003	2004	2005
Russian Federation	9.1	10.1	11.0	11.2	11.7	11.7
Estonia	5.3	5.9	6.3	6.5	7.9	8.4
Sweden	3.5	3.6	3.6	3.6	3.8	3.5
United Kingdom	1.4	1.5	1.5	1.5	1.7	1.7
Germany	1.3	1.4	1.4	1.4	1.5	1.6
Serbia and Montenegro	..	1.5	1.5	1.5	1.2	1.5
Turkey	1.0	1.1	1.2	1.3	1.3	1.4
Somalia	1.1	1.2	1.2	1.4	1.2	1.3
Thailand	0.6	0.7	0.8	0.9	1.1	1.2
China	0.7	0.8	0.8	1.0	1.1	1.2
Iraq	0.9	1.0	1.0	1.2	1.1	1.1
United States	0.8	0.9	0.9	0.9	0.9	0.9
Viet Nam	0.8	0.8	0.8	0.9	0.8	0.8
Bosnia and Herzegovina	0.7	0.8	0.7	0.8	0.8	0.7
Former Soviet Union	1.3	1.2	1.1	1.0	0.4	0.3
Other countries	12.9	12.9	12.5	12.5	13.5	15.7
Total	**41.4**	**45.4**	**46.3**	**47.6**	**50.0**	**53.0**

Note: For details on definitions and sources, please refer to the metadata at the end of the tables.

StatLink ⟪⟫ http://dx.doi.org/10.1787/020663313661

Table B.2.2. **Stock of foreign labour by nationality**

Thousands

FRANCE

	1996	1997	1998	1999	2000	2001	2002	2003	2004	2005
Portugal	359.0	342.5	316.0	325.7	353.1	371.0	376.8	334.0	350.9	303.5
Algeria	253.3	246.1	241.6	237.2	215.0	233.6	198.4	215.0	194.9	184.3
Morocco	203.1	205.0	229.6	226.9	204.3	186.0	199.6	194.6	193.5	180.5
Turkey	72.5	65.8	79.0	76.1	81.5	81.7	92.6	62.1	71.8	83.4
Tunisia	75.2	85.0	84.4	83.9	77.5	84.2	84.4	66.8	69.5	70.3
Italy	74.3	65.5	72.9	75.6	73.8	72.2	71.2	53.6	57.6	50.7
Spain	85.6	90.7	88.2	86.5	65.8	58.3	52.0	51.5	47.8	36.5
Poland	10.1	13.8	12.6	14.0	13.5	16.2	15.6	16.2	21.6	18.9
Other countries	471.5	455.4	462.5	467.9	493.1	514.5	533.2	533.0	533.4	528.1
Total	**1 604.7**	**1 569.8**	**1 586.7**	**1 593.9**	**1 577.6**	**1 617.6**	**1 623.8 |**	**1 526.8**	**1 541.1**	**1 456.4**

Note: For details on definitions and sources, please refer to the metadata at the end of the tables.

StatLink ⟪⟫ http://dx.doi.org/10.1787/020701034348

INTERNATIONAL MIGRATION OUTLOOK: SOPEMI 2007 EDITION – ISBN 978-92-64-03285-9 – © OECD 2007

Table B.2.2. **Stock of foreign labour by nationality**

Thousands

GERMANY

	1997	1999	2000	2001	2002	2003	2004	2005
Turkey	1 039.0	1 008.0	996.0	1 004.0	974.0	975.0	937.0	840.0
Italy	375.0	386.0	395.0	403.0	407.0	408.0	398.0	391.0
Greece	214.0	219.0	207.0	210.0	213.0	196.0	198.0	201.0
Croatia	215.0	189.0	195.0	193.0	185.0	173.0	186.0	195.0
Serbia and Montenegro	..	..	207.0	217.0	220.0	218.0	175.0	180.0
Poland	94.0	100.0	106.0	113.0	133.0	144.0	144.0	167.0
Bosnia and Herzegovina	169.0	103.0	100.0	96.0	98.0	104.0	114.0	149.0
Austria	123.0	118.0	110.0	116.0	113.0	118.0	124.0	135.0
Netherlands	63.0	63.0	63.0	61.0	63.0	74.0	83.0	86.0
Portugal	65.0	77.0	83.0	84.0	76.0	83.0	76.0	83.0
Spain	75.0	69.0	71.0	74.0	71.0	66.0	70.0	76.0
France	58.0	56.0	67.0	62.0	62.0	65.0	64.0	68.0
United Kingdom	76.0	65.0	71.0	74.0	72.0	78.0	73.0	62.0
United States	53.0	54.0	51.0	58.0	55.0	57.0	55.0	56.0
Other countries	956.0	1 038.0	824.0	851.0	892.0	944.0	1 004.0	1 134.0
Total	**3 575.0**	**3 545.0**	**3 546.0**	**3 616.0**	**3 634.0**	**3 703.0**	**3 701.0**	**3 823.0**

Note: For details on definitions and sources, please refer to the metadata at the end of the tables.

StatLink 🔗 http://dx.doi.org/10.1787/020536560767

Table B.2.2. **Stock of foreign labour by nationality**

Thousands

GREECE

	1998	1999	2000	2001	2002	2003	2004	2005
Albania	98.7	86.0	100.0	119.6	149.2	164.7	180.8	188.9
Bulgaria	4.7	5.3	6.2	7.9	13.8	13.3	18.8	20.9
Romania	3.5	4.8	3.8	4.8	10.0	10.7	12.1	13.4
Russian Federation	11.6	6.6	9.8	10.4	11.5	10.5	9.5	10.3
Poland	5.3	7.2	6.3	9.3	9.7	11.5	9.0	10.2
Georgia	3.9	3.7	2.9	5.6	6.4	5.3	8.3	9.9
Ukraine	3.2	4.3	1.9	4.4	8.7	7.8	10.7	9.7
Philippines	2.1	1.9	2.7	2.2	2.4	2.2	6.0	6.8
Pakistan	3.0	1.8	3.7	2.8	4.7	6.0	3.9	5.4
Armenia	3.2	2.4	0.9	2.5	2.9	2.2	5.0	4.2
Iraq	2.1	1.3	1.0	2.0	3.3	4.0	3.2	4.1
United Kingdom	1.5	2.4	2.2	2.8	1.9	3.7	2.4	3.3
Germany	2.5	2.4	2.5	1.7	0.8	1.1	1.6	2.6
Egypt	1.5	3.0	2.4	3.3	4.9	7.7	3.9	2.4
Cyprus	2.3	2.8	1.8	1.7	3.0	1.9	3.8	1.8
Other countries	20.7	21.4	20.9	23.9	25.6	22.1	30.5	30.7
Total	**169.8**	**157.3**	**169.1**	**204.8**	**258.9**	**274.5**	**309.6**	**324.6**

Note: For details on definitions and sources, please refer to the metadata at the end of the tables.

StatLink 🔗 http://dx.doi.org/10.1787/020722200651

Table B.2.2. **Stock of foreign labour by nationality**
Thousands
HUNGARY

	1996	1997	1998	1999	2000	2001	2002	2003	2004	2005
Romania	8.5	9.5	10.6	14.1	17.2	22.0	25.8	27.6	35.2	30.9
Slovak Republic	0.4	0.4	0.5	1.0	2.9	1.8	2.8	5.7	11.7	15.1
Ukraine	..	..	..	..	..	..	5.9	7.6	8.8	7.6
Serbia and Montenegro	..	..	..	..	..	..	0.9	0.9	1.1	1.3
China	0.5	0.7	1.1	1.4	2.1	1.1	1.0	0.9	0.9	1.1
Germany	..	..	..	..	..	..	..	..	0.8	1.0
Poland	1.0	1.1	1.0	0.5	0.3	0.3	0.3	0.3	0.6	0.6
Mongolia	..	..	..	..	..	..	..	..	0.7	0.6
Japan	..	..	..	..	..	..	..	..	0.4	0.5
France	..	..	..	..	..	..	..	..	0.1	0.3
United States	..	..	..	..	..	..	..	..	0.3	0.3
Austria	..	..	..	..	..	..	..	..	0.3	0.3
Viet Nam	0.1	0.2	0.3	0.4	0.7	0.4	0.3	0.2	0.2	0.2
Italy	..	..	..	..	..	..	..	..	0.2	0.2
Turkey	..	..	..	..	..	..	..	..	0.1	0.2
Other countries	8.2	8.5	9.0	11.0	11.8	13.0	5.6	5.3	4.6	2.5
Total	**18.8**	**20.4**	**22.4**	**28.5**	**35.0**	**38.6**	**42.7**	**48.7**	**66.1**	**62.9**

Note: For details on definitions and sources, please refer to the metadata at the end of the tables.

StatLink ⫘ http://dx.doi.org/10.1787/020724101786

Table B.2.2. **Stock of foreign labour by nationality**
Thousands
IRELAND

	2002
United Kingdom	62.2
United States	7.0
France	5.9
Germany	5.8
Spain	4.4
Philippines	4.2
Nigeria	4.1
Italy	3.8
Australia	3.6
South Africa	3.1
Romania	3.0
Netherlands	2.5
China	2.2
Latvia	2.2
Lithuania	2.2
Other countries	34.3
Total	**150.5**

Note: For details on definitions and sources, please refer to the metadata at the end of the tables.

StatLink ⫘ http://dx.doi.org/10.1787/020763481010

Table B.2.2. **Stock of foreign labour by nationality**

Thousands

ITALY

	1996	1997	1998	1999	2000	2001	2002	2003
Romania	17.6	17.8	19.2	41.5	47.0	52.7	56.6	194.4
Morocco	95.1	97.6	95.9	114.0	115.5	114.8	113.9	164.8
Albania	51.7	52.4	54.8	86.7	90.6	91.0	92.8	145.6
China	24.5	26.9	28.7	40.9	43.8	41.8	41.5	79.0
Philippines	48.6	49.1	49.4	56.0	53.2	54.1	51.1	60.7
Poland	14.4	13.1	12.1	16.6	17.0	17.0	17.4	45.8
Tunisia	32.9	33.2	31.6	35.5	34.2	38.6	36.2	45.5
Senegal	30.2	30.5	29.5	38.6	36.6	34.7	33.3	45.2
Ecuador	3.4	3.4	3.4	8.3	8.6	8.2	7.8	42.6
Peru	18.5	18.9	18.3	22.1	22.7	22.5	21.5	37.8
Egypt	18.8	18.6	18.0	26.9	25.2	24.0	22.3	37.1
Sri Lanka	19.6	19.6	19.8	22.6	23.4	25.3	23.4	30.7
India	10.9	11.4	11.0	14.8	16.1	16.2	16.6	30.3
Former Yugoslavia	26.1	24.2	23.9	23.8	24.6	23.0	22.2	27.9
Bangladesh	10.2	10.8	10.0	16.0	16.8	17.1	16.4	27.3
Other countries	234.1	232.7	235.0	263.4	262.7	260.0	256.7	464.9
Total	**656.6**	**660.3**	**660.6**	**827.6**	**837.9**	**841.0**	**829.8**	**1 479.4**

Note: For details on definitions and sources, please refer to the metadata at the end of the tables.

StatLink http://dx.doi.org/10.1787/020768807444

Table B.2.2. **Stock of foreign labour by nationality**

Thousands

JAPAN

	1996	1997	1998	1999	2000	2001	2002	2003	2004	2005
China	26.6	29.7	32.6	33.4	35.8	38.9	40.8	41.8	45.6	56.7
Philippines	18.1	20.3	25.7	28.6	45.6	46.9	48.8	52.9	53.2	26.7
United States	17.7	17.8	17.2	16.8	17.6	18.8	19.9	19.2	19.5	19.2
Korea	6.7	6.9	8.2	9.3	10.7	12.3	13.1	13.6	15.2	18.2
United Kingdom	6.1	6.8	7.0	7.4	8.1	9.1	9.8	9.3	9.0	8.5
India	2.1	2.5	2.9	3.1	3.5	4.5	5.3	5.7	6.2	7.1
Canada	4.5	5.0	5.2	5.3	5.8	6.6	7.1	7.0	6.9	6.5
Australia	2.6	3.0	3.5	3.9	4.6	5.7	6.3	6.2	6.0	5.8
Indonesia	0.3	0.4	0.6	0.8	1.4	1.7	1.8	2.2	2.5	3.3
France	1.5	1.6	1.7	1.7	2.0	2.2	2.4	2.4	2.5	2.6
Other countries	12.0	13.2	14.5	15.5	19.6	22.2	24.3	25.2	25.5	26.0
Total	**98.3**	**107.3**	**119.0**	**125.7**	**154.7**	**168.8**	**179.6**	**185.6**	**192.1**	**180.5**

Note: For details on definitions and sources, please refer to the metadata at the end of the tables.

StatLink http://dx.doi.org/10.1787/020817365860

Table B.2.2. **Stock of foreign labour by nationality**

Thousands

KOREA

	1996	1997	1998	1999	2000	2001	2002	2003	2004	2005
China	33.2	43.8	36.5	48.1	43.2	46.1	47.5	54.8	60.3	59.6
Philippines	10.1	12.0	6.9	9.2	9.8	12.2	12.4	22.0	21.0	20.1
Uzbekistan	1.0	2.1	1.9	2.2	3.5	3.6	2.8	13.0	10.4	9.3
United States	6.1	6.1	4.3	4.1	3.4	3.5	4.2	4.4	4.3	4.9
Canada	2.7	3.2	2.0	2.0	2.5	3.2	4.6	2.8	4.5	4.8
India	0.3	0.5	0.2	0.2	0.3	0.5	0.6	3.8	3.4	2.3
Russian Federation	0.4	0.6	0.5	1.0	1.9	2.3	2.7	1.9	2.5	1.4
Japan	1.7	1.9	1.3	1.3	1.0	1.1	1.1	2.8	1.2	1.2
United Kingdom	0.5	0.5	0.3	0.4	0.5	0.7	1.0	1.3	1.0	1.1
Australia	0.2	0.2	0.2	0.3	0.4	0.6	0.2	0.8	0.7	0.7
New Zealand	0.1	0.1	0.1	0.1	0.4	0.7	1.0	0.9	0.6	0.6
South Africa	0.1	0.1	0.1	0.1	0.1	0.3	0.4	0.8	0.3	0.3
Romania	0.1	0.0	0.0	0.0	0.0	0.1	0.0	0.4	0.4	0.3
France	0.2	0.2	0.2	0.2	0.2	0.2	0.2	0.6	0.2	0.2
Germany	0.2	0.3	0.2	0.2	0.2	0.2	0.9	0.5	0.2	0.2
Other countries	26.0	35.0	22.1	23.6	55.0	53.2	57.8	304.3	186.8	91.3
Total	**82.9**	**106.8**	**76.8**	**93.0**	**122.5**	**128.5**	**137.3 |**	**415.0**	**297.8**	**198.5**

Note: For details on definitions and sources, please refer to the metadata at the end of the tables.

StatLink ⌗ http://dx.doi.org/10.1787/020831720470

Table B.2.2. **Stock of foreign labour by nationality**

Thousands

LUXEMBOURG

	1996	1997	1998	1999	2000	2001	2002	2003	2004	2005
France	36.0	39.7	44.1	49.0	52.0	59.0	61.1	62.3	64.9	67.6
Portugal	27.8	28.3	29.5	30.5	32.0	32.2	33.3	34.5	35.5	36.8
Belgium	20.9	22.4	24.3	26.6	28.4	31.9	33.1	33.8	34.8	36.0
Germany	13.6	14.6	16.0	17.8	19.1	21.8	22.8	24.5	26.4	28.9
Italy	7.6	7.7	8.1	8.2	9.0	8.6	8.5	8.3	8.4	8.4
United Kingdom	1.4	1.4	1.5	1.6	1.8	1.9	1.8	1.7	1.7	1.8
Former Yugoslavia	1.5	1.5	1.6	1.6	1.8	1.9	2.2	2.3	2.0	1.4
Spain	1.0	1.0	1.1	1.1	1.2	1.2	1.2	1.2	1.3	1.3
Other countries	8.0	8.2	8.4	9.3	7.4	10.8	11.1	11.8	12.5	14.0
Total	**117.8**	**124.8**	**134.6**	**145.7**	**152.7**	**169.3**	**175.1**	**180.4**	**187.5**	**196.2**

Note: For details on definitions and sources, please refer to the metadata at the end of the tables.

StatLink ⌗ http://dx.doi.org/10.1787/021036881280

INTERNATIONAL MIGRATION OUTLOOK: SOPEMI 2007 EDITION – ISBN 978-92-64-03285-9 – © OECD 2007

Table B.2.2. **Stock of foreign labour by nationality**

Thousands

NETHERLANDS

	1996	1997	1998	1999	2000	2001	2002	2003	2004	2005
Germany	39.6	38.7	34.1	30.7	30.2	34.1	30.4	33.6	37.0	40.1
Turkey	36.6	33.6	34.7	26.7	56.8	54.5	48.9	53.3	42.4	36.8
Morocco	33.6	28.8	39.1	32.2	34.6	42.1	33.1	34.3	29.2	31.6
Belgium	23.8	22.2	17.4	19.3	16.9	19.2	25.7	16.7	20.7	20.7
United Kingdom	25.9	22.5	24.0	29.2	36.6	33.4	30.4	32.4	25.8	20.5
Italy	..	..	..	..	..	..	..	10.7	10.4	11.0
France	..	..	..	..	..	..	..	7.1	8.7	9.9
Spain	7.6	12.3	6.7	15.6	7.7	18.1	15.6	11.3	8.6	7.7
Other countries	113.4	116.9	113.4	113.9	117.3	101.1	111.8	117.8	116.5	109.2
Total	**280.5**	**275.2**	**269.5**	**267.5**	**300.1**	**302.6**	**295.9**	**317.2**	**299.4**	**287.5**

Note: For details on definitions and sources, please refer to the metadata at the end of the tables.

StatLink ⌸⌸⌸ http://dx.doi.org/10.1787/021043650164

Table B.2.2. **Stock of foreign labour by nationality**

Thousands

NORWAY

	1996	1997	1998	1999	2000	2001	2002	2003	2004	2005
Sweden	8.7	10.8	12.9	13.4	13.6	15.4	15.2	15.0	15.1	15.7
Denmark	9.1	9.5	9.9	9.1	9.0	10.7	10.6	10.5	10.4	10.3
Germany	2.4	2.7	3.0	4.3	4.4	5.6	5.9	6.2	6.7	7.3
Poland	0.6	0.6	0.7	2.7	2.8	3.4	3.8	4.0	4.8	6.7
Pakistan	1.8	1.7	1.7	4.8	4.9	5.8	5.9	6.0	6.2	6.4
United Kingdom	5.3	5.6	5.9	5.5	5.4	6.3	6.2	6.2	6.2	6.2
Sri Lanka	1.7	1.6	1.5	4.0	4.2	4.5	4.6	4.5	4.7	4.9
Turkey	1.0	1.0	1.0	2.9	3.1	3.5	3.8	3.8	4.1	4.4
Finland	2.0	2.3	2.8	3.6	3.7	4.4	4.3	4.2	4.0	3.8
Chile	1.3	1.2	1.3	2.8	2.9	3.4	3.3	3.3	3.4	3.5
United States	3.1	3.3	3.4	2.5	2.4	2.9	2.9	2.9	2.9	2.9
India	0.9	0.9	0.9	2.2	2.3	2.6	2.7	2.6	2.7	2.8
Netherlands	1.5	1.6	1.7	1.8	1.9	2.2	2.3	2.3	2.4	2.6
Other countries	15.3	17.2	20.2	45.1	50.6	63.1	66.8	69.0	75.4	81.7
Total	**54.8**	**59.9**	**66.9**	**104.6**	**111.2 |**	**133.7**	**138.4**	**140.7**	**149.0**	**159.3**

Note: For details on definitions and sources, please refer to the metadata at the end of the tables.

StatLink ⌸⌸⌸ http://dx.doi.org/10.1787/021073383880

Table B.2.2. **Stock of foreign labour by nationality**

Thousands

PORTUGAL

	1996	1997	1998	1999	2000	2001	2002	2003	2004	2005
Brazil	9.7	9.7	9.6	9.9	10.6	35.0	47.0	50.4	61.2	51.2
Ukraine	..	..	..	..	..	45.4	62.0	64.7	65.2	42.9
Cape Verde	22.2	22.1	21.9	22.0	23.1	29.8	32.3	33.1	33.8	36.8
Angola	8.2	8.2	8.2	8.4	9.7	15.4	18.3	18.8	19.1	17.7
Guinea-Bissau	7.2	7.2	7.2	7.8	8.9	12.7	13.9	14.9	15.1	14.2
Moldova	..	..	..	..	..	9.3	12.2	12.7	13.2	13.7
Romania	..	..	..	..	..	7.8	10.8	11.1	11.3	9.7
Spain	4.9	5.3	5.5	6.1	6.8	7.7	8.3	8.6	8.9	9.1
United Kingdom	5.6	5.8	6.0	6.3	6.5	6.8	7.0	7.1	7.4	7.6
Sao Tome and Principe	1.9	1.9	1.9	2.0	2.3	4.1	4.9	5.2	5.5	6.3
Germany	4.4	4.6	4.8	5.0	5.3	5.5	5.8	5.8	6.0	6.2
China	1.3	..	1.3	1.5	1.7	5.3	5.9	6.0	6.2	6.1
France	3.1	3.3	3.5	3.8	4.1	4.4	4.6	4.9	5.1	5.2
Russian Federation	..	..	..	..	..	5.8	7.2	7.3	7.6	4.6
United States	3.1	3.2	3.1	3.2	3.2	3.2	3.2	3.2	3.2	3.3
Other countries	15.1	16.7	15.7	15.7	17.8	38.4	44.8	46.9	47.1	36.7
Total	**86.8**	**87.9**	**88.6**	**91.6**	**99.8**	**236.6**	**288.3**	**300.8**	**315.8**	**271.4**

Note: For details on definitions and sources, please refer to the metadata at the end of the tables.

StatLink ⟨∎∎∎⟩ http://dx.doi.org/10.1787/021147332278

Table B.2.2. **Stock of foreign labour by nationality**

Thousands

SLOVAK REPUBLIC

	1996	1997	1998	1999	2000	2001	2002	2003	2004	2005
Czech Republic	1.5	1.7	2.2	2.3	2.2	1.9	2.0	2.3	0.5	0.9
France	..	..	..	0.1	0.1	0.1	0.1	0.1	0.2	0.9
Ukraine	0.6	0.7	0.7	0.4	0.4	0.3	0.3	0.3	0.3	0.6
Poland	0.5	0.6	0.7	0.2	0.2	0.2	0.1	0.1	0.2	0.6
Germany	..	..	..	0.2	0.3	0.3	0.4	0.4	0.2	0.4
United States	0.4	0.3	0.3	0.2	0.2	0.2	0.3	0.3	0.1	0.3
United Kingdom	..	..	..	0.2	0.2	0.2	0.2	0.2	0.1	0.2
Austria	0.1	0.1	0.1	0.1	0.1	0.1	0.1	0.2	0.1	0.2
Italy	..	..	..	0.1	0.1	0.1	0.1	0.1	0.1	0.1
Russian Federation	0.1	0.2	0.1	0.1	0.1	0.1	0.1	0.1	0.0	0.1
Croatia	0.1	0.1	0.1	0.0	0.0	0.0	0.0	0.0	0.0	0.1
Serbia and Montenegro	0.2	0.2	0.1	0.1	0.1	0.1	0.1	..	0.0	0.0
Viet Nam	0.0	0.0	0.0	0.0	0.0	0.0	0.0	0.0	0.0	0.0
Other countries	1.3	1.7	1.7	0.4	0.8	0.8	0.9	0.9	0.9	1.9
Total	**4.8**	**5.5**	**5.9**	**4.5**	**4.7**	**4.4**	**4.7**	**5.0**	**2.8**	**6.2**

Note: For details on definitions and sources, please refer to the metadata at the end of the tables.

StatLink ⟨∎∎∎⟩ http://dx.doi.org/10.1787/021163156812

INTERNATIONAL MIGRATION OUTLOOK: SOPEMI 2007 EDITION – ISBN 978-92-64-03285-9 – © OECD 2007

Table B.2.2. **Stock of foreign labour by nationality**

Thousands

SPAIN

	1996	1997	1998	1999	2000	2001	2002	2003	2004	2005
Ecuador	2.3	3.1	7.4	9.4	25.7	67.9	125.7	139.3	147.2	270.3
Morocco	61.6	68.8	76.9	80.4	101.8	124.2	148.1	173.8	172.7	239.9
Romania	1.1	1.5	2.4	3.0	8.3	18.2	38.2	46.3	60.8	156.0
Colombia	3.6	3.8	4.3	4.8	12.1	26.8	60.5	66.4	77.7	130.2
Peru	14.3	15.0	16.3	14.7	18.6	22.7	27.4	37.9	47.1	60.1
China	8.2	9.3	11.9	12.4	15.7	20.7	27.2	29.4	37.0	53.8
Argentina	7.8	6.6	4.9	3.9	7.0	9.9	16.9	24.1	30.8	53.4
Dominican Republic	12.4	12.3	13.2	11.0	12.3	13.2	14.6	17.0	18.7	25.3
Cuba	2.0	2.5	3.0	3.4	8.7	10.9	12.9	14.8	15.5	20.4
Uruguay	..	..	..	..	1.9	2.4	3.6	5.3	7.4	17.3
Algeria	3.3	3.7	4.0	4.2	7.0	8.8	11.0	13.6	13.2	17.3
Brazil	..	..	..	..	3.4	4.6	6.1	6.9	7.9	16.4
Senegal	3.9	4.3	4.7	5.0	5.2	7.0	8.1	9.9	10.2	15.7
Chile	2.8	..	..	..	2.8	3.7	4.8	6.5	8.4	13.1
Philippines	8.3	8.3	8.4	7.5	9.2	9.9	10.4	11.1	11.5	12.6
Other countries	34.7	39.6	39.8	40.0	214.9	256.2	316.2	380.0	410.9	586.7
Total	**166.5**	**178.7**	**197.1**	**199.8**	**454.6**	**607.1**	**831.7**	**982.4**	**1 076.7**	**1 688.6**

Note: For details on definitions and sources, please refer to the metadata at the end of the tables.

StatLink ᗉᐧᔑ http://dx.doi.org/10.1787/020634561556

Table B.2.2. **Stock of foreign labour by nationality**

Thousands

SWEDEN

	1996	1997	1998	1999	2000	2001	2002	2003	2004
Finland	57	54	52	52	50	53	53	52	49
Norway	19	18	17	19	17	16	17	16	17
Denmark	13	13	13	13	13	14	14	14	17
Former Yugoslavia	23	31	31	28	27	23	19	17	8
Turkey	7	7	5	4	10	7	5	5	6
Poland	7	7	7	8	8	10	8	8	5
Iran	10	10	9	8	5	4	4	4	4
Other countries	82	80	85	90	92	100	98	105	110
Total	**218**	**220**	**219**	**222**	**222**	**227**	**218**	**221**	**216**

Note: For details on definitions and sources, please refer to the metadata at the end of the tables.

StatLink ᗉᐧᔑ http://dx.doi.org/10.1787/021204776062

Table B.2.2. **Stock of foreign labour by nationality**

Thousands

SWITZERLAND

	1996	1997	1998	1999	2000	2001	2002	2003	2004	2005
Italy	202.5	191.7	184.4	179.3	177.4	172.3	..	177.8	172.9	168.4
Former Yugoslavia	136.2	138.2	142.8	148.3	154.5	133.9	..	166.2	164.2	161.2
Portugal	79.3	77.4	76.6	76.5	77.0	77.9	..	86.1	88.0	96.0
Germany	56.7	57.3	58.7	61.3	65.4	73.3	..	78.3	84.0	92.9
Spain	59.8	56.4	53.7	51.7	50.1	48.8	..	57.4	54.4	53.3
France	31.3	30.7	30.7	31.8	33.2	34.2	..	39.2	40.4	40.8
Austria	18.8	18.2	17.8	17.6	17.9	18.5	..	20.3	19.5	19.6
Other countries	124.5	122.9	126.4	134.7	141.8	179.9	829.4	189.2	194.1	197.9
Total	**709.1**	**692.8**	**691.1**	**701.2**	**717.3**	**738.8 |**	**829.4**	**814.5**	**817.4**	**830.1**

Note: For details on definitions and sources, please refer to the metadata at the end of the tables.

StatLink ▧ http://dx.doi.org/10.1787/020482446862

Table B.2.2. **Stock of foreign labour by nationality**

Thousands

UNITED KINGDOM

	1996	1997	1998	1999	2000	2001	2002	2003	2004	2005
Ireland	218.0	216.0	221.0	220.0	206.0	212.0	179.0	179.0	172.0	175.0
India	58.0	56.0	71.0	66.0	61.0	61.0	69.0	82.0	97.0	100.0
United States	46.0	53.0	63.0	55.0	61.0	75.0	52.0	62.0	68.0	61.0
Australia	32.0	35.0	31.0	36.0	54.0	46.0	57.0	55.0	63.0	58.0
France	27.0	33.0	49.0	44.0	48.0	47.0	60.0	59.0	51.0	58.0
Germany	30.0	32.0	39.0	44.0	33.0	35.0	32.0	39.0	48.0	50.0
Italy	42.0	42.0	52.0	43.0	55.0	58.0	58.0	53.0	67.0	45.0
Portugal	15.0	14.0	23.0	20.0	15.0	35.0	47.0	52.0	50.0	39.0
Pakistan	17.0	20.0	20.0	27.0	31.0	29.0	31.0	27.0	31.0	29.0
Spain	20.0	24.0	18.0	25.0	30.0	30.0	31.0	33.0	26.0	36.0
Bangladesh	12.0	18.0	16.0	17.0	14.0	19.0	14.0	11.0	26.0	18.0
New Zealand	26.0	21.0	30.0	23.0	25.0	25.0	39.0	29.0	29.0	31.0
Other countries	322.0	385.0	406.0	385.0	474.0	557.0	582.0	641.0	717.0	804.0
Total	**865.0**	**949.0**	**1 039.0**	**1 005.0**	**1 107.0**	**1 229.0**	**1 251.0**	**1 322.0**	**1 445.0**	**1 504.0**

Note: For details on definitions and sources, please refer to the metadata at the end of the tables.

StatLink ▧ http://dx.doi.org/10.1787/020720383458

INTERNATIONAL MIGRATION OUTLOOK: SOPEMI 2007 EDITION – ISBN 978-92-64-03285-9 – © OECD 2007

Metadata related to Tables A.2.3. and B.2.2. **Foreign labour force**

Country	Comments	Source
Austria	Annual average. The unemployed are included and the self-employed are excluded. Data on employment by nationality are from valid work permits. From 1994 on, EEA members no longer need work permits and are therefore no longer included. A person holding two permits is counted twice.	Ministry of Labour, Health and Social affairs.
Belgium	Including unemployed and self-employed.	National Institute of self employed's social insurances, National Office for Employment, National Bank of Belgium and National Institute of Statistics.
Czech Republic	Holders of a work permit and registered Slovak workers. Excluding holders of a trade licence. *Reference date:* 31 December (except 2004: 30 July).	Research Institute for Labour and Social Affairs.
Denmark	Data are from population registers. *Reference date:* 31 December.	Statistics Denmark.
Finland	Foreign labour force recorded in the population register. Includes persons of Finnish origin. *Reference date:* 31 December.	Statistics Finland.
France	Labour Force Survey. The survey has moved to a continuous one from 2003 on. Data are therefore not fully comparable with those of the previous years. *Reference date:* March of each year until 2002.	National Institute for Statistics and Economic Studies (INSEE).
Germany	Microcensus. Data include the unemployed and the self-employed. *Reference date:* April.	Federal Office of Statistics.
Greece	Labour Force Survey. Data refer to the employed and the unemployed.	National Statistical Service.
Hungary	Number of valid work permits. *Reference date:* 31 December.	Ministry of Labour.
Ireland	Estimates are from the Labour Force Survey. Data by nationality (Table B.2.2.) are issued from the 2002 Census and refer to persons aged 15 years and over in the labour force.	Central Statistics Office.
Italy	Figures refer to the number of foreigners with a valid work permit (including the self-employed, the unemployed, sponsored workers and persons granted a permit for humanitarian reasons). EU citizens do not need a work permit.	National Institute of Statistics (ISTAT).
Japan	Foreigners whose activity is restricted according to the Immigration Act (revised in 1990). Permanent residents, spouses or children of Japanese national, spouses or children of permanent residents and long-term residents have no restrictions imposed on the kind of activities they can engage in while in Japan and are excluded from the data.	Ministry of Justice, Immigration Bureau.
Korea	Data are based on registered foreign workers, which excludes short-term (under 90 days) workers. Trainees are included. The huge increase is mainly due to a number of undocumented workers who were given a legal worker status following a regularisation program in mid 2003.	Ministry of Justice.
Luxembourg	Number of work permits. Data cover foreigners in employment, including apprentices, trainees and cross-border workers. The unemployed are not included. *Reference date:* 1 October.	Social Security Inspection Bureau.
Netherlands	Data are from the Labour Force Survey and refer to the Labour force aged 15 and over. *Reference date:* March.	Labour Force Survey (Eurostat).
Norway	Data are from population registers. Excluding the self-employed until 2000. *Reference date:* Second quarter of each year (except in 1995, 1996, 1999 and 2000: 4th quarter).	Directorate of Immigration.
Portugal	Workers who hold a valid residence permit (including the unemployed). Including foreign workers who benefited from the 1992-1993, 1996 and 2001 regularisation programmes. Data for 2001, 2002 and 2003 include workers regularised following the 2001 programme. *Reference date:* 31 December.	Ministry of the Interior and National Statistical Office (INE).
Slovak Republic	Foreigners who hold a valid work permit. Czech workers do not need a work permit but they are registered through the Labour Offices.	Ministry of Labour and Social Affairs, National Labour Office.
Spain	Number of valid work permits. EU workers are not included. In 1996, the data include work permits delivered following the 1996 regularisation programme. From 2000 on, data relate to the number of foreigners who are registered in the Social Security system. A worker may be registered several times if he/she has several activities. Regularised workers are included in 2000 and 2001 data. *Reference date:* 31 December (data for 2003 are stocks on January 14th 2004).	Ministry of Labour and Social Security.

Metadata related to Tables A.2.3. and B.2.2. **Foreign labour force** (*Cont.*)

Country	Comments	Source
Sweden	Annual average from the Labour Force Survey.	Statistics Sweden.
Switzerland	Til 2001, data are counts of the number of foreigners with an annual residence permit or a settlement permit (permanent permit), who engage in gainful activity. Cross-border workers and seasonal workers are excluded.	Federal Office of Immigration, Integration and Emigration.
	Since the bilateral agreements signed with the European Union have come into force (1 June 2002), movements of EU workers can no longer be followed through the central register of foreigners. Data until 2001 are from the Central Register of Foreigners. Starting in 2002, data are from the Swiss Labour Force Survey.	
	Reference date: 31 December.	
United Kingdom	Estimates are from the Labour Force Survey. The unemployed are not included. There is a break in the serie as 2004 data are calculated using a new weighting system.	Home Office.

LIST OF SOPEMI CORRESPONDENTS

AUSTRALIA	Mr. G. MILLS Department of Immigration and Multicultural Affairs, Canberra
AUSTRIA	Ms. G. BIFFL Austrian Economic Institute, Vienna
BELGIUM	Ms. A. GEYSELS Service public fédéral Emploi, Travail et Concertation sociale, Brussels
BULGARIA	Ms. D. BOBEVA Bulgarian National Bank, Sofia
CANADA	Ms. M. JUSTUS Citizenship and Immigration Canada, Ottawa
CZECH REPUBLIC	Ms. J. MARESOVA Czech Statistical Office, Prague
DENMARK	Ms. A. MATHIESEN Ministry of Refugee, Immigration and Integration Affairs, Copenhagen
FINLAND	Ms. A.SAARTO Ministry of Labour, Helsinki
FRANCE	Ms. C. REGNARD Ministère de l'Emploi, de la Cohésion sociale et du Logement, Paris
GERMANY	Ms. B. FRÖHLICH Ministry of Labour and Social Affairs, Berlin
GREECE	Mr. S. ROBOLIS University of Athens
HUNGARY	Ms. V. ÁCS Ministry of Social Affairs and Labour, Budapest
IRELAND	Mr. P. O'CONNELL The Economic and Social Research Institute, Dublin
ITALY	Ms. C. COLLICELLI CENSIS, Rome Mr. J. CHALOFF CENSIS, Rome
JAPAN	Mr. J. HIROISHI Ministry of Justice, Tokyo Mr. T. OGATA Ministry of Health, Labour and Welfare, Tokyo
KOREA	Mr.Young-bum PARK Hansung University, Seoul

LITHUANIA	Ms. A. SIPAVICIENE
	Vilnius
LUXEMBOURG	Ms. C. MARTIN
	Commissaire du Gouvernement aux Etrangers
MEXICO	Mr. G. MOHAR
	Mexico
NETHERLANDS	Mr. G. ENGENSEN and Mr. E. SNEL
	Erasmus University, Rotterdam
NEW ZEALAND	Mr. B. LONG
	Department of Labour, Wellington
NORWAY	M. E. THORUD
	Royal Ministry of Local Government and Labour, Oslo
POLAND	Ms E. KEPINSKA
	University of Warsaw, Institute for Social Studies
PORTUGAL	Mr. J. MALHEIROS
	University of Lisbon
ROMANIA	Mr. D. GHEORGHIU
	National Institute for Statistics and Economic Studies, Bucarest
SLOVAK REPUBLIC	Ms. M. LUBYOVA
	Bratislava
SPAIN	Mr. A. IZQUIERDO ESCRIBANO
	Faculté des Sciences politiques et de sociologie, La Corunã
SWEDEN	Mr. M. HAGOS
	Ministry of Justice, Stockholm
SWITZERLAND	Ms. C. de COULON
	Federal Office of Migration, Berne
TURKEY	Mr. A. ICDUYGU
	Kok University, Istanbul
UNITED KINGDOM	Mr. J. SALT
	University College London, Department of Geography, London
UNITED STATES	MS. S. SMITH
	Washington

INTERNATIONAL MIGRATION OUTLOOK: SOPEMI 2007 EDITION – ISBN 978-92-64-03285-9 – © OECD 2007

LIST OF OECD SECRETARIAT MEMBERS INVOLVED IN THE PREPARATION OF THIS REPORT

Division of Non-Member Economies and International Migration Division

Jean-Pierre Garson, Head of Division

Georges Lemaître, Principal Administrator

Jean-Christophe Dumont, Principal Administrator

Thomas Liebig, Administrator

Gilles Spielvogel, Administrator

Cécile Thoreau, Statistical Assistant

Pauline Fron, Statistical Assistant

Sylviane Yvron-Solari, Assistant

Anne-Marie Gray, Assistant

Hélène Orain, ENA Trainee

Ozlem ATASEVER, Trainee

Health Division

Pascal Zurn, Consultant (Health Workforce Planning and Migration)

Christine le Thi, Statistical Assistant

OECD PUBLICATIONS, 2, rue André-Pascal, 75775 PARIS CEDEX 16
PRINTED IN FRANCE
(81 2007 12 1 P) ISBN 978-92-64-03285-9 – No. 55591 2007

Printed in the United States
100036LV00010B/52/A